Discovery and The Market Process
Toward an Understanding of the Business & Economic Environment

Barry Brownstein • Deborah Brownstein
University of Baltimore

The McGraw-Hill Companies, Inc.
College Custom Series

New York St. Louis San Francisco Auckland Bogotá
Caracas Lisbon London Madrid Mexico Milan Montreal
New Delhi Paris San Juan Singapore Sydney Tokyo Toronto

McGraw·Hill

A Division of The McGraw·Hill Companies

DISCOVERY AND THE MARKET PROCESS:
Toward an Understanding of the Business & Economic Environment

1 2 3 4 5 6 7 8 9 0 BKM BKM 9 0 9 8 7 6

ISBN 0-07-008515-3

Editor: Jean Laughlin
Cover Design: Maggie Lytle
Printer/Binder: Bookmart Press

TABLE OF CONTENTS

INTRODUCTION

Barry and Deborah Brownstein

Until recently economics and business curricula tended to be narrowly focused, compartmentalized subjects. In order to give students a systemic understanding of the field they are studying, innovative courses have begun to spring up that are more interdisciplinary in nature. We have designed this reader to be a resource for those who seek a systemic understanding of the role that free markets play in the economy and the ethical underpinnings of these markets. Now more than ever, such an integrative perspective is needed.

> To the layman untrained in economics, the market economy presents a bewildering face. It consists of numerous individuals each intent on his own goals, giving no concern to the overall social implications of his pursuits. No central coordinating agency controls or even monitors the innumerable independent production and exchange decisions made by these countless individuals. It is no wonder that the market economy seems to be nothing but a jungle of clashing discordant individual activities. From this perspective, government regulation fills a simple and obvious need: to introduce a modicum of coordination into these otherwise chaotic conditions.[1]

> —*Israel Kirzner*

Perhaps Israel Kirzner is being kind. Misunderstandings about the market process are not limited to "layman untrained in economics" but are also prevalent in academia, business and government. It is the admittedly ambitious, but attainable goal of this reader that a study of these essays will provide the reader a systemic understanding of the market process. While the chief perspective of the readings is economics, this collection of essays also draws on philosophical, political, and psychological theories. These essays will help the reader understand the effects of public policies as they impact, in intended and unintended ways, the domestic and global market-place. Perhaps more importantly the reader will gain insight into the ethical underpinnings of free markets and gain insights into their own beliefs about market. These readings will help uncover and make explicit assumptions that are often implicit in theories and in our own mental maps of the world. This challenges readers to know better their own minds and builds personal integrity. The approach taken here is consistent with emerging views in mainstream economics, particularly 1993 Nobel laureate Douglas North. "Economic choices are a function of how people perceive the world," said North. The *Wall Street Journal* further quotes North as saying, "people have subjective mental models" and that beliefs a society has in common aren't analyzed enough in traditional economics. We believe it is only by being aware and reflective about one's beliefs does one have the freedom to make mindful ethical choices and exercise personal responsibility.

Specifically the reader is designed to promote an understanding of:

- An ethical paradigm that stresses that the quality of an individual's decisions is affected by the quality of one's thinking and that belief and insight shape one's responses to life's challenges,

- The consequences of thought systems and beliefs as they effect issues of political-economy,

- The nature of rights, both human rights and property rights, and social justice,

- The role and impact of prices and profits in a market economy,

- The use of knowledge in society and the market conditions which promote the integration of knowledge,

- Entrepreneurial discovery which fuels dynamic change and adaptation in the market and the effects of government regulation on this discovery process,

- The effects of the growing volume of world trade, and

- Political-economy and ethical considerations in such issues as health care and environmental problems.

Without Friedrich Hayek's contributions to economics, this reader would not be possible. His seminal contributions resulted in his receiving the Nobel Prize in 1974. For the business or economics student Hayek's importance to understanding markets grows ever larger. Business guru Tom Peters writes of Hayek: "Why spend so much time on Hayek? Simple. To fail to appreciate—in the fullest sense of that term—the richness, passion and raggedness of the market mechanism is to be unprepared to lead a firm (or a regional or national economy)—especially in today's unhinged global marketplace."[2]

The first part of this reader is titled *The Individual, Property Rights and Society: The Basis for Free Markets* and begins with a psychological reading that explains the role of insight. With that reading and Emerson's classic essay "Self-Reliance," the reader understands that the individual is the decision maker and that the quality of one's decisions is affected by the quality of one's thinking. An understanding of insight has direct relevance to entrepreneurial discovery which is discussed later in the reader. Hayek's classic essay "Individualism: True and False" refutes "the silliest of the common misunderstandings (about individualism); the belief that individualism postulates (or bases its arguments on the assumptions of) the existence of isolated or self-contained individuals, instead of starting from men whose whole nature and character is determined by their existence in society." Emerson's essay has been subject to similar misunderstandings. "Cosmos and Taxis" introduces to the reader the contrast between spontaneous order and planned order. The careful reader will be forced to confront the core belief of many social scientists that the good order is one "which has been made by somebody putting the elements of a set in their places or directing their movements." From that point the reader introduces rights as a basis for any market using Rothbard's "Justice and Property Rights." Murray Rothbard writes: "For the free-market economy, as complex as the system appears to be on the surface, is yet nothing more than a vast network of voluntary and mutually agreed-upon two-person or two-party exchanges of property titles. . . ."[3] The importance of a clear and precise demarcation of property rights for the market economy . . . [is essential to] the allocation of resources and in preventing or compensating for unwanted imposition of 'external costs.' "[4] " 'Social' or Distributive Justice" which is from Hayek's *Law, Legislation and Liberty* discusses whether the role of government should be to rig outcomes or simply to insure fair rules to play the game. Hayek writes, "the enforcement of any image of 'social justice' inevitably destroys that freedom of personal decisions on which all morals must rest."[5] This rounds out a discussion of the ethical basis for free-markets. Armed with the understanding presented here, the reader begins to see that the government-business partnership accepted as axiomatic by many could be objected to on efficiency and equity grounds. The dichotomy Hayek presents between equity based on outcomes or conduct helps students see their own beliefs on "social justice" and traces through the systemic consequences of outcome based public policies. The next part of this reader focuses on efficiency considerations.

Perhaps Hayek's greatest and certainly most quoted contribution to economics is his seminal essay "The Use of Knowledge in Society." This essay is essential to understand that the core economic problem is "a problem of how to secure the best use of resources known to any of the members of society, for ends whose relative importance only those individuals know."[6] For those readers who have previous economic training this is obviously in stark contrast to neo-classical economics with its assumption of given knowledge and its reduction of the economic problem to allocative choices. In reading this essay the reader may find it useful to characterize centrally planned versus competitive systems in terms of (1) how the economic problem is defined, (2) the type of information that is used, and (3) how quickly it is used, in response to (4) how change in the economy is perceived by the relevant decision makers.

The readings in this section discuss the meaning of competition. We, along with many others, believe "the Austrian view of competition and entrepreneurship is critical to understanding the contemporary business environment. The conventional textbook model of perfect competition is incapable of producing real competitive behavior, because competition in the real world is a dynamic process of change and adaptation. . . . Anyone who claims that 'competitive firms' cut costs or introduce new products is implicitly employing a dynamic theory of competition."[7] The neo-classical model of perfect competition simply cannot produce this behavior.

A central theme in this reader is a discussion of the market process, the role of the entrepreneur and of discovery. In Kirzner's essays entrepreneurial discovery is compared and contrasted with neo-classical economics calculative economizing activity. He discusses the limits of rationality. He sets out the qualities of good entrepreneurship and describes how entrepreneurial alertness is fundamentally different from the resources ordinarily employed in decision making. Kirzner describes the impact that government regulation has on the entrepreneurial discovery process and economic growth.

Hayek describes in *The Road to Serfdom* the dangers to democracy of central planning. This reader includes two chapters from this 1944 work which Milton Friedman calls "a true classic" and Thomas Sowell calls "a landmark work." Useful to an understanding of the economic and business environment is Hayek's discussion of "the general interest." It is an impossibility to specify a complete system of human values upon which any defintion of "the general interest" depends. An understanding of the business environment is enhanced by understanding that the rule of law necessitates formal rules which limit the *ad hoc* powers of government. These are qualitatively distinct from substantive rules of government proposed by social planners.

Part III presents applications of the theoretical framework presented in Parts I and II. While the applications discussed are related to the environment, health care and international trade, the framework presented in these readings can be infinitely generalized. Indeed, a measure of the comprehension of these readings is the ability to generalize to other applications.

A Note on Reading the Reader

We have also designed this reader to build critical thinking skills. These skills include the ability to uncover and articulate hidden assumptions behind judgments, decisions and actions; to recognize faulty reasoning and biases in perceptions; to trace through cause and effect beyond primary effects to secondary effects and thus to analyze systems; to reframe a problem from many points of view and to synthesize ideas. The nature of the ideas presented will prompt the reader to reflect on their own beliefs and professional and ethical values. Readers will gain a deeper understanding of the mental models in their own minds and what is truly meaningful to them.

Reading original works instead of a textbook engages students in the great debates of our time and demonstrates that knowledge and beliefs change. We believe this sparks enthusiasm for life-long learning.

> The development of general ability for independent thinking and judgment should always be placed foremost.
>
> *—Albert Einstein*

> Some people will never learn anything for this reason: because they understand everything too soon.
>
> *—Alexander Pope*

For many this will be your initial exposure to reading original pieces of critical thinking as opposed to second or third hand textbook presentations. A few words about what to expect are in order. Initially you may find the readings difficult. You might long for the familiar formulas and graphs of a traditional textbook. Adam Robinson in his outstanding book, *What Smart Students Know,* tells the the story involving the famous physicist Nells Bohr. Bohr tells a scientist in his audience that "if he wasn't confused and bewildered by the presentation, he hadn't been paying attention."[8] While we hope these essays don't provoke such an extreme reaction, as Robinson writes, "if your brain isn't a little shaken up by something new, you've missed the point."[9]

We encourage the reader to have respect for the process of learning. For most readers several readings of the more difficult essays are necessary to begin to understand them. Hayek's prose which may be difficult at first encounter soon becomes a welcome treasure of rich ideas to return to again and again. Hayekian scholar Chiaki Nishiyama writes: "once readers master Hayekian terminology and his innovative way of thinking, they find it surprisingly easy to appreciate his arguments, none of which is self-evident at first glance. The so-called great discoveries and widely accepted 'truths' are almost without exception rather easy to understand. So it is with the Hayekian order of ideas."[10]

In the final analysis though this reader is a beginning not an end. To understand and learn is a lifetime's journey and because a central insight of Hayek's work is that an individual can never have the whole of knowledge this journey of understanding is ever unfolding.

Notes

1. Israel Kirzner, "Competition, Regulation, and the Market Process," *Policy Analysis* no. 18 (Cato Institute, Washington, DC 1982), p. 1.

2. Tom Peters, *Liberation Management* (New York: Alfred Knopf, 1992), p. 501.

3. Murray Rothbard, "Justice and Property Rights" in *Property in a Humane Society* (La Salle, Illinois: Open Court, 1974), p. 114.

4. Ibid., p. 102.

5. Friedrich Hayek, *Law, Legislation and Liberty,* V2 (Chicago: University of Chicago Press, 1976), p. 99.

6. Friedrich Hayek, "The Use of Knowledge in Society" in *Individualism and Economic Order* (Chicago: Henry Regnery Co., 1972), p. 78.

7. Professor Jerry Ellig of George Mason University.

8. Adam Robinson, *What Smart Students Know* (New York: Crown, 1993), p. 133.

9. Ibid.

10. Chiaki Nishiyama and Kurt Leube ed. *The Essence of Hayek* (Stanford: Hoover Institution Press, 1984), p. xxxviii.

ACKNOWLEDGMENTS

Part I

"Wisdom, Insight, and Psychological Change" by Rick Suarez, Roger Mills and Darlene Stewart from *Sanity, Insanity and Common Sense*. Copyright © 1980, 1982 by E.M. Suarez, Roger C. Mills and Darlene Stewart. Reprinted by permission of Ballantine Books, a Division of Random House, Inc.

"Self-Reliance" by Ralph Waldo Emerson from *Self-Reliance.*

"Individualism: True or False" by Friedrich Hayek from *The Essence of Hayek.* Copyright © 1948 by The University of Chicago.

"Cosmos and Taxis" by Friedrich A. Hayek from *Law, Legislation and Liberty*. Copyright © 1973 by F.A. Hayek. Reprinted by permission of The University of Chicago Press.

"Justice and Property Rights" by Murray N. Rothbard from *Property in a Humane Economy*. Copyright © 1974 by the Institute for Humane Studies, Inc.

" 'Social' or Distributive Justice" by Friedrich A. Hayek from *Law, Legislation and Liberty*. Copyright © 1976 by F.A. Hayek. Reprinted by permission of The University of Chicago Press.

Part II

"The Power of the Market" by Milton and Rose Friedman from *Free to Choose*. Copyright © 1980 by Harcourt Brace Javonovich, Inc., New York, pages 9-27. Reprinted with permission of the publisher.

"Violent Market-Injection Strategies" by Tom Peters from *Liberation Management: Necessary Disorganization for the Nanosecond Nineties*. Copyright © 1992 by Excel/, A California Limited Partnership. Published by Alfred A. Knopf, Inc.

"The Use of Knowledge in Society" by Friedrich Hayek from Individualism and Economic Order. Copyright © 1948 by The University of Chicago. 1972 Regnery Gateway edition reprinted by special permission of Regnery Gateway, Inc., Washington, D.C.

"The Meaning of Competition" by Friedrich Hayek from Individualism and Economic Order. Copyright © 1948 by The University of Chicago. 1972 Regnery Gateway edition reprinted by special permission of Regnery Gateway, Inc., Washington, D.C.

Part III

"Bureaucracy versus Environment" by Terry Anderson and Donald Leal from *Free Market Environmentalism*. Copyright © 1991 by Westview Press, Boulder, Colorado.

"Homesteading the Oceans" by Terry Anderson and Donald Leal from *Free Market Environmentalism*. Copyright © 1991 by Westview Press, Boulder, Colorado.

"A Market of Landscape Visions" by Karl Hess, Jr. from Visions Upon the Land: Man and Nature on the Western Range. Copyright © 1992 The Cato Institute.

"The Fair Trade Fraud" by James Bovard from *The Fair Trade Fraud*. Copyright © 1991 by James Bovard. Reprinted with St. Martin's Press, Incorporated.

"Tariffs and Other Border Land Mines" by James Bovard from *The Fair Trade Fraud*. Copyright © 1991 by James Bovard. Reprinted with St. Martin's Press, Incorporated.

"The Protectionist Mentality" by Robert W. McGee from *A Trade Policy for Free Societies: The Case Against Protectionism*. Copyright © 1994 Quorum Books.

"The Medical Monopoly" by Sue A. Blevins from *Policy Analysis*, December 15, 1995, No. 246. Published by The Cato Institute.

"The Law of the Microcosm and the End of Socialism" by George Gilder. Originally published in *The Cato Journal*, Vol. 11, no. 2. Cato Institute, 1991.

Thanks

Our appreciation to Jean Laughlin of McGraw-Hill and Karen Fuller of Architext for their expert assistance in completing this project.

Part I

THE INDIVIDUAL, PROPERTY RIGHTS AND SOCIETY: THE BASIS FOR FREE MARKETS

WISDOM, INSIGHT, AND PSYCHOLOGICAL CHANGE

Rick Suarez, Roger Mills and Darlene Stewart

Throughout time, humanity has sought to understand the words of the enlightened people of this world who have tried to improve the human condition. People have searched for the magic ingredient that would help them change conditions of mental disturbance and interpersonal conflict to conditions of mental health and cooperation. Such knowledge would be known by its results, but a look at human social and psychological conditions suggests that the desired change has come grudgingly over thousands of years and is microscopic. When progress in the human condition is compared to technological advancement, we find that our understanding of human psychological behavior has grown at a snail's pace. The words of the wise, which we revere, profess, and often quote, have remained words and have never become reality for most people. Why? What is missing?

The factor that has been missing in humanity's understanding has been the psychological recognition that perceptions, feelings, and behaviors are shaped by thoughts. As we have noted in earlier chapters, people have tried to understand life from the perspective of whatever thought system they acquired during their life. For this reason, it has been next to impossible for people to profit from what those who have achieved a deeper understanding of life have tried to convey. The reason for this is simple. At higher levels of consciousness, people see life in a simpler, less complex, and, in essence, more truthful way. These individuals, in touch with common sense, have a clearer picture of life. Now, someone who is in a different reality, one that is at a lower level of understanding, relatively devoid of common sense, would see the actions of the other as being wiser. This is why at many points in history, people with an extraordinary degree of common sense, relative to their contemporaries, have been referred to as being "wise." These wise men or women have been thought to possess something called "wisdom." So what is wisdom?

Wisdom and Mental Health

Wisdom is a level of intelligence, innate in every human being, which is deeper and more comprehensive than what we associate with an IQ score. Wisdom exists outside of individualized frames of reference, which is why it has not been more readily realized by a humanity that is wedded to fixed patterns of thinking and perceptions of reality. When wisdom is realized by an individual, it frees him from his own fixed views of life and guides that person toward the attainment of selfesteem, peace of mind, happiness, creativity, and productivity. In other words, wisdom shows the individual how to live in the state of mental health.

What we have begun to realize in the course of our studies is that wisdom is synonymous with understanding thought, reality, emotions, and levels of consciousness. Thus, when we read accounts of truly wise people, it becomes apparent that they were mentally healthy in a way that was so far beyond the realm of what was normal in their time, that their contemporaries (at varying levels of consciousness) either viewed them as a blessing or as a threat. In either case, people have always found it very difficult to listen to what the wise have said about how life works.

What we are saying is simply this: These wise people that we have revered were people who broke the barrier of humanity's thought-created reality and realized that humanity's problems were indeed thought-created. Wisdom, in essence, is mental health, and mental health, as we have noted, is a state of mind in which the human being understands the psychological principles of human reality. This is why the "wise," irrespective of culture, warned people about the perils of judging what is "out there." They were warning us about judging our own perceptions or misperceptions. They told people to look within for wisdom, noting that it did not exist in the realm of what mankind perceives to be real. And all pointed toward the feeling of love and goodwill as the route to a better reality.

Wisdom and Insight

The realization of wisdom occur in a very natural and spontaneous manner which is sometimes dramatic, but more frequently subtle. Sometimes wisdom is realized through an insight that breaks into our thought like a light being turned on in a dark room; other times wisdom appears quietly, as though a new thought crept silently into our awareness without our suspecting its importance at first, and later we cannot recall how it came. It was simply there, complete, obvious, relevant. When wisdom is realized, it reveals the unknown. It may show us a missing piece or an appropriate answer that seems so simple and obvious that we wonder how we could not see it before. The conscious state that provides the perspective to see obvious, positive answers is what we are calling common sense.

Everyone has had flashes of wisdom but some people have manifested it more consistently than others. The experience and expression of wisdom has been a haphazard affair because until now no one has understood this intelligence as a psychological factor. Most people have placed wisdom beyond the reach of their lives. Yet there are undeniable clues that wisdom is already within each human being. For example who could deny that a person in a mentally healthy state of mind acts wiser than when that person is in a lower state of mind. Who could deny that a person behaves wiser in a good mood than in a bad mood?

The beginning of wisdom is the realization that the human being has the ability to think. Everyone would agree of course, that human beings think. However, very few people realize that ability as a creative, voluntary function. People experience their ability to think as a passive review of data that is being imposed upon them. To see that the human mind has the ability to create thoughts and project them into forms that we call experience, is to understand that we can consciously nurture our mental health. Wisdom reveals to the individual that through the ability to think, that individual is creating the separate reality that becomes his life. Such understanding allows the individual to see beyond his personal frame of reference and find the common sense answers to life's questions.

The Experience of Insight

Wisdom cannot be realized through mental struggle or the intellectual process of trying to figure out our problems. The reason that wisdom is not more frequently recognized is that human beings have traditionally idolized intellectual and analytical reasoning, and wisdom does not come from these thought patterns. We have missed wisdom because we have learned to think in terms of our problems, to be "realistic," and to sort through our stored information for the answers that we seek. We have literally been looking for our answers in the wrong place without knowing it. All that we can think about is what is programmed into our biological computer.

This is not to say that our thought system has no use. Of course it does. As we have repeatedly noted, it is the perfect tool for accessing useful memory so that we don't forget our language or how to get to work, our telephone number or where to put the dishes when we take them out of the dishwasher. In other words, our thought system is our biological computer and it should be used to help us out in the same way that we utilize a personal computer. We would not consult our personal computer to tell us what to do when our teenager is taking drugs or how to make up with our sweetheart. This would be an obvious misuse of the computer. In the same way, we learn not to use our thought system for things that are beyond its capabilities.

When we realize knowledge that is beyond the software of our biological computer, this is called the experience of insight. Once we experience insight, we realize our capability to drop habits of anxiety, fear, insecurity, and worry. Once we do this we start to live in a more positive feeling level. This feeling level allows us to see things with clarity and objectivity. We regain our self-esteem and our sense of humor and move naturally into states of mind where we feel increased joy and appreciation for the simple things in life. Enjoying what we have opens us to beauty and possibilities that were unseen before. Gratitude for what we have increases the positive feelings which lead us deeper into states of mind where wisdom and insight are found.

Wisdom comes through insight, which is the act of seeing within ourselves and recognizing how our psychological functioning works. Wisdom is not to be found in information. Neither can wisdom depend on an idea, concept, theory, opinion, or belief because all of these things vary from individual to individual, theorist to theorist, profession to profession, culture to culture. Wisdom is not derived from the content of a frame of reference. Rather, the first step toward true wisdom involves the realization that other realities exist. Wisdom is the knowledge that beliefs and ideas are merely thoughts that can lock people into certain perceptions, feelings, and behaviors. Wisdom is a higher vantage point that is unobstructed by personal beliefs, attitudes, opinions, and biases. Wisdom is the intelligence of consciousness that exists before the creation of thought content. For this reason, wisdom cannot be taught to one person by another. It must be realized through the experience of insight. It is difficult, if not impossible, for one person to communicate insight to another person, because wisdom is not a thinking process. Wisdom is the spontaneous appearance of knowledge.

To understand wisdom, we can look at the two distinct approaches that people take in putting a jigsaw puzzle together. The more insecurity we have about completing the puzzle, the more we focus on the separate pieces of the puzzle and the more difficulty we have in putting the pieces together. When we lose sight of the overall picture we get lost in the parts. It is a simple case of not being able to see the forest for the trees. However, the moment that we relax and begin to enjoy the puzzle, the easier it becomes to see what pieces are out of place. As we begin to work, not so much with the separate pieces, but with the whole picture, our view becomes broader, more objective. As we find more missing pieces, the picture becomes more complete, and we are able to see each piece in relation to the whole picture. In states of wisdom, we have an objective clarity that guides us to see a bigger picture rather than to spend our time trying to figure out each piece. In an analogous way, wisdom helps us keep the details of life in perspective.

We ask our computer to do an impossible task when we ask it to tell us the meaning of life. The moment we see the futility of trying to use our thought system in this way, we cease to struggle, we relax, and our wisdom and common sense emerge naturally. We begin to know the experience of insight. It is insight that helps us realize facts about the workings of our thought systems, so we are able to see beyond our existing frames of reference. Insights show us how the conditioning process works. They show us what a thought is and what a belief is so that we are no longer at the mercy of perceptions resulting from beliefs and conditional thinking. Insights show us how we move from one belief system to another or, more to the point, how we move from one reality to another. Insights, similar to the ones that we used to learn a language when we were babies, show us the simplicity of life. Insights are a function of a higher level of consciousness, a level where we are guided by positive feeling and effortless knowing that allows us to live the lives that we want to have and to be successful and happy, regardless of the beliefs, opinions, or biases of the people around us.

By definition, an insight must be fresh, useful, and positive. An insight will never produce negativity or fear. Negativity is a sign that a person is responding to negative conditioning. Conditioning and insight are mutually exclusive and it is important to a person's mental health to be able to distinguish one from the other. A true insight will always show a better, more positive understanding than was previously seen. A true insight is a highlight, a purely pleasurable experience that increases our feelings of well-being and self-esteem. If a negative thought intrudes upon our awareness, bringing with it a feeling of repulsion, dread or fear, the negative feelings immediately tell us that we have tapped into conditioning from the past and are going in the opposite direction of our mental health.

A perfect example of an insight occurred in 1928. For nearly a century, researchers had been desperately searching for something that would kill the various kinds of bacteria that cause deadly infections. The scientific search for such a compound involved, among other things, growing colonies of the types of bacteria that were known to be pathogenic. One fateful day, while inspecting the cultures of bacteria growing in petri dishes, the director of a lab noticed that one of his dishes had been contaminated. Earlier that week he had opened that dish to extract some of the bacteria. When he did, some stray mold must have contaminated the bacterial colony. This was not an uncommon occurrence; it happened in all laboratories and all that a researcher could do was to contain his anger and frustration, discard the contaminated colony, and begin all over again. This particular researcher had experienced this same situation many times in his career. On this occasion, however, before discarding the dish as he was accustomed to doing, he held it up to the light and took another look at the green mold that had ruined his experiment. To his astonishment, he noted that for a considerable distance around the mold, the bacterial colony was undergoing lysis—something was dissolving the bacteria! The researcher, of course, was Alexander Fleming and the mold was penicillin. What had "ruined" this man's research was the answer he was seeking. One can only be grateful that on this one occasion, a human being took one look beyond his disappointment. So what began as a disaster, from the point of view of Fleming's conditioned thinking, ended up being one of the greatest scientific discoveries of the century.

While the above example shows how an insight can result in a breakthrough in the physical health of humanity, an insight can also assist an individual in attaining more mental health in everyday life, by shedding new light on his or her problems.

A person's conditioning might lead her to react negatively in a certain situation. Take, for example, a client named Ann, a teacher who had come to therapy because of job-related stress. On her way to therapy one day, Ann was caught in a rush hour traffic jam. As usual, she began to think the negative thoughts that were so familiar to her. She became tense, angry, and hostile toward other drivers. In her frustration, she began to honk her horn and make insulting comments to other drivers. All of a sudden, one of the drivers, a young man in the car next to hers, looked at her and said, "Lady, take it easy." Ann's initial reaction was to become enraged, but then she remembered where she was going. She realized she was late for a session where she hoped to find some peace of mind. Ann very quickly recognized that what she had been told by her therapist was not only applicable to the classroom, but also to her reality in her car. With this realization, Ann sat back, put some good music on her cassette player, and dropped all her thoughts of needing to hurry. She realized that if she was going to arrive late, she might as well arrive with her wellbeing intact. This was a turning point for Ann, who for the first time in her life began to see the difference between habit and insight. (As it turned out, Ann arrived 20 minutes late, but had to wait another 20 minutes, as her therapist was also stuck in traffic!)

The individual who experiences such an insight enters into a more positive reality than the one she lived in prior to the insight. What makes the examples of Alexander Fleming and Ann noteworthy is that both exemplify insight. So whether one achieves indirect relief through an insight of how to stop an infection or gains direct relief by realizing that one is inflicting oneself with negative thinking, the end result is the same: A new reality is found.

Adding the dimension of wisdom and insight to psychology is analogous to adding a third dimension to a two-dimensional geometry. It is a shift to a larger, more encompassing, more objective frame of reference. This broader frame of reference includes what was there before, and more. It gives a new meaning and significance to what was previously experienced.

Psychological Frames of Reference and Change

Before wisdom is realized, people live in their beliefs. A belief system is a psychological frame of reference that limits and distorts our vision of life, and leads to habitual behaviors. It is possible to make a horizontal shift within a frame of reference, which simply means moving from one belief system to another. A person's reality can be changed, to a new conditioned reality. This, of course, will change the pattern of behavior. It must be emphasized that this change is not to a new level of understanding reality, but is a shift at the same level to a different pattern. The process by which an individual is conditioned to a new set of beliefs without being aware of it is called a "conversion process." Such conversion processes do not involve any real change in the level of understanding, but are simply ways in which individuals transfer their insecurities from one thought pattern or set of beliefs to another.

If we look at conversion or reconditioning processes, we find that these processes always involve certain "commitment mechanisms" that ensure that people adhere to and identify with a particular ideology or belief system. In order to be converted to certain beliefs, people are subjected to initiations that involve highlighting their fears and inducing embarrassment, emotional catharsis, and emotional or physical exhaustion. These techniques are used to make people feel that they cannot have wellbeing or selfesteem without belonging to the group. These procedures foster a we/they mentality that excludes the rest of the world from their group. This intensifies the pressure to conform to the group's behavioral, moral, and attitudinal norms, or to face the insecurity of being rejected from the group. Conversions can never involve a shift to a higher level of understanding because this would obviate people attaching their well-being or security to a belief system.

On the other hand, there is another order of change, one that does not merely involve substituting one belief for another. This is the kind of shift that is involved in realizing wisdom or common sense. The shift to a psychological frame of reference of wisdom involves no conversion processing or reconditioning. This is a vertical shift that involves having an insight or realization about the existence and nature of the frames of reference of conditioned beliefs. When people have this realization, they move to a higher level or perspective where they are able to live outside of their conditioning. There is no need for individuals at these higher levels to attach themselves to any particular group, ideology, or movement, as they have little need to base their self-esteem or well-being on anything outside of themselves.

Moving from the psychological frame of reference created by a thought system to the frame of reference of wisdom is not a parallel movement across the same level, but a vertical transfer to a new level. This vertical shift can be compared to a change in understanding that happens in elementary school. In first grade, the teacher wanted us to learn the principle of addition. Since a principle cannot be articulated, the teacher presented us with example after example to show the result of the principle. At first, not knowing the principle of addition, we had no choice but to practice, drill, and memorize examples that were presented to us by the teacher. But at some point, we had an insight that showed us the comprehensive picture behind all the examples that the teacher had presented. From that moment on, we were able to add an endless variety of numbers, not from practice, but from a realization of the logical relationships involved in the problem. With this realization, we moved from a conditioned frame of reference to the larger, unconditioned frame of reference.

Learning the principle of addition is a recapitulation of learning to live life successfully. We are all taught to try to be loving, grateful, courteous, patient, fair, just, forgiving, understanding, and respectful of others. But how many people are successful at arriving at these correct answers when faced with the problems that they encounter in the course of their life? Very few. The reason for this is that these qualities are not techniques or causes, they are effects. They are the effects of living at a level of consciousness where one sees that every human being is acting according to the limits of his or her understanding. It is obvious that at any given moment, it is impossible for someone to be nonjudgmental, patient, loving, or forgiving if their level of consciousness is such that the reality they are feeling and perceiving is threatening, hurtful, harmful, or hostile. What few people realize is that all the positive attributes that people try so hard to live up to, as well as all those negative attributes which we try to suppress, are attributes of our level of consciousness rather than our beliefs. So the answer lies in raising one's level of consciousness above the level where we are constantly trying to be good by fighting off our negative desires. Figure 5 graphically depicts how our level of consciousness typically manifests itself. The upper half of this diagram denotes levels of consciousness where people see realities that are positive and thus elicit from them what most of us consider virtues, while the lower half denotes levels of consciousness where the realities that are perceived are more negative in nature and thus elicit all of humanity's shortcomings.

Insights are one of the natural outcomes of living in an unconditioned frame of reference. These insights give us working knowledge of the principles of thought, separate realities, levels of consciousness, and the role of feelings. As people advance through levels of consciousness, they learn to move through realities. True responsibility becomes a fact as individuals realize that the world is not what is really affecting them, but that they are, in fact, shaping their own experience in life through their own thinking. This is the beginning of wisdom, common sense, and mental health.

FIGURE 5: The Characteristics of Conditioned and Unconditioned Frames of Reference

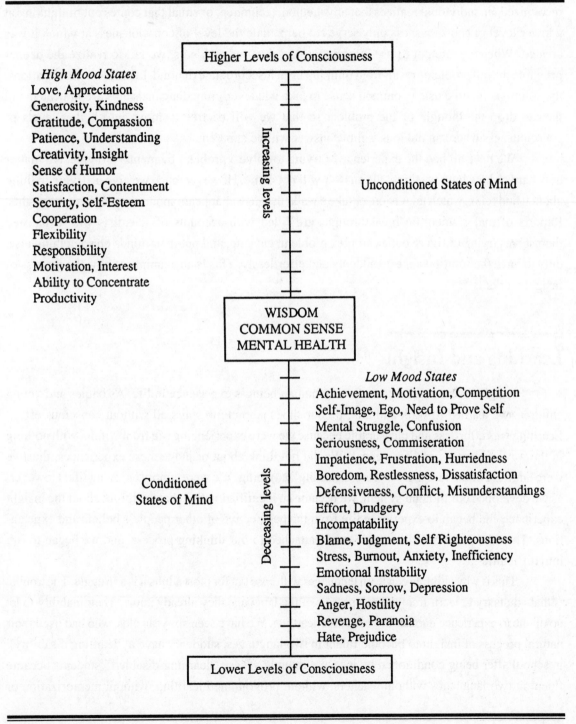

Higher Levels of Consciousness

High Mood States
Love, Appreciation
Generosity, Kindness
Gratitude, Compassion
Patience, Understanding
Creativity, Insight
Sense of Humor
Satisfaction, Contentment
Security, Self-Esteem
Cooperation
Flexibility
Responsibility
Motivation, Interest
Ability to Concentrate
Productivity

Increasing levels

Unconditioned States of Mind

WISDOM
COMMON SENSE
MENTAL HEALTH

Conditioned
States of Mind

Decreasing levels

Low Mood States
Achievement, Motivation, Competition
Self-Image, Ego, Need to Prove Self
Mental Struggle, Confusion
Seriousness, Commiseration
Impatience, Frustration, Hurriedness
Boredom, Restlessness, Dissatisfaction
Defensiveness, Conflict, Misunderstandings
Effort, Drudgery
Incompatability
Blame, Judgment, Self Righteousness
Stress, Burnout, Anxiety, Inefficiency
Emotional Instability
Sadness, Sorrow, Depression
Anger, Hostility
Revenge, Paranoia
Hate, Prejudice

Lower Levels of Consciousness

Wisdom, by the process of insight, reveals the futility of trying to solve a problem at the same level at which the problem was created by thought and perceived as reality. When this is recognized, an individual realizes that any method, technique, or ritual that comes out of thinking at a lower level of consciousness only serves to perpetuate the level of consciousness at which it was created. When we attempt to use information to solve our problems, we fail to realize the deeper principle that all problems result from thinking in an insecure state of mind. In problematic situations, the solutions involve using common sense to take whatever immediate measures are indicated and then to drop the thought of the problem so that we will be free to move into higher levels of consciousness where an obvious, simple answer will be apparent.

We have all had the experience of trying to solve a problem by mental struggle. No matter how hard or how long we think, the answer will not come. However, once we give up trying to think about it and relax, watch television, or take a walk, the answer appears spontaneously in our thoughts. Reports of major scientific breakthroughs are filled with accounts of scientists who exhausted themselves trying to figure out a complex problem, gave up, and put their minds on something else, only to have the solution appear suddenly and effortlessly. This is an example of how the process of insight works.

Learning and Insight

Insights are a natural part of every human being's experience in life. As babies and young children, we learned to walk and talk, tie our shoes, and climb stairs all without conscious effort. Learning was effortless and pleasurable because we were experiencing life from within, with nothing in the way of learning and enjoyment. We did not think about or judge these experiences; thus we were unaware of the fact that we were "learning" anything. We were simply enjoying life. However, as we developed our thought system, we became so identified with it that we forgot about the insight experience and began to experience life from the perspective of other people's beliefs and expectations. Then the process of learning became attached to our thinking process, and we began to run into difficulties.

This is why children can learn languages with ease but for most adults it is a struggle. The trouble is that adults try to learn from the perspective of the language they already know. Their inability to let go of one to experience another impedes their learning. We have seen six-year-olds, who had used their natural process of insight to become fluent in two languages, suddenly have a "learning disability" in school after being conditioned by insecure thought. These "learning-disabled" students became fluent in two languages without teachers, without programmed learning, without memorization or drill. Learning by insight, mastery of two languages was part of their play. But in the classroom, the function of insight is replaced by the memorization and utilization of information. When this happens, spontaneous learning is impede by compulsive thinking. We take the pleasure out of learning and make it difficult. From this point on, experiencing life from within—using insight—rather than from the thought system becomes the exception to the rule.

It takes some degree of courage to look at what we believe and to realize that much of what we believe to be true about how human beings function is based on misperceptions that have been handed down to us. But this realization must happen before we are willing to let go of the old to make way for something new. We have to be willing to do this before we can move into a larger realm of knowing that is not dependent on the stored information in our biological computer. Once we realize that there is more to life than what we think, our thought process softens, we become emotionally relaxed, and we discover new, positive feelings that indicate that we are in a state of mental health. These positive feelings bring us not only creativity, satisfaction, and happiness, but also a source of knowledge.

Wisdom has nothing to do with IQ scores or station in life. It has nothing to do with information or the ability to develop sophisticated or complex technology. In fact, many of our mental problems are a direct result of not being able to understand our own information and technologies. The deeper knowledge which we refer to as wisdom is not a thinking process. People who idolize their fixed forms of thinking will have difficulty accessing wisdom because thinking, and the insecurity that this thinking produces, is what actually obscures or denies the view within. When we return to the state of innocence of thought that we had as children, we will learn effortlessly, as we did then, all that is necessary for us to have happy, mentally healthy, and successful lives.

To date, very few individuals have even come close to understanding the words of the wise because the principle or essence of what the wise were trying to convey has been hidden by the separate reality of conditioned associations to the language they used—each using whatever words and terms were common to their culture. People have not been able to hear past language or culture. The link that has been missing is the psychological knowledge of thought, separate realities, levels of consciousness, and emotions. This knowledge is the necessary ingredient that begins to decipher the stories, parables, and statements of the wise. It allows the individual to listen beyond the cultural relativity of language to hear the universal wisdom behind the words. The beauty of wisdom, or true mental health, is that when any degree of wisdom is realized, one's level of sanity increases and one can never be as psychologically lost as before. Even more beautiful is the realization that no matter how wise one becomes, there is always more.

SELF-RELIANCE

Ralph Waldo Emerson

"Ne te quaesiveris extra."

Man is his own star; and the soul that can
Render an honest and a perfect man,
Commands all light, all influence, all fate;
Nothing to him falls early or too late.
Our acts our angels are, or good or ill,
Our fatal shadows that walk by us still.

Epilogue to Beaumont and Fletcher's Honest Man's Fortune.

Cast the bantling on the rocks,
Suckle him with the shewolf's teat,
Wintered with the hawk and fox,
Power and speed be hands and feet.

I read the other day some verses written by an eminent painter which were original and not conventional. The soul always hears an admonition in such lines, let the subject be what it may. The sentiment they instil is of more value than any thought they may contain. To believe your own thought, to believe that what is true for you in your private heart is true for all men — that is genius. Speak your latent conviction, and it shall be the universal sense; for the inmost in due time becomes the outmost, and our first thought is rendered back to us by the trumpets of the Last Judgment. Familiar as the voice of the mind is to each, the highest merit we ascribe to Moses, Plato and Milton is that they set at naught books and traditions, and spoke not what men, but what *they* thought. A man should learn to detect and watch that gleam of light which flashes across his mind from within, more than the lustre of the firmament of bards and sages. Yet he dismisses without notice his thought, because it is his. In every work of genius we recognize our own rejected thoughts; come back to us with a certain alienated majesty. Great works of art have no more affecting lesson for us than this. They teach us to abide by our spontaneous impression with good-humored inflexibility then most when the whole cry of voices is on the other side. Else tomorrow a stranger will say with masterly good sense precisely what we have thought and felt all the time, and we shall be forced to take with shame our own opinion from another.

There is a time in every man's education when he arrives at the conviction that envy is ignorance; that imitation is suicide; that he must take himself for better or worse as his portion; that though the wide universe is full of good, no kernel of nourishing corn can come to him but through his toil bestowed on that plot of ground which is given to him to till. The power which resides in him is new in nature, and none but he knows what that is which he can do, nor does he now until he has tried. Not for nothing one face, one character, one fact, makes much impression on him, and another none. This sculpture in the memory is not without preestablished harmony. The eye was placed where one ray should fall, that it might testify of that particular ray. We but half express ourselves, and are ashamed of that divine idea which each of us represents. It may be safely trusted as proportionate and of good issues, so it be faithfully imparted, but God will not have his work made manifest be cowards. A man is relieved and gay when he has put his heart into his work and done his best; but what he has said or done otherwise shall give him no peace. It is a deliverance which does not deliver. In the attempt his genius deserts him; no muse befriends; no invention, no hope.

Trust thyself: every heart vibrates to that iron string. Accept the place the divide providence has found for you, the society of your contemporaries, the connection of events. Great men have always done so, and confided themselves childlike to the genius of their age, betraying their perception that the absolutely trustworthy was seated at their heart, working through their hands, predominating in all their being. And we are now men, and must accept in the highest mind the same transcendent destiny; and not minors and invalids in a protected corner, not cowards fleeing before a revolution, but guides, redeemers and benefactors, obeying the Almighty effort and advancing on Chaos and the Dark.

What pretty oracles nature yields to us on this text in the face and behavior of children, babes, and even brutes! That divided and rebel mind, that distrust of a sentiment because our arithmetic has computed the strength and means opposed to our purpose, these have not. Their mind being whole, their eye is as yet unconquered; and when we look in their faces we are disconcerted. Infancy conforms to nobody; all conform to it; so that one babe commonly makes four or five out of the adults who prattle and play to it. So God has armed youth and puberty and manhood no less with its own piquancy and charm, and made it enviable and gracious and its claims not to be put by, if it will stand by itself. Do not think the youth has no force, because he cannot speak to you and me. Hark! in the next room his voice is sufficiently clear and emphatic. It seems he knows how to speak to his contemporaries. Bashful or bold then, he will know how to make us seniors very unnecessary.

The nonchalance of boys who are sure of a dinner, and would disdain as much as a lord to do or say aught to conciliate one, is the healthy attitude of human nature. A boy is in the parlor what the pit is in the playhouse; independent, irresponsible, looking out from his corner on such people and facts as pass by, he tries and sentences them on their merits, in the swift, summary way of boys, as good, bad, interesting, silly, eloquent, troublesome. He cumbers himself never about consequences, about interests; he gives an independent, genuine verdict. You must court him; he does not court you. But the man is as it were clapped into jail by his consciousness. As soon as he has once acted or spoken with *éclat* he is a committed person, watched by the sympathy or the hatred of hundreds, whose affections must now enter into his account. There is no Lethe for this. Ah, that he could pass again into his neutrality! Who can thus avoid all pledges and, having observed, observe again from the same unaffected, unbiased, unbribable, unaffrighted innocence—must always be formidable. He would utter opinions on all passing affairs, which being seen to be not private but necessary, would sink like darts into the ear of men and put them in fear.

These are the voices which we hear in solitude, but they grow faint and inaudible as we enter into the world. Society everywhere is in conspiracy against the manhood of every one of its members. Society is a joint-stock company, in which the members agree, for the better securing of his bread to each shareholder, to surrender the liberty and culture of the eater. The virtue in most request is conformity. Self-reliance is its aversion It loves not realities and creators, but names and customs.

Whoso would be a man, must be a nonconformist. He who would gather immortal palms must not be hindered by the name of goodness, but must explore if it be goodness. Nothing is at last sacred but the integrity of your own mind. Absolve you to yourself, and you shall have the suffrage of the world. I remember an answer which when quite young I was prompted to make to a valued adviser who was wont to importune me with the dear old doctrines of the church. On my saying, "What have I to do with the sacredness of traditions, if I live wholly from within?" my friend suggested—"But these impulses may be from below, not from above." I replied, "They do not seem to me to be such; but if I am the Devil's child, I will live then from the Devil." No law can be sacred to me but that of my nature. Good and bad are but names very readily transferable to that or this; the only right is what is after my constitution; the only wrong what is against it. A man is to carry himself in the presence of all opposition as if every thing were titular and ephemeral but he. I am ashamed to think how easily we capitulate to badges and names, to large societies and dead institutions. Every decent and well-spoken individual affects and sways me more than is right. I ought to go upright and vital, and speak the rude truth in all ways. If malice and vanity wear the coat of philanthropy, shall that pass? If an angry bigot assumes this bountiful cause of Abolition, and comes to me with his last news from Barbadoes, why should I not say to him, 'Go love thy infant; love thy wood-chopper; be good-natured and modest; have that grace; and never varnish your hard, uncharitable ambition with this incredible tenderness for black folk a thousand miles off. Thy love afar is spite at home.' Rough and graceless would be such greeting, but truth is handsomer than the affectation of love. Your goodness must have some edge to it else it is none. The doctrine of hatred must be preached, as the counteraction of the doctrine of love, when that pules and whines. I shun father and mother and wife and brother when my genius calls me. I would write on the lintels of the doorpost, *Whim*. I hope it is somewhat better than whim at last, but we cannot spend the day in explanation. Expect me not to show cause why I seek or why I exclude company. Then again, do not tell me, as a good man did today, of my obligation to put all poor men in good situations. Are they *my* poor? I tell thee, thou foolish philanthropist, that I grudge the dollar, the dime, the cent I give to such men as do not belong to me and to whom I do not belong. There is a class of persons to whom by all spiritual affinity I am bought and sold; for them I will go to prison if need be; but your miscellaneous popular charities; the education at college of fools; the building of meetinghouses to the vain end to which many now stand; alms to sots, and the thousand-fold Relief Societies; though I confess with shame I sometimes succumb and give the dollar, it is a wicked dollar, which by and by I shall have the manhood to withhold.

Virtues are, in the popular estimate, rather the exception than the rule. There is the man *and* his virtues. Men do what is called a good action, as some piece of courage or charity, much as they would pay a fine in expiation of daily nonappearance on parade. Their works are done as an apology or extenuation of their living in the world—as invalids and the insane pay a high board. Their virtues are penances. I do not wish to expiate, but to live. My life is for itself and not for a spectacle. I much prefer that it should be of a lower strain, so i be genuine and equal, than that it should be glittering and unsteady. I wish it to be sound and sweet, and not to need diet and bleeding. I ask primary evidence that you are a man, and refuse this appeal from the man to his actions. I know that for myself it makes no difference whether I do or forbear those actions which are reckoned excellent. I consent to pay for a privilege where I have intrinsic right. Few and mean as my gifts may be, I actually am, and do not need for my own assurance or the assurance of my fellows any secondary testimony.

What I must do is all that concerns me, not what the people think. This rule, equally arduous in actual and in intellectual life, may serve for the whole distinction between greatness and meanness.

It is the harder because you will always find those who think they know what is your duty better than you know it. It is easy in the world to live after the world's opinion; it is easy in solitude to live after our own; but the great man is he who in the midst of the crowd keeps with perfect sweetness the independence of solitude.

The objection to conforming to usages that have become dead to you is that it scatters your force. It loses your time and blurs the impression of your character. If you maintain a dead church, contribute to a dead Bible society, vote with a great party either for the government or against it, spread your table like base housekeepers—under all these screens I have difficulty to detect the precise man you are: and of course so much force is withdrawn from your proper life. But do your work, and I shall know you. Do your work, and you shall reinforce yourself. A man must consider what a blind-man's-bluff is this game of conformity. If I know your sect I anticipate your argument. I hear a preacher announce for his text and topic the expediency of one of the institutions of his church. Do I not know beforehand that not possibly can he say a new and spontaneous word? Do I not know that with all this ostentation of examining the grounds of the institution he will do no such thing? Do I not know that he is pledged to himself not to look but at one side, the permitted side, not as a man, but as a parish minister? He is a retained attorney, and these airs of the bench are the emptiest affectation. Well, most men have bound their eyes with one or another handkerchief, and attached themselves to some one of these communities of opinion. This conformity makes them not false in a few particulars, authors of a few lies, but false in all particulars. Their every truth is not quite true. Their two is not the real two, their four not the real four; so that every word they say chagrins us and we know not where to begin to set them right. Meantime nature is not slow to equip us in the prison uniform of the party to which we adhere. We come to wear one cut of face and figure, and acquire by degrees the gentlest asinine expression. There is a mortifying experience in particular, which does not fail to wreak itself also in the general history; I mean "the foolish face of praise," the forced smile which we put on in company where we do not feel at ease, in answer to conversation which does not interest us. The muscles, not spontaneously moved but moved by a low usurping willfulness, grow tight about the outline of the face, with the most disagreeable sensation.

For nonconformity the world whips you with its displeasure. And therefore a man must know how to estimate a sour face The bystanders look askance on him in the public street or in the friend's parlor. If this aversion had its origin in contempt and resistance like his own he might well go home with a sad countenance; but the sour faces of the multitude, like their sweet faces have no deep cause, but are put on and off as the wind blows and a newspaper directs. Yet is the discontent of the multitude more formidable than that of the senate and the college. It is easy enough for a firm man who knows the world to brook the rage of the cultivated classes. Their rage is decorous and prudent, for they are timid, as being very vulnerable themselves. But when to their feminine rage the indignation of the people is added, when the ignorant and the poor are aroused, when the unintelligent brute force that lies at the bottom of society is made to growl and mow, it needs the habit of magnanimity and religion to treat it godlike as a trifle of no concernment.

The other terror that scares us from self trust is our consistency; a reverence for our past act or word because the eyes of others have no other data for computing our orbit than our past acts, and we are loth to disappoint them.

But why should you keep your head over your shoulder? Why drag about this corpse of your memory, lest you contradict somewhat you have stated in this or that public place? Suppose you should contradict yourself; what then? It seems to be a rule of wisdom never to rely on your memory alone, scarcely even in acts of pure memory, but to bring the past for judgment into the thousand-eyed present, and live ever in a new day. In your metaphysics you have denied personality to the Deity, yet when the devout motions of the soul come, yield to them heart and life, though they should clothe God with shape and color. Leave your theory, as Joseph his coat in the hand of the harlot, and flee.

A foolish consistency is the hobgoblin of little minds, adored by little statesmen and philosophers and divines. With consistency a great soul has simply nothing to do. He may as well concern himself with his shadow on the wall. Speak what you think now in hard words and tomorrow speak what tomorrow thinks in hard words again, though it contradict every thing you said today. 'Ah, so you shall be sure to be misunderstood.' Is it so bad then to be misunderstood? Pythagoras was misunderstood, and Socrates, and Jesus, and Luther, and Copernicus, and Galileo, and Newton, and every pure and wise spirit that ever took flesh. To be great is to be misunderstood.

I suppose no man can violate his nature. All the sallies of his will are rounded in by the law of his being, as the inequalities of Andes and Himmaloh are insignificant in the curve of the sphere. Nor does it matter how you gauge and try him. A character is like an acrostic or Alexandrian stanza; read it forward, backward, or across, it still spells the same thing. In this pleasing contrite woodlife which God allows me, let me record day by day my honest thought without prospect or retrospect, and, I cannot doubt, it will be found symmetrical, though I mean it not and see it not. My book should smell of pines and resound with the hum of insects. The swallow over my window should interweave that thread or straw he carries in his bill into my web also. We pass for what we are. Character teaches above our wills. Men imagine that they communicate their virtue or vice only by overt actions, and do not see that virtue or vice emit a breath every moment.

There will be an agreement in whatever variety of actions, so they be each honest and natural in their hour. For of one will, the actions will be harmonious, however unlike they seem. These varieties are lost sight of at a little distance, at a little height of thought. One tendency unites them all. The voyage of the best ship is a zigzag line of a hundred tacks. See the line from a sufficient distance, and it straightens itself to the average tendency. Your genuine action will explain itself and will explain your other genuine actions. Your conformity explains nothing. Act singly, and what you have already done singly will justify you now. Greatness appeals to the future. If I can be firm enough today to do right and scorn eyes, I must have done so much right before as to defend me now. Be it how it will, do right now. Always scorn appearances and you always may. The force of character is cumulative. All the foregone days of virtue work their health into this. What makes the majesty of the heroes of the senate and the field, which so fills the imagination? The consciousness of a train of great days and victories behind. They shed a united light on the advancing actor. He is attended as by a visible escort of angels. This is it which throws thunder into Chatham's voice, and dignity into Washington's port, and America into Adam's eye. Honor is venerable to us because it is no ephemera. It is always ancient virtue.. We worship it today because it is not of today. We love it and pay it homage because it is not a trap for our love and homage, but is self-dependent, self derived, and therefore of an old immaculate pedigree, even if shown in a young person.

I hope in these days we have heard the last of conformity and consistency. Let the words be gazetted and ridiculous henceforward. Instead of the gong for dinner, let us hear a whistle from the Spartan fife. Let us never bow and apologize more. A great man is coming to eat at my house. I do not wish to please him; I wish that he should wish to please me. I will stand here for humanity, and though I would make it kind, I would make it true. Let us affront and reprimand the smooth mediocrity and squalid contentment of the times, and hurl in the face of custom and trade and office, the fact which is the upshot of all history, that there is a great responsible Thinker and Actor working wherever a man works; that a true man belongs to no other time or place, but is the centre of things. Where he is, there is nature. He measures you and all men and all events. Ordinarily every body in society reminds us of somewhat else, or of some other person. Character, reality, reminds you of nothing else; it takes place of the whole creation. The man must be so much that he must make all circumstances indifferent. Every true man is a cause, a country, and an age; requires infinite spaces and numbers and time fully to accomplish his design; and posterity seem to follow his steps as a train of clients. A man Caesar is born, and for ages after we have a Roman Empire. Christ is born, and millions of minds so grow and cleave to his genius that he is confounded with virtue and the possible of man. An institution is the lengthened shadow of one man; as, Monachism, of the Hermit Antony; the Reformation, of Luther; Quakerism, of Fox; Methodism, of Wesley; Abolition, of Clarkson. Scipio, Milton called "the height of Rome"; and all history resolves itself very easily into the biography of a few stout and earnest persons.

Let a man then know his worth, and keep things under his feet. Let him not peep or steal, or skulk up and down with the air of a charity boy, a bastard, or an interloper in the world which exists for him. But the man in the street, finding no worth in himself which corresponds to the force which built a tower or sculptured a marble god, feels poor when he looks on these. To him a palace, a statue, or a costly book have an alien and forbidding air, much like a gay equipage, and seem to say like that, "Who are you, Sir?" Yet they all are his, suitors for his notice, petitioners to his faculties that they will come out and take possession. The picture waits for my verdict; it is not to command me, but I am to settle its claims to praise. That popular fable of the sot who was picked up dead-drunk in the street, carried to the duke's house, washed and dressed and laid in the duke's bed, and, on his waking, treated with all obsequious ceremony like the duke, and assured that he had been insane, owes its popularity to the fact that it symbolizes so well the state of man, who is in the world a sort of sot, but now and then wakes up, exercises his reason and finds himself a true prince.

Our reading is mendicant and sycophantic. In history our imagination plays us false. Kingdom and lordship, power and estate, are a gaudier vocabulary than private John and Edward in a small house and common day's work; but the things of life are the same to both; the sum total of both is the same. Why all this deference to Alfred and Scanderbeg and Gustavus? Suppose they were virtuous; did they wear out virtue? As great a stake depends on your private act today as followed their public and renowned steps. When private men shall act with original views, the lustre will be transferred from the actions of kings to those of gentlemen.

The world has been instructed by its kings, who have so magnetized the eyes of nations. It has been taught by this colossal symbol the mutual reverence that is due from man to man. The joyful loyalty with which men have everywhere suffered the king, the noble, or the great proprietor to walk among them by a law of his own, make his own scale of men and things and reverse theirs, pay for benefits not with money but with honor, and represent the law in his person, was the hieroglyphic by which they obscurely signified their consciousness of their own right and comeliness, the right of every man.

The magnetism which all original action exerts is explained when we inquire the reason of self-trust. Who is the Trustee? What is the aboriginal Self, on which a universal reliance may be grounded? What is the nature and power of that science-baffling star, without parallax, without calculable elements, which shoots a ray of beauty even into trivial and impure actions, if the least mark of independence appear? The inquiry leads us to that source, at once the essence of genius, of virtue and of life, which we call Spontaneity or Instinct. We denote this primary wisdom as Intuition, whilst all later teachings are tuitions. In that deep force, the last fact behind which analysis cannot go, all things find their common origin. For the sense of being which in calm hours rises, we know not how, in the soul, is not diverse from things, from space, from light, from time, from man, but one with them and proceeds obviously from the same source whence their life and being also proceed. We first share the life by which things exist and afterwards see them as appearances in nature and forget that we have shared their cause. Here is the fountain of action and of thought. Here are the lungs of that inspiration which giveth man wisdom and which cannot be denied without impiety and atheism. We lie in the lap of immense intelligence, which makes us receivers of its truth and organs of its activity. When we discern justice, when we discern truth, we do nothing of ourselves, but allow a passage to its beams. If we ask whence this comes, if we seek to pry into the soul that causes, all philosophy is at fault. Its presence or its absence is all we can affirm. Every man discriminates between the voluntary acts of his mind and his involuntary perceptions, and knows that to his involuntary perceptions a perfect faith is due. He may err in the expression of them, but he knows that these things are so, like day and night, not to be disputed. My wilful actions and acquisitions are but roving; the idlest reverie, the faintest native emotion, command my curiosity and respect. Thoughtless people contradict as readily the statement of perceptions as of opinions, or rather much more readily; for they do not distinguish between perception and notion. They fancy that I choose to see this or that thing. But perception is not whimsical, but fatal. If I see a trait, my children will see it after me, and in course of time all mankind—although it may chance that no one has seen it before me. For my perception of it is as much a fact as the sun.

The relations of the soul to the divine spirit are so pure that it is profane to seek to interpose helps. It must be that when God speaketh he should communicate, not one thing, but all things; should fill the world with his voice; should scatter forth light, nature, time, souls, from the centre of the present thought; and new date and new create the whole. Whenever a mind is simple and receives a divine wisdom, old things pass away means, teachers, texts, temples fall; it lives now, and absorbs past and future into the present hour. All things are made sacred by relation to it one as much as another. All things are dissolved to their centre by their cause, and in the universal miracle petty and particular miracles disappear. If therefore a man claims to know and speak of God and carries you backward to the phraseology of some old mouldered nation in another country, in another world, believe him not. Is the acorn better than the oak to which is its fulness and completion? Is the parent better than the child into whom he has cast his ripened being? Whence then this worship of the past? The centuries are conspirators against the sanity and authority of the soul. Time and space are but physiological colors which the eye makes, but the soul is light: where it is, is day; where it was, is night; and history is an impertinence and an injury if it be any thing more than cheerful apologue or parable of my being and becoming.

Man is timid and apologetic; he is no longer upright; he dares not say 'I think,' 'I am,' but quotes some saint or sage. He is ashamed before the blade of grass or the blowing rose. These roses under my window make no reference to former roses or to better ones; they are for what they are; they exist with God today. There is no time to them. There is simply the rose; it is perfect in every moment of its existence. Before a leafbud has burst, its whole life acts; in the full-blown flower there is no more; in the leafless root there is no less. Its nature is satisfied and it satisfies nature in all moments alike. But man postpones or remembers; he does not live in the present, but with reverted eye laments the past, or, heedless of the riches that surround him, stands on tiptoe to foresee the future. He cannot be happy and strong until he too lives with nature in the present, above time.

This should be plain enough. Yet see what strong intellects dare not yet hear God himself unless he speak the phraseology of I know not what David, or Jeremiah, or Paul. We shall not always set so great a price on a few texts, on a few lives. We are like children who repeat by rote the sentences of grandames and tutors, and, as they grow older, of the men of talents and character they chance to see—painfully recollecting the exact words they spoke; afterwards, when they come into the point of view which those had who uttered these sayings, they understand them and are willing to let the words go; for at any time they can use words as good when occasion comes. If we live truly, we shall see truly. It is as easy for the strong man to be strong, as it is for the weak to be weak. When we have new perception, we shall gladly disburden the memory of its hoarded treasures as old rubbish. When a man lives with God, his voice shall be as sweet as the murmur of the brook and the rustle of the corn.

And now at last the highest truth on this subject remains unsaid; probably cannot be said; for all that we say is the far-off remembering of the intuition. That thought by what I can now nearest approach to say it, is this. When good is near you, when you have life in yourself, it is not by any known or accustomed way; you shall not discern the footprints of any other; you shall not see the face of man; you shall not hear any name; the way, the thought, the good, shall be wholly strange and new. It shall exclude example and experience. You take the way from man, not to man. All persons that ever existed are its forgotten ministers. Fear and hope are alike beneath it. There is somewhat low even in hope. In the hour of vision there is nothing that can be called gratitude, nor properly joy. The soul raised over passion beholds identity and eternal causation, perceives the self existence of Truth and Right, and calms itself with knowing that all things go well. Vast spaces of nature, the Atlantic Ocean, the South Sea; long intervals of time, years, centuries, are of no account. This which I think and feel underlay every former state of life and circumstances, as it does underlie my present, and what is called life and what is called death.

Life only avails, not the having lived. Power ceases in the instant of repose; it resides in the moment of transition from a past to a new state, in the shooting of the gulf, in the darting to an aim. This one fact the world hates; that the soul *becomes*; for that forever degrades the past, turns all riches to poverty, all reputation to a shame, confounds the saint with the rogue, shoves Jesus and Judas equally aside. Why then do we prate of self-reliance? Inasmuch as the soul is present there will be power not confident but agent. To talk of reliance is a poor external way of speaking. Speak rather of that which relies because it works and is. Who has more obedience than I masters me, though he should not raise his finger. Round him I must revolve by the gravitation of spirits. We fancy it rhetoric when we speak of eminent virtue. We do not yet see that virtue is Height, and that a man or a company of men, plastic and permeable to principles, by the law of nature must overpower and ride all cities, nations, kings, rich men, poets, who are not.

This is the ultimate fact which we so quickly reach on this as on every topic, the resolution of all into the ever-blessed ONE. Self-existence is the attribute of the Supreme Cause, and it constitutes the measure of good by the degree in which it enters into all lower forms. All things real are so by so much virtue as they contain. Commerce, husbandry, bunting, whaling, war eloquence, personal weight, are somewhat, and engage my respect as examples of its presence and impure action. I see the same law working in nature for conservation and growth. Power is, in nature, the essential measure of right. Nature suffers nothing to remain in her kingdoms which cannot help itself. The genesis and maturation of a planet, its poise and orbit, the bended tree recovering itself from the strong wind, the vital resources of every animal and vegetable, are demonstrations of the self sufficing and therefore self-relying soul.

Thus all concentrates: let us not rove; let us sit at home with the cause. Let us stun and astonish the intruding rabble of men and books and institutions by a simple declaration of the divine fact. Bid the invaders take the shoes from off their feet, for God is here within. Let our simplicity judge them, and our docility to our own law demonstrate the poverty of nature and fortune beside our native riches.

But now we are a mob. Man does not stand in awe of man, nor is his genius admonished to stay at home, to put itself in communication with the internal ocean, but it goes abroad to beg a cup of water of the urns of other men. We must go alone. I like the silent church before the service begins, better than any preaching. How far off, how cool, how chaste the persons look, begirt each one with a precinct or sanctuary! So let us always sit. Why should we assume the faults of our friend, or wife, or father, or child, because they sit around our hearth, or are said to have the same blood? All men have my blood and I all men's. Not for that will I adopt their petulance or folly, even to the extent of being ashamed of it. But your isolation must not be mechanical, but spiritual, that is, must be elevation. At times the whole world seems to be in conspiracy to importune you with emphatic trifles. Friend, client, child, sickness, fear, want, charity, all knock; at once at thy closet door and say—'Come out unto us.' But keep thy state; come not into their confusion. The power men possess to annoy me I give them by a weak curiosity. No man can come near me but through my act "What we love that we have, but by desire we bereave ourselves of the love."

If we cannot at once rise to the sanctities of obedience and faith, let us at least resist our temptations; let us enter into the state of war and wake Thor and Woden, courage and constancy, in our Saxon breasts. This is to be done in our smooth times by speaking the truth. Check this lying hospitality and lying affection. Live no longer to the expectation of these deceived and deceiving people with whom we converse. Say to them, 'O father, O mother, O wife, O brother, O friend, I have lived with you after appearances hitherto. Henceforward I am the truth's. Be it known unto you that henceforward I obey no law less than the eternal law. I will have no covenants but proximities. I shall endeavor to nourish my parents, to support my family, to be the chaste husband of one wife—but these relations I must fill after a new and unprecedented way. I appeal from your customs. I must be myself. I cannot break myself any longer for you, or you. If you can love me for what I am, we shall be the happier. If you cannot, I will still seek to deserve that you should. I will not hide my tastes or aversions. I will so trust that what is deep is holy, that I will do strongly before the sun and moon whatever inly rejoices me and the heart appoints. If you are noble, I will love you; if you are not, I will not hurt you and myself by hypocritical attentions. If you are true, but not in the same truth with me, cleave to your companions; I will seek my own. I do this not selfishly but humbly and truly. It is alike your interest, and mine, and all men's, however long we have dwelt in lies, to live in truth. Does this sound harsh today? You will soon love what is dictated by your nature as well as mine, and if we follow the truth it will bring us out safe at last.'—But so may you give these friends pain. Yes, but I cannot sell my liberty and my power, to save their sensibility. Besides, all persons have their moments of reason, when they look out into the region of absolute truth; then will they justify me and do the same thing.

The populace think that your rejection of popular standards is a rejection of all standard, and mere antinomianism; and the bold sensualist will use the name of philosophy to gild his crimes. But the law of consciousness abides. There are two confessionals, in one or the other of which we must be shriven. You may fulfil your round of duties by clearing yourself in the *direct*, or in the *reflex* way. Consider whether you have satisfied your relations to father, mother, cousin, neighbor, town, cat and dog—whether any of these can upbraid you. But I may also neglect this reflex standard and absolve me to myself. I have my own stern claims and perfect circle. It denies the name of duty to many offices that are called duties. But if I can discharge its debts it enables me to dispense with the popular code. If any one images that this law is lax, let him keep its commandment one day.

And truly it demands something godlike in him who has cast off the common motives of humanity and has ventured to trust himself for a taskmaster. High be his heart, faithful his will, clear his sight, that he may in good earnest be doctrine, society, law, to himself, that a simple purpose may be to him as strong as iron necessity is to others!

If any man consider the present aspects of what is called by distinction *society*, he will see the need of these ethics. The sinew and heart of man seem to be drawn out, and we are become timorous, desponding whimperers. We are afraid of truth, afraid of fortune, afraid of death, and afraid of each other. Our age yields no great and perfect persons. We want men and women who shall renovate life and our social state, but we see that most natures are insolvent, cannot satisfy their own wants, have an ambition out of all proportion to their practical force and do lean and beg day and night continually. Our housekeeping is mendicant, our arts, our occupations, our marriages, our religion we have not chosen, but society has chosen for us. We are parlor soldiers. We shun the rugged battle of fate, where strength is born.

If our young men miscarry in their first enterprises they lose all heart. If the young merchant fails, men say he is *ruined.* If the finest genius studies at one of our colleges and is not installed in an office within one year afterwards in the cities or suburbs of Boston or New York, it seems to his friends and to himself that he is right in being disheartened and in complaining the rest of his life. A sturdy lad from New Hampshire or Vermont, who in turn tries all the professions, who *teams it, farms it, peddles,* keeps a school, preaches, edits a newspaper, goes to Congress, buys a township, and so forth, in successive years, and always like a cat falls on his feet, is worth a hundred of these city dolls. He walks abreast with his days and feels no shame in not 'studying a profession,' for he does not postpone his life, but lives already. He has not one chance, but a hundred chances. Let a Stoic open the resources of man and tell men they are not leaning willows, but can and must detach themselves; that with the exercise of self-trust, new powers shall appear; that a man is the word made flesh, born to shed healing to the nations; that he should be ashamed of our compassion, and that the moment he acts from himself, tossing the laws, the books, idolatries and customs out of the window, we pity him no more but thank and revere him; and that teacher shall restore the life of man to splendor and make his name dear to all history.

It is easy to see that a greater self-reliance must work a revolution in all the offices and relations of men; in their religion; in their education; in their pursuits; their modes of living; their association; in their property; in their speculative views.

1. In what prayers do men allow themselves! That which they call a holy office is not so much as brave and manly. Prayer looks abroad and asks for some foreign addition to come through some foreign virtue, and loses itself in endless mazes of natural and supernatural, and mediatorial and miraculous. Prayer that craves a particular commodity, anything less than all good, is vicious. Prayer is the contemplation of the facts of life from the highest point of view. It is the soliloquy of a beholding and jubilant soul. It is the spirit of God pronouncing his works good. But prayer as a means to effect a private end is meanness and theft. It supposes dualism and not unity in nature and consciousness. As soon as the man is at one with God, he will not beg. He will then see prayer in all action. The prayer of the farmer kneeling in his field to weed it, the prayer of the rower kneeling with the stroke of his oar, are true prayers heard throughout nature, though for cheap ends. Caratach, in Fletcher's "Bonduca," when admonished to inquire the mind of the god Audate, replies—

> His hidden meaning lies in our endeavors;
> Our valors are our best gods.

Another sort of false prayers are our regrets. Discontent is the want of self-reliance: it is infirmity of will. Regret calamities if you can thereby help the sufferer; if not, attend your own work and already the evil begins to be repaired. Our sympathy is just as base. We come to them who weep foolishly and sit down and cry for company, instead of imparting to them truth and health in rough electric shocks, putting them once more in communication with their own reason. The secret of fortune is joy in our hands. Welcome evermore to gods and men is the self helping man. For him all doors are flung wide; him all tongues greet, all honors crown, all eyes follow with desire. Our love goes out to him and embraces him because he did not need it. We solicitously and apologetically caress and celebrate him because he held on his way and scorned our disapprobation. The gods love him because men hated him. "To the persevering mortal," said Zoroaster, "the blessed Immortals are swift."

As men's prayers are a disease of the will, so are their creeds a disease of the intellect. They say with those foolish Israelites, "Let not God speak to us, lest we die. Speak thou, speak any man with us, and we will obey." Everywhere I am hindered of meeting God in my brother, because he has shut his own temple doors and recites fables merely of his brother's, or his brother's God. Every new mind is a new classification. If it prove a mind of uncommon activity and power, a Locke, a Lavoisier, a Hutton, a Bentham, a Fourier, it imposes its classification on other men, and lo! a new system. In proportion to the depth of the thought, and so to the number of the objects it touches and brings within reach of the pupil, is his complacency. But chiefly is this apparent in creeds and churches, which are also classifications of some powerful mind acting on the elemental thought of duty and man's relation to the Highest. Such is Calvinism, Quakerism, Swedenborgism. The pupil takes the same delight in subordinating every thing to the new terminology as a girl who has just learned botany in seeing a new earth and new seasons thereby. It will happen for a time that the pupil will find his intellectual power has grown by the study of his master's mind. But in all unbalanced minds the classification is idolized, passes for the end and not for a speedily exhaustible means, so that the walls of the system blend to their eye in the remote horizon with the walls of the universe; the luminaries of heaven seem to them hung on the arch their master built. They cannot imagine how you aliens have any right to see how you can see; 'It must be somehow that you stole the light from us.' They do not yet perceive that light, unsystematic, indomitable, will break into any cabin, even into theirs. Let them chirp awhile and call it their own. If they are honest and do well, presently their neat new pinfold will be too strait and low, will crack, will lean, will rot and vanish, and the immortal light, all young and joyful, millionorbed, million colored, will beam over the universe as on the first morning.

2. It is for want of self culture that the superstition of Travelling, whose idols are Italy, England, Egypt, retains its fascination for all educated Americans. They who made England, Italy,

or Greece venerable in the imagination, did so by sticking fast where they were, like an axis of the earth. In manly hours we feel that duty is our place. The soul is no traveller; the wise man stays at home, and when his necessities, his duties, on any occasion call him from his house, or into foreign lands, he is at home still and shall make men sensible by the expression of his countenance that he goes, the missionary of wisdom and virtue, and visits cities and men like a sovereign and not like an interloper or a valet.

I have no churlish objection to the circumnavigation of the globe for the purposes of art, of study, and benevolence, so that the man is first domesticated, or does not go abroad with the hope of finding somewhat greater than he knows. He who travels to be amused, or to get somewhat which he does not carry, travels away from himself, and grows old even in youth among old things. In Thebes, in Palmyra, his will and mind have become old and dilapidated as they. He carries ruins to ruins.

Travelling is a fool's paradise. Our first journeys discover to us the indifference of places. At home I dream that at Naples at Rome, I can be intoxicated with beauty and lose my sadness. I pack my trunk, embrace my friends, embark on the sea and at last wake up in Naples, and there beside me is the stern fact, the sad self, unrelenting, identical, that I fled from. I seek the Vatican and the palaces. I affect to be intoxicated with sights and suggestions, but I am not intoxicated. My giant goes with me wherever I go.

3. But the rage of travelling is a symptom of a deeper unsoundness affecting the whole intellectual action. The intellect is a vagabond, and our system of education fosters restlessness. Our minds travel when our bodies are forced to stay at home. We imitate; and what is imitation but the travelling of the mind? Our houses are built with foreign taste; our shelves are garnished with foreign ornaments; our opinions, our tastes, our faculties, lean, and follow the Past and the Distant. The soul created the arts wherever they have flourished. It was in his own mind that the artist sought his model. It was an application of his own thought to the thing to be done and the conditions to be observed. And why need we copy the Doric or the Gothic model? Beauty, convenience, grandeur of thought and quaint expression are as near to us as to any, and if the American artist will study with hope and love the precise thing to be done by him, considering the climate, the soil, the length of the day, the wants of the people, the habit and form of the government, he will create a house in which all these will find themselves fitted, and taste and sentiment will be satisfied also.

Insist on yourself; never imitate. Your own gift you can present every moment with the cumulative force of a whole life's cultivation; but of the adopted talent of another you have only an extemporaneous half possession. That which each can do best, none but his Maker can teach him. No man yet knows what is, nor can, till that person has exhibited it. Where is the master who could have taught Shakespeare? Where is the master who could have instructed Franklin, or Washington, or Bacon, or Newton? Every great man is a unique. The Scipionism of Scipio is precisely that part he could not borrow. Shakespeare will never be made by the study of Shakespeare. Do that which is assigned to you, and you cannot hope too much or dare too much. There is at this moment for you an utterance brave and grand as that of the colossal chisel of Phidias, or trowel of the Egyptians, or the pen of Moses or Dante, but different from all these. Not possibly will the soul, all rich, all eloquent, with thousand-cloven tongue, deign to repeat itself; but if you can hear what these patriarchs say, surely you can reply to them in the same pitch of voice; for the ear and the tongue are two organs of one nature. Abide in the simple and noble regions of thy life, obey thy heart, and thou shalt reproduce the Foreworld again.

4. As our Religion, our Education, our Art look abroad, so does our spirit of society. All men plume themselves on the improvement of society, and no man improves.

Society never advances. It recedes as fast on one side as it gains on the other. It undergoes continual changes; it is barbarous, it is civilized, it is christianized, it is rich, it is scientific; but this change is not amelioration. For every thing that is given something is taken. Society acquires new arts and loses old instincts. What a contrast between the well-clad, reading, writing, thinking American, with a watch, a pencil and a bill of exchange in his pocket, and the naked New Zealander, whose property is a club, a spear, a mat and an undivided twentieth of a shed to sleep under! But compare the health of the two men and you shall see that the white man has lost his aboriginal strength. If the traveller tells us truly, strike the savage with a broad-axe and in a day or two the flesh shall unite and heal as if you struck the blow into soft pitch, and the same blow shall send the white to his grave.

The civilized man has built a coach, but has lost the use of his feet. He is supported on crutches, but lacks so much support of muscle. He has a fine Geneva watch, but he fails of the skill to tell the hour by the sun. A Greenwich nautical almanac he has, and so being sure of the information when he wants it, the man in the street does not know a star in the sky. The solstice he does not observe; the equinox he knows as little; and the whole bright calendar of the year is without a dial in his mind. His notebooks impair his memory; his libraries overload his wit; the insurance-office increases the number of accidents; and it may be a question whether machinery does not encumber; whether we have not lost by refinement some energy, by a Christianity, entrenched in establishments and forms, some vigor of wild virtue. For every Stoic was a Stoic; but in Christendom where is the Christian?

There is no more deviation in the moral standard than in the standard of height or bulk. No greater men are now than ever were. A singular equality may be observed between the great men of the first and of the last ages; nor can all the science, art, religion, and philosophy of the nineteenth century avail to educate greater men than Plutarch's heroes, three or four and twenty centuries ago.

Not in time is the race progressive. Phocion, Socrates, Anaxagoras, Diogenes, are great men, but they leave no class. He who is really of their class will not be called by their name, but will be his own man, and in his turn the founder of a sect. The arts and inventions of each period are only its costume and do not invigorate men. The harm of the improved machinery may compensate its good. Hudson and Behring accomplished so much in their fishing boats as to astonish Parry and Franklin, whose equipment exhausted the resources of science and art. Galileo, with an opera glass, discovered a more splendid series of celestial phenomena than any one since. Columbus found the New World in an undecked boat. It is curious to see the periodical disuse and perishing of means and machinery which were introduced with loud laudation a few years or centuries before. The great genius returns to essential man. We reckoned the improvements of the art of war among the triumphs of science, and yet Napoleon conquered Europe by the bivouac, which consisted of falling back on naked valor and disencumbering it of all aids. The Emperor held it impossible to make a perfect army, says Las Cases, "without abolishing our arms, magazines, commissaries and carriages, until, in imitation of the Roman custom, the soldier should receive his supply of corn, grind it in his hand-mill and bake his bread himself."

Society is a wave. The wave moves onward, but the water of which it is composed does not. The same particle does not rise from the valley to the ridge. Its unity is only phenomenal. The persons who make up a nation to-day, next year die, and their experience dies with them.

And so the reliance on Property, including the reliance on governments which protect it, is the want of self-reliance. Men have looked away from themselves and at things so long that they have come to esteem the religious, learned and civil institutions as guards of property, and they deprecate assaults on these, because they feel them to be assaults on property. They measure their esteem of each other by what each has, and not by what each is. But a cultivated man becomes ashamed of his property, out of new respect for his nature. Especially he a what he has if he see that is accidental—came to him by inheritance, or gift, or crime; then he feel that it is not having; it does not belong to him, has no root in him and merely lies there because no revolution or no robber takes it away. But which a man is, does always by necessity acquire; and the man acquires, is living property, which does not wait beck of rulers, or mobs, or revolutions, or fire, or storm, or bankruptcies, but perpetually renews itself wherever the man breathes. "Thy lot or portion of life," said the Caliph Ali, "is seeking after thee; therefore be at rest from seeking after it." Our dependence on these foreign goods leads us to our slavish respect for numbers. The political parties meet in numerous conventions; the greater the concourse and with each new uproar of announcement, The delegation from Essex! The Democrats from New Hampshire! The Whigs of Maine! the young patriot feels himself stronger than before by a new thousand of eyes and arms. In like manner the reformers summon conventions and vote and resolve in multitude. No so, O friends! will the God deign to enter and inhabit you, but by a method precisely the reverse. It is only as a man puts off all foreign support and stands alone that I see him to be strong and to prevail. He is weaker by every recruit to his banner. Is not a man better than a town? Ask nothing of men, and, in the endless mutation, thou only firm column must presently appear the upholder of all that surrounds thee. He who knows that power is inborn, that he is weak because he has looked for good out of him and elsewhere, and, so perceiving, throws himself unhesitatingly on his thought, instantly rights himself, stands in the erect position, commands his limbs, works miracles; just as a man who stands on his feet is stronger than a man who stands on his head.

So use all that is called Fortune. Most men gamble with her, and gain all, and lose all, as her wheel rolls. But do thou leave as unlawful these winnings, and deal with Cause and Effect, the chancellors of God. In the Will work and acquire, and thou hast chained the wheel of Chance, and shall sit hereafter out of fear from her rotations. A political victory, a rise of rents, the recovery of your sick or the return of your absent friend, or some other favorable event raises your spirits, and you think good days are preparing for you. Do not believe it. Nothing can bring you peace but yourself. Nothing can bring you peace but the triumph of principles.

INDIVIDUALISM: TRUE AND FALSE

Friedrich A. Hayek

Du dix-huitième siècle et de la révolution, comme d'une source
commune, étaient sortis deux fleuves: le premier conduisait les
hommes aux institutions libres, tandis que le second les menait
au pouvoir absolu.

—Alexis de Tocqueville

I

To advocate any clear-cut principles of social order is today an almost certain way to incur the stigma of being an unpractical doctrinaire. It has come to be regarded as the sign of the judicious mind that in social matters one does not adhere to fixed principles but decides each question "on its merits"; that one is generally guided by expediency and is ready to compromise between opposed views. Principles, however, have a way of asserting themselves even if they are not explicitly recognized but are only implied in particular decisions, or if they are present only as vague ideas of what is or is not being done. Thus it has come about that under the sign of "neither individualism nor socialism" we are in fact rapidly moving from a society of free individuals toward one of a completely collectivist character.

I propose not only to undertake to defend a general principle of social organization but shall also try to show that the aversion to general principles, and the preference for proceeding from particular instance to particular instance is the product of the movement which with the "inevitability of gradualness" leads us back from a social order resting on the general recognition of certain principles to a system in which order is created by direct commands.

After the experience of the last thirty years, there is perhaps not much need to emphasize that without principles we drift. The pragmatic attitude which has been dominant during that period, far from increasing our command over developments, has in fact led us to a state of affairs which nobody wanted; and the only result of our disregard of principles seems to be that we are governed by a logic of events which we are vainly attempting to ignore. The question now is not whether we need principles to guide us but rather whether there still exists a body of principles capable of general application which we could follow if we wished. Where can we still find a set of precepts which will give us definite guidance in the solution of the problems of our time? Is there anywhere a consistent philosophy to be found which supplies us not merely with the moral aims but with an adequate method for their achievement?

That religion itself does not give us definite guidance in these matters is shown by the efforts of the church to elaborate a complete social philosophy and by the entirely opposite results at which many arrive who start from the same Christian foundations. Though the declining influence of religion is undoubtedly one major cause or our present lack of intellectual and moral orientation, its revival would not much lessen the need for a generally accepted principle of social order. We still should require a political philosophy which goes beyond the fundamental but general precepts which religion or morals provide.

The title which I have chosen for this chapter shows that to me there still seems to exist such a philosophy—a set of principles which, indeed, is implicit in most of Western or Christian political tradition but which can no longer be unambiguously described by any readily understood term. It is therefore necessary to restate these principles fully before we can decide whether they can still serve us as practical guides.

The difficulty which we encounter is not merely the familiar fact that the current political terms are notoriously ambiguous or even that the same term often means nearly the opposite to different groups. There is the much more serious fact that the same word frequently appears to unite people who in fact believe in contradictory and irreconcilable ideals. Terms like "liberalism" or "democracy," "capitalism" or "socialism," today no longer stand for coherent systems of ideas. They have come to describe aggregations of quite heterogeneous principles and facts which historical accident has associated with these words but which have little in common beyond having been advocated at difficult times by the same people or even merely under the same name.

No political term has suffered worse in this respect than "individualism." It not only has been distorted by its opponents into an unrecognizable caricature—and we should always remember

---

that the political concepts which are today out of fashion are known to most of our contemporaries only through the picture drawn of them by their enemies—but has been used to describe several attitudes towards society which have as little in common among themselves as they have with those traditionally regarded as their opposites. Indeed, when in the preparation of this paper I examined some of the standard descriptions of "individualism," I almost began to regret that I had ever connected the ideals in which I believe with a term which has been so abused and so misunderstood. Yet, whatever "individualism" may have come to mean in addition to these ideals, there are two good reasons for retaining the term for the view I mean to defend: this view has always been known by that term, whatever else it may also have meant at different times, and the term has the distinction that the word "socialism" was deliberately coined to express its opposition to individualism.[1] It is with the system which forms the alternative to socialism that I shall be concerned.

II

Before I explain what I mean by true individualism, it may be useful if I give some indication of the intellectual tradition to which it belongs. The true individualism which I shall try to defend began its modern development with John Locke, and particularly with Bernard Mandeville and David Hume and achieved full stature for the first time in the work of Josiah Tucker, Adam Ferguson, and Adam Smith and in that of their great contemporary, Edmund Burke— the man whom Smith described as the only person he ever knew who thought on economic subjects exactly as he did without any previous communication having passed between them.[2] In the nineteenth century I find it represented most perfectly in the work of two of its greatest historians and political philosophers: Alexis de Tocqueville and Lord Acton. These two men seem to me to have more successfully developed what was best in the political philosophy of the Scottish philosophers, Burke, and the English Whigs than any other writers I know; while the classical economists of the nineteenth century, or at least the Benthamites or philosophical radicals among them, came increasingly under the influence of another kind of individualism of different origin.

This second and altogether different strand of thought, also known as individualism, is represented mainly by French and other Continental writers—a fact due, I believe, to the dominant role which Cartesian rationalism plays in its composition. The outstanding representatives of this tradition are the Encyclopedists, Rousseau, and the physiocrats; and, for reasons we shall presently consider, this rationalistic individualism always tends to develop into the opposite of individualism, namely, socialism or collectivism. It is because only the first kind of individualism is consistent that

I claim for it the name of true individualism, while the second kind must probably be regarded as a source of modern socialism as important as the properly collectivist theories.[3]

I can give no better illustration of the prevailing confusion about the meaning of individualism than the fact that the man who to me seems to be one of the greatest representatives of true individualism, Edmund Burke, is commonly (and rightly) represented as the main opponent of the so-called "individualism" of Rousseau, whose theories he feared would rapidly dissolve the commonwealth "into the dust and powder of individuality,"[4] and that the term "individualism" itself was first introduced into the English language through the translation of one of the works of another of the great representatives of true individualism, de Tocqueville, who uses it in his *Democracy in America* to describe an attitude which he deplores and rejects.[5] Yet there can no doubt that both Burke and de Tocqueville stand in all essentials close to Adam Smith, to whom nobody will deny the title of individualist, and that the "individualism" to which they are opposed is something altogether different from that of Smith.

III

What, then, are the essential characteristics of true individualism? The first thing that should be said is that it is primarily a *theory* of society, an attempt to understand the forces which determine the social life of man, and only in the second instance a set of political maxims derived from this view of society. This fact should by itself be sufficient to refute the silliest of the common misunderstandings: the belief that individualism postulates (or bases its arguments on the assumption of) the existence of isolated or self-contained individuals, instead of starting from men whose whole nature and character is determined by their existence in society.[6] If that were true, it would indeed have nothing to contribute to our understanding of society. But its basic contention is quite a different one; it is that there is no other way toward an understanding of social phenomena but through our understanding of individual actions directed toward other people and guided by their expected behavior.[7] This argument is directed primarily against the properly collectivist theories of society which pretend to be able directly to comprehend social wholes like society, etc., as entities *sui generis* which exist independently of the individuals which compose them. The next step in the individualistic analysis of society, however, is directed against the rationalistic pseudo-individualism which also leads to practical collectivism. It is the contention that, by tracing the combined effects of individual actions, we discover that many of the institutions on which human achievements rest have arisen and are functioning without a designing and directing mind; that, as Adam Ferguson expressed it, "nations stumble poll establishments, which are indeed the result of human action but not the result of human design";[8] and that the spontaneous collaboration of free men often creates things which are greater than their individual minds can ever fully comprehend. This is the great theme of Josiah Tucker and Adam Smith, of Adam Ferguson and Edmund Burke, the great discovery of classical political economy which has become the basis of our understnding not only of economic life but of most truly social phenomena.

The difference between this view, which accounts for most of order which we find in human affairs as the unforeseen result of individual actions, and the view which traces all discoverable order to deliberate design is the first great contrast between the true individualism of the British thinkers of the eighteenth century and the so-called "individualism" of the Cartesian school.[9] But it is merely one aspect of an even wider difference between a view which in general rates rather low the place which reason plays in human affairs, which contends that man has achieved what he has in spite of the fact that he is only partly guided by reason, and that his individual reason is very limited and imperfect, and a view which assumes that Reason, with a capital R, is always fully and equally available to all humans and that everything which man achieves is the direct result of, and therefore subject to, the control of individual reason. One might even say that the former is a product of an acute consciousness of the limitations of the individual mind which induces an attitude of humility toward the impersonal and anonymous social processes by which individuals help to create things greater than they know, while the latter is the product of an exaggerated belief in the powers of individual reason and of a consequent contempt for anything which has not been consciously designed by it or is not fully intelligible to it.

The antirationalistic approach, which regards man not as a highly rational and intelligent but as a very irrational and fallible being, whose individual errors are corrected only in the course of a social process, and which aims at making the best of a very imperfect material, is probably the most characteristic feature of English individualism. Its predominance in English thought seems to me due largely to the profound influence exercised by Bernard Mandeville, by whom the central idea was for the first time clearly formulated.[10]

I cannot better illustrate the contrast in which Cartesian or rationalistic "individualism" stands to this view than by quoting a famous passage from Part II of the *Discourse on Method*. Descartes argues that "there is seldom so much perfection in works composed of many separate parts, upon which different hands had been employed, as in those completed by a single master." He then goes on to suggest (after, significantly, quoting the instance of the engineer drawing up his plans) that "those nations which, starting from a semi-barbarous state and advancing to civilization by slow degrees, have had their laws successively determined, and, as it were, forced upon them simply by experience of the hurtfulness of particular crimes and disputes, would by this process come to be possessed of less perfect institutions than those which, from the commencement of their association as communities, have followed the appointment of some wise legislator." To drive this point home, Descartes adds that in his opinion "the past pre-eminence of Sparta was due not to the pre-eminence of each of its laws in particular . . . but to the circumstance that, originated by a single individual, they all tended to a single end."[11]

It would be interesting to trace further the development of this social contract individualism or the "design" theories of social institutions, from Descartes through Rousseau and the French Revolution down to what is still the characteristic attitude of the engineers to social problems.[12] Such a sketch would show how Cartesian rationalism has persistently proved a grave obstacle to an understanding of historical phenomena and that it is largely responsible for the belief in inevitable laws of historical development and the modern fatalism derived from this belief.[13]

All we are here concerned with, however, is that this view, though also known as "individualism," stands in complete contrast to true individualism on two decisive points. While it is perfectly true of this pseudo-individualism that "belief in spontaneous social products was logically impossible to any philosophers who regarded individual man as the starting point and supposed him to form societies by the union of his particular will with another in a formal contract,"[14] true individualism is the only theory which can claim to make the formation of spontaneous social products intelligible. And, while the design theories necessarily lead to the conclusion that social processes can be made to serve human ends only if they are subjected to the control of individual human reason, and thus lead directly to socialism, true individualism believes on the contrary that, if left free, men will often achieve more than individual human reason could design or foresee.

This contrast between the true, antirationalistic and the false, rationalistsic individualism permeates all social thought. But because both theories have become known by the same name, and partly because the classical economists of the nineteenth century, and particularly John Stuart Mill and Herbert Spencer, were almost as much influenced by the French as by the English tradition, all sorts of conceptions and assumptions completely alien to true individualism have come to be regarded as essential parts of its doctrine.

Perhaps the best illustration of the current misconceptions of the individualism of Adam Smith and his group is the common belief that they have invented the bogey of the "economic man" and that their conclusions are vitiated by their assumption of a strictly rational behavior or generally by a false rationalistic psychology. They were, of course, very far from assuming anything of the kind. It would be nearer the truth to say that in their view man was by nature lazy and indolent, improvident and wasteful, and that it was only by the force of circumstances that he could be made to behave economically or carefully to adjust his means to his ends. But even this would be unjust to the very complex and realistic view which these men took of human nature. Since it has become fashionable to deride smith and his contemporaries for their supposedly erroneous psychology, I may perhaps venture the opinion that for all practical purposes we can still learn more about the behavior of men from the *Wealth of Nations* than from most of the more pretentious modern treatises on "social psychology."

However that may be, the main point about which there can be little doubt is that Smith's chief concern was not so much with what man might occasionally achieve when he was at his best but that he should have as little opportunity as possible to do harm when he was at his worst. It would scarcely be too much to claim that the main merit of the individualism which he and his contemporaries advocated is that it is a system under which bad men can do least harm. It is a social system which does not depend for its functioning on our finding good men for running it, or on all men becoming better than they now are, but which makes use of men in all their given variety and complexity, sometimes good and sometimes bad, sometimes intelligent and more often stupid. Their aim was a system under which it should be possible to grant freedom to all, instead of restricting it, as their French contemporaries wished, to "the good and the wise."[15]

The chief concern of the great individualist writers was indeed to find a set of institutions by which man could be induced, by his own choice and from the motives which determined his ordinary conduct, to contribute as much as possible to the need of all others; and their discovery was that the system of private property did provide such inducements to a much greater extent than had yet been understood. They did not contend, however, that this system was incapable of further improvement and, still less, as another of the current distortions of their arguments will have it, that there existed a "natural harmony of interests" irrespective of the positive institutions. They were more than merely aware of the conflicts of individual interests and stressed the necessity of "well-constructed institutions" where the "rules and principles of contending interests and compromised advantages"[16] would reconcile conflicting interests without giving any one group power to make their views and interests always prevail over those of all others.

IV

There is one point in these basic psychological assumptions which it is necessary to consider somewhat more fully. As the belief that individualism approves and encourages human selfishness is one of the main reasons why so many people dislike it, and as the confusion which exists in this respect is caused by a real intellectual difficulty, we must carefully examine the meaning of the assumptions it makes. There can be no doubt, of course, that in the language of the great writers of the eighteenth century it was man's "self-love," or even his "selfish interests," which they represented as the "universal mover," and that by these terms they were referring primarily to a moral attitude, which they thought to be widely prevalent. These terms, however, did not mean egotism in the narrow sense of concern with only the immediate needs of one's proper person. The "self," for which alone people were supposed to care, did as a matter of course include their family and friends; and it would have made no difference to the anything if it had included anything for which people in fact did care.

Far more important than this moral attitude, which might be regarded as changeable, is an indisputable intellectual fact which nobody can hope to alter and which by itself is a sufficient basis for the conclusions which the individualist philosophers drew. This is the constitutional limitation of man's knowledge and interests, the fact that he *cannot* know more than a tiny part of the whole of society and that therefore all that can enter into his motives are the immediate effects which his actions will have in the sphere he knows. All the possible differences in men's moral attitudes amount to little, so far as their significance for social organization is concerned, compared with the fact that all man's mind can effectively comprehend are the facts of the narrow circle of which he is the center; that, whether he is completely selfish or the most perfect altruist, the human needs for which he *can* effectively care are an almost negligible fraction of the needs of all members of society. The real question therefore, is not whether man is, or ought to be, guided by selfish motives but whether we can allow him to be guided in his actions by those immediate consequences which he can know and care for or whether he ought to be made to do what seems appropriate to somebody else who is supposed to possess a fuller comprehension of the significance of these actions to society as a whole.

To the accepted Christian tradition that man must be free to follow *his* conscience in moral matters if his actions are to be of any merit, the economists added the further argument that he should be free to make full use of *his* knowledge and skill, that he must be allowed to be guided by his concern for the particular things of which *he* knows and for which *he* cares, if he is to make as great a contribution to the common purposes of society as he is capable of making. Their main problem was how these limited concerns, which did in fact determine people's actions, could be made effective inducements to cause them voluntarily to contribute as much as possible to needs which lay outside the range of their vision. What the economists understood for the first time was that the market as it had grown up was an effective way of making man take part in a process more complex and extended than he could comprehend and that it was through the market that he was made to contribute "to ends which were no part of his purpose."

It was almost inevitable that the classical writers in explaining their contention should use language which was bound to be misunderstood and that they thus earned the reputation of having extolled selfishness. We rapidly discover the reason when we try to restate the correct argument in simple language. If we put it concisely by saying that people are and ought to be guided in their actions by *their* interests and desires, this will at once be misunderstood or distorted into the false contention that they are or ought to be exclusively guided by their personal needs or selfish interests, while what we mean is that they ought to be allowed to strive for whatever *they* think desirable.

Another misleading phrase, used to stress an important point, is the famous presumption that each man knows his interests best. In this form the contention is neither plausible nor necessary for the individualist's conclusions. The true basis of his argument is that nobody can know *who* knows best and that the only way by which we can find out is through a social process in which everybody is allowed to try and see what he can do. The fundamental assumption, here as elsewhere, is the unlimited variety of human gifts and skills and the consequent ignorance of any single individual of most of what is known to all the other members of society taken together. Or, to put this fundamental contention differently, human Reason, with a capital *R*, does not exist in the singular, as given or available to any particular person, as the rationalist approach seems to assume, but must be conceived as an interpersonal process in which anyone's contribution is tested and corrected by others. This argument does not assume that all men are equal in their natural endowments and capacities but only that no man is qualified to pass final judgment on the capacities which another possesses or is to be allowed to exercise.

Here I may perhaps mention that only because men are in fact unequal can we treat them equally. If all men were completely equal in their gifts and inclinations, we should have to treat them differently in order to achieve any sort of social organization. Fortunately, they are not equal; and it is only owing to this that the differentiation of functions need not be determined by the arbitrary decision of some organizing will but that, after creating formal equality of the rules applying in the same manner to all, we can leave each individual to find his own level.

There is all the difference in the world between treating people equally and attempting to make them equal. While the first is the condition of a free society, the second means, as de Tocqueville described it, "a new form of servitude."[17]

V

From the awareness of the limitations of individual knowledge and from the fact that no person or small group of persons can know all that is known to somebody, individualism also derives its main practical conclusion: its demand for a strict limitation of all coercive or exclusive power. Its opposition, however, is directed only against the use of *coercion* to bring about organization or association, and not against association as such. Far from being opposed to voluntary association, the case of the individualist rests, on the contrary, on the contention that much of what in the opinion of many can be brought about only by conscious direction, can be better achieved by the voluntary and spontaneous collaboration of individuals. The consistent individualist ought therefore to be an enthusiast for voluntary collaboration—wherever and whenever it does not degenerate into coercion of others or lead to the assumption of exclusive powers.

True individualism is, of course, not anarchism, which is but another product of the rationalistic pseudo-individualism to which it is opposed. It does not deny the necessity of coercive power but wishes to limit it—to limit it to those fields where it is indispensable to prevent coercion by others and in order to reduce the total of coercion to a minimum. While all the individualist philosophers are probably agreed on this general formula, it must be admitted that they are not always very informative on its application in specific cases. Neither the much abused and much misunderstood phrase of "laissez faire" nor the still older formula of "the protection of life, liberty, and property" are of much help. In fact, in so far as both tend to suggest that we can just leave things as they are, they may be worse than no answer; they certainly do not tell us what are and what are not desirable or necessary fields of government activity. Yet the decision whether individualist philosophy can serve us as a practical guide must ultimately depend on whether it will enable us to distinguish between the agenda and the nonagenda of government.

Some general rules of this kind which are of very wide applicability seem to me to follow directly from the basic tenets of individualism: If each man is to use *his* peculiar knowledge and skill with the aim of furthering the aims for which *he* cares, and if, in so doing, he is to make as large a contribution as possible to needs which are beyond his ken, it is clearly necessary, first, that he should have a clearly delimited area of responsibility and, second, that the relative importance to him of the different results he can achieve must correspond to the relative importance to others of the more remote and to him unknown effects of his action.

Let us first take the problem of the determination of a sphere of responsibility and leave the second problem for later. If man is to remain free to make full use of his knowledge or skill, the delimination of spheres of responsibility must not take the form of an assignation to him of particular ends which he must try to achieve. This would be imposing a specific duty rather than delimiting a sphere of responsibility. Nor must it take the form of allocating to him specific resources selected by some authority, which would take the choice almost as much out of his hands as the imposition of specific tasks. If man is to exercise his own gifts, it must be as a result of his activities and planning that his sphere of responsibility is determined. The solution to this problem which men have gradually developed and which antedates government in the modern sense of the word is the acceptance of formal principles, "a standing rule to live by, common to every one of that society"[18]—of rules which, above all, enable man to distinguish between mine and thine, and from which he and his fellows can ascertain what is his and what is somebody else's sphere of responsibility.

The fundamental contrast between government by rules, whose main purpose is to inform the individual what is his sphere of responsibility within which he must shape his own life, and government by orders which impose specific duties has become so blurred in recent years that it is necessary to consider it a little further. It involves nothing less than the distinction between freedom under the law and the use of the legislative machinery, whether democratic or not, to abolish freedom. The essential point is not that there should be some kind of guiding principle behind the actions of the government but that government should be confined to making the individuals observe principles which they know and can take into account in *their* decisions. It means, further, that what the individual may or may not do, or what he can expect his fellows to do or not to do, must depend not on some remote and indirect consequences which his actions may have but on the immediate and readily recognizable circumstances which he can be supposed to know. He must have rules referring to typical situations, defined in terms of what can be known to the acting persons and without regard to the distant effects in the particular instance—rules which, if they are regularly observed, will in the majority of cases operate beneficially— even if they do not do so in the proverbial "hard cases which make bad law."

The most general principle on which an individualist system is based is that it uses the universal acceptance of general principles as the means to create order in social affairs. It is the opposite of such government by principles when, for example, a recent blueprint for a controlled economy suggests as "the fundamental principle of organization . . . that in any particular instance the means that serves society best should be the one that prevails."[19] It is a serious confusion thus to speak of principle when all that is meant is that no principle but only expediency should rule; when everything depends on what authority decrees to be "the interests of society." Principles are a means to prevent clashes between conflicting aims and not a set of fixed ends. Our submission to general principles is necessary because we cannot be guided in our practical action by full knowledge and evaluation of all the consequences. So long as men are not omniscient, the only way in which freedom can be given to the individual is by such general rules to delimit the sphere in which the decision is his. There can be no freedom if the government is not limited to particular kinds of action but can use its powers in any ways which serve particular ends. As Lord Acton pointed out long ago: "Whenever a single definite object is made the supreme end of the State, be it the advantage of a class, the safety or the power of the country, the greatest happiness of the greatest number or the support of any speculative idea, the State becomes for the time inevitably absolute."[20]

VI

But, if our main conclusion is that an individualist order must rest on the enforcement of abstract principles rather the on the enforcement of specific orders, this still leaves open the question of the kind of general rules which we want. It confines the exercise of coercive powers in the main to one method, but it still allows almost unlimited scope to human ingenuity in the designing of the most effective set of rules; and, though the best solutions of the concrete problems will in most instances have to be discovered by experience, there is a good deal more that we can learn from the general principles of individualism with regard to the desirable nature and contents of these rules. There is, in the first instance, one important corollary of what has already been said, namely, that the rules, because they are to serve as signposts to the individuals in making their own plans, should be designed to remain valid for long periods. Liberal or individualist policy must be essentially long-run policy; the present fashion to concentrate on short-run effects, and to justify this by the argument that "in the long run we are all dead," leads inevitably to the reliance on orders adjusted to the particular circumstances of the moment in the place of rules couched in terms of typical situations.

We need, and get from the basic principles of individualism, however, much more definite aid than this for the construction of a suitable legal system. The endeavor to make man by the pursuit of his interests contribute as much as possible to the needs of other men leads not merely to the general principle of "private property"; it also assists us in determining what the contents of property rights ought to be with respect to different kinds of things. In order that the individual in his decisions should take account of all the physical effects caused by these decisions, it is necessary that the "sphere of responsibility" of which I have been speaking be made to comprise as fully as possible all the direct effects which his actions have on the satisfactions which other people derive from the things under his control. This is achieved on the whole by the simple conception of property as the exclusive right to use a particular thing where mobile effects, or what the lawyer calls "chattels," are concerned. But it raises much more difficult problems in connection with land, where the recognition of the principle of private property helps us very little until we know precisely what rights and obligations ownership includes. And when we turn to such problems of more recent origin as the control of the air or of electric power, or of inventions and of literary or artistic creations, nothing short of going back to *rationale* of property will help us to decide what should be in the particular instance the sphere of control or responsibility of the individual.

I cannot here go further into the fascinating subject of a suitable legal framework for an effective individualist system or enter into discussion of the many supplementary functions, such as assistance in the spreading of information and in the elimination of genuinely avoidable uncertainty,[21] by which the government might greatly increase the efficiency of individual action. I mention them merely in order to stress that there are further (and noncoercive!) functions of government beyond the mere enforcement of civil and criminal law which can be fully justified on individualist principles.

There is still, however, one point left, to which I have already referred, but which is so important that I must give it further attention. It is that any workable individualist order must be so framed not only that the relative remunerations the individual can expect from the different uses of his abilities and resources correspond to the relative utility of the result of his efforts to others but also that these remunerations correspond to the objective results of his efforts rather than to their subjective merits. An effectively competitive market satisfies both these conditions. But it is in connection with the second that our personal sense of justice so frequently revolts against the impersonal decisions of the market. Yet, if the individual is to be free to choose it is inevitable that he should bear the risk attaching to that choice and that in consequence he be rewarded, not according to the goodness or badness of his intentions, but solely on the basis of the value of the results to others. We must face the fact that the preservation of individual freedom is incompatible with a full satisfaction of our views of distributive justice.

VII

While the theory of individualism has thus a definite contribution to make to the technique of constructing a suitable legal framework and of improving the institutions which have grown up spontaneously, its emphasis, of course, is on the fact that the part of our social order which can or ought to be made a conscious product of human reason is only a small part of all the forces of society. In other words, that the state, the embodiment of deliberately organized and consciously directed power, ought to be only a small part of the much richer organism which we call "society," and that the former ought to provide merely a framework within which free (and therefore not "consciously directed") collaboration of men has the maximum of scope.

This entails certain corollaries on which true individualism once more stands in sharp opposition to the false individualism of the rationalistic type. The first is that the organized state on the one side, and the individual on the other, far from being regarded as the only realities, while all the intermediate formations and associations are to be deliberately suppressed, as was the aim of the French Revolution, the noncompulsory conventions of social intercourse are considered as essential factors in preserving the orderly working of human society. The second is that the individual, in participating in the social processes, must be ready and willing to adjust himself to changes and to submit to conventions which are not the result of intelligent design, whose justification in the particular instance may not be recognizable, and which to him will often appear unintelligible and irrational.

I need not say much on the first point. That true individualism affirms the value of the family and all the common efforts of the small community and group, that it believes in local autonomy and voluntary associations, and that indeed its case rests largely on the contention that much for which the coercive action of the state is usually invoked can be done better by voluntary collaboration need not be stressed further. There can be no greater contrast to this than the false individualism which wants to dissolve all these smaller groups into atoms which have no cohesion other than the coercive rules imposed by the state, and which tries to make all social ties prescriptive, instead of using the state mainly as a protection of the individual against the arrogation of coercive powers by the smaller groups.

Quite as important for the functioning of an individualist society as these smaller groupings of men are the traditions and conventions which evolve in a free society and which, without being enforceable, establish flexible but normally observed rules that make the behavior of other people predictable in a high degree. The willingness to submit to such rules, not merely so long as one understands the reason for them but so long as one has no definite reasons to the contrary, is an essential condition for the gradual evolution and improvement of rules of social intercourse; and the readiness ordinarily to submit to the products of a social process which nobody has designed and the reasons for which nobody may understand is also an indispensable condition if it is to be possible to dispence with compulsion.[22] That the existence of common conventions and traditions among a group of people will enable them to work together smoothly and efficiently with much less formal organization and compulsion than a group without such common background, is, of course, a commonplace. But the reverse of this, while less familiar, is probably not less true: that coercion can probably only be kept to a minimum in a society where conventions and tradition have made the behavior of man to a large extent predictable.[23]

This brings me to my second point: the necessity, in any complex society in which the effects of anyone's action reach far beyond his possible range of vision, of the individual submitting to the anonymous society and seemingly irrational forces of society—a submission which must include not only the acceptance of rules of behavior as valid without examining what depends in the particular instance on their being observed but also a readiness to adjust himself to changes which may profoundly affect his fortunes and opportunities and the causes of which may be altogether unintelligible to him. It is against these that modern man tends to revolt unless their necessity can be shown to rest upon "reason made clear and demonstrable to every individual." Yet it is just here that the understandable craving for intelligibility produces illusory demands which no system can satisfy. Man in a complex society can have no choice but between adjusting himself to what to him must seem the blind forces of the social process and obeying the orders of a superior. So long as he knows only the hard discipline of the market, he may well think the direction by some other intelligent human brain preferable; but, when he tries it, he soon discovers that the former still leaves him at least some choice, while the latter leaves him none, and that it is better to have a choice between several unpleasant alternatives than being coerced into one.

The unwillingness to tolerate or respect any social forces which are not recognizable as the product of intelligent design, which is so important a cause of the present desire for comprehensive economic planning, is indeed only one aspect of a more general movement. We meet the same tendency in the field of morals and conventions, in the desire to substitute an artificial for the existing languages, and in the whole modern attitude toward processes which govern the growth of knowledge. The belief that only a synthetic system of morals, an artificial language, or even an artificial society can be justified in an age of science, as well as the increasing unwillingness to bow before any moral rules whose utility is not rationally demonstrated, or to conform with conventions whose rationale is not known, are all manifestations of the same basic view which wants all social activity to be recognizably part of a single coherent plan. They are the results of that same rationalistic "individualism" which wants to see in everything the product of conscious individual reason. They are certainly not, however, a result of true individualism and may even make the working of a free and truly individualistic system difficult or impossible. Indeed, the great lesson which the individualistic philosophy teaches us on this score is that, while it may not be difficult to destroy the spontaneous formations which are the indispensable bases of a free civilization, it may be beyond our power deliberately to reconstruct such a civilization once these foundations are destroyed.

VIII

The point I am trying to make is well illustrated by the apparent paradox that the Germans, though commonly regarded as very docile, are also often described as being particularly individualistic. With some truth this so-called German individualism is frequently represented as one of the causes why the Germans have never succeeded in developing free political institutions. In the rationalistic sense of the term, in their insistence on the development of "original" personalities which in every respect are the product of the conscious choice of the individual, the German intellectual tradition indeed favors a kind of "individualism" little known elsewhere. I remember well how surprised and even shocked I was myself when as a young student, on my first contact with English and American contemporaries, I discovered how much they were disposed to conform in all externals to common usage rather than, as seemed natural to me, to be proud to be different and original in most respects. If you doubt the significance of such an individual experience, you will find it fully confirmed in most German discussions of, for example, the English public school system, such as you will find in Dibelius'

well-known book on England.[24] Again and again you will find the same surprise about this tendency toward voluntary conformity and see it contrasted with the ambition of the young German to develop an "original personality," which in every respect expresses what he has come to regard as right and true. This cult of the distinct and different individuality has, of course, deep roots in the German intellectual tradition and, through the influence of some of its greatest exponents, especially Goethe and Wilhelm von Humboldt, has made itself felt far beyond Germany and is clearly seen in J. S. Mill's *Liberty*.

This sort of "individualism" not only has nothing to do with true individualism but may indeed prove a grave obstacle to the smooth working of an individualist system. It must remain an open question whether a free or individualistic society can be worked successfully if people are too "individualistic" in the false sense, if they are too unwilling voluntarily to conform to traditions and conventions, and if they refuse to recognize anything which is not consciously designed or which cannot be demonstrated as rational to every individual. It is at least understandable that the prevalence of this kind of "individualism" has often made people of good will despair of the possibility of achieving order in a free society and even made them ask for a dictatorial government with the power to impose on society the order which it will not produce itself.

In Germany, in particular, this preference for the deliberate organization and the corresponding contempt for the spontaneous and uncontrolled, was strongly supported by the tendency toward centralization which the struggle for national unity produced. In a country where what traditions it possessed were essentially local, the striving for unity implied a systematic opposition to almost everything which was a spontaneous growth and its consistent replacement by artificial creations. That, in what a recent historian has well described as a "desperate search for a tradition which they did not possess,"[25] the Germans should have ended by creating a totalitarian state which forced upon them what they felt they lacked should perhaps not have surprised us as much as it did.

IX

If it is true that the progressive tendency toward central control of all social processes is the inevitable result of an approach which insists that everything must be tidily planned and made to allow a recognizable order, it is also true that this tendency tends to create conditions in which nothing but an all-powerful central government can preserve order and stability. The concentration of all decisions in the hands of authority itself produces a state of affairs in which what structure society still possesses is imposed upon it by government and in which the individuals have become interchangeable units with no other definite or durable relations to one another than those determined by the all-comprehensive organization. In the jargon of the modern sociologists this type of society has come to be known as "mass society"—a somewhat misleading name, because the characteristic attributes of this kind of society are not so much the result of mere numbers as they are of the lack of any spontaneous structure other than that impressed upon it by deliberate organization, an incapacity to evolve its own differentiations, and a consequent dependence on a power which deliberately molds and shapes it. It is connected with numbers only in so far as in large nations the process of centralization will much sooner reach a point where deliberate organization from the top smothers those spontaneous formations which are founded on contacts closer and more intimate than those that can exist in the large unit.

It is not surprising that in the nineteenth century, when these tendencies first became clearly visible, the opposition to centralization became one of the main concerns of the individualist philosophers. This opposition is particularly marked in the writings of the two great historians whose names I have before singled out as the leading representatives of true individualism in the nineteenth century, de Tocqueville and Lord Acton; and it finds expression in their strong sympathies for the small countries and for the federal organization of large units. There is even more reason now to think that the small countries may before long become the last oases that will preserve a free society. It may already be too late to stop the fatal course of progressive centralization in the bigger countries which are well on the way to produce those mass societies in which despotism in the end comes to appear as the only salvation. Whether even the small countries will escape will depend on whether they keep free from the poison of nationalism, which is both an inducement to, and a result of, that same striving for a society which is consciously organized from the top.

The attitude of individualism to nationalism, which intellectually is but a twin brother of socialism, would deserve special discussion. Here I can only point out that the fundamental difference between what in the nineteenth century was regarded as liberalism in the English-speaking world and what was so called on the Continent is closely connected with their descent from true individualism and the false rationalistic individualism, respectively. It was only liberalism in the English sense that was generally opposed to centralization, to nationalism and to socialism, while the liberalism prevalent on the Continent favored all three. I should add, however, that, in this as in so many other respects, John Stuart Mill, and the later English liberalism derived from him, belong at least as much to the Continental as to the English tradition; and I know no discussion more illuminating of these basic differences than Lord Acton's criticism of the concessions Mill had made to the nationalistic tendencies of Continental liberalism.[26]

X

There are two more points of difference between the two kinds of individualism which are also best illustrated by the stand taken by Lord Acton and de Tocqueville by their views on democracy and equality toward trends which became prominent in their time. True individualism not only believes in democracy but can claim that democratic ideals spring from the basic principles of individualism. Yet, while individualism affirms that all government should be democratic, it has no superstitious belief in the omnicompetence of majority decisions, and in particular it refuses to admit that "absolute power may, by the hypothesis of popular origin, be as legitimate as constitutional freedom."[27] It believes that under a democracy, no less than under any other form of government, "the sphere of enforced command ought to be restricted within fixed limits";[28] and it is particularly opposed to the most fateful and dangerous of all current misconceptions of democracy—the belief that we must accept as true and binding for future developmental the views of the majority. While democracy is founded on the convention that the majority view decides on common action, it does not mean that what is today the majority view ought to become the generally accepted view—even if that were necessary to achieve the aims of the majority. On the contrary, the whole justification of democracy rests on the fact that in course of time what is today the view of a small minority may become the majority view. I believe, indeed, that one of the most important questions on which political theory will have to discover an answer in the near future is that of finding a line of demarcation between the fields in which the majority views must be binding for all and the fields in which on the contrary, the minority view ought to be allowed to prevail if it can produce results which better satisfy a demand of the public. I am, above all, convinced that, where the interests of a particular branch of trade are concerned, the majority view will always be the reactionary, stationary view and that the merit of competition is precisely that it gives the minority a chance to prevail. Where it can do so without any coercive powers, it ought always to have the right.

I cannot better sum up this attitude of true individualism toward democracy than by once more quoting Lord Acton: "The true democratic principle," he wrote, "that none shall have power over the people, is taken to mean that none shall be able to restrain or to elude its power. The true democratic principle, that the people shall not be made to do what it does not like, is taken to mean that it shall never be required to tolerate what it does not like. The true democratic principle, that every man's will shall be as unfettered as possible, is taken to mean that the free will of the collective people shall be fettered in nothing."[29]

When we turn to equality, however, it should be said at once that true individualism is not equalitarian in the modern sense of the word. It can see no reason for trying to make people equal as distinct from treating them equally. While individualism is profoundly opposed to all prescriptive privilege, to all protection, by law or force, of any rights not based on rules equally applicable to all persons, it also denies government the right to limit what the able or fortunate may achieve. It is equally opposed to any rigid limitation of the position individuals may achieve, whether this power is used to perpetuate inequality or to create equality. Its main principle is that no man or group of men should have power to decide what another man's status ought to be, and it regards this as a condition of freedom so essential that it must not be sacrificed to the gratification of our sense of justice or of our envy.

From the point of view of individualism there would not appear to exist even any justification for making all individuals start on the same level by preventing them from profiting by advantages which they have in no way earned, such as being born to parents who are more intelligent or more conscientious than the average. Here individualism is indeed less "individualistic" than socialism, because it recognizes the family as a legitimate unit as much as the individual; and the same is true with respect to other groups, such as linguistic or religious communities, which by their common efforts may succeed for long periods in preserving for their members material or moral standards different from those of the rest of the population. De Tocqueville and Lord Acton speak with one voice on this subject. "Democracy and socialism," de Tocqueville wrote, "have nothing in common but one word, equality. But notice the difference: while democracy seeks equality in liberty, socialism seeks equality in restraint and servitude."[30] And Acton joined him in believing that "the deepest cause which made the French revolution so disastrous to Liberty was its theory of equality"[31] and that "the finest opportunity ever given to the world was thrown away, because the passion for equality made vain the hope for freedom."[32]

XI

It would be possible to continue for a long time discussing further differences separating the two traditions of thought which, while bearing the same name, are divided by fundamentally opposed principles. But I must not allow myself to be diverted too far from my task of tracing to its source the confusion which has resulted from this and of showing that there is one consistent tradition which, whether you agree with me or not that it is "true" individualism, is at any rate the only kind of individualism which I am prepared to defend and, indeed, I believe, the only kind which can be defended consistently. So let me return, in conclusion, to what I said in the beginning: that the fundamental attitude of true individualism is one of humility toward the processes by which mankind has achieved things which have not been designed or understood by an individual and are indeed greater than individual minds. The great question at this moment is whether man's mind will be allowed to continue to grow as part of this process or whether human reason is to place itself in chains of its own making.

What individualism teaches us is that society is greater than the individual only in so far as it is free. In so far as it is controlled or directed, it is limited to the powers of the individual minds which control or direct it. If the presumption of the modern mind, which will not respect anything that is not consciously controlled by individual reason, does not learn in time where to stop, we may, as Edmund Burke warned us, "be well assured that everything about us will dwindle by degrees, until at length our concerns are shrunk to the dimensions of our minds."

Notes

1. Both the term "individualism" and the term "socialism" are originally the creation of the Saint-Simonians, the founders of modern socialism. They first coined the term "individualism" to describe the competitive society to which they were opposed and then invented the word "socialism" to describe the centrally planned society in which all activity was directed on the same principle that applied within a single factory. See on the origin of these terms the present author's article on "The Counter-Revolution of Science," *Economica*, VII (new ser., 1941), 146.

2. R. Bisset, *Life of Edmund Burke* (2d ed., 1800), 11, 429. Cf. also W. C. Dunn, "Adam Smith and Edmund Burke: Complimentary Contemporaries," *Southern Economic Journal* (University of North Carolina), Vol. VII, No. 3 (January, 1941).

3. Carl Menger, who was among the first in modern times consciously to revive the methodical individualism of Adam Smith and his school, was probably also the first to point out the connection between the design theory of social institutions and socialism. See his *Untersuchungen über die Methode der Sozialwissenschaften* (1883), esp. Book IV, chap.2, toward the end of which (p. 208) he speaks of "a pragmatism which, against the intention of its representatives, leads inevitably to socialism."

   It is significant that the physiocrats already were led from the rationalistic individualism from which they started, not only close to socialism (fully developed in their contemporary Morelly's *Le Code de la nature* [1755]), but to advocate the worst despotism. "L'État fait des hommes tout ce qu'il veut," wrote Bodeau.

4. Edmund Burke, *Reflections on the Revolution in France* (1790), in *Works* (World's Classics ed.), IV, 105: " Thus the commonwealth itself would, in a few generations, be disconnected into the dust and powder of individuality, and at length dispersed to all winds of heaven." That Burke (as A. M. Osborne points out in her book on *Rousseau and Burke* [Oxford, 1940], p. 23), after he had first attacked Rousseau for his extreme "individualism," later attacked him for his extreme collectivism was far from inconsistent but merely the result of the fact that in the case of Rousseau, as in that of all others, the rationalistic individualism which they preached inevitably led to collectivism.

5. Alexis de Tocqueville, *Democracy in America,* trans. Henry Reeve (London, 1864), Vol. II, Book II, chap. 2, where de Tocqueville defines individualism as "a mature and calm feeling, which disposes

each member of the community to sever himself from the mass of his fellows, and to draw apart with his family and friends; so that, after he has thus formed a little circle of his own, he willingly leaves society at large to itself." The translator in a note to this passage apologizes for introducing the French term "individualism" into English and explains that he knows "no English word exactly equivalent to the expression." As Albert Schatz pointed out in the book mentioned below, de Toc-queville's use of the well-established French term in this peculiar sense is entirely arbitrary and leads to serious confusion with the established meaning.

6.   In his excellent survey of the history of individualist theories the late Albert Schatz rightly concludes that "nous voyons tout d'abord avec évidence ce que l'individualisme n'est pas. C'est précisément ce qu'on croit communément qu'il est: un système d'isolèment dans l'estistence et une apologie de l'égoisme" (*L'Individualisme économique et social* [Paris 1907], p. 558). This book, to which I am much indebted, to be much more widely known as a contribution not only to the subject indicated by its title but to the history of economic theory in general.

7.   In this respect, as Karl Pribram has made clear, individualism is a necessary result of philosophical nomi-nalsim, while the collectivist theories have their roots in the "realist" or (as K. R. Popper now more appropriately calls it) "essentialist" tradition (Pribram, *Die Entstehung der individualistischen Sozial-philosophie* [Leipzig, 1912]) But this "nominalist" approach is characteristic only of true individual-ism while the false individualism of Rousseau and the physiocrats, in accordance with the Cartesian origin, is strongly "realist" or "essentialist."

8.   Adam Ferguson, *An Essay on the History of Civil Society* (1st ed., 1767), p. 187. Cf. also ibid.: "The forms of society are derived from an obscure and distant origin; they arise, long before the date of phi-losophy, from the instincts, not from the speculations of man.... We ascribe to a previous design, what came to be known only by experience, what no human wisdom could foresee, and what, without the concurring humour and disposition of his age, no authority could enable an individual to execute" (pp. 187 and 188).

It may be of interest to compare these passages with the similar statements in which Ferguson's contempo-raries expressed the same basic idea of the British economists:
 Josiah Tucker, *Elements of Commerce* (1756), reprinted in *Josiah Tucker: A Selection from His Economic and Political Writings*, ed. R. L. Schuyler (New York 1931), pp. 31 and 92: "The main point is neither to extinguish nor to enfeeble self-love, but to give it such a direction that it may pro-mote the public interest by promoting its own.... The proper design of this chapter is to show that the universal mover in human nature, self-love, may receive such a direction in this case (as in all others) as to promote the public interest by those efforts it shall make towards pursuing its own."

Adam Smith, *Wealth of Nations* (1776), ed. Cannan, I, 421: "By directing that industry in such a manner as its produce may be of the greatest value, he intends only his own gain, and he is in this, as in many other cases, led by an invisible hand to promote an end which was no part of his intention. Nor is it always the worse for the society that it was no part of it. By pursuing his own interest he frequently promotes that of the society more effectively than when he really intends to promote it." Cf. also *The Theory of Moral Sentiments* (1759), Part IV (9th ed., 1801), chap. i, p. 386.

Edmund Burke, *Thoughts and Details on Scarcity* (1795), in *Works* (World's classics ed.), VI, 9: "The benign and wise disposer of all things, who obliges men, whether they will or not, in pursuing their own selfish interests, to connect the general good with their own individual success."

After these statements have been held up for scorn and ridicule by the majority of writers for the last hundred years (C.E. Raven not long ago called the last-quoted statement by Burke a "sinister sentence"—see his *Christian Socialism* [1920], p. 34), it is interesting now to find one of the leading theorists of modern socialism adopting Adam Smith's conclusions. According to A. P. Lerner (*The Economics of Control* [New York, 1944], p. 67), the essential social utility of the price mechanism is that "if it is appropriately used it induces each member of society, while seeking his own benefit, to do that which is in the general social interest. Fundamentally this is the great discovery of Adam Smith and the Physiocrats."

9. Cf. Schatz, op. cit., pp 41- 42, 81, 378, 568-69, esp. the passage quoted by him (p. 41, n. 1) from an article by Albert Sorel ("Comment j'ai lu la 'Réforme sociale,' " in *Réforme sociale,* November 1, 1906, p. 614): "Quel que fut mon respect, assez commandé et indirect encore pour le *Discours de la methode,* je savais déja que de ce fameux discours il était sorti autant de déraison sociale et d'aberrations metaphysiques, d'abstractions et d'utopies, que de données positives, que s'il menait à Comte il avait aussie mené a Rousseau." On the influence of Descartes on Rousseau see further P. Janet, *Histoire de la science politique* (3d ed., 1887), p. 423; F. Bouillier, *Histoire de la philosophie cartésienne* (3d ed., 1868), p. 643 and H. Michel, *L'Idée de l'état* (3d ed., 1898), p. 68.

10. The decisive importance of Mandeville in the history of economics, long overlooked or appreciated only by a few authors (particularly Edwin Cannan and Albert Schatz), is now beginning to be recognized, thanks mainly to the magnificent edition of the *Fable of the Bees* which we owe to the late F. B. Kaye. Although the fundamental ideas of Mandeville's work are already implied in the original poem of 1705, the decisive elaboration and especially his full account of the origin of the division of labor, of money, and of language occur only in Part II of the *Fable* which was published in 1728 (see Bernard Mandeville, *The Fable of the Bees,* ed. F. B. Kaye [Oxford, 1924], II, 142, 287 - 88, 349 - 50). There is space here to quote only the crucial passage from his account of the development of the division of labor where he observes that "we often ascribe to the excellency of man's genius and the depth of his penetration, what is in reality owing to the length of time, and the experience of many generations, all of them very little differing from one another in natural parts and sagacity" (ibid., p. 142).

It has become usual to describe Giambattista Vico and his (usually wrongly quoted) formula, *homo non intelligendo fit omnia* (*Opere*, ed. G. Ferrari [2d ed.; Milan, 1854], V, 183), as the beginning of the antirationalistic theory of social phenomena, but it would appear that he has been both preceded and surpassed by Mandeville.

Perhaps it also deserves mention that not only Mandeville but also Adam Smith occupy honorable places in the development of the theory of language which in so many ways raises problems of a nature kindred to those of the other social sciences.

11. Réné Descartes, *A Discourse on Method* (Everyman's ed.), pp. 10 - 11.

12. On the characteristic approach of the engineer type of mind to economic phenomena compare the present author's study on "Scientism and the Study of Society," *Economica,* Vols. IX - Xl (new ser., 1942 - 44), esp Xl, 34 ff.

13. Since this lecture was first published I have become acquainted with an instructive article by Jerome Rosenthal on "Attitudes of Some Modern Rationalists to History (*Journal of the History of Ideas,* IV, No. 4, October 1943], 429-56), which shows in considerable detail the antihistorical attitude of Descartes and particularly his disciple Malebranche and gives interesting examples of the contempt expressed by Descartes in his *Recherche de la vérité par la lumière naturelle* for the study of history, languages, geography, and especially the classics.

14. James Bonar, *Philosophy and Political Economy* (1893), p. 85.

15. A. W. Benn, in his History of English Rationalism in the Nineteenth Century (1906), says rightly: "With Quesnay, following nature meant ascertaining by a study of the world about us and of its laws what conduct is most conducive to health and happiness; and the natural rights meant liberty to pursue the course so ascertained. Such liberty only belongs to the wise and good, and can only be granted to those whom the tutelary authority in the state is pleased to regard as such. With Adam Smith and his disciples, on the other hand, nature means the totality of impulses and instincts by which the individual members of society are animated; and their contentions is that the best arrangements result from giving free play to those forces in the confidence that partial failure will be more than compensated by successes elsewhere, and that the pursuit of his own interest by each will work out in the greatest happiness of all" (I, 289).

On this whole question see Elie Halevy, *The Growth of Philosophic Radicalism* (1928), esp. pp. 266 - 70.

The contrast of the Scottish philosophers of the eighteenth century with their French contemporaries is also brought out in Gladys Bryson's recent study on *Man and Society: The Scottish Enquiry of the Eighteenth Century* (Princeton, 1945), p. 145. She emphasizes that the Scottish philosophers "all wanted to break away from Cartesian rationalism, with its emphasis on abstract intellectualism and innate ideas," and repeatedly stresses the "anti-individualistic" tendencies of David Hume (pp. 106, 155)— using "individualistic" in what we call here the false, rationalistic sense. But she occasionally falls back into the common mistake of regarding them as "representative and typical of the thought of the century" (p. 176). There is still, largely as a result of an acceptance of the German conception of "the Enlightenment," too much inclination to regard the views of all the eighteenth-century philosophers as similar, whereas in many respects the differences between the English and the French philosophers of the period are much more important than the similarities. The common habit of lumping Adam Smith and Quesnay together, caused by the former belief that Smith was greatly indebted to the physiocrats, should certainly cease, now that this belief has been disproved by W. R. Scott's recent discoveries (see his *Adam Smith as Student and Professor* [Glasgow, 1937], p. 124). It is also significant that both Hume and Smith are reported to have been stimulated to their work by their opposition to Montesquieu.

Some suggestive discussion of the differences between the British and the French social philosophers of the eighteenth century, somewhat distorted, however, by the author's hostility toward the "economic liberalism" of the former, will be found in Rudolf Goldscheid, *Grundlinien zu einer Kritik der Willenskraft* (Vienna, 1905), pp. 32 - 37.

16. Edmund Burke, *Thoughts and Details on Scarcity* (1795), in *Works* (World's Classics ed.), VI, 15.

17. This phrase is used over and over again by de Tocqueville to describe the effects of socialism, but see particularly *Oeuvre complètes*, IX (1886), 541, where he says: "Si, en définitive, j'avais à trouver une formule générale pour exprimer ce que m'apparait le socialisme dans son ensemble, je dirais que c'est une nouvelle formule de la servitude." Perhaps I may be allowed to add that it was this phrase of de Tocqueville's which suggested to me the title of a recent book of mine.

18. John Locke, *Two Treatises of Government* (1690), Book II, chap. 4, §22: "Freedom of men under government is to have a standing rule to live by, common to every one of that society and made by the legislative power erected in it."

19. Lerner, op. cit., p. 5.

20. Lord Acton, "Nationality" (1862), reprinted in *The History of Freedom and Other Essays* (1907), p. 288.

21. The actions a government can expediently take to reduce really *avoidable* uncertainty for the individuals are a subject which has given rise to so many confusions that I am afraid to let the brief allusion to it in the text stand without some further explanation. The point is that, while it is easy to protect a particular person or group against the loss which might be caused by an unforeseen change, by preventing people from taking notice of the change after it has occurred, this merely shifts the loss onto other shoulders but does not prevent it. If, e.g., capital invested in very expensive plant is protected against obsolescence by new inventions by prohibiting the introduction of such new inventions, this increases the security of the owners of the existing plant but deprives the public of the benefit of the new inventions. Or, in other words, it does not really reduce uncertainty for society as a whole if we

make the behavior of the people more predictable by preventing them from adapting themselves to an unforeseen change in their knowledge of the world. The only genuine reduction of uncertainty consists in increasing its knowledge, but never in preventing people from making use of new knowledge.

22. The difference between the rationalistic and the true individualistic approach is well shown in the different views expressed by French observers on the apparent irrationality of English social institutions. While Henri de Saint-Simon, e.g., complains that "cent volumes *in folio*, de caractère plus fin, ne suffiraient pas pour rendre compte de toutes les inconséquences organiques qui existent en Angleterre" (*Oeuvres de Saint-Simon et d'Enfantin* [Paris, 1885 - 78], XXXVIII, 179), de Tocqueville retorts "que ces bizarreries des Anglais pussent avoir quelques rapports avec leurs libertés, c'est ce qui ne lui tombe point dans l'esprit" (*L'Ancien régime et la révolution* [7th ed.; Paris, 1866], p. 103).

23. Is it necessary to quote Edmund Burke once more to remind the reader how essential a condition for the possibility of a free society was to him the strength of moral rules? "Men are qualified for civil liberty," he wrote "in exact proportion to their disposition to put moral chains upon their own appetites; in proportion as their love of justice is above their rapacity; in proportion as their own soundness and sobriety of understanding is above their vanity and presumption; in proportion as they are more disposed to listen to the councils of the wise and good, in preference to the battery of knaves" (*A Letter to a Member of the National Assembly* [1791], in *Works* [World's Classics ed], IV, 319).

24. W. Dibelius, *England* (1923), pp. 464 - 68 of 1934 English translation.

25. E. Vermeil, *Germany's Three Reichs* (London, 1944), p. 224.

26. Lord Acton, "Nationality" (1862), reprinted in The History of Freedom, pp. 270 - 300.

27. Lord Acton, "Sir Erskine May's Democracy in Europe" (1878), reprinted in *The History of Freedom,* p. 78.

28. Lord Acton, *Lectures on Modern History* (1906), p. 10.

29. Lord Acton, "Sir Erskine May's Democracy in Europe," reprinted in *The History of Freedom*, pp. 93 - 94.

30. Alexis de Tocqueville, *Oeuvres complètes*, IX, 546.

31. Lord Acton, "Sir Erskine May's Democracy in Europe," reprinted in *The History of Freedom*, p. 88.

32. Lord Acton, "The History of Freedom in Christianity (1877), reprinted in *The History of Freedom,* p. 57.

COSMOS AND TAXIS

Friedrich A. Hayek

The man of system . . . seems to imagine that he can arrange the different members of a great society with as much ease as the hand arranges the different pieces upon a chessboard. He does not consider that the pieces upon the chessboard have no other principle of motion besides that which the hand impresses upon them; but that, in the great chessboard of human society, every single piece has a principle of motion of its own, altogether different from that which the legislature might choose to impress upon it. If those two principles coincide and act in the same direction, the game of human society will go on easily and harmoniously, and is very likely e opposite or different, the game will go on miserably a the highest degree of disorder.

—*Adam Smith**

The Concept of Order

The central concept around which the discussion of this book will turn is that of order, and particularly the distinction between two kinds of order which we will provisionally call 'made' and 'grown' orders. Order is an indispensable concept for the discussion of all complex phenomena, in which it must largely play the role the concept of law plays in the analysis of simpler phenomena.[1] There is no adequate term other than 'order' by which we can describe it, although 'system', 'structure' or 'pattern' may occasionally serve instead. The term 'order' has, of course, a long history in the social sciences,[2] but in recent times it has generally been avoided, largely because of the ambiguity of its meaning and its frequent association with authoritarian views. We cannot do without it, however, and shall have to guard against misinterpretation by sharply defining the general sense in which we shall employ it and then clearly distinguishing between the two different ways in which such order can originate.

By 'order' we shall throughout describe *a state of affairs in which a multiplicity of elements of various kinds are so related to each other that we may learn from our acquaintance with some spatial or temporal part of the whole to form correct expectations concerning the rest, or at least expectations which have a good chance of proving correct.*[3] It is clear that every society must in this sense possess an order and that such an order will often exist without having been deliberately created. As has been said by a distinguished social anthropologist, 'that there is some order, consistency and constancy in social life, is obvious. If there were not, none of us would be able to go about our affairs or satisfy our most elementary needs.'[4]

Living as members of society and dependent for the satisfaction of most of our needs on various forms of cooperation with others, we depend for the effective pursuit of our aims clearly on the correspondence of the expectations concerning the actions of others on which our plans are based with what they will really do. This matching of the intentions and expectations that determine the actions of different individuals is the form in which order manifests itself in social life; and it will be the question of how such an order does come about that will be our immediate concern. The first answer to which our anthropomorphic habits of thought almost inevitably lead us is that it must be due to the design of some thinking mind.[5] And because order has been generally interpreted as such a deliberate *arrangement* by somebody, the concept has become unpopular among most friends of liberty and has been favored mainly by authoritarians. According to this interpretation order in society must rest on a relation of command and obedience, or a hierarchical structure of the whole of society in which the will of superiors, and ultimately of some single supreme authority, determines what each individual must do.

This authoritarian connotation of the concept of order derives, however, entirely from the belief that order can be created only by forces outside the system (or 'exogenously'). It does not apply to an equilibrium set up from within[6] (or 'endogenously') such as that which the general theory of the market endeavours to explain. A spontaneous order of this kind has in many respects properties different from those of a made order.

The Two Sources of Order

The study of spontaneous orders has long been the peculiar task of economic theory, although, of course, biology has from its beginning been concerned with that special kind of spontaneous order which we call an organism. Only recently has there arisen within the physical sciences under the name of cybernetics a special discipline which is also concerned with what are called self-organizing or self-generating systems.[7]

The distinction of this kind of order from one which has been made by somebody putting the elements of a set in their places or directing their movements is indispensable for any understanding of the processes of society as well as for all social policy. There are several terms available for describing each kind of order. The made order which we have already referred to as an exogenous order or an arrangement may again be described as a construction, an artificial order or, especially where we have to deal with a directed social order, as an *organization*. The grown order, on the other hand, which we have referred to as a self-generating or endogenous order, is in English most conveniently described as a *spontaneous order*. Classical Greek was more fortunate in possessing distinct single words for the two kinds of order, namely *taxis* for a made order, such as, for example, an order of battle,[8] and *kosmos* for a grown order, meaning originally 'a right order in a state or a community'.[9] We shall occasionally avail ourselves of these Greek words as technical terms to describe the two kinds of order.

It would be no exaggeration to say that social theory begins with—and has an object only because of—the discovery that there exist orderly structures which are the product of the action of many men but are not the result of human design. In some fields this is now universally accepted. Although there was a time when men believed that even language and morals had been ''invented' by some genius of the past, everybody recognizes now that they are the outcome of a process of evolution whose results nobody foresaw or designed. But in other fields many people still treat with suspicion the claim that the patterns of interaction of many men can show an order that is of nobody's deliberate making; in the economic sphere, in particular, critics still pour uncomprehending ridicule on Adam Smith's expression of the 'invisible hand' by which, in the language of his time, he described how man is led 'to promote an end which was no part of his intentions'.[10] If indignant reformers still complain of the chaos of economic affairs, insinuating a complete absence of order, this is partly because they cannot conceive of an order which is not deliberately made, and partly because to them an order means something aiming at concrete purposes which is, as we shall see, what a spontaneous order cannot do.

We shall examine later (see volume 2, chapter 10) how that coincidence of expectations and plans is produced which characterizes the market order and the nature of the benefits we derive from it. For the moment we are concerned only with the fact that an order not made by man does exist and with the reasons why this is not more readily recognized. The main reason is that such orders as that of the market do not obtrude themselves on our senses but have to be traced by our intellect. We cannot see, or otherwise intuitively perceive, this order of meaningful actions, but are only able mentally to reconstruct it by tracing the relations that exist between the elements. We shall describe this feature by saying that it is an abstract and not a concrete order.

The Distinguishing Properties of Spontaneous Orders

One effect of our habitually identifying order with a made order or *taxis* is indeed that we tend to ascribe to all order certain properties which deliberate arrangements regularly, and with respect to some of these properties necessarily, possess. Such orders are relatively *simple* or at least necessarily confined to such moderate degrees of complexity as the maker can still survey; they are usually *concrete* in the sense just mentioned that their existence can be intuitively perceived by inspection; and, finally, having been made deliberately, they invariably do (or at one time did) *serve a purpose* of the maker. None of these characteristics necessarily belong to a spontaneous order or *kosmos*. Its degree of complexity is not limited to what a human mind can master. Its existence need not manifest itself to our senses but may be based on purely *abstract* relations which we can only mentally reconstruct. And not having been made it *cannot* legitimately be said to *have a particular purpose,* although our awareness of its existence may be extremely important for our successful pursuit of a great variety of different purposes.

Spontaneous orders are not necessarily complex, but unlike deliberate human arrangements, they may achieve any degree of complexity. One of our main contentions will be that very complex orders, comprising more particular facts than any brain could ascertain or manipulate, can be brought about only through forces inducing the formation of spontaneous orders.

Spontaneous orders need not be what we have called abstract, but they will often consist of a system of abstract relations between elements which are also defined only by abstract properties, and for this reason will not be intuitively perceivable and not recognizable except on the basis of a theory accounting for their character. The significance of the abstract character of such orders rests on the fact that they may persist while all the particular elements they comprise, and even the number of such elements, change. All that is necessary to preserve such an abstract order is that a certain structure of relationships be maintained, or that elements of a certain kind (but variable in number) continue to be related in a certain manner.

Most important, however, is the relation of a spontaneous order to the conception of purpose. Since such an order has not been created by an outside agency, the order as such also can have no purpose, although its existence may be very serviceable to the individuals which move within such order. But in a different sense it may well be said that the order rests on purposive action of its elements, when 'purpose' would, of course, mean nothing more than that their actions tend to secure the preservation or restoration of that order. The use of 'purposive' in this sense as a sort of 'teleological shorthand', as it has been called by biologists, is unobjectionable so long as we do not imply an awareness of purpose of the part of the elements, but mean merely that the elements have acquired regularities of conduct conducive to the maintenance of the order—presumably because those who did act in certain ways had within the resulting order a better chance of survival than those who did not. In general, however, it is preferable to avoid in this connection the term 'purpose' and to speak instead of 'function'.

Spontaneous Orders in Nature

It will be instructive to consider briefly the character of some spontaneous orders which we find in nature, since here some of their characteristic properties stand out most clearly. There are in the physical world many instances of complex orders which we could bring about only by availing ourselves of the known forces which tend to lead to their formation, and never by deliberately placing each element in the appropriate position. We can never produce a crystal or a complex organic compound by placing the individual atoms in such a position that they will form the lattice of a crystal or the system based on benzol rings which make up an organic compound. But we can create the conditions in which they will arrange themselves in such a manner.

What does in these instances determine not only the general character of the crystal or compound that will be formed but also the particular position of any one element in them? The important point is that the regularity of the conduct of the elements will determine the general character of the resulting order but not all the detail of its particular manifestation. The particular manner in which the resulting abstract order will manifest itself will depend, in addition to the rules which govern the actions of the elements, on their initial position and on all the particular circumstances of the immediate environment to which each of them will react in the course of the formation of that order. The order, in other words, will always be an adaptation to a large number of particular facts which will not be known in their totality to anyone.

We should note that a regular pattern will thus form itself not only if the elements all obey the same rules and their different actions are determined only by the different positions of the several individuals relatively to each other, but also, as is true in the case of the chemical compound, if there are different kinds of elements which act in part according to different rules. Whichever is the case, we shall be able to predict only the general character of the order that will form itself, and not the particular position which any particular element will occupy relatively to any other element.

Another example from physics is in some respects even more instructive. In the familiar school experiment in which iron filings on a sheet of paper are made to arrange themselves along some of the lines of force of a magnet placed below, we can predict the general shape of the chains that will be formed by the filings hooking themselves together; but we cannot predict along which ones of the family of an infinite number of such curves that define the magnetic field these chains will place themselves. This will depend on the position, direction, weight, roughness or smoothness of each of the iron filings and on all the irregularities of the surface of the paper. The forces emanating from the magnet and from each of the iron filings will thus interact with the environment to produce a unique instance of a general pattern, the general character of which will be determined by known laws, but the concrete appearance of which will depend on particular circumstances we cannot fully ascertain.

In Society, Reliance on Spontaneous Order Both Extends and Limits Our Powers of Control

Since a spontaneous order results from the individual elements adapting themselves to circumstances which directly affect only some of them, and which in their totality need not be known to anyone, it may extend to circumstances so complex that no mind can comprehend them all. Consequently, the concept becomes particularly important when we turn from mechanical to such 'more highly organized' or essentially complex phenomena as we encounter in the realms of life, mind and society. Here we have to deal with 'grown' structures with a degree of complexity which they have assumed and could assume only because they were produced by spontaneous ordering forces. They in consequence present us with peculiar difficulties in our effort to explain them as well as in any attempt to influence their character. Since we can know at most the rules observed by the elements of various kinds of which the structures are made up, but not all the individual elements and never all the particular circumstances in which each of them is placed, our knowledge will be restricted to the general character of the order which will form itself. And even where, as is true of a society of human beings, we may be in a position to alter at least some of the rules of conduct which the elements obey, we shall thereby be able to influence only the general character and not the detail of the resulting order.

This means that, though the use of spontaneous ordering forces enables us to induce the formation of an order of such a degree of complexity (namely comprising elements of such numbers, diversity and variety of conditions) as we could never master intellectually, or deliberately arrange, we will have less power over the details of such an order than we would of one which we produce by arrangement. In the case of spontaneous orders we may, by determining some of the factors which shape them, determine their abstract features, but we will have to leave the particulars to circumstances which we do not know. Thus, by relying on the spontaneously ordering forces, we can extend the scope or range of the order which we may induce to form, precisely because its particular manifestation will depend on many more circumstances than can be known to us—and in the case of a social order, because such an order will utilize the separate knowledge of all its several members, without this knowledge ever being concentrated in a single mind, or being subject to those processes of deliberate coordination and adaptation which a mind performs.

In consequence, the degree of power of control over the extended and more complex order will be much smaller than that which we could exercise over a made order or *taxis*. There will be many aspects of it over which we will possess no control at all, or which at least we shall not be able to alter without interfering with—and to that extent impeding—the forces producing the spontaneous order. Any desire we may have concerning the particular position of individual elements, or the relation between particular individuals or groups, could not be satisfied without upsetting the overall order. The kind of power which in this respect we would possess over a concrete arrangement or *taxis* we would not have over a spontaneous order where we would know, and be able to influence, only the abstract aspects.

It is important to note here that there are two different respects in which order may be a matter of degree. How well ordered a set of objects or events is depends on how many of the attributes of (or the relations between) the elements we can learn to predict. Different orders may in this respect differ from each other in either or both of two ways: the orderliness may concern only very few relations between the elements, or a great many; and, second, the regularity thus defined may be great in the sense that it will be confirmed by all or nearly all instances, or it may be found to prevail only in a majority of the instances and thus allow us to predict its occurrence only with a certain degree of probability. In the first instance we may predict only a few of the features of the resulting structure, but do so with great confidence; such an order would be limited but may still be perfect. In the second instance we shall be able to predict much more, but with only a fair degree of certainty. The knowledge of the existence of an order will however still be useful even if this order is restricted in either or both these respects; and the reliance on spontaneously ordering forces may be preferable or even indispensable, although the order towards which a system tends will in fact be only more or less imperfectly approached. The market order in particular will regularly secure only a certain probability that the expected relations will prevail, but it is, nevertheless, the only way in which so many activities depending on dispersed knowledge can be effectively integrated into a single order.

Spontaneous Orders Result from their Elements Obeying Certain Rules of Conduct

We have already indicated that the formation of spontaneous orders is the result of their elements following certain rules in their responses to their immediate environment. The nature of these rules still needs fuller examination, partly because the word 'rule' is apt to suggest some erroneous ideas, and partly because the rules which determine a spontaneous order differ in important respects from another kind of rules which are needed in regulating an organization or *taxis*.

On the first point, the instances of spontaneous orders which we have given from physics are instructive because they clearly show that the rules which govern the actions of the elements of such spontaneous orders need not be rules which are 'known' to these elements; it is sufficient that the elements actually behave in a manner which can be described by such rules. The concept of rules as we use it in this context therefore does not imply that such rules exist in articulated ('verbalized') forms, but only that it is possible to discover rules which the actions of the individuals in fact follow. To emphasize this we have occasionally spoken of 'regularity' rather than of rules, but regularity, of course, means simply that the elements behave according to rules.

That rules in this sense exist and operate without being explicitly known to those who obey them applies also to many of the rules which govern the actions of men and thereby determine a spontaneous social order. Man certainly does not know all the rules which guide his actions in the sense that he is able to state them in words. At least in primitive human society, scarcely less than in animal societies, the structure of social life is determined by rules of conduct which manifest themselves only by being in fact observed. Only when individual intellects begin to differ to a significant degree will it become necessary to express these rules in a form in which they can be communicated and explicitly taught, deviant behaviour corrected, and differences of opinion about appropriate behaviour decided. Although man never existed without laws that he obeyed, he did, of course, exist for hundreds of thousands of years without laws he 'knew' in the sense that he was able to articulate them.

What is of still greater importance in this connection, however, is that not every regularity in the behaviour of the elements does secure an overall order. Some rules governing individual behavior might clearly make altogether impossible the formation of an overall order. Our problem is what kind of rules of conduct will produce an order of society and what kind of order particular rules will produce.

The classical instance of rules of the behaviour of the elements which will not produce order comes from the physical sciences: it is the second law of thermodynamics or the law of enthropy, according to which the tendency of the molecules of a gas to move at constant speeds in straight lines produces a state for which the term 'perfect disorder' has been coined. Similarly, it is evident that in society some perfectly regular behaviour of the individuals could produce only disorder: if the rule were that any individual should try to kill any other he encountered, or flee as soon as he saw another, the result would clearly be the complete impossibility of an order in which the activities of the individuals were based on collaboration with others.

Society can thus exist only if by a process of selection rules have evolved which lead individuals to behave in a manner which makes social life possible. It should be remembered that for this purpose selection will operate as between societies of different types, that is, be guided by the properties of their respective orders, but that the properties supporting this order will be properties of the individuals, namely their propensity to obey certain rules of conduct on which the order of action of the group as a whole rests.

To put this differently: in a social order the particular circumstances to which each individual will react will be those known to him. But the individual responses to particular circumstances will result in an overall order only if the individuals obey such rules as will produce an order. Even a very limited similarity in their behaviour may be sufficient if the rules which they all obey are such as to produce an order. Such an order will always constitute an adaptation to the multitude of circumstances which are known to all the members of that society taken together but which are not known as a whole to any one person. This need not mean that the different persons will in similar circumstances do precisely the same thing; but merely that for the formation of such an overall order it is necessary that in some respects all individuals follow definite rules, or that their actions are limited to a certain range. In other words, the responses of the individuals to the events in their environment need be similar only in certain abstracts aspects to ensure that a determinate overall order will result.

The question which is of central importance as much for social theory as for social policy is thus what properties the rules must possess so that the separate actions of the individuals will produce an overall order. Some such rules all individuals of a society will obey because of the similar manner in which their environment represents itself to their minds. Other they will follow spontaneously because they will be part of their common cultural tradition. But there will be still others which they may have to be made to obey, since, although it would be in the interest of each to disregard them, the overall order on which the success of their actions depends will arise only if these rules are generally followed.

In a modern society based on exchange, one of the chief regularities in individual behaviour will result from the similarity of situations in which most individuals find themselves in working to earn an income; which means that they will normally prefer a larger return from their efforts to a smaller one, and often that they will increase their efforts in a particular direction if the prospects of return improve. This is a rule that will be followed at least with sufficient frequency to impress upon such a society an order of a certain kind. But the fact that most people will follow this rule will still leave the character of the resulting order very indeterminate, and by itself certainly would not be sufficient to give it a beneficial character. For the resulting order to be beneficial people must also observe some conventional rules, that is, rules which do not simply follow from their desires and their insight into relations of cause and effect, but which are normative and tell them what they ought to or ought not to do.

We shall later have to consider more fully the precise relation between the various kinds of rules which the people in fact obey and the resulting order of actions. Our main interest will then be those rules which, because we can deliberately alter them, become the chief instrument whereby we can affect the resulting order, namely the rules of law. At the moment our concern must be to make clear that while the rules on which a spontaneous order rests, may also be of spontaneous origin, this need not always be the case. Although undoubtedly an order originally formed itself spontaneously because the individuals followed rules which had not been deliberately made but had arisen spontaneously, people gradually learned to improve those rules; and it is at least conceivable that the formation of a spontaneous order relies entirely on rules that were de literately made. The spontaneous character of the resulting order must therefore be distinguished from the spontaneous origin of the rules on which it rests, and it is possible that an order which would still have to be described as spontaneous rests on rules which are entirely the result of deliberate design. In the kind of society with which we are familiar, of course, only some of the rules which people in fact observe, namely some of the rules of law (but never all, even of these) will be the product of deliberate design, while most of the rules of morals and custom will be spontaneous growths.

That even an order which rests on made rules may be spontaneous in character is shown by the fact that its particular manifestation will always depend on many circumstances which the designer of these rules did not and could not know. The particular content of the order will depend on the concrete circumstances known only to the individuals who obey the rules and apply them to facts known only to them. It will be through the knowledge of these individuals both of the rules and of the particular facts that both will determine the resulting order.

The Spontaneous Order of Society is Made Up of Individuals and Organizations

In any group of men of more than the smallest size, collaboration will always rest both on spontaneous order as well as on deliberate organization. There is no doubt that for many limited tasks organization is the most powerful method of effective coordination because it enables us to adapt the resulting order much more fully to our wishes, while where, because of the complexity of the circumstances to be taken into account, we must rely on the forces making for a spontaneous order, our power over the particular contents of this order is necessarily restricted.

That the two kinds of order will regularly coexist in every society of any degree of complexity does not mean, however, that we can combine them in any manner we like. What in fact we find in all free societies is that, although groups of men will join in organizations for the achievement of some particular ends, the coordination of the activities of all these separate organizations, as well as of the separate individuals, is brought about by the forces making for a spontaneous order. The family, the farm, the plant, the firm, the corporation and the various associations, and all the public institutions including government, are organizations which in turn are integrated into a more comprehensive spontaneous order. It is advisable to reserve the term 'society' for this spontaneous overall order so that we may distinguish it from all the organized smaller groups which will exist within it, as well as from such smaller and more or less isolated groups as the horde, the tribe, or the clan, whose members will at least in some respects act under a central direction for common purposes. In some instances it will be the same group which at times, as when engaged in most of its daily routine, will operate as a spontaneous order maintained by the observation of conventional rules without the necessity of commands, while at other times, as when hunting, migrating, or fighting, it will be acting as an organization under the directing will of a chief.

The spontaneous order which we call a society also need not have such sharp boundaries as an organization will usually possess. There will often be a nucleus, or several nuclei, of more closely related individuals occupying a central position in a more loosely connected but more extensive order. Such particular societies within the Great Society may arise as the result of spatial proximity, or of some other special circumstances which produce closer relations among their members. And different partial societies of this sort will often overlap and every individual may, in addition to being a member of the Great Society, be a member of numerous other spontaneous suborders or partial societies of this sort as well as of various organizations existing within the comprehensive Great Society.

Of the organizations existing within the Great Society one which regularly occupies a very special position will be that which we call government. Although it is conceivable that the spontaneous order which we call society may exist without government, if the minimum of rules required for the formation of such an order is observed without an organized apparatus for their enforcement, in most circumstances the organization which we call government becomes indispensable in order to assure that those rules are obeyed.

This particular function of government is somewhat like that of a maintenance squad of a factory, its object being not to produce any particular services or products to be consumed by the citizens, but rather to see that the mechanism which regulates the production of those goods and services is kept in working order. The purposes for which this machinery is currently being used will be determined by those who operate its parts and in the last resort by those who buy its products.

The same organization that is charged with keeping in order an operating structure which the individuals will use for their own purposes, will, however, in addition to the task of enforcing the rules on which that order rests, usually be expected also to render other services which the spontaneous order cannot produce adequately. These two distinct functions of government are usually not clearly separated; yet, as we shall see, the distinction between the coercive functions in which government enforces rules of conduct, and its service functions in which it need merely administer resources placed at its disposal, is of fundamental importance. In the second it is one organization among many and like the others part of a spontaneous overall order, while in the first it provides an essential condition for the preservation of that overall order.

In English it is possible, and has long been usual, to discuss these two types of order in terms of the distinction between 'society' and 'government'. There is no need in the discussion of these problems, so long as only one country is concerned, to bring in the metaphysically charged term 'state'. It is largely under the influence of continental and particularly Hegelian thought that in the course of the last hundred years the practice of speaking of the 'state' (preferably with a capital 'S'), where 'government' is more appropriate and precise, has come to be widely adopted. That which acts, or pursues a policy, is however always the organization of government; and it does not make for clarity to drag in the term 'state' where 'government' is quite sufficient. It becomes particularly misleading when 'the state' rather than 'government' is contrasted with 'society' to indicate that the first is an organization and the second a spontaneous order.

The Rules of Spontaneous Orders and the Rules of Organization

One of our chief contentions will be that, though spontaneous order and organization will always coexist, it is still not possible to mix these two principles of order in any manner we like. If this is not more generally understood it is due to the fact that for the determination of both kinds of order we have to rely on rules, and that the important differences between the kinds of rules which the two different kinds of order require are generally not recognized.

To some extent every organization must rely also on rules and not only on specific commands. The reason here is the same as that which makes it necessary for a spontaneous order to rely solely on rules: namely that by guiding the actions of individuals by rules rather than specific commands it is possible to make use of know ledge which nobody possesses as a whole. Every organization in which the members are not mere tools of the organizer will determine by commands only the function to be performed by each member, the purposes to be achieved, and certain general aspects of the methods to be employed, and will leave the detail to be decided by the individuals on the basis of their respective knowledge and skills.

Organization encounters here the problem which any attempt to bring order into complex human activities meets: the organizer must wish the individuals who are to cooperate to make use of knowledge that he himself does not possess. In none but the most simple kind of organization is it conceivable that all the details of all activities are governed by a single mind. Certainly nobody has yet succeeded in deliberately arranging all the activities that go on in a complex society. If anyone did ever succeed in fully organizing such a society, it would no longer make use of many minds but would be altogether dependent on one mind; it would certainly not be very complex but extremely primitive—and so would soon be the mind whose knowledge and will determined everything. The facts which could enter into the design of such an order could be only those which were known and digested by this mind; and as only he could decide on action and thus gain experience, there would be none of that interplay of many minds in which alone mind can grow.

What distinguishes the rules which will govern action within an organization is that they must be rules for the performance of assigned tasks. They presuppose that the place of each individual in a fixed structure is determined by command and that the rules each individual must obey depend on the place which he has been assigned and on the particular ends which have been indicated for him by the commanding authority. The rules will thus regulate merely the detail of the action of appointed functionaries or agencies of government.

Rules of organization are thus necessarily subsidiary to commands, filling in the gaps left by the commands. Such rules will be different for the different members of the organization according to the different roles which have been assigned to them, and they will have to be interpreted in the light of the purposes determined by the commands. Without the assignment of a function and the determination of the ends to be pursued by particular commands, the bare abstract rule would not be sufficient to tell each individual what he must do.

By contrast, the rules governing a spontaneous order must be independent of purpose and be the same, if not necessarily for all members, at least for whole classes of members not individually designated by name. They must, as we shall see, be rules applicable to an unknown and indeterminable number of persons and instances. They will have to be applied by the individuals in the light of their respective knowledge and purposes; and their application will be independent of any common purpose, which the individual need not even know.

In the terms we have adopted this means that the general rules of law that a spontaneous order rests on aim at an abstract order, the particular or concrete content of which is not known or foreseen by anyone; while the commands as well as the rules which govern an organization serve particular results aimed at by those who are in command of the organization. The more complex the order aimed at, the greater will be that part of the separate actions which will have to be determined by circumstances not known to those who direct the whole, and the more dependent control will be on rules rather than on specific commands. In the most complex types of organizations, indeed, little more than the assignment of particular functions and the general aim will be determined by command of the supreme authority, while the performance of these functions will be regulated only by rules—yet by rules which at least to some degree are specific to the functions assigned to particular persons. Only when we pass from the biggest kind of organization, government, which as organization must still be dedicated to a circumscribed and determined set of specific purposes, to the overall order of the whole of society, do we find an order which relies solely on rules and is entirely spontaneous in character.

It is because it was not dependent on organization but grew up as a spontaneous order that the structure of modern society has attained that degree of complexity which it possesses and which far exceeds any that could have been achieved by deliberate organization. In fact, of course, the rules which made the growth of this complex order possible were initially not designed in expectation of that result; but those people who happened to adopt suitable rules developed a complex civilization which then often spread to others. To maintain that we must deliberately plan modern society because it has become so complex is therefore paradoxical, and the result of a complete misunderstanding of these circumstances. The fact is, rather, that we can preserve an order of such complexity not by the method of directing the members, but only indirectly by enforcing and improving the rules conducive to the formation of a spontaneous order.

We shall see that it is impossible, not only to replace the spontaneous order by organization and at the same time to utilize as much of the dispersed knowledge of all its members as possible, but also to improve or correct this order by interfering in it by direct commands. Such a combination of spontaneous order and organization it can never be rational to adopt. While it is sensible to supplement the commands determining an organization by subsidiary rules, and to use organizations as elements of a spontaneous order, it can never be advantageous to supplement the rules governing a spontaneous order by isolated and subsidiary commands concerning those activities where the actions are guided by the general rules of conduct. This is the gist of the argument against 'interference' or 'intervention' in the market order. The reason why such isolated commands requiring specific actions by members of the spontaneous order can never improve but must disrupt that order is that they will refer to a part of a system of interdependent actions determined by information and guided by purposes known only to the several acting persons but not to the directing authority. The spontaneous order arises from each element balancing all the various factors operating on it and by adjusting all its various actions to each other, a balance which will be destroyed if some of the actions are determined by another agency on the basis of different knowledge and in the service of different ends.

What the general argument against 'interference' thus amounts to is that, although we can endeavour to improve a spontaneous order by revising the general rules on which it rests, and can supplement its results by the efforts of various organizations, we cannot improve the results by specific commands that deprive its members of the possibility of using their knowledge for their purposes.

We will have to consider throughout this book how these two kinds of rules have provided the model for two altogether different conceptions of law and how this has brought it about that authors using the same word 'law' have in fact been speaking about different things. This comes out most clearly in the contrast we find throughout history between those to whom law and liberty were inseparable[11] and those to whom the two were irreconcilable. We find one great tradition extending from the ancient Greeks and Cicero[12] through the Middle Ages[13] to the classical liberals like John Locke, David Hume, Immanuel Kant[14] and the Scottish moral philosophers, down to various American statesmen[15] of the nineteenth and twentieth centuries, for whom law and liberty could not exist apart from each other; while to Thomas Hobbes, Jeremy Bentham[16] and many French thinkers[17] and the modern legal positivists law of necessity means an encroachment on freedom. This apparent conflict between long lines of great thinkers does not mean that they arrived at opposite conclusions, but merely that they were using the word 'law' in different senses.

The Terms 'Organism' and 'Organization'

A few comments should be added on the terms in which the distinction examined in this chapter has most commonly been discussed in the past. Since the beginning of the nineteenth century the terms 'organism' and 'organization' have been frequently used to contrast the two types of order. As we have found it advisable to avoid the former term and to adopt the latter in a specific sense, some comments on their history may be appropriate.

It was natural that the organismal analogy should have been used since ancient times to describe the spontaneous order of society, since organisms were the only kinds of spontaneous order with which everybody was familiar. Organisms are indeed a kind of spontaneous order and as such show many of the characteristics of other spontaneous orders. It was therefore tempting to borrow such terms as 'growth', 'adaptation', and 'function' from them. They are, however, spontaneous orders of a very special kind, possessing also properties which by no means necessarily belong to all spontaneous orders; the analogy in consequence soon becomes more misleading than helpful.[18]

The chief peculiarity of organisms which distinguishes them from the spontaneous orders of society is that in an organism most of the individual elements occupy fixed places which, at least once the organism is mature, they retain once and for all. They also, as a rule, are more or less constant systems consisting of a fixed number of elements which, although some may be replaced by equivalent new ones, retain an order in space readily perceivable with the senses. They are, in consequence, in the terms we have used, orders of a more concrete kind than the spontaneous orders of society, which may be preserved although the total number of elements changes and the individual elements change their places. This relatively concrete character of the order of organisms shows itself in the fact that their existence as distinct wholes can be perceived intuitively by the senses, while the abstract spontaneous order of social structures usually can only be reconstructed by the mind.

The interpretation of society as an organism has almost invariably been used in support of hierarchic and authoritarian views to which the more general conception of the spontaneous order gives no support. Indeed, since Menenius Agrippa, on the occasion of the first secession of the Roman plebs, used the organismal metaphor to justify the privileges of a particular group, it must have been used innumerable times for similar purposes. The suggestion of fixed places assigned to particular elements according to their distinct 'functions', and the much more concrete determination of the biological structures as compared with the abstract character of the spontaneous structures of society, have indeed made the organismal conception of very questionable value for social theory. It has been abused even more than the term 'order' itself when interpreted as a made order or *taxis*, and has frequently been used to defend a hierarchical order, the necessity of 'degree', the relation of command and obedience, or the preservation of established positions of particular individuals, and for this reason has rightly become suspect.

The term 'organization', on the other hand, which in the nineteenth century was frequently used in contrast to 'organism' to express the distinction we have discussed,[19] and which we shall retain to describe a made order or *taxis*, is of comparatively recent origin. It seems to have come into general use at the time of the French Revolution, with reference to which Kant once observed that 'in a recently undertaken reconstruction of a great people into a great state the word *organization* has been frequently and appropriately used for the institution of the magistracies and even the whole state.'[20] The word became characteristic of the spirit of the Napoleonic period[21] and became the central conception in the plans for the 'reconstruction of society' of the chief founders of modern socialism, the Saint Simonians, and of Auguste Comte.[22] Until the term 'socialism' came into general, use 'the organization of society as a whole' was in fact the accepted way of referring to what we now describe as socialism.[23] Its central role, particularly for French thinking during the early part of the nineteenth century, was clearly seen by the young Ernest Renan, who in 1849 could speak of the ideal of a 'scientific organization of mankind as the last word of modern science and its daring but legitimate ambition'.[24]

In English, the word appears to have come into general use around 1790 as a technical term for a 'systematic arrangement for a definite purpose'.[25] But it was the Germans who adopted it with particular enthusiasm and to whom it soon appeared to express a peculiar capacity in which they believed themselves to excel other people. This even led to a curious rivalry between French and German scholars, who during the First World War conducted a slightly comic literary dispute across the fighting lines as to which of the two nations had the stronger claim to possessing the secret of organization.[26]

In confining the term here to a made order or *taxis* we follow what seems to have become the general use in sociology and especially in what is known as 'organization theory'.[27] The idea of organization in this sense is a natural consequence of the discovery of the powers of the human intellect and especially of the general attitude of constructivist rationalism. It appeared for a long time as the only procedure by which an order serviceable to human purposes could be deliberately achieved, and it is indeed the intelligent and powerful method of achieving certain known and foreseeable results. But as its development is one of the great achievements of constructivism, so is the disregard of its limits one of its most serious defects. What it overlooks is that the growth of that mind which can direct an organization, and of the more comprehensive order within which organizations function, rests on adaptations to the unforeseeable, and that the only possibility of transcending the capacity of individual minds is to rely on those superpersonal 'self-organizing' forces which create spontaneous orders.

Notes

*Adam Smith, *The Theory of Moral Sentiments* (London, 1759), Part 6, ch. 2, penultimate paragraph. It deserves to be noted that this passage contains some of the basic concepts and terms we shall have to use throughout this book: the conception of a spontaneous order of the *Great Society* as contrasted with a deliberate *arrangement* of the elements; the distinction between *coincidence* and *opposition* between the rules (*principles of motion*) inherent in the elements and those imposed upon them by legislation; and the interpretation of the social process as a *game* which will go on smoothly if the two kinds of rules are in concord but will produce *disorder* if they are in conflict.

1. See my essay on 'The theory of complex phenomena', in F. A. Hayek, *Studies in Philosophy, Politics and Economics* (London and Chicago, 1967, henceforth referred to as *S.P.P.E.*). It was in fact at first entirely the result of methodological considerations that led me to resume the use of the unpopular concept of 'order': see also F. A. Hayek, *The Counter Revolution of Science* (Chicago, 1952), p. 39: 'If social phenomena showed no order except in so far as they were consciously designed, there would indeed be no room for a theoretical science of society and there would be, as is often maintained, only problems of psychology.' In recent discussion the term 'system' is often used in much the same sense in which I use here 'order', which still seems to me preferable.

2. It would seem that the currency of the concept of order in political theory goes back to St Augustine. See in particular his dialogue *Ordo* in J. P. Migne (ed) *Patrologiae cursus completus sec. lat.* 32/47 (Paris, 1861-2), and in a German version *Die Ordnung*, trans. C. J. Peel, fourth edition (Paderborn, 1966).

3. See L. S. Stebbing, *A Modern Introduction to Logic* (London, 1933), p. 228: 'When we know how a set of elements is ordered, we have a basis for inference.' See also Immanuel Kant, *Werke* (Akademie Ausgabe), *Nachlass*, vol 6, p. 669: 'Ordnung ist die Zusammenfügung nach Regeln.'

4. See E. E. Evans Pritchard, *Social Anthropology* (London, 1951), p. 49; see also ibid., p. 19:

    It is evident that there must be uniformities and regularities in social life, that society must have some sort of order, or its members could not live together. It is only because people know the kind of behaviour expected of them, and what kind of behaviour to expect from others, in the various situations of life, and coordinate their activities in submission to rules and under the guidance of values that each and all are able to go about their affairs. They can make predictions, anticipate events, and lead their lives in harmony with their fellows because every society has a form or pattern which allows us to speak of it as a system, or structure, within which, and in accordance with which, its members live their lives.

5. See L. S. Stebbing, op. cit., p. 229: 'Order is most *apparent* where man has been at work.'

6. See J. Ortega y Gasset, *Mirabeau o el politico* (1927), in *Obras Completas* (Madrid, 1947) vol. 3, p. 603: 'Orden no es una presión que desde fuera se ejerce sobra la sociedad, sin un equilibrio que se suscita en su interior.'

7. See H. von Foerster and G. W. Zopf, Jr (eds) *Principles of Self-Organization* (New York, 1962) and, on the anticipation of the main conceptions of cybernetics by Adam Smith, cf. G. Hardin, *Nature and*

Man's Fate (New York, 1961), p. 54; and Dorothy Emmet, *Function, Purpose and Powers* (London, 1958), p. 90.

8. See H. Kuhn, 'Ordnung im Werden und Zerfall', in K. Ruhn and F. Wiedmann (eds), *Das Problem der Ordnung* (Sechster Deutscher Kongress für Philosophie, Munich, 1960, publ. Meisenheim am Glan, 1962), especially p. 17.

9. See Werner Jaeger, *Paideia: The Ideals of Greek Culture*, trans. G. Highet, vol. I, second edition (New York, 1945), p. 110, about 'Anaximander of Miletus transferring the concept of *diké* from the social life of the city-state to the realm of nature.... This is the original of the philosophical idea of cosmos: for the word originally signified the *right order* in a state or in a community'; and ibid., p. 179: 'So the physicist's cosmos became by a curious retrogression in thought, the pattern of anemia in human society.' See also the same author's 'Praise of law' in P. Sayre (ed), *Interpretations of Modern Legal Philosophies: Essays in Honor of Roscoe Pound* (New York, 1947), especially p. 358:

A world thus 'justified' could be called rightly by another term taken over from the social order, a cosmos. That word occurs for the first time in the language of the Ionian philosophers; by taking this step and extending the rule of *diké* to reality as a whole they clearly revealed the nature of Greek legal thought and showed that it was based on the relationship of justice to being.

And ibid., p. 361: 'The law on which it [the *polis*] was founded was not a mere decree but the *nomos,* which originally meant the sum total of that which was respected by all living custom with regard to what is right and wrong'; and ibid., p. 365 on the fact that even during the period of the dissolution of the old Greek faith in law: 'the strict relationship of the *nomos* to the nature of the cosmos was not universally questioned.'

For Aristotle, who connects *nomos* with *taxis* rather than *kosmos* (see *Politics*, 1287a 18 and especially 1326a, 30: *ho te gar nomos taxis tis esti*), it is characteristically inconceivable that the order resulting from the *nomos* should exceed what the orderer can survey, 'for who will command its over-swollen multitude in war? or who will serve as its herald, unless he had the lungs of Stentor?' The creation of order in such a multitude is for him a task only the gods can achieve. Elsewhere (*Ethics,* IX, x, §3) he even argues that a state, i.e. an ordered society, of a hundred thousand people is impossible.

10. Adam Smith, *Wealth of Nations*, edited by E. Cannan, vol. I, p. 421.

11. See G. Sartori, *Democratic Theory* (Detroit, 1962), p. 306:

Western man for two and a half millennia has sought liberty in the law.... [Yet] the widespread skepticism about the value of the juridical protection of liberty is not unjustified. The reason for this is that our conception of law has changed; and that, as a consequence, law can no longer give us the protection that it did give us in the past.

12. See Philo of Alexandria, *Quod omnis probus liber sit,* 452, 45, Loeb edition, vol. IX, p. 36: *'hosoi de meta nomou zosin, eleuteroi'*. On freedom in ancient Greece see in particular Max Pohlenz, *The Idea of Freedom in Greek Life and Thought* (Dordrecht, 1962). On Cicero and the Roman concept of liberty generally see U. von Lübtow, *Blüte und Verfall der römischen Freikeit* (Berlin, 1953); Theo Mayer-Maly, 'Rechtsgeschichte der Freiheitsidee in Antike und Mittelalter', *Österreichische Zeitschrift für öffentliches Recht,* N.F. VI, 1956; and G. Crifo, 'Su alcuni aspetti della libertà in Roma', *Archivio Giuridico 'Filippo Serafini'*, sesta serie, xxiii, 1958.

13. See R. W. Southern, *The Making of the Middle Ages* (New Haven, 1953), p. 107 *et seq.:*

The hatred of that which was governed, not by rule, but by will, went very deep in the Middle Ages.... The higher one rose towards liberty, the more the area of action was covered by law, the less it was subject by will.... Law was not the enemy of freedom; on the contrary, the outline of liberty was traced by the bewildering variety of law which was slowly evolved during our period.... High and low alike sought liberty by insisting on enlarging the number of rules under which they lived.... It was only when the quality of freedom was articulated by being attached to the status of knight, burgess or baron that it could be observed, analysed and measured.... Liberty is a creation of law, and law is reason in action; it is reason which makes men, as we should say, ends in themselves. Tyranny, whether of King John or of the Devil, is a manifestation of the absence of law.

14. Most emphatically, perhaps, Adam Ferguson, *Principles of Moral and Political Science* (Edinburgh, 1792), vol. 2, p. 258 *et seq.:*

Liberty or freedom is not, as the origin of the name may seem to imply, an exemption from all restraint, but rather the most effectual application of every just restraint to all the members of a free state, whether they be magistrates or subjects.

It is under just restraints only that every person is safe, and cannot be invaded, either in the freedom of his person, his property, or innocent action.... The establishment of a just and effectual government is of all circumstances in civil society the most essential to freedom: that everyone is justly said to be free in proportion as the government under which he resides is sufficiently powerful to protect him, at the same time that it is sufficiently restrained and limited to prevent the abuse of this power.

15. Daniel Webster is credited with the statement that 'Liberty is the creature of law, essentially different from the authorized licentiousness that trespasses on right'; and Charles Evans Hughes with that 'Liberty and Law are one and inseparable'. There are many similar statements by continental legal scholars of the last century, e.g. Charles Beudant, *Le Droit individuel et l'état* (Paris, 1891), p. 5: 'Le

Droit, au sens le plus général du mot, est la science de la liberté'; and Karl Binding who argued somewhere that 'Das Recht ist eine Ordnung menschlicher Freiheit.'

16. See J. Bentham, 'Principles of the civil code', in *Theory of Legislation,* edited by C. K. Ogden (London, 1931), p. 98: 'Laws cannot be made except at the expense of liberty.' Also in *Deontology* (London and Edinburgh, 1834), vol. 2, p. 59:

There are few words which, with its derivations, have been more mischievous than this word liberty. When it means anything beyond mere caprice and dogmatism, it means good government; and if good government had had the good fortune to occupy the same place in the public mind which has been occupied by liberty, the crimes and follies which have disgraced and retarded the progress of political improvement would hardly have been committed. The usual definition of liberty—that it is the right to do everything that the law does not forbid—shows with what carelessness words are used in ordinary discourse or composition; for if the laws are bad, what becomes of liberty? and if the laws are good, where is its value? Good laws have a definite intelligible meaning; they pursue an evidently useful end by obviously appropriate means.

17. See for example, Jean Salvaire, *Autorité et liberté* (Montpellier, 1932), p. 65 *et seq.*, who argues that 'the complete realization of liberty is, in fact, nothing else but the complete abolition of law.... Law and liberty are mutually exclusive'.

18. Edmund Burke, 'Letter to W. Elliot' (1795), in *Works* (London, 1808), vol. 7, p. 366:

These analogies between bodies natural and politick, though they may sometimes illustrate arguments, furnish no arguments for themselves. They are but too often used under the colour of a specious philosophy, to find apologies for the despair of laziness and pusillanimity, and to excuse the want of all manly efforts when the exigencies of our country call for them the more loudly.

19. For a characteristic use of the contrast between 'organism' and 'organization' see Adolf Wagner, *Grundlegung der politischen Ökonomie, I. Grundlagen der Volkswirtschaft* (Leipzig, 1876), § § 149 and 299.

20. See Immanuel Rant, *Kritik der Urteilshraft* (Berlin, 1790), Part 2 section I, § 6sn.: 'So hat man sich bei einer neuerlich unternommenen gänzlichen Umbildung eines grossen Volkes zu einem Staat des Wortes *Organisation* haüfig für Einrichtung der Magistraturen usw. und selbst des ganzen Staatskörpers sehr schicklich bedient.'

21. See H. Balzac, *Autre étude de femme*, in *La Comédie Humaine*, Pleiade edition, vol. 3, p. 226: 'Organiser, par example, est un mot de l'Empire et qui contient Napoléon tout entier.'

22. See, for example, the journal edited by H. de Saint Simon and Auguste Comte called *Organisateur,* reprinted in *Oeuvres de Saint Simon et d'Enfantin* (Paris, 1865-78), vol. 20, especially p. 220, where the aim of the work is described as 'D'imprimer au XIX siècle le caractère organisateur'.

23. See in particular Louis Blanc, *Organisation du travail* (Paris, 1839), and H. Ahrens, *Rechtsphilosophie,* fourth edition (Vienna, 1852) on 'organization' as the magic word of the communists and socialists; see also Francis Lieber, 'Anglican and Gallican liberty' (1848), in *Miscellaneous Writings* (Philadelphia, 1881), vol 2, p. 385:

> The fact that Gallican liberty expects everything from *organization*, while Anglican liberty inclines to development, explains why we see in France so little improvement and expansion of institutions; but when improvements are attempted, a total abolition of the preceding state of things—a beginning *ab ovo*—a rediscussion of the first elementary principles.

24. See Ernest Renan, *L'Avenir de la Science* (1890), in *Oeuvres complètes* (Paris, 1949), vol. 3, p. 757: 'ORGANISER SCIENTIFIQUEMENT L'HUMANITE, tel est donc le dernier mot de la science moderne, telle est son audacieuse mais légitime prétention.'

25. See *Shorter Oxford Dictionary*, s.v. 'organization', which shows, however, that the term was already used by John Locke.

26. Jean Labadie (ed), *L'Allemagne, a -t-elle secret de l'organisation?* (Paris, 1916).

27. See Dwight Waldo, 'Organization theory: an elephantine problem', *Public Administration Review,* xxx, 1961, and reprinted in *General Systems, Yearbook of the Society for General System Research,* VII 1962, the preceding volume of which contains a useful collection of, articles on the theory of organization.

JUSTICE AND PROPERTY RIGHTS

Murray N. Rothbard

I. The Failure of Utilitarianism

Until very recently, free-market economists paid little attention to the entities actually being exchanged on the very market they have advocated so strongly. Wrapped up in the workings and advantages of freedom of trade, enterprise, investment, and the price system, economists tended to lose sight of the things being exchanged on that market. Namely, they lost sight of the fact that when $10,000 is being exchanged for a machine, or $1 for a hula loop, what is actually being exchanged is the *title of ownership* to each of these goods. In short, when I buy a hula hoop for a dollar, what I am actually doing is exchanging my title of ownership to the dollar in exchange for the ownership title to the hula hoop; the retailer is doing the exact opposite.[1] But this means that economists' habitual attempts to be *Wertfrei*, or at the least to confine their advocacy to the processes of trade and exchange, cannot be maintained; for if I and the retailer are indeed to be free to trade the dollar for the hula hoop without coercive interference by third parties, then this can only be done if these economists will proclaim the justice and the propriety of my original ownership of the dollar and the retailer's ownership of the hula hoop.

In short, for an economists to say that X and Y should be free to trade Good A for Good B unmolested by third parties, he must *also* say that X legitimately and properly owns Good A and that Y legitimately owns Good B. But this means that the free-market economist must have some sort of theory of justice in property rights; he can scarcely say that X properly owns Good A without asserting some sort of theory of justice on behalf of such ownership.

Suppose, for example, that as I am about to purchase the hula hoop, the information arrives that the retailer had really stolen the hoop from Z. Surely not even the supposed *Wertfrei* economist can continue to endorse blithely the proposed exchange of ownership titles between myself and the retailer. For now we find that retailer Y's title of ownership is improper and unjust and that he must be forced to return the hoop to Z, the original owner. The economist can then only endorse the proposed exchange between myself and Z, rather than Y, for the hula hoop, since he has to acknowledge Z as the proper owner of title to the hoop.

In short, we have two mutually exclusive claimants to the ownership of the hoop. If the economist agrees to endorse only Z's sale of the hoop, then he is implicitly agreeing that Z has the just, and Y the unjust, claim to the hoop. And even if he continues to endorse the sale by Y, then he is implicitly maintaining *another* theory of property titles: namely, that theft is justified. Whichever way he decides, the economist cannot escape a judgment, a theory of justice in the ownership of property. Furthermore, the economist is not really finished when he proclaims the injustice of theft and endorses Z's proper title. For what is the justification for Z's title to the hoop? Is it only because he is a nonthief?

In recent years, free-market economists Ronald Coase and Harold Demsetz have begun to redress the balance and to focus on the importance of a clear and precise demarcation of property rights for the market economy. They have demonstrated the importance of such demarcation in the allocation of resources and in preventing or compensating for unwanted imposition of "external costs" from the actions of individuals. But Coase and Demsetz have failed to develop any theory of justice in these property rights; or rather, they have advanced two theories: one, that it "doesn't matter" *how* the property titles are allocated, so long as they are allocated precisely; and two, that the titles should be allocated to minimize "total social transaction costs," since a minimization of costs is supposed to be a *Wertfrei* way of benefitting all of society.

There is no space here for a detailed critique of the Coase-Demsetz criteria. Suffice it to say that even if, say, in a conflict over property titles between a rancher and a farmer for the same piece of land, even if the allocation of title "doesn't matter" for the allocation of resources (a point which itself could be challenged), it certainly matters from the point of view of the rancher and the farmer. And secondly, that it is impossible to weigh "total social costs" if we fully realize that all costs are subjective to the individuals and therefore cannot be compared interpersonally.[2] Here the important point is that Coase and Demsetz, along with all other utilitarian free-market economists, implicitly or explicitly leave it to the hands of government to define and allocate the titles to private property.

It is a curious fact that utilitarian economists, generally so skeptical of the virtues of government intervention, are so content to leave the fundamental underpinning of the market process—the definition of property rights and the allocation of property titles—wholly in the hands of government. Thus, if Smith, Jones, and Doe each own property and are about to exchange their titles, utilitarians simply assert that if these titles are *legal* (i.e., if the government puts the stamp of approval upon them), then they consider those titles to be justified; it is only if someone violates the government's definition of legality (e.g., in the case of Y, the thieving retailer) that utilitarians are willing to agree with the general and the governmental view of the injustice of such action. But this means, of course, that once again, the utilitarians have failed in their wish to escape having a theory of justice in property; actually they do have such a theory, and it is the surely simplistic one that *whatever government denies as legal is right.*

As in so many other areas of social philosophy, then, we see that utilitarians, in pursuing their vain goal of being *Wertfrei*, of "scientifically" abjuring any theory of justice, actually *have* such a theory, namely, putting their stamp of approval on whatever the process by which the government arrives at its allocation of property titles. Furthermore, we find that, as on many similar occasions, utilitarians in their vain quest for the *Wertfrei*, really conclude by endorsing as right and just whatever the government happens to decide, that is, by blindly apologizing for the *status quo*.[3]

Let us consider the utilitarian stamp of approval on government allocation of property titles. Can this approval possibly achieve en the limited utilitarian goal of certain and precise allocation of property titles? Suppose that the government endorses the existing titles to their property held by Smith, Jones, and Doe. Suppose then that a faction of government calls for the confiscation of these titles and redistribution of that property to Roe, Brown, and Robinson. The reasons for this program may stem from any number of social theories or even from the brute fact that Roe, Brown, and Robinson have greater political power than the original trio of owners. The reaction to this proposal by free-market economists and other utilitarians is predictable: they will oppose this proposal on the ground that definite and certain property rights, so socially beneficial, are being endangered. But suppose that the government, ignoring the protests of our utilitarians, proceeds anyway and redistributes these titles to property. Roe, Brown, and Robinson are *now* defined by the government as the proper and legal owners, while any claims to that property by the original trio of Smith, Jones, and Doe are considered improper and illegitimate, if not subversive. What now will be the reaction of our utilitarians?

It should be clear that since the utilitarians base their theory of justice in property only on *whatever the government defines* as legal, they can have no groundwork whatever for any call for restoring the property in question to its original owners. They can only, willy-nilly, and despite any emotional reluctance on their part, simply endorse the new allocation of property titles as defined and endorsed by government. Not only must utilitarians endorse the *status quo* of property titles, they must endorse whatever *status quo* exists and however rapidly the government decides to shift and redistribute such titles. Furthermore, considering the historical record, we may indeed say that relying upon government to be the guardian of property rights is like placing the proverbial fox on guard over the chicken coop.

We see, therefore, that the supposed defense of the free market and of property rights by utilitarians and free-market economists is a very weak reed indeed. Lacking a theory of justice that goes beyond the existing *imprimatur* of government, utilitarians can only go along with every change and shift of government allocation after the occur, no matter how arbitrary, rapid, or politically motivated such shifts might be. And since they provide no firm roadblock for governmental reallocations of property, the utilitarians, in the final analysis, can offer no real defense of property rights themselves. Since governmental redefinitions can and will be rapid and arbitrary, they cannot provide long-run certainty for property rights, and therefore they cannot even ensure the very social and economic efficiency which they themselves seek.[4] All this is implied in the pronouncements of utilitarians that any future free society must confine itself to whatever definitions of property titles the government may happen to be endorsing at that moment.

Let us consider a hypothetical example of the failure of utilitarian defense of private property. Suppose that somehow government becomes persuaded of the necessity to yield to a clamor for a free-market, *laissez-faire* society. Before dissolving itself, however, it redistributes property titles: granting the owernship of the entire territory of New York to the Rockefeller family, of Massachusetts to the Kennedy family, etc. It then dissolves, ending taxation and all other forms of government intervention in the economy. However, while taxation has been abolished, the Rockefeller, Kennedy, etc., families proceed to dictate to all the residents in what is now "their" territory, exacting what are now called "rents" over all the inhabitants.[5] It seems clear that our utilitarians could have no intellectual armor with which to challenge this new dispensation; indeed, they would have to endorse the Rockefeller, Kennedy, etc., holdings as "private property" equally deserving of support as the ordinary property titles which they had endorsed only a few months previously. All this because the utilitarians have no theory of justice in property beyond endorsement of whatever *status quo* happens to exist.

Consider, furthermore, the grotesque box in which the utilitarian proponent of freedom places himself in relation to the institution of human slavery. Contemplating that institution and the "free" market that once existed in buying, selling, and renting slaves, the utilitarian who must rely on the legal definition of property can only endorse slavery on the ground that the slave masters had purchased their slave titles legally and in good faith. Surely, any endorsement of a "free" market in

as in 1999?

slavery

slaves indicates the inadequacy of utilitarian concepts of property and the need for a theory of justice to provide a groundwork for property rights and a critique of existing official titles to property.

II. Toward a Theory of Justice in Property

We conclude that utilitarianism cannot be supported as a groundwork for property rights or, *a fortiori*, for the free-market economy. A theory of justice must be arrived at which goes beyond government allocations of property titles and which can therefore serve as a basis for criticizing such allocations. Obviously, in this space I can only outline what I consider to be the correct theory of justice in property rights. This theory has two fundamental premises: (a) the absolute property right of each individual in his own person, his own body: this may be called the *right of self-ownership;* and (b) the absolute right in material property of the person who first finds an unused material resource and then in some way occupies or transforms that resource by the use of his personal energy. This might be called the *homestead principle*—the case in which someone, in the phrase of John Locke, has "mixed his labour" with an unused resource. Let Locke summarize these principles:

> ...every man has a *property* in his own *person*. This nobody has any right to but himself. The *labour* of his body and the *work* of his hands, we may say, are properly his. Whatsoever, then, he removes out of the state that nature hath provided and left it in, he hath mixed his labour with it, and joined to it something that is his own, and thereby makes it his property. It being by him removed from the common state nature placed it in, it hath by this labour something annexed to it that excludes the common right of other men.[6]

Let us consider the first principle: the right to self-ownership. This principle asserts the absolute right of each man, by virtue of his (or her) being a human being, to "own" his own body; that is, to control that body free of coercive interference. Since the nature of man is such that each individual must use his mind to learn about himself and the world, to select values, and to choose ends and means in order to survive and flourish, the right to self-ownership gives each man the right to perform these vital activities without being hampered and restricted by coercive molestation.

Consider, then, the alternatives—the consequences of *denying* each man the right to own his own person. There are only two alternatives: either (1) a certain class of people, A, have the right to own another class, B; or (2) everyone has the right to own his equal quotal share of everyone else. The first alternative implies that while Class A deserves the rights of being human, Class B is in reality subhuman and therefore deserves no such rights. But since they *are* indeed human beings, the first alternative contradicts itself in denying natural human rights to one set of humans. Moreover, allowing Class A to own Class B means that the former is allowed to exploit, and therefore to live parasitically, at the expense of the latter; but, as economics can tell us, this parasitism itself violates the basic economic requirement for human survival: production and exchange.

The second alternative, which we might call "participatory communalism" or "communism," holds that every man should have the right to own his equal quotal share of everyone else. If there are three billion people in the world, then everyone has the right to own a three-billionth of every other person. In the first place, this ideal itself rests upon an absurdity: proclaiming that every man is entitled to own a part of everyone else and yet is not entitled to *own himself*. Secondly, we can picture the viability of such a world: a world in which *no* man is free to take any action whatever without prior approval or indeed command by *everyone else* in society. It should be clear that in that sort of "communist" world, no one would be able to do anything, and the human race would quickly perish. But if a world of zero self-ownership and 100 percent other-ownership spells death for the human race, then any steps in that direction also contravene the natural law of what is best for man and his life on earth.

Finally, however, the participatory communist world *cannot* be put into practice. For it is physically impossible for everyone to keep continual tabs on everyone else and thereby to exercise his equal quotal share of partial ownership over every other man. In practice, then, any attempt to institute universal and equal other-ownership is utopian and impossible, and supervision, and therefore control and ownership of others, would necessarily devolve upon a specialized group of people, who would thereby become a "ruling class." Hence, in practice, any attempt at communist society will automatically become class rule, and we would be back at our rejected first alternative.

We conclude, then, with the premise of absolute universal right of self-ownership as our first principle of justice in property. This principle, of course, automatically rejects slavery as totally incompatible with our primary right.[7]

Let us now turn to the more complex case of property in material objects. For even if every man has the right to self-ownership, people are not floating wraiths; they are not self-subsistent entities; they can only survive and flourish by grappling with the earth around them. They must, for example, *stand* on land areas; they must also, in order to survive, transform the resources given by nature into "consumer goods," into objects more suitable for their use and consumption. Food must be grown and eaten; minerals must be mined and then transformed into capital and finally into useful consumer goods, etc. Man, in other words, must own not only his own person, but also material objects for his control and use. How, then, should property titles in these objects be allocated?

Let us consider, as our first example, the case of a sculptor fashioning a work of art out of clay and other materials; and let us simply assume for the moment that he owns these materials while waiving the question of the justification for their ownership. Let us examine the question: *who* should own the work of art, as it emerges from the sculptor's fashioning? The sculpture is, in fact, the sculptor's "creation," not in the sense that he has created matter *de novo*, but in the sense that he has transformed nature-given matter—the clay—into another form dictated by his own ideas and fashioned by his own hands and energy. Surely, it is a rare person who, with the case put thus, would say that the sculptor does *not* have the property right in his own product. For if every man has the right to his own body, and if he must grapple with the material objects of the world in order to survive, then the sculptor has the right to own the product which he has made, by his energy and effort, a veritable *extension* of his own personality. He has placed the stamp of his person upon the raw material, by "mixing his labor" with the clay.

As in the case of the ownership of people's bodies, we again have three logical alternatives: (1) either the transformer, the "creator," has the property right in his creation; or (2) another man or set of men have the right to appropriate it by force without the sculptor's consent; or (3) the "communal" solution—every individual in the world has an equal, quotal share in the ownership of the sculpture. Again, put badly, there are very few who would not concede the monstrous injustice of confiscating the sculptor's property, either by one or more others, or by the world as whole. For by what right do they do so? By what right do they appropriate to themselves the product of the creator's mind and energy? (Again, as in the case of bodies, any confiscation in the supposed name of the world as a whole would in practice devolve into an oligarchy of confiscators.)

But the case of the sculptor is not qualitatively different from *all* cases of "production." The man or men who extracted the clay from the ground and sold it to the sculptor were *also* "producers;" they too mixed their ideas and their energy and their technological knowhow with the nature-given material to emerge with a useful product. As producers, the sellers of the clay and of the sculptor's tools also mixed their labor with natural materials to transform them into more useful goods and services. All the producers are therefore entitled to the ownership of their product.

The chain of material production logically reduces back, then, back from consumer goods and works of art to the first producers who gathered or mined the nature-given soil and resources to use and transform them by means of their personal energy. And use of the soil logically reduces back to the legitimate ownership by first users of previously unowned, unused, virginal, nature-given resources. Let us again quote Locke:

> He that is nourished by the acorns he picked up under an oak, or the apples he gathered from the trees in the wood, has certainly appropriated them to himself. Nobody can deny but the nourishment is his. I ask then, when did they begin to be his? When he digested? or when he ate? or when he boiled? or when he brought them home? or when he picked them

up? And 'tis plain, if the first gathering made them not his, nothing else could. That labour put the distinction between them and common. That added something to them more than Nature, the common mother of all, had done, and so they became his private right. And will any one say he had no right to those acorns or apples he thus appropriated because he had not the consent of all mankind to make them his? Was it a robbery thus to assume to himself what belonged to all in common? If such a consent as that was necessary, man had starved, notwithstanding the plenty God had given him.... Thus, the grass my horse has bit, the turfs my servant has cut, and the ore I have digged in my place, where I have a right to them in common with others, become my property without the assignation or consent of any body. The labour that was mine, removing them out of that common state they were in, hath fixed my property in them.[8]

If every man owns his own person and therefore his own labor, and if by extension he owns whatever material property he has "created" or gathered out of the previously unused, unowned "state of nature," then what of the logically final question: who has the right to own or control the earth *itself*? In short, if the gatherer has the right to own the acorns or berries he picks, or the farmer the right to own his crop of wheat or peaches, *who* has the right to own the land on which these things have grown? It is at this point that Henry George and his followers, who would have gone all the way so far with our analysis, leave the track and deny the individual's right to own the piece of land itself, the ground on which these activities have taken place. The Georgists argue that, while every man should own the goods which he produces or creates, since Nature or God created the land itself, no individual has the right to assume ownership of that land. Yet again we are faced with our three logical alternatives: either the land itself belongs to the pioneer, the first user, the man who first brings it into production; *or* it belongs to a group of others; *or* it belongs to the world as a whole, with every individual owning an equal quotal part of every acre of land. George's option for the last solution hardly solves his moral problem: for if the land itself should belong to God or Nature, then why is it more moral for every acre in the world to be owned by the world as a whole, than to concede individual ownership? In practice, again, it is obviously impossible for every person in the world to exercise his ownership of his three-billionth portion of every acre of the world's surface; in practice a small oligarchy would do the controlling and owning rather than the world as a whole.

But apart from those difficulties in the Georgist position, our proposed justification for the ownership of ground land is the same as the justification for the original ownership of all other property. For, as we have indicated, no producer *really* "creates" matter; he takes nature-given matter and transforms it by his personal energy in accordance with his ideas and his vision. But *this* is precisely what the pioneer—the "homesteader"—does when he brings previously unused land into his private ownership. Just as the man who makes steel out of iron and transforms that ore out of his knowhow and with his energy, and just as the man who takes the iron out of the ground does the same, so too does the homesteader who clears, fences, cultivates or builds upon the land. The homesteader, too, has transformed the character and usefulness of the nature-given soil by his labor and his personality. The homesteader is just as legitimately the owner of the property as the sculptor or the manufacturer; he is just as much a "producer" as the others.

Moreover, if the producer is *not* entitled to the fruits of his labor, who is? It is difficult to see why a newborn Pakistani baby should have a moral claim to a quotal share of ownership of a piece of Iowa land that someone has just transformed into a wheatfield—and vice versa of course for an Iowan baby and a Pakistani farm. Land in its original state is unused and unowned. Georgists and other land communalists may claim that the entire world population "really" owns it, but if no one has yet used it, it is in the real sense owned and controlled by no one. The pioneer, the homesteader, the first user and transformer of this land, is the man who first brings this simple valueless thing into production and use. It is difficult to see the justice of depriving him of ownership in favor of people who have never gotten within a thousand miles of the land and who may not even know of the existence of the property over which they are supposed to have a claim. It is even more difficult to see the justice of a group of outside oligarchs owning the property, and at the expense of expropriating the creator or the homesteader who had originally brought the product into existence.

Finally, no one can produce *anything* without the cooperation of ground land, if only to be used as standing room. No man can produce or create anything by his labor alone; he must have the cooperation of land and other natural raw material. Man comes into the world with just himself and the world around him—the land and natural resources given him by nature. He takes these resources and transforms them by his labor and mind and energy into goods more useful to man. Therefore, if an individual cannot own original land, neither can he in the full sense own any of the fruits of his labor. Now that this labor has been inextricably mixed with the land, he cannot be deprived of one without being deprived of the other.

The moral issue involved here is even clearer if we consider the case of animals. Animals are "economic land," since they are original nature-given resources. Yet will anyone deny full title to a horse to the man who finds and domesticates it? This is no different from the acorns and berries which are generally conceded to the gatherer. Yet in land, too, the homesteader takes the previously wild, undomesticated land, and tames it by putting it to productive use. Mixing his labor with land sites should give him just as clear a title as in the case of animals.

From our two basic axioms: the right of every man to self-ownership; and the right of every man to own previously unused natural resources that he first appropriates or transforms by his labor—the entire system of justification for property rights can be deduced. For if anyone justly owns the land himself and the property which he finds and creates, then he of course has the right to

---

exchange that property for the similarly acquired just property of someone else. This establishes the right of free exchange of property, as well as the right to give one's property away to someone who agrees to receive it. Thus, X may own his person and labor and the farm he clears on which he grows wheat; Y owns the fish he catches; Z owns the cabbages he grows and the land under it. But then X has the right to exchange some of his wheat for some of Y's fish (if Y agrees) or Z's cabbages. And when X and Y make a voluntary agreement to exchange wheat for fish, then that fish becomes X's justly acquired property to do with what he wishes, and the wheat becomes Y's just property in precisely the same way. Further, a man may of course exchange not only the tangible objects he owns but also his own labor, which of course he owns as well. Thus, Z may sell his labor services of teaching farmer X's children in return for some of the farmer's produce.

We have thus established the property-right justification for the free-market process. For the free-market economy, as complex as the system appears to be on the surface, is yet nothing more than a vast network of voluntary and mutually agreed upon two-person or two-party exchanges of property titles, such as we have seen occurs between wheat and cabbage farmers, or between the farmer and the teacher. In the developed free-market economy, the farmer exchanges his wheat for money; the wheat is bought by the miller who processes and transforms the wheat into flour; the baker sells the bread to the wholesaler, who in turn sells it to the retailer, who finally sells it to the consumer. In the case of the sculptor, he buys the clay and the tools from the producers who dug the clay out of the ground or those who bought the clay from the original miners; and he bought his tools from the manufacturers who in turn purchased the raw material from the miners of iron ore.

How "money" enters the equation is a complex process; but it should be clear here that conceptually the use of money is equivalent to any useful commodity that is exchanged for wheat, flour, etc. Instead of money, the commodity exchanged could be cloth, iron or whatever. At each step of the way, mutually beneficial exchanges of property titles—to goods, services, or money—are agreed upon and transacted.

And what of the capital-labor relationship? Here, too, as in the case of the teacher selling his services to the farmer, the laborer sells his services to the manufacturer who has purchased the iron ore or to the shipper who has bought logs from the loggers. The capitalist performs the function of saving money to buy the raw material, and then pays the laborers in advance of sale of the product to the eventual customers.

Many people, including such utilitarian free-market advocates as John Stuart Mill, have been willing to concede the propriety and the justice (if they are not utilitarians) of the producer owning and earning the fruits of his labor. But they balk at one point: inheritance. If Roberto Clemente is ten times as good and "productive" a ballplayer as Joe Smith, they are willing to concede the justice of Clemente's earning ten times the amount; but what, they ask, is the justification for someone whose only merit is being born a Rockefeller inheriting far more wealth than someone born a Rothbard?

There are several answers that could be given to this question: for example, the natural fact that every individual must, of necessity, be born into a different condition, at a different time or place, and to different parents. Equality of birth or rearing, therefore, is an impossible chimera. But in the context of our theory of justice in property rights, the answer is to focus *not* on the recipient, not on the child Rockefeller or the child Rothbard, but to concentrate on the *giver*, the man who bestows the inheritance. For if Smith and Jones and Clemente have the right to their labor and their property and to exchange the titles to this property for the similarly obtained property of others, then they *also* have the right to give their property to whomever they wish. The point is not the right of "inheritance" but the right of *bequest*, a right which derives from the title to property itself. If Roberto Clemente owns his labor and the money he earns from it, then he has the right to give that money to the baby Clemente.

Armed with a theory of justice in property rights, let us now apply it to the often vexing question of how we should regard existing titles to property.

III. Toward a Critique of Existing Property Titles

Among those who call for the adoption of a free market and a free society, the utilitarians, as might be expected, wish to validate all existing property titles, as so defined by the government. But we have seen the inadequacy of this position, most clearly in the case of slavery, but similarly in the validation that it gives to *any* acts of governmental confiscation or redistribution, including our hypothetical Kennedy and Rockefeller "private" ownership of the territorial area of a state. But how much of a redistribution from existing titles would be implied by the adoption of our theory of justice in property, or of any attempt to put that theory into practice? Isn't it true, as some people charge, that all existing property titles, or at least all land titles, were the result of government grants and coercive redistribution? Would *all* property titles therefore be confiscated in the name of justice? And who would be granted these titles?

Let us first take the easiest case: where existing property has been stolen, as acknowledged by the government (and therefore by utilitarians) as well as by our theory of justice. In short, suppose that Smith has stolen a watch from Jones; in that case, there is no difficulty in calling upon Smith to relinquish the watch and to give it back to the true owner, Jones. But what of more difficult cases—in short, where existing property titles are ratified by state confiscation of a previous victim? This could apply either to money or especially to land titles, since land is a constant, identifiable, fixed quotal share of the earth's surface.

Suppose, first, for example, that the government has either taken land or money from Jones by coercion (either by taxation or its imposed redefinition of property) and has granted the land to Smith, or alternatively, has ratified Smith's direct act of confiscation. What would our policy of justice say then? We would say, along with the general view of crime, that the aggressor and unjust owner, Smith, must be made to disgorge the property title (either land or money) and give it over to its true owner, Jones. Thus, in the case of an identifiable unjust owner and the identifiable victim or just owner, the case is clear: a restoration to the victim of his rightful property. Smith, of course, must not be compensated for this restitution, since compensation would either be enforced unjustly on the victim himself or on the general body of taxpayers. Indeed, there is a far better case for the additional punishment of Smith, but there is no space here to develop the theory or punishment for crime or aggression.

Suppose, next, a second case, in which Smith has stolen a piece of land from Jones but that Jones has died; he leaves, however, an heir, Jones II. In that case, we proceed as before; there is still the identifiable aggressor, Smith, and the identifiable heir of the victim, Jones II, who now is the inherited just owner of the title. Again, Smith must be made to disgorge the land and turn it over to Jones II.

But suppose, a third, more difficult case; Smith is still the thief, but Jones and his entire family and heirs have been wiped out, either by Smith himself or in the natural course of events. Jones is intestate; what then should happen to the property? The first principle is that Smith, being the thief, cannot keep the fruits of his aggression; but in that case, the property becomes unowned and becomes up for grabs in the same way as any piece of unowned property. The "homestead principle" becomes applicable, in the sense that the first user or occupier of the newly declared unowned property becomes the just and proper owner. The only stipulation is that Smith himself, being the thief, is not eligible for this homesteading.[9]

Suppose now a fourth case, and one generally more relevant to problems of land title in the modern world. Smith is not a thief, nor has he directly received the land by government grant; but his *title* is derived from his ancestor who *did* so unjustly appropriate title to the property; the ancestor, Smith I, let us say, stole the property from Jones I, the rightful owner. What should be the disposition of the property now? The answer, in our view, completely depends on whether or not Jones' heirs, the surrogates of the identifiable victims, still exist. Suppose, for example, that Smith VI legally "owns" the land, but that Jones VI is still extant and identifiable. Then we would have to say that, while Smith VI himself is not a thief and not punishable as such, his *title* to the land, being solely derived from inheritance passed down from Smith I, does not give him true ownership, and that he too must disgorge the land—without compensation—and yield it into the hands of Jones VI.

But, it might protested, what of the improvements that Smiths II-VI may have added to the land? Doesn't Smith VI deserve compensation for these legitimately owned additions to the original land received from Jones I? The answer depends on the moveability or separability of these improvements. Suppose, for example, that Smith steals a car from Jones and sells it to Robinson. When the car is apprehended, then Robinson, though he purchased it in good faith from Jones, has no title better than Smith's which was nil, and therefore he must yield up the car to Jones without compensation. (He has been defrauded by Smith and must try to extract compensation out of Smith, *not* out of the victim Jones.) But suppose that Robinson, in the meantime, has improved the car? The answer depends on whether these improvements are separable from the car itself. If, for example, Robinson has installed a new radio which did not exist before, then he should certainly have the right to take it out before handing the car back to Jones. Similarly, in the case of land, to the extent that Smith VI has simply improved the land itself and mixed his resources inextricably with it, there is nothing he can do; but if, for example, Smith VI or his ancestors built new buildings upon the land, then he should have the right to demolish or cart away these buildings before handing the land over to Jones VI.

But what if Smith I did indeed steal the land from Jones I, but that all of Jones' descendants or heirs are lost in antiquity and cannot be found? What should be the status of the land then? In that case, since Smith VI is not himself a thief, he becomes the *legitimate* owner of the land on the basis of our homestead principle. For if the land is "unowned" and up for grabs, then Smith VI himself has been occupying and using it, and therefore he becomes the just and rightful owner on the homestead basis. Furthermore, all of his descendants have clear and proper title on the basis of being his heirs.

It is clear, then, that *even* if we can show that the origin of most existing land titles are in coercion and theft, the existing owners are still just and legitimate owners if (a) they themselves did not engage in aggression, and (b) if no identifiable heirs of the original victims can be found. In most cases of current land title this will probably be the case. *A fortiori*, of course, if we simply *don't know* whether the original land titles were acquired by coercion, then our homestead principle gives the current property owners the benefit of the doubt and establishes them as just and proper owners as well. Thus, the establishment of our theory of justice in property titles will not usually lead to a wholesale turnover of landed property.

In the United States, we have been fortunate enough to have largely escaped continuing aggression in land titles. It is true that originally the English Crown gave land titles unjustly to favored persons (e.g., the territory roughly of New York State to the ownership of the Duke of York), but fortunately these grantees were interested enough in quick returns to subdivide and sell their lands to the actual settlers. As soon as the settlers purchased their land, their titles were legitimate, and so were the titles of all those who inherited or purchased them. Later on, the U.S. government unfortunately laid claim to all virgin land as the "public domain," and then unjustly sold the land to speculators who had not earned a homestead title. But eventually these speculators sold the land to the actual settlers, and from then on the land title was proper and legitimate.[10]

In South America and much of the undeveloped world, however, matters are considerably different. For here, in many areas, an invading state conquered the lands of peasants and then parcelled out such lands to various warlords as their private fiefs, from then on to extract rent from the hapless peasantry. The descendants of the *conquistadores* still presume to own the land tilled by the descendants of the original peasants, people with a clearly just claim to ownership of the land. In this situation, justice requires the vacating of the land titles by these feudal or coercive landholders, (who are in a position equivalent to our hypothetical Rockefellers and Kennedys) and the turning over of the property titles without compensation to the individual peasants who are the true owners of their land.

Much of the drive for "land reform" by the peasantry of the undeveloped world is precisely motivated by an instinctive application of our theory of justice: by the apprehension of the peasants that the land they have tilled for generations is *their* land and that the landlord's claim is coercive and unjust. It is ironic, that, in these numerous cases, the only response of utilitarian free-market advocates is to defend existing land titles, regardless of their injustice, and to tell the peasants to keep quiet and "respect private property." Since the peasants are convinced that the property is *their* private title, it is no wonder that they fail to be impressed; but since they find the supposed champions of property rights and free-market capitalism to be their staunch enemies, they generally are forced to turn to the only organized groups that at least rhetorically champion their claims and are willing to carry out the required rectification of property titles—the socialists and communists. In short, from simply a utilitarian consideration of consequences, the utilitarian free-marketeers have done very badly in the undeveloped world, the result of their ignoring the fact that others than themselves, however inconveniently, *do* have a passion for justice. Of course, after socialists or communists take power, they do their best to collectivize peasant land, and one of the prime struggles of socialist society is that of the state *versus* the peasantry. But even those peasants who are aware of socialists duplicity on the land question may still feel that with the socialists and communists they *at least* have a fighting chance. And sometimes, of course, the peasants have been able to win and to force communist regimes to keep hands off their newly gained private property: notably in the cases of Poland and Yugoslavia.

The utilitarian defense of the *status quo* will then be *least* viable—and therefore the least utilitarian—in those situations where the *status quo* is the most glaringly unjust. As often happens, far more than utilitarians will admit, justice and genuine utility are here linked together.

To sum up: all existing property titles may be considered just under the homestead principle, *provided* (a) that there may never be any property in *people*; (b) that the existing property owner did not himself steal the property; and particularly (c) that any identifiable just owner (the original victim of theft or his heir) must be accorded his property.

It might be charged that our theory of justice in property titles is deficient because in the real world most landed (and even other) property has a past history so tangled that it becomes *impossible* to identify who or what has committed coercion and therefore who the current just owner may be. But the point of the "homestead principle" is that if we *don't know* what crimes have been committed in acquiring the property in the past, or if we don't know the victims or their heirs, then the current owner becomes the legitimate and just owner on homestead grounds. In short, if Jones owns a piece of land at the present time, and we don't know what crimes were committed to arrive at the current title, then Jones, as the current owner, becomes as fully legitimate a property owner of this land as he does over his own person. Overthrow of existing property title only becomes legitimate if the victims or their heirs can present an authenticated, demonstrable, and specific claim to the property. Failing such conditions, existing landowners possess a fully moral right to their property.

Notes

1. Economists failed to heed the emphasis on titles of ownership underlying exchange stressed by the social philosopher Spencer Heath. Thus: "Only those things which are *owned* can be exchanged or used as instruments of service or exchange. This exchange is not transportation; it is the transfer of ownership or title. This is a social and not a physical process." Spencer Heath, *Citadel, Market and Altar* (Baltimore: Science of Society Foundation, 1957), p. 48.

2. For a welcome recent emphasis on the subjectivity of cost, see James N. Buchanan, *Cost and Choice* (Chicago: Markham Pub. Co., 1969).

3. I do not mean to imply here that *no* social science of economic analysis can be *Wertfrei,* only that any attempt whatever to apply the analysis to the political arena, however remote, *must* involve and imply some sort of ethical position.

4. On the arbitrariness and uncertainty of all legislative law, see Bruno Leoni, *Freedom and the Law* (Los Angeles: Nash Pub. Co., 1972).

5. The point here is not, of course, to criticize all rents *per se,* but rather to call into question the legitimacy of property titles (here landed property) derived from the coercive actions of government.

6. John Locke, *An Essay Concerning the True, Original, Extent and End of Civil Government*, in E. Barker, ed., *Social Contract* (New York: Oxford University Press, 1948), pp. 17-18.

7. Equally to be rejected is a grotesque proposal by Professor Kenneth E. Boulding, which however is a typical suggestion of a market-oriented utilitarian economist. This is a scheme for the government to allow only a certain maximum number of baby-permits per mother, but then to allow a "free" market in the purchase and sale of these baby rights. This plan, of course, denies the right of every mother over her own body. Boulding's plan may be found in Kenneth E. Boulding, *The Meaning of the 20th Century* (New York: Harper & Row, 1964). For a discussion of the plan, see Edwin G. Dolan, *TAN-STAAFL: The Economic Strategy for Environmental Crisis* (New York: Holt, Rinehart & Winston, 1971), p. 64.

8. Locke, *Civil Government*, p. 18.

9. Neither is the government eligible. There is no space here to elaborate our view that government can never be the just owner of property. Suffice it to say here that the government gains its revenue from tax appropriation from production rather than from production itself, and hence that the concept of just property can never apply to government.

10. This legitimacy, of course, does not apply to the vast amount of land in the West still owned by the federal government which it refuses to throw open to homesteading. Our response to this situation must be that the government should throw open all of its public domain to private homesteading without delay.

'SOCIAL' OR DISTRIBUTIVE JUSTICE

Friedrich A. Hayek

> So great is the uncertainty of merit, both from its natural obscurity, and from the self-conceit of each individual, that no determinate rule of conduct could ever follow from it.
>
> —*David Hume**

> Welfare, however, has no principle, neither for him who receives it, nor for him who distributes it (one will place it here and another there); because it depends on the material content of the will, which is dependent upon particular facts and thereby incapable of a general rule.
>
> —*Immanuel Kant**

The Concept of 'Social Justice'

While in the preceding chapter I had to defend the conception of justice as the indispensable foundation and limitation of all law, I must now turn against an abuse of the word which threatens to destroy the conception of law which made it the safeguard of individual freedom. It is perhaps not surprising that men should have applied to the joint effects of the actions of many people, even where these were never foreseen or intended, the conception of justice which they had developed with respect to the conduct of individuals towards each other. 'Social' justice (or sometimes 'economic' justice) came to be regarded as an attribute which the 'actions' of society, or the 'treatment' of individuals and groups by society, ought to possess. As primitive thinking usually does when first noticing some regular processes, the results of the spontaneous ordering of the market were interpreted as if some thinking being deliberately directed them, or as if the particular benefits or harm different persons derived from them were determined by deliberate acts of will, and could therefore be guided by moral rules. This conception of 'social' justice is thus a direct consequence of that anthromorphism or personification on by which naive thinking tries to account for all self-ordering processes. It is a sign of the immaturity of our minds that we have not yet outgrown these primitive concepts and still demand from an impersonal process which brings about a greater satisfaction of human desires than any deliberate human organization could achieve, that it conform to the moral precepts men have evolved for the guidance of their individual actions.[1]

The use of the term 'social justice' in this sense is of comparatively recent date, apparently not much older than a hundred years. The expression was occasionally used earlier to describe the organized efforts to enforce the rules of just individual conduct,[2] and it is to the present day sometimes employed in learned discussion to evaluate the effects of the existing in situations of society.[3] But the sense in which it is now generally used and constantly appealed to in public discussion, and in which it will be examined in this chapter, is essentially the same as that in which the expression 'distributive justice' had long been employed. It seems to have become generally current in this sense at the time when (and perhaps partly because) John Stuart Mill explicitly treated the two terms as equivalent in such statements as that

> society should treat all equally well who have deserved equally well of it, that is, who have deserved equally well absolutely. This is the highest abstract standard of social and distributive justice; towards which all institutions, and the efforts of all virtuous citizens should be made in the utmost degree to converge.[4]

or that

> it is universally considered just that each person should obtain that (whether good or evil) which he deserves; and unjust that he should obtain a good, or be made to undergo an evil, which he does not deserve. This is perhaps the clearest and most emphatic form in which the idea of justice is conceived by the general mind. As it involves the idea of desert, the questions arises of what constitutes desert.[5]

It is significant that the first of these two passages occurs in the description of one of five meanings of justice which Mill distinguishes, of which four refer to rules of just individual conduct

---

THE INDIVIDUAL, PROPERTY RIGHTS AND SOCIETY

while this one defines a factual state of affairs which may but need not have been brought about by deliberate human action. Yet Mill appears to have been wholly unaware of the circumstance that in this meaning it refers to situations entirely different from those to which the other four meanings apply, or that this conception of 'social justice' leads straight to full- fledged socialism.

Such statements which explicitly connect 'social and distributive justice' with the 'treatment' by the society of the individuals according to their 'deserts' bring out most clearly its difference from plain justice, and at the same time the cause of the vacuity of the concept: the demand for 'social justice' is addressed not to the individual but to society—yet society, in the strict sense in which it must be distinguished from the apparatus of government, is incapable of acting for specific purpose, and the demand for 'social justice' therefore becomes a demand that the members of society should organize themselves in a manner which makes it possible to assign particular shares of the product of society to the different individuals or groups. The primary question then becomes whether there exists a moral duty to submit to a power which can co-ordinate the efforts of the members of society with the aim of achieving a particular pattern of distribution regarded as just.

If the existence of such power is taken for granted, the question of how the available means for the satisfaction of needs ought to be shared out becomes indeed a question of justice—though not a question to which prevailing morals provide an answer. Even the assumption from which most of the modern theorists of 'social justice' start, namely that it would require equal shares for all in so far as special considerations do not demand a departure from this principle, would then appear to be justified.[6] But the prior question is whether it is moral that men be subjected to the powers of direction that would have to be exercised in order that the benefits derived by the individuals could be meaningfully described as just or unjust.

It has of course to be admitted that the manner in which the benefits and burdens are apportioned by the market mechanism would in many instances have been regarded as very unjust *if* it were the result of a deliberate allocation to particular people. But this is not the case. Those shares are the outcome of a process the effect of which on particular people was neither intended nor foreseen by anyone when the institutions first appeared—institutions which were then permitted to continue because it was found that they improve for all or most the prospects of having their needs satisfied. To demand justice from such a process is clearly absurd, and to single out some people in such a society as entitled to a particular share evidently unjust.

What does it mean?

The Conquest of Public Imagination By 'Social Justice'

The appeal to 'social justice' has nevertheless by now become the most widely used and most effective argument in political discussion. Almost every claim for government action on behalf of particular groups is advanced in its name, and if it can be made to appear that a certain measure is demanded by 'social justice', opposition to it will rapidly weaken. People may dispute whether or not the particular measure is required by 'social justice'. But that this is the standard which ought to guide political action, and that the expression has a definite meaning, is hardly ever questioned. In consequence, there are today probably no political movements of politicians who do not readily appeal to 'social justice' in support of the particular measures which they advocate.

It also can scarcely be denied that the demand for 'social justice' has already in a great measure transformed the social order and is continuing to transform it in a direction which those who called for it never forsaw. Though the phase has undoubtably helped occasionally to make the law more equal for all, whether the demand for justice in distribution has in any sense made society juster or reduced discontent must remain doubtful.

The expression of course described from the beginning the aspirations which were at the heart of socialism. Although classical socialism has usually been defined by its demand for the socialization of the means of production, this was for it chiefly a means thought to be essential in order to bring about a 'just' distribution of wealth; and since socialists have later discovered that this redistribution could in great measure, and against less resistance, be brought about by taxation (and government services financed by it), and have in practice often shelved their earlier demands, the realization of 'social justice' has become their chief promise. It might indeed be said that the main difference between the order of society at which classic liberalism aimed and the sort of society into which it is now being transformed is that the former was governed by principles of just individual conduct while the new society is to satisfy the demands for 'social justice'—or, in other words, that the former demanded just action by the individuals while the latter more and more places the duty of justice on authorities with power to command people what to do.

The phrase could exercise this effect because it has gradually been taken over from the socialist not only by all the other political movements but also by most teachers and preachers of morality. It seems in particular to have been embraced by a large section of the clergy of all Christian denominations, who, while increasingly losing their faith in a supernatural revelation, appear to have sought a refuge and consolation in a new 'social' religion which substitutes a temporal for a celestial promise of justice, and who hope that they can thus continue their striving to do good. The Roman Catholic church especially has made the aim of 'social justice' part of its official doctrine;[7] but the ministers of most Christian denominations appear to vie with each other with such offers of more mundane aims—which also seem to provide the chief foundation for renewed ecumenical efforts.

The various modern authoritarian or dictatorial governments have of course no less proclaimed 'social justice' as their chief aim. We have it on the authority of Mr. Andrei Sakharov that millions of men in Russia are the victims of a terror that 'attempts to conceal itself behind the slogan of social justice'.

The commitment to 'social justice' has in fact become the chief outlet for moral emotion, the distinguishing attribute of the good man, and the recognized sign of the possession of a moral conscience. Though people may occasionally be perplexed to say which of the conflicting claims advanced in its name are valid, scarcely anyone doubts that the expression has a definite meaning, describes a high ideal, and points to grave defects of the existing social order which urgently call for correction. Even though until recently one would have vainly sought in the extensive literature for an intelligible definition of the term,[8] there still seems to exist little doubt, either among ordinary people or among the learned, that the expression has a definite and well understood sense.

But the near-universal acceptance of a belief does not prove that it is valid or even meaningful any more than the general belief in witches or ghosts proved the validity of these concepts. What we have to deal with in the case of 'social justice' is simply a quasi-religious superstition of the kind which we should respectfully leave in peace so long as it merely makes those happy who hold it, but which we must fight when it becomes the pretext of coercing other men. And the prevailing belief in 'social justice' is at present probably the gravest threat to most other values of a free civilization.

Whether Edward Gibbon was wrong or not, there can be no doubt that moral and religious beliefs can destroy a civilization and that, where such doctrines prevail, not only the most cherished beliefs but also the most revered moral leaders, sometimes saintly figures whose unselfishness is beyond question, may become grave dangers to the values which the same people regard as unshakeable. Against this threat we can protect ourselves only by subjecting even our dearest dreams of a better world to ruthless rational dissection.

It seems to be widely believed that 'social justice' is just a new moral value which we must add to those that were recognized in the past, and that it can be fitted within the existing framework of moral rules. What is not sufficiently recognized is that in order to give this phrase meaning a complete change of the whole character of the social order will have to be effected, and that some of the values which used to govern it will have to be sacrificed. It is such a transformation of society into one of a fundamentally different type which is currently occurring piecemeal and without awareness of the outcome to which it must lead. It was in the belief that something like 'social justice' could thereby be achieved, that people have placed in the hands of government powers which it can now not refuse to employ in order to satisfy the claims of the ever increasing number of special interests who have learnt to employ the open sesame of 'social justice'.

I believe that 'social justice' will ultimately be recognized as a will-o'-the-wisp which has lured men to abandon many of the values which in the past have inspired the development of civilization—an attempt to satisfy a craving inherited from the traditions of the small group but which is meaningless in the Great Society of free men. Unfortunately, this vague desire which has become one of the strongest bonds spurring people of good will to action, not only is bound to be disappointed. This would be sad enough. But, like most attempts to pursue an unattainable goal, the striving for it will also produce highly undesirable consequences, and in particular lead to the destruction of the indispensible environment in which the traditional moral values alone can flourish, namely personal freedom.

The Inapplicability of the Concept of Justice to the Results of a Spontaneous Process

It is now necessary clearly to distinguish between two wholly different problems which the demand for social justice raises in a market order.

The first is whether within an economic order based on the market the concept of 'social justice' has any meaning or content whatever.

The second is whether it is possible to preserve a market order while imposing upon it (in the name of 'social justice' or any other pretext) some pattern of remuneration based on the assessment of the performance or the needs of different individuals or groups by an authority possessing the power to enforce it.

The answer to each of the questions is a clear no.

Yet it is the general belief in the validity of the concept of 'social justice' which drives all contemporary societies into greater and greater efforts of the second kind and which has a peculiar self-accelerating tendency the more dependent the position of the individuals or groups is seen to become on the actions of government, the more they will insist that the governments aim at some recognizable scheme of distributive justice and the more governments try to realize some preconceived pattern of desirable distribution, the more they must subject the position of the different individuals and groups to their control. So long as the belief in 'social justice' governs political action, this process must progressively approach nearer and nearer to a totalitarian system.

We shall at first concentrate on the problem of the meaning, or rather lack of meaning, of the term 'social justice', and only later consider the effects which the efforts to impose *any* preconceived pattern of distribution must have on the structure of the society subjected to them.

The contention that in a society of free men (as distinct from any compulsory organization) the concept of social justice is strictly empty and meaningless will probably appear as quite unbelievable to most people. Are we not all constantly disquited by watching how unjustly life treats different people and by seeing the deserving suffer and the unworthy prosper? And do we not all have a sense of fitness, and watch it with satisfaction, when we recognize a reward to be appropriate to effort or sacrifice?

The first insight which should shake this certainty is that we experience the same feelings also with respect to differences in human fates for which clearly no human agency is responsible and which it would therefore clearly be absurd to call injustice. Yet we do cry out against the injustice when a succession of calamities befalls one family while another steadily prospers, when a meritorious effort is frustrated by some unforseeable accident, and particularly if of many people whose endeavours seem equally great, some succeed brilliantly while others utterly fail. It is certainly tragic to see the failure of the most meritorious efforts of parents to bring up their children, of young men to build a career, or of an explorer or scientist pursuing a brilliant idea. And we will protest against such a fate although we do not know anyone who was to blame for it, or any way in which such disappointments can be prevented.

It is no different with regard to the general feeling of injustice about the distribution of material goods in a society of free men. Though we are in this case less ready to admit it, our complaints about the outcome of the market as unjust do not really assert that somebody has been unjust; and there is no answer to the question of *who* has been unjust. Society has simply become the new deity to which we complain and clamour for redress if it does not fulfil the expectations it has created. There is no individual and no cooperating group of people against which the sufferer would have a just complaint, and there are no conceivable rules of just individual conduct which would at the same time secure a functioning order and prevent such disappointments.

The only blame implicit in those complaints is that we tolerate a system in which each is allowed to choose his occupation and therefore nobody can have the power and the duty to see that the results correspond to our wishes. For in such a system in which each is allowed to use his knowledge for his own purposes[9] the concept of 'social justice' is necessarily empty and meaning-less, because in it nobody's will can determine the relative incomes of the different people, or prevent that they can be partly dependent on accident. 'Social justice' can be giving a meaning only in a directed or 'command' economy (such as an army) in which the individuals are ordered what to do; and any particular conception of 'social justice' could be realized only is such a centrally directed system. It presupposes that people are guided by specific directions and not by rules of just individual contact. Indeed, no system of rules of just individual conduct, and therefore no free action of the individuals, could produce results satisfying any principle of distributive justice.

We are of course not wrong in perceiving that the effects of the processes of a free society on the fates of the different individuals are not distributed according to some recognizable principle of justice. Where we go wrong is in concluding from this that they are unjust and that somebody is to be blamed for this. In a free society in which the position of the different individuals and groups is not the result of anybody's design—or could, within such a society, be altered in accordance with a generally applicable principle—the differences in reward simply cannot meaningfully be described as just or unjust. There are, no doubt, many kinds of individual action which are aimed at affecting particular remunerations and which might be called just or unjust. But there are no principles of individual conduct which would produce a pattern of distribution which as such could be called just, and therefore also no possibility for the individual to know what he would have to do to secure a just remuneration of his fellows.

The Rationale of the Economic Game in Which Only the Conduct of the Players But Not the Result Can Be Just

We have seen earlier that justice is an attribute of human conduct which we have learnt to exact because a certain kind of conduct is required to secure the formation and maintenance of a beneficial order of actions. The attribute of justice may thus be predicated about the intended results of human action but not about circumstances which have not deliberately been brought about by men. Justice requires that in the 'treatment' of another person or persons, i.e. in the intentional actions affecting the well-being of other persons, certain uniform rules of conduct be observed. It clearly has no application to the manner in which the impersonal process of the market allocates command over goods and services to particular people: this can be neither just nor unjust, because the results are not intended or foreseen, and depend on a multitude of circumstances not known in their totality to anybody. The conduct of the individuals in that process may well be just or unjust; but since their wholly just actions will have consequences for others which were neither intended nor foreseen, these effects do not thereby become just or unjust.

The fact is simply that we consent to retain, and agree to enforce, uniform rules for a procedure which has greatly improved the chances of all to have their wants satisfied, but at the price of all individuals and groups incurring the risk of unmerited failure. With the acceptance of this procedure the recompense of different groups and individuals becomes exempt from deliberate control. It is the only procedure yet discovered in which information widely dispersed among millions of men can be effectively utilized for the benefit of all—and used by assuring to all an individual liberty desirable for itself on ethical grounds. It is a procedure which of course has never been 'designed' but which we have learnt gradually to improve after we had discovered how it increased the efficiency of men in the groups who had evolved it.

It is a procedure which, as Adam Smith (and apparently before him the ancient Stoics) understood,[10] in all important respects (except that normally it is not pursued solely as a diversion) is wholly analogous to a game, namely a game partly of skill and partly of chance. We shall later describe it as the game of catallaxy. It proceeds, like all games, according to rules guiding the actions of individual participants whose aims, skills, and knowledge are different, with the consequence that the outcome will be unpredictable and that there will regularly be winners and losers. And while, as in a game, we are right in insisting that it be fair and that nobody cheat, it would be nonsensical to demand that the results for the different players be just. They will of necessity be determined partly by skill and partly by luck. Some of the circumstances which make the services of a person more or less valuable to his fellows, or which may make it desirable that he change the direction of his efforts, are not of human design or foreseeable by men.

We shall in the next chapter have to return to the rationale of the discovery procedure which the game of competition in a market in effect constitutes. Here we must content ourselves with emphasizing that the results for the different individuals and groups of a procedure for utilizing more information than any one person or agency can possess, must themselves be unpredictable, and must often be different from the hopes and intentions which determined the direction and intensity of their striving; and that we can make effective use of that dispersed knowledge only if (as Adam Smith was also one of the first to see clearly)[11] we allow the principle of negative feedback to operate, which means that some must suffer unmerited disappointment.

We shall also see later that the importance for the functioning of the market order of particular prices or wages, and therefore of the incomes of the different groups and individuals, is not due chiefly to the effects of the prices on all of those who receive them, but to the effects of the prices on those for whom they act as signals to change the direction of their efforts. Their function is not so much to reward people for what they *have* done as to tell them what in their own as well as in general interest they *ought* to do. We shall then also see that, to hold out a sufficient incentive for those movements which are required to maintain a market order, it will often be necessary that the return of people's efforts do *not* correspond to recognizable merit, but should show that, in spite of the best efforts of which they were capable, and for reasons they could not have known, their efforts were either more or less successful than they had reason to expect. In a spontaneous order the question of whether or not someone has done the 'right' thing cannot always be a matter of merit, but must be determined independently of whether the persons concerned ought or could have known what was required.

The long and the short of it all is that men can be allowed to decide what work to do only if the remuneration they can expect to get for it corresponds to the value their services have to those of their fellows who receive them; and that *these values which their services will have to their fellows will often have no relations to their individual merits or needs.* Reward for merit earned and indication of what a person should do, both in his own and in his fellows' interest, are different things. It is not good intentions or needs but doing what in fact most benefits others, irrespective of motive, which will secure the best reward. Among those who try to climb Mount Everest or to reach the Moon, we also honour not those who made the greatest efforts, but those who got there first.

The general failure to see that in this connection we cannot meaningfully speak of the justice or injustice of the results is partly due to the misleading use of the term 'distribution' which inevitably suggests a personal distributing agent whose will or choice determines the relative position of the different persons or groups.[12] There is of course no such agent, and we use an impersonal process to determine the allocation of benefits precisely because through its operation we can bring about a structure of relative prices and remunerations that will determine a size and composition of the total output which assures that the real equivalent of each individual's share that accident or skill assigns to him will be as large as we know to make it.

It would serve little purpose to enquire here at greater length into the relative importance of skill and luck in actually determining relative incomes. This will clearly differ a great deal between different trades, localities and times, and in particular between highly competitive and less enterprising societies. I am on the whole inclined to believe that within any one trade or profession the correspondence between individual ability and industry is higher than is commonly admitted, but that the relative position of all the members of a particular trade or profession compared with others will more often be affected by circumstances beyond their control and knowledge. (This may also be one reason why what is called 'social' injustice is generally regarded as a graver fault of the existing order than the corresponding misfortunes of individuals.)[13] But the decisive point is not that the price mechanism does on the whole bring it about that rewards are proportioned to skill and effort, but that even where it is clear to us that luck plays a great part, and we have no idea why some are regularly luckier in guessing than others, it is still in the general interest to proceed on the presumption that the past success of some people in picking winners makes it probable that they will also do so in the future, and that it is therefore worthwhile to induce them to continue their attempts.

The Alleged Necessity of a Belief in the Justice of Rewards

It has been argued persuasively that people will tolerate major inequalities of the material positions only if they believe that the different individuals get on the whole what they deserve, that they did in fact support the market order only because (and so long as) they thought that the differences of remuneration corresponded roughly to differences of merit, and that in consequence the maintenance of a free society presupposes the belief that some sort of 'social justice' is being done.[14] The market order, however, does not in fact owe its origin to such beliefs, nor was originally justified in this manner. This order could develop, after its earlier beginnings had decayed during the middle ages and to some extent been destroyed by the restrictions imposed by authority, when a thousand years of vain efforts to discover substantively just prices or wages were abandoned and the late schoolmen recognized them to be empty formulae and taught instead that the prices determined by just conduct of the parties in the market, i.e. the competitive prices arrived at without fraud, monopoly and violence, was all that justice required.[15] It was from this tradition that John Locke and his contemporaries derived the classical liberal conception of justice for which, as has been rightly said, it was only 'the way in which competition was carried on, not its results',[16] that could be just or unjust.

It is unquestionably true that, particularly among those who were very successful in the market order, a belief in a much stronger moral justification of individual success developed, and that, long after the basic principles of such an order had been fully elaborated and approved by catholic moral philosophers, it had in the Anglo-Saxon world received strong support from Calvinist teaching. It certainly is important in the market order (or free enterprise society, misleadingly called 'capitalism') that the individuals believe that their well-being depends primarily on their own efforts and decisions. Indeed, few circumstances will do more to make a person energetic and efficient than the belief that it depends chiefly on him whether he will reach the goals he has set himself. For this reason this belief is often encouraged by education and governing opinion—it seems to me, generally much to the benefit of most of the members of the society in which it prevails, who will owe many important material and moral improvements to persons guided by it. But it leads no doubt also to an exaggerated confidence in the truth of this generalization which to those who regard themselves (and perhaps are) equally able but have failed must appear as a bitter irony and severe provocation.

It is probably a misfortune that, especially in the USA, popular writers like Samuel Smiles and Horatio Alger, and later the sociologist W.G. Sumner, have defended free enterprise on the ground that it regularly rewards the deserving, and it bodes ill for the future of the market order that this seems to have become the only defence of it which is understood by the general public. That it has largely become the basis of the self-esteem of the businessman often gives him an air of self-righteousness which does not make him more popular.

It is therefore a real dilemma to what extent we ought to encourage in the young the belief that when they really try they will succeed, or should rather emphasize that inevitably some unworthy will succeed and some worthy fail—whether we ought to allow the views of those groups to prevail with whom the over-confidence in the appropriate reward of the able and industrious is strong and who in consequence will do much that benefits the rest, and whether without such partly erroneous beliefs the large numbers will tolerate actual differences in rewards which will be based only partly on achievement and partly on mere chance.

There is No 'Value to Society'

The futile medieval search for the just price and just wage, finally abandoned when it was recognized that only that 'natural' price could be regarded as just which would be arrived at in a competitive market where it would be determined not by any human laws or decrees but would depend on so many circumstances that it could be known beforehand only by God,[17] was not the end of the search for that philosophers' stone. It was revived in modern times, not only by the general demand for 'social justice,' but also by the long and equally abortive efforts to discover criteria of justice in connection with the procedures for reconciliation or arbitration in wage disputes. Nearly a century of endeavours by public spirited men and women in many parts of the world to discover principles by which just wage rates could be determined have, as more and more of them acknowledge, produced not a single rule which would do this.[18] It is somewhat surprising in view of this when we find an experienced arbitrator like Lady Wootton, after admitting that arbitrators are 'engaged in the impossible task of attempting to do justice in an ethical vacuum,' because 'nobody knows in this context what justice is,' drawing from it the conclusion that the criteria should be determined by legislation, and explicitly demand a political determination of all wages and incomes.[19] One can hardly carry any further the illusion that Parliament can determine what is just, and I don't suppose the writer would really wish to defend the atrocious principle implied that all rewards should be determined by political power.

Another source of the conception that the categories of just and unjust can be meaningfully applied to the remunerations determined by the market is the idea that the different services have a determined and ascertainable 'value to society,' and that the actual remuneration frequently differs from the value. But though the conception of a 'value to society' is sometimes carelessly used even by economists, there is strictly no such thing and the expression implies the same sort of anthropomorphism or personification of society as the term 'social justice.' Services can have value only to particular people (or an organization), and any particular service will have very different values for different members of the same society. To regard them differently is to treat society not as a spontaneous order of free men but as an organization whose members are all made to serve a single hierarchy of ends. This would necessarily be a totalitarian system in which personal freedom would be absent.

Although it is tempting to speak of a 'value to society' instead of a man's value to his fellows, it is in fact highly misleading if we say, e.g., that a man who supplies matches to millions and thereby earns $200,000 a year is worth more 'to society' than a man who supplies great wisdom or exquisite pleasure to a few thousand and thereby earns $20,000 a year. Even the performance of a Beethoven sonata, a painting by Leonardo or a play by Shakespeare have no 'value to society' but a value only to those who know and appreciate them. And it has little meaning to assert that a boxer or a crooner is worth more to society than a violin virtuoso or a ballet dancer if the former renders services to millions and the latter to a much smaller group. The point is not that the true values are different, but that the values attached to the different services by different groups of people are incommensurable; all that these expressions mean is merely that one in fact receives a larger aggregate sum from a larger number of people than the other.[20]

Incomes earned in the market by different persons will normally not correspond to the relative values of their services to any one person. Although, in so far as any one of a given group of different commodities is consumed by any one person, he or she will buy so much of each that the relative values to them of the last units bought will correspond to their relative prices, many pairs of commodities will never by consumed by the same person: the relative price of articles consumed only by men and of articles consumed only by women will not correspond to the relative values of these articles to anybody.

The remunerations which the individuals and groups receive in the market are thus determined by what these services are worth to those who receive the (or, strictly speaking, to the last pressing demand for them which can still be satisfied by the available supply) and not by some fictitious 'value to society.'

Another source of the complaint about the alleged injustice of this principle of remuneration is that the remuneration thus determined will often be much higher than would be necessary to induce the recipient to render those services This is perfectly true but necessary if all who render the same service are to receive the same remuneration, if the kind of service in question is to be increased so long as the price still exceeds costs, and if anyone who wishes to buy or set it at the current price is to be able to do so. The consequence must be that all but the marginal sellers make a gain in excess of what was necessary to induce them to render the services in question—just as all but the marginal buyers will get what they buy for less than they were prepared to pay. The remuneration of the market will therefore hardly ever seem just in the sense in which somebody might endeavour justly to compensate others for the efforts and sacrifice incurred for his benefit.

The consideration of the different attitudes which different groups will take to the remuneration of different services incidentally also shows that the large numbers by no means grudge all the incomes higher than theirs, but generally only those earned by activities the functions of which they do not understand or which they even regard as harmful. I have never known ordinary people grudge the very high earnings of the boxer or torero, the football idol or the cinema star or the jazz king—they seem often even to revel vicariously in the display of extreme luxury and waste of such figures compared with which those of industrial magnates or financial tycoons pale. It is where most people do not comprehend the usefulness of an activity, and frequently because they erroneously regard it as harmful (the 'speculator'—often combined with the belief that only dishonest activities can bring so much money), and especially where the large earnings are used to accumulate a fortune (again out of the erroneous belief that it would be desirable that it should be spent rather than invested) that the outcry about the injustice of it arises. Yet the complex structure of the modern Great Society would clearly not work if the remunerations of all the different activities were determined by the opinion which the majority holds of their value—or indeed if they were dependent on any one person's understanding or knowledge of the importance of all the different activities required for the functioning of the system.

The main point is not that the masses have in most instances no idea of the values which a man's activities have to his fellows, and that it is necessarily their prejudices which would determine the use of the government's power. It is that nobody knows except in so far as the market tells him. It is true enough that our esteem of particular activities often differs from the value given to them by the market; and we express this feeling by an outcry about the injustice of it. But when we ask what ought to be the relative remunerations of a nurse and a butcher, of a coal miner and a judge at a high court, of the deep sea diver or the cleaner of sewers, of the organizer of a new industry and a jockey, of the inspector of taxes and the inventor of a life-saving drug, of the jet pilot or the professor of mathematics, the appeal to 'social justice' does not give us the slightest help in deciding—and if we use it it is no more than an insinuation that the others ought to agree with our view without giving any reason for it.

It might be objected that, although we cannot give the term 'social justice' a precise meaning, this need not be a fatal objection because the position may be similar to that which I have earlier contended exists with regard to justice proper: we might not know what is 'socially just' yet know quite well what is 'socially unjust'; and by persistently eliminating 'social injustice' whenever we encounter it, gradually approach 'social justice.' This, however, does not provide a way out of the basic difficulty. There can be no test by which we can discover what is 'socially unjust' because there is no subject by which such an injustice can be committed, and there are no rules of individual conduct the observance of which in the market order would secure to the individuals and groups the position which as such (as distinguished from the procedure by which it is determined) would appear just to us.[21] It does not belong to the categeory of error but to that of nonsense, like the term 'a moral stone'.

The Meaning of 'Social'

One might hope to get some help in the search for the meaning of 'social justice' by examining the meaning of the attribute 'social'; but the attempt to do so soon leads into a quagmire of confusion nearly as bad as that which surrounds 'social justice' itself.[22] Originally 'social' had of course a clear meaning (analogous to formations like 'national', 'tribal', or 'organizational'), namely that of pertaining to, or characteristic of the structure and operations of society. In this sense justice clearly is a social phenomenon and the addition of 'social' to the noun a pleonasm[23] such as if we spoke of 'social language'—though in occasional early uses it might have been intended to distinguish the generally prevailing views of justice from that held by particular persons or groups.

But 'social justice' as used today is not 'social' in the sense of 'social norms', i.e. something which has developed as a practice of individual action in the course of social evolution, not a product of society or of a social process, but a conception to be imposed upon society. It was the reference of 'social' to the whole of society, or to the interests of all its members, which led to its gradually acquiring a predominant meaning of moral approbation. When it came into general use during the third quarter of the last century it was meant to convey an appeal to the still ruling classes to concern themselves more with the welfare of the much more numerous poor whose interests had not received adequate consideration.[24] The 'social question' was posed as an appeal to the conscience of the upper classes to recognize their responsibility for the welfare of the neglected sections of society whose voices had till then carried little weight in the councils of government. 'Social policy' (or *Social-politik* in the language of the country then leading in the movement) became the order of the day, the chief concern of all progressive and good people, and 'social' came increasingly to displace such terms as 'ethical' or simply 'good'.

But from such an appeal to the conscience of the public to concern themselves with the unfortunate ones and recognize them as members of the same society, the conception gradually came to mean that 'society' ought to hold itself responsible for the particular material position of all its members, and for assuring that each received what was 'due' to him. It implied that the processes of society should be deliberately directed to particular results and, by personifying society, represented it as a subject endowed with a conscious mind, capable of being guided in its operation by moral principles.[25] 'Social' became more and more the description of the pre-eminent virtue, the attribute in which the good man excelled and the ideal by which communal action was to be guided.

But while this development indefinitely extended the field of application of the term 'social', it did not give it the required new meaning. It even so much deprived it of its original descriptive meaning that American sociologists have found it necessary to coin the new term 'societal' in its place. Indeed, it has produced a situation in which 'social' can be used to describe almost any action as publicly desirable and has at the same time the effect of depriving any terms with which it is combined of clear meaning. Not only 'social justice' but also 'social democracy', 'social market economy'[26] or the 'social state of law' (or rule of law—in German *sozialer Rechtsstaat*) are expressions which, through justice, democracy, the market economy or the *Rechtsstaat* have by themselves perfectly good meanings, the addition of the adjective 'social' makes them capable of meaning almost anything one likes. The word has indeed become one of the chief sources of confusion of political discourse and can probably no longer be reclaimed for a useful purpose.

There is apparently no end to the violence that will be done to language to further some ideal and the example of 'social justice' has recently given rise to the expression 'global justice'! Its negative, 'global injustice', was defined by an ecumenical gathering of American religious leaders as 'characterized by a dimension of sin in the economic, political, social, sexual, and class structures and systems of global society'![27] It would seem as if the conviction that one is arguing in a good cause produced more sloppy thinking and even intellectual dishonesty than perhaps any other cause.

'Social Justice' and Equality

The most common attempts to give meaning to the concept of 'social justice' resort to egalitarian considerations and argue that every departure from equality of material benefits enjoyed has to be justified by some recognizable common interest which these differences serve.[28] This is based on a specious analogy with the situation in which some human agency has to distribute rewards, in which case indeed justice would require that these rewards be determined in accordance with some recognizable rule of general applicability. But earnings in a market system, though people tend to regard them as rewards, do not serve such a function. Their rationale (if one may use this term for a role which was not designed but developed because it assisted human endeavour without people understanding how), is rather to indicate to people what they ought to do if the order is to be maintained on which they all rely. The prices which must be paid in a market economy for different kinds of labour and other factors of production if individual efforts are to match, although they will be affected by effort, diligence, skill, need, etc., cannot conform to any one of these magnitudes; and considerations of justice just do not make sense[29] with respect to the determination of a magnitude which does not depend on anyone's will or desire, but on circumstances which nobody knows in their totality.

The contention that all differences in earnings must be justified by some corresponding difference in deserts is one which would certainly not have been thought to be obvious in a community of farmers or merchants or artisans, that is, in a society in which success or failure were clearly seen to depend only in part on skill and industry, and in part on pure accident which might hit anyone—although even in such societies individuals were known to complain to God or fortune about the injustice of their fate. But, though people resent that their remuneration should in part depend on pure accident, that is in fact precisely what it must if the market order is to adjust itself promptly to the unavoidable and unforeseen changes in circumstances, and the individual is to be allowed to decide what to do. The now prevalent attitude could arise only in a society in which large numbers worked as members of organizations in which they were remunerated at stipulated rates for time worked. Such communities will not ascribe the different fortunes of its members to the operation of an impersonal mechanism which serves to guide the directions of efforts, but to some human power that ought to allocate shares according to merit.

The postulate of material equality would be a natural starting point only if it were a necessary circumstance that the shares of the different individuals or groups were in such a manner determined by deliberate human decision. In a society in which this were an unquestioned fact, justice would indeed demand that the allocation of the means for the satisfaction of human needs were effected according to some uniform principle such as merit or need (or some combination of these), and that, where the principle adopted did not justify a difference, the shares of the different individuals should be equal. The prevalent demand for material equality is probably often based on the belief that the existing inequalities are the effect of somebody's decision—a belief which would be wholly mistaken in a genuine market order and has still only very limited validity in the highly interventionist 'mixed' economy existing in most countries today. This now prevalent form of economic order has in fact attained its character largely as a result of governmental measures aiming at what was thought to be required by 'social justice'.

When the choice, however, is between a genuine market order, which does not and cannot achieve a distribution corresponding to any standard of material justice, and a system in which government uses its powers to put some such standard into effect, the question is not whether government ought to exercise, justly or unjustly, powers it must exercise in any case, but whether government should possess and exercise additional powers which can be used to determine the shares

---

of the different members of society. The demand for 'social justice', in other words, does not merely require government to observe some principle of action according to uniform rules in those actions which it must perform in any case, but demands that it undertake additional activities, and thereby assume new responsibilities—tasks which are not necessary for maintaining law and order and providing for certain collective needs which the market could not satisfy.

The great problem is whether this new demand for equality does not conflict with the equality of the rules of conduct which government must enforce on all in a free society. There is, of course, a great difference between government treating all citizens according to the same rules in all the activities it undertakes for other purposes, and government doing what is required in order to place the different citizens in equal (or less unequal) material positions. Indeed, there may arise a sharp conflict between these two aims. Since people will differ in many attributes which government cannot alter, to secure for them the same material position would require that government treat them very differently. Indeed, to assure the same material position to people who differ greatly in strength, intelligence, skill, knowledge and perseverance as well as in their physical and social environment, government would clearly have to treat them very differently to compensate for those disadvantages and deficiencies it could not directly alter. Strict equality of those benefits which government could provide for all, on the other hand, would clearly lead to inequality of the material positions.

This, however, is not the only and not even the chief reason why a government aiming to secure for its citizens equal material positions (or any determined pattern of material welfare) would have to treat them very unequally. It would have to do so because under such a system it would have to undertake to tell people what to do. Once the rewards the individual can expect are no longer an appropriate indication of how to direct their efforts to where they are most needed, because these rewards correspond not to the value which their services have for their fellows, but to the moral merit or desert the persons are deemed to have earned, they lose the guiding function they have in the market order and would have to be replaced by the commands of the directing authority. A central planning office would, however, have to decide on the tasks to be allotted to the different groups or individuals wholly on grounds of expedience or efficiency and, in order to achieve its ends, would have to impose upon them very different duties and burdens. The individuals might be treated according to uniform rules so far as their rewards were concerned, but certainly not with respect to the different kinds of work they would have to be made to do. In assigning people to their different tasks, the central planning authority would have to be guided by considerations of efficiency and expediency and not by principles of justice or equality. No less than in the market order would the individuals in the common interest have to submit to great inequality—only these inequalities would be determined not by the interaction of individual skills in an impersonal process, but by the uncontradictable decision of authority.

As is becoming clear in ever increasing fields of welfare policy, an authority instructed to achieve particular results for the individuals must be given essentially arbitrary powers to make the individuals do what seems necessary to achieve the required result. Full equality for most cannot but mean the equal submission of the great masses under the command of some elite who manages their affairs. While an equality of rights under a limited government is possible and an essential condition of individual freedom, a claim for equality of material position can be met only by a government with totalitarian powers.[30]

We are of course not wrong when we perceive that the effects on the different individuals and groups of the economic processes of a free society are not distributed according to some recognizable principle of justice. Where we go wrong is in concluding from this that they are unjust and that somebody is responsible and to be blamed for this. In a free society in which the position of the different individuals and groups is not the result of anybody's design—or could within such a society not be altered in accordance with a principle of general applicability—the differences in rewards cannot meaningfully be described as just or unjust. There are, no doubt, many kinds of individual actions which are aimed at affecting particular remunerations and which might be regarded as unjust. But there are no principles of individual conduct which would produce a pattern of distribution which as such could be called just, and therefore also no possibility for the individual to know what he would have to do to secure a just remuneration of his fellows.

Our whole system of morals is a system of rules of individual conduct, and in a Great Society no conduct guided by such rules, or by decisions of the individuals guided by such rules, could produce for the individuals results which would appear to us as just in the sense in which we regard designed rewards as just or unjust: simply because in such a society nobody has the power or the knowledge which would enable him to ensure that those affected by his actions will get what he thinks right for them to get. Nor could anyone who is assured remuneration according to some principle which is accepted as constituting 'social justice' be allowed to decide what he is to do: remuneration indicating how urgent it was that a certain work should be done could not be just in this sense, because the need for work of a particular kind would often depend on unforeseeable accidents and certainly not on the good intentions or efforts of those able to perform it. And an authority that fixed remunerations with the intention of thereby reducing the kind and number of people thought necessary in each occupation could not make these remunerations 'just', i.e. proportionate to desert, or need, or the merits of any other claim of the persons concerned, but would have to offer what was necessary to attract or retain the number of people wanted in each kind of activity.

'Equality of Opportunity'

It is of course not to be denied that in the existing market order not only the results but also the initial chances of different individuals are often very different; they are affected by circumstances of their physical and social environment which are beyond their control but in many particular respects might be altered by some governmental action. The demand for equality of opportunity or equal starting conditions (*Startgerechtigkeit*) appeals to, and has been supported by, many who in general favour the free market order. So far as this refers to such facilities and opportunities as are of necessity affected by governmental decisions (such as appointments to public office and the like), the demand was indeed one of the central points of classical liberalism, usually expressed by the French phrase 'la carrière ouverte aux talents'. There is also much to be said in favour of the government providing on an equal basis the means for the schooling of minors who are not yet fully responsible citizens, even though there are grave doubts whether we ought to allow government to administer to them.

But all this would still be very far from creating real equality of opportunity, even for persons possessing the same abilities. To achieve this government would have to control the whole physical and human environment of all persons, and have to endeavour to provide at least equivalent chances for each; and the more government succeeded in these endeavours, the stronger would become the legitimate demand that, on the same principle, any still remaining handicaps must be removed—or compensated for by putting extra burden on the still relatively favoured. This would have to go on until government literally controlled every circumstance which could affect any person's well-being. Attractive as the phrase of equality of opportunity at first sounds, once the idea is extended beyond the facilities which for other reasons have to be provided by government, it becomes a wholly illusory ideal, and any attempt concretely to realize it apt to produce a nightmare.

'Social Justice' and Freedom under the Law

The idea that men ought to be rewarded in accordance with the assessed merits or deserts of their services 'to society' presupposes an authority which not only distributes these rewards but also assigns to the individuals the tasks for the performance of which they will be rewarded. In other words, if 'social justice' is to be brought about, the individuals must be required to obey not merely general rules but specific demands directed to them only. The type of social order in which the individuals are directed to serve a single system of ends is the organization and not the spontaneous order of the market, that is, not a system in which the individual is free because bound only be general rules of just conduct, but a system in which all are subject to specific directions by authority.

It appears sometimes to be imagined that a mere alteration of the rules of individual conduct could bring about the realization of 'social justice'. But there can be no set of such rules, no principles by which the individuals could so govern their conduct that in a Great Society the joint effect of their activities would be a distribution of benefits which could be described as materially just, or any other specific and intended allocation of advantages and disadvantages among particular people or groups. In order to achieve *any* particular pattern of distribution through the market process, each producer would have to know, not only whom his efforts will benefit (or harm), but also how well off all the other people (actually or potentially) affected by his activities will be as the result of the services they are receiving from other members of the society. As we have seen earlier, appropriate rules of conduct can determine only the formal character of the order of activities that will form itself, but not the specific advantages particular groups or individuals will derive from it.

This rather obvious fact still needs to be stressed since even eminent jurists have contended that the substitution of 'social' or distributive for individual or commutative justice need not destroy the freedom under the law of the individual. Thus the distinguished German legal philosopher Gustav Radbruch explicitly maintained that 'the socialist community would also be a *Rechtsstaat* [i.e., the Rule of Law would prevail there], although a *Rechtsstaat* governed not by commutative but by distributive justice.'[31] And of France it is reported that 'it has been suggested that some highly placed administrators should be given the permanent task of "pronouncing" on the distribution of national income, as judges pronounce on legal matters.'[32] Such beliefs, however, overlook the fact that no specific pattern of distribution can be achieved by making the individuals obey rules of conduct, but that the achievement of such particular pre-determined results require deliberate co-ordination of all the different activities in accordance with the concrete circumstances of time and place. It precludes, in other words, that the several individuals act on the basis of their own knowledge and in the service of their own ends, which is the essence of freedom, but requires that they be made to act in the manner which according to the knowledge of the directing authority is required for the realization of the ends chosen by that authority.

The distributive justice at which socialism aims is thus irreconcilable with the rule of law, and with that freedom under the law which the rule of law is intended to secure. The rules of distributive justice cannot be rules for the conduct towards equals, but must be rules for the conduct of superiors towards their subordinates. Yet though some socialists have long ago themselves drawn the inevitable conclusion that 'the fundamental principles of formal law by which every case must be judged according to general rational principles...obtains only for the competitive phase of capitalism,'[33] and the communists, so long as they took socialism seriously, had even proclaimed that 'communism means not the victory of socialist law, but the victory of socialism over any law, since with the abolition of classes with antagonistic interests, law will disappear altogether',[34] when, more than thirty years ago, the present author made this the central point of a discussion of the political effects of socialist economic policies,[35] it evoked great indignation and violent protests. But the crucial point is implied even in Radbruch's own emphasis on the fact that the transition from commutative to distributive justice means a progressive displacement of prive by public law,[36] since public law consists not of rules of conduct for private citizens but of rules of organization for public officials. It is, as Radbruch himself stresses, a law that subordinates the citizens to authority.[37] Only if one understands by law not the general rules of just conduct only but any command issued by authority (or any authorization of such commands by a legislature), can the measures aimed at distributive justice be represented as compatible with the rule of law. But this concept is thereby made to mean mere legality and ceases to offer the protection of individual freedom which it was originally intended to serve.

There is no reason why in a free society government should not assure to all protection against severe deprivation in the form of an assured minimum income, or a floor below which nobody need to descend. To enter into such an insurance against extreme misfortune may well be in the interest of all; or it may be felt to be a clear moral duty of all to assist, within the organized community, those who cannot help themselves. So long as such a uniform minimum income is provided outside the market to all those who, for any reason, are unable to earn in the market an adequate maintenance, this need not lead to a restriction of freedom, or conflict with the Rule of Law. The problems with which we are here concerned arise only when the remuneration for services rendered is determined by authority, and the impersonal mechanism of the market which guides the direction of individual efforts is thus suspended.

Perhaps the acutest sense of grievance about injustice inflicted on one, not by particular persons but by the 'system', is that about being deprived of opportunities for developing one's abilities which others enjoy. For this any difference of environment, social or physical, may be responsible, and at least some of them may be unavoidable. The most important of these is clearly inseparable from the institution of the family. This not only satisfies a strong psychological need but in general serves as an instrument for the transmission of important cultural values. There can be no doubt that those who are either wholly deprived of this benefit, or grew up in unfavourable conditions, are gravely handicapped; and few will question that it would be desirable that some public institution so far as possible should assist such unfortunate children when relatives and neighbours fail. Yet few will seriously believe (although Plato did) that we can fully make up for such a deficiency, and I trust even fewer that, because this benefit cannot be assured to all, it should, in the interest of equality, be taken from those who now enjoy it. Nor does it seem to me that even material equality could compensate for those differences in the capacity of enjoyment and of experiencing a lively interest in the cultural surroundings which a suitable upbringing confers.

There are of course many other irremediable inequalities which must seem as unreasonable as economic inequalities but which are less resented than the latter only because they do not appear to be man-made or the consequence of institutions which could be altered.

The Spatial Range of 'Social Justice'

There can be little doubt that the moral feelings which express themselves in the demand for 'social justice' derive from an attitude which in more primitive conditions the individual developed towards the fellow members of the small group to which he belonged. Towards the personally known member of one's own group it may well have been a recognized duty to assist him and to adjust one's actions to his needs. This is made possible by the knowledge of his person and his circumstances. The situation is wholly different in the Great or Open Society. Here the products and services of each benefit mostly persons he does not know. The greater productivity of such a society rests on a division of labour extending far beyond the range any one person can survey. This extension of the process of exchange beyond relatively small groups, and including large numbers of persons not known to each other, has been made possible by conceding to the stranger and even the foreigner the same protection of rules of just conduct which apply to the relations to the known members of one's own small group.

This application of the same rules of just conduct to the relations to all other men is rightly regarded as one of the great achievements of a liberal society. What is usually not understood is that this extension of the same rules to the relations to all other men (beyond the most intimate group such as the family and personal friends) requires an attenuation at least of some of the rules which are enforced in the relations to other members of the smaller group. If the legal duties towards strangers or foreigners are to be the same as those towards the neighbours or inhabitants of the same village or town, the latter duties will have to be reduced to such as can also be applied to the stranger. No doubt men will always wish to belong also to smaller groups and be willing voluntarily to assume greater obligations towards self-chosen friends or companions. But such moral obligations towards some can never become enforced duties in a system of freedom under the law, because in such a system the selection of those towards whom a man wishes to assume special moral obligations must be left to him and cannot be determined by law. A system of rules intended for an Open Society and, at least in principle, meant to be applicable to all others, must have a somewhat smaller content than one to be applied in a small group.

Especially a common agreement on what is the due status or material position of the different members is likely to develop only in the relatively small group in which the members will be familiar with the character and importance of each other's activities. In such small communities the opinion about appropriate status will also still be associated with a feeling about what one self owes to the other, and not be merely a demand that somebody provide the appropriate reward. Demands for the realization of 'social justice' are usually as a matter of course, though often only tacitly, addressed to national governments as the agencies which possess the necessary powers. But it is doubtful whether in any but the smallest countries standards can be applied nationally which are derived from the condition of the particular locality with which the individual is familiar, and fairly certain that few men would be willing to concede to foreigners the same right to a particular income that they tend to recognize in their fellow citizens.

It is true that in recent years concern about the suffering of large numbers in the poor countries has induced the electorates of the wealthier nations to approve substantial material aid to the former; but it can hardly be said that in this considerations of justice played a significant role. It is indeed doubtful whether any substantial help would have been rendered if competing power groups had not striven to draw as many as possible of the developing countries into their orbit. And it deserves notice that the modern technology which has made such assistance possible could develop only because some countries were able to build up great wealth while most of the world saw little change.

Yet the chief point is that, if we look beyond the limits of our national states, and certainly if we go beyond the limits of what we regard as our civilization, we no longer even deceive ourselves that we know what would be 'socially just', and that those very groups within the existing states which are loudest in their demands for 'social justice', such as the trade unions, are regularly the first to reject such claims raised on behalf of foreigners. Applied to the international sphere, the complete lack of a recognized standard of 'social justice', or of any known principles on which such a standard could be based, becomes at once obvious; while on a national scale most people still think that what on the level of the face-to-face society is to them a familiar idea must also have some validity for national politics or the use of the powers of government. In fact, it becomes on this level a humbug—the effectiveness of which with well-meaning people the agents of organized interests have learnt successfully to exploit.

There is in this respect a fundamental difference between what is possible in the small group and in the Great Society. In the small group the individual can know the effects of his actions on his several fellows, and the rules may effectively forbid him to harm them in any manner and even require him to assist them in specific ways. In the Great Society many of the effects of a person's actions on various fellows must be unknown to him. It can, therefore, not be the specific effects in the particular case, but only rules which define kinds of actions as prohibited or required, which must serve as guides to the individual. In particular, he will often not know who the individual people will be who will benefit by what he does, and therefore not know whether he is satisfying a great need or adding to abundance. He cannot aim at just results if he does not know who will be affected.

Indeed the transition from the small group to the Great or Open Society—and the treatment of every other person as a human being rather than as either a known friend or an enemy—requires a reduction of the range of duties we owe to all others.

If a person's legal duties are to be the same towards all, including the stranger and even the foreigner (and greater only where he has voluntarily entered into obligations, or is connected by physical ties as between parents and children), the legally enforceable duties to neighbour and friend must not be more than those towards the stranger. That is, all those duties which are based on personal acquaintance and familiarity with individual circumstances must cease to be enforceable. The extension of the obligation to obey certain rules of just conduct to wider circles and ultimately to all men must thus lead to an attenuation of the obligation towards fellow members of the same small group. Our inherited or perhaps in part even innate moral emotions are in part inapplicable to Open Society (which is an abstract society), and the kind of 'moral socialism' that is possible in the small group and often satisfies a deeply ingrained instinct may well be impossible in the Great Society. Some altruistic conduct aimed at the benefit of some known friend that in the small group might be highly desirable, need not be so in the Open Society, and may there even be harmful (as e.g. the requirement that members of the same trade refrain from competing with each other).[38]

It may at first seem paradoxical that the advance of morals should lead to a reduction of specific obligations towards others: yet whoever believes that the principle of equal treatment of all men, which is probably the only chance for peace, is more important than special help to visible suffering, must wish it. It admittedly means that we make our rational insight dominate over our inherited instincts. But the great moral adventure on which modern man has embarked when he launched into the Open Society is threatened when he is required to apply to all his fellowmen rules which are appropriate only to the fellow members of a tribal group.

[handwritten margin note: rational insight over instinct]

Claims for Compensation for Distasteful Jobs

The reader will probably expect me now to examine in greater detail the particular claims usually justified by the appeal to 'social justice'. But this, as bitter experience has taught me, would be not only an endless but also a bootless task. After what has been said already, it should be obvious that there are no practicable standards of merit, deserts, or needs, on which in a market order the distribution of material benefits could be based, and still less any principle by which these different claims could be reconciled. I shall therefore confine myself to considering two arguments in which the appeal to 'social justice' is very commonly used. The first case is usually quoted in theoretical argument to illustrate the injustice of the distribution by the market process, though little is done about it in practice, while the second is probably the most frequent type of situation in which the appeal to social justice leads to government action.

The circumstance which is usually pointed out to demonstrate the injustice of the existing market order is that the most unpleasant jobs are commonly also the worst paid. In a just society, it is contended, those who have to dig coal underground or to clean chimneys or sewers, or who perform other unclean or menial tasks, should be remunerated more highly than those whose work is pleasurable.

It is of course true that it would be unjust if persons, although equally able as others to perform other tasks, were without special compensation assigned by a superior to such distasteful duties. If, e.g., in such an organization as an army, two men of equal capacity were made to perform different tasks, one of which was attractive and the other very unpleasant, justice would clearly require that the one who had regularly to perform the unpleasant duty should in some way be specially compensated for it.

The situation is entirely different, however, where people earn their living by selling their services to whoever pays best for them. Here the sacrifice brought by a particular person in rendering the service is wholly irrelevant and all that counts is the (marginal) value the services have to those to whom they are rendered. The reason for this is not only that the sacrifices different people bring in rendering the same kind of service will often be very different, or that it will not be possible to take account of the reason why some will be capable of rendering only less valuable services than others. But those whose aptitudes, and therefore also remunerations, will be small in the more attractive occupations will often find that they can earn more than they could otherwise by undertaking unpleasant tasks that are scorned by their more fortunate fellows. The very fact that the more unpleasant occupations will be avoided by those who can render services that are valued more highly by the buyers, will open to those whose skills are little valued opportunities to earn more than they otherwise could.

That those who have to offer to their fellows little that is valuable may have to incur more pain and effort to earn even a pittance than others who perhaps actually enjoy rendering services for which they are well paid, is a necessary concomitant of any system in which remuneration is based on the values the services have to the user and not an assessment of merit earned. It must therefore prevail in any social order in which the individual is free to choose whatever occupation he can find and is not assigned to one by authority.

The only assumption on which it could be represented as just that the miner working underground, or the scavenger, or slaughter-house workers, should be paid more highly than those engaged in more pleasant occupations, would thus be that this was necessary to induce a sufficient number of persons to perform these tasks, or that they are by some human agency deliberately assigned to these tasks. But while in a market order it may be a misfortune to have been born and bred in a village where formost the only chance of making a living is fishing (or for the women the cleaning of fish), it does not make sense to describe this as unjust. Who is supposed to have been unjust?—especially when it is considered that, if these local opportunities had not existed, the people in question would probably never have been born at all, as most of the population of such a village will probably owe its existence to the opportunities which enabled their ancestors to produce and rear children.

The Resentment of the Loss of Accustomed Positions

The appeal to 'social justice' which in practice has probably had the greatest influence is not one which has been much considered in literary discussion. The considerations of a supposed 'social injustice' which have led to the most far-reaching interference with the functioning of the market order are based on the idea that people are to be protected against an unmerited descent from the material position to which they have become accustomed. No other consideration of 'social justice' has probably exercised as widespread an influence as the 'strong and almost universal belief that it is unjuust to disappoint legitimate expectations of wealth. When differences of opinion arise, it is always on the question of what expectations are legitimate.' It is believed, as the same author says, 'that it is legitimate even for the largest classes to expect that no very great and sudden changes will be made to their detriment.'[39]

The opinion that long established positions create a just expectation that they will continue serves often as a substitute for more substantial criteria of 'social justice'. Where expectations are disappointed, and in consequence the rewards of effort often disproportionate to the sacrifice incurred, this will be regarded as an injustice without any attempt to show that those affected had a claim in justice to the particular income which they expected. At least when a large group of people find their income reduced as a result of circumstances which they could not have altered or foreseen, this is commonly regarded as unjust.

The frequent recurrence of such undeserved strokes of misfortune affecting some group is, however, an inseparable part of the steering mechanism of the market: it is the manner in which the cybernetic principle of negative feedback operates to maintain the order of the market. It is only through such changes which indicate that some activities ought to be reduced, that the efforts of all can be continuously adjusted to a greater variety of facts than can be known to any one person or agency, and that that utilization of dispersed knowledge is achieved on which the well-being of the Great Society rests. We cannot rely on a system in which the individuals are induced to respond to events of which they do not and cannot know without changes of the values of the services of different groups occurring which are wholly unrelated to the merits of their members. It is a necessary part of that process of constant adaptation to changing circumstances on which the mere maintenance of the existing level of wealth depends that some people should have to discover by bitter experience that they have misdirected their efforts and are forced to look elsewhere for a remunerative occupation. And the same applies to the resentment of the corresponding undeserved gains that will accrue to others for whom things have turned out better than they had reason to expect.

The sense of injury which people feel when an accustomed income is reduced or altogether lost is largely the result of a belief that they have morally deserved that income and that, therefore, so long as they work as industriously and honestly as they did before, they are in justice entitled to the continuance of that income. But the idea that we have morally deserved what we have honestly earned in the past is largely an illusion. What is true is only that it would have been unjust if anybody had taken from us what we have in fact acquired while observing the rules of the game.

It is precisely because in the cosmos of the market we all constantly receive benefits which we have not deserved in any moral sense that we are under an obligation also to accept equally undeserved diminutions of our incomes. Our only moral title to what the market gives us we have earned by submitting to those rules which makes the formation of the market order possible. These rules imply that nobody is under an obligation to supply us with a particular income unless he has specifically contracted to do so. If we were all to be consistently deprived, as the socialists propose to do, of all 'unearned benefits' which the market confers upon us, we would have to be deprived of most of the benefits of civilization.

It is clearly meaningless to reply, as is often done, that, since we owe these benefits to 'society', 'society' should also be entitled to allocate these benefits to those who in its opinion deserve them. Society, once more, is not an acting person but an orderly structure of actions resulting from the observation of certain abstract rules by its members. We all owe the benefits we receive from the operation of this structure not to anyone's attention to confer them on us, but to the members of society generally obeying certain rules in the pursuit of their interests, rules which include the rule that nobody is to coerce others in order to secure for himself (or for third persons) a particular income. This imposes upon us the obligation to abide by the results of the market also when it turns against us.

The chance which any individual in our society has of earning an income approximating that which he has now is the consequence of most individuals obeying the rules which secure the formation of that order. And though this order provides for most good prospects for the successful employment of their skills, this success must remain dependent also on what from the point of view of the individual must appear as mere luck. The magnitude of the chances open to him are not of his making but the result of others submitting to the same rules of the game. To ask for protection against being displaced from a position one has long enjoyed, by others who are now favoured by new circumstances, means to deny to them the chances to which one's own present position is due.

Any protection of an accustomed position is thus necessarily a privilege which cannot be granted to all and which, if it had always been recognized, would have prevented those who now claim it from ever reaching the position for which they now demand protection. There can, in particular, be no right to share equally in a general increase of incomes if this increase (or perhaps even their maintenance at the existing level) is dependent on the continuous adjustment of the whole structure of activities to new and unforeseen circumstances that will alter and often reduce the contributions some groups can make to the needs of their fellows. There can thus be in justice no such claims as, e.g., those of the American farmer for 'parity', or of any other group to the preservation of their relative or absolute position.

The satisfaction of such claims by particular groups would thus not be just but eminently unjust, because it would involve the denial to some of the chances to which those who make this claim owe their position. For this reason it has always been conceded only to some powerfully organized groups who were in the position to enforce their demands. Much of what is today done in the name of 'social justice' is thus not only unjust but also highly unsocial in the true sense of the word: it amounts simply to the protection of entrenched interests. Though it has come to be regarded as a 'social problem' when sufficiently large numbers clamour for protection of their accustomed position, it becomes a serious problem chiefly because, camouflaged as a demand for 'social justice', it can engage the sympathy of the public. We shall see in volume 3 why, under the existing type of democratic institutions, it is in practice inevitable that legislatures with unlimited powers yield to such demands when made by sufficiently large groups. This does not alter the fact that to represent such measures as satisfying 'social justice' is little more than a pretext for making the interest of the particular groups prevail over the general interest of all. Though it is now usual to regard every claim of an organized group as a 'social problem', it would be more correct to say that, though the long run interests of the several individuals mostly agree with the general interest, the interests of the organized groups almost invariably are in conflict with it. Yet it is the latter which are commonly represented as 'social'.

Conclusions

The basic contention of this chapter, namely that in a society of free men whose members are allowed to use their own knowledge for their own purposes the term 'social justice' is wholly devoid of meaning or content, is one which by its very nature cannot be *proved*. A negative assertion never can. One may demonstrate for any number of particular instances that the appeal to 'social justice' in no way assists the choices we have to make. But the contention that in a society of free men the term has no meaning whatever can only be issues as a challenge which will make it necessary for others to reflect on the meaning of the words they use, and as an appeal not to use phrases the meaning of which they do not know.

So long as one assumes that a phrase so widely used must have some recognizable meaning one may endeavour to prove that attempts to enforce it in a society of free individuals must make that society unworkable. But such efforts become redundant once it is recognized that such a society lacks the fundamental precondition for the application of the concept of justice to the manner in which material benefits are shared among its members, namely that this is determined by a human will—or that the determination of rewards by human will could produce a viable market order. One does not have to prove that something is impracticable which cannot exist.

What I hope to have made clear is that the phrase 'social justice' is not, as most people probably feel, an innocent expression of good will towards the less fortunate, but that it has become a dishonest insinuation that one ought to agree to a demand of some special interest which can give no real reason for it. If political discussion is to become honest it is necessary that people should recognize that the term is intellectually disreputable, the mark of demagogy or cheap journalism which responsible thinkers ought to be ashamed to use because, once its vacuity is recognized, its use is dishonest. I may, as a result of long endeavours to trace the destructive effect which the invocation of 'social justice' has had on our moral sensitivity, and of again and again finding even eminent thinkers thoughtlessly using the phrase,[40] have become unduly allergic to it, but I have come to feel strongly that the greatest service I can still render to my fellow men would be that I could make the speakers and writers among them thoroughly ashamed ever again to employ the term 'social justice'.

That in the present state of the discussion the continued use of the term is not only dishonest and the source of constant political confusion, but destructive of moral feeling, is shown by the fact that again and again thinkers, including distinguished philosophers,[41] after rightly recognizing that the term justice in its now predominant meaning of distributive (or retributive) justice is meaningless, draw from this the conclusion that the concept of justice itself is empty, and who in consequence jettison one of the basic moral conceptions on which the working of a society of free men rests. But it is justice in this sense which courts of justice administer and which is the original meaning of justice and must govern men's conduct if peaceful coexistence of free men is to be possible. While the appeal to 'social justice' is indeed merely an invitation to give moral approval to demands that have no moral justification, and which are in conflict with that basic rule of a free society that only such rules as can be applied equally to all should be enforced, justice in the sense of rules of just conduct is indispensable for the intercourse of free men.

We are touching here upon a problem which with all its ramifications is much too big to try to be examined here systematically, but which must at least be mentioned briefly. It is that we can't have any morals we like or dream of. Morals, to be viable, must satisfy certain requirements, requirements which we may not be able to specify but may only be able to find out by trial and error. What is required is not merely consistency, or compatibility of the rules as well as the acts demanded by them. A system of morals also must produce a functioning order, capable of maintaining the apparatus of civilization which it presupposes.

We are not familiar with the concept of non-viable systems of morals and certainly cannot observe them anywhere in practice since societies which try them rapidly disappear. But they are being preached, often by widely revered saintly figures, and the societies in decay which we can observe are often societies which have been listening to the teaching of such moral reformers and still revere the destroyers of their society as good men. More often, however, the gospel of 'social justice' aims at much more sordid sentiments: the dislike of people who are better off than oneself, or simply envy, that 'most anti-social and evil of all passions' as John Stuart Mill called it,[42] that animosity towards great wealth which represents it as a 'scandal' that some should enjoy riches while others have basic needs unsatisfied, and camouflages under the name of justice what has nothing to do with justice. At least all those who wish to despoil the rich, not because they expect that some more deserving might enjoy that wealth, but because they regard the very existence of the rich as an outrage, not only cannot claim any moral justification for their demands, but indulge in a wholly irrational passion and in fact harm those to whose rapacious instincts they appeal.

There can be no moral claim to something that would not exist but for the decision of others to risk their resources on its creation. What those who attack great private wealth do not understand is that it is neither by physical effort nor by the mere act of saving and investing, but by directing resources to the most productive uses that wealth is chiefly created. And there can be no doubt that most of those who have built up great fortunes in the form of new industrial plants and the like have thereby benefited more people through creating opportunities for more rewarding employment than if they had given their superfluity away to the poor. The suggestion that in these cases those to whom in fact the workers are most indebted do wrong rather than greatly benefit them is an absurdity. Though there are undoubtedly also other and less meritorious ways of acquiring large fortunes (which we can hope to control by improving the rules of the game), the most effective and important is by directing investment to points where they most enhance the productivity of labour—a task in which governments notoriously fail, for reasons inherent in non-competitive bureaucratic organizations.

But it is not only by encouraging malevolent and harmful prejudices that the cult of 'social justice' tends to destroy genuine moral feelings. It also comes, particularly in its more egalitarian forms, into constant conflict with some of the basic moral principles on which any community of free men must rest. This becomes evident when we reflect that the demand that we should equally esteem all our fellow men is irreconcilable with the fact that our whole moral code rests on the approval or disapproval of the conduct of others; and that similarly the traditional postulate that each capable adult is primarily responsible for his own and his dependents' welfare, meaning that he must not through his own fault become a charge to his friends or fellows, is incompatible with the idea that 'society' or government owes each person an appropriate income.

Though all these moral principles have also been seriously weakened by some pseudo-scientific fashions of our time which tend to destroy all morals—and with them the basis of individual freedom—the ubiquitous dependence on other people's power, which the enforcement of any image of 'social justice' creates, inevitably destroys that freedom of personal decisions on which all morals must rest.[43] In fact, that systematic pursuit of the *ignis fatuus* of 'social justice' which we call socialism is based throughout on the atrocious idea that political power ought to determine the material position of the different individuals and groups—an idea defended by the false assertion that this must always be so and socialism merely wishes to transfer this power from the privileged to the most numerous class. It was the great merit of the market order as it has spread during the last two centuries that it deprived everyone of such power which can be used only in arbitrary fashion. It had indeed brought about the greatest reduction of arbitrary power ever achieved. This greatest triumph of personal freedom the seduction of 'social justice' threatens again to take from us. And it will not be long before the holders of the power to enforce 'social justice' will entrench themselves in their position by awarding the benefits of 'social justice' as the remuneration for the conferment of that power and in order to secure to themselves the support of a praetorian guard which will make it certain that their view of what is 'social justice' will prevail.

Before leaving the subject I want to point out once more that the recognition that in such combinations as 'social', 'economic', 'distributive' or 'retributive' justice the term 'justice' is wholly empty should not lead us to throw the baby out with the bath water. Not only as the basis of the legal rules of just conduct is the justice which the courts of justice administer exceedingly important; there unquestionably also exists a genuine problem of justice in connection with the deliberate design of political institutions, the problem to which Professor John Rawls has recently devoted an important book. The fact which I regret and regard as confusing is merely that in this connection he employs the term 'social justice'. But I have no basic quarrel with an author who, before he proceeds to that problem, acknowledges that the task of selecting specific systems or distributions of desired things as just must be 'abandoned as mistaken in principle, and it is, in any case, not capable of a definite answer. Rather, the principles of justice define the crucial constraints which institutions and joint activities must satisfy if persons engaging in them are to have no complaints against them. If these constraints are satisfied, the resulting distribution, whatever it is, may be accepted as just (or at least not unjust).'[44] This is more or less what I have been trying to argue in this chapter.

Appendix to Chapter Nine:
Justice And Individual Rights

The transition from the negative conception of justice as defined by rules of individual conduct to a 'positive' conception which makes it a duty of 'society' to see that individuals have particular things, is often effected by stressing the *rights* of the individual. It seems that among the younger generation the welfare institutions into which they have been born have engendered a feeling that they have a claim in justice on 'society' for the provision of particular things which it is the duty of that society to provide. However strong this feeling may be, its existence does not prove that the claim has anything to do with justice, or that such claims can be satisfied in a free society.

There is a sense of the noun 'right' in which every rule of just individual conduct creates a corresponding right of individuals. So far as rules of conduct delimit individual domains, the individual will have a right to his domain, and in the defence of it will have the sympathy and the support of his fellows. And where men have formed organizations such as government for enforcing rules of conduct, the individual will have a claim in justice on government that his right be protected and infringements made good.

Such claims, however, can be claims in justice, or rights, only in so far as they are directed towards a person or organization (such as government) which can act, and which is bound in its actions by rules of just conduct. They will include claims on people who have voluntarily incurred obligations, or between people who are connected by special circumstances (such as the relations between parents and children). In such circumstances the rules of just conduct will confer on some persons rights and on others corresponding obligations. But rules as such, without the presence of the particular circumstances to which they refer, cannot confer on anyone a right to a particular sort of thing. A child has a right to be fed, clad, and housed because a corresponding duty is placed on the parents or guardians, or perhaps a particular authority. But there can be no such right in the abstract determined by a rule of just conduct without the particular circumstances being stated which determine on whom the corresponding obligation rests. Nobody has a right to a particular state of affairs unless it is the duty of someone to secure it. We have no right that our houses do not burn down, nor a right that our products or services find a buyer, nor that any particular goods or services be provided for us. Justice does not impose on our fellows a general duty to provide for us; and a claim to such a provision can exist only to the extent that we are maintaining an organization for that purpose. It is meaningless to speak of a right to a condition which nobody has the duty, or perhaps even the power, to bring about. It is equally meaningless to speak of right in the sense of a claim on a spontaneous order, such as society, unless this is meant to imply that somebody has the duty of transforming that cosmos into an organization and thereby to assume the power of controlling its results.

Since we are all made to support the organization of government, we have by the principles determining that organization certain rights which are commonly called political rights. The existence of the compulsory organization of government and its rules of organization does create a claim in justice to shares in the services of government, and may even justify a claim for an equal share in determining what government shall do. But it does not provide a basis for a claim on what government does not, and perhaps could not, provide for all. We are not, in this sense, members of an organization called society, because the society which produces the means for the satisfaction of most of our needs is not an organization directed by a conscious will, and could not produce what it does if it were.

The time-honored political and civil rights which have been embodied in formal Bills of Right constitute essentially a demand that so far as the power of government extends it ought to be used justly. As we shall see, they all amount to particular applications of, and might be effectively replaced by, the more comprehensive formula that no coercion must be used except in the enforcement of a generic rule applicable to an unknown number of future instances. It may well be desirable that these rights should become truly universal as a result of all governments submitting to them. But so long as the powers of the several governments are at all limited, these rights cannot produce a duty of the governments to bring about a particular state of affairs. What we can require is that so far as government acts it ought to act justly; but we cannot derive from them any positive powers government ought to have. They leave wholly open the question whether the organization for coercion which we call government can and ought in justice be used to determine the particular material position of the several individuals or groups.

To the negative rights which are merely a complement of the rules protecting individual domains and which have been institutionalized in the charters of organization of governments, and to the positive rights of the citizens to participate in the direction of this organization, there have recently been added new positive 'social and economic' human rights for which an equal or even higher dignity is claimed.[45] These are claims to particular benefits to which every human being as such is presumed to be entitled without any indication as to who is to be under the obligation to provide those benefits or by what process they are to be provided.[46] Such positive rights, however, demand as their counterpart a decision that somebody (a person or organization) should have the duty of providing what the others are to have. It is, of course, meaningless to describe them as claims on 'society' because 'society' cannot think, act, value, or 'treat' anybody in a particular way. If such claims are to be met, the spontaneous order which we call society must be replaced by a deliberately directed organization; the cosmos of the market would have to be replaced by a taxis whose members would have to do what they are instructed to do. They could not be allowed to use their knowledge for their own purposes but would have to carry out the plan which their rulers have designed to meet the needs to be satisfied. From this it follows that the old civil rights and the new social and economic rights cannot be achieved at the same time but are in fact incompatible; the new rights could not be enforced by law without at the same time destroying that liberal order at which the old civil rights aim.

The new trend was given its chief impetus through the proclamation by President Franklin Roosevelt of his 'Four Freedoms' which included 'freedom *from* want' and 'freedom *from* fear' together with the old 'freedom *of* speech' and 'freedom *of* worship'. But it found its definite embodiment only in the *Universal Declaration of Human Rights* adopted by the General Assembly of the United Nations in 1948. This document is admittedly an attempt to fuse the rights of the Western liberal tradition with the altogether different conception deriving from the Marxist Russian Revolution.[47] It adds to the list of the classical civil rights enumerated in its first twenty-one articles seven further guarantees intended to express the new 'social and economic rights'. In these additional clauses 'every one, as a member of society' is assured the satisfaction of positive claims to particular benefits without at the same time placing on anyone the duty or burden of providing them. The document also completely fails to define these rights in such a manner that a court could possibly determine what their contents are in a particular instance. What, for instance, can be the legal meaning of the statement that every one 'is entitled to the realization . . . of the economic, social, and cultural rights indispensible for his dignity and free development of his personality' (Art. 22)? Against whom is 'every one' to have a claim to 'just and favourable conditions of work' (Art. 23 (I)) and to 'just and favourable employment' (Art. 23 (3))? What are the consequences of the requirement that every one should have the right 'freely to participate in the cultural life of the community and to share in the scientific advances and its benefits' (Art. 27 (I))? 'Every one' is even said to be 'entitled to a social and international order in which the rights and freedoms set forth in this Declaration are fully realized' (Art. 28)—on the assumption apparently that not only is this possible but that there exists now a known method by which these claims can be satisfied for all men.

It is evident that all these 'rights' are based on the interpretation of society as a deliberately made organization by which everybody is employed. They could not be made universal within a system of rules of just conduct based on the conception of individual responsibility, and so require that the whole of society be converted into a single organization, that is, made totalitarian in the fullest sense of the word. We have seen that rules of just conduct which apply to everybody alike but subject nobody to the commands of a superior can never determine what particular things any person is to have. They can never take the form of 'everybody must have so and so.' In a free society what the individual will get must always depend in some measure on particular circumstances which nobody can foresee and nobody has the power to determine. Rules of just conduct can therefore never confer on any person as such (as distinct from the members of a particular organization) a claim to particular things; they can bring about only opportunities for the acquiring of such claims.

It apparently never occurred to the authors of the Declaration that not everybody is an employed member of an organization whose right 'to just and favourable remuneration, including reasonable limitations of working hours and periodic holidays with pay' (Art. 24) can be guaranteed. The conception of a 'universal right' which assures to the peasant, to the Eskimo, and presumably to the Abominable Snowman, 'periodic holidays with pay' shows the absurdity of the whole thing. Even the slightest amount of ordinary common sense ought to have told the authors of the document that what they decreed as universal rights were for the present and for any foreseeable future utterly impossible of achievement, and that solemnly to proclaim them as rights was to play an irresponsible game with the concept of 'right' which could result only in destroying the respect for it.

The whole document is indeed couched in that jargon of organization thinking which one has learnt to expect in the pronouncement of trade union officials or the International Labour Organization and which reflects an attitude business employees share with civil servants and the organization men of the big corporations, but which is altogether inconsistent with the principles on which the order of a Great Society rests. If the document were merely the production of an international group of social philosophers (as in origin it is), it would constitute only somewhat disturbing evidence of the degree to which organization thinking has permeated the thinking of these social philosophers and how much they have become total strangers to the basic ideals of a free society. But its acceptance by a body of presumably responsible statesmen, seriously concerned with the creation of a peaceful international order, gives cause for much greater apprehension.

Organization thinking, largely as a result of the sway of the rationalist constructivism of Plato and his followers, has long been the besetting vice of social philosophers; perhaps it should therefore not surprise us that academic philosophers in their sheltered lives as members of organizations should have lost all understanding of the forces which hold the Great Society together and, imagining themselves to be Platonic philosopher-kings, should propose a reorganization of society on totalitarian lines. If it should be true, as we are told, that the social and economic rights of the Universal Declaration of Human Rights would today be 'accepted by the vast majority of American and British moralists,'[48] this would merely indicate a sorry lack of critical acumen on the part of these thinkers.

The spectacle, however, of the General Assembly of the United Nations solemnly proclaiming that *every* individual (!), 'keeping this Declaration constantly in mind' (!), should strive to insure the universal observation of those human rights, would be merely comic if the illusions which this creates were not so profoundly tragic. To see the most comprehensive authority which man has yet created undermining the respect it ought to command by giving countenance to the naive prejudice that we can create any state of affairs which we think to be desirable by simply decreeing that it ought to exist, and indulging in the self-deception that we can benefit from the spontaneous order of society and at the same time mould it to our own will, is more than merely tragic.[49]

The fundamental fact which these illusions disregard is that the availability of all those benefits which we wish as many people as possible to have depends on these same people using for their production their own best knowledge. To establish enforceable rights to the benefits is not likely to produce them. If we wish everybody to be well off, we shall get closest to our goal, not by commanding by law that this should be achieved, or giving everybody a legal claim to what we think he ought to have, but by providing inducements for all to do as much as they can that will benefit others. To speak of rights where what are in question are merely aspirations which only a voluntary system can fulfill, not only misdirects attention from what are the effective determinants of the wealth which we wish for all, but also debases the word 'right', the strict meaning of which it is very important to preserve if we are to maintain a free society.

Notes

*The first quotation is taken from David Hume, *An Enquiry Concerning the Principles of Morals,* sect. III, part II, *Works* IV, p. 187, and ought to be given here in its context: the

most obvious thought would be, to assign the largest possessions to the most extensive virtue, and give every one the power of doing good proportioned to his inclination.... But were mankind to execute such a law; so great is the uncertainty of merit, both from its natural obscurity, and from the self-conceit of each individual, that no determinate rule of conduct would ever follow from it; and the total dissolution of society must be the immediate consequence.

*The second quotation is translated from Immanuel Kant (*Der Streit der Fakultäten* (1798), sect. 2, para. 6, note 2) and reads in the original: 'Wohlfahrt aber hat kein Prinzip, weder für den der sie empfängt, noch für den der sie austeilt (der eine setzt sie hierin, der andere darin); well es dabei auf das *Materiale* des Willens ankommt, welches empirisch und so einer allgemeinen Regel unfähig ist.' An English translation of this essay in which the passage is rendered somewhat differently will be found in *Kant's Political Writings*, ed. H. Reiss, trs. H. B. Nisbett (Cambridge, 1970), p. 183, note.

1. Cf. P. H. Wicksteed, *The Common Sense of Political Economy* (London, 1910), p. 184: 'It is idle to assume that ethically desirable results will necessarily be produced by an ethically indifferent instrument.'

2. Cf. G. del Vecchio, *Justice* (Edinburgh, 1952), p. 37. In the eighteenth century the expression 'social justice' was occasionally used to describe the enforcement of rules of just conduct within a given society, so e.g. by Edward Gibbon, *Decline and Fall of the Roman Empire*, chapter 41 (World's Classics edn, vol. IV, p. 367).

3. E.g. by John Rawls, *A Theory of Justice* (Harvard, 1971).

4. John Stuart Mill, *Utilitarianism* (London, 1861), chapter 5, p.92; in H. Plamenatz, ed., *The English Utilitarians* (Oxford, 1949), p. 225.

5. *Ibid.*, pp. 66 and 208 respectively. Cf. also J. S. Mill's review of F. W. Newman, *Lectures on Political Economy*, originally published in 1851 in the *Westminster Review* and republished in *Collected Works*, vol. v (Toronto and London, 1967), p. 444: 'the distinction between rich and poor, so slightly connected as it is with merit and demerit, or even with exertion and want of exertion, is obviously unjust.' Also *Principles of Political Economy*, book II, ch. I, §, ed. W. J. Ashley (London, 1909), pp. 211ff.: 'The proportioning of remuneration to work done is really just only in so far as the more or less of the work is a matter of choice: when it depends on natural differences of strength and capacity, this principle of remuneration is itself an injustice, it gives to those who have.'

6. See e.g. A. M. Honoré, 'Social Justice' in *McGill Law Journal*, VIII, 1962 and revised version in R. S. Summers, ed., *Essays in Legal Philosophy* (Oxford, 1968), p. 62 of the reprint: 'The first [of the two propositions of which the principle of social justice consists] is the contention that *all men considered merely as men and apart from their conduct or choice have a claim to an equal share in all those things, here called advantages, which are generally desired and are in fact conducive to well-being.*' Also W. G. Runciman, *Relative Deprivation and Social Justice* (London, 1966), p. 261.

7. Cf. especially the encyclicals *Quadragesimo Anno* (1931) and *Divini Redemptoris* (1937) and Johannes Messner, 'Zum Begriff der sozialen Gerechtigkeit' in the volume *Die soziale Frage und der Katholizismus* (Paderborn, 1931) issued to commemorate the fortieth anniversary of the encyclical *Rerum Novarum*.

8. The term 'social justice' (or rather its Italian equivalent) seems to have been first used in its modern sense by Luigi Taparelli d'Azeglio, *Saggio teoretico di diritto naturale* (Palermo, 1840) and to have been made more generally known by Antonio RosminiSerbati, *La costitutione secondo la giustizia sociale* (Milan, 1848). For more recent discussions cf. N. W. Willoughby, *Social Justice* (New York, 1909); Stephen Leacock, *The Unsolved Riddle of Social Justice* (London and New York, 1920); John A. Ryan, *Distributive Justice* (New York, 1916); L. T. Hobhouse, *The Elements of Social Justice* (London and New York, 1922); T. N. Carver, *Essays in Social Justice* (Harvard, 1922); W. Shields, *Social Justice, The History and Meaning of the Term* (Notre Dame Ind. 1941); Benevuto Donati 'che cosa è giustizia sociale?', *Archivio giuridico,* vol. 134, 1947; C. de Pasquier, 'La notion de justice sociale', *Zeitschrift für Schweizerisches Recht,* 1952; P. Antoine, 'Qu-est-ce la justice sociale?', *Archives de Philosophie,* 24, 1961; For a more complete list of this literature see G. del Vecchio, *op. cit.,* pp. 379.

In spite of the abundance of writings on the subject, when about ten years ago I wrote the first draft of this chapter, I found it still very difficult to find any serious discussion of what people meant when they were using this term. But almost immediately afterwards a number of serious studies of the subject appeared, particularly the two works quoted in note 6 above as well as R. W. Baldwin, *Social Justice* (Oxford and London, 1966), and R. Rescher, *Distributive Justice* (Indianapolis, 1966). Much the most acute treatment of the subject is to be found in a German work by the Swiss economist Emil Küng, *Wirtschaft und Gerechtigkeit* (Tübingen, 1967) and many sensible comments in H. B. Acton, *The Morals of the Market* (London, 1971), particularly p. 71: 'Poverty and misfortune are evils but not injustices'. Very important is also Bertrand de Jouvenel, *The Ethics of Redistribution* (Cambridge, 1951) as well as certain passages in his *Sovereignty* (London, 1957), two of which may here be quoted. P. 140: 'The justice now recommended is a quality not of a man and a man's actions, but of a certain configuration of things in social geometry, no matter by what means it is brought about. Justice is now something which exists independently of just men.' P. 164: 'No proposition is likelier to scandalise our contemporaries than this one: it is impossible to establish a just social order. Yet it flows logically from the very idea of justice, on which we have, not without difficulty, thrown light. To do justice is to apply, when making a share-out, the relevant serial order. But it is impossible for the human intelligence to establish a relevant serial order for all resources in all respects. Men have needs to satisfy, merits to reward, possibilities to actualize; even if we consider these three aspects only and assume that—what is not the case—there are precise *indicia* which we can apply to these aspects, we still could not weight correctly among themselves the three sets of *indicia* adopted.'

The at one time very famous and influential essay by Gustav Schmoller on 'Die Gerechtigkeit in der Volkswirtschaft' in that author's *Jahrbuch für Volkswirtschaft etc.,* vol. v, 1895 is intellectually most disappointing—a pretentious statement of the characteristic muddle of the do-gooder foreshadowing some unpleasant later developments. We know now what it means if the great decisions are to be left to the 'jeweilige Volksbewusstsein nach der Ordnung der Zwecke, die im Augenblick als die richtige erscheint' !

9. Cf. note 7 to chapter VII above.

10. Cf. Adam Smith, *The Theory of Moral Sentiments* (London, 1801), vol. II, part VII, sect. ii, ch. I, p. 198: 'Human life the Stoics appear to have considered as a game of great skill, in which, however, there was a mixture of chance or of what is vulgarly understood to be chance.' See also Adam Ferguson, *Principles of Moral and Political Science* (Edinburgh 1792) vol. I p. 7: 'The Stoics conceived of human life under the image of a Game, at which the entertainment and merit of the players consisted in playing attentively and well whether the stake was great or small.' In a note Ferguson refers to the *Discourses of Epictetus* preserved by Arrian, book II, ch. 5.

11. Cf. G. Hardin, *Nature and Man's Fate* (New York, 1961), p. 55: 'In a free market, says Smith in effect, prices are regulated by negative feedback.' The much ridiculed 'miracle' that the pursuit of self-interest serves the general interest reduces to the self-evident proposition that an order in which the action of the elements is to be guided by effects of which they cannot know can be achieved only if they are induced to respond to signals reflecting the effects of those events. What was familiar to Adam Smith has belatedly been rediscovered by scientific fashion under the name of 'self-organizing systems'.

12. See L. von Mises, *Human Action* (Yale, 1949), p. 255 note: 'There is in the operation of the market economy nothing which could properly be called distribution. Goods are not first produced and then distributed, as would be the case in a socialist state.' Cf. also M. R. Rothbard, 'Towards a Reconstruction of Utility and Welfare Economics' in M. Sennholz (ed.), *On Freedom and Free Enterprise* (New York, 1965), p. 231.

13. Cf. W. G. Runciman, *op. cit.*, p. 274: 'Claims for social justice are claims on behalf of a group, and the person relatively deprived within an individual category will, if he is the victim of an unjust inequality, be a victim only of individual injustice.'

14. See Irving Kristol, 'When Virtue Loses all Her Loveliness—Some Reflections on Capitalism and "The Free Society"', *The Public Interest,* no. 21 (1970), reprinted in the author's *On the Democratic Idea in America* (New York, 1972), as well as in Daniel Bell and Irving Kristol (eds), *Capitalism Today* (New York, 1970).

15. Cf. J. Höffner, *Wirtschaftsethik und Monopole im 15. und 16. Fahrhundert* (Jena, 1941) und 'Der Wettbewerb in der Scholastik', *Ordo*, V, 1953; also Max Weber, *On Law in Economy and Society*, ed. Max Rheinstein (Harvard, 1954) pp. 295ff., but on the latter also H. M. Robertson, *Aspects on the Rise of Economic Individualism* (Cambridge, 1933) and B. Groethuysen, *Origines de l'esprit bourgeois en France* (Paris, 1927). For the most important expositions of the conception of a just price by the late sixteenth century Spanish Jesuits see particularly L. Molina, *De iustitia et de iure,* vol. 2, *De Contractibus* (Cologne, 1594), disp. 347, no. 3 and especially disp. 348, no. 3, where the just price is

defined as that which will form 'quando absque fraude, monopoliis, atque aliis versutiies, commu-niter res aliqua vendi consuevit pretio in aliqua regione, aut loco, it habendum est pro mensura et reg-ula judicandi pretium iustum rei illius in ea regione.' About man's inability to determine beforehand what a just price would be see also particularly Johannes de Salas, *Commentarii in Secundum Secun-dae D. Thomas de Contractibus* (Lyon, 1617), *Tr. de empt. et Vend.* IV, n. 6, p. 9: '. . . quas exacte comprehendere, et ponderare Dei est, not hominum'; and J. de Lugo, *Disputationes de Iustitia et Iure* (Lyon, 1643), vol. II d. 26 s. 4, n. 40; 'pretium iustum matematicum, licet sold Deo notum.' See also L. Molina, *op. cit.*, disp. 365, no. 9: 'omnesque rei publicae parses ius habent conscendendi ad gradum superiorem, si cuiusque sors id tulerit, neque cuiquam certus quidam gradus debitur, qui de-scendere et conscendere possit.' It would seem that H. M. Robertson (*op. cit.*, p. 164) hardly exagger-ates when he writes 'It would not be difficult to claim that the religion which favoured the spirit of capitalism was Jesuitry, not Calvinism.'

16.   John W. Chapman, 'Justice and Fairness', *Nomos VI, Justice* (New York, 1963), p. 153. This Lockean conception has been preserved even by John Rawls, at least in his earlier work, 'Constitutional Lib-erty and the Concept of Justice', *Nomos VI, Justice* (New York, 1963), p. 117, note: 'If one assumes that law and government effectively act to keep markets competitive, resources fully employed, prop-erty and wealth widely distributed over time, and maintains a reasonable social minimum, then, if there is equality of opportunity, the resulting distribution will be just or at least not unjust. It will have resulted from the working of a just system . . . a social minimum is simply a form of rational in-surance and prudence.'

17.   See passages quoted in note 15 above.

18.   See M. Fogarty, *The Just Wage* (London, 1961).

19.   Barbara Wootton, *The Social Foundation of Wage Policy* (London, 1962), pp. 120 and 162, and now also her *Incomes Policy, An Inquest and a Proposal* (London, 1974).

20.   Surely Samuel Butler (Hudibras, II, I) was right when he wrote

For what is worth in any thing
But so much money as 'twill bring.

21.   On the general problem of remuneration according to merit, apart from the passages by David Hume and Immanuel Kant placed at the head of this chapter, see chapter VI of my book *The Constitution of Lib-erty* (London and Chicago, 1960) and cf. also Maffeo Pantaleoni, 'L'atto economico' in *Erotemi di Economia* (2 vols, Padua, 1963), vol. I, p. 101:

E tre sono le proposizioni che conviene comprendere bene:
La prima è che il merito è una parole vuota di senso.

La seconda è che il concetto di giustizia è un polisenso che si presta a quanti paralogismi si vogliono ex amphibologia.

La terza è che la remunerazione non può essere commisurata da una produttività (marginale) capace di determinazione isolamente, cioè senza la simultanea determinazione della produttività degli altri fattori con i quali entra in una combinazione di complimentarità.

22. On the history of the term 'social' see Karl Wasserrab, *Sozialwissenschaft und soziale Frage* (Leipzig, 1903); Leopold von Wiese, *Der Liberalismus in Vergangenheit und Zukunft* (Berlin, 1917), and *Sozial, Geistig, Kulturell* (Cologne, 1936); Waldemar Zimmermann, 'Das "Soziale" im geschichtlichen Sinn- und Begriffswandel' in *Studien zur Soziologie, Festgabe für L. von Wiese* (Mainz, 1948); L. H. A. Geck, *Über das Eindringen des Wortes 'sozial' in die deutsche Sprache* (Göttingen, 1963); and Ruth Crummemerl Zur Wortgeschichte von 'sozial' bis zur englischen Aufklärung', unpublished essay for the State examination in philology (Bonn, 1963). Cf. also my essay 'What is "Social"? What does it Mean?' in a corrected English version in my *Studies in Philosophy, Politics and Economics* (London and Chicago, 1967).

23. Cf. G. del Vecchio, *op. cit.,* p. 37.

24. Very instructive on this is Leopold von Wiese, D*er Liberalismus in Vergangenheit und Zukunft* (Berlin, 1917) pp. 115ff.

25. Characteristic for many discussions of the issue by social philosophers is W. A. Frankena, 'The Concept of Social Justice', in *Social Justice,* ed. R. B. Brandt (New York, 1962), p. 4, whose argument rests on the assumption that 'society' *acts* which is a meaningless term if applied to a spontaneous order. Yet this anthropomorphic interpretation of society seems to be one to which utilitarians are particularly prone, although this is not often as naively admitted as by J. W. Chapman in the statement quoted before in note 21 to chapter VII.

26. I regret this usage though by means of it some of my friends in Germany (and more recently also in England) have apparently succeeded in making palatable to wider circles the sort of social order for which I am pleading.

27. Cf. the 'Statement of Conscience' received by the 'Aspen Consultation on Global Justice', an 'ecumenical gathering of American religious leaders' at Aspen, Colorado, 4-7 June 1974, which recognized that 'global injustice is characterised by a dimension of sin in the economic, political, social, racial, sexual and class structures and systems of global society.' *Aspen Institute Quarterly* (New York), no. 7, third quarter, 1974, p. 4.

28. See particularly A. M. Honoré, *op. cit.* The absurdity of the contention that in a Great Society it needs moral justification if *A* has more than *B,* as if this were the result of some human artifice, becomes obvious when we consider not only the elaborate and complex apparatus of government which would

be required to prevent this, but also that this apparatus would have to possess power to direct the efforts of all citizens and to claim the products of those efforts.

29.   One of the few modern philosophers to see this clearly and speak out plainly was R. G. Collingwood. See his essay on 'Economics as a philosophical science,' *Ethics* 36, 1926, esp. p. 74: 'A just price, a just wage, a just rate of interest, is a contradiction in terms. The question of what a person ought to get in return for his goods and labour is a question absolutely devoid of meaning.'

30.   If there is any one fact which all serious students of the claims for equality have recognized it is that material equality and liberty are irreconcilable. Cf. A. de Tocqueville, *Democracy in America,* book II, ch. I (New York, edn 1946, vol. II, p. 87): democratic communities 'call for equality in freedom, and if they cannot obtain that, they still call for equality in slavery'; William S. Sorley, *The Moral Life and the Moral Worth* (Cambridge, 1911) p. 110: 'Equality is gained only by constant interference with liberty'; or more recently Gerhard Leibholz, 'Die Bedrohung der Freiheit durch die Macht der Gesetzgeber', in *Freiheit der Personlichkeit* (Stuttart, 1958), p. 80: 'Freiheit erzeugt notwendig Ungleichheit und Gleichheit notwendig Unfreiheit', are merely a few instances which I readily find in my notes. Yet people who claim to be enthusiastic supporters of liberty still clamour constantly for material equality.

31.   Gustav Radbruch, *Rechtsphilosophie* (Stuttgart, 1956), p. 87: 'Auch das sozialistische Gemeinwesen wird also ein Rechtsstaat sein, ein Rechtsstaat freilich, der statt von der ausgleichenden von der austeilenden Gerechtigkeit beherrscht wird.'

32.   See M. Duverger, *The Idea of Politics* (Indianapolis, 1966), p. 201.

33.   Karl Mannheim, *Man and Society in an Age of Reconstruction* (London, 1940), p. 180.

34.   P. J. Stuchka (President of the Soviet Supreme Court) in *Encyclopedia of State and Law* (in Russian, Moscow, 1927), quoted by V. Gsovski, *Soviet Civil Law* (Ann Arbor, Michigan, 1948), I, p. 70. The work of E. Paschukanis the Soviet author who has most consistently developed the idea of the disappearance of law under socialism, has been described by Karl Korsch in *Archiv sozialistischer Literatur*, III, (Frankfurt, 1966) as the only consistent development of the teaching of Karl Marx.

35.   *The Road to Serfdom* (London and Chicago, 1944), chapter IV. For discussions of the central thesis of that book by lawyers see W. Friedmann, *The Planned State and the Rule of Law* (Melbourne, 1948), reprinted in the same author's *Law and Social Change in Contemporary Britain* (London, 1951). Hans Kelsen, 'The Foundations of Democracy', *Ethics* 66, 1955; Roscoe Pound, 'The Rule of Law and the Modern Welfare State', *Vanderbilt Law Review*, 7, 1953; Harry W. Jones, 'The Rule of Law and the Modern Welfare State', *Columbia Law Review*, 58, 1958; A. L. Good hart, 'The Rule of Law and Absolute Sovereignty', *University of Pennsylvania Law Review*, 106, 1958.

36.   G. Radbruch, *op. cit.,* p. 126.

37. Radbruch's conceptions of these matters are concisely summed up by Roscoe Pound (in his introduction to R. H. Graves, *Status in the Common Law*, London, 1953, p. XI): Radbruch

   starts with a distinction between commutative justice, a correcting justice which gives back to one what has been taken away from him or gives him a substantial substitute, and distributive justice, a distribution of the goods of existence not equally but according to a scheme of values. Thus there is a contrast between coordinating law, which secures interests by reparation and the like, treating all individuals as equal, and subordinating law, which prefers some or the interests of some according to its measure of value. Public law, he says, is a law of subordination, subordinating individual to public interests but not the interests of other individuals with those public interests.

38. Cf. Bertrand de Jouvenel, *Sovereignty* (Chicago, 1957), p. 136:

   The small society, as the milieu in which man is first found, retains for him an infinite attraction; he undoubtedly goes to it to renew his strength; but . . . any attempt to graft the same features on a large society is utopian and leads to tyranny. With that admitted, it is clear that as social relations become wider and more various, the common good conceived as reciprocal trustfulness cannot be sought in methods which the model of the small, closed society inspires; such a model is, in the contrary, entirely misleading.

39. Edwin Cannan, *The History of Local Rates in England*, 2nd edn (London, 1912), p. 162.

40. While one has become used to find the confused minds of social philosophers talking about 'social justice', it greatly pains me if I find a distinguished thinker like the historian Peter Geyl (*Encounters in History*, London, 1963, p. 358) thoughtlessly using the term. J. M. Keynes (*The Economic Consequences of Mr. Churchill,* London, 1925, *Collected Writings,* vol. IX, p. 223) also writes unhesitatingly that 'on grounds of social justice no case can be made for reducing the wages of the miners.'

41. Cf. e.g. Walter Kaufmann, *Without Guilt and Justice* (New York, 1973) who, after rightly rejecting the concepts of distributive and retributive justice, believes that this must lead him to reject the concept of justice altogether. But this is not surprising after even *The Times* (London) in a thoughtful leading article (I March 1957) apropos the appearance of an English translation of Josef Pieper's *Justice* (London, 1957) had observed that 'roughly, it may be said that in so far as the notion of justice continues to influence political thinking, it has been reduced to the meaning of the phrase "distributive justice" and that the idea of commutative justice has almost entirely ceased to influence our calculations except in so far it is embodied in laws and customs—in the maxims for instance of the Common Law— which are preserved from sheer conservatism.' Some contemporary social philosophers indeed beg the whole issue by so *defining* 'justice' that it includes only distributive justice. See e.g. Brian M. Barry, 'Justice and the Common Good', *Analysis*, 19, 1961, p. 80: 'although Hume uses the expression "rules of justice" to cover such things as property rules, *"justice" is now analytically tied to*

"desert" and "need", so that one could quite properly say that some of what Hume calls "rules of justice" were unjust' (italics added). Cf. *ibid.*, p. 89.

42. J. S. Mill, *On Liberty*, ed. McCallum (Oxford, 1946), p. 70.

43. On the destruction of moral values by scientific error see my discussion in my inaugural lecture as Visiting Professor at the University of Salzburg, *Die Irrtümer des Konstruktivismus und die Grundlagen legitimer Kritik gesellschaftlicher Gebilde* (Munich, 1970, now reprinted for the Walter Eucken Institute at Freiburg i.Brg. by J. C. B. Mohr, Tübingen, 1975).

44. John Rawls, 'Constitutional Liberty and the Concept of Justice', *Nomos IV, Justice* (New York, 1963), p. 102 where the passage quoted is preceded by the statement that 'It is the system of institutions which has to be judged and judged from a general point of view.' I am not aware that Professor Rawls' later more widely read work *A Theory of Justice* (Harvard, 1971) contains a comparatively clear statement of the main point, which may explain why this work seems often, but as it appears to me wrongly, to have been interpreted as lending support to socialist demands, e.g. by Daniel Bell, 'On Meritocracy and Equality', *Public Interest,* Autumn 1972, p. 72, who describes Rawls' theory as 'the most comprehensive effort in modern philosophy to justify a socialistic ethic.'

Appendix To Chapter Nine
This appendix has been published as an article in the 75th anniversary issue of the Norwegian journal *Farmand* (Oslo, 1966).

45. For discussions of the problem cf. the papers assembled in the *Philosophical Review,* April 1955 and in D. D. Raphael (ed.), *Political Theory and the Rights of Man* (London, 1967).

46. See the *Universal Declaration of Human Rights* adopted by the General Assembly of the United Nations on 10 December 1948. It is reprinted, and the intellectual background of this document can be found, in the volume entitled *Human Rights, Comments and Interpretations*, a symposium edited by UNESCO (London and New York, 1945). It contains in the Appendix not only a 'Memorandum Circulated by UNESCO on the Theoretical Bases of the Rights of Men' (pp. 251-4), but also a 'Report of the UNESCO Committee on the Theoretical Bases of the Human Rights' (in other places described as the 'UNESCO Committee on the Principles of the Rights of Men'), in which it is explained that their efforts were directed towards reconciling the two different 'complementary' working concepts of human rights, of which one 'started, from the premises of inherent individual rights . . . while the other was based on Marxist principles', and at finding 'some common measure of the two tendencies'. 'This common formulation,' it is explained, 'must by some means reconcile the various divergent or opposing formulations now in existence'! (The British representatives on that committee were Professors H. J. Laski and E. H. Carr!).

47. *Ibid.*, p. 22, Professor E. H. Carr, the chairman of the UNESCO Committee of experts, explains that 'If the new declaration of the rights of man is to include provisions for social services, for maintenance in childhood, in old age, in incapacity or in unemployment, it becomes clear that no society can guarantee the enjoyment of such rights unless it in turn has the right to call upon and direct the productive capacities of the individuals enjoying them'!

48. G. Vlastos, 'Justice', *Revue Internationale de la Philosophie,* 1957, p. 331.

49. On the whole document cf. Maurice Cranston, 'Human Rights, Real and Supposed' in the volume edited by D. D. Raphael quoted in note 45 above, where the author argues that 'a philosophically respectable concept of human rights has been muddied, obscured, and debilitated in recent years by an attempt to incorporate in it specific rights of a different logical category.' See also the same author's *Human Rights Today* (London, 1955).

Part II

UNDERSTANDING THE USE OF KNOWLEDGE IN SOCIETY, COMPETITION, THE MARKET PROCESS, DISCOVERY AND REGULATION

THE POWER OF THE MARKET

Milton and Rose Friedman

Every day each of us uses innumerable goods and services—to eat, to wear, to shelter us from the elements, or simply to enjoy. We take it for granted that they will be available when we want to buy them. We never stop to think how many people have played a part in one way or another in providing those goods and services. We never ask ourselves how it is that the corner grocery store—or nowadays, supermarket—has the items on its shelves that we want to buy, how it is that most of us are able to earn the money to buy those goods.

It is natural to assume that someone must give orders to make sure that the "right" products are produced in the "right" amounts and available at the "right" places. That is one method of coordinating the activities of a large number of people—the method of the army. The general gives orders to the colonel, the colonel to the major, the major to the lieutenant, the lieutenant to the sergeant, and the sergeant to the private.

But that command method can be the exclusive or even principal method of organization only in a very small group. Not even the most autocratic head of a family can control every act of other family members entirely by order. No sizable army can really be run entirely by command. The general cannot conceivably have the information necessary to direct every movement of the lowliest private. At every step in the chain of command, the soldier, whether officer or private, must have discretion to take into account information about specific circumstances that his commanding officer could not have. Commands must be supplemented by voluntary cooperation—a less obvious and more subtle, but far more fundamental, technique of coordinating the activities of large numbers of people.

Russia is the standard example of a large economy that is supposed to be organized by command—a centrally planned economy. But that is more fiction than fact. At every level of the economy, voluntary cooperation enters to supplement central planning or to offset its rigidities—sometimes legally, sometimes illegally.

In agriculture, full-time workers on government farms are permitted to grow food and raise animals on small private plots in their spare time for their own use or to sell in relatively free markets. These plots account for less than 1 percent of the agricultural land in the country, yet they are said to provide nearly a third of total farm output in the Soviet Union (are "said to" because it is likely that some products of government farms are clandestinely marketed as if from private plots).

In the labor market individuals are seldom ordered to work at specific jobs; there is little actual direction of labor in this sense. Rather, wages are offered for various jobs, and individuals apply for them—much as in capitalist countries. Once hired, they may subsequently be fired or may leave for jobs they prefer. Numerous restrictions affect who may work where, and, of course, the laws prohibit anyone from setting up as an employer—although numerous clandestine workshops serve the extensive black market. Allocation of workers on a large scale primarily by compulsion is just not feasible; and neither, apparently, is complete suppression of private entrepreneurial activity.

The attractiveness of different jobs in the Soviet Union often depends on the opportunities they offer for extralegal or illegal moonlighting. A resident of Moscow whose household equipment fails may have to wait months to have it repaired if he calls the state repair office. Instead, he may hire a moonlighter—very likely someone who works for the state repair office. The householder gets his equipment repaired promptly; the moonlighter gets some extra income. Both are happy.

These voluntary market elements flourish despite their inconsistency with official Marxist ideology because the cost of eliminating them would be too high. Private plots could be forbidden—but the famines of the 1930s are a stark reminder of the cost. The Soviet economy is hardly a model of efficiency now. Without the voluntary elements it would operate at an even lower level of effectiveness. Recent experience in Cambodia tragically illustrates the cost of trying to do without the market entirely.

Just as no society operates entirely on the command principle, so none operates entirely through voluntary cooperation. Every society has some command elements. These take many forms. They may be as straightforward as military conscription or forbidding the purchase and sale of heroin or cyclamates or court orders to named defendants to desist from or perform specified actions. Or, at the other extreme, they may be as subtle as imposing a heavy tax on cigarettes to discourage smoking—a hint, if not a command, by some of us to others of us.

It makes a vast difference what the mix is—whether voluntary exchange is primarily a clandestine activity that flourishes because of the rigidities of a dominant command element, or whether voluntary exchange is the dominant principle of organization, supplemented to a smaller or larger extent by command elements. Clandestine voluntary exchange may prevent a command economy from collapsing, may enable it to creak along and even achieve some progress. It can do little to undermine the tyranny on which a predominantly command economy rests. A predominantly voluntary exchange economy, on the other hand, has within it the potential to promote both prosperity and human freedom. It may not achieve its potential in either respect, but we know of no society that has ever achieved prosperity and freedom unless voluntary exchange has been its dominant principle of organization. We hasten to add that voluntary exchange is not a sufficient condition for prosperity and freedom. That, at least, is the lesson of history to date. Many societies organized predominantly by voluntary exchange have not achieved either prosperity or freedom, though they have achieved a far greater measure of both than authoritarian societies. But voluntary exchange is a necessary condition for both prosperity and freedom.

Cooperation through Voluntary Exchange

A delightful story called "I, Pencil: My Family Tree as Told to Leonard E. Read" dramatizes vividly how voluntary exchange enables millions of people to cooperate with one another. Mr. Read, in the voice of the "Lead Pencil—the ordinary wooden pencil familiar to all boys and girls and adults who can read and write," starts his story with the fantastic statement that *"not a single person... knows how to make me."* Then he proceeds to tell about all the things that go into the making of a pencil. First, the wood comes from a tree, "a cedar of straight grain that grows in Northern California and Oregon." To cut down the tree and cart the logs to the railroad siding requires "saws and trucks and rope and...countless other gear." Many persons and numberless skills are involved in their fabrication:in "the mining of ore, the making of steel and its refinement into saws, axes, motors; the growing of hemp and bringing it through all the stages to heavy and strong rope; the logging camps with their beds and mess halls...untold thousands of persons had a hand in every cup of coffee the loggers drink!"

And so Mr. Read goes on to the bringing of the logs to the mill, the millwork involved in converting the logs to slats, and the transportation of the slats from California to Wilkes-Barre, where the particular pencil that tells the story was manufactured. And so far we have only the outside wood of the pencil. The "lead" center is not really lead at all. It starts as graphite mined in Ceylon. After many complicated processes it ends up as the lead in the center of the pencil.

The bit of metal—the ferrule—near the top of the pencil is brass. "Think of all the persons," he says, "who mine zinc and copper and those who have the skills to make shiny sheet brass from these products of nature."

What we call the eraser is known in the trade as "the plug." It is thought to be rubber. But Mr. Read tells us the rubber is only for binding purposes. The erasing is actually done by "Factice," a rubberlike product made by reacting rape seed oil from the Dutch East Indies (now Indonesia) with sulfur chloride.

After all of this, says the pencil, "Does anyone wish to challenge my earlier assertion that no single person on the face of this earth knows how to make me?"

None of the thousands of persons involved in producing the pencil performed his task because he wanted a pencil. Some among them never saw a pencil and would not know what it is for. Each saw his work as a way to get the goods and services he wanted—goods and services we produced in order to get the pencil we wanted. Every time we go to the store and buy a pencil, we are exchanging a little bit of our services for the infinitesimal amount of services that each of the thousands contributed toward producing the pencil.

It is even more astounding that the pencil was ever produced. No one sitting in a central office gave orders to these thousands of people. No military police enforced the orders that were not given. These people live in many lands, speak different languages, practice different religions, may even hate one another—yet none of these differences prevented them from cooperating to produce a pencil. How did it happen? Adam Smith gave us the answer two hundred years ago.

The Role of Prices

The key insight of Adam Smith's *Wealth of Nations* is misleadingly simple: if an exchange between two parties is voluntary, it will not take place unless both believe they will benefit from it. Most economic fallacies derive from the neglect of this simple insight, from the tendency to assume that there is a fixed pie, that one party can gain only at the expense of another.

This key insight is obvious for a simple exchange between two individuals. It is far more difficult to understand how it can enable people living all over the world to cooperate to promote their separate interests.

The price system is the mechanism that performs this task without central direction, without requiring people to speak to one another or to like one another. When you buy your pencil or your daily bread, you don't know whether the pencil was made or the wheat was grown by a white man or a black man, by a Chinese or an Indian. As a result, the price system enables people to cooperate peacefully in one phase of their life while each one goes about his own business in respect of everything else.

Adam Smith's flash of genius was his recognition that the prices that emerged from voluntary transactions between buyers and sellers—for short, in a free market—could coordinate the activity of millions of people, each seeking his own interest, in such a way as to make everyone better off. It was a startling idea then, and it remains one today, that economic order can emerge as the unintended consequence of the actions of many people, each seeking his own interest.

The price system works so well, so efficiently, that we are not aware of it most of the time. We never realize how well it functions until it is prevented from functioning, and even then we seldom recognize the source of the trouble.

The long gasoline lines that suddenly emerged in 1974 after the OPEC oil embargo, and again in the spring and summer of 1979 after the revolution in Iran, are a striking example. On both occasions there was a sharp disturbance in the supply of crude oil from abroad. But that did not lead to gasoline lines in Germany or Japan, which are wholly dependent on imported oil. It led to long gasoline lines in the United States, even though we produce much of our own oil, for one reason and one reason only: because legislation, administered by a government agency, did not permit the price system to function. Prices in some areas were kept by command below the level that would have equated the amount of gasoline available at the gas stations to the amount consumers wanted to buy at that price. Supplies were allocated to different areas of the country by command, rather than in response to the pressures of demand as reflected in price. The result was surpluses in some areas and shortages plus long gasoline lines in others. The smooth operation of the price system—which for many decades had assured every consumer that he could buy gasoline at any of a large number of service stations at his convenience and with a minimal wait—was replaced by bureaucratic improvisation.

Prices perform three functions in organizing economic activity: first, they transmit information; second, they provide an incentive to adopt those methods of production that are least costly and thereby use available resources for the most highly valued purposes; third, they determine who gets how much of the product—the distribution of income. These three functions are closely interrelated.

Transmission of Information

Suppose that, for whatever reason, there is an increased demand for lead pencils—perhaps because a baby boom increases school enrollment. Retail stores will find that they are selling more pencils. They will order more pencils from their wholesalers. The wholesalers will order more pencils from the manufacturers. The manufacturers will order more wood, more brass, more graphite—all the varied products used to make a pencil. In order to induce their suppliers to produce more of these items, they will have to offer higher pries for them. The higher prices will induce the suppliers to increase their work force to be able to meet the higher demand. To get more workers they will have to offer higher wages or better working conditions. In this way ripples spread out over ever widening circles, transmitting the information to people all over the world that there is a greater demand for pencils—or, to be more precise, for some product they are engaged in producing, for reasons they may not and need not know.

The price system transmits only the important information and only to the people who need to know. The producers of wood, for example, do not have to know whether the demand for pencils has gone up because of a baby boom or because 14,000 more government forms have to be filled out in pencil. They don't even have to know that the demand for pencils has gone up. They need to know only that someone is willing to pay more for wood and that the higher price is likely to last long enough to make it worthwhile to satisfy the demand. Both items of information are provided by market prices—the first by the current price, the second by the price offered for future delivery.

A major problem in transmitting information efficiently is to make sure that everyone who can use the information gets it without clogging the "in" baskets of those who have no use for it. The price system automatically solves this problem. The people who transmit the information have an incentive to search out the people who can use it and they are in a position to do so. People who can use the information have an incentive to get it and they are in a position to do so. The pencil manufacturer is in touch with people selling the wood he uses. He is always trying to find additional suppliers who can offer him a better product or a lower price. Similarly, the producer of wood is in touch with his customers and is always trying to find new ones. On the other hand, people who are not currently engaged in these activities and are not considering them as future activities have no interest in the price of wood and will ignore it.

The transmission of information through prices is enormously facilitated these days by organized markets and by specialized communication facilities. It is a fascinating exercise to look through the price quotations published daily in, say the *Wall Street Journal*, not to mention the numerous more specialized trade publications. These prices mirror almost instantly what is happening all over the world. There is a revolution in some remote country that is a major producer of copper, or there is a disruption of copper production for some other reason. The current price of copper will shoot up at once. To find out how long knowledgeable people expect the supplies of copper to be affected, you need merely examine the prices for future delivery on the same page.

Few readers even of the *Wall Street Journal* are interested in more than a few of the prices quoted. They can readily ignore the rest. The *Wall Street Journal* does not provide this information out of altruism or because it recognizes how important it is for the operation of the economy. Rather, it is led to provide this information by the very price system whose functioning it facilitates. It has found that it can achieve a larger or a more profitable circulation by publishing these prices—information transmitted to it by a different set of prices.

Prices not only transmit information from the ultimate buyers to retailers, wholesalers, manufacturers, and owners of resources; they also transmit information the other way. Suppose that a forest fire or strike reduces the availability of wood. The price of wood will go up. That will tell the manufacturer of pencils that it will pay him to use less wood, and it will not pay him to produce as many pencils as before unless he can sell them for a higher price. The smaller production of pencils will enable the retailer to charge a higher price, and the higher price will inform the final user that it will pay him to wear his pencil down to a shorter stub before he discards it, or shift to a mechanical pencil. Again, he doesn't need to know why the pencil has become more expensive, only that it has.

Anything that prevents prices from expressing freely the conditions of demand or supply interferes with the transmission of accurate information. Private monopoly—control over a particular commodity by one producer or a cartel of producers—is one example. That does not prevent the transmission of information through the price system, but it does distort the information transmitted. The quadrupling of the price of oil in 1973 by the oil cartel transmitted very important information. However, the information it transmitted did not reflect a sudden reduction in the supply of crude oil, or a sudden discovery of new technical knowledge about future supplies of oil, or anything else of a physical or technical character bearing on the relative availability of oil and other sources of energy. It simply transmitted the information that a group of countries had succeeded in organizing a price-fixing and market-sharing arrangement.

Price controls on oil and other forms of energy by the U.S. government in their turn prevented information about the effect of the OPEC cartel from being transmitted accurately to users of petroleum. The result both strengthened the OPEC cartel, by preventing a higher price from leading U.S. consumers to economize on the use of oil, and required the introduction of major command elements in the United States in order to allocate the scarce supply (by a Department of Energy spending in 1979 about $10 billion and employing 20,000 people).

Important as private distortions of the price system are, these days the government is the major source of interference with a free market system—through tariffs and other restraints on international trade, domestic action fixing or affecting individual prices, including wages (see Chapter 2), government regulation of specific industries (see Chapter 7), monetary and fiscal policies producing erratic inflation (see Chapter 9), and numerous other channels.

One of the major adverse effects of erratic inflation is the introduction of static, as it were, into the transmission of information through prices. If the price of wood goes up, for example, producers of wood cannot know whether that is because inflation is raising all prices or because wood is now in greater demand or lower supply relative to other products than it was before the price hike. The information that is important for the organization of production is primarily about *relative* prices—the price of one item compared with the price of another. High inflation, and particularly highly variable inflation, drowns that information in meaningless static.

Incentives

Act on info

Distribute income

The effective transmission of accurate information is wasted unless the relevant people have an incentive to act, and act correctly, on the basis of that information. It does no good for the producer of wood to be told that the demand for wood has gone up unless he has some incentive to react to the higher price of wood by producing more wood. One of the beauties of a free price system is that the prices that bring the information also provide both an incentive to react to the information and the means to do so.

This function of prices is intimately connected with the third function—determining the distribution of income—and cannot be explained without bringing that function into the account. The producer's income—what he gets for his activities—is determined by the difference between the amount he receives from the sale of his output and the amount he spends in order to produce it. He balances the one against the other and produces an output such that producing a little more would add as much to his costs as to his receipts. A higher price shifts this margin.

In general, the more he produces, the higher the cost of producing still more. He must resort to wood in less accessible or otherwise less favorable locations; he must hire less skilled workers or pay higher wages to attract skilled workers from other pursuits. But now the higher price enables him to bear these higher costs and so provides both the incentive to increase output and the means to do so.

Prices also provide an incentive to act on information not only about the demand for output but also about the most efficient way to produce a product. Suppose one kind of wood becomes scarcer and therefore more expensive than another. The pencil manufacturer gets that information through a rise in the price of the first kind of wood. Because his income, too, is determined by the difference between sales receipts and costs, he has an incentive to economize on that kind of wood. To take a different example, whether it is less costly for loggers to use a chain saw or handsaw depends on the price of the chain saw and the handsaw, the amount of labor required with each, and the wages of different kinds of labor. The enterprise doing the logging has an incentive to acquire the relevant technical knowledge and to combine it with the information transmitted by prices in order to minimize costs.

Or take a more fanciful case that illustrates the subtlety of the price system. The rise in the price of oil engineered by the OPEC cartel in 1973 altered slightly the balance in favor of the handsaw by raising the cost of operating a chain saw. If that seems far-fetched, consider the effect on the use of diesel-powered versus gasoline-powered trucks to haul logs out of the forests and to the sawmill.

To carry this example one step further, the higher price of oil, insofar as it was permitted to occur, raised the cost of products that used more oil relative to products that used less. Consumers had an incentive to shift from the one to the other. The most obvious examples are shifts from large cars to small ones and from heating by oil to heating by coal or wood. To go much further afield to more remote effects: insofar as the relative price of wood was raised by the higher cost of producing it or by the greater demand for wood as a substitute source of energy, the resulting higher price of lead pencils gave consumers an incentive to economize on pencils! And so on in infinite variety.

We have discussed the incentive effect so far in terms of producers and consumers. But it also operates with respect to workers and owners of other productive resources. A higher demand for wood will tend to produce a higher wage for loggers. This is a signal that labor of that type is in greater demand than before. The higher wage gives workers an incentive to act on that information. Some workers who were indifferent about being loggers or doing something else may now choose to become loggers. More young people entering the labor market may become loggers. Here, too, interference by government, through minimum wages, for example, or by trade unions, through restricting entry, may distort the information transmitted or may prevent individuals from freely acting on that information (see Chapter 8).

Information about prices—whether it be wages in different activities, the rent of land, or the return to capital from different uses—is not the only information that is relevant in deciding how to use a particular resource. It may not even be the most important information, particularly about how to use one's own labor. That decision depends in addition on one's own interests and capacities— what the great economist Alfred Marshall called the whole of the advantages and disadvantages of an occupation, monetary and nonmonetary. Satisfaction in a job may compensate for low wages. On the other hand, higher wages may compensate for a disagreeable job.

Distribution of Income

The income each person gets through the market is determined, as we have seen, by the difference between his receipts from the sales of goods and services and the costs he incurs in producing those goods and services. The receipts consist predominantly of direct payments for the productive resources we own—payments for labor or the use of land or buildings or other capital. The case of the entrepreneur—like the manufacturer of pencils—is different in form but not in substance. His income, too, depends on how much of each productive resource he owns and on the price that the market sets on the services of those resources, though in his case the major productive resource he owns may be the capacity to organize an enterprise, coordinate the resources it uses, assume risks, and so on. He may also own some of the other productive resources used in the enterprise, in which case part of his income is derived from the market price for their services. Similarly, the existence of the modern corporation does not alter matters. We speak loosely of the "corporation's income" or of "business" having an income. That is figurative language. The corporation is an intermediary between its owners—the stockholders—and the resources other than the stockholders' capital, the services of which it purchases. Only people have incomes and they derive them through the market from the resources they own, whether these be in the form of corporate stock, or of bonds, or of land, or of their personal capacity.

In countries like the United States the major productive resource is personal productive capacity—what economists call "human capital." Something like three-quarters of all income generated in the United States through market transactions takes the form of the compensation of employees (wages and salaries plus supplements), and about half the rest takes the form of the income of proprietors of farms and nonfarm enterprises, which is a mixture of payment for personal services and for owned capital.

The accumulation of physical capital—of factories, mines, office buildings, shopping centers; highways, railroads, airports, cars, trucks, planes, ships; dams, refineries, power plants; houses, refrigerators, washing machines, and so on and on in endless variety—has played an essential role in economic growth. Without that accumulation the kind of economic growth that we have enjoyed could never have occurred. Without the maintenance of inherited capital the gains made by one generation would be dissipated by the next.

But the accumulation of human capital—in the form of increased knowledge and skills and improved health and longevity—has also played an essential role. And the two have reinforced one another. The physical capital enabled people to be far more productive by providing them with the tools to work with. And the capacity of people to invent new forms of physical capital, to learn how to use and get the most out of physical capital, and to organize the use of both physical and human capital on a larger and larger scale enabled the physical capital to be more productive. Both physical and human capital must be cared for and replaced. That is even more difficult and costly for human than for physical capital—a major reason why the return to human capital has risen so much more rapidly than the return to physical capital.

chance
or choice

The amount of each kind of resource each of us owns is partly the result of chance, partly of choice by ourselves or others. Chance determines our genes and through them affects our physical and mental capacities. Chance determines the kind of family and cultural environment into which we are born and as a result our opportunities to develop our physical and mental capacity. Chance determines also other resources we may inherit from our parents or other benefactors. Chance may destroy or enhance the resources we start with. But choice also plays an important role. Our decisions about how to use our resources, whether to work hard or take it easy, to enter one occupation or another, to engage in one venture or another, to save or spend—these may determine whether we dissipate our resources or improve and add to them. Similar decisions by our parents, by other benefactors, by millions of people who may have no direct connection with us will affect our inheritance.

The price that the market sets on the services of our resources is similarly affected by a bewildering mixture of chance and choice. Frank Sinatra's voice was highly valued in twentieth-century United States. Would it have been highly valued in twentieth-century India, if he had happened to be born and to live there? Skill as a hunter and trapper had a high value in eighteenth- and nineteenth-century America, a much lower value in twentieth-century America. Skill as a baseball player brought much higher returns than skill as a basketball player in the 1920s; the reverse is true in the 1970s. These are all matters involving chance and choice—in these examples, mostly the choices made by consumers of services that determine the relative market prices of different items. But the price we receive for the services of our resources through the market also depends on our own choices—where we choose to settle, how we choose to use those resources, to whom we choose to sell their services, and so on.

What skills are valuable today

In every society, however it is organized, there is always dissatisfaction with the distribution of income. All of us find it hard to understand why we should receive less than others who seem no more deserving—or why we should be receiving more than so many others whose needs seem as great and whose deserts seem no less. The farther fields always look greener—so we blame the existing system. In a command system envy and dissatisfaction are directed at the rulers. In a free market system they are directed at the market.

One result has been an attempt to separate this function of the price system—distributing income—from its other functions—transmitting information and providing incentives. Much government activity during recent decades in the United States and other countries that rely predominantly on the market has been directed at altering the distribution of income generated by the market in order to produce a different and more equal distribution of income. There is a strong current of opinion pressing for still further steps in this direction. We discuss this movement at greater length in Chapter 5.

distribution of income

However we might wish it otherwise, it simply is not possible to use prices to transmit information and provide an incentive to act on that information without using prices also to affect, even if not completely determine, the distribution of income. If what a person gets does not depend on the price he receives for the services of his resources, what incentive does he have to seek out information on prices or to act on the basis of that information? If Red Adair's income would be the same whether or not he performs the dangerous task of capping a runaway oil well, why should he undertake the dangerous task? He might do so once, for the excitement. But would he make it his major activity? If your income will be the same whether you work hard or not, why should you work hard? Why should you make the effort to search out the buyer who values most highly what you have to sell if you will not get any benefit from doing so?If there is no reward for accumulating capital, why should anyone postpone to a later date what he could enjoy now?Why save?How would the existing physical capital ever have been built up by the voluntary restraint of individuals?If there is no reward for maintaining capital, why should people not dissipate any capital which they have either accumulated or inherited? If prices are prevented from affecting the distribution of income, they cannot be used for other purposes. The only alternative is command. Some authority would have to decide who should produce what and how much. Some authority would have to decide who should sweep the streets and who manage the factory, who should be the policeman and who the physician.

The intimate connection among the three functions of the price system has manifested itself in a different way in the communist countries. Their whole ideology centers on the alleged exploitation of labor under capitalism and the associated superiority of a society based on Marx's dictum: "to each according to his needs, from each according to his ability." But the inability to run a pure command economy has made it impossible for them to separate income completely from prices.

For physical resources—land, buildings, and the like—they have been able to go farthest by making them the property of the government. But even here the effect is a lack of incentive to maintain and improve the physical capital. When everybody owns something, nobody owns it, and nobody has a direct interest in maintaining or improving its condition. That is why buildings in the Soviet Union—like public housing in the United States—look decrepit within a year or two of their construction, why machines in government factories break down and are continuously in need of repair, why citizens must resort to the black market for maintaining the capital that they have for their personal use.

For human resources the communist governments have not been able to go as far as with physical resources, though they have tried to. Even they have had to permit people to own themselves to some extent and to let them make their own decisions, and have had to let prices affect and guide those decisions and determine the income received. They have, of course, distorted those prices, prevented them from being free market prices, but they have been unable to eliminate market forces.

The obvious inefficiencies that have resulted from the command system have led to much discussion by planners in socialist countries—Russia, Czechoslovakia, Hungary, China—of the possibility of making greater use of the market in organizing production. At a conference of economists from East and West, we once heard a brilliant talk by a Hungarian Marxist economist. He had rediscovered for himself Adam Smith's invisible hand—a remarkable if somewhat redundant intellectual achievement. He tried, however, to improve on it in order to use the price system to transmit information and organize production efficiently but not to distribute income. Needless to say, he failed in theory, as the communist countries have failed to practice.

A Broader View

Adam Smith's "invisible hand" is generally regarded as referring to purchases or sales of goods or services for money. But economic activity is by no means the only area of human life in which a complex and sophisticated structure arises as an unintended consequence of a large number of individuals cooperating while each pursues his own interests.

Consider, for example, language. It is a complex structure that is continually changing and developing. It has a well-defined order, yet no central body planned it. No one decided what words should be admitted into the language, what the rules of grammar should be, which words should be adjectives, which nouns. The French Academy does try to control changes in the French language, but that was a late development. It was established long after French was already a highly structured language and it mainly serves to put the seal of approval on changes over which it has no control. There have been few similar bodies for other languages.

How did language develop? In much the same way as an economic order develops through the market—out of the voluntary interaction of individuals, in this case seeking to trade ideas or information or gossip rather than goods and services with one another. One or another meaning was attributed to a word, or words were added as the need arose. Grammatical usages developed and were later codified into rules. Two parties who want to communicate with one another benefit from coming to a common agreement about the words they use. As a wider and wider circle of people find it advantageous to communicate with one another, a common usage spreads and is codified in dictionaries. At no point is there any coercion, any central planner who has power to command, though in more recent times government school systems have played an important role in standardizing usage.

Another example is scientific knowledge. The structure of disciplines—physics, chemistry, meteorology, philosophy, humanities, sociology, economics—was not the product of a deliberate decision by anyone. Like Topsy, it "just growed." It did so because scholars found it convenient. It is not fixed, but changes as different needs develop.

Within any discipline the growth of the subject strictly parallels the economic marketplace. Scholars cooperate with one another because they find it mutually beneficial. They accept from one another's work what they find useful. They exchange their findings—by verbal communication, by circulating unpublished papers, by publishing in journals and books. Cooperation is worldwide, just as in the economic market. The esteem or approval of fellow scholars serves very much the same function that monetary reward does in the economic market. The desire to earn that esteem, to have their work accepted by their peers, leads scholars to direct their activities in scientifically efficient directions. The whole becomes greater than the sum of its parts, as one scholar builds on another's work. His work in turn becomes the basis for further development. Modern physics is as much a product of a free market in ideas as a modern automobile is a product of a free market in goods. Here again, developments have been much influenced, particularly recently, by government involvement, which has affected both the resources available and the kinds of knowledge that have been in demand. Yet government has played a secondary role. Indeed, one of the ironies of the situation is that many scholars who have strongly favored government central planning of economic activity have recognized very clearly the danger to scientific progress that would be imposed by central government planning of science, the danger of having priorities imposed from above rather than emerging spontaneously from the gropings and explorations of individual scientists.

A society's values, its culture, its social conventions—all these develop in the same way, through voluntary exchange, spontaneous cooperation, the evolution of a complex structure through trial and error, acceptance and rejection. No monarch ever decreed that the kind of music that is enjoyed by residents of Calcutta, for example, should differ radically from the kind enjoyed by residents of Vienna. These widely different musical cultures developed without anyone's "planning" them that way, through a kind of social evolution paralleling biological evolution—though, of course, individual sovereigns or even elected governments may have affected the direction of social evolution by sponsoring one or another musician or type of music, just as wealthy private individuals did.

The structures produced by voluntary exchange, whether they be language or scientific discoveries or musical styles or economic systems, develop a life of their own. They are capable of taking many different forms under different circumstances. Voluntary exchange can produce uniformity in some respects combined with diversity in others. It is a subtle process whose general principles of operation can fairly readily be grasped but whose detailed results can seldom be foreseen.

These examples may suggest not only the wide scope for voluntary exchange but also the broad meaning that must be attached to the concept of "self-interest." Narrow preoccupation with the economic market has led to a narrow interpretation of self-interest as myopic selfishness, as exclusive concern with immediate material rewards. Economics has been berated for allegedly drawing far-reaching conclusions from a wholly unrealistic "economic man" who is little more than a calculating machine, responding only to monetary stimuli. That is a great mistake. Self-interest is not myopic selfishness. It is whatever it is that interests the participants, whatever they value, whatever goals they pursue. The scientist seeking to advance the frontiers of his discipline, the missionary seeking to convert infidels to the true faith, the philanthropist seeking to bring comfort to the needy—all are pursuing their interests, as they see them, as they judge them by their own values...

VIOLENT MARKET-INJECTION STRATEGIES

Tom Peters

> The thematic terms are . . . *autonomy, experiment,* and *diversity.* . . . The underlying source of the West's ability to attract the lightning of economic revolutions was a unique use of experiment in technology and organization.... The key elements of the system were the wide diffusion of the authority and resources necessary to experiment; an absence of more than rudimentary political and religious restrictions on experiment; and incentives which combined ample rewards for success . . . with the risk of severe penalties for failing to experiment.
>
> —*Nathan Rosenberg and L. E. Birdzell, Jr.*
> *How the West Grew Rich*

In the title of this section, you'll find markets *first*, innovation *second*. It's increasingly clear to me that in a topsy-turvy world, where all goods are more or less fashion goods, only egging on the market to fully buffet each and every part of the firm will increase (to a satisfactory level—maybe!) the possibility of corporate survival, and, occasionally, excellence.

Exalter of Untidiness

F. A. Hayek was that rare economist who was also a first-rate historian. And to the faithful economic historian, like the meritorious novelist, the mess is the story. Hayek describes fitful economic (and human) progress as a direct function of rich, volatile, unpredictable experimentation in the marketplace. (He calls the global economy "the most complex structure in the universe"—inherently incomprehensible.) It's not pretty, but it's increasingly clear that it works far better than any alternative.

Tumbling into Hayck—yes, I started reading him by accident, appropriately enough—was a profoundly exhilarating experience. He mustered hard empirical evidence to buttress his case (in those 22 volumes of collected works—I'm not through all of them yet). My introduction to Hayek made me vow that I'd never again accede to the forces of order—the dogmatic strategic planners, the hierarchists, the central controllers who try to convince us that order and success are handmaidens (oh, what a comforting illusion, as Hayek points out so eloquently); that if we can just get the plan right, goodness will surely follow. To revel in disorder and the joys of accidental discovery. That's the magic of Madison Avenue and of Hollywood. Of Silicon Valley and once, long ago, of Detroit.

Where's the Mess?

> After two years I have not been able to get rid of the smell of central planning.
>
> *—Vladimir Dloughy, Minister of the Economy, Czechoslovakia, on the offices he inherited from the Communist regime in 1988*

> There is no hope for the state enterprises.
>
> *—Anonymous Chinese economist, quoted in The New York Times December 18, 1991*

In 1991, I glanced at *Marketing Strategy: A Customer-driven Approach,* by Professor Steven P. Schnaars. Then I dug in. It's a useful brook, neatly summarizing the important positions taken by today's marketing and business strategy gurus: the successes and stumbles of the Boston Consulting Group's market share/"experience curve" approach in the 1970s; the pros and cons of Harvard professor Michael Porter's three "generic strategies"; the strengths and weaknesses of the PIMS (profit impact of market strategies) database. And so on.

I took notes. Then, as I prepared to write this section, I reviewed my scribblings on Hayek one last time—and ripped up my notes on *Marketing Strategy* with anguish, anger, even disgust.

Why? Nowhere in those tidy pages (presented as a primer for business students) was there even a hint of the richness, messiness, and uncertainty of markets. Of the disorder, fun, and enthusiasm—and agony and despair—of markets. (No, not untidiness "of" markets. Untidiness *is* markets.) To the contrary, the possibility of conquering markets with a sound plan and a little more market research could be found on any page. Not in *these* pages. You'll quickly find that messiness is the message here.

F. A. Hayek: The Mess is the Message

To understand innovation in a frantic world, like it or not, we need to go back to the economic basics. Not the dull basics of supply and demand curves that you and I first learned, but the real basics—the hurly-burly of economic life. Friedrich August von Hayek long ago dismissed traditional macroeconomic thinking, for he was the exceptional observer who examines the raw essence of markets. Consider the circumstances that led to the emergence of markets, upon which Hayek speculates in *The Fatal Conceit:*

> Only a few, relatively small localities would have provided small bands of hunters and gatherers all that even the most primitive tool-using groups need for a settled existence.... Without support from fellows elsewhere, most humans would find the places they wished to occupy either uninhabitable or able to be settled only very thinly. Those few relatively self-sustaining niches that did exist would likely be the first in any particular area to be permanently occupied and defended against intruders. Yet people living there would come to know of neighboring places that provided most but not all of their needs, and which would lack some substances that they would require only occasionally: flint, strings for their bows....
>
> Confident that such needs could be met by infrequent return visits to their present homes, they would stride out from their groups, and occupy some of these neighboring places, or other new territory even further away in other parts of the thinly populated continents on which they lived. The importance of these early movements of persons and of necessary goods cannot be gauged by volume alone. Without the availability of imports, even if they formed only an insignificant fraction of what was currently being consumed in any particular place, it would have been impossible for early settlers to maintain themselves, let alone to multiply. Return visits to replenish supplies would raise no difficulty so long as the migrants were still known to those who had remained at home.
>
> Within a few generations, however, descendants of these original groups would begin to seem strangers to one another; and those inhabiting the original more self-sustaining

localities would often begin to defend themselves and their supplies in various ways. To gain permission to enter the original territory for the purpose of obtaining whatever special substances could be obtained only there, visitors would, to herald their peaceful intentions and to tempt desires of its occupants, have had to bring presents. To be more effective, these gifts had best not satisfy everyday needs readily met locally, but would need to be enticingly new and unusual ornaments or delicacies. This is one reason why objects offered on one side of such transactions were, in fact, so often "luxuries"—which hardly means that the objects exchanged were not necessities to the other side. Initially, regular connections involving exchange of presents would probably have developed between families with mutual obligations of hospitality....

The transition from the practice of giving presents to such family members and relations to the appearance of more impersonal institutions of hosts or "brokers" who routinely sponsored such visitors and gained for them permission to stay long enough to obtain what they needed, and on to the practice of exchanging particular things at rates determined by their relative scarcity, was no doubt slow. But from the recognition of a minimum still regarded as appropriate, and of a maximum at which the transaction seemed no longer worthwhile, specific prices for particular objects will gradually have emerged.

In this description, the complexity of what Hayek calls the "extended [economic] order" appears. And along with it, and quickly at that, the "unknowability" in any exhaustive sense, of even the simplest extended order. The connections have already become far too rich and too dense to map.

Extended trade, Hayek observes, emerged before agriculture—in the Paleolithic Age some 30,000 years ago. To move trade beyond the narrow immediate locale, some small number of guiding traditions and rules proved essential. (It is important to note at the outset that those "rules" were not, as the term might imply the product of planning. Some societies accidentally fell into such practices, Hayek asserts. They prospered. The practices—"rules"—they had stumbled upon were copied and spread.) Above all, he avers, private property was the cornerstone for all that followed, the very basis for organized trade and thence the painful movement from small, isolated savage bands or tribes to widespread interdependent modern civilization.

The "extended order" began around the Mediterranean. Societies there were the first, according to Hayek, to accept a "person's rights to dispose [of property], thus allowing individuals to develop a dense network of commercial relations." Private property, Hayek insists, also enshrines, by definition, the primacy of decentralization. The right to dispose of one's assets provides the basis for dealing with—or not dealing with—others of one's choosing (the most fundamental definition of decentralization).

The intellectual problem that was Hayek's preoccupation (and amply illustrated by the long extract) is this: The dense, decentralized network that emerges quickly becomes unknowable. Moreover, the chief vehicle which moves economies and civilization forward is unplanned experimentation by and among millions of individuals (billions today) who do not know one another. Along the way, successful experiments are emulated. (Some very few experiments are immediately successful, for the "right" reasons—i.e., according to "plan." The rest that are successful emerge, over time, for the "wrong" —i.e., unplanned, unimagined, mostly unimaginable—reasons.) Unsuccessful experiments, the vast majority, simply drop by the wayside. Thus the process of economic expansion is humbling, irrational, and—in principle—not amenable to centralized planning and control. "Order generated without design," Hayek wrote, "can far outstrip plans men consciously contrive." He adds that the "extended [economic] order resulted not from human design or intention but spontaneously.... Evolution leads us ahead precisely in bringing about much that we could not intend or foresee."

(Hayek's use of "evolution" and terms derived from evolutionary theory such as "blind variation," "adaptation" and "selection" is no accident. Indeed, he takes pains to point out that Darwin was singularly influenced, 20 years prior to publication of *Origin of the Species,* by reading Adam Smith's *The Wealth of Nations.* The proper credit for evolutionary theory may lie almost as much with Smith's brilliant notion of the "invisible hand" as with Darwin's rich observations during the voyage of the *Beagle.*)

But those, yesterday or today, who are under the spell of the invisible hand are faced with a dilemma: First, they/we cannot fully "understand" how the market works, given its extensive nature. Second, the market serves no purpose "that one can specify fully in advance." And third, it produces results that are "not immediately observable" (i.e., results clouded by those tangles of causes and effects). But these three properties, Hayek points out, are *the* defining bases of testable, modern scientific hypotheses. That is, this extended, unknowable, unplannable, unspecifiable market order flies squarely in the face of the Enlightenment, of Cartesian logic and of scientific reasoning—all that has defined intellectual "progress" for the last several hundred years.

Part of the problem is egocentrism. "Intelligent people," Hayek wrote, ". . . tend to over-value intelligence and to suppose that we must owe all advantages and opportunities that civilization offers to deliberate design." To the contrary, Hayek insists, for instance, that Europe's "extraordinary expansion in the Middle Ages" was a product of "political anarchy." The anarchy per se produced the diversity which led directly to modern economic "order." The rowdy capitalist towns of the Renaissance in northern Italy, southern Germany, the Low Countries, and England were an inexplicable new species—which launched modern market economics.

Joyous Anarchy

So much of economic success—Silicon Valley, Taipei, Hong Kong, Guangdong, Hollywood—has to do with anarchy. The "magic" of Silicon Valley lies as much in the bars and the squash courts as in Stanford University's fertile labs. It is the anarchy itself that "produces" the high volume of chance connections, the oft-told motivational fables. It is the energy from the critical mass—a statistical artifact, product of the law of large numbers—that makes Silicon Valley what it is, and makes it almost uncopyable. You could physically construct a Silicon Brasilia, but you'd be hard-pressed to initiate the wild, untrammeled growth that created California's matchless economic hot spot.

On the one hand, Hayek argues persuasively that rules are imperative to progress (in very small number: private property, enforceability of contracts). On the other hand, freedom is maximized—as is wealth and the fruits of civilization in general—precisely because these rules are *impersonal*. They guide vast numbers of relationships among large numbers of people unknown to one another; their content and minimalist nature spawn decentralization rather than centralization. And maximizing decentralization, Hayek claims, by definition maximizes experiments—thereby maximizing the number of "blind variations" (the evolutionary model) from which unpredictable but useful outcomes (called "selective retention") can occasionally occur.

Hayek further claims that "all evolution rest[s] on competition.... [Useful knowledge] arises in a process of experimental interaction of widely dispersed, different and even conflicting beliefs of millions of individuals.... [Rules aimed at] repressing differentiation due to luck . . . would have scotched most discoveries." Hayek cites the preeminent philosopher of science, Karl Popper, who wrote in *Conjectures and Refutations* that there can be no final knowledge, only "suggestions" (hypotheses or conjectures) which are supported for a time, then subsequently overturned (refuted) by better but still necessarily inconclusive "suggestions"/conjectures. "Our aim," Popper added in a passage admiringly quoted by Hayek, "must be to make our successive mistakes as quickly as possible."

Which leads us back to Hayek's disdain for modern macroeconomic reasoning. He contends that it "conceals the character of competition as a discovery process." (Some maintain that the connection of markets and spontaneous discovery is Hayek's most profound contribution.) Hayek hammers away at the importance of disorderly decentralization as "the only way to make use of [widely] dispersed information in its great variety.... Decentralized control of resources, . . . through [privately owned] property, leads to the generation and use of more information than is possible under central direction. [As Popper said,] 'To the naive mind, that conceives of order only as product of deliberate arrangement, it may seem absurd that in complex condtions order and adaptation to the unknown can be achieved more effective by decentralizing decisions.' "

Yet another problem for rationalists, Hayek says, is that diversity wants/tastes/values— which directly creates relative scarcity, and indirectly creates the price mechanism—is "not an attribute or physical property possessed by things." It is completely subjective. (Fashion!) The creation of products, markets, and trade itself is "simply" a by-product of playing up to different tastes among different individuals. "To serve a constantly changing scale of values," Hayek acknowledges, "may indeed seem repulsive." Economists, he asserts, have wrongheadedly regarded the daily elbowing among merchants in the marketplace as "superfluous . . . a methodological mistake . . . Activities that appear to add to available wealth 'out of nothing,' without physical creation and by merely rearranging what already exists, stink of sorcery."

Why spend so much time on Hayek? Simple. To fail to appreciate—in the fullest sense of that term—the richness, passion, and raggedness of the market mechanism is to be unprepared to lead a firm (or a regional or national economy)—especially in today's unhinged global marketplace. There is doubt that economists and planners don't much like bawdy capitalists. There's no place in the Chase Econometrics Model (or the General Motors strategic plan) for destabilizers like today's Steve Jobs, Ted Turner, Al Neuharth, or yesterday's Thomas Edison, J. P. Morgan, Andrew Carnegie.

Propositions from Hayek

- Liberty/wealth ("civilization") is due to "extended order"—i.e., trade over distance where producers and distributors and buyers are *not known to one another*.

- The extended order is based on a few overarching "rules"—e.g., private property, enforceable contracts. (The rules did not emerge as the product of planning!)

- Following a few uniform, impersonal rules maximizes variety. Variety (the product of competition/decentralization) in turn is the key to discovery and hence the creation of wealth.

- *Intangibles*—money and banking, differing tastes—are *the* basis for the extended order. *All* value (trade) is a function of intangibles/human relationships, *not* physical properties (e.g., intrinsic "quality" of the objects per se).

- Value stems from rearrangement/rearrangers. Brokers, etc., are *more* important than "producers."

- Growth stems from trial and error, competition, the survival of (and imitation of) the successful. (The successful seldom know they will be successful. Success invariably stems from unintended consequences, from endless strings of unpredictable causes and effects.)

- Decentralization/decentralized processing of information (and the trial-and-error, often "lucky" discovery of preferences/tastes) is the key to the extended order. More information, *by far*, can be processed more quickly in a "disorganized" (decentralized) system—i.e., more chance, unpredictable-in-advance connections occur, which lead to more "blind variations," thence, eventually, more "selective retention." (Not for sure, of course. "Selective retention" is a probabilities game.)

- Success doesn't necessarily come to those who "deserve it" and is not a matter of "fairness"—because of the complexity of the system, which leads to long chains of unintended consequences, with *long-term* effects which can rarely if ever be anticipated at the moment by even the most brilliant prognosticator.

THE USE OF KNOWLEDGE IN SOCIETY*

Friedrich A. Hayek

1

What is the problem we wish to solve when we try to construct a rational economic order? On certain familiar assumptions the answer is simple enough. *If* we possess all the relevant information, *if* we can start out from a given system of preferences, and *if* we command complete knowledge of available means, the problem which remains is purely one of logic. That is, the answer to the question of what is the best use of the available means is implicit in our assumptions. The conditions which the solution of this optimum problem must satisfy have been fully worked out and can be stated best in mathematical form:put at their briefest, they are that the marginal rates of substitution between any two commodities or factors must be the same in all their different uses.

This, however, is emphatically *not* the economic problem which society faces. And the economic calculus which we have developed to solve this logical problem, though an important step toward the solution of the economic problem of society, does not yet provide an answer to it. The reason for this is that the "data" from which the economic calculus starts are never for the whole society "given" to a single mind which could work out the implications and can never be so given.

The peculiar character of the problem of a rational economic order is determined precisely by the fact that the knowledge of the circumstances of which we must make use never exists in the concentrated or integrated form but solely as the dispersed bits of incomplete and frequently contradictory knowledge which all the separate individuals possess. The economic problem of society is thus not merely a problem of how to allocate "given" resources—if "given" is taken to mean given to a single mind which deliberately solves the problem set by these "data." It is rather a problem of how to secure the best use of resources known to any of the members of society, for ends whose relative importance only these individuals know. Or, to put it briefly, it is a problem of the utilization of knowledge which is not given to anyone in its totality.

This character of the fundamental problem has, I am afraid, been obscured rather than illuminated by many of the recent refinements of economic theory, particularly by many of the uses made of mathematics. Though the problem with which I want primarily to deal in this paper is the problem of a rational economic organization, I shall in its course be led again and again to point to its close connections with certain methodological questions. Many of the points I wish to make are indeed conclusions toward which diverse paths of reasoning have unexpectedly converged. But, as I now see these problems, this is no accident. It seems to me that many of the current disputes with regard to both economic theory and economic policy have their common origin in a misconception about the nature of the economic problem of society. This misconception in turn is due to an erroneous transfer to social phenomena of the habits of thought we have developed in dealing with the phenomena of nature.

2

In ordinary language we describe by the word "planning" the complex of interrelated decisions about the allocation of our available resources. All economic activity is in this sense planning; and in any society in which many people collaborate, this planning, whoever does it, will in some measure have to be based on knowledge which, in the first instance, is not given to the planner but to somebody else, which somehow will have to be conveyed to the planner. The various ways in which the knowledge on which people base their plans is communicated to them is the crucial problem for any theory explaining the economic process, and the problem of what is the best way of utilizing knowledge initially dispersed among all the people is at least one of the main problems of economic policy—or of designing an efficient economic system.

The answer to this question is closely connected with that other question which arises here, that of *who* is to do the planning. It is about this question that all the dispute about "economic planning" centers. This is not a dispute about whether planning is to be done or not. It is a dispute as to whether planning is to be done centrally, by one authority for the whole economic system, or is to be divided among many individuals. Planning in the specific sense in which the term is used in contemporary controversy necessarily means central planning—direction of the whole economic system according to one unified plan. Competition, on the other hand, means decentralized planning by many separate persons. The halfway house between the two, about which many people talk but which few like when they see it, is the delegation of planning to organized industries, or, in other words, monopolies.

Which of these systems is likely to be more efficient depends mainly on the question under which of them we can expect that fuller use will be made of the existing knowledge. This, in turn, depends on whether we are more likely to succeed in putting at the disposal of a single central authority all the knowledge which ought to be used but which is initially dispersed among many different individuals, or in conveying to the individuals such additional knowledge as they need in order to enable them to dovetail their plans with those of others.

3

It will at once be evident that on this point the position will be different with respect to different kinds of knowledge. The answer to our question will therefore largely turn on the relative importance of the different kinds of knowledge: those more likely to be at the disposal of particular individuals and those which we should with greater confidence expect to find in the possession of an authority made up of suitably chosen experts. If it is today so widely assumed that the latter will be in a better position, this is because one kind of knowledge, namely, scientific knowledge, occupies now so prominent a place in public imagination that we tend to forget that it is not the only kind that is relevant. It may be admitted that, as far as scientific knowledge is concerned, a body of suitably chosen experts may be in the best position to command all the best knowledge available—though this is of course merely shifting the difficulty to the problem of selecting the experts. What I wish to point out is that, even assuming that this problem can be readily solved, it is only a small part of the wider problem.

Today it is almost heresy to suggest that scientific knowledge is not the sum of all knowledge. But a little reflection will show that there is beyond question a body of very important but unorganized knowledge which cannot possibly be called scientific in the sense of knowledge of general rules: the knowledge of the particular circumstances of time and place. It is with respect to this that practically every individual has some advantage over all others because he possesses unique information of which beneficial use might be made, but of which use can be made only if the decisions depending on it are left to him or are made with his active co-operation. We need to remember only how much

---

we have to learn in any occupation after we have completed our theoretical training, how big a part of our working life we spend learning particular jobs, and how valuable an asset in all walks of life is knowledge of people, of local conditions, and of special circumstances. To know of and put to use a machine not fully employed, or somebody's skill which could be better utilized, or to be aware of a surplus stock which can be drawn upon during an interruption of supplies, is socially quite as useful as the knowledge of better alternative techniques. The shipper who earns his living from using otherwise empty or half-filled journeys of tramp-steamers, or the estate agent whose whole knowledge is almost exclusively one of temporary opportunities, or the *arbitrageur* who gains from local differences of commodity prices—are all performing eminently useful functions based on special knowledge of circumstances of the fleeting moment not know to others.

It is a curious fact that this sort of knowledge should today be generally regarded with a kind of contempt and that anyone who by such knowledge gains an advantage over somebody better equipped with theoretical or technical knowledge is thought to have acted almost disreputably. To gain an advantage from better knowledge of facilities of communication or transport is sometimes regarded as almost dishonest, although it is quite as important that society make use of the best opportunities in this respect as in using the latest scientific discoveries. This prejudice has in a considerable measure affected the attitude toward commerce in general compared with that toward production. Even economists who regard themselves as definitely immune to the crude materialist fallacies of the past constantly commit the same mistake where activities directed toward the acquisition of such practical knowledge are concerned—apparently because in their scheme of things all such knowledge is supposed to "given." The common idea now seems to be that all such knowledge should as a matter of course be readily at the command of everybody, and the reproach of irrationality leveled against the existing economic order is frequently based on the fact that it is not so available. This view disregards the fact that the method by which such knowledge can be made as widely available as possible is precisely the problem to which we have to find an answer.

4

If it is fashionable to minimize the importance of the knowledge of the particular circumstances of time and place, this is closely connected with the smaller importance which is now attached to change as such. Indeed, there are few points on which the assumptions made (usually only implicitly) by the "planners" differ from those of their opponents as much as with regard to the significance and frequency of changes which will make substantial alterations of production plans necessary. Of course, if detailed economic plans could be laid down for fairly long periods in advance and then closely adhered to, so that no further economic decisions of importance would be required, the task of drawing up a comprehensive plan governing all economic activity would be much less formidable.

It is, perhaps, worth stressing that economic problems arise always and only in consequence of change. As long as things continue as before, or at least as they were expected to, there arise no new problems requiring a decision, no need to form a new plan. The belief that changes, or at least day-to-day adjustments, have become less important in modern times implies the contention that economic problems also have become less important. This belief in the decreasing importance of change is, for that reason, usually held by the same people who argue that the importance of economic considerations has been driven into the background by the growing importance of technological knowledge.

Is it true that, with the elaborate apparatus of modern production, economic decisions are required only at long intervals, as when a new factory is to be erected or a new process to be introduced? Is it true that, once a plant has been built, the rest is all more or less mechanical, determined by the character of the plant, and leaving little to be changed in adapting to the ever changing circumstances of the moment?

The fairly widespread belief in the affirmative is not, as far as I can ascertain, borne out by the practical experience of the businessman. In a competitive industry at any rate—and such an industry alone can serve as a test—the task of keeping cost from rising requires constant struggle, absorbing a great part of the energy of the manager. How easy it is for an inefficient manager to dissipate the differentials on which profitability rests and that it is possible, with the same technical facilities, to produce with a great variety of costs are among the commonplaces of business experience which do not seem to be equally familiar in the study of the economist. The very strength of the desire, constantly voiced by producers and engineers, to be allowed to proceed untrammeled by considerations of money costs, is eloquent testimony to the extent to which these factors enter into their daily work.

One reason why economists are increasingly apt to forget about the constant small changes which make up the whole economic picture is probably their growing preoccupation with statistical aggregates, which show a very much greater stability than the movements of the detail. The comparative stability of the aggregates cannot, however, be accounted for—as the statisticians occasionally seem to be inclined to do—by the "law of large numbers" or the mutual compensation of random changes. The number of elements with which we have to deal is not large enough for such accidental forces to produce stability. The continuous flow of goods and services is maintained by constant deliberate adjustments, by new dispositions made every day in the light of circumstances not known the day before, by B stepping in at once when A fails to deliver. Even the large and highly

---

mechanized plant keeps going largely because of an environment upon which it can draw for all sorts of unexpected needs:tiles for its roof, stationery or its forms, and all the thousand and one kinds of equipment in which it cannot be self-contained and which the plans for the operation of the plant require to be readily available in the market.

This is, perhaps, also the point where I should briefly mention the fact that the sort of knowledge with which I have been concerned is knowledge of the kind which by its nature cannot enter into statistics and therefore cannot be conveyed to any central authority in statistical form. The statistics which such a central authority would have to use would have to be arrived at precisely by abstracting from minor differences between the things, by lumping together, as resources of one kind, items which differ as regards location, quality, and other particulars, in a way which may be very significant for the specific decision. It follows from this that central planning based on statistical information by its nature cannot take direct account of these circumstances of time and place and that the central planner will have to find some way or other in which the decisions depending on them can be left to the "man on the spot."

5

If we can agree that the economic problem of society is mainly one of rapid adaptation to changes in the particular circumstances of time and place, it would seem to follow that the ultimate decisions must be left to the people who are familiar with these circumstances, who know directly of the relevant changes and of the resources immediately available to meet them. We cannot expect that this problem will be solved by first communicating all this knowledge to a central board which, after integrating all knowledge, issues its orders. We must solve it by some form of decentralization. But this answers only part of our problem. We need decentralization because only thus can we insure that the knowledge of the particular circumstances of time and place will be promptly used. But the "man on the spot" cannot decide solely on the basis of his limited but intimate knowledge of the facts of his immediate surrounding. There still remains the problem of communicating to him such further information as he needs to fit his decisions into the whole pattern of changes of the larger economic system.

How much knowledge does he need to do so successfully? Which of the events which happened beyond the horizon of his immediate knowledge are of relevance to his immediate decision, and how much of them need he know?

There is hardly anything that happens anywhere in the world that *might* not have an effect on the decision he ought to make. But he need not know of these events as such, nor of *all* their

---

effects. It does not matter for him *why* at the particular moment more screws of one size than of another are wanted, *why* paper bags are more readily available than canvas bags, or *why* skilled labor, or particular machine tools, have for the moment become more difficult to obtain. All that is significant for him is *how much more or less* difficult to procure they have become compared with other things with which he is also concerned, or how much more or less urgently wanted are the alternative things he produces or uses. It is always a question of the relative importance of the particular things with which he is concerned, and the causes which alter their relative importance are of no interest to him beyond the effect on those concrete things of his own environment.

It is in this connection that what I have called the "economic calculus" (or the Pure Logic of Choice) helps us, at least by analogy, to see how this problem can be solved, and in fact is being solved, by the price system. Even the single controlling mind, in possession of all the data for some small, self-contained economic system, would not—every time some small adjustment in the allocation of resources had to be made—go explicitly through all the relations between ends and means which might possibly be affected. It is indeed the great contribution of the Pure Logic Choice that it has demonstrated conclusively that even such a single mind could solve this kind of problem only be constructing and constantly using rates of equivalence (or "values," or "marginal rates of substitution"), that is, by attaching to each kind of scarce resource a numerical index which cannot be derived from any property possessed by that particular thing, but which reflects, or in which is condensed, its significance in view of the whole means-end structure. In any small change he will have to consider only these quantitative indices (or "values") in which all the relevant information is concentrated; and, by adjusting the quantities one by one, he can appropriately rearrange his dispositions without having to solve the whole puzzle *ab initio* or without needing at any stage to survey it at once in all its ramifications.

Fundamentally, in a system in which the knowledge of the relevant facts is dispersed among many people, prices can act to co-ordinate the separate actions of different people in the same way as subjective values help the individual to co-ordinate the parts of his plan. It is worth contemplating for a moment a very simple and commonplace instance of the action of the price system to see what precisely it accomplishes. Assume that somewhere in the world a new opportunity for the use of some raw material, say, tin, has arisen, or that one of the sources of supply of tin has been eliminated. It does not matter for our purpose—and it is significant that it does not matter—which of these two causes has made tin more scarce. All that the users of tin need to know is that some of the tin they used to consume is now more profitably employed elsewhere and that, in consequence, they must economize tin. There is no need for the great majority of them even to know where the more urgent need has arisen, or in favor of what other needs they ought to husband the supply. If only some of them know directly of the new demand, and switch resources over to it, and if the people who are aware of the new gap thus created in turn fill it from still other sources, the effect will rapidly spread throughout the whole economic system and influence not only all the uses of tin but also those of its substitutes and the substitutes of these substitutes, the supply of all the things made of tin, and their substitutes, and so on, and all this without the great majority of those instrumental in bringing about these substitutions knowing anything at all about the original cause of these changes. The whole acts as one market, not because any of its members survey the whole field, but because their limited individual fields of vision sufficiently overlap so that through many intermediaries the relevant information is communicated to all. The mere fact that there is one price for any commodity—or rather that local prices are connected in a manner determined by the cost of transport, etc.—brings about the solution which (it is just conceptually possible) might have been arrived at by one single mind possessing all the information which is in fact dispersed among all the people involved in the process.

6

We must look at the price system as such a mechanism for communicating information if we want to understand its real function—a function which, of course, it fulfils less perfectly as prices grow more rigid. (Even when quoted prices have become quite rigid, however, the forces which would operate through changes in price still operate to a considerable extent through changes in the other terms of the contract.) The most significant fact about this system is the economy of knowledge with which it operates, or how little the individual participants need to know in order to be able to take the right action. In abbreviated form, by a kind of symbol, only the most essential information is passed on and passed on only to those concerned. It is more than a metaphor to describe the price system as a kind of machinery for registering change, or a system of telecommunications which enables individual producers to watch merely the movement of a few pointers, as an engineer might watch the hands of a few dials, in order to adjust their activities to changes of which they may never know more than is reflected in the price movement.

Of course, these adjustments are probably never "perfect" in the sense in which the economist conceives of them in his equilibrium analysis. But I fear that our theoretical habits of approaching the problem with the assumption of more or less perfect knowledge on the part of almost everyone has made us somewhat blind to the true function of the price mechanism and led us to apply rather misleading standards in judging its efficiency. The marvel is that in a case like that of a scarcity of one raw material, without an order being issued, without more than perhaps a handful of people knowing the cause, tens of thousands of people whose identity could not be ascertained by months of investigation, are made to use the material or its products more sparingly; that is, they move in the right direction. This is enough of a marvel even if, in a constantly changing world, not all will hit off so perfectly that their profit rates will always be maintained at the same even or "normal" level.

I have deliberately used the word "marvel" to shock the reader out of the complacency with which we often take the working of this mechanism for granted. I am convinced that if it were the result of deliberate human design, and if the people guided by the price changes understood that their decisions have significance far beyond their immediate aid, this mechanism would have been acclaimed as one of the greatest triumphs of the human mind. Its misfortune is the double one that it is not the product of human design and that the people guided by it usually do not know why they are made to do what they do. But those who clamor for "conscious direction"—and who cannot believe that anything which has evolved without design (and even without our understanding it) should solve problems which we should not be able to solve consciously—should remember this: The problem is precisely how to extend the span of our utilization of resources beyond the span of the control of any one mind; and, therefore, how to dispense with the need of conscious control and how to provide inducements which will make the individuals do the desirable things without anyone having to tell them what to do.

The problem which we meet here is by no means peculiar to economics but arises in connection with nearly all truly social phenomena, with language and with most of our cultural inheritance, and constitutes really the central theoretical problem of all social science. As Alfred Whitehead has said in another connection, "It is a profoundly erroneous truism, repeated by all copy-books and by eminent people when they are making speeches, that we should cultivate the habit of thinking what we are doing. The precise opposite is the case. Civilization advances by extending the number of important operations which we can perform without thinking about them." This is of profound significance in the social field. We make constant use of formulas, symbols, and rules whose meaning we do not understand and through the use of which we avail ourselves of the assistance of knowledge which individually we do not possess. We have developed these practices and institutions by building upon habits and institutions which have proved successful in their own sphere and which have in turn become the foundation of the civilization we have built up.

The price system is just one of those formations which man has learned to use (though he is still very far from having learned to make the best use of it) after he had stumbled upon it without understanding it. Through it not only a division of labor but also a co-ordinated utilization of resources based on an equally divided knowledge has become possible. The people who like to deride any suggestion that this may be so usually distort the argument by insinuating that it asserts that by some miracle just that sort of system has spontaneously grown up which is best suited to modern civilization. It is the other way round: man has been able to develop that division of labor on which our civilization is based because he happened to stumble upon a method which made it possible. Had he not done so, he might still have developed some other, altogether different, type of civilization, something like the "state" of the termite ants, or some other altogether unimaginable type. All that we can say is that nobody has yet succeeded in designing an alternative system in which certain features of the existing one can be preserved which are dear even to those who most violently assail it—such as particularly the extent to which the individual can choose his pursuits and consequently freely use his own knowledge and skill.

7

It is in many ways fortunate that the dispute about the indispensability of the price system for any rational calculation in a complex society is now no longer conducted entirely between camps holding different political views. The thesis that without the price system we could not preserve a society based on such extensive division of labor as ours was greeted with a howl of derision when it was first advanced by von Mises twenty-five years ago. Today the difficulties which some still find in accepting it are no longer mainly political, and this makes for an atmosphere much more conducive to reasonable discussion. When we find Leon Trotsky arguing that "economic accounting is unthinkable without market relations"; when Professor Oscar Lange promises Professor von Mises a statue in the marble halls of the future Central Planning Board; and when Professor Abba P. Lerner rediscovers Adam Smith and emphasizes that the essential utility of the price system consists in inducing the individual, while seeking his own interest, to do what is in the general interest, the differences can indeed no longer be ascribed to political prejudice. The remaining dissent seems clearly to be due to purely intellectual, and more particularly methodological, differences.

A recent statement by Joseph Schumpeter in his *Capitalism, Socialism, and Democracy* provides a clear illustration of one of the methodological differences which I have in mind. Its author is pre-eminent among those economists who approach economic phenomena in the light of a certain branch of positivism. To him these phenomena accordingly appear as objectively given quantities of commodities impinging directly upon each other, almost, it would seem, without any intervention of human minds. Only against this background can I account for the following (to me startling) pronouncement. Professor Schumpeter argues that the possibility of a rational calculation in the absence of markets for the factors of production follows for the theorist "from the elementary proposition that consumers in evaluating ('demanding') consumers' goods *ipso facto* also evaluate the means of production which enter into the production of these goods."[1]

Taken literally, this statement is simply untrue. The consumers do nothing of the kind. What Professor Schumpeter's "*ipso facto*" presumably means is that the valuation of the factors of production is implied in, or follows necessarily from, the valuation of consumers' goods. But this, too, is not correct. Implication is a logical relationship which can be meaningfully asserted only of propositions simultaneously present to one and the same mind. It is evident, however, that the values of the factors of production do not depend solely on the valuation of the consumers' goods but also on the conditions of supply of the various factors of production. Only to a mind to which all these facts were simultaneously known would the answer necessarily follow from the facts given to it. The practical problem, however, arises precisely because these facts are never so given to a single mind, and because, in consequence, it is necessary that in the solution of the problem knowledge should be used that is dispersed among many people.

The problem is thus in no way solved if we can show that all the facts, *if* they were known to a single mind (as we hypothetically assume them to be given to the observing economist), would uniquely determine the solution; instead we must show how a solution is produced by the interactions of people each of whom possesses only partial knowledge. To assume all the knowledge to be given to a single mind in the same manner in which we assume it to be given to us as the explaining economists is to assume the problem away and to disregard everything that is important and significant in the real world.

That an economist of Professor Schumpeter's standing should thus have fallen into a trap which the ambiguity of the term "datum" sets to the unwary can hardly be explained as a simple error. It suggests rather that there is something fundamentally wrong with an approach which habitually disregards an essential part of the phenomena with which we have to deal: the unavoidable imperfection of man's knowledge and the consequent need for a process by which knowledge is constantly communicated and acquired. Any approach, such as that of much of mathematical economics with its simultaneous equations, which in effect starts from the assumption that people's *knowledge* corresponds with the objective *facts* of the situation, systematically leaves out what is our main task to explain. I am far from denying that in our system equilibrium analysis has a useful function to perform. But when it comes to the point where it misleads some of our leading thinkers into believing that the situation which it describes has direct relevance to the solution of practical problems, it is high time that we remember that it does not deal with the social process at all and that is no more than a useful preliminary to the study of the main problem.

Notes

*Reprinted from the *American Economic Review*, XXXV, No. 4 (September, 1945), 519-30.

1. *Capitalism, Socialism, and Democracy* (New York: Harper & Bros., 1942), p. 175. Professor Schumpeter is, I believe, also the original author of the myth that Pareto and Barone have "solved" the problem of socialist calculation. What they, and many others, did was merely to state the conditions which a rational allocation of resources would have to satisfy and to point out that these were essentially the same as the conditions of equilibrium of a competitive market. This is something altogether different from showing how the allocation of resources satisfying these conditions can be found in practice. Pareto himself (from whom Barone has taken practically everything he has to say), far from claiming to have solved the practical problem, in fact explicitly denies that it can be solved without the help of the market. See his *Manuel d'economie pure* (2d ed., 1927), pp. 233-34. The relevant passage is quoted in an English translation at the beginning of my article on "Socialist Calculation: The Competitive 'Solution,'" in *Economica*, VIII, No. 26 (new ser., 1940), 125; reprinted below as chapter viii.

THE MEANING OF COMPETITION*

Friedrich A. Hayek

1

There are signs of increasing awareness among economists that what they have been discussing in recent years under the name of "competition" is not the same thing as what is thus called in ordinary language. But, although there have been some valiant attempts to bring discussion back to earth and to direct attention to the problems of real life, notably by J.M. Clark and F. Machlup,[1] the general view seems still to regard the conception of competition currently employed by economists as the significant one and to treat that of the businessman as an abuse. It appears to be generally held that the so-called theory of "perfect competition" provides the appropriate model for judging the effectiveness of competition in real life and that, to the extent that real competition differs from that model, it is undesirable and even harmful.

For this attitude there seems to me to exist very little justification. I shall attempt to show that what the theory of perfect competition discusses has little claim to be called "competition" at all and that its conclusions are of little use as guides to policy. The reason for this seems to me to be that this theory throughout assumes that state of affairs already to exist which, according to the truer view of the older theory, the process of competition tends to bring about (or to approximate) and that, if the state of affairs assumed by the theory of perfect competition ever existed, it would not only deprive of their scope all the activities which the verb "to compete" describes but would make them virtually impossible.

If all this affected only the use of the word "competition," it would not matter a great deal. But it seems almost as if economists by this peculiar use of language were deceiving themselves into the belief that, in discussing "competition," they are saying something about the nature and significance of the process by which the state of affairs is brought about which they merely assume to exist. In fact, this moving force of economic life is left almost altogether undiscussed.

I do not wish to discuss here at any length the reasons which have led the theory of competition into this curious state. As I have suggested elsewhere in this volume,[2] the tautological method which is appropriate and indispensable for the analysis of individual action seems in this instance to have been illegitimately extended to problems in which we have to deal with a social process in which the decisions of many individuals influence one another and necessarily succeed one another in time. The economic calculus (or the Pure Logic of Choice) which deals with the first kind of problem consists of an apparatus of classification of possible human attitudes and provides us with a technique for describing the interrelations of the different parts of a single plan. Its conclusions are implicit in its assumptions:the desires and the knowledge of the facts, which are assumed to be simultaneously present to a single mind, determine a unique solution. The relations discussed in this type of analysis are logical relations, concerned solely with the conclusions which follow for the mind of the planning individual from the given premises.

When we deal, however, with a situation in which a number of persons are attempting to work out their separate plans, we can no longer assume that the data are the same for all the planning minds. The problem becomes one of how the "data" of the different individuals on which they base their plans are adjusted to the objective facts of their environment (which includes the actions of the other people). Although in the solution of this type of problem we still must make use of our technique for rapidly working out the implications of a given set of data, we have now to deal not only with several separate sets of data of the different persons but also—and this is even more important—with a process which necessarily involves continuous changes in the data for the different individuals. As I have suggested before, the causal factor enters here in the form of the acquisition of new knowledge by the different individuals or of changes in their data brought about by the contacts between them.

The relevance of this for my present problem will appear when it is recalled that the modern theory of competition deals almost exclusively with a state of what is called "competitive equilibrium" in which it is assumed that the data for the different individuals are fully adjusted to each other, while the problem which requires explanation is the nature of the process by which the data are thus adjusted. In other words, the description of competitive equilibrium does not even attempt to say that, if we find such and such conditions, such and such consequences fill follow, but confines itself to defining conditions in which its conclusions are already implicitly contained and which may conceivably exist but of which it does not tell us how they can ever be brought about. Or, to anticipate our main conclusion in a brief statement, competition is by its nature a dynamic process whose essential characteristics are assumed away by the assumptions underlying static analysis.

2

That the modern theory of competitive equilibrium *assumes* the situation to exist which a true explanation ought to account for as the effect of the competitive process is best shown by examining the familiar list of conditions found in any modern textbook. Most of these conditions, incidentally, not only underlie the analysis of "perfect" competition but are equally assumed in the discussion of the various "imperfect" or "monopolistic" markets, which throughout assume certain unrealistic "perfections." For our immediate purpose, however, the theory of perfect competition will be the most instructive case to examine.

While different authors may state the list of essential conditions of perfect competition differently, the following is probably more than sufficiently comprehensive for our purpose, because, as we shall see, those conditions are not really independent of each other. According to the generally accepted view, perfect competition presupposes:

Perfect Competition generally accepted view

1. A homogeneous commodity offered and demanded by a large number of relatively small sellers or buyers, none of whom expects to exercise by his action a perceptible influence on price.

2. Free entry into the market and absence of other restraints on the movement of prices and resources.

3. Complete knowledge of the relevant factors on the part of all participants in the market.

We shall not ask at this stage precisely for what these conditions are required or what is implied if they are assumed to be given. But we must inquire a little further about their meaning, and in this respect it is the third condition which is the critical and obscure one. The standard can evidently not be perfect knowledge of everything affecting the market on the part of every person taking part in it. I shall here not go into the familiar paradox of the paralyzing effect really perfect knowledge and foresight would have on all action.[4] It will be obvious also that nothing is solved when we assume everybody to know everything and that the real problem is rather how it can be brought about that as much of the available knowledge as possible is used. This raises for a competitive society the question, not how we can "find" the people who know best, but rather what institutional arrangements are necessary in order that the unknown persons who have knowledge specially suited to a particular task are most likely to be attracted to that task. But we must inquire a little further what sort of knowledge it is that is supposed to be in possession of the parties of the market.

If we consider the market for some kind of finished consumption goods and start with the position of its producers or sellers, we shall find, first, that they are assumed to know the lowest cost at which the commodity can be produced. Yet this knowledge which is assumed to be given to begin with is one of the main points where it is only through the process of competition that the facts will be discovered. This appears to me one of the most important of the points where the starting-point of the theory of competitive equilibrium assumes away the main task which only the process of competition can solve. The position is somewhat similar with respect to the second point on which the producers are assumed to be fully informed:the wishes and desires of the consumers, including the kinds of goods and services which they demand and the prices they are willing to pay. These cannot properly be regarded as given facts but ought rather to be regarded as problems to be solved by the process of competition.

The same situation exists on the side of the consumers or buyers. Again the knowledge they are supposed to possess in a state of competitive equilibrium cannot be legitimately assumed to be at their command before the process of competition starts. Their knowledge of the alternatives before them is the result of what happens on the market, of such activities as advertising, etc.; and the whole organization of the market serves mainly the need of spreading the information on which the buyer is to act.

The peculiar nature of the assumptions from which the theory of competitive equilibrium starts stands out very clearly if we ask which of the activities that are commonly designated by the verb "to compete" would still be possible if those conditions were all satisfied. Perhaps it is worth recalling that, according to Dr. Johnson, competition is "the action of endeavoring to gain what another endeavors to gain at the same time." Now, how many of the devices adopted in ordinary life to that end would still be open to a seller in a market in which so-called "perfect competition" prevails?I believe that the answer is exactly none. Advertising, undercutting, and improving ("differentiating") the goods or services produced are all excluded by definition—"perfect" competition means indeed the absence of all competitive activities.

Especially remarkable in this connection is the explicit and complete exclusion from the theory of perfect competition of all personal relationships existing between the parties.[5] In actual life the fact that our inadequate knowledge of the available commodities or services is made up for by our experience with the persons or firms supplying them—that competition is in a large measure competition for reputation or good will—is one of the most important facts which enables us to solve our daily problems. The function of competition is here precisely to teach us *who* will serve us well:

which grocer or travel agency, which department store or hotel, which doctor or solicitor, we can expect to provide the most satisfactory solution for whatever particular personal problem we may have to face. Evidently in all these fields competition may be very intense, just because the services of the different persons or firms will never be exactly alike, and it will be owing to this competition that we are in a position to be served as well as we are. The reasons competition in this field is described as imperfect have indeed nothing to do with the competitive character of the activities of these people; it lies in the nature of the commodities or services themselves. If no two doctors are perfectly alike, this does not mean that the competition between them is less intense but merely that any degree of competition between them will not produce exactly those results which it would if their services were exactly alike. This is not a purely verbal point. The talk about the defects or competition when we are in fact talking about the necessary difference between commodities and services conceals a very real confusion and leads on occasion to absurd conclusions.

While on a first glance the assumption concerning the perfect knowledge possessed by the parties may seem the most startling and artificial of all those on which the theory of perfect competition is based, it may in fact be no more than a consequence of, and in part even justified by, another of the presuppositions on which it is founded. If, indeed, we start by assuming that a large number of people are producing the same commodity and command the same objective facilities and opportunities for doing so, then indeed it might be made plausible (although this has, to my knowledge, never been attempted) that they will in time all be led to know most of the facts relevant for judging the market of that commodity. Not only will each producer by his experience learn the same facts as every other but also he will thus come to know what his fellows know and in consequence the elasticity of the demand for his own product. The condition where different manufacturers produce the identical product under identical conditions is in fact the most favorable for producing that state of knowledge among them which perfect competition requires. Perhaps this means no more than that the commodities can be identical in the sense in which it is alone relevant for our understanding human action only if people hold the same views about them, although it should also be possible to state a set of physical conditions which is favorable to all those who are concerned with a set of closely interrelated activities learning the facts relevant for their decisions.

However that be, it will be clear that the facts will not always be as favorable to this result as they are when many people are at least in a position to produce the same article. The conception of the economic system as divisible into distinct markets for separate commodities is after all very largely the product of the imagination of the economist and certainly is not the rule in the field of manufacture and of personal services, to which the discussion about competition so largely refers. In fact, it need hardly be said, no products of two producers are ever exactly alike, even if it were only because, as they leave his plant, they must be at different places. These differences are part of the facts which create our economic problem, and it is little help to answer it on the assumption that they are absent.

The belief in the advantages of perfect competition frequently leads enthusiasts even to argue that a more advantageous use of resources would be achieved if the existing variety of products were reduced by *compulsory* standardization. Now, there is undoubtedly much to be said in many fields for assisting standardization by agreed recommendations or standards which are to apply unless different requirements are explicitly stipulated in contracts. But this is something very different from the demands of those who believe that the variety of people's tastes should be disregarded and the constant experimentation with improvements should be suppressed in order to obtain the advantages of perfect competition. It would clearly not be an improvement to build all houses exactly alike in order to create a perfect market for houses, and the same is true of most other fields where differences between the individual products prevent competition from ever being perfect.

3

We shall probably learn more about the nature and significance of the competitive process if for a while we forget about the artificial assumptions underlying the theory of perfect competition and ask whether competition would be any less important if, for example, no two commodities were ever exactly alike. If it were not for the difficulty of the analysis of such a situation, it would be well worth while to consider in some detail the case where the different commodities could not be readily classed into distinct groups, but where we had to deal with a continuous range of close substitutes, every unit somewhat different from the other but without any marked break in the continuous range. The result of the analysis of competition in such a situation might in many respects be more relevant to the conditions of real life than those of the analysis of competition in a single industry producing a homogeneous commodity sharply differentiated from all others. Or, if the case where no two commodities are exactly alike be thought to be too extreme, we might at least turn to the case where no two producers produce exactly the same commodity, as is the rule not only with all personal services but also in the markets of many manufactured commodities, such as the markets for books or musical instruments.

For our present purpose I need not attempt anything like a complete analysis of such kinds of markets but shall merely ask what would be the role of competition in them. Although the result would, of course, within fairly wide margins be indeterminate, the market would still bring about a set of prices at which each commodity sold just cheap enough to outbid its potential close substitutes—and this in itself is no small thing when we consider the unsurmountable difficulties of discovering even such a system of prices by any other method except that of trial and error in the market, with the individual participants gradually learning the relevant circumstances. It is true, of course, that in such a market correspondence between prices and marginal costs is to be expected only to the degree that elasticities of demand for the individual commodities approach the conditions assumed by the theory of perfect competition or that elasticities of substitution between the different commodities approach infinity. But the point is that in this case this standard of perfection as something desirable or to be aimed at is wholly irrelevant. The basis of comparison, on the grounds of which the achievement of competition ought to be judged, cannot be a situation which is different from the objective facts and which cannot be brought about by any known means. It ought to be the situation as it would exist if competition were prevented from operating. Not the approach to an unachievable and meaningless ideal but the improvement upon the conditions that would exist without competition should be the test.

In such a situation how would conditions differ, if competition were "free" in the traditional sense, from those which would exist if, for example, only people licensed by authority were allowed to produce particular things, or prices were fixed by authority, or both? Clearly there would be not only no likelihood that the different things would be produced by those who knew best how to do it and therefore could do it at lowest cost but also no likelihood that all those things would be produced at all which, if the consumers had the choice, they would like best. There would be little relationship between actual prices and the lowest cost at which somebody would be able to produce these commodities; indeed, the alternatives between which both producers and consumers would be in a position to choose, their data, would be altogether different from what they would be under competition.

The real problem in all this is not whether we will get *given* commodities or services at *given* marginal costs but mainly by what commodities and services the needs of the people can be most cheaply satisfied. The solution of the economic problem of society is in this respect always a voyage of exploration into the unknown, an attempt to discover new ways of doing things better than they have been done before. This must always remain so as long as there are any economic problems to be solved at all, because all economic problems are created by unforeseen changes which require adaptation. Only what we have not foreseen and provided for requires new decisions. If no such adaptations were required, if at any moment we knew that all change had stopped and things would forever go on exactly as they are now, there would be no more questions of the use of resources to be solved.

A person who possesses the exclusive knowledge or skill which enables him to reduce the cost of production of a commodity by 50 per cent still renders an enormous service to society if he enters its production and reduces its price by only 25 per cent—not only through that price reduction but also through his additional saving of cost. But it is only through competition that we can assume that these possible savings of cost will be achieved. Even if in each instance prices were only just low enough to keep out producers which do not enjoy these or other equivalent advantages, so that each commodity were produced as cheaply as possible, though many may be sold at prices considerably above costs, this would probably be a result which could not be achieved by any other method than that of letting competition operate.

4

That in conditions of real life the position even of any two producers is hardly ever the same is due to facts which the theory of perfect competition eliminates by its concentration on a long-term equilibrium which in an ever changing world can never be reached. At any given moment the equipment of a particular firm is always largely determined by historical accident, and the problem is that it should make the best use of the given equipment (including the acquired capacities of the members of its staff) and not what it should do if it were given unlimited time to adjust itself to constant conditions. For the problem of the best use of the given durable but exhaustible resources the long-term equilibrium price with which a theory discussing "perfect" competition must be concerned is not only not relevant; the conclusions concerning policy to which preoccupation with this model leads are highly misleading and even dangerous. The idea that under "perfect" competition prices should be equal to long-run costs often leads to the approval of such antisocial practices as the demand for an "orderly competition" which will secure a fair return on capital and for the destruction of excess capacity. Enthusiasm for perfect competition in theory and the support of monopoly in practice are indeed surprisingly often found to live together.

This is, however, only one of the many points on which the neglect of the time element makes the theoretical picture of perfect competition so entirely remote from all that is relevant to an understanding of the process of competition. If we think of it, as we ought to, as a succession of events, it becomes even more obvious that in real life there will at any moment be as a rule only one producer who can manufacture a given article at the lowest cost and who may in fact sell below the cost of his next successful competitor, but who, while still trying to extend his market, will often be overtaken by somebody else, who in turn will be prevented from capturing the whole market by yet another, and so on. Such a market would clearly never be in a state of perfect competition, yet competition in it might not only be as intense as possible but would also be the essential factor in bringing about the fact that the article in question is supplied at any moment to the consumer as cheaply as this can be done by any known method.

When we compare an "imperfect" market like this with a relatively "perfect" market as that of, say, grain, we shall now be in a better position to bring out the distinction which has been

---

underlying this whole discussion—the distinction between the underlying objective facts of a situation which cannot be altered by human activity and the nature of the competitive activities by which men adjust themselves to the situation. Where, as in the latter case, we have a highly organized market of a fully standardized commodity produced by many producers, there is little need or scope for competitive activities because the situation is such that the conditions which these activities might bring about are already satisfied to begin with. The best ways of producing the commodity, its character and uses, are most of the time known to nearly the same degree to all members of the market. The knowledge of any important change spreads so rapidly and the adaptation to it is so soon effected that we usually simply disregard what happens during these short transition periods and confine ourselves to comparing the two states of near equilibrium which exist before and after them. But it is during this short and neglected interval that the forces of competition operate and become visible, and it is the events during this interval which we must study if we are to "explain" the equilibrium which follows it.

It is only in a market where adaptation is slow compared with the rate of change that the process of competition is in continuous operation. And though the reason why adaptation is slow *may* be that competition is weak, e.g., because there are special obstacles to entry into the trade, or because of some other factors of the character of natural monopolies, slow adaptation does by no means necessarily mean weak; competition. When the variety of near-substitutes is great and rapidly changing, where it takes a long time to find out about the relative merits of the available alternatives, or where the need for a whole class of goods or services occurs only discontinuously at irregular intervals, the adjustment must be slow even if competition is strong and active.

The confusion between the objective facts of the situation and the character of the human responses to it tends to conceal from us the important fact that competition is the more important the more complex or "imperfect" are the objective conditions in which it has to operate. Indeed, far from competition being beneficial only when it is "perfect," I am inclined to argue that the need for competition is nowhere greater than in fields in which the nature of the commodities or services makes it impossible that it ever should create a perfect market in the theoretical sense. The inevitable actual imperfections of competition are as little an argument against competition as the difficulties of achieving a perfect solution of any other task are an argument against attempting to solve it at all, or as little as imperfect health is an argument against health.

In conditions where we can never have many people offering the same homogeneous product or service, because of the ever changing character of our needs and our knowledge, or of the infinite variety of human skills and capacities, the ideal state cannot be one requiring an identical character of large numbers of such products and services. The economic problem is a problem of making the best use of what resources we have, and not one of what we should do if the situation were different from what it actually is. There is no sense in talking of a use of resources "as if" a perfect market existed, if this means that the resources would have to be different from what they are, or in discussing what somebody with perfect knowledge would do if our task must be to make the best use of the knowledge the existing people have.

5

The argument in favor of competition does not rest on the conditions that would exist if it were perfect. Although, where the objective facts would make it possible for competition to approach perfection, this would also secure the most effective use of resources, and, although there is therefore every case for removing human obstacles to competition, this does not mean that competition does not also bring about as effective a use of resources as can be brought about by any known means where in the nature of the case it must be imperfect. Even where free entry will secure no more than that at any one moment all the goods and services for which there would be an effective demand if they were available are in fact produced at the least current[6] expenditure of resources at which, in the given historical situation, they can be produced, even though the price the consumer is made to pay for them is considerably higher and only just below the cost of the next best way in which his need could be satisfied, this, I submit, is more than we can expect from any other known system. The decisive point is still the elementary one that it is most unlikely that, without artificial obstacles which government activity either creates or can remove, any commodity or service will for any length of time be available only at a price at which outsiders could expect a more than normal profit if they entered the field.

The practical lesson of all this, I think, is that we should worry much less about whether competition in a given case is perfect and worry much more whether there is competition at all. What our theoretical models of separate industries conceal is that in practice a much bigger gulf divides competition from no competition than perfect from imperfect competition. Yet the current tendency in discussion is to be intolerant about the imperfections and to be silent about the prevention of competition. We can probably still learn more about the real significance of competition by studying the results which regularly occur where competition is deliberately suppressed than by concentrating on the shortcomings of actual competition compared with an ideal which is irrelevant for the given facts. I say advisedly "where competition is deliberately suppressed" and not merely "where it is absent," because its main effects are usually operating, even if more slowly, so long as it is not outright suppressed with the assistance or the tolerance of the state. The evils which experience has shown to be the regular consequence of a suppression of competition are on a different plane from those which the imperfections of competition may cause. Much more serious than the fact that prices may not correspond to marginal cost is the fact that, with an intrenched monopoly, costs are likely to be much higher than is necessary. A monopoly based on superior efficiency, on the other hand, does comparatively little harm so long as it is assured that it will disappear as soon as anyone else becomes more efficient in providing satisfaction to the consumers.

In conclusion I want for a moment to go back to the point from which I started and restate the most important conclusion in a more general form. Competition is essentially a process of the formation of opinion: by spreading information, it creates that unity and coherence of the economic system which we presuppose when we think of it as one market. It creates the views people have about what is best and cheapest, and it is because of it that people know at least as much about possibilities and opportunities as they in fact do. It is thus a process which involves a continuous change in the data and whose significance must therefore be completely missed by any theory which treats these data as constant.

Notes

*This essay reproduces the substance of the Stafford Little Lecture delivered at Princeton University on May 20, 1946.

1. J.M. Clark, "Toward a Concept of Workable Competition," *American Economic Review,* Vol. XXX (June, 1940); F. Machlup, "Competition, Pliopoly, and Profit," *Economica,* Vol. IX (new ser.; February and May, 1942).

2. See the second and fourth chapters.

3. Particularly the assumptions that *at all times* a uniform price must rule for a given commodity throughout the market and that sellers know the shape of the demand curve.

4. See O. Morgenstern, "Vollkommene Voraussicht und wirtschaftliches Gleichgewicht," *Zeitschrift für Nationalokonomic,* Vol. VI (1935).

5. Cf. G.J. Stigler, *The Theory of Price* (1946), p. 24: "Economic relationships are never perfectly competitive if they involve any personal relationships between economic units" (see also *ibid.,* p. 226).

6. "Current" cost in this connection excludes all true bygones but includes, of course, "user cost."

THE BUTTERFLY EFFECT

James Gleick

> Physicists like to think that all you have to do is say,
> these are the conditions, now what happens next?
>
> —*Richard P. Feynman*

The sun beat down through a sky that had never seen clouds. The winds swept across an earth as smooth as glass. Night never came, and autumn never gave way to winter. It never rained. The simulated weather in Edward Lorenz's new electronic computer changed slowly but certainly, drifting through a permanent midday midseason, as if the world had turned into Camelot, or some particularly bland version of southern California.

Outside his window Lorenz could watch real weather, the early-morning fog creeping along the Massachusetts Institute Technology campus or the low clouds slipping over the rooftops from the Atlantic. Fog and clouds never arose in the model running on his computer. The machine, a Royal McBee, was a thicket of wiring and vacuum tubes that occupied an ungainly portion of Lorenz's office, made a surprising and irritating noise, and broke down every week or so. It had neither the speed nor the memory to manage a realistic simulation of the earth's atmosphere and oceans. Yet Lorenz created a toy weather in 1960 that succeeded in mesmerizing his colleagues. Every minute the machine marked the passing of a day by printing a row of numbers across a page. If you knew how to read the printouts, you would see a prevailing westerly wind swing now to the north, now to the south, now back to the north. Digitized cyclones spun slowly around an idealized globe. As word spread through the department, the other meteorologists would gather around with the graduate students making bets on what Lorenz's weather would do next. Somehow, nothing ever happened the same way twice.

Lorenz enjoyed weather—by no means a prerequisite for a research meteorologist. He savored its changeability. He appreciated the patterns that come and go in the atmosphere, families of eddies and cyclones, always obeying mathematical rules, yet never repeating themselves. When he looked at clouds, he thought he saw a kind of structure in them. Once he had feared that studying the science of weather would be like prying a jack-in-the-box apart with a screwdriver. Now he wondered whether science would be able to penetrate the magic at all. Weather had a flavor that could not be expressed by talking about averages. *The daily high temperature in Cambridge, Massachusetts, averages 75 degrees in June. The number of rainy days in Riyadh, Saudi Arabia, averages ten a year.* Those were statistics. The essence was the way patterns in the atmosphere changed over time, and that was what Lorenz captured on the Royal McBee.

He was the god of this machine universe, free to choose the laws of nature as he pleased. After a certain amount of undivine trial and error, he chose twelve. They were numerical rules—equations that expressed the relationships between temperature and pressure, between pressure and wind speed. Lorenz understood that he was putting into practice the laws of Newton, appropriate tools for a clockmaker deity who could create a world and set it running for eternity. Thanks to the determinism of physical law, further intervention would then be unnecessary. Those who made such models took for granted that, from present to future, the laws of motion provide a bridge of mathematical certainty. Understand the laws and you understand the universe. That was the philosophy behind modeling weather on a computer.

Indeed, if the eighteenth century philosophers imagined their creator as a benevolent noninterventionist, content to remain behind the scenes, they might have imagined someone like Lorenz. He was an odd sort of meteorologist. He had the worn face of a Yankee farmer, with surprising bright eyes that made him seem to be laughing whether he was or not. He seldom spoke about himself or his work, but he listened. He often lost himself in a realm of calculation or dreaming that his colleagues found inaccessible. His closest friends felt that Lorenz spent a good deal of his time off in a remote outer space.

As a boy he had been a weather bug, at least to the extent of keeping close tabs on the maxmin thermometer recording the day's highs and lows outside his parents' house in West Hartford Connecticut. But he spent more time inside playing with mathematical puzzle books than watching the thermometer. Sometimes he and his father would work out puzzles together. Once they came upon a particularly difficult problem that turned out to be insoluble. That was acceptable, his father told him: you can always try to solve a problem by proving that no solution exists. Lorenz liked that, as he always liked the purity of mathematics, and when he graduated from Dartmouth College, in 1938, he thought that mathematics was his calling. Circumstance interfered, however, in the form of World War II, which put him to work as a weather forecaster for the Army Air Corps. After the war Lorenz decided to stay with meteorology, investigating the theory of it, pushing the mathematics a little further forward. He made a name for himself by publishing work on orthodox problems, such as the general circulation of the atmosphere. And in the meantime he continued to think about forecasting.

To most serious meteorologists, forecasting was less than science. It was a seat-of-the-pants business performed by technicians who needed some intuitive ability to read the next day's weather in the instruments and the clouds. It was guesswork. At centers like M.I.T., meteorology favored problems that had solutions. Lorenz understood the messiness of weather prediction as well as anyone, having tried it firsthand for the benefit of military pilots, but he harbored an interest in the problem—a mathematical interest.

Not only did meteorologists scorn forecasting, but in the 1960s virtually all serious scientists mistrusted computers. These souped-up calculators hardly seemed like tools for theoretical science. So numerical weather modeling was something of a bastard problem Yet the time was right for it. Weather forecasting had been waiting two centuries for a machine that could repeat thousands of calculations over and over again by brute force. Only a computer could cash in the Newtonian promise that the world unfolded along a deterministic path, rule-bound like the planets, predictable like eclipses and tides. In theory a computer could let meteorologists do what astronomers had been able to do with pencil and slide rule: reckon the future of their universe from its initial conditions and the physical laws that guide its evolution. The equations describing the motion of air and water were as well known as those describing the motion of planets. Astronomers did not achieve perfection and never would, not in a solar system tugged by the gravities of nine planets, scores of moons and thousands of asteroids, but calculations of planetary motion were so accurate that people forgot they were forecasts. When an astronomer said, "Comet Halley will be back this way in seventy six years," it seemed like fact, not prophecy. Deterministic numerical forecasting figured accurate courses for spacecraft and missiles. Why not winds and clouds?

Weather was vastly more complicated, but it was governed by the same laws. Perhaps a powerful enough computer could be the supreme intelligence imagined by Laplace, the eighteenth century philosopher-mathematician who caught the Newtonian fever like no one else: "Such an intelligence," Laplace wrote, "would embrace in the same formula the movements of the greatest bodies of the universe and those of the lightest atom; for it, nothing would be uncertain and the future, as the past, would be present to its eyes." In these days of Einstein's relativity and Heisenberg's uncertainty, Laplace seems almost buffoon-like in his optimism, but much of modern science has pursued his dream. Implicitly, the mission of many twentieth century scientists—biologists, neurologists, economists—has been to break their universes down into the simplest atoms that will obey scientific rules. In all these sciences, a kind of Newtonian determinism has been brought to bear. The fathers of modern computing always had Laplace in mind, and the history of computing and the history of forecasting were intermingled ever since John von Neumann designed his first machines at the Institute for Advanced Study in Princeton, New Jersey, in the 1950s. Von Neumann recognized that weather modeling could be an ideal task for a computer.

There was always one small compromise, so small that working scientists usually forgot it was there, lurking in a corner of their philosophies like an unpaid bill. Measurements could never be perfect. Scientists marching under Newton's banner actually waved another flag that said something like this: Given an *approximate* knowledge of a system's initial conditions and an understanding of natural law, one can calculate the *approximate* behavior of the system. This assumption lay at the philosophical heart of science. As one theoretician liked to tell his students: "The basic idea of Western science is that you don't have to take into account the falling of a leaf on some planet in another galaxy when you're trying to account for the motion of a billiard ball on a pool table on earth. Very small influences can be neglected. There's a convergence in the way things work, and arbitrarily small influences don't blow up to have arbitrarily large effects." Classically, the belief in approximation and convergence was well justified. It worked. A tiny error in fixing the position of Comet Halley in 1910 would only cause a tiny error in predicting its arrival in 1986, and the error would stay small for millions of years to come. Computers rely on the same assumption in guiding spacecraft: approximately accurate input gives approximately accurate output. Economic forecasters rely on this assumption, though their success is less apparent. So did the pioneers in global weather forecasting.

With his primitive computer, Lorenz had boiled weather down to the barest skeleton. Yet, line by line, the winds and temperatures in Lorenz's printouts seemed to behave in a recognizable earthly way. They matched his cherished intuition about the weather, his sense that it repeated itself, displaying familiar patterns over time, pressure rising and falling, the airstream swinging north and south He discovered that when a line went from high to low without a bump, a double bump would come next, and he said, "That's the kind of rule a forecaster could use." But the repetitions were never quite exact. There was pattern, with disturbances. An orderly disorder.

To make the patterns plain to see, Lorenz created a primitive kind of graphics. Instead of just printing out the usual lines of digits, he would have the machine print a certain number of blank spaces followed by the letter a. He would pick one variable— perhaps the direction of the airstream. Gradually the a's marched down the roll of paper, swinging back and forth in a wavy line, making a long series of hills and valleys that represented the way the west wind would swing north and south across the continent. The orderliness of it, the recognizable cycles coming around again and again but never twice the same way, had a hypnotic fascination. The system seemed slowly to be revealing its secrets to the forecaster's eye.

One day in the winter of 1961, wanting to examine one sequence at greater length, Lorenz took a shortcut. Instead of starting the whole run over, he started midway through. To give the machine its initial conditions, he typed the numbers straight from the earlier printout. Then he walked down the hall to get away from the noise and drink a cup of coffee. When he returned an hour later, he saw something unexpected, something that planted a seed for a new science.

This new run should have exactly duplicated the old. Lorenz had copied the numbers into the machine himself. The program had not changed. Yet as he stared at the new printout, Lorenz saw his weather diverging so rapidly from the pattern of the last run that, within just a few months, all resemblance had disappeared. He looked at one set of numbers, then back at the other. He might as well have chosen two random weathers out of a hat. His first thought was that another vacuum tube had gone bad.

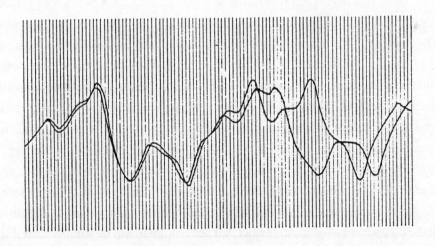

How Two Weather Patterns Diverge. From nearly the same starting point, Edward Lorenz saw his computer weather produce patterns that grew farther and farther apart until all resemblance disappeared. (From Lorenz's 1961 printouts.)

Suddenly he realized the truth. There had been no malfunction. The problem lay in the numbers he had typed. In the computer's memory, six decimal places were stored: .506127. On the printout, to save space, just three appeared: .506. Lorenz had entered the shorter, rounded-off numbers, assuming that the difference—one part in a thousand—was inconsequential.

It was a reasonable assumption. If a weather satellite can read ocean-surface temperature to within one part in a thousand, its operators consider themselves lucky. Lorenz's Royal McBee was implementing the classical program. It used a purely deterministic system of equations. Given a particular starting point, the weather would unfold exactly the same way each time. Given a slightly different starting point, the weather should unfold in a slightly different way. A small numerical error was like a small puff of wind—surely the small puffs faded or canceled each other out before they could change important, large-scale features of the weather. Yet in Lorenz's particular system of equations, small errors proved catastrophic.

He decided to look more closely at the way two nearly identical runs of weather flowed apart. He copied one of the wavy lines of output onto a transparency and laid it over the other, to inspect the way it diverged. First, two humps matched detail for detail. Then one line began to lag a hairsbreadth behind. By the time the two runs reached the next hump, they were distinctly out of phase. By the third or fourth hump, all similarity had vanished.

It was only a wobble from a clumsy computer. Lorenz could have assumed something was wrong with his particular machine or his particular model—probably *should* have assumed. It was not as though he had mixed sodium and chlorine and got gold. But for reasons of mathematical intuition that his colleagues would begin to understand only later, Lorenz felt a jolt: something was philosophically out of joint. The practical import could be staggering. Although his equations were gross parodies of the earth's weather, he had a faith that they captured the essence of the real atmosphere. That first day, he decided that long-range weather forecasting must be doomed.

"We certainly hadn't been successful in doing that anyway and now we had an excuse," he said. "I think one of the reasons people thought it would be possible to forecast so far ahead is that there are real physical phenomena for which one can do an excellent job of forecasting, such as eclipses, where the dynamics of the sun, moon, and earth are fairly complicated, and such as oceanic tides. I never used to think of tide forecasts as prediction at all—I used to think of them as statements of fact—but of course, you are predicting. Tides are actually just as complicated as the atmosphere. Both have periodic components—you can predict that next summer will be warmer than this winter. But with weather we take the attitude that we knew that already. With tides, it's the predictable part that we're interested in, and the unpredictable part is small, unless there's a storm.

"The average person, seeing that we can predict tides pretty well a few months ahead would say, why can't we do the same thing with the atmosphere, it's just a different fluid system, the laws are about as complicated. But I realized that *any* physical system that behaved nonperiodically would be unpredictable."

The fifties and sixties were years of unreal optimism about weather forecasting. Newspapers and magazines were filled with hope for weather science, not just for prediction but for modification and control. Two technologies were maturing together, the digital computer and the space satellite. An international program was being prepared to take advantage of them, the Global Atmosphere Research Program. There was an idea that human society would free itself from weather's turmoil and become its master instead of its victim. Geodesic domes would cover cornfields. Airplanes would seed the clouds. Scientists would learn how to make rain and how to stop it.

The intellectual father of this popular notion was Von Neumann, who built his first computer with the precise intention, among other things, of controlling the weather. He surrounded himself with meteorologists and gave breathtaking talks about his plans to the general physics community. He had a specific mathematical reason for his optimism. He recognized that a complicated dynamical system could have points of instability—critical points where a small push can have large consequences, as with a ball balanced at the top of a hill. With the computer up and running, Von Neumann imagined that scientists would calculate the equations of fluid motion for the next few days. Then a central committee of meteorologists would send up airplanes to lay down smoke screens or seed clouds to push the weather into the desired mode. But Von Neumann had overlooked the possibility of chaos, with instability at every point.

By the 1980s a vast and expensive bureaucracy devoted itself to carrying out Von Neumann's mission, or at least the prediction part of it. America's premier forecasters operated out of an unadorned cube of a building in suburban Maryland, near the Washington beltway, with a spy's nest of radar and radio antennas on the roof. Their supercomputer ran a model that resembled Lorenz's only in its fundamental spirit. Where the Royal McBee could carry out sixty multiplications each second, the speed of a Control Data Cyber 205 was measured in megaflops, millions of floating point operations per second. Where Lorenz had been happy with twelve equations, the modern global model calculated systems of 500,000 equations. The model understood the way moisture moved heat in and out of the air when it condensed and evaporated. The digital winds were shaped by digital mountain ranges. Data poured in hourly from every nation on the globe, from airplanes, satellites, and ships. The National Meteorological Center produced the world's second best forecasts.

The best came out of Reading, England, a small college town an hour's drive from London. The European Centre for Medium Range Weather Forecasts occupied a modest tree-shaded building in a generic United Nations style, modern brick-and-glass architecture, decorated with gifts from many lands. It was built in the heyday of the all-European Common Market spirit, when most of the nations of western Europe decided to pool their talent and resources in the cause of weather prediction. The Europeans attributed their success to their young, rotating staff—no civil service— and their Cray supercomputer, which always seemed to be one model ahead of the American counterpart.

Weather forecasting was the beginning but hardly the end of the business of using computers to model complex systems. The same techniques served many kinds of physical scientists and social scientists hoping to make predictions about everything from the small-scale fluid flows that concerned propeller designers to the vast financial flows that concerned economists. Indeed, by the seventies and eighties, economic forecasting by computer bore a real resemblance to global weather forecasting. The models would churn through complicated, somewhat arbitrary webs of equations, meant to turn measurements of initial conditions—atmospheric pressure or money supply—into a simulation of future trends The programmers hoped the results were not too grossly distorted by the many unavoidable simplifying assumptions. If a model did anything too obviously bizarre—flooded the Sahara or tripled interest rates—the programmers would revise the equations to bring the output back in line with expectation. In practice, econometric models proved dismally blind to what the future would bring, but many people who should have known better acted as though they believed in the results. Forecasts of economic growth or unemployment were put forward with an implied precision of two or three decimal places. Governments and financial institutions paid for such predictions and acted on them, perhaps out of necessity or for want of anything better. Presumably they knew that such variables as "consumer optimism" were not as nicely measurable as "humidity" and that the perfect differential equations had not yet been written for the movement of politics and fashion. But few realized how fragile was the very process of modeling flows on computers, even when the data was reasonably trustworthy and the laws were purely physical, as in weather forecasting.

Computer modeling had indeed succeeded in changing the weather business from an art to a science. The European Centre's assessments suggested that the world saved billions of dollars each year from predictions that were statistically better than nothing. But beyond two or three days the world's best forecasts were speculative, and beyond six or seven they were worthless.

The Butterfly Effect was the reason. For small pieces of weather—and to a global forecaster, small can mean thunderstorms and blizzards—any prediction deteriorates rapidly. Errors and uncertainties multiply, cascading upward through a chain of turbulent features, from dust devils and squalls up to continent size eddies that only satellites can see.

The modern weather models work with a grid of points on the order of sixty miles apart, and even so, some starting data has to be guessed, since ground stations and satellites cannot see everywhere. But suppose the earth could be covered with sensors spaced one foot apart, rising at-one-foot intervals all the way the top of the atmosphere. Suppose every sensor gives perfectly accurate readings of temperature, pressure, humidity, and a other quantity a meteorologist would want. Precisely at noon an infinitely powerful computer takes all the data and calculates what will happen at each point at 12:01, then 12:02, then 12:03 . . .

The computer will still be unable to predict whether Princeton, New Jersey, will have sun or rain on a day one month away. At noon the spaces between the sensors will hide fluctuations that the computer will not know about, tiny deviations from the average. By 12:01, those fluctuations will already have created small errors one foot away. Soon the errors will have multiplied to the ten-foot-scale, and so on up to the size of the globe.

Even for experienced meteorologists, all this runs against intuition. One of Lorenz's oldest friends was Robert White, a fellow meteorologist at M.I.T. who later became head of the National Oceanic and Atmospheric Administration. Lorenz told him about the Butterfly Effect and what he felt it meant for long-rangeprediction. White gave Von Neumann's answer. "Prediction, nothing," he said. "This is weather control." His thought was that small modifications, well within human capability, could cause desired large-scale changes.

Lorenz saw it differently. Yes, you could change the weather. You could make it do something different from what it would otherwise have done. But if you did, then you would never *know* what it would otherwise have done. It would be like giving an extra shuffle to an already well-shuffled pack of cards. You know it will change your luck, but you don't know whether for better or worse.

PROFIT AND LOSS*

Ludwig Von Mises

A. The Economic Nature of Profit and Loss

1. The Emergence of Profit and Loss

In the capitalist system of society's economic organization the entrepreneurs determine the course of production. In the performance of this function they are unconditionally and totally subject to the sovereignty of the buying public, the consumers. If they fail to produce in the cheapest and best possible way those commodities which the consumers are asking for most urgently, they suffer losses and are finally eliminated from their entrepreneurial position. Other men who know better how to serve the consumers replace them.

If all people were to anticipate correctly the future state of the market, the entrepreneurs would neither earn any profits nor suffer any losses. They would have to buy the complementary factors of production at prices which would, already at the instant of the purchase, fully reflect the future prices of the products. No room would be left either for profit or for loss. What makes profit emerge is the fact that the entrepreneur who judges the future prices of the products more correctly than other people do buys some or all of the factors of production at prices which, seen from the point of view of the future state of the market, are too low. Thus the total costs of production—including interest on the capital invested—lag behind the prices which the entrepreneur receives for the product. This difference s entrepreneurial profit.

On the other hand, the entrepreneur who misjudges the future prices of the products allows for the factors of production prices which, seen from the point of view of the future state of the market, are too high. His total costs of production exceed the prices at which he can sell the product. This difference is entrepreneurial loss.

Thus profit and loss are generated by success or failure in adjusting the course of production activities to the most urgent demand of the consumers. Once this adjustment is achieved, they disappear. The prices of the complementary factors of production reach a height at which total costs of production coincide with the price of the product. Profit and loss are ever present features only on account of the fact that ceaseless change in the economic data makes again and again new discrepancies, and consequently the need for new adjustments originate.

2. The Distinction Between Profits and Other Proceeds

Many errors concerning the nature of profit and loss were caused by the practice of applying the term profit to the totality of the residual proceeds of an entrepreneur.

Interest on the capital employed is not a component part of profit. The dividends of a corporation are not profit. They are interest on the capital invested plus profit or minus loss.

The market equivalent of work performed by the entrepreneur in the conduct of the enterprise's affairs is entrepreneurial quasi-wages but not profit.

If the enterprise owns a factor on which it can earn monopoly prices, it makes a monopoly gain. If this enterprise is a corporation, such gains increase the dividend. Yet they are not profit proper.

Still more serious are the errors due to the confusion of entrepreneurial activity and technological innovation and improvement.

The maladjustment the removal of which is the essential function of entrepreneurship may often consist in the fact that new technological methods have not yet been utilized to the full extent to which they should be in order to bring about the best possible satisfaction of consumers' demand. But this is not necessarily always the case. Changes in the data, especially in consumers' demand, may require adjustments which have no reference at all to technological innovations and improvements. The entrepreneur who simply increases the production of an article by adding to the existing production facilities a new outfit without any change in the technological method of production is no less an entrepreneur than the man who inaugurates a new way of producing. The business of the entrepreneur is not merely to experiment with new technological methods, but to select from the multitude of technologically feasible methods those which are best fit to supply the public in the cheapest way with the things they are asking for most urgently. Whether a new technological procedure is or is not fit for this purpose is to be provisionally decided by the entrepreneur and will be finally decided by the conduct of the buying public. The question is not whether a new method is to be considered as a more "elegant" solution of a technological problem. It is whether, under the given state of economic data, it is the best possible method of supplying the consumers in the cheapest way.

The activities of the entrepreneur consist in making decisions. He determines for what purpose the factors of production should be employed. Any other acts which an entrepreneur may perform are merely accidental to his entrepreneurial function. It is this that laymen often fail to realize. They confuse the entrepreneurial activities with the conduct of the technological and administrative affairs of a plant. In their eyes not the stockholders, the promotors and speculators, but hired employees are the real entrepreneurs. The former are merely idle parasites who pocket the dividends.

Now nobody ever contended that one could produce without working. But neither is it possible to produce without capital goods, the previously produced factors of further production. These capital goods are scarce, i.e., they do not suffice for the production of all things which one would like to have produced. Hence the economic problem arises: to employ them in such a way that only those goods should be produced which are fit to satisfy the most urgent demands of the consumers. No good should remain unproduced on account of the fact that the factors required for its production were used—wasted—for the production of another good for which the demand of the public is less intense. To achieve this is under capitalism the function of entrepreneurship that determines the allocation of capital to the various branches of production. Under socialism it would be a function of the state, the social apparatus of coercion and oppression. The problem whether a socialist directorate, lacking any method of economic calculation, could fulfill this function is not to be dealt with in this essay.

There is a simple rule of thumb to tell entrepreneurs from non-entrepreneurs. The entrepreneurs are those on whom the incidence of losses on the capital employed falls. Amateur-economists may confuse profits with other kinds of intakes. But it is impossible to fail to recognize losses on the capital employed.

3. Non-Profit Conduct of Affairs

What has been called the democracy of the market manifests itself in the fact that profit-seeking business is unconditionally subject to the supremacy of the buying public.

Non-profit organizations are sovereign unto themselves. They are, within the limits drawn by the amount of capital at their disposal, in a position to defy the wishes of the public.

A special case is that of the conduct of government affairs, the administration of the social apparatus of coercion and oppression, viz. the police power. The objectives of government, the protection of the inviolability of the individuals' lives and health and of their efforts to improve the material conditions of their existence, are indispensable. They benefit all and are the necessary prerequisite of social cooperation and civilization. But they cannot be sold and bought in the way merchandise is sold and bought; they have therefore no price on the market. With regard to them there cannot be any economic calculation. The costs expended for their conduct cannot be confronted with a price received for the product. This state of affairs would make the officers entrusted with the administration of governmental activities irresponsible despots if they were not curbed by the budget system. Under this system the administrators are forced to comply with detailed instructions enjoined upon them by the sovereign, be it a self-appointed autocrat or the whole people acting through elected representatives. To the officers limited funds are assigned which they are bound to spend only for those purposes which the sovereign has ordered. Thus the management of public administration becomes bureaucratic, i. e., dependent on definite detailed rules and regulations.

Bureaucratic management is the only alternative available where there is no profit and loss management.[1]

4. The Ballot of the Market

The consumers by their buying and abstention from buying elect the entrepreneurs in a daily repeated plebiscite as it were. They determine who should own and who not, and how much each owner should own.

As is the case with all acts of choosing a person—choosing holders of public office, employees, friends or a consort—the decision of the consumers is made on the ground of experience and thus necessarily always refers to the past. There is no experience of the future. The ballot of the market elevates those who in the immediate past have best served the consumers. However, the choice is not unalterable and can daily be corrected. The elected who disappoints the electorate is speedily reduced to the ranks.

Each ballot of the consumers adds only a little to the elected man's sphere of action. To reach the upper levels of entrepreneurship he needs a great number of votes, repeated again and again over a long period of time, a protracted series of successful strokes. He must stand every day a new trial, must submit anew to reelection as it were.

It is the same with his heirs. They can retain their eminent position only by receiving again and again confirmation on the part of the public. Their office is revocable. If they retain it, it is not on account of the deserts of their predecessor, but on account of their own ability to employ the capital for the best possible satisfaction of the consumers.

The entrepreneurs are neither perfect nor good in any metaphysical sense. They owe their position exclusively to the fact that they are better fit for the performance of the functions incumbent upon them than other people are. They earn profit not because they are clever in performing their tasks, but because they are more clever or less clumsy than other people are. They are not infallible and often blunder. But they are less liable to error and blunder less than other people do. Nobody has the right to take offense at the errors made by the entrepreneurs in the conduct of affairs and to stress the point that people would have been better supplied if the entrepreneurs had been more skillful and prescient. If the grumbler knew better, why did he not himself fill the gap and seize the opportunity to earn profits? It is easy indeed to display foresight after the event. In retrospect all fools become wise.

A popular chain of reasoning runs this way: The entrepreneur earns profit not only on account of the fact that other people were less successful than he in anticipating correctly the future state of the market. He himself contributed to the emergence of profit by not producing more of the article concerned; but for intentional restriction of output on his part, the supply of this article would have been so ample that the price would have dropped to a point at which no surplus of proceeds over costs of production expended would have emerged. This reasoning is at the bottom of the spurious doctrines of imperfect and monopolistic competition. It was resorted to a short time ago by the American Administration when it blamed the enterprises of the steel industry for the fact that the steel production capacity of the United States was not greater than it really was.

Certainly those engaged in the production of steel are not responsible for the fact that other people did not likewise enter this field of production. The reproach on the part of the authorities would have been sensible if they had conferred on the existing steel corporations the monopoly of steel production. But in the absence of such a privilege, the reprimand given to the operating mills is not more justified than it would be to censure the nation's poets and musicians for the fact that there are not more and better poets and musicians. If somebody is to blame for the fact that the number of people who joined the voluntary civilian defense organization is not larger, then it is not those who have already joined but only those who have not.

That the production of a commodity p is not larger than it really is, is due to the fact that the complementary factors of production required for an expansion were employed for the production of other commodities. To speak of an insufficiency of the supply of p is empty rhetoric if it does not indicate the various products m which were produced in too large quantities with the effect that their production appears now, i.e., after the event, as a waste of scarce factors of production. We may assume that the entrepreneurs who instead of producing additional quantities of p turned to the production of excessive amounts of m and consequently suffered losses, did not intentionally make their mistake.

Neither did the producers of p intentionally restrict the production of p. Every entrepreneur's capital is limited; he employs it for those projects which, he expects, will, by filling the most urgent demand of the public, yield the highest profit.

An entrepreneur at whose disposal are 100 units of capital employs, for instance, 50 units for the production of p and 50 units for the production of q. If both lines are profitable, it is odd to blame him for not having employed more, e. g., 75 units, for the production of p. He could increase the production of p only by curtailing correspondingly the production of q. But with regard to q the same fault could be found by the grumblers. If one blames the entrepreneur for not having produced more p, one must blame him also for not having produced more q. This means: one blames the entrepreneur for the facts that there is a scarcity of the factors of production and that the earth is not a land of Cockaigne.

Perhaps the grumbler will object on the ground that he considers p a vital commodity, much more important than q, and that therefore the production of p should be expanded and that of q restricted. If this is really the meaning of his criticism, he is at variance with the valuations of the consumers. He throws off his mask and shows his dictatorial aspirations. Production should not be directed by the wishes of the public but by his own despotic discretion.

But if our entrepreneur's production of q involves a loss, it is obvious that his fault was poor foresight and not intentional.

Entrance into the ranks of the entrepreneurs in a market society, not sabotaged by the interference of government or other agencies resorting to violence, is open to everybody. Those who know how to take advantage of any business opportunity cropping up will always find the capital required. For the market is always full of capitalists anxious to find the most promising employment for their funds and in search of the ingenious newcomers, in partnership with whom they could execute the most remunerative projects.

People often failed to realize this inherent feature of capitalism because they did not grasp the meaning and the effects of capital scarcity. The task of the entrepreneur is to select from the multitude of technologically feasible projects those which will satisfy the most urgent of the not yet satisfied needs of the public. Those projects for the execution of which the capital supply does not suffice must not be carried out. The market is always crammed with visionaries who want to float such impracticable and unworkable schemes. It is these dreamers who always complain about the blindness of the capitalists who are too stupid to look after their own interests. Of course, the investors often err in the choice of their investments. But these faults consist precisely in the fact that they preferred an unsuitable project to another that would have satisfied more urgent needs of the buying public.

People often err very lamentably in estimating the work of the creative genius. Only a minority of men are appreciative enough to attach the right value to the achievement of poets, artists and thinkers. It may happen that the indifference of his contemporaries makes it impossible for a genius to accomplish what he would have accomplished if his fellow-men had displayed better judgment. The way in which the poet laureate and the philosopher *á la mode* are selected is certainly questionable.

But it is impermissible to question the free market's choice of the entrepreneurs. The consumers' preference for definite articles may be open to condemnation from the point of view of a philosopher's judgment. But judgments of value are necessarily always personal and subjective. The consumer chooses what, as he thinks, satisfies him best. Nobody is called upon to determine what could make another man happier or less unhappy. The popularity of motor cars, television sets and nylon stockings may be criticized from a "higher" point of view. But these are the things that people are asking for. They cast their ballots for those entrepreneurs who offer them this merchandise of the best quality at the cheapest price.

In choosing between various political parties and programs for the commonwealth's social and economic organization most people are uninformed and groping in the dark. The average voter lacks the insight to distinguish between policies suitable to attain the ends he is aiming at and those unsuitable. He is at a loss to examine the long chains of aprioristic reasoning which constitute the philosophy of a comprehensive social program. He may at best form some opinion about the short-run effects of the policies concerned. He is helpless in dealing with the long run effects. The socialists and communists in principle often assert the infallibility of majority decisions. However, they belie their own words in criticizing parliamentary majorities rejecting their creed, and in denying to the people, under the one party system, the opportunity to choose between different parties.

But in buying a commodity or abstaining from its purchase there is nothing else involved than the consumer's longing for the best possible satisfaction of his instantaneous wishes. The consumer does not—like the voter in political voting—choose between different means whose effects appear only later. He chooses between things which immediately provide satisfaction. His decision is final.

An entrepreneur earns profit by serving the consumers, the people, as they are and not as they should be according to the fancies of some grumbler or potential dictator.

5. The Social Function of Profit and Loss

Profits are never normal. They appear only where there is a maladjustment, a divergence between actual production and production as it should be in order to utilize the available material and mental resources for the best possible satisfaction of the wishes of the public. They are the prize of those who remove this maladjustment; they disappear as soon as the maladjustment is entirely removed. In the imaginary construction of an evenly rotating economy there are no profits. There the sum of the prices of the complementary factors of production, due allowance being made for time preference, coincides with the price of the product.

The greater the preceding maladjustments, the greater the profit earned by their removal. Maladjustments may sometimes be called excessive. But it is inappropriate to apply the epithet "excessive" to profits.

People arrive at the idea of excessive profits by confronting the profit earned with the capital employed in the enterprise an measuring the profit as a percentage of the capital. This method is suggested by the customary procedure applied in partnerships and corporations for the assignment of quotas of the total profit to the individual partners and shareholders. These men have contributed to a different extent to the realization of the project and share in the profits and losses according to the extent of their contribution.

But it is not the capital employed that creates profits and losses. Capital does not "beget profit" as Marx thought. The capital goods as such are dead things that in themselves do not accomplish anything. If they are utilized according to a good idea, profit results. If they are utilized according to a mistaken idea, no profit or losses result. It is the entrepreneurial decision that creates either profit or loss. It is mental acts, the mind of the entrepreneur, from which profits ultimately originate. Profit is a product of the mind, of success in anticipating the future state of the market. It is a spiritual and intellectual phenomenon.

The absurdity of condemning any profits as excessive can easily be shown. An enterprise with a capital of the amount c produced a definite quantity of p which it sold at prices that brought a surplus of proceeds over costs of s and consequently a profit of n per cent. If the entrepreneur had been less capable, he would have needed a capital of $2c$ for the production of the same quantity of p. For the sake of argument we may even neglect the fact that this would have necessarily increased costs of production as it would have doubled the interest on the capital employed, and we may assume that s would have remained unchanged. But at any rate s would have been confronted with $2c$ instead of c and thus the profit would have been only $n/2$ per cent of the capital employed. The "excessive" profit would have been reduced to a "fair" level. Why? Because the entrepreneur was less efficient and because his lack of efficiency deprived his fellow-men of all the advantages they could have got if an amount c of capital goods had been left available for the production of other merchandise.

In branding profits as excessive and penalizing the efficient entrepreneurs by discriminatory taxation, people are injuring themselves. Taxing profits is tantamount to taxing success in best serving the public. The only goal of all production activities is to employ the factors of production in such a way that they render the highest possible output. The smaller the input required for the production of an article becomes, the more of the scarce factors of production is left for the production of other articles. But the better an entrepreneur succeeds in this regard, the more is he vilified and the more is he soaked by taxation. Increasing costs per unit of output, that is, waste, is praised as a virtue.

The most amazing manifestation of this complete failure to grasp the task of production and the nature and functions of profit and loss is shown in the popular superstition that profit is an addendum to the costs of production, the height of which depends uniquely on the discretion of the seller. It is this belief that guides governments in controlling prices. It is the same belief that has prompted many governments to make arrangements with their contractors according to which the price to be paid for an article delivered is to equal costs of production expended by the seller increased by a definite percentage. The effect was that the purveyor got a surplus the higher, the less he succeeded in avoiding superfluous costs.

Contracts of this type enhanced considerably the sums the United States had to expend in the two World Wars. But the bureaucrats, first of all the professors of economics who served in the various war agencies, boasted of their clever handling of the matter.

All people, entrepreneurs as well as nonentrepreneurs, look askance upon any profits earned by other people. Envy is a common weakness of men. People are loath to acknowledge the fact that they themselves could have earned profits if they had displayed the same foresight and judgment the successful businessman did. Their resentment is the more violent, the more they are subconsciously aware of this fact.

There would not be any profits but for the eagerness of the public to acquire the merchandise offered for sale by the successful entrepreneur. But the same people who scramble for these articles vilify the businessman and call his profit illgot.

The semantic expression of this enviousness is the distinction between earned and unearned income. It permeates the textbooks, the language of the laws and administrative procedure. Thus, for instance, the official Form 201 for the New York State Income Tax Return calls "Earnings" only the compensation received by employees and, by implication, all other income, also that resulting from the exercise of a profession, unearned income. Such is the terminology of a state whose governor is a Republican and whose state assembly has a Republican majority.

Public opinion condones profits only as far as they do not exceed the salary paid to an employee. All surplus is rejected as unfair. The objective of taxation is, under the ability-to-pay principle, to confiscate this surplus.

Now one of the main functions of profits is to shift the control of capital to those who know how to employ it in the best possible way for the satisfaction of the public. The more profits a man earns, the greater his wealth consequently becomes, the more influential does he become in the conduct of business affairs. Profit and loss are the instruments by means of which the consumers pass the direction of production activities into the hands of those who are best fit to serve them. Whatever is undertaken to curtail or to confiscate profits, impairs this function. The result of such measures is to loosen the grip the consumers hold over the course of production. The economic machine becomes, from the point of view of the people, less efficient and less responsive.

The jealousy of the common man looks upon the profits of the entrepreneurs as if they were totally used for consumption. A part of them is, of course, consumed. But only those entrepreneurs attain wealth and influence in the realm of business who consume merely a fraction of their proceeds and plough back the much greater part into their enterprises. What makes small business develop into big business is not spending, but saving and capital accumulation.

6. *Profit and Loss in the Progressing and in the Retrogressing Economy*

We call a stationary economy an economy in which the per head quota of the income and wealth of the individuals remains unchanged. In such an economy what the consumers spend more for the purchase of some articles must be equal to what they spend less for other articles. The total amount of the profits earned by one part of the entrepreneurs equals the total amount of losses suffered by other entrepreneurs.

A surplus of the sum of all profits earned in the whole economy above the sum of all losses suffered emerges only in a progressing economy, that is in an economy in which the per head quota of capital increases. This increment is an effect of saving that adds new capital goods to the quantity already previously available. The increase of capital available creates maladjustments insofar as it brings about a discrepancy between the actual state of production and that state which the additional capital makes possible. Thanks to the emergence of additional capital, certain projects which hitherto could not be executed become feasible. In directing the new capital into those channels in which it satisfies the most urgent among the previously not satisfied wants of the consumers, the entrepreneurs earn profits which are not counterbalanced by the losses of other entrepreneurs.

The enrichment which the additional capital generates goes only in part to those who have created it by saving. The rest goes, by raising the marginal productivity of labor and thereby wage rates, to the earners of wages and salaries and, by raising the prices of definite raw materials and food stuffs, to the owners of land, and, finally, to the entrepreneurs who integrate this new capital into the most economical production processes. But while the gain of the wage earners and of the landowners is permanent, the profits of the entrepreneurs disappear once this integration is accomplished. Profits of the entrepreneurs are, as has been mentioned already, a permanent phenomenon only on account of the fact that maladjustments appear daily anew by the elimination of which profits are earned.

Let us for the sake of argument resort to the concept of national income as employed in popular economics. Then it is obvious that in a stationary economy no part of the national income goes into profits. Only in a progressing economy is there a surplus of total profits over total losses. The popular belief that profits are a deduction from the income of workers and consumers is entirely fallacious. If we want to apply the term deduction to the issue, we have to say that this surplus of profits over losses as well as the increments of the wage earners and the landowners is deducted from the gains of those whose saving brought about the additional capital. It is their saving that is the vehicle of economic improvement, that makes the employment of technological innovations possible and raises productivity and the standard of living. It is the entrepreneurs whose activity takes care of the most economical employment of the additional capital. As far as they themselves do not save, neither the workers nor the landowners contribute anything to the emergence of the circumstances which generate what is called economic progress and improvement. They are benefited by other peoples' saving that creates additional capital on the one hand and by the entrepreneurial action that directs this additional capital toward the satisfaction of the most urgent wants on the other hand.

A retrogressing economy is an economy in which the per head quota of capital invested is decreasing. In such an economy the total amount of losses incurred by entrepreneurs exceeds the total amount of profits earned by other entrepreneurs.

7. The Computation of Profit and Loss

The originary praxeological categories of profit and loss are psychic qualities and not reducible to any interpersonal description in quantitative terms. They are intensive magnitudes. The difference between the value of the end attained and that of the means applied for its attainment is profit if it is positive and loss if it is negative.

Where there are social division of efforts and cooperation as well as private ownership of the means of production, economic calculation in terms of monetary units becomes feasible and necessary. Profit and loss are computable as social phenomena. The psychic phenomena of profit and loss, from which they are ultimately derived, remain, of course, incalculable intensive magnitudes.

The fact that in the frame of the market economy entrepreneurial profit and loss are determined by arithmetical operations has misled many people. They fail to see that essential items that enter into this calculation are estimates emanating from the entrepreneur's specific understanding of the future state of the market. They think that these computations are open to examination and verification or alteration on the part of a disinterested expert. They ignore the fact that such computations are as a rule an inherent part of the entrepreneur's speculative anticipation of uncertain future conditions.

For the task of this essay it suffices to refer to one of the problems of cost accounting. One of the items of a bill of costs is the establishment of the difference between the price paid for the acquisition of what is commonly called durable production equipment and its present value. This present value is the money equivalent of the contribution this equipment will make to future earnings. There is no certainty about the future state of the market and about the height of these earnings. They can only be determined by a speculative anticipation on the part of the entrepreneur. It is preposterous to call in an expert and to substitute his arbitrary judgment for that of the entrepreneur. The expert is objective insofar as he is not affected by an error made. But the entrepreneur exposes his own material well-being.

Of course, the law determines magnitudes which it calls profit and loss. But these magnitudes are not identical with the economic concepts of profit and loss and must not be confused with them. If a tax law calls a magnitude profit, it in effect determines the height of taxes due. It calls this magnitude profit because it wants to justify its tax policy in the eyes of the public. It would be more correct for the legislator to omit the term profit and simply to speak of the basis for the computation of the tax due.

The tendency of the tax laws is to compute what they call profit as high as possible in order to increase immediate public revenue. But there are other laws which are committed to the tendency to restrict the magnitude they call profit. The commercial codes of many nations were and are guided by the endeavor to protect the rights of creditors. They aimed at restricting what they called profit in order to prevent the entrepreneur from withdrawing to the prejudice of creditors too much from the firm or corporation for his own benefit. It was these tendencies which were operative in the evolution of the commercial usages concerning the customary height of depreciation quotas.

There is no need today to dwell upon the problem of the falsification of economic calculation under inflationary conditions. All people begin to comprehend the phenomenon of illusory profits, the offshoot of the great inflations of our age.

Failure to grasp the effects of inflation upon the customary methods of computing profits originated the modern concept of *profiteering*. An entrepreneur is dubbed a profiteer if his profit and loss statement, calculated in terms of a currency subject to a rapidly progressing inflation, shows profits which other people deem "excessive." It has happened very often in many countries that the profit and loss statement of such a profiteer, when calculated in terms of a noninflated or less inflated currency, showed not only no profit at all but considerable losses.

Even if we neglect for the sake of argument any reference to the phenomenon of merely inflation induced illusory profits, it is obvious that the epithet profiteer is the expression of an arbitrary judgment of value. There is no other standard available for the distinction between profiteering and earning fair profits than that provided by the censor's personal envy and resentment.

It is strange indeed that an eminent logician, the late L. Susan Stebbing, entirely failed to perceive the issue involved. Professor Stebbing equated the concept of profiteering to concepts which refer to a clear distinction of such a nature that no sharp line can be drawn between extremes. The distinction between excess profits or profiteering, and "legitimate profits," she declared, is clear, although it is not a sharp distinction.[2] Now this distinction is clear only in reference to an act of legislation that defines the term excess profits as used in its context. But this is not what Stebbing had in mind. Se explicitly emphasized that such legal definitions are made "in an arbitrary manner for the practical purposes of administration." She used the term *legitimate* without any reference to legal statutes and their definitions. But is it permissible to employ the term legitimate without reference to any standard from the point of view of which the thing in question is to be considered as legitimate? And is there any other standard available for the distinction between profiteering and legitimate profits than one provided by personal judgments of value?

Professor Stebbing referred to the famous *acervus* and *calvus* arguments of the old logicians. Many words are vague insofar as they apply to characteristics which may be possessed in varying degrees. It is impossible to draw a sharp line between those who are bald and those who are not. It is impossible to define precisely the concept of baldness. But what Professor Stebbing failed to notice is that the characteristic according to which people distinguish between those who are bald and those who are not is open to a precise definition. It is the presence or the absence of hair on the head of a person. This is a clear and unambiguous mark of which the presence or absence is to be established by observation and to be expressed by propositions about existence. What is vague is merely the determination of the point at which nonbaldness turns into baldness. People may disagree with regard to the determination of this point. But their disagreement refers to the interpretation of the convention that attaches a certain meaning to the word baldness. No judgments of value are implied. It may, of course, happen that the difference of opinion is in a concrete case caused by bias. But this is another thing.

The vagueness of words like bald is the same that is inherent in the indefinite numerals and pronouns. Language needs such terms as for many purposes of daily communication between men an exact arithmetical establishment of quantities is superfluous and too bothersome. Logicians are badly mistaken in attempting to attach to such words whose vagueness is intentional and serves definite purposes the precision of the definite numerals. For an individual who plans to visit Seattle the information that there are many hotels in this city is sufficient. A committee that plans to hold a convention in Seattle needs precise information about the number of hotel beds available.

Professor Stebbing's error consisted in the confusion of existential propositions with judgments of value. Her unfamiliarity with the problems of economics, which all her otherwise valuable writings display, led her astray. She would not have made such a blunder in a field that was better known to her. She would not have declared that there is a clear distinction between an author's "legitimate royalties" and "illegitimate royalties." She would have comprehended that the height of the royalties depends on the public's appreciation of a book and that an observer who criticizes the height of royalties merely expresses his personal judgment of value.

B. The Condemnation of Profit

1. Economics and the Abolition of Profit

Those who spurn entrepreneurial profit as "unearned" mean that it is lucre unfairly withheld either from the workers or from the consumers or from both. Such is the idea underlying the alleged "right to the whole produce of labor" and the Marxian doctrine of exploitation. It can be said that most governments—if not all—and the immense majority of our contemporaries by and large endorse this opinion although some of them are generous enough to acquiesce in the suggestion that a fraction of profits should be left to the "exploiters."

There is no use in arguing about the adequacy of ethical precepts. They are derived from intuition; they are arbitrary and subjective. There is no objective standard available with regard to which they could be judged. Ultimate ends are chosen by the individual's judgments of value. They cannot be determined by scientific inquiry and logical reasoning. If a man says, "This is what I am aiming at whatever the consequences of my conduct and the price I shall have to pay for it may be," nobody is in a position to oppose any arguments against him. But the question is whether it is really true that this man is ready to pay any price for the attainment of the end concerned. If this latter question is answered in the negative, it becomes possible to enter into an examination of the issue involved.

If there were really people who are prepared to put up with all the consequences of the abolition of profit, however detrimental they may be, it would not be possible for economics to deal with the problem. But this is not the case. Those who want to abolish profit are guided by the idea that this confiscation would improve the material well-being of all non-entrepreneurs. In their eyes the abolition of profit is not an ultimate end but a means for the attainment of a definite end, viz., the enrichment of the non-entrepreneurs. Whether this end can really be attained by the employment of this means and whether the employment of this means does not perhaps bring about some other effects which may to some or to all people appear more undesirable than conditions before the employment of this means, these are questions which economics is called upon to examine.

2. The Consequences of the Abolition of Profit

The idea to abolish profit for the advantage of the consumers involves that the entrepreneur should be forced to sell the products at prices not exceeding the costs of production expended. As such prices are, for all articles the sale of which would have brought profit, below the potential market price, the available supply is not sufficient to make it possible for all those who want to buy at these prices to acquire the articles. The market is paralyzed by the maximum price decree. It can no longer allocate the products to the consumers. A system of rationing must be adopted.

The suggestion to abolish the entrepreneur's profit for the benefit of the employees aims not at the abolition of profit. It aims at wresting it from the hands of the entrepreneur and handing it over to his employees.

Under such a scheme the incidence of losses incurred falls upon the entrepreneur, while profits go to the employees. It is probable that the effect of this arrangement would consist in making losses increase and profits dwindle. At any rate, a greater part of the profits would be consumed and less would be saved and ploughed back into the enterprise. No capital would be available for the establishment of new branches of production and for the transfer of capital from branches which—in compliance with the demand of the customers—should shrink into branches which should expand. For it would harm the interests of those employed in a definite enterprise or branch to restrict the capital employed in it and to transfer it into another enterprise or branch. If such a scheme had been adopted half a century ago, all the innovations accomplished in this period would have been rendered impossible. If, for the sake of argument, we were prepared to neglect any reference to the problem of capital accumulation, we would still have to realize that giving profit to the employees must result in rigidity of the once attained state of production and preclude any adjustment, improvement and progress.

In fact, the scheme would transfer ownership of the capital invested into the hands of the employees. It would be tantamount to the establishment of syndicalism and would generate all the effects of syndicalism, a system which no author or reformer ever had the courage to advocate openly.

A third solution of the problem would be to confiscate all the profits earned by the entrepreneurs for the benefit of the state. A one hundred per cent tax on profits would accomplish this task. It would transform the entrepreneurs into irresponsible administrators of all plants and workshops. They would no longer be subject to the supremacy of the buying public. They would just be people who have the power to deal with production as it pleases them.

The policies of all contemporary governments which have not adopted outright socialism apply all these three schemes jointly. They confiscate by various measures of price control a part of the potential profits for the alleged benefit of the consumers. They support the labor unions in their endeavors to wrest, under the ability-to-pay principle of wage determination, a part of the profits from the entrepreneurs. And, last but not least, they are intent upon confiscating, by progressive income taxes, special taxes on corporation income and "excess profits" taxes, an ever increasing part of profits for public revenue. It can easily be seen that these policies if continued will very soon succeed in abolishing entrepreneurial profit altogether.

The joint effect of the application of these policies is already today rising chaos. The final effect will be the full realization of socialism by smoking out the entrepreneurs. Capitalism cannot survive the abolition of profit. It is profit and loss that force the capitalists to employ their capital for the best possible service to the consumers. It is profit and loss that make those people supreme in the conduct of business who are best fit to satisfy the public. If profit is abolished, chaos results.

3. The Anti-Profit Arguments

All the reasons advanced in favor of an anti-profit policy are the outcome of an erroneous interpretation of the operation of the market economy.

The tycoons are too powerful, too rich and too big. They abuse their power for their own enrichment. They are irresponsible tyrants. Bigness of an enterprise is in itself an evil. There is no reason why some men should own millions while others are poor. The wealth of the few is the cause of the poverty of the masses.

Each word of these passionate denunciations is false. The businessmen are not irresponsible tyrants. It is precisely the necessity of making profits and avoiding losses that gives to the consumers a firm hold over the entrepreneurs and forces them to comply with the wishes of the people. What makes a firm big is its success in best filling the demands of the buyers. If the bigger enterprise did not better serve the people than a smaller one, it would long since have been reduced to smallness. There is no harm in a businessman's endeavors to enrich himself by increasing his profits. The businessman has in his capacity as a businessman only one task: to strive after the highest possible profit. Huge profits are the proof of good service rendered in supplying the consumers. Losses are the proof of blunders committed, of failure to perform satisfactorily the tasks incumbent upon an entrepreneur. The riches of successful entrepreneurs is not the cause of anybody's poverty; it is the consequence of the fact that the consumers are better supplied than they would have been in the absence of the entrepreneur's effort. The penury of millions in the backward countries is not caused by anybody's opulence; it is the correlative of the fact that their country lacks entrepreneurs who have acquired riches. The standard of living of the common man is highest in those countries which have the greatest number of wealthy entrepreneurs. It is to the foremost material interest of everybody that control of the factors of production should be concentrated in the hands of those who know how to utilize them in the most efficient way.

It is the avowed objective of the policies of all present-day governments and political parties to prevent the emergence of new millionaires. If this policy had been adopted in the United States fifty years ago, the growth of the industries producing new articles would have been stunted. Motorcars, refrigerators, radio sets and a hundred other less spectacular but even more useful innovations would not have become standard equipment of most of the American family households.

The average wage earner thinks that nothing else is needed to keep the social apparatus of production running and to improve and to increase output than the comparatively simple routine work assigned to him. He does not realize that the mere toil and trouble of the routinist is not sufficient. Sedulousness and skill are spent in vain if they are not directed toward the most important goal by the entrepreneur's foresight and are not aided by the capital accumulated by capitalists. The American worker is badly mistaken when he believes that his high standard of living is due to his own excellence. He is neither more industrious nor more skillful than the workers of Western Europe. He owes his superior income to the fact that his country clung to "rugged individualism" much longer than Europe. It was his luck that the United States turned to an anti-capitalistic policy as much as forty or fifty years later than Germany. His wages are higher than those of the workers of the rest of the world because the capital equipment per head of the employee is highest in America and because the American entrepreneur was not so much restricted by crippling regimentation as his colleagues in other areas. The comparatively greater prosperity of the United States is an outcome of the fact that the New Deal did not come in 1900 or 1910, but only in 1933.

If one wants to study the reasons for Europe's backwardness, it would be necessary to examine the manifold laws and regulations that prevented in Europe the establishment of an equivalent of the American drug store and crippled the evolution of chain stores, department stores, super markets and kindred outfits. It would be important to investigate the German Reich's effort to protect the inefficient methods of traditional *Handwerk* (handicraft) against the competition of capitalist business. Still more revealing would be an examination of the Austrian *Gewerbepolitik*, a policy that from the early eighties on aimed at preserving the economic structure of the ages preceding the Industrial Revolution.

The worst menace to prosperity and civilization and to the material well-being of the wage earners is the inability of union bosses, of "union economists" and of the less intelligent strata of the workers themselves to appreciate the role entrepreneurs play in production. This lack of insight has found a classical expression in the writings of Lenin. As Lenin saw it all that production requires besides the manual work of the laborer and the designing of the engineers is "control of production and distribution," a task that can easily be accomplished "by the armed workers." For this accounting and control "have been *simplified* by capitalism to the utmost, till they have become the extraordinarily simple operations of watching, recording and issuing receipts, within the reach of everybody who can read and write and knows the first four rules of arithmetic."[3] No further comment is needed.

4. The Equality Argument

In the eyes of the parties who style themselves progressive and leftist the main vice of capitalism is the inequality of incomes and wealth. The ultimate end of their policies is to establish equality. The moderates want to attain this goal step by step; the radicals plan to attain it at one stroke, by a revolutionary overthrow of the capitalist mode of production.

However, in talking about equality and asking vehemently for its realization, nobody advocates a curtailment of his own present income. The term equality as employed in contemporary political language always means upward levelling of one's income, never downward levelling. It means getting more, not sharing one's own affluence with people who have less.

If the American automobile worker, railroadman or compositor says equality, he means expropriating the holders of shares and bonds for his own benefit. He does not consider sharing with the unskilled workers who earn less. At best, he thinks of equality of all American citizens. It never occurs to him that the peoples of Latin America, Asia and Africa may interpret the postulate of equality as world equality and not as national equality.

The political labor movement as well as the labor union movement flamboyantly advertise their internationalism. But this internationalism is a mere rhetorical gesture without any substantial meaning. In every country in which average wage rates are higher than in any other area, the unions advocate insurmountable immigration barriers in order to prevent foreign "comrades" and "brothers"' from competing with their own members. Compared with the anti-immigration laws of the European nations, the immigration legislation of the American republics is mild indeed because it permits the immigration of a limited number of people. No such normal quotas are provided in most of the European laws.

All the arguments advanced in favor of income equalization within a country can with the same justification or lack of justification also be advanced in favor of world equalization. An American worker has no better title to claim the savings of the American capitalist than has any foreigner. That a man has earned profits by serving the consumers and has not entirely consumed his funds but ploughed back the greater part of them into industrial equipment does not give anybody a valid title to expropriate this capital for his own benefit. But if one maintains the opinion to the contrary, there is certainly no reason to ascribe to anybody a better right to expropriate than to anybody else. There is no reason to assert that only Americans have the right to expropriate other Americans. The big shots of American business are the scions of people who immigrated to the United States from England, Scotland, Ireland, France, Germany and other European countries. The people of their country of origin contend that they have the same title to seize the property acquired by these men as the American people have. The American radicals are badly mistaken in believing that their social program is identical or at least compatible with the objectives of the radicals of other countries. It is not. The foreign radicals will not acquiesce in leaving to the Americans, a minority of less than 7% of the world's total population, what they think is a privileged position. A world government of the kind the American radicals are asking for would try to confiscate by a world income tax all the surplus an average American earns above the average income of a Chinese or Indian worker. Those who question the correctness of this statement, would drop their doubts after a conversation with any of the intellectual leaders of Asia.

There is hardly any Iranian who would qualify the objections raised by the British Labor Government against the confiscation of the oil wells as anything else but a manifestation of the most reactionary spirit of capitalist exploitation. Today governments abstain from virtually expropriating—by foreign exchange control, discriminatory taxation and similar devices—foreign investments only if they expect to get in the next years more foreign capital and thus to be able in the future to expropriate a greater amount.

The disintegration of the international capital market is one of the most important effects of the antiprofit mentality of our age. But no less disastrous is the fact that the greater part of the world's population looks upon the United States—not only upon the American capitalists but also upon the American workers—with the same feelings of envy, hatred, and hostility with which, stimulated by the socialist and communist doctrines, the masses everywhere look upon the capitalists of their own nation.

5. Communism and Poverty

A customary method of dealing with political programs and movements is to explain and to justify their popularity by referring to the conditions which people found unsatisfactory and to the goals they wanted to attain by the realization of these programs.

However, the only thing that matters is whether or not the program concerned is fit to attain the ends sought. A bad program and a bad policy can never be explained, still less justified by pointing to the unsatisfactory conditions of its originators and supporters. The sole question that counts is whether or not these policies can remove or alleviate the evils which they are designed to remedy.

Yet almost all our contemporaries declare again and again: If you want to succeed in fighting communism, socialism and interventionism, you must first of all improve peoples' material conditions. The policy of *laissez faire* aims precisely at making people more prosperous. But it cannot succeed as long as want is worsened more and more by socialist and interventionist measures.

In the very short run the conditions of a part of the people can be improved by expropriating entrepreneurs and capitalists and by distributing the booty. But such predatory inroads, which even the *Communist Manifesto* described as "despotic" and as "economically insufficient and untenable," sabotage the operation of the market economy, impair very soon the conditions of all the people and frustrate the endeavors of entrepreneurs and capitalists to make the masses more prosperous. What is good for a quickly vanishing instant, (i.e., in the long run) result in most detrimental consequences.

Historians are mistaken in explaining the rise of Nazism by referring to real or imaginary adversities and hardships of the German people. What made the Germans support almost unanimously the twenty-five points of the "unalterable" Hitler program was not some conditions which they deemed unsatisfactory, but their expectation that the execution of this program would remove their complaints and render them happier. They turned to Nazism because they lacked common sense and intelligence. They were not judicious enough to recognize in time the disasters that Nazism was bound to bring upon them.

The immense majority of the world's population is extremely poor when compared with the average standard of living of the capitalist nations. But this poverty does not explain their propensity to adopt the communist program. They are anti-capitalitic because they are blinded by envy, ignorant and too dull to appreciate correctly the causes of their distress. There is but one means to improve their material conditions, namely, to convince them that only capitalism can render them more prosperous.

The worst method to fight communism is that of the Marshall Plan. It gives to the recipients the impression that the United States alone is interested in the preservation of the profit system while their own concerns require a communist regime. The United States, they think, is aiding them because its people have a bad conscience. They themselves pocket this bribe but their sympathies go to the socialist system. The American subsidies make it possible for their governments to conceal partially the disastrous effects of the various socialist measures they have adopted.

Not poverty is the source of socialism, but spurious ideological prepossessions. Most of our contemporaries reject beforehand, without having ever studied them, all the teachings of economics as aprioristic nonsense. Only experience, they maintain, is to be relied upon. But is there any experience that would speak in favor of socialism?

Retorts the socialist: But capitalism creates poverty; look at India and China. The objection is vain. Neither India nor China has ever established capitalism. Their poverty is the result of the absence of capitalism.

What happened in these and other underdeveloped countries was that they were benefited from abroad by some of the fruits of capitalism without having adopted the capitalist mode of production. European, and in more recent years also American, capitalists invested capital in their areas and thereby increased the marginal productivity of labor and wage rates. At the same time these peoples received from abroad the means to fight contagious diseases, medications developed in the capitalist countries. Consequently mortality rates, especially infant mortality, dropped considerably. In the capitalist countries this prolongation of the average length of life was partially compensated by a drop in the birth rate. As capital accumulation increased more quickly than population, the per head quota of capital invested grew continuously. The result was progressing prosperity. It was different in the countries which enjoyed some of the effects of capitalism without turning to capitalism. There the birth rate did not decline at all or not to the extent required to make the per head quota of capital invested rise. These nations prevent by their policies both the importation of foreign capital and the accumulation of domestic capital. The joint effect of the high birth rate and the absence of an increase in capital is, of course, increasing poverty.

There is but one means to improve the material well-being of men, viz., to accelerate the increase in capital accumulated as against population. No psychological lucubrations, however sophisticated, can alter this fact. There is no excuse whatever for the pursuit of policies which not only fail to attain the ends sought, but even seriously impair conditions.

6. *The Moral Condemnation of the Profit Motive*

As soon as the problem of profits is raised, people shift it from the praxeological sphere into the sphere of ethical judgments of value. Then everybody glories in the aureole of a saint and an ascetic. He himself does not care for money and material well-being. He serves his fellowmen to the best of his abilities unselfishly. He strives after higher and nobler things than wealth. Thank God, he is not one of those egoistic profiteers.

The businessmen are blamed because the only thing they have in mind is to succeed. Yet everybody—without any exception—in acting aims at the attainment of a definite end. The only alternative to success is failure; nobody ever wants to fail. It is the very essence of human nature that man consciously aims at substituting a more satisfactory state of affairs for a less satisfactory. What distinguishes the decent man from the crook is the different goals they are aiming at and the different means they are resorting to in order to attain the ends chosen. But they both want to succeed in their sense. It is logically impermissible to distinguish between people who aim at success and those who do not.

Practically everybody aims at improving the material conditions of his existence. Public opinion takes no offense at the endeavors of farmers, workers, clerks, teachers, doctors, ministers, and people from many other callings to earn as much as they can. But it censures the capitalists and entrepreneurs for their greed. While enjoying without any scruples all the goods business delivers, the consumer sharply condemns the selfishness of the purveyors of this merchandise. He does not realize that he himself creates their profits by scrambling for the things they have to sell.

Neither does the average man comprehend that profits are indispensable in order to direct the activities of business into those channels in which they serve him best. He looks upon profits as if their only function were to enable the recipients to consume more than he himself does. He fails to realize that their main function is to convey control of the factors of production into the hands of those who best utilize them for his own purposes. He did not, as he thinks, renounce becoming an entrepreneur out of moral scruples. He chose a position with a more modest yield because he lacked the abilities required for entrepreneurship or, in rare cases indeed, because his inclinations prompted him to enter upon another career.

Mankind ought to be grateful to those exceptional men who out of scientific zeal, humanitarian enthusiasm or religious faith sacrificed their lives, health and wealth, in the service of their fellow-men. But the philistines practice self deception in comparing themselves with the pioneers of medical X-ray application or with nuns who attend people afflicted with the plague. It is not self-denial that makes the average physician choose a medical career, but the expectation of attaining a respected social position and a suitable income.

Everybody is eager to charge for his services and accomplishments as much as the traffic can bear. In this regard there is no difference between the workers, whether unionized or not, the ministers and teachers on the one hand and the entrepreneurs on the other hand. Neither of them has the right to talk as if he were Francis d'Assisi.

There is no other standard of what is morally good and morally bad than the effects produced by conduct upon social cooperation. A—hypothetical—isolated and self-sufficient individual would not in acting have to take into account anything else than his own well-being. Social man must in all his actions avoid indulging in any conduct that would jeopardize the smooth working of the system of social cooperation. In complying with the moral law man does not sacrifice his own concerns to those of a mythical higher entity, whether it is called class, state, nation, race or humanity. He curbs some of his own instinctive urges, appetites and greed, that is his shortrun concerns, in order to serve best his own—rightly understood or long-run—interests. He foregoes a small gain that he could reap instantly lest he miss a greater but later satisfaction. For the attainment of all human ends, whatever they may be, is conditioned by the preservation and further development of social bonds and interhuman cooperation. What is an indispensable means to intensify social cooperation and to make it possible for more people to survive and to enjoy a higher standard of living is morally good and socially desirable. Those who reject this principle as un-Christian ought to ponder over the text: "That thy days may be long upon the land which the Lord thy God giveth thee." They can certainly not deny that capitalism has made man's days longer than they were in the precapitalistic ages.

There is no reason why capitalists and entrepreneurs should be ashamed of earning profits. It is silly that some people try to defend American capitalism by declaring: "The record of American business is good; profits are not too high." The function of entrepreneurs is to make profits; high profits are the proof that they have well performed their task of removing maladjustments of production.

Of course, as a rule capitalists and entrepreneurs are not saints excelling in the virtue of self-denial. But neither are their critics saintly. And with all the regard due to the sublime self-effacement of saints, we cannot help stating the fact that the world would be in a rather desolate condition if it were peopled exclusively by men not interested in the pursuit of material well-being.

7. The Static Mentality

The average man lacks the imagination to realize that the conditions of life and action are in a continual flux. As he sees it, there is no change in the external objects that constitute his well-being. His world view is static and stationary. It mirrors a stagnating environment. He knows neither that the past differed from the present nor that there prevails uncertainty about future things.

He is at a complete loss to conceive the function of entrepreneurship because he is unaware of this uncertainty. Like children who take all the things the parents give them without asking any questions, he takes all the goods business offers him. He is unaware of the efforts that supply him with all he needs. He ignores the role of capital accumulation and of entrepreneurial decisions. He simply takes it for granted that a magic table appears at a moment's notice laden with all he wants to enjoy.

This mentality is reflected in the popular idea of socialization. Once the parasitic capitalists and entrepreneurs are thrown out, he himself will get all that they used to consume. It is but the minor error of this expectation that it grotesquely overrates the increment in income, if any, each individual could receive from such a distribution. Much more serious is the fact that it assumes that the only thing required is to continue in the various plants production of those goods they are producing at the moment of the socialization in the ways they were hitherto produced. No account is taken of the necessity to adjust production daily anew to perpetually changing conditions. The dilettante-socialist does not comprehend that a socialization effected fifty years ago would not have socialized the structure of business as it exists today but a very different structure. He does not give a thought to the enormous effort that is needed in order to transform business again and again to render the best possible service.

This dilettantish inability to comprehend the essential issues of the conduct of production affairs is not only manifested in the writings of Marx and Engels. It permeates no less the contributions of contemporary psuedo-economics.

The imaginary construction of an evenly rotating economy is an indispensable mental tool of economic thinking. In order to conceive the function of profit and loss, the economist constructs the image of a hypothetical, although unrealizable, state of affairs in which nothing changes, in which tomorrow does not differ at all from today and in which consequently no maladjustments can arise and no need for any alteration in the conduct of business emerges. In the frame of this imaginary construction there are no entrepreneurs and no entrepreneurial profits and losses. The wheels turn spontaneously as it were. But the real world in which men live and have to work can never duplicate the hypothetical world of this mental makeshift.

Now one of the main shortcomings of the mathematical economists is that they deal with this evenly rotating economy—they call it the static state—as if it were something really existing. Prepossessed by the fallacy that economics is to be treated with mathematical methods, they concentrate their efforts upon the analysis of static states which, of course, allow a description in sets of simultaneous differential equations. But this mathematical treatment virtually avoids any reference to the real problems of economics. It indulges in quite useless mathematical play without adding anything to the comprehension of the problems of human acting and producing. It creates the misunderstanding as if the analysis of static states were the main concern of economics. It confuses a merely ancillary tool of thinking with reality.

The mathematical economist is so blinded by his epistemological prejudice that he simply fails to see what the tasks of economics are. He is anxious to show us that socialism is realizable under static conditions. As static conditions, as he himself admits, are unrealizable, this amounts merely to the assertion that in an unrealizable state of the world socialism could be realizable. A very valuable result, indeed, a hundred years of the joint work of hundreds of authors, taught at all universities, publicized in innumerable textbooks and monographs and in scores of allegedly scientific magazines!

There is no such thing as a static economy. All the conclusions derived from preoccupation with the image of static states and static equilibrium are of no avail for the description of the world as it is and will always be.

C. The Alternative

A social order based on private control of the means of production cannot work without entrepreneurial action and entrepreneurial profit and, of course, entrepreneurial loss. The elimination of profit, whatever methods may be resorted to for its execution, must transform society into a senseless jumble. It would create poverty for all.

In a socialist system there are neither entrepreneurs nor entrepreneurial profit and loss. The supreme director of the socialist commonwealth would, however, have to strive in the same way after a surplus of proceeds over costs as the entrepreneurs do under capitalism. It is not the task of this essay to deal with socialism. Therefore it is not necessary to stress the point that, not being able to apply any kind of economic calculation, the socialist chief would never know what the costs and what the proceeds of his operations are.

What matters in this context is merely the fact that there is no third system feasible. There cannot be any such thing as a nonsocialist system without entrepreneurial profit and loss. The endeavors to eliminate profits from the capitalist system are merely destructive. They disintegrate capitalism without putting anything in its place. It is this that we have in mind in maintaining that they result in chaos.

Men must choose between capitalism and socialism. They cannot avoid this dilemma by resorting to a capitalist system without entrepreneurial profit. Every step toward the elimination of profit is progress on the way toward social disintegration.

In choosing between capitalism and socialism people are implicitly also choosing between all the social institutions which are the necessary accompaniment of each of these systems, its "superstrucure" as Marx said. If control of production is shifted from the hands of entrepreneurs, daily anew elected by a plebiscite of the consumers, into the hands of the supreme commander of the "industrial armies" (Marx and Engels) or of the "armed workers" (Lenin), neither representative government nor any civil liberties can survive. Wall Street, against which the self-styled idealists are battling, is merely a symbol. But the walls of the Soviet prisons within which all dissenters disappear forever are a hard fact.

Notes

*A paper prepared for the meeting of the Mont Pèlerin Society held in Beauvallon, France, September 9 to 16, 1951. Available same year in English as separate booklet from Libertarian Press—out of print.

1.   Cf. Mises, *Human Action*, Yale University Press, 1949, pages 305-307; *Bureaucracy*, Yale University Press, 1944, Pages 40-73.

2.   Cf. L. Susan Stebbing, *Thinking to Some Purpose*. (Pelican Books A44), pages 185-187.

3.   Lenin, *State and Revolution*, 1917 (Edition by International Publishers, New York, pages 83-84). The italics are Lenin's (or the communist translator's).

THE ENIGMA OF ENTERPRISE

George Gilder

America's entrepreneurs live in a world with 4 billion poor people. Vulnerable men and women, these leaders of business command little political power or means of defense. Democratic masses or military juntas could take their wealth at will. Why, on a planet riven with famine, poverty, and disease, should this tiny minority be allowed to control riches thousands of times greater than their needs for subsistence and comfort? Why should a few thousand families command wealth far exceeding the endowments of most nations?

More specifically, why should William Kluge, the broadcasting tycoon, have $7 billion, and Suzie Saintly, the social worker, make $15,000 a year? Or why should Harry Helmsley command a fortune worth over a billion dollars and Harry Homeless live on a rug on a grate? Why should Bill Gates, the chairman of Microsoft, be worth over $7 billion while Dan Bricklin, the inventor of the pioneering Visicalc spreadsheet, is still working out of his home with one employee. And why should Michael Milken have ruled tides of billions while the president of the United States earns $200,000 a year?

Does any of this make sense?

In statistical terms, the issue arises just as starkly. Why should the top 1 percent of families own 20 percent of the nation's wealth, while the bottom 20 percent, awash in debts, have no measurable net worth at all?

On a global level, the disparity assumes a deadly edge. Why should even this bottom fifth of Americans be able to throw away enough food to feed a continent, while a million Ethiopians die of famine?Why should the dogs and cats of American eat far better than the average citizen on this unfair planet?

We all know that life is not fair, but to many people, this is ridiculous. These huge disparities seem to defy every measure of proportion and property. They apparently correspond neither to need nor to virtue nor to IQ, nor to credentials, nor to education, nor to social contribution.

Most observers now acknowledge that capitalism generates prosperity. But the rich seem a caricature of capitalism. Look at the "Forbes Four Hundred" list of America's wealthiest people, for example, and hold your nose. Many of them are short and crabby, beaked and mottled, fat and foolish. At least 10 never finished high school and only 240 out of the 304 who went to college managed to graduate. A society may tolerate an aristocracy certified by merit. But capitalism exalts a strange riffraff with no apparent rhyme or reason.

Couldn't we create a system of capitalism without fat cats? Wouldn't it be possible to contrive an economy that is just as prosperous, but with a far more just and appropriate distribution of wealth?

Wouldn't it be a better world if rich entrepreneurs saw their winnings capped at, say $15 million? Surely Sam Walton's heirs, or Harry and Leona Helmsley, could make do on a million dollars or so a year of annual income, four or five times the salary of the president.

Most defenders of capitalism say no. They contend that the bizarre inequalities we see are an indispensable reflection of the processes that create wealth. They imply capitalism doesn't make sense, morally or rationally, but it does make wealth. So, they say, don't knock it.

The usual case for capitalism maintains that greed may drive Leona Helmsley or Ivan Boesky to behavior that attracts the scrutiny of official investigators. But, runs the argument, greed also makes the system go. Because greed is less trammeled in the United States than in Ethiopia, Harry on the grate eats better than the middle class of Addis Ababa.

This was essentially the argument of Adam Smith, the first and still most quoted apologist of capitalism. He declared that it is only from the entrepreneur's "luxury and caprice," his desire for "all the different baubles and trinkets in the economy of greatness," that the poor "derive that share of the necessities of life, which they would in vain have expected from his humanity or his justice."

In perhaps his most famous lines, Smith wrote of entrepreneurs:

> · In spite of their natural selfishness and rapacity, though they mean only their own
> conveniency, though the sole end which they proposed from the labours of all the thousands
> they employ, be the gratification of their own vain and insatiable desires...they are led by an
> invisible hand...and without intending it, without knowing it, advance the interest of society.

Thus did capitalism's greatest defender write of the rich of his day. But more recent writers, from John Kenneth Galbraith to Robert Kuttner, speak of the rich wallowing in their riches and implicitly bilking the poor of the necessities of life.

What slanderous garbage it all is! This case for capitalism as a Faustian pact, by which we trade greed for wealth, is simple hogwash. America's entrepreneurs are not more greedy than Harry Homeless or Suzie Saintly. Even without making comparison to their opportunities for indolence, one can see that they work fanatically hard. In proportion to their holdings or their output, and their contributions to the human race, they consume less than any other group of people in the history of the world.

Far from being greedy, America's leading entrepreneurs—with some unrepresentative exceptions—display discipline and self-control, hard work and austerity that excel that in any college of social work, Washington think tank, or congregation of bishops. They are a strange riffraff, to be sure, because they are chosen not according to blood, credentials, education, or services rendered to the establishment. They are chosen for performance alone, for service to the people as consumers.

Greed is an appetite for unneeded and unearned wealth and power. The truly greedy seek comfort and security first. They seek goods and clout they have not earned. Because the best and safest way to gain unearned pay is to get the state to take it from others, greed leads, as by an invisible hand, toward ever more government action—to socialism, not capitalism. Socialism is in practice a conspiracy of the greedy to exploit the productive. To confuse the issue, the beneficiaries of government transfers of wealth smear their betters with the claim of avarice that they themselves deserve.

The rich in general have earned their money by contributions to the common weal that far exceed their income, or have inherited fortunes from forebears who did likewise. What is more, most entrepreneurs continue their work to enrich the world. Let us hail them and their wealth.

Greed is actually less a characteristic of Bill Gates than of Harry Homeless. Harry may seem pitiable. But he and his advocates insist that he occupy—and devalue—some of the planet's most valuable real estate. From the beaches of Santa Monica to the center of Manhattan, he wants to live better than most of the population of the world throughout human history but he does not want to give back anything whatsoever to the society that sustains him. He wants utterly unearned wealth. That is the essence of avarice. If you want to see a carnival of greed, watch Jesse Jackson regale an audience of welfare mothers on the "economic violence" of capitalism, or watch a conference of leftist college professors denouncing the economic system that provides their freedom, tenure, long vacations, and other expensive privileges while they pursue their Marxist ego-trip at the expense of capitalism.

America's entrepreneurs in no way resemble the plutocrats of socialist and feudal realms who get government to steal their winnings for them and then revel in their palaces with eunuchs and harems. The American rich, in general, cannot revel in their wealth because most of it is not liquid. It has been given to others in the form of investments. It is embodied in a vast web of enterprise that retains its worth only through constant work and sacrifice.

Bill Gates and most of the others live modestly. They give prodigally of themselves and their work. They reinvest their profits in productive enterprise that employs and enriches the world.

Nonetheless, the reason for the disparities between the Four Hundred and the Four Billion is not that the entrepreneurs work harder or better or forgo more consumption. Dismissing the charge that the Four Hundred engage in a carnival of greed, we do not explain the real reasons for their huge wealth.

Since Adam Smith, a host of theories have been offered in answer to the great enigma of capitalist inequality. There is the argument of rights: the creators of great wealth have a right to it. But the assertion of rights to vast fortunes created by thousands of people and protected by the state only repeats the enigma in more abstract terms.

Then there is the argument of carrots and sticks: Sam Walton's billions offered him a necessary incentive in the expansion of his stores through the South; Harry on the grate offers a cautionary message to passer-by to work hard and obediently. But the critics can plausibly answer, "Sure, we all need incentives...but $7 billion?" Finally, some apologists will say that Sam's billions were a reward for his brilliant entrepreneurship, while penury is the just outcome of alcoholism and improvidence. But Suzy Saintly, Dan Bricklin, and George Bush are neither improvident, nor necessarily less brilliant than Sam was.

All these arguments, too, are beside the point. The distributions of capitalism make sense, but not because of the virtue or greed of entrepreneurs or the invisible hand of the market. The reason is not carrots and sticks, or just deserts. The reason capitalism works is that the creators of wealth are granted the right and burden of reinvesting it—of choosing the others who are given it in the investment process.

The very process of creating wealth is the best possible education for creating more wealth. Every enterprise is an experimental test of an entrepreneurial idea. If it succeeds it yields a twofold profit: a financial increase and an enlargement of knowledge and learning. An economy can continue to grow only if its profits are joined with entrepreneurial knowledge. In general, wealth can grow only if the people who create it control it. Divorce the financial profits from the learning process and the economy stagnates. Like a tree or a garden, an economy grows by photosynthesis. Without the light of new knowledge and the roots of ownership, it withers.

The riches of the Four Hundred all ultimately stem from this entrepreneurial process. Well over half of them received no significant inherited wealth and most of the rest gained their fortunes from entrepreneurial parents.

Entrepreneurial knowledge has very little to do with certified expertise of advanced degrees or the learning of establishment schools. It has little to do with the gregarious charm or the valedictory scope of the students judged most likely to succeed in every high school class. The fashionably educated and cultivated spurn the kind of fanatically focused learning commanded by the Four Hundred. Wealth usually comes from doing what other people consider insufferably boring.

The treacherous intricacies of building codes or garbage routes or software languages or groceries, the mechanics of butchering sheep and pigs or frying and freezing potatoes, the mazes of high-yield bonds and low-collateral companies, the murky lore of petroleum leases or housing deeds or Far Eastern electronics supplies, the ways and means of pushing pizzas or insurance policies or hawking hosiery or pet supplies, the grind of grubbing for pennies in fast-food unit sales, the chemistry of soap or candy or the silicon/silicon dioxide interface, the endless round of motivating workers and blandishing union bosses and federal inspectors and the IRS and EPA: all are considered tedious and trivial by the established powers.

Most people think they are above learning the gritty and relentless details of life that allow the creation of great wealth. They leave it to the experts. But in general you join the Four Hundred not by leaving it to the experts but by creating new expertise, not by knowing what the experts know but by learning what they think is beneath them.

Because entrepreneurship overthrows establishments rather than undergirds them, the entrepreneurial tycoons mostly begin as rebels and outsiders. Often they live in out-of-the-way places—like Bentonville, Arkansas; Omaha, Nebraska; or Mission Hills, Kansas—mentioned in New York, at all, as the punch lines of comedy routines. When these entrepreneurs move into high society, they are usually inheritors on the way down.

In a sense, entrepreneurship is the launching of surprises. What bothers many critics of capitalism is that a group like the Forbes Four Hundred is too full of surprises. Sam Walton opens a haberdashery and it goes broke. He opens another and it works. He launches a shopping center empire in the rural South and becomes America's richest man. Who would have thunk it? Forrest Mars goes bankrupt, fails twice in other ventures, then builds a fortune in candy bars. Bill Gates drops out of Harvard and founds a software company that brings IBM into personal computers. J.R. Simplot makes his fortune in potatoes and then takes a flyer in his eighties on microchip technology, chipping in another $100 million to his portfolio.

This process of wealth creation is offensive to levelers and because it yields mountains of new wealth in ways that could not possibly be planned. But unpredictability is fundamental to free human enterprise. It defies every econometric model and socialist scheme. It makes no sense to most professors, who their positions by the systematic acquisition of credentials pleasing to the establishment above them. By definition, innovations cannot be planned. Leading entrepreneurs—from Jack Simplot to Michel Milken—did not ascend a hierarchy; they created a new one. They did not climb to the top of anything. They were pushed to the top by their own success. They did not capture the pinnacle, they became it.

This process creates wealth. But to maintain and increase it is nearly as difficult. A pot of honey attracts flies as well as bears. Bureaucrats, politicians, bishops, raiders, robbers, revolutionaries, short-sellers, managers, business writers, and missionaries all think they could invest money better than its owners. Owners are besieged on all sides by aspiring spenders—debauchers of wealth and purveyors of poverty in the name of charity, idealism, envy, or social change. In fact, of all the people on the face of the globe it is only the legal owners of businesses who have a clear interest in building wealth for others rather than spending it on themselves.

Leading entrepreneurs in general consume only a tiny portion of their holdings. Usually they are owners and investors. As owners, they are the ones damaged most by mismanagement or the exploitation or waste of their assets.

As long as Bill Gates is in charge of Microsoft, it will probably grow in value. But if you put Harry Homeless in charge of Microsoft—or if as Harry's proxy you put a government bureaucrat in charge—within minutes the company would be worth half its former value. As other software firms, such as Oracle and Lotus, discovered in the early 1990s, a software stock can lose most of its worth in minutes if fashions shift or investors distrust the management.

As a Harvard Business School study recently showed, even if you put "professional management" at the helm of great wealth, value is likely to grow less rapidly than if you give owners the real control. A manager of Microsoft might benefit from stealing from it or turning it into his own special preserve, making self-indulgent "investments" in company planes and playgrounds or favored foundations that were in fact his own disguised consumption. It is only Gates who would see his own wealth drop catastrophically if he began to focus less on his customers than on his own consumption. The key to his wealth is his resolution neither to spend nor to abandon it. In a sense, Gates is as much the slave as the master of Microsoft.

The government could not capture America's wealth even if it wished to. As Marxist despots and tribal socialists from Cuba to Angola have discovered to their huge disappointment, governments can expropriate wealth, but cannot appropriate it or redistribute it. In the United States as well, a left ward administration could destroy the value of the Four Hundred's property but could not seize it or pass it on. In general, the confiscated banks and savings and loans of recent years accelerated their losses under government management and regulation.

Under capitalism, wealth is less a stock of goods than a flow of ideas. Joseph Schumpeter propounded the basic rule when he declared capitalism a "form of change" that "never can be stationary." The landscape of capitalism may seem solid and settled and thus seizable; but capitalism is really a mindscape.

Volatile and shifting ideas, not heavy and entrenched establishments, constitute the source of wealth. There is no bureaucratic net or tax web that can catch the fleeting thoughts of Gordon Moore of Intel or Michael Milken, lately of Pleasanton.

Nonetheless, in this mindscape of capitalism, all riches finally fall into the gap between thoughts and things. Governed by mind but caught in matter, to retain its value an asset must afford an income stream that is expected to continue. The expectation can shift as swiftly as thought, but the things, alas, are all too solid and slow to change.

Sam Walton's shopping centers, Bill Gate's software copyrights, John Kluge's TV stations, Lester Crown's skyscrapers, David Packard's chip factories, Fred Trammel Crow's building projects, the Hunt brothers' oil and real estate, Warren Buffett's media stocks, Craig McCaw's cellular franchises, David Rockefeller's real estate and banking interests all could become shattered monuments of Ozymandias tomorrow. "Look on my works, ye Mighty and despair!" Shelley wrote in the voice of the king whose empires became mere mounds in the desert sands. Like the deep gas of Oklahoma, the commercial real estate of Houston, the steel mills of Pittsburgh, the railroad grid of New England, the great printing presses of a decade ago, the supercomputers of a year ago, the giant nuclear plants of yesteryear, or the sartorial rage of last week, the physical base of the Four Hundred can be a trap of wealth, not a treasure chest.

In recent years, for example, Arthur Rock's venture holdings, Austin Furst's videocassette rights, Ken Pontikes's computer leases, Roy Speer and Lowell Paxon's Home Shopping Network all tumbled out of the mindscape of value. Earlier years saw the demise of scores of oil and real estate fortunes in Texas and Oklahoma. The underlying oil and buildings did not change. In all these cases, the *things* stayed pretty much the same. But *thoughts* about them changed. Much of what was supremely valuable in 1980 plunged to near worthlessness by 1990.

Overseas interests could buy the buildings and the rapidly obsolescing equipment and patents of high-technology firms. But they would probably fail to reproduce the leadership, savvy, and loyalty lost in the sale. If the Japanese or Arabs bought all of Silicon Valley, for example, they might well do best by returning it to the production of apricots, oranges, and bedrooms for San Francisco. Capturing the worth of a company is incomparably more complex and arduous a task than purchasing it.

In the Schumpeterian mindscape of capitalism, the entrepreneurial owners are less captors than captives of their wealth. If they try to take it or exploit it, it will tend to evaporate. As Bill Gates puts it, he is "tied to the mast" of Microsoft. David Rockefeller devoted a lifetime of sixty hour weeks to his own enterprises. Younger members of the family wanted to get at the wealth, and now after the sale of Rockefeller Center to Mitsubishi they command much of it. But they will discover that they can keep it only to the extent that they serve it, and thereby serve others, rather than themselves.

Wealth is valuable only to the extent others think it will be valuable in the future. Its value depends on running a fortune for the needs of the customers rather than for the interests of the owners. Its worth will collapse overnight if the market believes that the firm is chiefly serving its owner rather than he serving it, or that it is chiefly being run for the managers rather than for the people who buy its wares. The minds of the customers are ultimately sovereign even over the mindscape of America's entrepreneurs.

In feudal and socialist realms, in the third world or behind the increasingly porous boundaries of communism, a register of the holdings of material things could capture a fixed distribution of wealth. There, riches reside chiefly in land, natural resources, police powers, and party offices, often held in perpetuity. Under socialism, a Forbes Four Hundred might represent a dominant establishment, combining both political and economic clout.

Socialist regimes try to guarantee the value of things rather than the ownership of them. Thus they tend to destroy the value, which depends on dedicated ownership. In the United States, however, the government guarantees only the right to property, not the worth of it.

The belief that wealth consists not in ideas, attitudes, moral codes, and mental disciplines, but in definable and static things that can be seized and redistributed, is the materialist superstition. It stultified the works of Marx and other prophets of violence and envy. It betrays every person who seeks to redistribute wealth by coercion. It balks every socialist revolutionary who imagines that by seizing the socalled means of production he can capture the crucial capital of an economy. It baffles nearly every conglomerator who believes he can safely enter new industries by buying rather than by learning them. The means of production of entrepreneurs are not land, labor, or capital, but minds and hearts.

The reason for the huge wealth gap between John Kluge and Suzie Saintly, between Harry Helmsley and Harry Homeless, between all the Four Hundred and George Bush, or between Bill Gates and inventor Dan Bricklin or any number of other worthy men and women, is entrepreneurial knowledge and commitment. Most of the richest individuals are bound to the masts of their fortunes. They are allowed to keep their wealth only as long as they give it to others in the form of investments. They know how to maintain and expand their holdings and the market knows of their knowledge. Thus they increase the wealth of America and the opportunities of even the poorest.

The wealth of America is not an inventory of goods; it is an organic, living entity, a fragile pulsing fabric of ideas, expectations, loyalties, moral commitments, visions. To vivisect it for redistribution would eventually kill it. As President Mitterand's French Technocrats discovered in the 1980s, the proud new socialist owners of complex systems of wealth soon learn that they are administering an industrial corpse rather than a growing corporation.

The single most important question for the future of America is how we treat our entrepreneurs. If we smear, harass, overtax, and over regulate them, our liberal politicians will be shocked and horrified to discover how swiftly the physical tokens of the means of production collapse into so much corroded wire, eroding concrete, scrap metal, and jungle rot. They will be amazed how quickly the wealth of America flees to other countries.

Most American entrepreneurs would stay in America. But the new global ganglion of telecommunications would allow them to invest their liquid funds elsewhere at the speed of light down a fiber-optic line. Young entrepreneurs, once determined to start in America the fortunes of future decades, instead would begin them overseas, or not begin them at all, clutching instead to the corpse of a stagnant establishment. Their own worth and the wealth of the United States would decline sharply in the process. But within a few years, other countries would begin to thrive where America once flourished. During recent decades, the secrets of the wealthy have been spreading across the increasingly global mindscape of capitalism.

Even the prospects of the poor in the United States and around the world above all depend on the treatment of the rich. If the rich are immobilized by socialism, the poor will suffer everywhere. High tax rates and oppressive regulations do not keep anyone from being rich. They prevent poor people from getting rich. But if the rich are respected and allowed to risk their wealth—and new rebels are allowed to rise up and challenge them—America will continue to be the land where the last regularly become first by serving others.

This is the spirit of enterprise—but it is best embodied not in the theory of a writer but in the life of an entrepreneur, a story that leads from the old frontier to the new.

PRIVATE CORPOCRACY

Michael Rothschild

In business, the groups that join together to form an enterprise—investors, managers, and employees—must all benefit from their relationships if the organization is to remain healthy and competitive in its market. Unfair, exploitive relationships among the parties weaken the organization. Managers who exploit workers with below market wages and dangerous working conditions cause high employee turnover, shoddy workmanship, absenteeism, and strikes. Workers who exploit management through restrictive work rules and job featherbedding cause high costs, defective products, and poor customer service.

Exploitive labor/management relationships afflict many firms. And, generally speaking, firms that fail to remedy exploitive internal relationships eventually are forced out of business by competitors who enjoy predominantly mutualistic relationships. Poor labor/management relations inside American steel and auto firms accelerated their loss of market share to Japanese firms, which carefully cultivate mutualistic corporate cultures. Whether they wear the hat of management or of labor, unchecked internal parasites can kill off their host organizations.

In fact, although exploitive worker/manager relationships traditionally have received the most attention, the real problem area in the United States today is the relationship between a company's owners its shareholders and its management. Parasitism tends to afflict the very largest companies far more often than it affects smaller firms. Corporate behemoths, like elephants that harbor huge tapeworms, are so immense that they can endure decades of parasitic damage. Smaller firms, struggling for survival in hotly competitive niches, tend to die off quickly when weakened by parasitism.

A corporation's shareholders depend on management to organize the company's people and equipment. Ideally, a mutualistic relationship exists. Executives are paid high salaries and benefits in exchange for delivering sufficient profits on the capital invested by the shareholders. If the shareholders fail to compensate the executives well enough, they jump ship to other firms where the shareholders are more appreciative. By the same token, if the executives fail to manage the company's resources effectively, the shareholders fire them and bring in new managers. Excessive demands by either shareholders or executives are kept in check by the alternatives available in the marketplaces for investment capital and executive talent.

While this system works pretty well in small and medium size corporations, it often breaks down in extremely large companies. As a firm grows into a giant, the original investors, who monitored management carefully, sell off their shares to thousands of small shareholders. Effective ownership power dissipates. A "commons problem" emerges because no single shareholder has a strong proprietary interest.

The small shareholder realizes that she owns far too little of the firm to be influential in its affairs. Consequently, most small shareholders pay no attention to what's going on inside the companies whose shares they own. As long as the company's stock price keeps rising, the small shareholder is happy. If the price falls, she usually becomes disenchanted, sells her shares, and puts the money into another firm's stock. By selling out, she avoids further losses. But the problems that caused the stock price to decline often go unremedied. One of the fundamental tenets of capitalism breaks down. Owners do not attempt to nurture the growth of their capital.

Under corporate law, a company's board of directors is obligated to protect the financial interests of the shareholders. But where no shareholder is wealthy enough to own more than a sliver of the company, board members usually are nominated by the company's top manager, the chief executive officer (CEO). So-called "inside" board members are senior executives who work for the CEO. "Outside" directors typically are attorneys, bankers, and consultants who do not work directly for the CEO but whose firms depend in part on the CEO's willingness to do business with them. Quite often, outside board members are simply old friends and supporters of the CEO.

The market-feedback loop that keeps management responsive to shareholders breaks down. A two-way mutualistic relationship—high pay, "perks," and power for executives in exchange for excellent returns on investment for shareholders—is transformed into a one-sided, parasitic relationship. In the absence of effective shareholder power, all real authority is ceded to top management. Rather than playing the role of managers hired to perform a job, subject to dismissal for poor results, executives atop large companies gain de facto control over the shareholders. The balance of power between owners and managers shifts decisively and allows the top executive group—sometimes called a "corpocracy"—to sink a hook into the shareholders. Like a tapeworm, a corpocracy can feed undetected for decades on the wealth of a great corporation.

Among the many American firms infected with this silent, parasitic disease was Walt Disney Productions, the multibillion-dollar business empire built by Mickey Mouse, Donald Duck, Snow White, and the other well-loved denizens of the Magic Kingdom. The roots of the company's corpocracy problem can be traced back to Walt Disney's unexpected death in 1966. Disney, a storytelling wizard and marketing genius, was one of those rare entrepreneurial personalities who, by virtue of talent, drive, and ambition, constructed a fabulously successful enterprise almost single-handedly. His untimely death left his company without its prime creative force and business visionary.

His death also left the company with a power vacuum at the top. Because Walt and his family members held the controlling interest in the firm, Walt wielded all power. His decisions were law. The board of directors was a rubber stamp. When Walt died, the board did not even attempt to search for a CEO talented enough to replace him. Instead, Card Walker, Disney's senior marketing executive, a man with no filmmaking experience, grabbed the top spot and the board of directors went along.

The financial momentum built up while Disney was still at the helm obscured the impact of his death and carried the company through the 1970s. Walt Disney World, the enormous theme park in Florida that Walt conceived and designed, was opened to the public in 1971. Its constantly climbing attendance levels, along with the continuing growth of Disneyland in southern California, drove the company's revenues and profits higher year after year.

But the Disney movie studio, the heart and soul of the company, had become the laughing-stock of Hollywood. By 1984, the studio had gone 15 years since its last live action hit—The *Love Bug*. Throughout the 1970s, the studio churned out insipid formula films like *The Boatniks*, *The Shaggy D.A.*, and *The Unidentified Flying Oddball*. A flourishing center of filmmaking ingenuity under Walt's leadership, the studio had become hopelessly outdated, producing "fresh-scrubbed, wholesome family entertainment" for a society that had changed dramatically since the 1960s. While George Lucas and Steven Spielberg produced such immensely profitable movies as *Star Wars* and *E.T.*—films that the Disney studio should have made—Card Walker kept asking himself, "What would Walt have done?"The public's tastes had changed, but Disney's corpocrats could do no better than crank out mindless imitations of products the market no longer wanted.

The studio had accounted for more than half of total company revenues before Walt Disney World opened, but by 1979 it generated less than 20 percent of sales. And half of that came from regular reissues of the great Disney animated classics like *Snow White*, *Bambi*, *Pinocchio*, and

Fantasia. Stifled by management's aversion to innovation, talented young animators quit the studio for places where they were allowed to do challenging work. With each passing year, Disney made fewer films and its share of the movie market dwindled, but the costs of maintaining the studio did not. Consequently, the profits of the film division slipped from $35 million in 1981 to $20 million in 1982, and 1983 saw a loss of $33 million.

Despite rising attendance at the theme parks, the studio's loss caused a drop in overall profits, and falling profits finally awakened Wall Street to the company's profound troubles. Many investors feared that without successful films keeping the Disney magic alive, attendance at the theme parks eventually would decline. As pessimism about Disney's long-term viability took hold, many investors dumped their shares, and the price of Disney stock headed south. In one year, the stock's price slumped from $80 to $50.

At the annual shareholders' meeting in February 1984, one man stood up and pleaded to the top executives assembled on the dais:

> My mother asked me what stocks to invest in and I advised her to buy Disney when it was at $85. It started going down, and she keeps calling me and asking me why, and I say, "Don't worry, Mother. It will come back up; it's a great company." I'm tired of answering her questions now, so if I give you her number, will you call her and explain what's going on so she will get off my back?

This shareholder's dismay was nothing compared to that of Walt's nephew, Roy E. Disney, the company's largest single largest shareholder. With more than a million Disney shares in his portfolio, the drop from $80 to $50 a share had cost him a paper loss of more than $30 million. Yet, with nearly 35 million shares of stock on the market, Roy's shares accounted for only 3 percent of total ownership. Ousting top management would require the support of 51 percent of the shares. With share ownership so widely dispersed among thousands of investors, Roy was powerless.

Card Walker consistently had ignored Roy's advice to reinvigorate the studio. Ron Miller, Walt's son-in-law and the number two man in the company hierarchy, was more sympathetic, but he did little to improve the studio. "Card would listen but not hear; Ron would listen but not act," said one former executive. Roy Disney knew that his chances of rescuing the Magic Kingdom from its corpocracy were practically nil.

As is typically the case, the parasitism of the Disney corpocracy was not overt. Disney executives did not pay themselves outrageous salaries or provide perks out of line with normal practices. In fact, salaries were modest by Hollywood standards. Card Walker and Ron Miller were not evil or malicious people. By all accounts, they were fine human beings trying to do the very best job they could.

The problem was that their best wasn't good enough. Top managers, like professionals in any field, must be measured against the best talent available. Card Walker and Ron Miller just didn't have the "right stuff." Being born without the talents of Walt Disney is no sin, but clinging to powerful positions that demand extraordinary ability becomes a parasitic act once the organization's financial results show that performance consistently falls short of reasonable investor expectations.

The steep drop in Disney's stock price attracted the attention of several corporate raiders, the top predators in the corporate jungle. Always on the lookout for weakened prey, they target firms that cannot keep pace with the herd. Not always, but quite often, these financial strugglers are organizations whose profits are being drained away by a parasitic corpocracy. In an environment where large companies frequently are parasitized by incompetent managements, there are hundreds of diseased firms from which to choose. The rational raider—and they all are remorselessly rational—targets the firm he believes will yield the richest profits for the risks involved in the takeover chase.

Saul Steinberg, a Wall Street raider known for getting rid of the managements in the companies he takes over, decided to take a close look at the Disney situation. He began by having his staff prepare an exhaustive evaluation of the company's assets. Essentially, Disney was comprised of three parts. The first was the library of hundreds of cartoons, movies, and TV shows that had been produced since the company began in 1923. The second piece consisted of the two theme park Disneyland and Walt Disney World. The third was 17,000 acres of undeveloped land in Florida surrounding Walt Disney World.

While the stock market consensus of buyers and sellers valued the ongoing operations of the company at $50 a share, or roughly $1.75 billion ($50 a share times 35 million shares), Steinberg's appraisal of the three pieces totaled about $3.5 billion, or 100 a share. Instead of the whole company being worth more than the sum of its parts—the economic rationale for any organization—because of mismanagement the business was worth less than its physical assets. In short, the Disney corporation was worth twice as much dead as alive.

But knowing that a property is a fantastic bargain does not necessarily mean you have the wherewithal to acquire it Even the very wealthiest investors do not have the cash to buy up a 51 percent controlling interest in a firm that, even at a depressed stock price, was still worth nearly $2 billion. For this reason, the sheer enormity of companies such as Disney protected them from raiders even when, economically speaking, they deserved to die. The fiercest lion is still too puny to bring down the most parasitized bull elephant. By infesting organizations too huge to be attacked by predators, the corpocracies kept safe and snug, beyond the reach of predators eager to dismember their hosts—and them.

Only a major economic innovation could upset these bionomic relationships and make these lumbering giants vulnerable to corporate predators. In 1977, just such an economic mutation took place when the "junk bond" was invented by Michael Milken of the Wall Street firm Drexel Burnham Lambert. Although Milken and Drexel Burnham later would be convicted and bankrupted for violating U.S. securities laws, the invention of junk bonds took place well before those transgressions and is regarded by experts as a major contribution to the field of corporate finance.

Simply put, a bond is a loan agreement. Like a mortgage or a promissory note, a bond is an IOU, a piece of paper signed by a borrower that promises to repay the loan with interest. A "junk" bond is nothing more than a bond that promises to pay the lender an unusually high rate of interest—say, 15 percent when U.S. government bonds are paying 10 percent. There's nothing magical about junk bonds—it's just that in the hidebound world of high finance, no one had ever arranged such financings before Milken began doing it.

Wall Street tradition said that bonds could be issued only at normal interest rates by blue-chip companies. But Milken realized that hundreds of smaller corporations—companies snubbed by Wall Street as "junk," too risky to lend to—were perfectly sound and legitimately needed to borrow money to finance expansion. Milken believed that if high interest loans were made to enough of these up-and-coming firms, the investors—wealthy individuals, banks, pension funds, corporations, and mutual funds—could be protected from the risk of default. A few of these small companies would go bankrupt and not pay back their loans, but the great majority would pay back, and the extra interest earned on a diversified portfolio of junk bonds would more than offset the incremental risk to investors.

It took some time for junk bonds to catch on, but by 1983, they had grown to represent about 5 percent of the $400 billion American corporate bond market. As the middleman between borrowers who needed cash and investors who wanted high interest rates, Milken and his firm collected a fee of 3 to 4 percent of the bonds they sold. Milken and his firm grew fabulously rich in this previously unoccupied niche of the market for capital.

With investors clamoring for more high-yield bonds, Milken began to search for other kinds of borrowers, people who needed billions and whose projects could tolerate the hefty fees and interest charges. In an adjacent niche of the corporate finance market—a niche populated by smart but puny predators and parasitized corporate behemoths—Milken found his new borrowers.

Corporate raiders, such as Saul Steinberg, were perfect borrowers for the capital source that Milken had tapped. Milken's junk bonds worked like an instantaneous supergrowth hormone, turning individuals into economic giants able to devour the largest corporate prey. Almost overnight, the availability of junkbond financing set off the feeding frenzy of hostile takeovers that reshaped much of corporate America in the 1980s.

Steinberg's plan to buy up 51 percent of Disney's shares on the open stock market would absorb more than $1 billion of borrowed money. After gaining control of Disney, Steinberg planned to sell off enough of the company's assets to pay off the junk bonds. Steinberg and the shareholders who chose to hold onto their shares would wind up owning downsized Disney. Steinberg's plan for the company is the plan behind most hostile takeovers.

In accordance with federal law, Steinberg publicly announced that he had purchased several million shares of Disney. He then offered to buy all the additional shares he needed at a premium over the stock-market price. The premium represented an immediate profit for shareholders willing to sell. A board of directors looking out for the interests of shareholders at least might have considered the offer. After all, it would, have benefited the shareholders, whose interests the board was legally bound to protect.

But Disney's executives didn't want to lose control of "their" company. They rejected Steinberg's offer and, with the board's support began a series of anti takeover maneuvers. After decades of inaction management suddenly decided that the time was right to buy a Florida land development company—the Arvida Corporation. They paid for Arvida by issuing new shares of Disney stock to the Bass brothers, the owners of Arvida. With more Disney shares outstanding, Steinberg's recently purchased 12 percent position shrank to 11 percent.

Through intermediaries, Disney executives made it clear to Steinberg that they would use every legal technique to keep him from snatching control of the company. They announced plans for another major acquisition—Gibson Greeting Cards. If this deal went through, Steinberg's ownership position would be diluted further. But Steinberg knew before he started his attack that a vigorous defense was likely. Like any shrewd businessman, he had a fallback position.

Steinberg continued buying up Disney shares while simultaneously offering to sell his shares back to the company at a premium over the market price. In essence, Steinberg offered to abandon the chase and leave the company alone if the corpocracy paid him off. After much pious soul-searching, Disney's board of directors, at the urging of top management, did exactly that. Using company funds—the property of the shareholders—Disney's management bought back Steinberg's stock, leaving him with a $32 million "greenmail" profit.

"It's an outrage. They have raped the shareholders," fumed one livid Wall Street trader. In a torrent of articles, speeches, and editorials, the investment community and the press pilloried Disney's management and Saul Steinberg. Shareholders launched lawsuits. Congress held hearings. But it was all perfectly legal. Under corporate law, a company can buy back shares owned by one shareholder at a price not offered to all shareholders. Without a shareholder vote, the board of directors has the power to use company money—again, shareholders' money—to pay a threatening shareholder to go away.

But Steinberg's profitable retreat did not end the Disney takeover battle. In fact, his attack set the stage for a takeover campaign led by Roy Disney, who had been waiting in the wings. In a complex series of moves and counter moves, the Roy Disney forces assembled a coalition of major shareholders. The most important among them were the Bass brothers, formerly the owners of Arvida, who now owned a large chunk of Disney. Together, these shareholding allies had the concentrated ownership power needed to overthrow Disney's executives. With effective shareholder power restored, the days of Disney's corpocracy were numbered. Realizing the game was lost, Card Walker and Ron Miller quit, and the Roy Disney/Bass brothers coalition replaced them with a team led by Michael Eisner and Frank Wells. Eisner had been president of Paramount Pictures, and Wells had been president of Warner Brothers. Both had outstanding track records in Hollywood.

Within months of their ascension to top spots at Disney, Eisner and Wells revitalized the company, attracting new talent to the long neglected studio. In 1988, Disney became the leader in box-office receipts among all Hollywood studios, with hits such as *Who Framed Roger Rabbit?*; *Good Morning, Vietnam*; and *Three Men and a Baby*. Only four years earlier, Disney had finished last at the box office. The videocassette of Pinocchio became one of the best-selling videos ever released. Disney's network television show, "The Wonderful World of Disney," which had been canceled in 1983 after 29 years on the air, reappeared as "The Disney Sunday Movie." George Lucas, Francis Ford Coppola, and Michael Jackson were brought in to create a new Disneyland and Epcot attraction called Captain EO.

Revenues and profits soared. Investors expressed their renewed confidence in the company's future by bidding its stock up to $145 in March 1986, just two years after Saul Steinberg began buying up shares at $50. Riding a wave of enthusiasm about Disney's long-term prospects, the company whose stock the market thought was worth $1.75 billion had nearly tripled to $5 billion in just 24 months.

Despite the storybook ending that saved the Magic Kingdom from demolition, the Disney takeover battle left the general public and lawmakers with a distorted perception of the problems that had set off the battle in the first place. Most media attention focused on the $32 million that Saul Steinberg had reaped from 90 days of jousting with Disney's management. Many were outraged by Steinberg's plan to break up "a national treasure." A *Los Angeles Times* columnist wrote, "Breaking up Disney to cash in on its assets would be on the order of smashing a Tiffany vase to get at a penny that fell inside." No one acknowledged that a silent, parasitic disease had been devouring this national treasure from within for two decades.

The sudden, bloody acts of predators—from a lion's dismemberment of a parasitized water buffalo to a corporate raider's breakup of a familiar-yet-diseased company—affront our sensibilities. But, like top predators in an ecosystem, corporate predators serve a vital economic role. They weed out weak firms that mismanage people and resources. Predators kill for their own profit, but, in so doing, they begin the process of recycling scarce skills and equipment back into healthy and productive organizations. It is parasitism by corpocracies, not predation by takeover artists, that weakens an economy. The real enemy of efficiency, growth, and innovation is inept and shortsighted management.

Saul Steinberg was not a parasite because he had no "hook." After risking $265 million to buy 11 percent of the Disney shares, he had to go ahead and purchase another 40 percent or sit around and hope that something would boost the value of his holdings. He never had the power to extract a quick profit. Only the Disney board of directors had that legal power. A capable and confident board, acting in the interests of the shareholders instead of the corpocrats, would have welcomed Steinberg as a savvy shareholder with worthwhile ideas. But Steinberg knew that Disney's corpocrats would use their "hook" into the shareholders' purse to extract a bribe.

Steinberg's fast $32 million is the kind of number that draws attention. Few realize that the long-term ineptitude of Disney's top management cost the shareholders far more. The difference between the $50 share price under the Card Walker/Ron Miller regime and the $145 stock price under Michael Eisner/Frank Wells amounted to about $3.3 billion. Compared to the $32 million "green mail" crumb tossed to Steinberg, two decades of unobtrusive, persistent parasitism by an entrenched corpocracy had cost Disney's shareholders more than 100 times as much.

Because Disney is such a well-known company, its takeover saga sparked a surge of interest in "reforming" corporate takeover law. In 1985 alone, more than 50 bills were introduced in Congress to deal with the sudden surge in takeover activity. More than 20 hearings were held by nine committees. The testimony of the experts was divided over whether hostile takeovers are good or bad for the economy, and not one piece of legislation came close to passing. America's lawmakers were baffled. Should society limit the ability of corporate raiders to buy stock in public companies and wrest control away from their current managements?

Legislative confusion stemmed from the fact that attention was focused on the symptoms rather than the cause of the disease. Many lawmakers wanted to stamp out the "epidemic of takeovers," but few understood the conditions that had spawned them. At the state level, several legislatures wrote laws dealing with takeover tactics that had created a whole new business vocabulary—"greenmail," "poison pill," "shark repellent," "golden parachute," "Pac-Man defense," and "crown jewels lockup." For the most part, changes in state laws further entrenched management power. Not one addressed the erosion in shareholder power that had created corpocracies, weakened companies, and caused hostile takeovers to become economically sensible.

Difficult public-policy questions arise whenever the parasitic/mutualistic qualities of an economic activity are unclear. To keep the law in step with a fast evolving economy, lawmakers need to understand precisely which new economic phenomena are parasitic and which are not. In the search for a parasite, the only reliable clue is finding its economic "hook." Legislators who ignore the hook and focus on takeover tactics are like doctors who treat the stomach pains of a tapeworm victim by prescribing an antacid. No cure is possible unless the parasite's hook is purged from the host.

In America's corporate world, the hook is the nearly invulnerable power of the corpocracies. At present, company managements nominate new directors and draft the resolutions mailed to shareholders. Dissident shareholders must overcome several legal hurdles to get their views printed on proxy statements. Managements control shareholder mailing lists. Managements even count shareholder votes. Voting does indeed take place, but the result is a foregone conclusion in all except the rarest of situations.

In the United States, the laws governing the relationships between shareholders and managements are written at the state level. Since choosing the state of incorporation seems like a technical legal matter, shareholders rarely object to the state selected by management. But the choice of a corporation's state of legal residence makes an enormous difference in the balance of power between shareholders and management. The favorite state of corpocracies is Delaware. To attract such lucrative legal business, the Delaware legislature has doubled over backward to make the rules absurdly favorable to management. More than half of the Fortune 500 firms are registered in tiny Delaware. Shareholders trying to block an unfair action by the management of a "Delaware" corporation are out of luck.

But Delaware is not the only state that abuses shareholder rights. Across the country, under the guise of protecting workers' jobs, state legislatures have passed laws that further strengthen the powers of top management. Legislators understandably are anxious to help constituents threatened with the loss of jobs in takeovers led by "rapacious Wall Street predators." With little hesitation, they pass laws authorizing new anti-takeover defenses. These lawmakers fail to recognize that the only true protection for jobs is companies that are consistently well managed and intensely competitive. Only independent boards of directors that aggressively represent the interests of shareholders can force managements to work to their fullest potential.

Political realism suggests that the managements running America's largest firms will be able to thwart the reforms that would strengthen the independence of corporate boards. Unlike worker/management battles, this isn't the kind of issue that excites the passions of voters. Consequently, many of America's largest companies, weakened by inept managements, will continue losing contests with foreign competitors, while lawmakers remain oblivious to the fact that existing corporate laws condemn the nation's largest firms, and the millions who depend on them, to slow death by parasitism.

The only bright spot in this otherwise-dismal picture is the growing power of pension funds, which manage the retirement savings of millions of American workers. Today, the funds own about one third of the stock of all public companies—nearly twice as much as they held in 1970. The professional money managers who vote the stocks owned by these funds are strictly regulated by federal pension law and are obliged to earn the highest possible return for their worker-owners. In the last few years, fund managers have begun to assert themselves, demanding that managements and directors act in the best interests of shareholders.

Pension funds are now opposing management proposals that would further erode corporate democracy and shareholder rights. They are voting against the plans of some corpocracies that want to entrench themselves further by issuing new stock that carries no voting rights. In this pivotal but virtually unreported battle for economic power, pension funds are insisting that the "one share, one vote" principle be maintained.

Now that working people are on the verge of accumulating the dominant ownership position in America's largest corporations, executives in these companies want to abolish the fundamental link between the ownership of and power over capital. Ironically, it is America's workers who, through their pension funds, are fighting to protect the most basic property rights of the capitalist system. Genuine corporate democracy—where shareholders have the power to hire and fire the managers running their companies—seems cruelly unfair to a corpocratic clique grown accustomed to the perquisites of the parasitic life.

No one can accurately calculate the damage done to the American economy by corpocracies. One guess puts the total cost of corpocracy at more than $800 billion per year. At 16 percent of America's GNP, this estimate probably is way too high. But whatever the invisible cost of corpocracy, it certainly dwarfs the annual $13 billion damage done by all the highly publicized parasitic acts of robbery, burglary, larceny, and auto theft.

How much more efficient and internationally competitive would America's corporations be if all executives were held to reasonable performance standards? Would America have lost the automobile industry to Japan if Detroit's Big Three had not been so hopelessly paralyzed by corporate bureaucracy? Just a 5 percent increase in the sales of America's 500 largest firms would yield a $150 billion rise in GNP and several hundred thousand new jobs.

Without question, our standard of living would rise significantly if the corpocracies were purged from corporate America. In all likelihood, however, the required reforms will not be implemented. Like enormous tapeworms, these persistent, unobtrusive parasites will be sapping our economic strength for a very long time to come.

PUBLIC BUREAUCRACY

Michael Rothschild

I t's hard to believe that America might be infected by an even more devastating form of economic parasitism than corpocracy. But, sadly large-scale exploitation is not limited to the domain of private enterprise. Economic parasitism exists wherever an organization has the power to attach itself to a host. Whether the parasite and host happen to be in the private or the public sector is irrelevant.

Without question, the most debilitating case of public sector parasitism involves America's public schools. Few interpret the demise of these schools as an example of economic parasitism, but all the usual symptoms of this organizational disease are readily apparent. The sole objective of a public school system is to produce a well educated citizenry. But, as exhaustive studies have shown and the personal experiences of millions of Americans can attest, the U.S. public-school system is a catastrophic failure. For the last three decades, the organization charged by American society with responsibility for preparing literate, economically competent adults has been in an appalling tailspin.

For a democratic society seriously challenged by powerful foreign economic competitors, the litany of public-school failures is ominous. More than 25 percent of American high-school students drop out before graduation. Of those who remain in school, only one in five eleventh graders is able to write a note applying for a summer job at a swimming pool. Only one in five young adults is able to read a schedule well enough to figure out when a bus will arrive at a terminal. Less than 40 percent of Americans in the twenty-one to twenty-five-year old bracket are able to read well enough to interpret an article by a newspaper columnist. Among blacks, the ratios fall to just one in ten.

Less than one-third of high-school seniors know in which half century the Civil War occurred, what the Magna Carta was, what the Reformation was, or that the Declaration of Independence is the document that marked the separation of the American colonies from Great Britain or that Lincoln wrote the Emancipation Prolamation.

Even the performance of America's very best students has collapsed. In international rankings of top high-school students, America's advanced science students were near the bottom in chemistry and physics. In biology, they came in dead last, behind such nations as Singapore and Thailand.

Just half the nation's 17-year-olds can solve math problems at the junior-high level, and fewer than one in 15 can cope with problems at the high-school level that require several steps or involve algebra or geometry. In a calculus and algebra test comparing the best students in 11 industrial countries, the top 5 percent of U.S. high-school seniors came in last. In fact, America's top math students scored below Japan's *average* 17 year-olds. Among fifth graders, the situation is even worse. The *lowest* math and science test scores in Japan are higher than the *highest* scores in comparable American schools.

While Japanese kids spend about 1,100 hours each year in actual study time at school (240 days a year at 4.7 hours a day), American kids put in only about 500 hours per year (180 days a year at 2.8 hours a day). After the typical Japanese student gets home, he puts in at least two hours a day on homework, while his American counterpart exerts no more than 30 minutes of effort. One education expert comments "People often say that our best and brightest can compare with Japan's best and brightest, who only memorize. But it's simply not true." One need look no farther than the nearest classroom to explain America's accelerating decline and Japan's emerging dominance.

Americans worry that too many new jobs are low-pay and low-skill, but our schools simply are not turning out enough graduates capable of performing in high skill occupations. Recently, more than 80 percent of the applicants taking a simple test for entry level jobs at New York Telephone flunked. While the newspapers are filled with listings for high-skill jobs that go begging for qualified applicants, the flood of dropouts and functional illiterates disgorged by the public school system swells a pool of 30 million illiterate adults already trapped in menial jobs.

Without question, student performance has been hurt by the social ills of shattered families, violence, and drugs. But these plagues cannot account for the whole problem. After years of intense publicity, Americans have concluded that the public school system desperately needs fixing. Democracy is imperiled in a nation that has forgotten its heritage. With intensifying global economic competition and advancing technological complexity, good jobs will not go to near illiterates just because they happen to be *American* near-illiterates. But the problem, as always, is to figure out what pragmatic steps can reverse the decline. The advice of the education establishment—teachers' unions, school boards, superintendents, and colleges of education—is not surprising. In short, their response to the crisis is, "Give us more money and we'll do a better job."

But, contrary to common perceptions, the resources devoted to public education have climbed rapidly during the 30 years of the system's performance collapse. In 1950, public schools consumed 2 percent of America's GNP to educate its school-age population. By 1986, it took 3.5 percent for the same portion of the population. If private and public colleges are included, America now spends more on education than it spends on its other grotesquely bloated system—defense.

On a per-student basis, the United States spends more on its public schools than any nation except Switzerland. Adjusted for inflation, one year of public school for one student cost $1,200 in 1952; by 1989, it cost $4,400. During the same period, average scores on Scholastic Aptitude Tests collapsed. In short, while the quality of American education disintegrated, the price society paid to the public school system to produce one student year nearly *quadrupled*. The claim that inadequate spending is the problem simply does not hold water.

Clearly, something is profoundly wrong with an organization that consumes ever more resources to produce an ever more pitiful product. Indeed, the record of the American public school system shows a negative "learning curve"—ever higher costs for deteriorating performance. One clue to the cause of this disease can be seen in the shift in the mix of spending by public schools. In 1955, nearly 55 percent of school operating budgets went to teacher salaries. By 1985, just 40 percent went to pay teachers. This shift was not caused by fewer teachers. In fact, since 1965, as the number of students fell 8 percent, the number of teachers grew 29 percent. An expanding teacher population absorbed a declining portion of public-school budgets, because the number of administrators and other nonteaching staffers grew even faster—jumping to 102 percent.

Of course, every sizable organization needs people in administrative jobs. There is nothing "wrong" with administration per se. Rules and procedures must be established and maintained if an organization is to run smoothly. Policies need to be decided and communicated. But every new rule or regulation becomes the basis of a new exception. Administrative edicts, like all other forms of information, have an inherent tendency to evolve to greater complexity.

Because the number of rules tends to grow, the number of rule makers must grow with it. The only force powerful enough to counter the inherent tendency of organizations to add administrative overhead is the pressure of competition. Only organizations whose very survival is threatened by high costs have the fortitude to slash unnecessary administrative expenses. Organizations that have no competitors—monopolies—grow immensely inefficient and bureaucratic, because their waste of resources carries with it no threat to organizational survival.

By virtually every measure, the bureaucracy running the Chicago Public Schools system is among the worst in America. Student performance is consistently at the bottom in nationwide rankings. School buildings are in shambles, classes lack funds for basic supplies, and money for teacher raises is unavailable. But the 3,000 bureaucrats who work in the Chicago Board of Education's newly renovated headquarters listen to piped-in music, walk on plush carpets, and enjoy a panoramic view of the city from their well-appointed offices.

Prior to a recent reorganization, Chicago's 514 school principals reported up through a chain of command that included layer after layer of assistant superintendents, associate superintendents, directors, coordinators, and facilitators. Deputy and associate superintendents are still paid $70,000 to $80,000 a year, yet no one is quite sure what they do. Chicago School Superintendent Manford Byrd was paid $110,000 a year but admitted that he didn't know what to do about the city's chronically ailing school system, or why the system's children didn't perform better on standardized tests. When asked about leaking roofs and lacking supplies, he responded, "Money is hard to come by."

Like all other parasites, a bureaucracy lacks the capacity to do anything but grow and reproduce itself. A bureaucracy—that portion of an administrative apparatus that exceeds what is necessary for essential coordinating functions—does not contribute to its host organization. Indeed, a bureaucracy's drain on resources and its excessive rule-making cripples the efficiency of its host. The only way to prevent an administrative group from growing into a bureaucracy is by denying it the money to hire more "administrators." In a market environment, where the organization's survival depends on its efficiency, managers are forced to pare expenses and contain the growth of bureaucracy.

But wherever organizations, private or public, are insulated from competition, there is little to stop the growth of bureaucracy. The bureaucracy becomes the non competing organization's tapeworm, consuming scarce resources and giving nothing back in return. Just as it is impossible for the human immune system to detect a tapeworm ensconced in the intestines, it seems impossible for organization leaders to distinguish clearly between necessary administration and damaging bureaucracy. When it comes to America's public schools, the wildly disproportionate growth in "administrative" spending over the last 30 years shows that the education bureaucracy has mushroomed into a massive parasite. It has absorbed immense quantities of public money, frustrated dedicated teachers, and destroyed the futures of millions of Americans.

Because America's public education bureaucracy is so deeply entrenched and politically potent, the education reform campaign of the last few years has not directly challenged it. Until recently, reformers have limited themselves to changes that the bureaucracy can tolerate—more spending and more new programs to be administered. Teachers' salaries have been increased.

Teacher competency exams have been instituted to weed out the very worst teachers. More money has been granted to establish computerized learning centers and "magnet" schools. Reading and mathematics remedial programs have been launched. Students are being tested more frequently and thoroughly to determine what they have learned. In many states, students now must demonstrate competence in basic skills before being granted a high school diploma. All these reforms are helpful, but they do not strike the schools' disease at its source.

For all the additional spending and new programs, improvement since the early 1980s has been slight. College-entrance-exam scores are up a bit, but they appear to be flattening out again. Dropout rates are higher than ever. Unmistakable signs of a dramatic recovery, indicators of the rapid progress so urgently needed, are nowhere to be found. Such a turnaround will remain elusive, because school reforms, like anti-takeover laws, have addressed the symptoms of parasitism instead of the cause. If the parasitic bureaucracy that has infested America's public schools is to be expelled, its hook must be purged.

The hook is the legal monopoly of America's public school bureaucracies. Except for the 11 percent of children whose parents are wealthy enough to send them to private schools, American kids are subject to the monopoly power of their local school districts. Almost without exception, state laws grant each local school district an exclusive right to provide educational services to the children living within its geographic boundaries. Under penalty of law, children must attend the schools in their district. They must swallow the product their local school district dishes out, however unpalatable. For most, the only real option is dropping out—an arguably rational act for the hundreds of thousands condemned to the nation's worst schools.

Because state laws grant monopolies to each of America's 16,000 local school districts, these organizations do not compete with each other. Regardless of how badly it performs, no district faces the prospect of being put out of business. And even though hundreds of well-run school districts do exist, the problem is that high quality school districts are exceptional. If the system were competitive rather than monopolistic, high quality schools would be the norm.

The only way to cure the parasitic infestation of the American public school system is to sever the parasite from the student body at its point of attachment. Despite all the claims made for other remedies, no other reform can revive American public education. Students and parents, like shareholders, must be granted the power of choice. They must be transformed from captives into consumers. School districts, like all other efficient providers of service, must be forced to compete with each other for customers. The parasitic, involuntary relationship between school district and student must be converted into a mutualistic, voluntary relationship. If, and only if, this reform takes place will radical improvement in education quality occur.

Remarkably, there is hope for real reform. One state, Minnesota, already has recognized that consumer choice and school-district competition are the keys to progress. In May 1988, after a few years of experimentation, Minnesota's legislature passed a bill that stripped school districts of monopoly power. Under the law, students are permitted to leave the school districts in which live and apply for admission to another. The law does not *force* school districts to admit "foreign" students, but once a school board decides that its schools have seats available for a g number of students, it cannot pick and choose among applicants. If too many students want too fe spaces, a lottery determines which students "immigrate" into the district.

Traditionally, the state of Minnesota, like the other 49 states, automatically paid $3,600 directly to the resident school district of every child attending school. Now, the state's money travels with the student. The state funnels the money to whichever school district the student decides to attend. Simply by allowing students to emigrate and backing up their choices with state funds, Minnesota has utterly transformed the relationship between education producers and consumers.

In the new market environment, educational quality, as measured by the performance of students, ultimately will determine the survival of the organization running a school district. If a district fails to deliver a quality education, it will lose $3,600 each time a student transfers out. If the district's schools fail to improve, continuing emigration will force the district to close more and more of its facilities. Ineffective administrators and teachers will lose their jobs. On the other hand, school districts that produce a quality educational product will gain $3,600 with each new customer. If a district has classroom space available, the state's $3,600 is profitable revenue, since each extra student generates only a few hundred dollars in direct costs for books and supplies.

Districts that attract students can reinvest their "profits" however they see fit. Some will use the funds to create programs tailored to the special needs of student customers. Others may boost salaries to recruit outstanding teachers. Whatever decisions are made, they will be driven by the desire to improve performance, because for the first time, job security and organizational survival will be linked directly to student performance. The incentive system that propels the responsiveness of private firms will be replicated in the public domain. Customer satisfaction will become the key to school district survival.

In a society built on freedom of choice, the idea of school choice seems radical only because Americans have grown used to having no choice over their children's schools. But Dr. Ruth Randall, until recently Minnesota's Commissioner of Education, asks:

> Why shouldn't we be able to choose? We can choose our spouse, our church or synagogue or wherever we get our values from. We can choose where we live, our car, the food we eat. We can choose our preschool up to age five. We can choose our college after age 18. Why, between the ages of five and 18, should we not be allowed choice?

In hearings before the Minnesota legislature, school administrators opposed choice largely on the grounds that it would harm minority students. They claimed that some minority students would get left behind in crumbling schools as others headed off to the best suburban districts. But, much to the administrators' embarrassment, black parents vigorously supported the idea of choice. They argued that while middle-class parents can afford to rescue their children by moving to tolerable suburban districts, they are left behind to endure the disastrous schools foisted on them by urban school district bureaucracies. Without the power of consumer choice, they have no leverage over their local schools.

Because the implementation of Minnesota's "open enrollment" plan is so recent, fully documented results will not be available for several years. But a few years earlier, Minnesota launched a trial program—the Secondary Options Program—which allows eleventh- and twelfth-grade high-school students to attend any public or private college in the state. Within months, Minnesota's Secondary Options Program unleashed all the evolutionary phenomena common to market environments—competition, cooperation, innovation cost reduction, and specialization. Now, with choice becoming available at all grade levels in all public schools, these organic processes will take hold and utterly transform Minnesota's schools during the 1990s.

When introduced in the state legislature, the Secondary Options Program was opposed vigorously by the most powerful groups in the state's education establishment—the Minnesota Education Association (the largest teachers' union), the Minnesota Association of School Administrators, and the Minnesota School Board Association. At first, they argued that thousands of kids would abandon their high schools for college. But only a small number of the eligible students actually shifted to colleges. The opposition then contended that the brightest kids would desert the high schools, leaving behind only the poor students.

But analysis showed that the top high-school students didn't move to the colleges. These kids were content where they were. Most transfers were among average students who weren't happy with their education. Opponents then argued that average kids should not be allowed to leave because they would do terribly in college. But, despite the tendency of these students to select rigorous courses, they out performed average Minnesota college freshmen. In fact, several hundred of the participating students were former dropouts who decided to return to school once they were given some control over their lives.

Threatened for the first time by competition from colleges, Minnesota's high schools didn't sit around waiting for students to desert them. Like organizations trying to survive in any market, the schools began offering what their customers had long said they wanted—more challenging courses. In just two years, the number of college-credit advanced placement courses offered by

Minnesota high schools quadrupled. Several districts established new cooperative relationships with nearby universities to offer college-level courses inside the high schools.

Encouraged by these early signs of success, Minnesota Governor Rudy Perpich, the leader of the school-choice movement, set up an advisory panel to recommend legislation that would spread choice to every grade level and public school in the state. After a year and a half of negotiations, the advisory group hammered out draft legislation that sailed through both houses of the state legislature in early 1987. Under this law, school districts could, but did not have to, allow their students to emigrate. One year later, the legislature changed the law to mandate open enrollment for every school district by 1991.

The impact of the legislation was immediate. Ken Zastrow, former director of the Open Enrollment Program for Minnesota's Department of Education, recalled a conversation with the superintendent of a district in northern Minnesota just one month into the program. "Already I notice a difference at the school board meetings, and in our meetings with principals and teachers," the superintendent said. "For a long time the board opposed spending any money on new programs. Now they say things like, 'Maybe we should get involved with that new early childhood, family education program [where mothers come to school with their babies for special classes]. Otherwise someone else is going to do it, and the kids are going to leave and go over to the other district. If we can get the parents involved early on, they'll be supportive of us.' " "You know," the superintendent commented, "those kinds of discussions weren't happening before."

As in the private market, Minnesota school districts are pursuing a strategy of specialization to minimize the impact of head-to-head competition. The "one-size-fits-all" school is beginning to be replaced by an array of alternatives. Some schools focus on "fundamentals," where basic skills are taught in a highly structured classroom setting. Others position themselves as "continuous progress" schools, where students learn at their own pace using computers and programmed learning texts. Certain schools emphasize strong math/science curricula, others specialize in classes for those "gifted and talented" in music and arts, and still others are built around the "open-classroom" concept. Individual students learn in different ways. Some teachers are more effective in one setting than in others. Choice stimulates variety and allows students and teachers to work in classrooms suited to their individual needs. The "take-it-or-leave-it" style of education-by-monopoly is vanishing in Minnesota.

Fearing the loss of students to urban schools large enough to offer a variety of special courses, small rural districts are beginning to cooperate. In one case, two districts have agreed that one district will manage all the elementary schools while the other handles the junior highs. By combining student populations, they will be large enough to offer a broad range of courses. Like small companies that merge to achieve competitive size, school districts are finding ways to make better use of limited resources. Over time, they will move people out of redundant administrative jobs and devote the savings to programs that improve student performance.

Open enrollment is also beginning to reshape Minnesota's housing market. Before choice, the purchase of a home was linked to the selection of a school system. Now the housing and school decisions are unbundled. Price differentials are disappearing between identical homes on opposite sides of a school district boundary. A family that likes a neighborhood, but doesn't like the local schools, isn't forced to move to a high-price neighborhood for the well-being of the children. The implications for neighborhood and school desegregation are far-reaching.

"White flight" is the result of both racism and the fear of poor urban schools. School choice empowers minority parents to demand real improvements. Unless the worst urban school districts reform, their students will abandon them. As urban school quality improves, there will be less motivation for whites to transfer to suburban districts. White families may decide not to flee the cities, and neighborhoods will not become as segregated. Perhaps the historical lack of school choice has been an unrecognized factor in the vicious cycle of "white flight" and forced school busing. If so, school choice may well do more to encourage the voluntary reintegration of America's cities than any other conceivable program.

Ironically, the Minnesota teachers' union, which strenuously fought against choice, now sees possible benefits in what is taking place. A lobbyist for the Minnesota Education Association said, "We are starting to see it as a teacher empowerment bill. You can't really talk about improving schools if it doesn't matter what the labor force does. Now, the superintendent and principal are the most threatened if a large number of students opt to leave a district or a school. Teacher input will be much greater to avert or stem such a flow." Just as competition forces firms to listen to their skilled employees, choice is causing power to shift from the bureaucrats to the teachers.

Now that most of those who opposed choice are busy adjusting to the realities of the market, a new and unexpected source of opposition is springing up. Some wealthy parents who have been sending their kids to expensive private schools are pulling them out and registering them in public schools. In some cases, these kids take the demandig courses now available in the public high schools. In others, they transfer into colleges. Either way, it's free.

Minnesota's Roman Catholic schools also are witnessing a decline in enrollments as neighboring public schools boost their quality. In effect the monopoly that created awful public schools simultaneously enlarged the market for high-quality private and parochial schools. Now that the public schools have lost their monopoly power and are turning into effective competitors, the private/parochial-school market is shrinking. Not long ago, the archbishop of Minneapolis telephoned Governor Perpich and complained, "This is not good. Can't you find some way to make our schools eligible for open enrollment?"

These dynamics show that the conflict between public and private, which plagues so much of America's political discourse, is entirely misplaced. The issue isn't public versus private; it's choice versus lack of choice. It's a struggle between economic relationships founded on voluntary association and relationships based upon legal coercion. As soon as the power of consumer choice is injected into the domain of publicly provided goods, public solutions to social problems acquire the best characteristics of the private market.

Lacking a "hook," an organization—public or private—must behave as an efficient mutualist. It must control the inexorable tendency of necessary administration to turn into parasitic bureaucracy. Conversely, any organization that has a hook inevitably will be infected by the bureaucracy parasite, wasting scarce economic resources. Parasitic private corpocracies and public bureaucracies flourish wherever effective choice is denied to their hosts, whether those hosts are shareholders attempting to grow financial capital or students trying to acquire human capital.

The concept of public-school choice is just beginning to catch on. But Dan Loritz, Governor Perpich's aide, says that although the concept is incredibly simple, it's difficult to get across:

> The rest of the country doesn't yet understand what we've done. They think choice is always private. They have it confused with magnet schools or vouchers or whatever. They don't understand that the districts are sovereign on the way in. Districts can choose to accept nobody, or take a hundred. But they can't discriminate among those trying to get into their district. We don't promise students they can get in anywhere. But the districts can't stop them from leaving.

Governor Perpich compares the traditional American school district monopoly to the emigration policies of the Soviet Union it's forbidden. The people simply have to accept the situation as it is, like it or not. Dan Loritz says,

> We don't expect a lot of students to switch districts. Just because the boundaries of the United States are open, we don't expect everyone to leave. They just feel better knowing that they can. And there's a reason for people who want to provide services to them to do a good job so they won't leave, instead of relying on a law so they can't get out.

By surgically removing the monopoly's hook, Minnesota has taken the crucial reform step. Follow-on measures already underway will enhance the ability of students and parents to use their consumer power intelligently. The Minnesota Department of Education plans to publish school-by-school, grade-by-grade statistics reporting student performance levels. Parents and students will be able to judge from these "consumer reports" which schools merit their patronage.

Minnesota's schools will not be revolutionized overnight. Thoroughgoing institutional reform takes time. But, by establishing a market like environment, profound change at the grass roots becomes inevitable. Freed from the bureaucracy's hook, the state's education consumers will demand and get a radical improvement in the quality and variety of public-school offerings.

Progress will cost money, but most of it won't come from higher spending. As in other well-managed, intelligent organizations, the learning curve will allow more to be accomplished with the same resources. Consolidations, reorganizations, school closures, and new cooperatives will hack away at previously impervious layers of bureaucracy. Savings recovered through reduced waste will fund quality improvements. As they struggle to protect their jobs in an environment that permits organization death, capable teachers and administrators will gain the upper hand against their inept colleagues. School-by-school and classroom-by-classroom, the able will force out the incompetent. As the results of thousands of microscopic decisions accumulate, true reform will unfold.

If only one system in American society can be rescued from the depredations of bureaucratic parasitism, it must be the public-education system. Unless America's 16,000 public-school districts are forced to rid themselves of their bloated bureaucratic parasites, Americans will not be able to compete for decent jobs in the twenty-first century's global economy.

The damage already done by the education bureaucracy must run into the trillions of dollars in forgone economic growth. Because this parasite has so grievously damaged America's most vital resource, its costs dwarf even those caused by corpocracy. Revamping the public schools must be America's number one economic and social priority. Unless this monopoly is eradicated, the nation will not rebound from its slide into economic and political oblivion.

As dismal as America's public-school situation is at present, there is hope. Our democracy works. In their 1989 conference on school reform, the president and the governors declared school choice to be one of their key objectives. Minnesota has shown the way and its success will inspire others. Massachusetts, Colorado, Wisconsin, and California already are in the process of switching to schools-by-choice.

From their daily experience with the cornucopia of quality goods and services provided by the private sector, the American people know the power of choice and competition. It may well prove impossible to build public support for the reforms needed to purge the corpocracies infesting our largest corporations. Few voters can be rallied to demand arcane amendments to corporate govern-ance procedures. But the American people are more than ready for meaningful school reform. Recent polls show that 60 percent of Americans support the concept of school choice. Despite its awesome political clout, the education bureaucracy soon will be overwhelmed by an exasperated public.

COMPETITION AS A DISCOVERY PROCEDURE

Friedrich A. Hayek

1

It is difficult to defend economists against the charge that for some 40 to 50 years they have been discussing competition on assumptions that, *if* they were true of the real world, would make it wholly uninteresting and useless. If anyone really knew all about what economic theory calls the data, competition would indeed be a very wasteful method of securing adjustment to these facts. It is thus not surprising that some people have been led to the conclusion that we can either wholly dispense with the market, or that its results should be used only as a first step towards securing an output of goods and services which we can then manipulate, correct, or redistribute in any manner we wish. Others, who seem to derive their conception of competition solely from modern textbooks, have not unnaturally concluded that competition does not exist.

Against this, it is salutary to remember that, *wherever* the use of competition can be rationally justified, it is on the ground that we do *not* know in advance the facts that determine the actions of competitors. In sports or in examinations, no less than in the award of government contracts or of prizes for poetry, it would clearly be pointless to arrange for competition, if we were certain beforehand who would do best. As indicated in the title of this lecture, I propose to consider competition as a procedure for the discovery of such facts as, without resort to it, would not be known to anyone, or at least would not be utilised.[1]

This may at first appear so obvious and incontestable as hardly to deserve attention. Yet, some interesting consequences that are not so obvious immediately follow from the explicit formulation of the above apparent truism. One is that competition is valuable *only* because, and so far as, its results are unpredictable and on the whole different from those which anyone has, or could have, deliberately aimed at. Further, that the generally beneficial effects of competition must include disappointing or defeating some particular expectations or intentions.

Closely connected with this is an interesting methodological consequence. It goes far to account for the discredit into which the micro-economic approach to theory has fallen. Although this theory seems to me to be the only one capable of explaining the role of competition, it is no longer understood, even by some professed economists. It is therefore worthwhile to say at the outset a few words about the methodological peculiarity of any theory of competition, because it has made its conclusions suspect to many of those who habitually apply an over-simplified test to decide what they are willing to accept as scientific. The necessary consequence of the reason why we use competition is that, *in those cases in which it is interesting*, the validity of the theory can never be tested empirically. We can test it on conceptual models, and we might conceivably test it in artificially created real situations, where the facts which competition is intended to discover are already known to the observer. But in such cases it is of no practical value, so that to carry out the experiment would hardly be worth the expense. If we do not know the facts we hope to discover by means of competition, we can never ascertain how effective it has been in discovering those facts that might be discovered. All we can hope to find out is that, on the whole, societies which rely for this purpose on competition have achieved their aims more successfully than others. This is a conclusion which the history of civilisation seems eminently to have confirmed.

The peculiarity of competition—which it has in common with scientific method—is that its performance cannot be tested in particular instances where it is significant, but is shown only by the fact that the market will prevail in comparison with any alternative arrangements. The advantages of accepted scientific procedures can never be proved scientifically, but only demonstrated by the common experience that, on the whole, they are better adapted to delivering the goods than alternative approaches.[2]

The difference between economic competition and the successful procedures of science consists in the fact that the former is a method of discovering particular facts relevant to the achievement of specific, temporary purposes, while science aims at the discovery of what are sometimes called 'general facts', which are regularities of events. Science concerns itself with unique, particular facts only to the extent that they help to confirm or refute theories. Because these refer to general, permanent features of the world, the discoveries of science have ample time to prove their value. In contrast, the benefits of particular facts, whose usefulness competition in the market discovers, are in a great measure transitory. So far as the theory of scientific method is concerned, it would be as easy to discredit it on the ground that it does not lead to testable predictions about what science will discover, as it is to discredit the theory of the market on the ground that it fails to predict particular results the market will achieve. This, in the nature of the case, the theory of competition cannot do in any situation in which it is sensible to employ it. As we shall see, its capacity to predict is necessarily limited to predicting the kind of pattern, or the abstract character of the order that will form itself, but does not extend to the prediction of particular facts.[3]

II

Having relieved myself of this pet concern, I shall return to the central subject of this lecture, by pointing out that economic theory sometimes appears at the outset to bar its way to a true appreciation of the character of the process of competition, because it starts from the assumption of a 'given' supply of scarce goods. But which goods are scarce goods, or which things are goods, and how scarce or valuable they are—these are precisely the things which competition has to discover. Provisional results from the market process at each stage alone tell individuals what to look for. Utilisation of knowledge widely dispersed in a society with extensive division of labour cannot rest on individuals knowing all the particular uses to which well known things in their individual environment might be put. Prices direct their attention to what is worth finding out about market offers for various things and services. This means that the, in some respects always unique, combinations of individual knowledge and skills, which the market enables them to use, will not merely, or even in the first instance, be such knowledge of facts as they could list and communicate if some authority asked them to do so. The knowledge of which I speak consists rather of a capacity to find out particular circumstances, which becomes effective only if possessors of this knowledge are informed by the market which kinds of things or services are wanted, and how urgently they are wanted.[4]

This must suffice to indicate what kind of knowledge I am referring to when I call competition a discovery procedure. Much would have to be added to clothe the bare bones of this abstract statement with concrete flesh, so as to show its full practical importance. But I must be content with thus briefly indicating the absurdity of the usual procedure of starting the analysis with a situation in which all the facts ate supposed to be known. This is a *state* of affairs which economic theory curiously calls 'perfect competition'. It leaves no room whatever for the activity called competition, which is presumed to have already done its task. However, I must hurry on to examine a question, on which there exists even more confusion—namely, the meaning of the contention that the market adjusts activities spontaneously to the facts it discovers—or the question of the purpose for which it uses this information.

The prevailing confusion here is largely due to mistakenly treating the order which the market produces as an 'economy' in the strict sense of the word, and judging results of the market process by criteria which are appropriate only to such a single organised community serving a given hierarchy of ends. But such a hierarchy of ends is not relevant to the complex structure composed of countless individual economic arrangements. The latter, unfortunately, we also describe by the same word 'economy,' although it is something fundamentally different, and must be judged by different standards. An economy in the strict sense of the word, is an organization or arrangement in which someone deliberately allocates resources to a unitary order of ends. Spontaneous order produced by the market is nothing of the kind; and in important respects it does not behave like an economy proper. In particular, such spontaneous order differs because it does *not* ensure that what general opinion regards as more important needs are always satisfied before the less important ones. This is the chief reason why people object to it. Indeed, the whole of socialism is nothing but a demand that the market order (or catallaxy, as I like to call it, to prevent confusion with an economy proper)[5] should be turned into an economy in the strict sense, in which a common scale of importance determines which of the various needs are to be satisfied, and which are not to be satisfied.

The trouble with this socialist aim is a double one. As is true of every deliberate organisation, only the knowledge of the organiser can enter into the design of the economy proper, and all the members of such an economy, conceived as a deliberate organisation, must be guided in their actions by the unitary hierarchy of ends which it serves. On the other hand, advantages of the spontaneous order of the market, or the catallaxy, are correspondingly two. Knowledge that is used in it is that of all its members. Ends that it serves are the separate ends of those individuals, in all their variety and contrariness.

Out of this fact arise certain intellectual difficulties which worry not only socialists, but all economists who want to assess the accomplishments of the market order; because, if the market order does not serve a definite order of ends, indeed if, like any spontaneously formed order, it cannot legitimately be said to *have* particular ends, it is also not possible to express the value of the results as a sum of its particular individual products. What, then, do we mean when we claim that the market order produces in some sense a maximum or optimum?

The fact is, that, though the existence of a spontaneous order made for a particular purpose cannot be properly said to have a purpose, it may yet be highly conducive to the achievement of many different individual purposes not known as a whole to any single person, or relatively small group of persons. Indeed, rational action is possible only in a fairly orderly world. Therefore it clearly makes sense to try to produce conditions under which the chances for any individual taken at random

---

to achieve his ends as effectively as possible will be very high—even if it cannot be predicted which particular aims will be favoured, and which not.

As we have seen, the results of a discovery procedure are in their nature unpredictable; and all we can expect from the adoption of an effective discovery procedure is to improve the chances for unknown people. The only common aim which we can pursue by the choice of this technique of ordering social affairs is the general kind of pattern, or the abstract character, of the order that will form itself.

III

Economists usually ascribe the order which competition produces as an equilibrium—a somewhat unfortunate term, because such an equilibrium presupposes that the facts have already all been discovered and competition therefore has ceased. The concept of an 'order' which, at least for the discussion of problems of economic policy, I prefer to that of equilibrium, has the advantage that we can meaningfully speak about an order being approached to various degrees, and that order can be preserved throughout a process of change. While an economic equilibrium never really exists, there is some justification for asserting that the kind of order of which our theory describes an ideal type, is approached in a high degree.

This order manifests itself in the first instance in the circumstance that the expectations of transactions to be effected with other members of society, on which the plans of all the several economic subjects are based, can be mostly realised. This mutual adjustment of individual plans is brought about by what, since the physical sciences have also begun to concern themselves with spontaneous orders, or 'self-organising systems', we have learnt to call 'negative feedback'. Indeed, as intelligent biologists acknowledge, 'long before Claude Bernard, Clerk Maxwell, Walter B. Cannon, or Norbert Wiener developed cybernetics, Adam Smith has just as clearly used the idea in *The Wealth of Nations*. The 'invisible hand' that regulated prices to a nicety is clearly this idea. In a free market, says Smith in effect, prices are regulated by negative feedback'.[6]

We shall see that the fact that a high degree of coincidence of expectations is brought about by the systematic disappointment of some kind of expectations is of crucial importance for an understanding of the functioning of the market order. But to bring about a mutual adjustment of individual plans is not all that the market achieves. It also secures that whatever is being produced will be produced by people who can do so more cheaply than (or at least as cheaply as) anybody who does not produce it (and cannot devote his energies to produce something else comparatively even more cheaply), and that each product is sold at a price lower than that at which anybody who in fact

---

does not protect it could supply it. This, of course, does not exclude that some may make considerable profits over their costs if these costs are much lower than those of the next efficient potential producer. But it does mean that of the combination of commodities that is in fact produced, as much will be produced as we know to bring about by any known method. It will of course not be as much as we might produce if all the knowledge anybody possessed or can acquire were commanded by some one agency, and fed into a computer (the cost of finding out would, however be considerable). Yet we do injustice to the achievement of the market if we judge it, as it were, from above, by comparing it with an ideal standard which we have no known way of achieving. If we judge it, as we ought to, from below, that is, if the comparison in this case is made against what we could achieve by any other method—especially against what would be produced if competition were prevented, so that only those to whom some authority had conferred the right to produce or sell particular things were allowed to do so. All we need to consider is how difficult it is in a competitive system to discover ways of supplying to consumers better or cheaper goods than they already get. Where such undeveloped opportunities seem to exist we usually find that they remain undeveloped because their use is either prevented by the power of authority (including the enforcement of patent privileges), or by some private misuse of power which the law ought to prohibit.

It must not be forgotten that in this respect the market only brings about an approach towards some point on that n-dimensional surface, by which pure economic theory represents the horizon of all possibilities to which the production of any one proportional combination of commodities and services could conceivably be carried. The market leaves the particular combination of goods, and its distribution among individuals, largely to unforeseeable circumstances—and, in this sense, to accident. It is, as Adam Smith already understood,[7] as if we had agreed to play a game, partly of skill and partly of chance. This competitive game, at the price of leaving the share of each individual in some measure to accident, ensures that the real equivalent of whatever his share turns out to be, is as large as we know how to make it. The game is, to use up-to-date language, not a zero sum game, but one through which, by playing it according to the rules, the pool to be shared is enlarged, leaving individual shares in the pool in a great measure to chance. A mind knowing all the facts could select any point he liked on the surface and distribute this product in the manner he thought right. But the only point on, or tolerably near, the horizon of possibilities which we know how to reach is the one at which we shall arrive if we leave its determination to the market. The so-called 'maximum' which we thus reach naturally cannot be defined as a sum of particular things, but only in terms of the chances it offers to unknown people to get as large a real equivalent as possible for their relative shares, which will be determined partly by accident. Simply because its results cannot be assessed in terms of a single scale of values, as is the case in an economy proper, it is very misleading to assess the results of a catallaxy as if it were an economy.

IV

Misinterpretation of the market order as an economy that can and ought to satisfy different needs in a certain order of priority, shows itself particularly in the efforts of policy to correct prices and incomes in the interest of what is called 'social justice'. Whatever meaning social philosophers have attached to this concept, in the practice of economic policy it has almost always meant one thing, and one thing only: the protection of certain groups against the necessity to descend from the absolute or relative material position which they have for some time enjoyed. Yet this is not a principle on which it is possible to act generally without destroying the foundations of the market order. Not only continuous increase, but in certain circumstances even mere maintenance of the existing level of incomes, depends on adaptation to unforeseen changes. This necessarily involves the relative, and perhaps even the absolute, share of some having to be reduced, although they are in no way responsible for the reduction.

The point to keep constantly in mind is that *all* economic adjustment is made necessary by unforeseen changes; and the whole reason for employing the price mechanism is to tell individuals that what they are doing, or can do, has for some reason for which they are not responsible become less or more demanded. Adaptation of the whole order of activities to changed circumstances rests on the remuneration derived from different activities being changed, without regard to the merits or faults of those affected.

The term 'incentives' often used in this connection with somewhat misleading connotations, as if the main problem were to include people to exert themselves sufficiently. However, the chief 'guidance which prices offer is not so much how to act, but *what to do*. In a continuously changing world even mere maintenance of a given level of wealth requires incessant changes in the direction of the efforts of some, which will be brought about only if there numeration of some activities is increased and that of others decreased. With these adjustments, which under relatively stable conditions are needed merely to maintain the income stream, no 'surplus' is available which can be used to compensate those against whose prices turn. Only in a rapidly growing system can we hope to avoid absolute declines in the position of some groups.

Modern economists seem in this connection often to overlook that even the relative stability shown by many of those aggregates which macro-economics treats as data, is itself the result of a micro-economic process, of which changes in relative prices are an essential part. It is only thanks to the market mechanism that someone else is induced to step in and fill the gap caused by the failure of anyone to fulfill the expectations of his partners. Indeed, all those aggregate demand and supply curves with which we like to operate are not really objectively given facts, but results of the process of competition going on all the time. Not can we hope to learn from statistical information what

---

changes in prices or incomes are necessary in order to bring about adjustments to the inevitable changes.

The chief point, however, is that in a democratic society it would be wholly impossible by commands to bring about changes which are not felt to be just, and the necessity of which could never be clearly demonstrated. Deliberate regulation in such a political system must always aim at securing prices which appear to be just. This means in practice preservation of the traditional structure of incomes and prices. An economic system in which each gets what others think he deserves would necessarily be a highly inefficient system—quite apart from its being also an intolerably oppressive system. Every 'incomes policy' is therefore more likely to prevent than to facilitate those changes in the price and income structures that are required to adapt the system to new circumstances.

It is one of the paradoxes of the present world that the communist countries are probably freer from the incubus of 'social justice', and more willing to let those bear the burden against whom developments turn, than are the 'capitalist' countries. For some Western countries at least the position seems hopeless, precisely because the ideology dominating their politics makes changes impossible that are necessary for the position of the working class to rise sufficiently fast to lead to the disappearance of this ideology.

V

If even in highly developed economic systems competition is important as a process of exploration in which prospectors search for unused opportunities that, when discovered, can also be used by others, this is to an even greater extent true of underdeveloped societies. My first attention has been deliberately given to problems of preserving an efficient order for conditions in which most resources and techniques are generally known, and constant adaptations of activities are made necessary only by inevitably minor changes, in order to maintain a given level of incomes. I will not consider here the undoubted role competition plays in the advance of technological knowledge. But I do want to point out how much more important it must be in countries where the chief task is to discover yet unknown opportunities of a society in which in the past competition has not been active. It may not be altogether absurd, although largely erroneous, to believe that we can foresee and control the structure of society which further technological advance will produce in already highly developed countries. But it is simply fantastic to believe that we can determine in advance the social structure in a country where the chief problem still is to discover what material and human resources are available, or that for such a country we can predict the particular consequences of any measures we may take.

Apart from the fact that there is in such countries so much more to be discovered, there is still another reason why the greatest freedom of competition seems to be even more important there than in more advanced countries. This is that required changes in habits and customs will be brought about only if the few willing and able to experiment with new methods can make it necessary for the many to follow them, and at the same time to show them the way. The required discovery process will be impeded or prevented, if the many are able to keep the few to the traditional ways. Of course, it is one of the chief reasons for the dislike of competition that it not only shows how things can be done more effectively, but also confronts those who depend for their incomes on the market with the alternative of imitating the more successful or losing some or all of their income. Competition produces in this way a kind of impersonal compulsion which makes it necessary for numerous individuals to adjust their way of life in a manner that no deliberate instructions or commands could bring about. Central direction in the service of so-called 'social justice' may be a luxury rich nations can afford, perhaps for a long time, without too great an impairment of their incomes. But it is certainly not a method by which poor countries can accelerate their adaptation to rapidly changing circumstances, on which their growth depends.

Perhaps it deserves mention in this connection that possibilities of growth are likely to be greater the more extensive are a country's yet unused opportunities. Strange though this may seem at first sight, a high rate of growth is more often than not evidence that opportunities have been neglected in the past. Thus, a high rate of growth can sometimes testify to bad policies of the past rather than good policies of the present. Consequently it is unreasonable to expect in already highly developed countries as high a rate of growth as can for some time be achieved in countries where effective utilisation of resources was previously long prevented by legal and institutional obstacles.

From all I have seen of the world the proportion of private persons who are prepared to try new possibilities, if they appear to them to promise better conditions, and if they are not prevented by the pressure of their fellows, is much the same everywhere. The much lamented absence of a spirit of enterprise in many of the new countries is not an unalterable characteristic of the individual inhabitants, but the consequence of restraints which existing customs and institutions place upon them. This is why it would be fatal in such societies for the collective will to be allowed to direct the efforts of individuals, instead of governmental power being confined to protecting individuals against the pressures of society. Such protection for private initiatives and enterprise can only ever be achieved through the institution of private property and the whole aggregate of libertarian institutions of law.

Notes

1. Since I wrote this my attention has been drawn to a paper by Leopold Von Wiese on 'Die Konkurrenz, vorwiegend in soziologisch-systematischer Betrachtung', *Verhandlungen des 6. Deutschen Soziologentages,* 1929), where, on p. 27, he discusses the 'experimental' nature of competition.

2. Cf. the interesting studies of the late Michael Polanyi in *The Logic of Liberty*, London, 1951, which show how he has been led from the study of scientific method to the study of competition in economic affairs; and see also K. R. Popper, *The Logic of Scientific Discovery*, London, 1959.

3. On the nature of 'pattern prediction' see my essay on 'The theory of complex phenomena' in *Studies in Philosophy, Politics and Economics,* London and Chicago, 1967.

4. Cf. Samuel Johnson in J. Boswell, *Life of Samuel Johnson*, L.F. Powell's revision of G. B. Hill's edition, Oxford, 1934, vol. II, p. 365 (18 April 1775): 'Knowledge is of two kinds. We know a subject ourselves, or we know where we can find information about it'.

5. For a fuller discussion see now my *Law, Legislation and Liberty,* vol. II, *The Mirage of Social Justice*, London and Chicago, 1976, pp. 107-20.

6. G. Hardin, *Nature and Man's Fate* (1951), Mentor ed. 1961, p 54.

7. Adam Smith, *The Theory of Moral Sentiments,* London, 1759, part VI, chapter 2, penultimate paragraph, and part VII, section II, chapter 1.

UNCERTAINTY, DISCOVERY, AND HUMAN ACTION

A STUDY OF THE ENTREPRENEURIAL PROFILE IN THE MISESIAN SYSTEM

Israel M. Kirzner

A central element in the economics of Ludwig von Mises is the role played by the entrepreneur and the function fulfilled by entrepreneurship in the market process. The character of that process for Mises is decisively shaped by the leadership, the initiative, and the driving activity displayed and exercised by the entrepreneur. Moreover, in an intellectual edifice built systematically on the notion of individual *human action*—on the manner in which reasoning human beings interact while seeking to achieve their individual purposes—it is highly significant that Mises found it of relevance to emphasize that each human actor is always, in significant respects, an entrepreneur.[1] The present paper seeks to explore the character of Misesian entrepreneurship, with special reference to the influence exercised by the inescapable uncertainty that pervades economic life. Both at the level of isolated individual human action and at the level of entrepreneurial activity in market context, I shall be concerned to determine the extent to which the Misesian entrepreneur owes his very existence and his function to the unpredictability of his environment and to the ceaseless tides of change that undergird that unpredictability.

On the face of it, this question may not seem worthy of new research. Mises, it may be pointed out, expressed himself quite clearly on numerous occasions to the effect that the entrepreneurial function is inseparable from speculation with respect to an uncertain future. For example he wrote that "the entrepreneur is always a speculator."[2] Or again, he wrote that "entrepreneur means acting man in regard to the changes occurring in the data of the market."[3] Moreover, when Mises points out that every individual acting man is an entrepreneur, this is because "every action is embedded in the flux of time and thus involves a speculation."[4] In other words, the entrepreneurial element cannot be abstracted from the notion of individual human action, because the "uncertainty of the future is already implied in the very notion of action. That man acts and that the future is uncertain are by no means two independent matters, they are only two different modes of establishing one thing."[5]

Thus it might seem that the essentiality of uncertainty for the Misesian entrepreneur hardly needs to be established anew. Certainly any thought of questioning that essentiality must, it might appear, be quickly dismissed.

What I shall argue in this chapter is not that the role of uncertainty in the function of the Misesian entrepreneur may be any less definitive than these clear-cut statements imply, but that this role is a more subtle one than may on the surface appear to be the case. It is this subtlety in the role played by uncertainty in the Misesian system, I believe, that sets that system apart in significant respects from the views of other economists (such as Knight or Shackle) who have emphasized the phenomenon of uncertainty in the context of the market.

The Background of the Present Exploration

In earlier forays into the field of the Misesian entrepreneur, I developed an interpretation of the entrepreneurial function in which the role of uncertainty, while recognized and certainly not denied, was not emphasized. This failure to emphasize uncertainty was quite deliberate and was indeed explicitly acknowledged.[6] Instead of emphasizing the uncertainty in which entrepreneurial activity is embedded, these earlier treatments stressed the element of *alertness to hitherto unperceived opportunities* that is, I argued, crucial for the Misesian concept of entrepreneurship.[7] Since my position explicitly recognized the element of change and uncertainty while it claimed to be able to explicate the elusive quality of entrepreneurship without need to emphasize the uncertainty element, it is perhaps not surprising that my treatment has drawn fire from two different perspectives. A number of critics have felt rather strongly that failure to emphasize the role of uncertainty renders my understanding of entrepreneurship fundamentally defective. At least one critic, on the other hand, has been persuaded by my exposition of entrepreneurship to the point that even my frugal references to uncertainty as an inescapable characteristic of the entrepreneurial scene appear altogether unnecessary and are seen as producing confusion. Since all these critics are basically in agreement with me, I believe, on the broad accuracy of the general entrepreneurial character of the market process that I ascribe to Mises, it has for some time been my hope to delve into these questions more thoroughly. Some further brief recapitulation of these earlier discussions seems in order as an introduction to our present exploration.

My emphasis on alertness to hitherto unperceived opportunities as the decisive element in the entrepreneurial function stemmed from my pursuit of a didactic purpose. This purpose was to distinguish the analysis of the market *process* (a process in which the entrepreneur plays the crucial role) as sharply as possible from the analysis of equilibrium states (in which all scope for entrepreneurial activity has been assumed away). In equilibrium, it turns out, all market decisions have somehow come already into complete mutual coordination. Market participants have been assumed to be making their respective decisions with perfectly correct information concerning the decisions that all other participants are making at the same time.[8] So long as the underlying present consumer attitudes and production possibilities prevail, it is clear that we can rely on the very same set of decisions being made in each of an indefinite number of future periods. On the other hand, in the absence of such complete equilibrium coordination of decisions, a market process is set in motion in which market participants are motivated to learn to anticipate more accurately the decisions of others; in this process the entrepreneurial, profit-motivated discovery of the gaps in mutual coordination of decisions is a crucial element. Entrepreneurial activity drives this market process of mutual discovery by a continually displayed alertness to profit opportunities (into which the market automatically translates the existing gaps in coordination). Whereas entrepreneurial activity is indeed speculative, the pursuit of profit opportunities is a purposeful and deliberate one, the "emphasis on the element of alertness in action [was] intended to point out that, far from being numbed by the inescapable uncertainty of our world, men *act upon their judgments of* what opportunities have been left unexploited by others."[9]

In developing this aspect of entrepreneurship I was led to emphasize the capture of pure entrepreneurial profit as reducible essentially to the exploitation of arbitrage opportunities. Imperfect mutual awareness on the part of other market participants had generated the emergence of more than one price for the same bundle of economic goods; the entrepreneur's alertness to the profit opportunity presented by this price discrepancy permits him to win these profits (and, in so doing, tends to nudge the prices into closer adjustment with each other). In so emphasizing the arbitrage character of pure profit, emphasis was deliberately withdrawn from the speculative character of entrepreneurial activity that wins pure profit by correctly anticipating *future* price movements.[10]

A number of (otherwise friendly) critics expressed serious reservations concerning my deliberate lack of stress on the speculative character of entrepreneurial activity. Henry Hazlitt pointed out that my repeated references to the entrepreneur's perceiving of opportunities fail to make clear that at best the entrepreneur *thinks* that he perceives opportunities: that what an entrepreneur "acts on may not be a perception but a *guess*."[11] Murray Rothbard has endorsed a discussion by Robert Hébert in which my definition of the entrepreneur is sharply distinguished from that of Mises: "Mises conceives of the entrepreneur as the uncertainty bearer.... To Kirzner, on the other hand, entrepreneurship becomes reduced to the quality of *alertness*; and uncertainty seems to have little to do with the matter."[12] Although conceding that my treatment of the entrepreneur has "a certain amount of textual justification in Mises," Rothbard sees this not as providing genuine support for my reading of the Misesian entrepreneur but as being the result of a "certain uncharacteristic lack of clarity in Mises' discussion of entrepreneurship."[13]

In a most thoughtful paper several years ago, Lawrence H. White too deplored my deliberate failure to emphasize uncertainty in the analysis of entrepreneurship. This treatment, White argues, fosters neglect of important features of entrepreneurial activity that arise precisely from the passage of time and from the uncertainty generated by the prospect of unanticipated changes bound to occur during the journey to the future. To compress entrepreneurial activity into an arbitrage box is, in particular, to fail to recognize the highly important part played by entrepreneurial *imagination*.[14]

On the other hand, my treatment of entrepreneurship has been criticized by J. High from a diametrically opposite point of view. High accepts the definition of entrepreneurship in terms of alertness to opportunities for pure profit. He proceeds to point out that "nothing in this definition requires uncertainty. The definition requires ignorance, because the opportunity has not been discovered earlier: it requires error, because the opportunity could have been discovered earlier, but the definition does not require uncertainty."[15] High is therefore critical of passages in which uncertainty is linked specifically with entrepreneurship.[16]

Clearly the role of uncertainty in the entrepreneurial environment, and in particular its relationship to the entrepreneur's alertness to error, demands further explication. What follows may not satisfy my critics (from both wings). I trust, however, that my discussion of some of the perhaps less obvious links between uncertainty and alertness will, if it does not quite absolve me of the charge of intransigence, at least bear witness to my grateful acknowledgment of the very deep importance of the problems raised by my critics.

Our inquiry will be facilitated by a careful examination of the sense in which each individual engaging in human action is, as already cited from Mises, exercising entrepreneurship.[17] Or to put the issue somewhat differently, it will be helpful to explore more precisely what it is that distinguishes human action from purely calculative, allocative, economizing activity.

I have argued in earlier work that the concept of human action emphasized by Mises includes an ineradicable entrepreneurial element that is absent from the notion of economizing, of the allocation of scarce resources among competing ends, that was articulated by Lord Robbins.[18] On the face of it there appear to be two distinct aspects of Misesian human action that might be considered to set it apart from Robbinsian economizing activity. We shall have to ask whether these are indeed two distinct aspects of human action and how they relate to the entrepreneurial element that human action contains (but which Robbinsian allocative activity does not). These two aspects of human action (not present in economizing activity) may be identified as (1) the element in action that is beyond the scope of "rationality" as an explanatory tool, and (2) the element in action that constitutes discovery of error. Let us consider these in turn.

The Limits of Rationality

Perhaps the central feature of purely economizing activity is that it enables us to explain behavior by reference to the postulate of rationality. With a given framework of ranked goals sought, and of scarce resources available to be deployed, rationality (in the narrow sense of consistency of behavior with the relevant given ranking of ends) ensures a unique pattern of resource allocation; decision making can be fully understood in the light of the given ends-means framework. There is no part of the decision that cannot be accounted for; given the framework, the decision taken is fully determined (and therefore completely explained); any other decision would have been simply unthinkable.

On the other hand, the notion of Msesian human action embraces the very adoption of the ends means framework to be considered relevant. The adoption of any particular ends-means framework is a step which is logically (although not necessarily chronologically) prior to that of allocating means consistently with the given ranking of ends. If the human decision is to be perceived as including the selection of the ends-means framework, then we have an element in that decision that cannot, of course, be explained by reference to rationality. Consistency in action is not sufficient to account for that ranking of ends in terms of which consistency itself is to be defined. Thus the totality of human action cannot, even in principle, be explained on the basis of rationality. A science of human action cannot fail to acknowledge—even after full recognition of the formidable explanatory power of the postulate of rationality—that human history, depending as it does on unexplained adoption of goals and awareness of means, contains a strong element of the unexplained and even the spontaneous. These are themes that have, of course, been extensively developed by G. L. S. Shackle: "Choice and reason are things different in nature and function, reason *serves* the chosen purposes, not performs the selection of them."[19] "A man can be supposed to act always in rational response to his 'circumstances' but those 'circumstances' can, *and must*, be in part the creation of his own mind.... In this loose-textured history, men's choices of action being choices action being choices among thoughts which spring indeterminately in their minds, we can deem them to *initiate* trains of events in some real sense."[20]

In an earlier era, much criticism of the role of the rationality postulate in economic theory focused on the place of apparently nonrational behavior, behavior arising out of impetuous impulse or out of unthinking habit.[21] It is simply unrealistic, these criticisms ran, to assume that economic activity represents the exclusive result of deliberation. Man acts all too often without careful deliberation; he does not weigh the costs and benefits of his actions. This is not the place to evaluate these criticisms or deal with the debates that they engendered three-quarters of a century ago and more. But it is perhaps important to point out that limits of rationality discussed in this section have little to do with the arguments based on impulsiveness and on habit bondage. It is not at all being argued here that human action involves the *thoughtless* selection of goals. Human decision making may of course involve the most agonizingly careful appraisal of alternative courses of action to choose what seems likely to offer the most estimable of outcomes. In emphasizing that the rationality postulate is unable to explain the selection of the relevant ends-means framework, I am not suggesting that that selection occurs without deliberation, but merely that the results of that deliberation cannot be predicted on the basis of the postulate of consistency; that deliberation is essentially creative. One may predict the answer that a competent mathematician will arrive at when he tackles a given problem in computation (in the same way that one may know in advance the answer to that problem that will be yielded by an electronic computer); but one cannot, in the same way, predict which computational problem the mathematician will deliberately choose to tackle (as one may not be able to predict which problems will be selected to be fed into the electronic computer).

The matter may be presented in an alternative version. One may always distinguish, within each human decision, an element into which thought enters in self-aware fashion from an element into which thought enters without self awareness. A man desires a specific goal with great eagerness; but deliberation persuades him, let us imagine, that it is in his interest not to reveal that eagerness to others (say, because others might then spitefully wish to deny that goal to him). The studied nonchalance with which he masks his pursuit of the goal exhibits scope for both element: (1) his apparent nonchalance is indeed deliberate and studied, he knows precisely the reason why it is important that he pretend lack of interest; but (2) he may not be at all self-aware as to how he arrived at this judgment to act on the assumption that others may spitefully seek to frustrate his achievement. He simply decides to act. His decision is to refrain from naively pursuing with evident eagerness what he eagerly desires; but his decision is yet naive in the sense that he has not, for example, sought (as reasons having to do with long-term strategy might well suggest) to ostentatiously pretend unawareness of the spitefulness of the others. No matter how calculative a man's behavior may be, it seems impossible to avoid having accepted, without calculation, some framework within which to self-consciously engage in cost-benefit comparisons. A man decides to display behavior a. We may call the mental activity of making that decision activity b. Now the man *may* have decided (in the course of decision-making activity c) to engage in decision making activity b (or he may have simply and impulsively engaged in decision-making activity b). But even if engaging in decision-making activity b (as a result of which behavior a was chosen) was itself the outcome of "higher" decisions, at some level our decision maker's highest decision was made quite unselfconsciously.

This extra-Robbinsian aspect of human action, the aspect which involves the creative, unpredictable selection of the ends-means framework, can also be usefully stated in terms of *knowledge*. Given his knowledge of the relevant ends-means framework, man's decision can be predicted without doubt; it is simply a matter of computation. To the extent, however, that man must "decide" what it is, so to speak, that he knows, and that this determination is not in general based ineluctably on other knowledge unambiguously possessed, man's behavior is not at all predictable. What a man believes himself to know is not itself the result of a calculative decision.[22] This expression of the notion of the existence of limits to rationality will facilitate our insight into the important linkage that exists between these limits and the phenomenon of uncertainty.

In the absence of uncertainty it would be difficult to avoid the assumption that each individual does in fact already know the circumstances surrounding his decision. Without uncertainty, therefore, decision making would no longer call for any imaginative, creative determination of what the circumstances really are. Decision making would call merely for competent calculation. Its results could, in general, be predicted without doubt. Human judgment would have no scope. "With uncertainty absent, man's energies are devoted altogether to doing things; . . . in a world so built . . . it seems likely that . . . all organisms [would be] automata."[23] "If man knew the future, he would not have to choose and would not act. He would be like an automaton, reacting to stimuli without any will of its own."[24] Thus the extra-Robbinsian aspect of human action, the aspect responsible for rendering human action unpredictable and incompletely explainable in terms of rationality, arises from the inherent uncertainty of human predicament. If, then, one chooses to identify entrepreneurship with the function of making decisions in the face of an uncertain present or future environment, it certainly appears that Misesian human action does (while Robbinsian economizing does not) include an entrepreneurial element.

But before making up our minds on this point, we must consider that second element, mentioned at the end of the preceding section, that distinguishes Misesian human action from Robbinsian allocative decision making.

The Discovery of Error

To draw attention to this element in human action I shall draw on an earlier paper in which I attempted to identify what might represent "entrepreneurial profit" in successful individual action in a Crusoe context.[25] Entrepreneurial profit in the Crusoe context, it turned out, can be identified only where Crusoe discovers that he has up until now attached an erroneously low valuation to resources over which he has command. Until today Crusoe has been spending his time catching fish with his bare hands. Today he has realized that he can use his time far more valuably by building a boat or making a net. "He has discovered that he had placed an incorrectly low value on his time. His reallocation of his labor time from fishing to boat-building is an entrepreneurial decision and, assuming his decision to be a correct one, yields pure profit in the form of additional value discovered to be forthcoming from the labor time applied."[26] This (Crusonian) pure profit arises from the circumstance that at the instant of entrepreneurial discovery Menger's law is violated. Menger's law teaches that men value goods according to the value of the satisfactions that depend on possession of those goods. This law arises from man's propensity to attach the value of ends to the means needed for their achievement. At the moment of entrepreneurial discovery Crusoe realizes that the ends achievable with his labor time have higher value than the ends he had previously sought to achieve:

> The value Crusoe has until now attached to his time is *less* than the value of the ends he now seeks. This discrepancy is, at the level of the individual, pure profit.... Once the old ends-means framework has been completely and unquestionably replaced by the new one, of course, it is the value of the new ends that Crusoe comes to attach to his means.... But, during the instant of an entrepreneurial leap of faith . . . there is scope for the discovery that, indeed, the ends achieved are more valuable than had hitherto been suspected. *This*, is the discovery of pure (Crusonian) entrepreneurial profit.[27]

Scope for entrepreneurship thus appears to be grounded in the possibility of discovering error. In the market context, the state of general equilibrium, providing as it does absolutely no scope for the discovery of profitable discrepancies between prices and costs, affords no opportunity for entrepreneurial discovery and turns out to be populated entirely by Robbinsian maximizers. In the same way, it now appears, the situation in which Crusoe is errorlessly allocating his resources—with the value of ends being fully and faultlessly attached to the relevant means in strict accordance with Menger's law— affords no scope for the entrepreneurial element in human action. Human action, without scope for the discovery of error, collapses into Robbinsian allocative activity.

Clearly this way of identifying the entrepreneurial element that is present in Misesian human action but absent in Robbinsian economizing activity fits in well with the approach that defines entrepreneurship as alertness to hitherto unperceived opportunities.[28] In the market context entrepreneurship is evoked by the presence of as yet unexploited opportunities for pure profit. These opportunities are evidence of the failure of market participants, up until now, to correctly assess the realities of the market situation. At the level of the individual too, it is then attractive to argue, an entrepreneurial element in action is evoked by the existence of as yet unexploited private opportunities. To act entrepreneurially is to identify situations overlooked until now because of error.

Uncertainty and/or Discovery

Our discussion has led us to identify two apparently distinct elements in human action, each of which possesses plausible claims as constituting that entrepreneurial element in action that sets it apart from purely calculative economizing activity: (1) On the one hand we saw that it appears plausible to associate entrepreneurship with the department within human action in which the very framework for calculative economizing activity is, in an open-ended, uncertain world, selected as being relevant. It is here that we would find scope for the unpredictable, the creative, the imaginative expressions of the human mind—expressions that cannot themselves be explained in terms of the postulate of consistency. Thus entrepreneurship, at the Crusoe level, arises uniquely and peculiarly from the circumstance that, as a result of the inescapable uncertainty of the human predicament, acting man cannot be assumed to be sure of the framework relevant for calculative activity. He must, using whatever entrepreneurial gifts he can display, *choose* a framework. (2) On the other hand, as we have seen, it appears perhaps equally plausible to associate entrepreneurship with that aspect of human action in which the alert individual realizes the existence of opportunities that he has up until now somehow failed to notice. Scope for entrepreneurship, at the Crusoe level, arises then not from the present uncertainty that must now be grappled with in decision making but from earlier error from which entrepreneurial discovery must now provide protection.

I must emphasize that these alternative identifications of the entrepreneurial element in action do appear, at least on a first scrutiny, to be genuinely different from one another. It is of course true that past error (from which, on the one view, we look to entrepreneurial discovery to provide a rescue) may be attributed to the pervasive uncertainty that characterizes our world (and to the inevitably kaleidic changes responsible for that uncertainty). But to discover hitherto unnoticed opportunities (unnoticed because of past failure to pierce correctly the fog of uncertainty) does not at all seem to be the same task as that of selecting between alternative present scenarios for the future within which calculative activity is to be undertaken. Moreover, whatever the possible reasons for past error, error itself implies merely ignorance, not necessarily uncertainty.[29] To escape ignorance is one thing; to deal with uncertainty is another.

This tension that we have discovered at the level of human action in the Crusoe context, between present uncertainty and earlier error as sources of entrepreneurship, is clearly to be linked immediately with our more general exploration in this chapter. This chapter is concerned with determining the extent to which the Misesian entrepreneur is to be perceived as the creature of uncertainty. The tension we have now discovered between present uncertainty and earlier error corresponds exactly to the disagreement we encountered between those who see the Misesian entrepreneur as essentially the bearer of market uncertainty and those who see him as the discoverer of earlier market errors. It is my contention that our awareness of this apparent tension can in fact shed light on certain subtleties in the concept of entrepreneurship likely otherwise to be overlooked. My procedure to develop this claim will be as follows: I will seek to show that, on a deeper understanding of the meaning of uncertainty and of the discovery of error at the level of individual action, the tension between them dissolves in a way that will reveal the full significance of entrepreneurial alertness at the level of the individual. Thereafter I will pursue the analogy between the scope of entrepreneurship at the individual level and that of entrepreneurship at the level of the market, drawing on this analogy to identify precisely the relative roles, in market entrepreneurship, of uncertainty and of alertness.

Action and Alertness

Man acts, in the light of the future as he envisages it, to enhance his position in that future. The realized consequences of man's actions, however, flow from the impact of those actions on the actual (as contrasted with the envisaged) course of future events. The extent to which man's plans for the enhancement of his prospects are fulfilled depends on the extent to which the future as he has envisaged it corresponds to the future as it in fact occurs. There is no natural set of forces or constraints assuring correspondence between the envisaged future and the realized future. The two may, it seems at first glance, diverge from one another with complete freedom. The future course of events is in general certainly not constrained by past forecasts; nor, unfortunately, are forecasts constrained by the actual future events these forecasts seek to foretell. On the face of it, then, with nothing to guarantee correspondence between the actual future and the future as it is envisaged, it might seem as if successful action were entirely a matter of good fortune. Indeed, if man is aware of this apparent lack of ability to envisage the future correctly except as a matter of sheer good fortune, it is not clear why (apart from the joys of gambling itself) man bothers to act at all. But of course the overwhelming fact of human history is that man does act, and his choices are made in terms of an envisaged future that, although by no means a photographic image of the future as it will actually unfold, is yet not entirely without moorings in regard to that realized future. "To be genuine, choice must be neither random nor predetermined. There must be some grounds for choosing, but they must be inadequate; there must be some possibility of predicting the consequences of choice, but none of perfect prediction."[30] "The essence of the situation is action according to *opinion*, . . . neither entire ignorance nor complete and perfect information, but partial knowledge."[31] The genuine choices that do, I am convinced, make up human history express man's conviction that the future as he envisages it does hold correspondence, in some degree, to the future as it will in fact unfold. The uncertainty of the future reflects man's awareness that this correspondence is far from complete; the fact that he acts and chooses at all reflects his conviction that this correspondence is far from negligible. Whence does this correspondence, incomplete though it may be, arise? If there are no constraints assuring correspondence, how is successful action anything but the sheerest good fortune?

The answer to this dilemma surely lies in the circumstance that man is *motivated* to formulate the future as he envisages it, as accurately as possible. It is not a matter of two unfolding tapestries, one the realized future, the second a fantasized series of pictures of what the first might look like. Rather, acting man really does try to construct his picture of the future to correspond to the truth as it will be realized. He really does try to glimpse the future, to peer through the fog. He is thus motivated to *bring about* correspondence between the envisaged and the realized futures. Not only are man's purposeful efforts to better his condition responsible for his choices as constructed against a given envisaged future, that purposefulness is, perhaps even more importantly, responsible for the remarkable circumstance that that envisaged future does overlap significantly with the future as it actually unfolds. (Of course, these forecasts need not be made, explicitly, prior to action; they are embedded, possibly without self-awareness, in action itself.) I call this motivated propensity of man to formulate an image of the future man's alertness. Were man totally lacking in alertness, he could not act at all: his blindness to the future would rob him of any framework for action. (In fact, were man totally lacking in potential for *alertness*, it would be difficult to identify a notion of error altogether: were unalert man to act, it would not be on the basis of an erroneously forecast future. It would be on the basis of no relevant forecast at all. Not recognizing that he might— had he been more alert—have avoided the incorrect picture of the future, he could not in any meaningful sense blame himself for having erred.)

It will surely be acknowledged that this alertness— which provides the only pressure to constrain man's envisaged future toward some correspondence with the future to be realized—is what we are searching for under the phrase "the entrepreneurial element in human action."

Robbinsian allocation activity contains no such element, because within the assigned scope of such defined activity no possible divergence between a future as envisaged and a future to be realized is considered. What is incomplete in the notion of purely allocative activity is surely to be found precisely in this abstraction from the desperately important element of entrepreneurship in human action.

It should be observed that the entrepreneurial alertness we have identified does not consist merely in "seeing" the unfolding of the tapestry of the future in the sense of seeing a preordained flow of events. Alertness must, importantly, embrace the awareness of the ways the human agent can, by imaginative, bold leaps of faith, and determination, in fact *create* the future for which his present acts are designed. As I shall argue in a subsequent section, this latter expression of entrepreneurial alertness does not affect its essential formal character—which remains that of ensuring a tendency for the future context envisaged as following present action to bear some realistic resemblance to the future as it will be realized.

In understanding this entrepreneurial element in human action, we must notice, two aspects of it: (1) We note what provides the scope for entrepreneurship. This scope is provided by the complete freedom with which the future as envisaged might, without entrepreneurial alertness, diverge from the future as it will in fact be. Entrepreneurial alertness has a function to perform. (2) We note what provides the incentive that switches on entrepreneurial alertness. This incentive is provided by the lure of pure entrepreneurial profit to be grasped in stepping from a less accurately envisaged future to a more accurately envisaged one. Each step taken in moving toward a vision of the future that overlaps more significantly with the truth is not merely a step toward truth (that is, a positive entrepreneurial success); it is also a profitable step (that is, a step that enhances the value of the sources with which action is available to be taken).

Viewed from this perspective, the tension between the uncertainty environment in which action occurs, on the one hand, and the discovery-of-error aspect of action, on the other, can be seen to dissolve at a glance. These two aspects of action can be seen immediately as merely two sides of the same entrepreneurial coin. If uncertainty were merely an unpleasant condition of life to which man must passively adjust, then it would be reasonable to distinguish between the quite separate activities of bearing uncertainty on the one hand and of discovering error on the other. Escaping from current errors is one thing; grappling with the uncertainty of the future is another. But, as we have noticed, to choose means to *endeavor*, under the incentive to grasp pure profit, to identify a more truthful picture of the future. Dealing with uncertainty is motivated by the profit to be won by avoiding error. In this way of viewing the matter the distinction be seen escaping current enor and avoiding potential future error is unimportant. The discovery of error is an interesting feature of action because it offers incentive. It is this incentive that inspires the effort to pierce the fog of uncertainty that shrouds the future. To deal with uncertainty means to seek to overcome it by more accurate prescience; to discover error is merely that aspect of this endeavor that endows it with incentive attraction. The imagination and creativity with which man limits his envisaged future are inspired by the pure gains to be won in ensuring that that envisaged future is in fact no less bright than that which can be made the truth.

We shall find in the next section that these insights surrounding entrepreneurship at the level of individual action have their exact counterparts in entrepreneurship in the market context. It will be useful to summarize briefly the key points we have learned about individual entrepreneurship:

1. Entrepreneurship in individual action consists of the endeavor to secure greater corre-spondence between the individual's future as he envisages it and his future as it will in fact unfold. This endeavor consists in the individual's alertness to whatever can provide clues to the future. This alertness, broadly conceived, embraces those aspects of imagination and creativity through which the individual may himself *ensure* that his envisaged future will be realized.

2. Scope for entrepreneurship is provided by the uncertainty of the future. For our purposes uncertainty means that, in the absence of entrepreneurial alertness, an individual's view of the future may diverge with total freedom from the realized future. In the absence of entrepreneurial alertness it is only sheer chance that can be responsible for successful action.

3. Incentive for the "switching on" of entrepreneurial alertness is provided by the pure gain (or avoidance of loss) to be derived from replacing actions based on less accurate prescience by action based on the more realistically envisaged future. The avoidance of entrepreneurial error is not merely a matter of being more truthful, it happens also to be profitable.

Entrepreneurship in the Market

Our examination of the entrepreneurial element in individual action permits us to see the role of entrepreneurship in the market in a fresh light. We shall discover, in the market context, elements that correspond precisely to their analogues in the individual context. Let us consider what happens in markets.

In a market, exchanges occur between market participants.[32] In the absence of perfect mutual knowledge, many of the exchanges are inconsistent with one another. Some sales are made at low prices when some buyers are buying at high prices. Some market participants are not buying at all because they are unaware of the possibility of buying at prices low enough to be attractive; some are refraining from selling because they are unaware of the possibility of selling at prices high enough to be attractive. Clearly the actions of these buyers and sellers are, from the perspective of omniscience, uncoordinated and inconsistent. We notice that, although the assumption of perfect knowledge that is necessary for market equilibrium would constrain different transactions in the market to complete mutual consistency, the actuality of imperfect knowledge permits these different transactions in different parts of the market to diverge with apparently complete freedom. What alone tends to introduce a modicum of consistency and coordination into this picture, preventing a situation in which even the slightest degree of coordination could exist only as a matter of sheerest chance, is market entrepreneurship, inspired by the lure or pure market profit. We are now in a position to identify, in the market context, elements that correspond to key features already identified in the context of individual entrepreneurship.

Corresponding to uncertainty as it impinges on individual action, we have market discoordination. The freedom with which an individual's envisaged future may diverge from the future to be realized corresponds precisely to the freedom with which transactions made in one part of the market may diverge from transactions made elsewhere. In the absence of entrepreneurship it is only out of the purest chance that market transactions by different pairs of buyers and sellers are made on anything but the most wildly inconsistent terms. There is nothing that constrains the mutually satisfactory price bargain reached between one pair of traders to bear any specific relation to corresponding bargains reached between other pairs of traders.

Corresponding to error at the level of the individual, we have price divergence at the level of the market. Perfect knowledge (such as in Robbinsian individual allocative activity) precludes error. Market equilibrium (implied by universal perfect knowledge) precludes price divergences.

The individual entrepreneurial element permits the individual to escape from the distressing freedom with which divergences between envisaged futures and realized futures may occur; the entrepreneur fulfills the same function for the market. The function of the entrepreneur is to bring different parts of the market into coordination with each other. The market entrepreneur bridges the gaps in mutual knowledge, gaps that would otherwise permit prices to diverge with complete freedom.

Corresponding to the incentive for individual entrepreneurship provided by more realistic views of the future, we have at the market level the incentive provided by opportunities for pure entrepreneurial profit. Market profit consists in the gap between prices generated by error and market inconsistency—just as the source for private gain is to be discovered in a present divergence between the imagined and the actual future.

The following are propositions, in the context of the market, that concern entrepreneurship; they correspond precisely to those stated at the conclusion of the preceding section.[33]

1°. Entrepreneurship in the market consists in the function of securing greater consistency between different parts of the market. It expresses itself in entrepreneurial alertness to what transactions are in fact available in different parts of the market. It is only such alertness that is responsible for any tendency toward keeping these transactions in some kind of mutual consistency.

2°. Scope for market entrepreneurship is provided by the imperfect knowledge that permits market transactions to diverge from what would be a mutually consistent pattern.

3°. Incentive for market entrepreneurial activity is provided by the pure gain to be won by noticing existing divergences between the prices at which market transactions are available in different parts of the market. It is the lure of market profits that inspires entrepreneurial alertness.

Time, Uncertainty, and Entrepreneurship

My analogy between entrepreneurship at the level of the individual and entrepreneurship in the market emphasized only the most salient respects of the analogy. Certain additional features of the entrepreneurial function in the market need to be dealt with more extensively. In the individual context the divergence (which it is the function of entrepreneurship to limit) was a divergence between anticipated and realized future. Its source in uncertainty was immediately apparent. In the market context the divergence (which it is the function of entrepreneurship to limit) was a divergence between the transactions in different parts of the market. Its source was stated in terms of imperfect mutual knowledge among market participants. Its relationship to uncertainty was not asserted. This requires both amplification and modification.

My statements concerning market entrepreneurship were couched in terms of the market for a single commodity within a single period. It should be clear that nothing essential is lost when our picture of the market is expanded to include many commodities and, in particular, the passage of time. This should of course not be understood to mean that the introduction of the passage of time does not open up scope for additional insights. I merely argue that the insights we have gained in the single-period context for entrepreneurship are not to be lost sight of in the far more complex multiperiod case.

When we introduce the passage of time, the dimensions along which mutual ignorance may develop are multiplied. Market participants in one part of today's market not only may be imperfectly aware of the transactions available in another part of that market, they also may be imperfectly aware of the transactions that will be available in next year's market. Absence of consistency between different parts of today's market is seen as a special case of a more general notion of inconsistency that also includes inconsistency between today's transactions and those to be transacted next year. A low price today may be in this sense inconsistent with the high prices that will prevail next year. Scope for market entrepreneurship, in the context of the passage of time, arises then from the need to coordinate markets also across time. Incentive for market entrepreneurship along the intertemporal dimension is provided not by arbitrage profits generated by imperfectly coordinated present markets but, more generally, by the speculative profits generated by the as yet imperfectly coordinated market situations in the sequence of time. And, of course, the introduction of entrepreneurial activity to coordinate markets through time introduces, for individual entrepreneurs engaged in market entrepreneurship, precisely the considerations concerning the uncertain future that we have, until now, considered only in the context of the isolated individual.

It is because of this last circumstance that we must acknowledge that the introduction of the passage of time, although leaving the overall formal function of market entrepreneurship unchanged, will of course introduce substantial modification into the way we must imagine entrepreneurship to be exercised concretely. It is still the case, as noted, that the entrepreneurial function is that of bringing about a tendency for transactions in different parts of the market (conceived broadly now as including transactions entered into at different times) to be made in greater mutual consistency. But whereas in the case of entrepreneurship in the single-period market (that is, the case of the entrepreneur as arbitrageur) entrepreneurial alertness meant alertness to present facts, in the case of multi period entrepreneurship alertness must mean alertness to the future. It follows that market entrepreneurship in the multiperiod case introduces uncertainty as facing the entrepreneur not only as in the analogy offered in the preceding section—where the market analogue for uncertainty turned out to be the freedom with which transactions in different parts of today's market may unconstrainedly diverge from being mutually consistent—but also in the simple sense of the entrepreneur's awareness of the freedom with which his own envisaged future (concerning future market transactions) may diverge from the realized future. In particular the futurity that entrepreneurship must confront introduces the possibility that the entrepreneur may, by his own creative actions, in fact *construct* the future as *he* wishes it to be. In the singleperiod case alertness can at best discover hitherto overlooked current facts. In the multiperiod case entrepreneurial alertness must include the entrepreneur's perception of the way creative and imaginative action may vitally shape the kind of transactions that will be entered into in future market periods.

Thus the exercise of entrepreneurial alertness in the multiperiod market context will indeed call for personal and psychological qualifications that were unneeded in the single-period case. To be a successful entrepreneur one must now possess those qualities of vision, boldness, determination, and creativity that we associated earlier with the entrepreneurial element in isolated individual action with respect to an uncertain future. There can be no doubt that in the concrete fulfillment of the entrepreneurial function these psychological and personal qualities are of paramount importance. It is in this sense that so many writers are undoubtedly correct in linking entrepreneurship with the courage and vision necessary to *create* the future in an uncertain world (rather than with merely seeing what stares one in the face).

However, the function of market entrepreneurship in the multiperiod context is nonetheless still that spelled out in the preceding section. What market entrepreneurship accomplishes is a tendency for transactions in different parts of the market (including the market at different dates) to become coordinated. The incentive that inspires this entrepreneurial coordination is the lure of pure profit—the difference in market values resulting from hitherto less complete coordination. These insights remain true for the multiperiod case no less than for the arbitrage case. For some purposes it is no doubt important to draw attention to the concrete psychological requirements on which successful entrepreneurial decision making depends. But for other purposes such emphasis is not required; in fact such emphasis may divert attention from what is, from the perspective of the overall functioning of the market system, surely the essential feature of entrepreneurship: its market-coordinative properties.

Let us recall that at the level of the individual, entrepreneurship involved not merely bearing uncertainty but also overcoming uncertainty. Uncertainty is responsible for what would, in the absence of entrepreneurship, be a failure to perceive the future in a manner sufficiently realistic to permit action. Entrepreneurship, so to speak, pushes aside to some extent the swirling fogs of uncertainty, permitting meaningful action. It is this function of entrepreneurship that must be kept in view when we study the market process. The uncertainty that characterizes the environment within which market entrepreneurship plays its coordinative role must be fully recognized; without it there would be no need and no scope for entrepreneurship. But an understanding of what entrepreneurship accomplishes requires us to recognize not so much the extent to which uncertainty is the ineradicable feature of human existence as the extent to which both individual action and social coordination through the market can occur significantly despite the uncertainty of the future (and in spite also of the uncertainty analogue that would, in the absence of the arbitrageur, fog up even the single-period market).

Further Reflections on Uncertainty and Alertness

Thus we can see how those writers who have denied that the pure entrepreneurial role involves the bearing of uncertainty were both correct and yet at least partly irrelevant. Both J. A. Schumpeter[34] and J. B. Clark insisted that only the capitalist bears the hazards of business; the pure entrepreneur has, by definition, nothing to lose.[35] No doubt all this is true, as far as it goes, but what is important about linking the entrepreneur with the phenomenon of uncertainty is not that it is the entrepreneur who accepts the disutilities associated with the assumption of the hazards of business in an uncertain world. What is important is that the entrepreneur, motivated by the lure of pure profits, attempts to pierce these uncertainties and endeavors to see the truth that will permit profitable action on his part.

A number of economists may be altogether unwilling to accept the notion of alertness with respect to uncertain future. In fact many may wish to reject the very formulation I have employed to schematize the uncertainty of the future. For me uncertainty means the essential freedom with which the envisaged future may diverge from the realized future. Entrepreneurial alertness means the ability to impose constraints on that freedom, so that the entrepreneur's vision of the future may indeed overlap, to some significant extent, with that future he is attempting to see. But many will be unwilling to treat the future as something to be seen at all. "The present is uniquely determined. It can be seen by the eyewitness.... What is the future but the void? To call it the future is to concede the presumption that it is already 'existent' and merely waiting to appear. If that is so, if the world is determinist, then it seems idle to speak of choice."[36] Similarly, many are unwilling to see the entrepreneur as "alert to opportunities" if this terminology implies that future opportunities already "exist" and are merely waiting to be grasped. "Entrepreneurial projects are not waiting to be sought out so much as to be thought up."[37]

What perhaps needs to be emphasized once again is that in using phrases such as "grasping future opportunities," "seeing the future correctly or incorrectly," or the "divergence between the envisaged future and the realized future" I do not wish to imply any determinacy regarding the future. No doubt, to say that one sees the future (with greater or lesser accuracy) is to employ a metaphor. No doubt that future that one "sees" is a future that may in fact be constructed significantly by one's action, which is supposed to be informed by that very vision. But surely these metaphors are useful and instructive. To dream realistically in a way that inspires successful, creative action is to "see correctly" as compared with the fantasies that inspire absurd ventures or the cold water poured by the unduly timid pessimist that stunts all efforts at improvement. "The future, " we have learned, "is unknowable, though not unimaginable."[38] To acknowledge the unknowability of the future is to acknowledge the essential indeterminacy and uncertainty surrounding human existence. But surely in doing so we need not consign human existence to wholly uncoordinated chaos. To speak of entrepreneurial vision is to draw attention, by use of metaphor, to the formidable and benign coordinative powers of the human imagination. Austrian economists have, in principled fashion, refused to see the world as wholly knowable, as suited to interpretation by models of equilibrium from which uncertainty has been exhausted. It would be most unfortunate if, in pursuing this refusal, economists were to fall into a no less serious kind of error. This error would be the failure to understand how entrepreneurial individual actions, and the systematic market forces set in motion by freedom for entrepreneurial discovery and innovation, harness the human imagination to achieve no less a result than the liberation of mankind from the chaos of complete mutual ignorance. Mises's concept of human action and his analysis of the role of entrepreneurial market processes surely remain, in this regard, unique and as yet insufficiently appreciated contributions to the profound understanding of human society.

Notes

1. L. von Mises, *Human Action* (New Haven: Yale University Press, 1949), p. 253.

2. Ibid., p. 288.

3. Ibid., p. 255.

4. Ibid., p. 254.

5. Ibid., p. 105.

6. Israel M. Kirzner, *Competition and Entrepreneurship,* (Chicago: University of Chicago Press, 1973), pp. 86-87.

7. Ibid., chap.2. See also Israel M. Kirzner, *Perception, Opportunity, and Profit* (Chicago: University of Chicago Press, 1979), chap. 10.

8. F. A. Hayek, *Individualism and Economic Order* (London: Routledge and Kegan Paul, 1949), p. 42.

9. Kirzner, *Competition and Entrepreneurship,* pp. 86-87 (italics in original).

10. Such activity was subsumed under arbitrage by pointing out the formal similarity between (1) buying and selling in different markets today and (2) buying and selling in different markets at different dates (see Kirzner, *Competition and Entrepreneurship,* pp. 85-86).

11. Henry Hazlitt, review of *Competition and Entrepreneurship*, in *Freeman* 24 (December 1974: 759. Similar concerns seem to be expressed in a review of *Competition and Entrepreneurship* by Percy L. Greaves, Jr., in *Wertfrei* no. 2 (Spring 1974), esp. pp. 18-19.

12. See unpublished paper by Murray N. Rothbard, "Professor Hébert on Entrepreneurship," pp. 1-2. Quoted with permission.

13. Ibid., p. 7.

14. L. H. White, "Entrepreneurship, Imagination, and the Question of Equilibrium," unpublished paper (1976). See also L. H. White, "Entrepreneurial Price Adjustment" (paper presented at Southern Economic Association meetings, Washington, D.C., November 1978), p. 36, n. 3.

15. J. High, review article on *Perception, Opportunity, and Profit* in *Austrian Economics Newsletter 2*, 3 (Spring 1980): 14.

16. High's criticisms of my references to uncertainty as a characteristic of the entrepreneurial environment focus most specifically on what he believes to be my use of uncertainty to "serve as the distinguishing characteristic between entrepreneurship and luck" (ibid.). Here there seems to be a definite misunderstanding of my position. Far from the presence of the uncertainty surrounding entrepreneurship being what separates entrepreneurial profit from the lucky windfall, almost the exact reverse is the case. What marks entrepreneurial profit as different from the lucky windfall is that the former was, despite the (inevitable) uncertainty that might have discouraged the entrepreneur, in fact deliberately pursued. Where luck confers gain it may well reflect the circumstance that the uncertainty of this gain deterred the actor from even dreaming of winning it. High's reading apparently resulted from his understanding a passage that he cites (from Kirzner, *Perception, Opportunity, and Profit,* pp. 159-60) to represent the case of a purely lucky gain. In fact the passage cited does not refer to luck at all. If one knows that one's labor can convert low-valued leisure into high-valued apples, the apples one so gains through one's hard work do not constitute a lucky windfall. The point of the cited passages is that Menger's law shows there is no value gain at all derived from that labor, since one would already have attached the higher value of the ends to the available means. My discussion in this chapter, however, proceeds on the assumption that High's unhappiness at my treatment of uncertainty in entrepreneurship does not rest solely on the validity of the way I distinguish entrepreneurial profits from windfall gains.

17. Mises, *Human Action*, p. 253.

18. See Kirzner, *Competition and Entrepreneurship*, pp. 32-35. See also Kirzner, *Perception, Opportunity, and Profit*, pp. 166-68.

19. G.L.S. Shackle, *Epistemics and Economics* (Cambridge: Cambridge University Press, 1972), p. 136 (italics in original).

20. Ibid., p. 351.

21. See also Israel M. Kirzner, *The Economic Point of View* (Princeton: Van Nostrand, 1960), p. 167.

22. See also Kirzner, *Perception, Opportunity, and Profit*, chap. 9.

23. F.H. Knight, *Risk, Uncertainty and Profit* (New York: Houghton Mifflin, 1921), p. 268.

24. Mises, *Human Action*, p. 105.

25. See Kirzner, *Perception, Opportunity, and Profit,* chap. 10, esp. pp. 158-64.

26. Ibid, p. 162.

27. Ibid., p. 163.

28. See, for example, Kirzner, *Competition and Entrepreneurship*, p. 39.

29. See note 15 of this chapter.

30. B.J. Loasby, *Choice, Complexity and Ignorance* (Cambridge: Cambridge University Press, 1976), p. 5.

31. Knight, *Risk, Uncertainty and Profit,* p. 199.

32. Our discussion proceeds in terms of the market for a single commodity. It could be couched, without altering the essentials in any respect, in more general terms. See also the subsequent section of this chapter.

33. The three pairs of statements may be viewed as additions to the two lists of twelve statements developing the analogy between the individual and the market provided in Kirzner, *Perception, Opportunity, and Profit*, chap. 10, pp. 170-72, 173-75.

34. J.A. Schumpeter, *The Theory of Economic Development* (Cambridge: Harvard University, 1934), p. 137; J.A. Schumpeter, *History of Economic Analysis* (Oxford: Oxford University, 1954), p. 556. See also S.M. Kanbur, "A Note on Risk Taking, Entrepreneurship and Schumpeter," *History of Political Economy* 12 (Winter 1980): 489-98.

35. J.B. Clark, "Insurance and Business Profit," *Quarterly Journal of Economics* 7 (October 1892): 46 (cited in Knight, *Risk, Uncertainty, and Profit*, p. 38).

36. Shackle, *Epistemics and Economics,* p. 122.

37. White, "Entrepreneurship, Imagination," p. 7.

38. L.M. Lachmann, "From Mises to Shackle: An Essay," *Journal of Economic Literature* 14 (March 1976): 59.

COMPETITION

Ludwig von Mises

In nature there prevail irreconcilable conflicts of interests. The means of subsistence are scarce. Proliferation tends to outrun subsistence. Only the fittest plants and animals survive. The antagonism between an animal starving to death and another that snatches the food away from it is implacable.

Social cooperation under the division of labor removes such antagonisms. It substitutes partnership and mutuality for hostility. The members of society are united in a common venture.

The term competition as applied to the conditions of animal life signifies the rivalry between animals which manifests itself in their search for food. We may call this phenomenon *biological competition*. Biological competition must not be confused with *social competition*, i.e., the striving of individuals to attain the most favorable position in the system of social cooperation. As there will always be positions which men value more highly than others, people will strive for them and try to outdo rivals. Social competition is consequently present in every conceivable mode of social organization. If we want to think of a state of affairs in which there is no social competition, we must construct the image of a socialist system in which the chief in his endeavors to assign to everybody his place and task in society is not aided by any ambition on the part of his subjects. The individuals are entirely indifferent and do not apply for special appointments. They behave like the stud horses which do not try to put themselves in a favorable light when the owner picks out the stallion to impregnate his best brood mare. But such people would no longer be acting men.

Catallactic competition is emulation between people who want to surpass one another. It is not a fight, although it is usual to apply to it in a metaphorical sense the terminology of war and internecine conflict, of attack and defense, of strategy and tactics. Those who fail are not annihilated; they are removed to a place in the social system that is more modest, but more adequate to their achievements than that which they had planned to attain.

In a totalitarian system, social competition manifests itself in the endeavors of people to court the favor of those in power. In the market economy, competition manifests itself in the fact that the sellers must outdo one another by offering better or cheaper goods and services, and that the buyers must outdo one another by offering higher prices. In dealing with this variety of social competition which may be called *catallactic competition*, we must guard ourselves against various popular fallacies.

The classical economists favored the abolition of all trade barriers preventing people from competing on the market. Such restrictive laws, they explained, result in shifting production from those places in which natural conditions of production are more favorable to places in which they are less favorable. They protect the less efficient man against his more efficient rival. They tend to perpetuate backward technological methods of production. In short they curtail production and thus lower the standard of living. In order to make all people more prosperous, the economists argued, competition should be free to everybody. In this sense they used the term *free competition*. There was nothing metaphysical in their employment of the term *free*. They advocated the nullification of privileges barring people from access to certain trades and markets. All the sophisticated lucubrations caviling at the metaphysical connotations of the adjective *free* as applied to competition are spurious; they have no reference whatever to the catallactic problem of competition.

As far as natural conditions come into play, competition can only be "free" with regard to those factors of production which are not scarce and therefore not objects of human action. In the catallactic field competition is always restricted by the inexorable scarcity of the economic goods and services. Even in the absence of institutional barriers erected to restrict the number of those competing, the state of affairs is never such as to enable everyone to compete in all sectors of the market. In each sector only comparatively small groups can engage in competition.

Catallactic competition, one of the characteristic features of the market economy, is a social phenomenon. It is not a right, guaranteed by the state and the laws, that would make it possible for every individual to choose ad libitum the place in the structure of the division of labor he likes best. To assign to everybody his proper place in society is the task of the consumers. Their buying and abstention from buying is instrumental in determining each individual's social position. Their supremacy is not impaired by any privileges granted to the individuals qua producers. Entrance into a definite branch of industry is virtually free to newcomers only as far as the consumers approve of this branch's expansion or as far as the newcomers succeed in supplanting those already occupied in it by filling better or more cheaply the demands of the consumers. Additional investment is reasonable only to the extent that it fills the most urgent among the not yet satisfied needs of the consumers. If the existing plants are sufficient, it would be wasteful to invest more capital in the same industry. The structure of market prices pushes the new investors into other branches.

It is necessary to emphasize this point because the failure to grasp it is at the root of many popular complaints about the impossibility of competition. Some sixty years ago people used to declare: You cannot compete with the railroad companies; it is impossible to challenge their position by starting competing lines; in the field of land transportation there is no longer competition. The truth was that at that time the already operating lines were by and large sufficient. For additional capital investment the prospects were more favorable in improving the serviceableness of the already operating lines and in other branches of business than in the construction of new railroads. However, this did not interfere with further technological progress in transportation technique. The bigness and the economic "power" of the railroad companies did not impede the emergence of the motor car and the airplane.

Today people assert the same with regard to various branches of big business: You cannot challenge their position, they are too big and too powerful. But competition does not mean that anybody can prosper by simply imitating what other people do. It means the opportunity to serve the consumers in a better or cheaper way without being restrained by privileges granted to those whose vested interests the innovation hurts. What a newcomer who wants to defy the vested interests of the old established firms needs most is brains and ideas. If his project is fit to fill the most urgent of the unsatisfied needs of the consumers or to purvey them at a cheaper price than their old purveyors, he will succeed in spite of the much talked of bigness and power of the old firms.

Catallactic competition must not be confused with prize fights and beauty contests. The purpose of such fights and contests is to discover who is the best boxer or the prettiest girl. The social function of catallactic competition is, to be sure, not to establish who is the smartest boy and to reward the winner by a title and medals. Its function is to safeguard the best satisfaction of the consumers attainable under the given state of the economic data.

Equality of opportunity is a factor neither in prize fights and beauty contests nor in any other field of competition, whether biological or social. The immense majority of people are by the physiological structure of their bodies deprived of a chance to attain the honors of a boxing champion or a beauty queen. Only very few people can compete on the labor market as opera singers and movie stars. The most favorable opportunity to compete in the field of scientific achievement is provided to the university professors. Yet, thousands and thousands of professors pass away without leaving any trace in the history of ideas and scientific progress, while many of the handicapped outsiders win glory through marvelous contributions.

It is usual to find fault with the fact that catallactic competition is not open to everybody in the same way. The start is much more difficult for a poor boy than for the son of a wealthy man. But the consumers are not concerned about the problem of whether or not the men who shall serve them start their careers under equal conditions. Their only interest is to secure the best possible satisfaction of their needs. As the system of hereditary property is more efficient in this regard, they prefer it to other less efficient systems. They look at the matter from the point of view of social expediency and social welfare, not from the point of view of an alleged, imaginary, and unrealizable "natural" right of every individual to compete with equal opportunity. The realization of such a right would require placing at a disadvantage those born with better intelligence and greater will power than the average man. It is obvious that this would be absurd.

The term competition is mainly employed as the antithesis of monopoly. In this mode of speech the term monopoly is applied in different meanings which must be clearly separated.

The first connotation of monopoly, very frequently implied in the popular use of the term, signifies a state of affairs in which the monopolist, whether an individual or a group of individuals, exclusively controls one of the vital conditions of human survival. Such a monopolist has the power to starve to death all those who do not obey his orders. He dictates and the others have no alternative but either to surrender or to die. With regard to such a monopoly there is no market or any kind of catallactic competition. The monopolist is the master and the rest are slaves entirely dependent on his good graces. There is no need to dwell upon this kind of monopoly. It has no reference whatever to a market economy. It is enough to cite one instance. A world embracing socialist state would exercise such an absolute and total monopoly; it would have the power to crush its opponents by starving them to death.[1]

The second connotation of monopoly differs from the first in that it describes a state of affairs compatible with the conditions of a market economy. A monopolist in this sense is an individual or a group of individuals, fully combining for joint action, who has the exclusive control of the supply of a definite commodity. If we define the term monopoly in this way, the domain of monopoly appears very vast. The products of the processing industries are more or less different from one another. Each factory turns out products different from those of the other plants. Each hotel has a monopoly on the sale of its services on the site of its premises. The professional services rendered by a physician or a lawyer are never perfectly equal to those rendered by any other physician or lawyer. Except for certain raw materials, foodstuffs, and other staple goods, monopoly is everywhere on the market.

However, the mere phenomenon of monopoly is without any significance and relevance for the operation of the market and the determination of prices. It does not give the monopolist any advantage in selling his products. Under copyright law every rhymester enjoys a monopoly in the sale of his poetry. But this does not influence the market. It may happen that no price whatever can be realized for his stuff and that his books can only be sold at their waste paper value.

Monopoly in this second connotation of the term becomes a factor in the determination of prices only if the demand curve for the monopoly good concerned is shaped in a particular way. If conditions are such that the monopolist can secure higher net proceeds by selling a smaller quantity of his product at a higher price than by selling a greater quantity of his supply at a lower price, there emerges a *monopoly price* higher than the potential market price would have been in the absence of monopoly. Monopoly prices are an important market phenomenon, while monopoly as such is only important if it can result in the formation of monopoly prices.

It is customary to call prices which are not monopoly prices *competitive prices*. While it is questionable whether or not this terminology is expedient, it is generally accepted and it would be difficult to change it. But one must guard oneself against its misinterpretation. It would be a serious blunder to deduce from the antithesis between monopoly price and competitive price that the monopoly price is the outgrowth of the absence of competition. There is always catallactic competition on the market. Catallactic competition is no less a factor in the determination of monopoly prices than it is in the determination of competitive prices. The shape of the demand curve that makes the appearance of monopoly prices possible and directs the monopolists' conduct is determined by the competition of all other commodities competing for the buyers' dollars. The higher the monopolist fixes the price at which he is ready to sell, the more potential buyers turn their dollars toward other vendible goods. On the market every commodity competes with all other commodities.

There are people who maintain that the catallactic theory of prices is of no use for the study of reality because there has never been "free" competition or because, at least today, there is no longer any such thing. All these doctrines are wrong.[2] They misconstrue the phenomena and simply do not know what competition really is. It is a fact that the history of the last decades is a record of policies aiming at the restriction of competition. It is the manifest intention of these schemes to grant privileges to certain groups of producers by protecting them against the competition of more efficient competitors. In many instances these policies have brought about the conditions required for the emergence of monopoly prices. In many other instances this was not the case and the result was only a state of affairs preventing many capitalists, entrepreneurs, farmers, and workers from entering those branches of industry in which they would have rendered the most valuable services to their fellow citizens. Catallactic competition has been seriously restricted, but the market economy is still in operation although sabotaged by government and labor union interference. The system of catallactic competition is still functioning although the productivity of labor has been seriously reduced.

It is the ultimate end of these anticompetition policies to substitute for capitalism a socialist system of planning in which there is no catallactic competition at all. While shedding crocodile tears about the decline of competition, the planners want to abolish this "mad" competitive system. They have attained their goal in some countries. But in the rest of the world they have only restricted competition in some branches of business by increasing the number of people competing in other branches.

The forces aiming at a restriction of competition play a great role in our day. It is an important task of the history of our age to deal with them. Economic theory has no need to refer to them in particular. The fact that there are trade barriers, privileges, cartels, government monopolies and labor unions is merely a datum of economic history. It does not require special theorems for its interpretation.

Notes

1. Cf. Trotsky (1937) as quoted by Hayek, *The Road to Serfdom* (London, 1944), p. 89.

2. For a refutation of the fashionable doctrines of imperfect and of monopolistic competition cf. F.A. Hayek, *Individualism and Economic Order* (Chicago, 1948), pp. 92118.

GOVERNMENT POLICY AND THE MARKET

Friedrich A. Hayek

> The pure market economy assumes that government, the social apparatus of compulsion and coercion, is intent upon preserving the operation of the market system, abstains from hindering its functioning, and protects it against encroachment on the part of other people.
>
> —*Ludwig von Mises**

The Advantages of Competition Do Not Depend On It Being 'Perfect'[1]

In certain conditions competition will bring about an allocation of the resources for the production of the different commodities and services which leads to an output of that particular combination of products as large as that which could be brought about by a single mind who knew all those facts actually known only to all the people taken together, and who was fully capable of utilizing this knowledge in the most efficient manner. The special case in which these results follow from the competitive market process has been found intellectually so satisfying by economic theorists that they have tended to treat it as paradigmatic. The case for the competition has in consequence regularly been stated as if competition were desirable because as a rule it achieves these results, or even as if it were desirable only when in fact it does so. From basing the argument for the market on this special case of 'perfect' competition it is, however, not far to the realization that it is an exceptional case approached in only a few instances, and that, in consequence, if the case for competition rested on what it achieves under those special conditions, the case for it as a general principle would be very weak indeed. The setting of a wholly unrealistic, over-high standard of what competition should achieve thus often leads to an erroneously low estimate of what in fact it does achieve.

This model of perfect competition rests on assumptions of facts which do not exist except in a few sectors of economic life and which in many sectors it is not in our power to create and would sometimes not even be desirable to create if we could. The crucial assumption on which that model is based is that any commodity of service that differs significantly from others can be supplied to most consumers at the same cost by a large number of producers, with the result that none of the latter can deliberately determine the price because, if he tried to change more than his marginal costs, it would be in the interests of others to undersell him. This ideal case, in which for each competitor the price is given, and where his interests will induce him to increase his production until the marginal costs are equal to price, came to be regarded as the model and was used as a standard by which the achievement of competition in the real world was judged.

It is true that, if we could bring about such a state, it would be desirable that the production of each article should be extended to the point where prices equalled marginal costs because, so long as this was not so, a further increase of production of the commodity in question would mean that the factors of production required would be used more productively than elsewhere. This, however, does not mean that where we have to use the process of competition to find out what the different people want and are able to do, we are also in a position to bring about the ideal state, or that the results even of 'imperfect' competition will not be preferable to any condition we can bring about by any other known method such as direction by government.

It is evidently neither desirable nor possible that every commodity or service that is significantly different from others should be produced by a large number of producers, or that there should always be a large number of producers capable of producing any particular thing at the same cost. As a rule there will exist at any one time not only an optimum size of the productive unit, below and above which costs will rise, but also special advantages of skill, location, traditions, etc. which only some but not all enterprises will possess. Frequently a few enterprises or perhaps only a single one will be able to supply as much of a particular commodity as can be sold at prices covering its costs which may be cheaper than those of any other firm. In this case a few firms (or the single firm) will not be under the necessity of bringing their prices down to the marginal costs, or of producing such a quantity of their product that they can be sold only at prices just covering its marginal costs.

All that their interests will induce the firm to do will be to keep prices below the figure at which new producers would be tempted to enter the market. Within this range such firms (or such a firm) would indeed be free to act as monopolists or obligopolists and to fix their prices (or the quantities of goods produced) at the level which would bring them the highest profits, limited only by the consideration that they must be low enough to keep out others.

In all such instances an omniscient dictator could indeed improve the use of the available resources by requiring the firms to expand production until prices only just covered marginal costs. On this standard, habitually applied by some theorists, most of the markets in the existing world are undoubtedly very imperfect. For all practical problems, however, this standard is wholly irrelevant, because it rests on a comparison. not with some other state that could be achieved by some known procedure, but with one that might have been achieved if certain facts which we cannot alter were other that they in fact are. To use as a standard by which we measure the actual achievement of competition the hypothetical arrangements made by an omniscient dictator comes naturally to the economist whose analysis must proceed on the fictitious assumption that *he* knows all the facts which determine the order of the market. But it does not provide us with a valid test which can meaningfully be applied to the achievements of practical policy. The test should not be the degree of approach towards an unachievable result, but should be whether the results of a given policy exceed or fall short of the results of other available procedures. The real problem is how far we can raise efficiency above the preexisting level, *not* how close we can come to what would be desirable if the fact were different.

That standard for judging the performance of competition, in other words, must not be the arrangements which would be made by somebody who had complete knowledge of all the facts, but the probability which only competition can secure that the different things will be done by those who thereby produce more of what the others want than they would do otherwise.

Competition as a Discovery Procedure

Quite generally outside as well as inside the economic sphere, competition is a sensible procedure to employ only if we do not know beforehand who will do best. In examinations or in sport meetings as well as on the market, it will tell us, however, only who did best on the particular occasion, and not necessarily that each did as well as he could have done—though it also provides one of the most effective spurs to achievement. It will produce an inducement to do better than the next best, but if this next best is far behind, the range within which the better one will be free to decide how much to exert himself may be very wide. Only if the next best is pressing on his heels and he himself does not know how much better he really is, will he find it necessary to exert himself to the full. And only if there is a more or less continuous graduation of capacities, and each anxious to achieve as good a place as he can, will each be kept on tiptoe and be looking over his shoulder to see whether the next best is catching up with him.

Competition is thus, like experimentation in science, first and foremost a discovery procedure. No theory can do justice to it which starts from the assumption that the facts to be discovered are already known.[2] There is no predetermined range of known or given facts which will ever all be taken into account. All we can hope to secure is a procedure that is on the whole likely to bring about a situation where more of the potentially useful objective facts will be taken into account than would be done in any other procedure which we know. It is the circumstances which makes so irrelevant for the choice of a desirable policy all evaluation of the results of competition that starts from the assumption that all the relevant facts are known to some single mind. The real issue is how we can best assist the optimum utilization of the knowledge, skills and opportunities to acquire knowledge, that are dispersed among hundreds of thousands of people, but given to nobody in their entirety. Competition must be seen as a process in which people acquire and communicate knowledge; to treat it as if all this knowledge were available to any one person at the outset is to make nonsense of it. And it is as nonsensical to judge the concrete results of competition by some preconception of the products it 'ought' to bring forth as it would be to judge the results of scientific experimentation by their correspondence with what had been expected. As is true of the results of scientific experimentation we can judge the value of the results only by the conditions under which it was conducted, not by the results. It therefore cannot be said of competition any more than of any other sort of experimentation that it leads to a maximization of any measurable results. It merely leads, under favourable conditions, to the use of more skill and knowledge than any other known procedure. Though every successful use of skill and knowledge can be regarded as a gain, and therefore each additional act of exchange in which both parties prefer what they get for what they give can be regarded as an advantage, we can never say by what aggregate amount the net benefits available to the people have increased. We have not to deal with measurable or additive magnitudes, but must accept as the possible optimum the results of those general conditions which are most likely to lead to the discovery of the largest number of opportunities.

How any individual will act under the pressure of competition, what particular circumstance he will encounter in such conditions, is not known before even to him and must be still more unknown to anyone else. It is therefore literally meaningless to require him to act 'as if' competition existed, or as if it were more complete than it is. We shall see in particular that one of the chief sources of error in this field is the conception derived from the fictitious assumption that the individual's 'cost curves' are an objectively given fact ascertainable by inspection, and not something which can be determined only on the basis of his knowledge and judgment—a knowledge which will be wholly different when he acts in a highly competitive market from what it would be if he were the sole producer or one of a very few.

Though to explain the results of competition is one of the chief aims of economic theory (or catallactics), the facts we have considered greatly restrict the extent to which this theory can predict the particular results of competition in the kind of situation in which we are practically interested. Indeed, competition is of value precisely because it constitutes a discovery procedure which we would not need if we could predict its results. Economic theory can elucidate the operation of this discovery procedure by constructing models in which it is assumed that the theoretician possesses all the knowledge which guides all the several individuals whose interaction his model represents. We are interested in such a model only because it tells how a system of this sort will work. But we have to apply it to actual situations in which we do not possess that knowledge of the particulars. What the economist alone can do is to derive from mental models in which he assumes that, as it were, he can look into the cards of all the individual players, certain conclusions about the general character of the result, conclusions which he may perhaps be able to test on artificially constructed models, but which are interesting only in the instances where he cannot test them because he does not possess that knowledge which he would need.

If the Factual Requirements of 'Perfect' Competition are Absent, it is Not Possible to Make Firms Act 'As If' It Existed

Competition as a discovery procedure must rely on the self-interest of the producers, that is it must allow them to use their knowledge for their purposes, because nobody else possesses the information on which they must base their decision. Where the conditions of 'perfect' competition are absent, some will find it profitable to sell their products at prices above their marginal costs, though they could still make an adequate profit by selling at lower prices. It is this that those object to who regard the condition of perfect competition as the standard. They contend that producers in such conditions ought to be made to act as if perfect competition existed, although their self-interest will not lead them to do so. But we rely on self-interest because only through it can we induce producers to use knowledge which we do not possess, and to take actions the effects of which only they can determine. We cannot at the same time rely on their self-interest to find the most economical method of production and not allow them to produce the kinds and quantities of goods by the methods which best serve their interest. The inducement to improve the manner of production will often consist in the fact that whoever does so first will thereby gain a temporary profit. Many of the improvements of production are due to each striving for such profits even though he knows that they will only be temporary and last only so long as he leads.

If the future costs of production of any producer (and particularly his marginal costs of any additional quantity produced) were an objectively ascertainable magnitude which could unambiguously be determined by a supervising authority, it might be meaningful to demand that producers should be made to sell at marginal costs. But, though we are in the habit of arguing in theory as if costs were a 'datum', that is, given knowledge, the lowest costs at which a thing can be produced are exactly what we want competition to discover. They are not necessarily known to anyone but to him who has succeeded in discovering them—and even he will often not be aware what it is that enables him to produce more cheaply than others can.

It is, therefore, generally also not possible for an outsider to establish objectively whether a large excess of price over costs, manifesting itself in high profits and due to some improvement in technique or organization, is merely an 'adequate' return on investment. 'Adequate' in this connection must mean a return the expectation of which was sufficient to justify the risk incurred. In technologically advanced production the cost of a particular product will quite generally not be an objectively ascertainable fact, but will in a large measure depend on the opinion of the producer about probable future developments. The success of the individual enterprise and its long-run efficiency will depend on the degree of correctness of the expectations which are reflected in the entrepreneur's estimate of costs.

Whether a firm that has made large investments in improving its plant should at once extend production to the point where prices will fall to its new marginal costs will thus depend on judgment about the probability of future developments. It clearly is desirable that some investment in new and more efficient plant should be undertaken that will be profitable only if for some time after they come into operation prices will remain above the cost of operating the already existing plant. The construction of a new plant will only be justified if it is expected that the prices at which the product can be sold will remain sufficiently above marginal costs to provide not only amortization of the capital sunk in it but also to compensate for the risk of creating it. Who can say how great this risk did appear, or ought to have appeared, to those who in the first instance made the decision to build the plant? It would clearly make the running of such risks impossible if, after the venture had proved successful, the firm were required to reduce prices to what would then appear as its long-run marginal costs. Competitive improvement of productive techniques rests largely on the endeavour of each to gain temporary monopolistic profits so long as he leads; and it is in a great measure out of such profits that the successful obtain the capital for further improvements.

Nor is it unreasonable that in such situations some of the benefits which the producers could offer to the consumers will still be served better by the producer with the new equipment than by anybody else, and that is all we can demand so long as we rely on his use of his knowledge. Not to do as well as one could cannot be treated as an offence in a free society in which each is allowed to choose the manner of employing his person and property.

Quite apart from the practical difficulty of ascertaining whether such a *de facto* monopolist does extend his production to the point at which prices will only just cover marginal costs, it is by no means clear that to require him to do so could be reconciled with the general principles of just conduct on which the market order rests. So far as his monopoly is a result of his superior skill or of the possession of some factor of production uniquely suitable for the product in question, this would hardly be equitable. At least so long as we allow persons possessing special skills or unique objects not to use them at all, it would be paradoxical that as soon as they use them for commercial purposes, they should be required to use them to the greatest possible extent. We have no more justification for prescribing how intensively anyone must use his skill or his possessions than we have for prohibiting him from using his skill for solving crossword puzzles or his capital for acquiring a collection of postage stamps. Where the source of a monopoly position is a unique skill, it would be absurd to punish the possessor for doing better than anyone else by insisting that he should do as well as he can. And even where the monopoly position is the result of the possession of some object conferring a unique advantage, such as a particular site, it would seem hardly any less absurd to allow somebody to use for his private swimming pool a spring of water which would provide unique advantages for a brewery or whisky distillery, and then, once he turns it to such purpose, insist that he must not make a monopoly profit from it.

The power to determine the price or the quality of a product at the figure most profitable to the owner of such a rare resource used in its production is a necessary consequence of the recognition of private property in particular things, and cannot be eliminated without abandoning the institution of private property. There is in this respect no difference between a manufacturer or merchant who has built up a unique organization, or acquired a uniquely suitable site, and a painter who limits his output to what will bring him the largest income. There exists no more an argument in justice, or a moral case, against such a monopolist making a monopoly profit than there is against anyone who decides that he will work no more than he finds worth his while.

We shall see that the situation is wholly different where 'market power' consists in a power of preventing others from serving the customers better. In certain circumstances it is true that even the power over prices, etc. may confer upon a monopolist the power of influencing the market behaviour of others in a manner which protects him against unwelcome competition. We shall see that in such cases there is indeed a strong argument for preventing him from doing so.

Sometimes, however, the appearance of a monopoly (or of an obligopoly) may even be a desirable result of competition, that is, competition will have done its best when, for the time being,

---

it has led to a monopoly. Although, except in a special case which we shall consider later, production is not likely to be more efficient *because* it is conducted by a monopoly, it will often be conducted most effectively by one particular enterprise that for some special reason is more efficient than other existing ones.[3] While this does not provide a justification for protecting monopolistic positions or assisting their preservation, it makes it desirable not only to tolerate monopolies but even to allow them to exploit their monopolistic positions—so long as they maintain them solely by serving their customers better than anyone else, and not by preventing those who think they could do still better from trying to do so. So long as any producer is in a monopoly position because he can produce at costs lower than anybody else can, and sells at prices which are lower than those which anybody else can sell, that is all we can hope to achieve—even though we can in theory conceive of a better use of resources which, however, we have no way of realizing.

If such a position appears objectionable to many people this is chiefly due to the false suggestion of the word monopoly that it constitutes a privilege. But the bare fact that one producer (or a few producers) can meet the demand at prices which nobody else can match, does not constitute a privilege so long as the inability of others to do the same is not due to their being prevented from trying. The term privilege is used legitimately only to describe a right conferred by special decree (*privi-legium*) which others do not have, and not for an objective possibility which circumstances offer to some but not others.

So far as monopoly does not rest on privilege in the strict sense, it is indeed always objectionable when it depends on people being prevented from trying to do better than others. But those monopolies or obligopolies of which we have spoken in this section do not rest upon any such discrimination. They rest on the fact that men and things are not perfectly alike and that often a few or even only one of them will possess certain advantages over all others. We know how to induce such individuals or organizations to serve their fellows better than anyone else can do. But we have no means of always making them serve the public as well as they could.

The Achievements of the Free Market

What, then, is it that we want competition to bring about and which it normally does bring about if it is not prevented from doing so? It is a result so simple and obvious that most of us are inclined to take it for granted; and we are wholly unaware that it is a remarkable thing which is brought about and which never could be achieved by any authority telling the individual producer what to do. Competition, if not prevented, tends to bring about a state of affairs in which: *first,* everything will be produced which somebody knows how to produce and which he can sell profitably at a price at which buyers will prefer it to the available alternatives; *second*, everything that is being produced is produced by persons who can do so at least as cheaply as anybody else who in fact is not producing it;[4] and *third*, that everything will be sold at prices lower than, or at least as low as, those at which it could be sold by anybody who in fact does not do so.

There are three points which have to be considered if one wants to see the significance of such a state in its proper light: first, that this is a state of affairs which no central direction could ever bring about; second, that this state is approached remarkably closely in all fields where competition is not prevented by government or where governments do not tolerate such prevention by private persons or organizations; third, that in very large sectors of economic activity this state has never been closely approached because governments have restricted competition or allowed and often assisted private persons or organizations to restrict competition.

Modest as these accomplishments of competition may at first appear, the fact is that we do not know of any other method that would bring about better results; and wherever competition is prevented or impeded the conditions for their achievement are usually very far from being satisfied. Considering that competition has always been prevented in many fields by the deliberate policies of government from achieving this, while the result is very closely approximated wherever competition is allowed to operate, we should certainly be more concerned to make it generally possible than to make it operate in accordance with an unachievable standard of 'perfection'.

To what a great extent in a normally functioning society the result described is in fact achieved in all sectors where competition is not prevented is demonstrated by the difficulty of discovering opportunities for making a living by serving the customers better than is already being done. We know only too well how difficult this in fact is and how much ingenuity is needed in a functioning catallaxy to discover such opportunities.[5] It is also instructive to compare in this respect the situation in a country which possesses a large commercially alert class where most of the existing opportunities will have been taken advantage of, and in a country where people are less versatile or enterprising and which in consequence will often offer to one with a different outlook great opportunities for rapid gain.[6] The important point here is that a highly developed commercial spirit is itself as much the product as the condition of effective competition, and that we know of no other method of producing it than to throw competition open to all who want to take advantage of the opportunities it offers.

Competition and Rationality

Competition is not merely the only method which we know for utilizing the knowledge and skills that other people may possess, but it is also the method by which we all have been led to acquire much of the knowledge and skills we do possess. This is not understood by those who maintain that the argument for competition rests on the assumption of rational behaviour of those who take part in it. But rational behaviour is not a premise of economic theory, though it is often presented as such. The basic contention of theory is rather that competition will make it necessary for people to act rationally in order to maintain themselves. It is based not on the assumption that most or all the participants in the market process are rational, but, on the contrary, on the assumption that it will in general be through competition that a few relatively more rational individuals will make it necessary for the rest to emulate them in order to prevail.[7] In a society in which rational behaviour confers an advantage on the individual, rational methods will progressively be developed and be spread by imitation. It is no use being more rational than the rest if one is not allowed to derive benefits from being so. And it is therefore in general not rationality which is required to make competition work, but competition, or traditions which allow competition, which will produce rational behaviour.[8] The endeavour to do better than can be done in the customary manner is the process in which that capacity for thinking is developed which will later manifest itself in argument and criticism. No society which has not first developed a commercial group within which the improvement of the tools of thought has brought advantage to the individual has ever gained the capacity of systematic rational thinking.

This should be remembered particularly by those who are inclined to argue that competition will not work among people who lack the spirit of enterprise: let merely a few rise and be esteemed and powerful because they have successfully tried new ways, even if they may be in the first instance foreign intruders, and let those tempted to imitate them be free to do so, however few they may be in the first instance, and that spirit of enterprise will emerge by the only method which can produce it. Competition is as much a method for breeding certain types of mind as anything else: the very cast of thinking of the great entrepreneurs would not exist but for the environment in which they developed their gifts. The same innate capacity to think will take a wholly different turn according to the task it is set.

Such a development will be possible only if the traditionalist majority does not have power to make compulsory for everyone those traditional manners and mores which would prevent the experimentation with new ways inherent in competition. This means that the powers of the majority must be limited to the enforcement of such general rules as will prevent the individuals from encroaching on the protected domains of their fellows, and should not extend to positive prescriptions of what the individuals must do. If the majority view, or any *one* view, is made generally to prevail concerning how things must be done, such developments as we have sketched by which the more rational procedures gradually replace the less rational ones become impossible. The intellectual growth of a community rests on the views of a few gradually spreading, even to the disadvantage of those who are reluctant to accept them; and though nobody should have the power to force upon them new views because he thinks they are better, if success proves that they are more effective, those who stick to their old ways must not be protected against a relative or even absolute decline in their position. Competition is, after all, always a process in which a small number makes it necessary for larger numbers to do what they do not like, be it to work harder, to change habits, or to devote a degree of attention, continuous application, or regularity to their work which without competition would not be needed.

If in a society in which the spirit of enterprise has not yet spread, the majority has power to prohibit whatever it dislikes, it is most unlikely that it will allow competition to arise. I doubt whether a functioning market has ever newly arisen under an unlimited democracy, and it seems at least likely that unlimited democracy will destroy it where it has grown up. To those with whom others compete, the fact that they have competitors is always a nuisance that prevents a quiet life; and such direct effects of competition are always much more visible than the indirect benefits which we derive from it. In particular, the direct effects will be felt by the members of the same trade who see how competition is operating, while the consumer will generally have little idea to whose actions the reduction of prices or the improvement of quality is due.

Size, Concentration and Power

The misleading emphasis on the influence of the individual firm on prices, in combination with the popular prejudice against bigness as such, with various 'social' considerations supposed to make it desirable to preserve the middle class, the independent entrepreneur, the small craftsman or shopkeeper, or quite generally the existing structure of society, has acted against changes caused by economic and technological development. The 'power' which large corporations can exercise is represented as in itself dangerous and as making necessary special governmental measures to restrict it. This concern about size and power of individual corporations more often than perhaps any other consideration produces essentially antiliberal conclusions drawn from liberal premises.

We shall presently see that there are two important respects in which monopoly may confer on its possessor harmful power. But neither size in itself, nor ability to determine the prices at which all can buy their product is a measure of their harmful power. More important still, there is no possible measure or standard by which we can decide whether a particular enterprise is too large. Certainly the bare fact that one big firm in a particular industry 'dominates' the market because the other firms of the industry will follow its price leadership, is no proof that this position can in fact be improved upon in any way other than by the appearance of an effective competitor—an event which we may hope for, but which we cannot bring about so long as nobody is available who does enjoy the same (or other compensating) special advantages as the firm that is now dominant.

The most effective size of the individual firm is as much one of the unknowns to be discovered by the market process as the prices, quantities or qualities of the goods to be produced and sold. There can be no general rule about what is the desirable size since this will depend on the ever-changing technological and economic conditions; and there will always be many changes which will give advantages to enterprises of what on past standards will appear to be an excessive size. It is not to be denied that the advantages of the size will not always rest on facts which we cannot alter, such as the scarcity of certain kinds of talents or resources (including such accidental and yet unavoidable facts as that somebody has been earlier in the field and therefore has had more time to acquire experience and special knowledge); they will often be determined by institutional arrangements which happen to give an advantage to size which is artificial in the sense that it does not secure smaller social costs of the unit of output. In so far as tax legislation, the law of corporations, or the greater influence on the administrative machinery of government, give to the larger unit differential advantages which are not based on genuine superiority of performance, there is indeed every reason for so altering the framework as to remove such artificial advantages of bigness. But there is as little justification for discrimination by policy against large size as such as there is for assisting it.

The argument that mere size confers harmful power over the market behaviour of competitors possesses a degree of plausibility when we think in terms of one 'industry' within which there may indeed sometimes be room only for one specialized big firm. But the growth of the giant corporation has made largely meaningless the conception of separate industries which one corporation, because of the magnitude of its resources, can dominate. One of the unforeseen results of the increase of size of the individual corporations which the theorists have not yet quite digested is that large size has brought diversification far beyond the bounds of any definable industry. In consequence, the size of the corporations in other industries has become the main check on the power which size might give a single large corporation in one industry. It may well be that, say in the electrical industry of one country, no other corporation has the strength or staying power to 'take on' an established giant intent upon defending its *de facto* monopoly of some of the products. But as the development of the great automobile or chemical concerns in the USA shows, they have no compunction about encroaching on such fields in which the backing of large resources is essential to make the prospects of entry promising. Size has thus become the most effective antidote to the power of size: what will control the power of large aggregations of capital are other large aggregations of capital, and such control will be much more effective than any supervision by government, whose permission of an act carries its authorization, if not outright protection. As I cannot repeat too often, government-supervised monopoly always tends to become government-protected monopoly; and the fight against bigness only too often results in preventing those very developments through which size becomes the antidote of size.

I do not intend to deny that there are real social and political (as distinct from merely economic) considerations which make a large number of small enterprises appear as more desirable or 'healthy' structures than a smaller number of large ones. We have already had occasion to refer to the danger arising from the fact that constantly increasing numbers of the population work in ever larger corporations, and as a result are familiar with the organizational type of order but strangers to the working of the market which co-ordinates the activities of the several corporations. Considerations like this are often advanced in justification of measures designed to curb the growth of individual enterprise or to protect the less efficient smaller firms against their displacement or absorption into a big one.

Yet, even granting that such measures might in some sense be desirable, it is one of those things which, even though in themselves desirable, cannot be achieved without conferring a discretionary and arbitrary power on some authority, and which therefore must give way to the higher consideration that no authority should be given such power. We have already stressed that such a limitation on all power may make impossible the achievement of some particular aims which may be desired by a majority of the people, and that generally, to avoid greater evils, a free society must deny itself certain kinds of power even if the foreseeable consequences of its exercise appear only beneficial and constitute perhaps the only available method of achieving that particular result.

The Political Aspects of Economic Power

The argument that the great size of an individual corporation confers great power on its management, and that such power of a few men is politically dangerous and morally objectionable, certainly deserves serious consideration. Its persuasiveness derives, however, in a great measure from a confusion of the different meanings of the word 'power', and from a constant shifting from one of the senses in which the possession of great power is desirable to another in which it is objectionable: power over material things and power over the conduct of other men. These two kinds of power are not necessarily connected and can to a large extent be separated. It is one of the ironies of history that socialism, which gained influence by promising the substitution of the administration of things for the power over men, inevitably leads to an unbounded increase of the power exercised by men over other men.

So long as large aggregations of material resources make it possible to achieve better results in terms of improved or cheaper products or more desirable services than smaller organizations provide, every extension of this kind of power must be regarded as in itself beneficial. The fact that large aggregations of resources under a single direction often increase power of this kind more than in proportion to size is often the reason for the development of very large enterprises. Although size is not an advantage in every respect, and though there will always be a limit to the increase of size which still brings an increase of productivity, there will at all times exist fields in which technological change gives an advantage to units larger than those which have existed before. From the replacement of the cottage weaver by the factory to the growth of the continuous process in steel production and to the supermarket, advances in technological knowledge have again and again made larger units more efficient. But if such increase in size leads to more effective use of resources, it does not necessarily increase the power over the conduct of the people, except the limited power which the head of an enterprise wields over those who join it for their benefit. Even though a mail-order house like Sears Roebuck & Co. has grown to be one of the 100 largest corporations in the world and far exceeds in size any comparable enterprise, and although its activities have profoundly affected the standards and habits of millions, it cannot be said to exercise power in any sense other than that of offering services which people prefer when they become available. Nor would a single corporation gain power over the conduct of other men if it were so efficient in the production of a piece of mechanical equipment as universally employed as, say, ball bearings, that it would drive out all competition: so long as it stood ready to supply everyone awaiting its product on the same terms, even though it thereby made a huge profit, not only would all its customers be better off for its existence, but they could also not be said to be dependent on its power.

In modern society it is not the size of the aggregate of resources controlled by an enterprise which gives it power over the conduct of other people, so much as its capacity to withhold services on which people are dependent. As we shall see in the next section, it is therefore also not only simply power over the price of their products but the power to exact different terms from different customers which confers power over conduct. This power, however, is not directly dependent on size and not even an inevitable product of monopoly—although it will be possessed by the monopolist of any essential product, whether he be big or small, so long as he is free to make a sale dependent on terms not exacted from all customers alike. We shall see that it is not only the power of the monopolist to discriminate, together with the influence he may exercise on government possessing similar powers, which is truly harmful and ought to be curbed. But this power, although often associated with large size, is neither a necessary consequence of size nor confined to large organizations. The same problem arises when some small enterprise, or a labour union. which controls an essential service can hold the community to ransom by refusing to supply it.

Before we consider further the problem of checking these harmful actions of monopolists we must, however, consider some other reasons why size as such is often regarded as harmful.

The fact that the welfare of many more people is affected by the decisions of a big enterprise rather than by those of a small one does not mean that other considerations should enter into those decisions, or that it is desirable or possible in the case of the former to safeguard against mistakes by some sort of public supervision. Much of the resentment against the big corporations is due to the belief that they do not take consequences into account which we think that they could because they are big, although a smaller firm admittedly could not do so: if a large concern closes down an unprofitable local plant, there will be an outcry because it 'could have afforded' to run it at a loss in order to preserve the jobs, while if the same plant had been an independent enterprise everybody would accept its closing down as inevitable. It is, however, no less desirable that an uneconomical plant be closed down if it belongs to a large concern, although it could be kept going out of the profits of the rest of the concern, than if it is an enterprise which cannot draw on such other sources of revenue.

There exists a widespread feeling that a big corporation, because it is big, should take more account of the indirect consequences of its decisions, and that it should be required to assume responsibilities not imposed upon smaller ones. But it is precisely here that there lies the danger of a big enterprise acquiring objectionably large powers. So long as the management has the one overriding duty of administering the resources under its control as trustees for the shareholders and for their benefit, its hands are largely tied; and it will have no arbitrary power to benefit this or that particular interest. But once the management of a big enterprise is regarded as not only entitled but even obliged to consider in its decisions whatever is regarded as the public or social interest, or to support good causes and generally to act for the public benefit, it gains indeed an uncontrollable power—a power which could not long be left in the hands of private managers but would inevitably be made the subject of increasing public control.[9]

In so far as corporations have power to benefit groups of individuals, mere size will also become a source of influencing government, and thus beget power of a very objectionable kind. We shall see presently that such influence, much more serious when it is exerted by the organized interests of groups than when exerted by the largest single enterprise, can be guarded against only by depriving government of the power of benefiting particular groups.

We must finally mention another instance in which it is undeniable that the mere fact of bigness creates a highly undesirable position: namely where, because of the consequences of what happens to a big enterprise, government cannot afford to let such an enterprise fail. At least in so far as the expectation that it will thus be protected makes investment in very big corporations appear less risky than investment in smaller ones, this will produce one of the 'artificial' advantages of bigness which are not based on better performance and which policy ought to eliminate. It seems clear that this can be done only by effectively depriving government of the power of providing such protection, for as long as it has such power it is vulnerable to pressure.

The chief point to remember, which is often obscured by the current talk about monopoly, is that it is not monopoly as such but only the prevention of competition which is harmful. These are so very far from being the same thing that it ought to be repeated that a monopoly that rests entirely on superior performance is wholly praiseworthy—even if such a monopolist keeps prices at a level at which he makes large profits and only just low enough to make it impossible for others to compete with him successfully, because he still uses a smaller amount of resources than others would do if they produced the same quantity of the product. Nor can there be a legitimate claim that such a monopolist is under a moral obligation to sell his product as cheaply as he still could while making a 'normal' profit—as little as we are under a moral obligation to work as hard as possible, or to sell a rare object at a moderate gain. Just as nobody dreams of attacking the monopoly price of the unique skill of an artist or surgeon, so there is no wrong in the 'monopoly' profit of an enterprise capable of producing more cheaply than anybody else.

That it is not monopoly but only the prevention of competition (and all prevention of competition, whether it leads to monopoly or not) which is morally wrong should be specially remembered by those 'neo-liberals' who believe that they must show their impartiality by thundering against all enterprise monopoly as much as against labour monopolies, forgetting that much enterprise monopoly is the result of better performance, while all labour monopoly is due to the coercive suppression of competition. Where enterprise monopoly is based on a similar prevention of competition, it is as reprehensible and in as much need of prevention as those of labour and ought to be severely dealt with. But neither the existence of monopoly nor size as such are on economic or moral grounds undesirable or comparable with any acts aiming at the prevention of competition.

When Monopoly Becomes Harmful

We leave out here deliberately one model case in which it must be admitted that monopolies are likely to arise—the case of scarce and exhaustible resources such as the deposits of certain ores and the like. The reason for the omission is that the problems which arise in this connection are much too complex for any brief discussion to be useful. We need merely note that this one case in which the development of a monopoly may be inevitable is also a case in which it is by no means clear that a monopoly is harmful, since such a monopoly is likely only to spread over a longer period the exploitation of the resource in question, but not to lead to any permanent withholding of goods or services at the expense of the total output.

Quite generally it can probably be said that what is harmful is not the existence of monopolies that are due to greater efficiency or to the control of particular limited resources, but the ability of some monopolies to protect and preserve their monopolistic position after the original cause of their superiority has disappeared. The main reason for this is that such monopolies will be able to use their power, not only over the prices which they charge uniformly to all, but over the prices which it can charge to particular customers. This power over the prices they will charge particular customers, or the power to discriminate, can in many ways be used to influence the market behaviour of these others, and particularly to deter or otherwise influence potential competitors.

It is probably not much of an exaggeration to say that almost all really harmful power of non-privileged monopolies rests on this power of discrimination because it alone, short of violence, gives them power over potential competitors. So long as a monopolist enjoys a monopolistic position because he offers to all better terms than anybody else can, even if these terms are not as favourable as those he could offer, everybody is better off for his existence. But if, because he can supply most people at better terms than anyone else, no other firm is ready to supply the product in question, anyone to whom he refuses to supply at those terms will have no alternative opportunity to satisfy his needs. Though the majority of the people may still be better off for the existence of such a monopolist, anyone may be at his mercy in so far as the nature of the product or service makes aimed discrimination possible and the monopolist chooses to practice it in order to make the buyer behave in some respect in a manner that suits the monopolist. He can, in particular, use this power to keep out a potential competitor by offering specially favourable terms to customers only in that limited region in which a newcomer at first will be able to compete.

The task of preventing such use of discrimination is especially difficult because certain kinds of discrimination by a monopolist will often be desirable. We have already mentioned that there is one case in which a monopolist may render better services *because* he is a monopolist. This is the case where his power to discriminate between different users of his product enables him to cover most of his fixed costs from those who can pay a relatively higher price and then to supply others at little more than variable costs. In such fields as transport and public utilities it is at least possible that some services could not be supplied at all at a profit if it were not for the possibility of discrimination such as monopoly confers.

The problem can therefore not be solved by imposing upon all monopolists the obligation to serve all customers alike. Yet since the power of the monopolist to discriminate can be used to coerce particular individuals or firms, and is likely to be used to restrict competition in an undesirable manner, it clearly ought to be curbed by appropriate rules of conduct. Though it would not be desirable to make all discrimination illegal, aimed discrimination intended to enforce a certain market conduct should clearly be prohibited. It is doubtful, however, whether it would be effectively achieved by making it a punishable offence rather than merely the basis of a claim for damages. The knowledge required here in order to prosecute successfully is not the kind of knowledge that any authority is likely to possess.

The Problem of Anti-Monopoly Legislation

It would seem more promising to give potential competitors a claim to equal treatment where discrimination cannot be justified on grounds other than the desire to enforce a particular market conduct, and to hold out an inducement for enforcing such claims in the form of multiple damages to all who feel they have been unreasonably discriminated against. Thus to set potential competitors as watchdogs over the monopolist and to give them a remedy against the use of price discrimination would seem a more promising check on such practices than to place enforcement in the hands of a supervising authority. Particularly if the law explicitly authorized that a part of the damages awarded might be collected by the lawyers conducting such cases, in lieu of fees and expenses, highly specialized legal consultants would probably soon grow up who, since they would owe the whole of their business to such suits, would not be inhibited through fear of offending the big corporations.

The same applies largely to the case where not a single monopolist but small groups of firms acting in concert to control the market are concerned. It is generally thought necessary to prohibit such monopolistic combinations or cartels by prohibiting them under penalties. The example set in the USA by Section One of the Sherman Act 1890 has been widely imitated. It seems also that this provision of the Act has been remarkably successful in creating in the business world a climate of opinion which regards as improper such explicit agreements to restrict competition. I have no doubt that such a general prohibition of all cartels, if it were consistently carried through, would be preferable to any discretionary power given to authorities for the purpose of merely preventing 'abuses'. The latter leads to a distinction between good and bad monopolies and usually to governments becoming more concerned with protecting the good monopolies than with combating the bad ones. There is no reason to believe that any monopolistic organization deserves protection against threatening competition, and much reason to believe that some wholly voluntary organizations of firms that do not rely on compulsion are not only not harmful but actually beneficial. It would seem that prohibition under penalties cannot be carried out without a discretionary power of granting exemptions, or of imposing upon courts the difficult task of deciding whether a particular agreement is, or is not, in the public interest. Even in the USA, under the Sherman Act and its various amendments and supplements, a situation has in consequence arisen of which it could be said that 'the law tells some businessmen that they must not cut prices, others that they must not raise prices, and still others that there is something evil in similar prices'.[10] It seems to me, therefore, that a third possibility, less far-reaching than prohibition under penalties, but more general than discretionary surveillance to prevent abuses, would be both more effective and more in conformity with the rule of law than either. This would be to declare invalid and legally unenforceable all agreement in restraint of trade, without any exceptions, and to prevent all attempts to enforce them by aimed discrimination or the like by giving those upon whom such pressures were brought a claim for multiple damages as suggested above.

We need not here again consider the misconception that this would be contrary to the principle of freedom of contract. Freedom of contract, like any other freedom, means merely that what kind of contract is enforceable in the courts depends only on the general rules of law and not on the previous approval by authority of the particular contents of the contract. Many kinds of contracts, such as gambling contracts, or contracts for immoral purposes, or contracts for life-long service, have long been held invalid and unenforceable. There is no reason why the same should not also apply to all contracts in restraint of trade, and no reason why all attempts to make someone, by the threat of withholding usual services, conform to certain rules of conduct should not be treated as unwarranted interference in this private domain which entitles him to damages. The practical solution of our problem may be much facilitated by the necessity which, as we shall see later, will arise of imposing special limitations upon the power of 'legal persons' (corporations and all other formal or informal organizations) which do not apply to private individuals.

The reason why such a modest aim of the law seems to me to promise greater results is that it can be applied universally without exceptions, while all the more ambitious attempts are generally emasculated by so many exceptions that they become not nearly so effective than the general application of a less far-reaching rule would be—not to mention the wholly undesirable discretionary power which, under the first system confers on government the power of determining the character of economic activity.

There is probably no better illustration of the failure of the more ambitious attempt than the German Federal Republic's law against restriction of competition.[11] It begins with a sweeping provision which, wholly in the sense of what has been suggested, declares as invalid all agreements in restraint of competition. But after it has also made such agreements a punishable offence, it ends up by perforating the general rule with so many exceptions, which wholly exempt various kinds of contracts, or confer upon authorities discretionary powers to permit them, and finally confines the application of the law to such a limited sector of the economy, that it deprives the whole of most of its effectiveness. There would have been no need for most of if not for all of these exceptions if the law had confined itself to what it provided in the first paragraph and had not added to the declaration of the invalidity of agreements in restraint of trade a prohibition under penalties.

As there exist undoubtedly all kinds of understandings on standards and the like which are to apply unless other terms are explicitly agreed upon in the particular instances, and which are wholly beneficial so long as adherence to them is purely voluntary and no pressure can be brought on those who find it in their interest to divert from them, any outright prohibition of such agreements would be harmful. Both as regards types of products and terms of the contract the establishment of such norms as it would be in the interest of most to observe in ordinary instances would produce considerable economies. In such instances it will, however, be not so much that the norm is obligatory as that it pays the individual to adhere to an established standard practice which will bring about his conformity. The necessary check on such agreements on standards becoming obstructive will be provided by any individual firms being free explicitly to deviate from the norm in making a contract whenever this is to the interest of both parties to the contract.

Before leaving this particular subject a few words may be added on the curiously contradictory attitude of most governments towards monopoly. While in recent times they have generally endeavoured to control monopolies in the production and distribution of manufactured goods, and have in this field often applied overly rigorous standards, they have at the same time in much larger fields—in transport, public utilities, labour, agriculture, and, in many countries, also finance—deliberately assisted monopoly or used it as an instrument of policy. Also, the anti-cartel or anti-trust legislation has mostly been aimed at the combination of a few big firms and has rarely effectively touched the restrictive practices of the large groups of smaller firms organized in trade associations and the like. If we add to this the extent to which monopolies have been assisted by tariffs, industrial patents, some features of the law of corporations and the principles of taxation, one may well ask whether, if government had merely refrained from favouring monopolies, monopoly would ever have been a serious problem. Though I do believe that it should be one of the aims of the development of law to reduce private power over the market conduct of others, and that some beneficial results would follow from this, it does not appear to me that this compares in importance with what could be achieved by government refraining from assisting monopoly by discriminatory rules or measures of policy.

Not Individual But Group Selfishness is the Chief Threat

While public indignation and in consequence also legislation has been directed almost entirely against the selfish actions of single monopolists, or of a few conspicuous enterprises acting in concert, what is chiefly threatening to destroy the market order is not the selfish action of individual firms but the selfishness of organized groups. These have gained their power largely through the assistance government has given them to suppress those manifestations of individual selfishness which would have kept their action in check. The extent to which the functioning of the market order has already been impeded, and threatens to become progressively more inoperative, is a result not so much of the rise of large productive units as of the deliberately furthered organization of the units for collective interests. What is increasingly suspending the working of the spontaneous forces of the market is not what the public has in mind when it complains about monopolies, but the ubiquitous associations and unions of the different 'trades'. They operate largely through the pressure they can bring on government to 'regulate' the market in their interest.

It was a misfortune that these problems became acute for the first time in connection with labour unions when widespread sympathy with their aims led to the toleration of methods which certainly could not be generally permitted, and which even in the field of labour will have to be curbed, though most workers have come to regard them as their hard-earned and sacred rights. One need merely ask what the results would be if the same techniques were generally used for political instead of economic purposes (as indeed they sometimes already are) in order to see that they are irreconcilable with the preservation of what we know as a free society.

The very term 'freedom of organization,' hallowed by its use as a battle cry not only by labour but also by those political organizations which are indispensable for democratic government, carries overtones which are not in accord but in conflict with the reign of law on which a free society rests. Certainly any control of these activities through a discretionary supervision by government would be incompatible with a free order. But 'freedom of organization' should no more than 'freedom of contract' be interpreted to mean that the activities of organizations must not be subject to rules restricting their methods, or even that the collective action of organizations should not be restricted by rules which do not apply to individuals. The new powers created by the perfection of organizational techniques, and by the right conceded to them by existing laws, will probably require limitations by general rules of law far more narrow than those it has been found necessary to impose by law on the actions of private individuals.

It is easy to see why the weak individual will often derive comfort from the knowledge that he is a member of an organized group comprising individuals with common aims and which, as an organized group, is stronger than the strongest individual. It is an illusion, however, to believe that he would benefit, or that generally the many will benefit at the expense of the few, if all interests were so organized. The effect of such organization on society as a whole would be to make power not less but more oppressive. Though groups may then count for more than individuals, small groups may still be more powerful than large ones, simply because the former are more organizable, or the whole of their produce more indispensable than the whole of the produce of larger groups. And even though to the individual his single most important interest may be enhanced by joining an organization, this single most important interest that is organizable may still be less important to him than the sum of all his other interests which will be encroached upon by other organizations and which he himself cannot defend by joining a corresponding number of other organizations.

The importance attached and the respect paid to the collective bodies is a result of an understandable though erroneous belief that the larger the group becomes the more its interests will correspond to the interest of all. The term 'collective' has become invested with much the same aura of approval which the term 'social' commands. But far from the collective interests of the various groups being nearer to the interests of society as a whole, the exact opposite is true. While as a rough approximation it can legitimately be said that individual selfishness will in most instances lead the individual to act in a manner conducive to the preservation of the spontaneous order of society, the selfishness of a closed group, or the desire of its members to become a closed group, will always be in opposition to the true common interest of the members of a Great Society.[12]

That is what classical economics had already clearly brought out and modern marginal analysis has put into a more satisfying form. The importance of any particular service which any individual renders to the members of society is always only that of the last (or marginal) additions he makes to all the services of that kind; and if, whatever any member of society takes out of the pool of products and services is to leave as much as possible to the others, this requires that not the groups as such but the separate individuals composing them, by their free movement between the groups, strive to make their respective incomes as large as possible. The common interest of the members of any organized group will, however, be to make the value of their services correspond, not to the importance of the last increment, but to the importance which the aggregate of the services rendered by the group has for the users. The producers of food or electrical energy, of transport or medical services, etc., will therefore aim to use their joint power of determining the volume of such services to achieve a price that will be much higher than that which the consumers would be prepared to pay for the last increment. There exists no necessary relationship between the importance of a kind of commodity or service as a whole and the importance of the last addition that is still provided. If to have some food is essential for survival, this does not mean that the last addition to the supply of food is also more important than the production of an additional quantity of some frivolity, or that the production of food should be better remunerated than the production of things whose existence is certainly much less important than the availability of food as such.

The special interest of the producers of food, or electricity, or transport, or medical services will be, however, to be remunerated not merely according to the marginal value of the kind of services they render, but according to the value that the total supply of the services in question has to the users. Public opinion, which still sees the problem in terms of the importance of this kind of service as such, therefore tends to give some support to such demands because it is felt that remuneration should be appropriate to the absolute importance of the commodity in question. It is only through the efforts of the marginal producers who can earn a living by rendering their services much below the value which the consumers would be prepared to pay if the total supply were smaller, that we are assured of plenty and that the chances of all are improved. The collective interests of the organized groups, on the other hand, will always be opposed to this general interest and aim at preventing those marginal individuals from adding to the total supply.

Any control wielded by the members of a trade or profession over the total amount of goods or services to be supplied will therefore always be opposed to the true general interest of society, while the selfish interests of the individual will normally drive them to make those marginal contributions which will cost approximately as much as the price at which they can be sold.

It is a wholly mistaken conception that a bargaining between groups in which the producers and the consumers of each of the different commodities or services respectively are combined would lead to a state of affairs which secures either efficiency in production or a kind of distribution which from any point of view would appear to be just. Even if all the separate interests (or even all 'important' interests) could be organized (which, as we shall see they cannot), the sort of balance between the strengths of different organized groups which some people expect as the necessary or even desirable outcome of the developments which have been going on for some time, would in fact produce a structure which would be demonstrably irrational and inefficient, and unjust to the extreme in the light of any test of justice which requires a treatment of all according to the same rules.

The decisive reason for this is that in negotiations between existing organized groups the interests of those who bring about the required adjustments to changes, namely those who could improve their position by moving from one group to another, are systematically disregarded. So far as the group to which they wish to move is concerned, it will be its chief aim to keep them out. And the groups they wish to leave will have no incentive to assist their entry into what will often be a great variety of other groups. Thus, in a system in which the organizations of the existing producers of the various commodities and services determine prices and quantities to be produced, those who would bring about the continuous adjustment to change would be deprived of influence on events. It is not true, as the argument in support of the various syndicalist or corporativist systems assumes, that anybody's interest is bound up with the interest of all others who produce the same goods. It may be much more important to some to be able to shift to another group, and these movements are certainly most important for the preservation of the overall order. Yet it is these changes which, possible in a free market, agreements between organized groups will aim to prevent.

The organized producers of particular commodities or services will in general attempt to justify the exclusive policies by pleading that they can still meet the whole demand, and that, if and when they are not able to do so, they will be fully prepared to let others enter the trade. What they do not say is that this means merely that they can meet the demand at prevailing prices which give them what they regard as adequate profits. What is desirable, however, is that the demand be satisfied at the lower prices at which others might be able to supply—leaving those now in the trade perhaps only an income reflecting the fact that their particular skill is no longer scarce, or their equipment no longer up-to-date. In particular, though it should be as profitable for those in possession to introduce improvements in technique as it is for any newcomers, this will involve for the former risks and often the necessity of raising outside capital which will disturb their comfortable established position and seem not worth while unless their position is threatened by those not content with theirs. To allow the established producers to decide when new entrants are to be permitted would normally lead simply to the *status quo* being preserved.

Even in a society in which all the different interests were organized as separate closed groups, this would therefore lead merely to a freezing of the existing structure and as a result, to a gradual decline of the economy as it became progressively less adjusted to the changed conditions. It is therefore not true that such a system is unsatisfactory and unjust only so long as not all groups are equally organized. The belief of such authors as G. Myrdal and J. K. Galbraith[13] that the defects of the existing order are only those of a transitory kind which will be remedied when the process of organization is completed, is therefore erroneous. What makes most Western economies still viable is that the organization of interests is yet only partial and incomplete. If it were complete, we would have a deadlock between these organized interests, producing a wholly rigid economic structure which no agreement between the established interests and only the force of some dictatorial power could break.

The Consequences of a Political Determination of the Incomes of the Different Groups

The interest which is common to all members of a society is not the sum of the interests which are common to the members of the existing groups of producers, but only the interest in the continuous adaptation to changing conditions which some particular groups will always find it in their interests to prevent. The interest of the organized producers is therefore always contrary to the one permanent interest of all the individual members of society, namely the interest in the continuous adaptation to unpredictable changes, an adaptation necessary even if only the existing level of production is to be maintained (cf. chapters 8 and 10). The interest of organized producers is always to prevent the influx of others who want to share their prosperity or to avoid being driven out from a group by the more efficient producers when demand should decline. By this all strictly economic decisions, that is all new adjustments to unforeseen changes, will be impeded. The viability of a society, however, depends on the smooth and continuous execution of such gradual changes and their not being blocked by obstacles which can only be broken down when sufficient pressure accumulates. All the benefits we receive from the spontaneous order of the market are the results of such changes, and will be maintained only if the changes are allowed to continue. But every change of this kind will hurt some organized interests; and the preservation of the market order will therefore depend on those interests not being allowed to prevent what they dislike. All the time it is thus the interest of most that some be placed under the necessity of doing something they dislike (such as changing their jobs or accepting a lower income), and this general interest will be satisfied only if the principle is recognized that each has to submit to changes when circumstances nobody can control determine that he is the one who is placed under such a necessity. This risk itself is inseparable from the occurrence of unforeseen changes; and the only choice we have is either to allow the effects of such changes to fall, through the impersonal mechanism of the market, on the individuals whom the market will require to make the change or to accept a reduction of income, or to decide, arbitrarily or by a power struggle, who are to be those who must bear the burden which in this case will necessarily be greater than it would have been if we had let the market bring about the necessary change.

The deadlock to which the political determination of prices and wages by organized interests has already led has produced in some countries the demand for an 'incomes policy' which is to substitute an authoritative fixing of the remuneration of the different factors of production for their determination by the market. The demand is based on the recognition that if wages and other incomes are no longer determined by the market but by the political force of the organized groups, some deliberate co-ordination becomes necessary—and particularly that, if such political determination is to be effected with regard to wages, where the political determination had become most conspicuous, this would be possible to achieve only if a similar control was applied to all other incomes also.

The immediate danger which led to the demand for an 'incomes policy' was, however, the process of inflation which the competitive pressure for an increase of all incomes produced. As a means of curbing this upward movement of all money incomes, these 'incomes policies' were bound to fail. And the inflationary policies by which we are at present attempting to overcome those 'rigidities' are no more than palliatives that in the long run will not solve the problem but merely make it worse: because the temporary escape which they provide from the difficulties only allows the rigidities to grow stronger and stronger. No wage and price stop can alter the basic malaise, and every attempt to bring about the necessary alterations in relative prices by authoritative decision must fail, not only because no authority can know which prices are appropriate, but even more because such authority must, in whatever it does, endeavour to appear to be just, though the changes that will be required will have nothing whatever to do with justice. In consequence, all the measures of 'incomes policy' that have been taken have not even come near to solving the really central problem, that of restoring the process by which the relative incomes of the different groups are adjusted to changing conditions; and by treating this as a matter of political decisions they have, if anything, made matters only worse. As we have seen, the only definite content that can be given to the concept of 'social justice' is the preservation of the relative positions of the different groups; but these are what must be altered if adjustment to changed conditions is to be achieved. If change can be brought about only by political decision, the effect can only be, since there exists no basis for real agreement, an increasing rigidity of the whole economic structure.

Since Great Britain was the only big country which, at a time when a thorough readaptation of the deployment of her resources was required, found itself in the grip of extreme rigidity produced by an essentially politically determined wage structure, the resulting difficulties have come to be known as the 'English disease'. But in many other countries, where the situation is not very different, similar methods are now being tried in vain to solve the same kind of difficulties.

What is not yet generally recognized is that the real exploiters in our present society are not egotistic capitalists or entrepreneurs, and in fact not separate individuals, but organizations which derive their power from the moral support of collective action and the feeling of group loyalty. It is the built-in bias of our existing institutions in favour of organized interests which gives these organizations an artificial preponderance over the market forces and which is the main cause of real injustice in our society and of distortion of its economic structure. More real injustice is probably done in the name of group loyalty than from any selfish individual motives. Once we recognize that the degree of organizability of an interest has no relation to its importance from any social point of view, and that interests can be effectively organized only if they are in a position to exercise anti-social powers of coercion, the naive conception that, if the power of organized interests is checked by 'countervailing power',[14] this will produce a viable social order, appears as an absurdity. If by 'regulatory mechanism', of which the chief expounder of these ideas speaks, is meant a mechanism conducive to the establishment of an advantageous or rational order, 'countervailing powers' certainly produces no such mechanism. The whole conception that the power of organized interests can or will be made innocuous by 'countervailing power' constitutes a relapse into the methods of settling conflicts which once prevailed among individuals and from which the development and enforcement of rules of just conduct has gradually freed us. The problem of developing similar rules of just conduct for organized groups is still largely a problem for the future, and the main concern in the efforts to solve it will have to be the protection of the individuals against group pressure.

Organizable and Non-Organizable Interests

During the last half century or so the dominant opinion which has guided policy has been that the growth of organized interests for the purpose of bringing pressure on government is inevitable, and that its obviously harmful effects are due to the fact that only some interests are yet so organized; this defect, it is thought, will disappear as soon as all important interests are equally organized so as to balance each other. Both views are demonstrably false. In the first instance, it is worth bringing pressure on government only if government has the power to benefit particular interests and this power exists only if it has authority to lay down and enforce aimed and discriminatory rules. In the second instance, as has been shown in an important study by M. Olson,[15] except in the case of relatively small groups, the existence of common interests will normally *not* lead to the spontaneous formation of a comprehensive organization of such interests, and has in fact done so only when government either positively assisted the efforts to organize all members of such groups, or has at least tolerated the use of coercion or discrimination to bring about such organization. It can be shown that these methods, however, can never bring about a comprehensive organization of all important interests but will always produce a condition in which the non-organizable interests will be sacrificed to and exploited by the organizable interests.

Olson's demonstration that, *first*, only relatively small groups will in general spontaneously form an organization, *second,* that the organizations of the great economic interests which today dominate government to a large extent have come about only with the help of the power of that government, and, *third*, that it is impossible in principle to organize all interests and that in consequence the organization of certain large groups assisted by government leads to a persistent exploitation of unorganized and unorganizable groups is here of fundamental importance. To the latter seem to belong such important groups as the consumers in general, the taxpayers, the women, the aged, and many others who together constitute a very substantial part of the population. All these groups are bound to suffer from the power of organized group interests.

Notes

* Ludwig von Mises, *Human Action: A Treatise on Economics* (Yale University Press, 1949), p. 239.

1. This chapter, written in more or less the present form about ten years ago and partly published, after having been used for public lectures at Chicago and Kiel, as 'Der Wettbewerb als Entdeckungsverfahren' in *Kieler Vorträge,* No. 56 (Kiel, 1969) and in English more recently in my *New Studies in Philosophy, Politics, Economics and the History of Ideas* (London and Chicago, 1977), I have let stand largely unchanged since it already occupies an undue amount of space in the present context and any attempt to deal with more recent developments would in this place have been inappropriate. I should, however, refer here at least to some of the works which have substantially developed the conceptions here sketched, such as Murray Rothbard, *Power and Market* (Menlo Park,1970), John S. MacGee, *In Defence of Industrial Concentration* (New York, 1971), D. T. Armentano, *The Myth of Antitrust* (New Rochelle. N.Y., 1972), and particularly Israel Kirzner, *Competition and Entrepreneurship* (Chicago, 1973) and a number of German essays by Erich Hoppmann, especially 'Missbrauch der Missbrauchaufsicht', *Mitteilungen der List Gesellschaft*, May 1976, and 'Preisunelastizität der Nachfrage als Quelle von Marktbeherrschung', in H. Gutzler and J. H. Kaiser (eds), *Wetztewerb im Wandel* (Baden-Baden, 1976).

2. Among the few who have seen this is the sociologist Leopold von Wiese. See his lecture on 'Die Konkurrenz, vorwiegend in soziologisch-systematischer Betrachtung', *Verhandlungen des 6. Deutschen Soziologentages*, 1929.

3. This seems to have been confused by J. A. Schumpeter, *Capitalism, Socialism, and Democracy* (New York, 1942), p. 101 where he contends that:

    there are superior methods available to the monopolist which either are not available to a crowd of competitors or are not available to them so readily: for their advantages which, though not strictly available on the competitive level of enterprise, are as a matter of fact secured only on the monopoly level, for instance, because monopolization may increase the share of influence of the better, and decrease the share of influence of the inferior brains.

    Such a situation may indeed lead to monopoly, but it would not be monopoly but perhaps size which would give the better brains greater influence.

4. Where in both cases we must count as part of these costs of production the alternative products which the particular person or firm could produce instead. It would therefore be compatible with these conditions that somebody who could produce some commodity more cheaply than anybody else will in fact not do so and produce something else instead with respect to which his comparative advantage over other producers is even greater.

5. It may be instructive if I illustrate the kind of obstacles into which one who believes he has discovered a ,possibility of improving upon existing routines is likely to encounter in modern conditions. The instance of such a frustration which many years I had the opportunity to watch in detail was the case of an American building contractor who, after looking at the prices and rents of houses, the wages and the prices of building materials in a European city, felt convinced that he could provide better houses at a considerably lower price and still make a substantial profit. What made him in the end give up his plan was that building regulations, trade union rules, cartellized prices of special building equipment and the cost of the bureaucratic procedure of obtaining all the required permissions and approvals precluded the economies in production on which he had based his calculations. I cannot say now whether the obstacles raised directly by government or those due to its toleration of restrictive practices or producers and trade unions were more decisive. What was obvious was that the reason why well-tried possibilities of reducing the costs of houses could not be applied were that those who knew how to use them were not allowed to do so.

6. It deserves observation that an economy in which it is easy to make large profits rapidly, although it is one in which there exist possibilities of rapid growth because there is much that can be quickly remedied, is one which almost certainly has been in a very unsatisfactory state and where the aim of exploiting the obvious opportunities will soon be achieved. This shows, incidentally, how absurd it is to judge relative performance by rate of growth, which is as often as not evidence of past neglect rather than of present achievement. In many respects it is easier and not more difficult for an undeveloped country to grow rapidly once an appropriate framework has been secured.

7. Even the statement of the problem as one of utilizing knowledge dispersed among hundreds of thousands of individuals still over-simplifies its character. It is not merely a task of utilizing information about particular concrete facts which the individuals already possess, but one of using their abilities of discovering such facts as will be relevant to their purposes in the particular situation. This is the reason why all the information accessible to (rather than already possessed by) the individuals can never be put at the disposal of some other agency but can be used only if those who know where the relevant information is to be found are called upon to make the decisions. Every person will discover what he knows or can find out only when faced with a problem where this will help, but can never pass on all the knowledge he commands and still less all the knowledge he knows how to acquire if needed by somebody else.

8. Cf. W. Mieth, 'Unsicherheitsbereiche beim wirtschafts-politischen Sachurteil als Quelle volkswirtschaftlicher Vorurteile' in W. Strzelewicz (ed.), *Das Vorurteil als Bildungsbarriere* (Göttingen, 1965), p. 192.

9. This has been repeatedly emphasized by Milton Friedman, see, for example, *his Capitalism and Freedom* (Chicago, 1962).

10. W. L. Letwin, *Law and Economic Policy in America* (New York, 1965), p. 281.

11. The *Gesetz gegen Wettbewerbsbeschränkungen* of 27 July 1957.

12. On all this and the issues discussed in the following paragraphs see Mancur Olson Jr, *The Logic of Collective Action* (Harvard University Press, 1973).

13. Gunner Myrdal, *An International Economy* (New York, 1956) and J. K. Galbraith, *The Affluent Society* (Boston, 1969).

14. J. K. Galbraith, *op. cit.*

15. Mancur Olson Jr, *op. cit.*

THE PERILS OF REGULATION: A MARKET-PROCESS APPROACH

Israel M. Kirzner

Introduction

Economists have for at least two centuries debated the merits of government regulation of the market economy. In recent decades, however, this debate appeared to die down, and for a number of years it seemed that economists, with very few exceptions, subscribed to (and indeed helped propagate) a strongly approving view of extensive government intervention in the marketplace. Only recently has the pendulum of professional opinion begun to swing away from a definitely interventionist position, permitting a renewal of the classic debate about government regulation of the economy.

The position in favor of extensive government regulation of the market, of course, must be sharply distinguished from the views of radical critics of capitalism. The interventionist position, unlike that of radical critics, in general thoroughly appreciates the role of the market system in the efficient allocation of resources. The interventionist position fully accepts the central theorem of welfare economics concerning the Pareto optimality achieved, on appropriate assumptions, by the competitive market in general equilibrium. Intervention, however, is said to be required by the real-world impossibility of fulfilling the assumptions needed to hold for a perfectly competitive equilibrium to prevail. Because of chronic "market failure" attributable to the violation of these assumptions, the interventionist position deems it essential that government actively modify the operation of the free market by extensive, even massive, doses of intervention and regulation. The interventionist position holds that the market economy, suitably modified by a judicious combination of government controls on prices, quality of outputs, and the organization of industry, can achieve reasonably satisfactory results. This position came to be so entrenched in professional opinion that, supported (as it always has been) by the layman's intuition, interventionism became a virtually unchallenged orthodoxy.

Only recently has this orthodoxy begun to crumble. Both the layman and the economist have come to suspect that government interventions, especially those limiting competition and controlling prices, are consistently responsible for undesirable consequences. Confidence in the ability of government officials to construct a useful program of controls that would correct "market failure" without generating new problems attributable to government action itself has been rather thoroughly shaken. For many members of the public, and even for many economists, the crumbling of orthodoxy has come as a sharp surprise, if not a jarring shock. Economists now must rethink the theory of the market. They have begun to see that the assumption that the market can approximate a competitive equilibrium is more robust than hitherto believed. They have argued that government regulation produces its own undesirable distortions in market outcomes. Finally, economists have begun to understand that the political economy of regulation tends to ensure that market interventions are far more likely to be undertaken to further the well-being of special interests (not excepting those of the regulators themselves) than of the public at large.

This essay, too, draws attention to problems that appear to be the inescapable results of government regulation of the market. However, the approach taken here differs substantially from those just mentioned in that it does not postulate instantaneous or even rapid achievement of a general equilibrium in the free market; nor does it emphasize the undesirable distortions in equilibrium conditions introduced by government regulation. And to simplify matters, the discussion will relate to controls assumed to be deliberately introduced and enforced by legislators and officials intent on nothing but the welfare of the consuming public. The position developed here argues that intervention tends to interfere harmfully in the *entrepreneurial process* upon which the most basic of the market's virtues (conceded in principle by its interventionist critics) must surely depend.

To avoid misunderstanding, it should be emphasized that I do not wish to minimize the impact of those implications of regulation upon which my own argument does not rest. There can be little doubt that much regulation has been inspired, consciously or not, by considerations other than the goal of contributing to the public weal.[1] And the propensity of government interventions to generate tendencies toward suboptimal equilibrium configurations has certainly been amply demonstrated by economists from Bastiat to Friedman.[2] I merely contend that, valid though these approaches to a critique of interventionism undoubtedly are, they do not exhaust the phenomena to be explained. To sharpen the presentation of the approach taken here, regulations are assumed to be introduced and enforced with only the public welfare in mind. Many of regulation's undesirable consequences undoubtedly can be attributed to the tendency for regulation to serve the interests of regulators. I maintain that, quite apart from such difficulties, regulation generates economic confusion and inefficiency. This confusion and inefficiency are perceived more clearly by assuming, for the sake of argument, that those *other* difficulties (arising out of the regulators' self-interest) are absent.

Interventionism and Socialism: A Parallel

The surprise and dismay experienced today by so many economists and others at the manifest failure of well-meaning interventionist measures to create anything but inefficiencies of their very own is reminiscent in many ways of the surprise and disquiet experienced some sixty years ago when Mises first demonstrated on theoretical grounds, the inability of a socialized economy to perform the economic calculation needed for social efficiency. It is instructive to pursue this parallel further, for properly understood, Mises's theoretical argument regarding the socialist (that is, nonmarket) economy suggests useful insights into the problems of the hampered (that is, regulated) market economy. It was the earlier failure (by Mises's readers) to understand the operation and function of the market economy that led them to assume uncritically that a socialist society, in principle, need encounter no difficulty in the attainment of social efficiency. The realization that this assumption was far from obviously justified occasioned the surprise and disquiet following Mises's famous article. The now crumbling orthodoxy upon which the interventionist approach until very recently has rested reflects misunderstandings concerning the operation and function of markets. And those misunderstandings bear a remarkable likeness to those pointed out by Mises, and later by Hayek. These deep-rooted misunderstandings, in turn, appear responsible for the surprise and dismay occasioned by the realization that government regulation may itself be the problem rather than the solution it had so obviously seemed to be.

The hampered, regulated market, of course, is not at all the same thing as the fully socialized economy which Mises and Hayek studied. In the socialized economy there is no market at all, free or otherwise, for the services of material factors. In the socialized economy, therefore, there can be no market prices for such factor services. This absence of market prices is crucial to the Mises-Hayek critique of socialism. The regulated market economy, on the other hand, no matter how hampered it may be, *is* unquestionably a market economy, in which prices emerge through the interplay of profit-seeking market transactions. The Mises-Hayek critique of socialism, therefore, is certainly not applicable, as it stands, to the regulated market.

A brief review of the Mises-Hayek critique of socialism nonetheless proves helpful for a critical appraisal of regulation. For the Mises-Hayek discussion offers an appreciation for the operation of the market process by revealing the enormous difficulties confronting socialist planners trying to emulate the market economy's achievements without a market. This discussion also reveals the hazards besetting the path of regulators seeking to improve on the market's performance. Just as the attempt to seek social efficiency through central planning rather than through the spontaneous market process, in the Mises-Hayek view, must necessarily fail, so too, for essentially similar reasons, must attempts to control the outcomes of the spontaneous market by deliberate, extra market, regulatory action necessarily tend to generate unexpected and wholly undesired consequences.

I turn, therefore, to a brief review of the debate on socialist economic calculation, drawing particular attention to a widespread failure to appreciate fully certain important elements in the Mises-Hayek critique. It is these important elements, indeed, that will be found to be the basis for this essay's critical analysis of government regulation of the market economy. These elements underlie our perception of the parallel between a critique of the regulated market on the one hand and of socialism, without any market at all, on the other.

Mises and Hayek on Socialism

Mises's demonstration of the economic calculation problem facing the socialist planning authorities was first presented in 1920.[3] The demonstration was subsequently repeated in more or less similar terms (with critical attention paid to the attempts of socialist writers to respond to his challenge) in several of Mises's later works.[4] Hayek first addressed the problem in two essays, which respectively introduced and summed up the debate concerning socialist calculation (in the volume of essays on the subject that he edited in 1935).[5] An important third essay, published in 1940, contains Hayek's most complete appraisal of the issues.[6] Many writers on the Continent, in England, and in the United States attempted to meet Mises's arguments, the best known socialist contribution being that of Oskar Lange.[7] A thorough survey of the state of literature at the onset of World War II, provided by a Norwegian economist, was made available in English in 1949.[8]

For Mises, the defining element in socialism lies in its collective ownership of the means of production, in particular land and capital. It follows, therefore, that under socialism there exists no market for these factors of production or for their services; without private ownership, there can be no market exchanges between individual owners; and without market exchanges, of course, there can be no ratios of exchange—that is, there can be no market prices. Mises finds in the absence of factor prices the essence of the difficulty. Without prices, socialist decision makers (the central planners and their subordinates, the managers of socialized enterprises) do not have available relevant indicators (prices) of the relative economic importance of the various factor services in their various alternative uses. Socialist planners cannot know whether the allocation of a unit of a particular resource to a specific line of production is more or less desirable than its replacement by some quantity of another resource which is technologically capable of substituting for the first. Planners cannot know in advance where efficiency is likely to be attained, nor do they have any way of assessing ex post whether or to what extent such efficiency may have been achieved.

Professor Armentano illustrates Mises's point by imagining a socialist director choosing between the construction of a power plant that uses fossil fuel and one that uses nuclear fuel. Since the state owns all of the resources, no objective money prices exist for any of the alternative projects' required resources. The socialist planner has no way of knowing which project is cheaper, which promises the greater return on investment, which, in sum, offers the most efficient way to produce electricity. "If and when the power plant is built at a particular point with particular resources, it will represent an 'arbitrary' and not an economic decision."[9]

Hayek's most complete discussion of the problem of socialist calculation appeared in 1940 as a review article analyzing particularly the contributions of two socialist economists, Oskar Lange and H. D. Dickinson.[10] Both Lange and Dickinson conceded that economic calculation is unthinkable without factor prices.[11] They pointed out, however, that a price need not mean merely an exchange ratio established in a market; the notion of price, they maintained, can be understood more broadly as "the terms on which alternatives are offered." Using price in this broader sense, they argued, there is every possibility for setting up a socialist economy in which "prices" are announced by the planning authorities and are used as guides in the decisions of socialist managers (who are instructed to obey specified rules in which these "prices" appear). These writers believed the authorities could handle the adjustment of prices on the basis of trial and error, with the relation between perceived supply and demand indicating to the authorities where adjustments should be made. In this fashion, the socialist writers held, a socialist economy could achieve an efficient allocation of resources without markets in the material factors of production, and without profit-maximizing entrepreneurial decisions.

Hayek's critique of the Lange-Dickinson proposals was long and detailed. He considered their approach to be a vast improvement as compared with the earlier socialist reactions to Mises, in which the nature of the problem was hardly perceived at all. Yet he continued to find the Lange-Dickinson proposals seriously deficient both in their perception of the problem to be solved and of the practical difficulties confronting the suggested solution. The difference, Hayek wrote, between the "system of regimented prices" proposed by the socialist economists "and a system of prices determined by the market seems to be about the same as that between an attacking army in which every unit and every man could move only by special command and by the exact distance ordered by headquarters and an army in which every unit and every man can take advantage of every opportunity offered to them."[12]

Some Thoughts on the Socialist Calculation Literature

Despite Hayek's powerful critique of the Lange-Dickinson proposals, the postwar textbook literature, curiously, came to present the results of the interwar debate as if Mises's original claim (to have demonstrated the impossibility of economic calculation under socialism) had been decisively refuted by Lange, Dickinson, and Lerner.[13] Several writers have noted that this view conveyed by the literature is seriously mistaken.[14] A careful review of the debate surely reveals that the Lange-Dickinson Lerner solution hardly comes to grips with the difficulties that Mises and Hayek explained. The textbook literature did not so much ignore the arguments of Mises and Hayek *as it failed to understand the view of the market process, which underlies their critique of socialist calculation.* Indeed, the authors of the socialist proposals themselves offered their solution from a perspective on the nature and function of the market economy that differed sharply from the "Austrian" perspective shared by Mises and Hayek. My purpose in drawing attention to this defective view of the market reflected in the Lange-Dickinson literature is not merely to throw light on the socialist calculation debate (an issue only tangentially relevant to our own theme of efficiency in the regulated market economy); for the insights into the market process expressed in the Mises-Hayek view and overlooked in the Lange-Dickinson proposal become crucial to a critique of the economics of regulation.

Lange's response to Mises placed much emphasis on the *"parametric function of prices,* i.e., on the fact that. . . each individual separately regards the actual market prices as given data to which he has to adjust himself."[15] For Lange, each person in the market treats prices as if they were equilibrium prices to which he must adjust himself passively. If the market prices happen *not* to be equilibrium prices, then these market prices must somehow change "by a series of successive trials"—prices rising where demand exceeds supply, and so on.[16] Lange does not address the question of *how* market prices actually change if each person at all times considers prices as given data to which he must silently adjust himself.

For Lange, indeed, the function that prices play in the efficiency of markets is simply the function that the equilibrium set of prices would fill. Prices, that is, provide the parameters to guide market participants in engaging in the set of activities that are consistent with equilibrium conditions. Lange understandably held that this function of prices could be simulated in a socialist economy.

Socialist managers can be given lists of "prices" to which they can react according to well-defined rules (analogous to, but of course not identical with, the "rule" that capitalist decision makers are assumed to follow: that is, to maximize profits), Lange believed the task of ensuring that the lists of "prices" would be those required to ensure overall efficiency in the socialist economy could be fulfilled by again simulating (what he thought to be) the market trial and error procedure.

But here lies Lange's cardinal misunderstanding: he assumed that there exists in the market a procedure (involving "a series of successive trials") whereby prices are somehow adjusted toward equilibrium *without essentially altering the "parametric" character and function of prices* (that is, without departing from the supposition that each person separately regards market prices as given data, which he is unable to change). The market process through which prices are adjusted toward equilibrium, however, is a process in which prices are *not* treated as given parameters but are themselves hammered out in the course of vigorous and rivalrous bidding.

In emphasizing exclusively the "parametric" function of market prices. Lange misunderstood the central role of the market. The primary function of the market is *not* to offer an arena within which market participants can have their decentralized decisions smoothly coordinated through attention to the appropriate list of given prices. The market's essential function, rather, is to offer an arena in which market participants, by entrepreneurial exploitation of the profit opportunities offered by disequilibrium prices, can nudge prices in the direction of equilibrium. In this entrepreneurial process prices are *not* treated as parameters. Nor, in this process, are prices changed impersonally in response to excess demand or supply. It is one thing for Lange to assume that socialist managers can be motivated to follow rules with respect to centrally promulgated given "prices" (in the way capitalist decision makers can be imagined to treat given equilibrium market prices).[17] It is quite another to assume that the *non*-parametric function of price in the market system, the function dependent on entrepreneurial alertness to opportunities for pure profit, can be simulated in a system from which the entrepreneurial function has been wholly excised.

That Lange did not understand this nonparametric function of prices must certainly be attributed to a perception of the market system's operation primarily in terms of perfectly competitive equilibrium. (Indeed, it is this textbook approach to price theory that Lange explicitly presents as his model for socialist pricing.[18]) Within this paradigm, as is now well recognized, the role of the entrepreneurial quest for pure profit, as the key element in bringing about price adjustment, is completely ignored. It is not difficult to see how Lange could conclude that such a (nonentrepreneurial) system might be simulated under socialism.

Mises and Hayek, by contrast, saw the price system under capitalism from a totally different—an Austrian— perspective. For these writers, the essence of the market process lies not in the "parametric" function of price, and not in the perfectly competitive state of equilibrium, but in the rivalrous activity of entrepreneurs taking advantage of disequilibrium conditions. The debate between Lange-Dickinson on the one hand and Mises-Hayek on the other can best be understood as a clash between two conflicting views of the price system. Mises's views on the market as a process have been expounded extensively in a number of his works.[19] The idea of the market as a *dynamic process* is at the very heart of his system. Hayek's perception of the price system was articulated (during the same period in which his critical essays on socialist calculation were written) in a remarkable series of papers on the role of knowledge and discovery in market processes.[20]

That the postwar textbooks incorrectly presented the debate on socialist calculation as having been decisively won by Lange must be attributed not to ideological bias (although this may not have been entirely absent) but to an utter failure to understand the flaws in Lange's discussion (flaws that Hayek indeed had identified). Not recognizing the Austrian background of Hayek's critique, Anglo-American economists saw in Lange a cogent application of standard price theory; Hayek's critique simply was not understood.

The Market Process: An Austrian View[21]

Before returning to the theme of efficiency in the regulated economy, it is useful to review some Austrian lessons to be drawn from the socialist calculation debate. The Austrian understanding of the market as a dynamic process of discovery generated by the entrepreneurial-competitive scramble for pure profit may be spelled out in terms of a brief discussion of several key concepts. A sensitive appreciation of these ideas will alert us to problems raised by government regulation of the market that might otherwise easily be overlooked. It is partly because the terms convenient for the exposition of these concepts also are used in non-Austrian contexts, with rather different meanings, that the ideas developed here are so often misunderstood and therefore require brief elaboration.

Competition. What keeps the market process in motion is competition—*not* competition in the sense of "perfect competition," in which perfect knowledge is combined with very large numbers of buyers and sellers to generate a state of perennial equilibrium—but competition as the rivalrous activities of market participants trying to win profits by offering the market better opportunities than are currently available. The existence of rivalrous competition requires *not* large numbers of buyers and sellers but simply *freedom of entry*. Competition places pressure on market participants to discover where and how better opportunities, as yet unnoticed, *might* be offered to the market. The competitive market process occurs because equilibrium has not yet been attained. This process is thwarted whenever nonmarket barriers are imposed blocking entry to potential competitors.

Knowledge and Discovery. As Hayek has emphasized, the competitive market process is a discovery procedure.[22] If all that needed to be known were already known, then the market would already have attained full equilibrium, the state in which all decisions correctly anticipate all other decisions being made within the market. An institutional device for social organization that mobilizes existing knowledge and brings it to bear upon decision makers is necessary because realistically people never do have command even over all the information that is already known somewhere.[23] Market equilibrium is thinkable only if we can presuppose the full mobilization of existing knowledge; so also centralized economic control would be thinkable (whether by Lange-Dickinson—Lerner proposals or other devices) if we could assume existing knowledge already to be fully mobilized. It is just because, without a market, such prior mobilization is so difficult to assume that a market is seen to be a prerequisite for economic calculation.

The competitive market process is needed not only to mobilize existing knowledge, but also to generate awareness of opportunities whose very existence until now has been known to no one at all.[24] The entrepreneurial process, moreover, disseminates existing information through the market. The process itself is a continual one of the discovery of opportunities. The discoverer of these opportunities himself, at least, has had no inkling whatever of their very existence. The market, in other words, is not merely a process of search for information of the need for which men had previously been aware; it is a discovery procedure that tends to correct ignorance where the discoverers themselves were totally unaware that they indeed were ignorant. A realization that the market yields knowledge—the sort of knowledge that people do not at present even know they need—should engender among would-be social engineers who seek to replace or to modify the results of the free market a very definite sense of humility. To announce that one can improve on the performance of the market, one must also claim know in advance what the market will reveal. This knowledge is clearly impossible in all circumstances. Indeed, where the market process has been thwarted, in general it will not be possible to point with certainty to what *might* have been discovered that has now been lost.

Profit and Incentives. In standard treatments of price theory, decision makers are assumed to maximize utility or "profit." The profit for which entrepreneurs are so eager (and which for Austrians drives the market process) is not that "profit" maximized by the firm in the standard theory of the firm. The standard theory assumes that the firm confronts definitely known and given cost and revenue possibilities. For the theory of the firm, therefore, to maximize profits does not mean to *discover* an opportunity for pure gain; it means merely to perform the mathematical calculations required to exhaust the *already fully perceived* opportunity for gain that the given revenue and cost curves might present. The urge of would-be entrepreneurs to grasp profit, by contrast, is the force which *itself reveals* the existence of gaps between costs and revenues. This distinction is of considerable importance.

It is elementary to the theory of the market that the market performs its functions by virtue of the *incentives* it offers to those who make "correct" decisions. For example, the incentive of the higher wages offered by industries in which the marginal productivity of labor is greatest attracts labor to more important uses. Such incentives tend to ensure that once a superior use for a given factor (or group of factors) is discovered, it becomes worthwhile for factor owners to forgo alternative ways of putting their factors to work. This is well understood. What is not always understood is that the market also offers incentives for the *discovery* of new opportunities (for the most useful employment of factors), that is, for the exploitation of opportunities that until now have remained unexploited. These opportunities have remained unexploited *not* because of high costs, and not even because of the high cost of searching for them. They have remained unexploited simply because of sheer oversight, possibly including oversight of the opportunity to find them through deliberate search. Pure entrepreneurial profit is the market form in which *this* kind of incentive presents itself. The availability of pure entrepreneurial profit has the function not of outweighing the costs associated with withdrawing inputs from alternative uses, but of alerting decision makers to the present error of committing factors to uses less valuable to the markets than others waiting and able to be served.

Market Prices. Market prices in the Austrian view are not primarily approximations to the set of equilibrium prices. Instead, they are (disequilibrium) exchange ratios worked out between entrepreneurial market participants. On the one hand, these exchange ratios with all their imperfections reflect the discoveries made up until this moment by profit-seeking entrepreneurs. On the other hand, these ratios express entrepreneurial errors currently being made. Market prices, therefore, offer opportunities for pure profit. And we can rely on these opportunities to create a tendency for market prices to be changed through the rivalrous bidding of alert entrepreneurs. The course of market prices, in other words, is closely bound up, in *two* distinct ways, with the incentive system of pure entrepreneurial profit. First, the configuration of market prices at any given moment must be attributed to the pure profit incentives that have until now determined bids and offers. Second, this present configuration of market prices, together with existing and future conditions of supply and demand, is responsible for the opportunities for pure profit. The discovery and exploitation of these opportunities will constitute the course of the market process in the immediate future. From this perspective on market prices it is not difficult to perceive how small must be the resemblance to them of any centrally promulgated set of socialist "prices." The entrepreneurial drive for pure profit plays no role at all in the determination of socialist "prices."

Regulated Market Economy

I shall assume, as noted at the outset of this essay, that government regulation of the market economy is generated by dissatisfaction with market outcomes. Legislators or other government officials (perhaps in response to public outcry, or in anticipation thereof) are disturbed either by the high price that certain would-be purchasers are asked to pay in the market or by the low price (for example, farm prices or the wages of labor) received by certain sellers in the market; or they are disturbed by the quality of goods or services being offered for sale (for example, because of the absence of safety devices) or by the unavailability in the market of goods or services that they believe to be important. They are disturbed by the conditions under which workers are expected to work, or they are disturbed by the pattern of income distribution generated by the market, by unemployment, or by "profiteering," or by the side effects (such as environmental pollution, or spread of disease, or exposure of the young to pornography) generated by uncontrolled market activity.

Hoping to correct what are perceived to be unsatisfactory conditions, the government intervenes in the market. It seeks to replace the outcomes expected to result from unchecked market transactions by a preferred configuration of prices and outputs, to be achieved not, as under socialism, by replacing the market by central ownership of factors, but by imposing appropriate regulations and controls. The laissez-faire market is replaced by the regulated market. Price ceilings and price and wage floors, transfers of incomes, imposed safety standards, child labor laws, zoning laws, prohibited industrial integration, tariff protection, prohibited competition, imposed health warnings, compulsory old age pensions, and prohibited drugs are all examples of the countless controls that well-meaning public officials impose.

In the face of these controls, regulations, and interventions there remains, nonetheless, a genuine market both for factor services and for consumer products. Government controls constrain and constrict; they rearrange and repattern the structure of incentives; they redistribute incomes and wealth and sharply modify both the processes of production and the composition of consumption. Yet within the limits that such controls impose, buying and selling continue, and the constant effort to capture pure entrepreneurial gain keeps the market in perpetual motion. Government regulations drastically alter and disturb opportunities for entrepreneurial gain, but they do not eliminate them. These controls thoroughly influence the prices that emerge from the interplay of entrepreneurial competition. But unless directly mandated prices are involved, exchange ratios still reflect the outcome to date of the entrepreneurial process.

Traditionally, criticism of government intervention involves one of more of several general lines of argument.[25] First, critics may argue that the admitted failure of market outcomes to meet successfully the aspirations of regulators is a result not of market failure to achieve peak efficiency, but of inescapable scarcity. If costs are fully taken into account, efforts to improve outcomes must be found to be doomed to failure or to lead to even less preferable outcomes. Second, critics may agree that from the viewpoint of the value system adopted by the would-be regulators market outcomes might be improved upon. But, these critics maintain that the market faithfully reflects consumers' values. Regulation in such circumstances therefore must violate consumer sovereignty, if not consumer freedom.

Third, critics may argue that the unwished-for market outcomes are to be attributed not to the free market, but to earlier government interventions in the market which have hindered the corrective forces of the market from doing their work. Additional regulation, it is then pointed out, either may be unnecessary (since the earlier interventions can simply be eliminated) or may compound the problems. Fourth, critics may argue that whether or not the undesirable outcomes of the market are (in the sense appropriate to economic science and not necessarily from the viewpoint of the regulators' values) to be regretted, government regulation is simply incapable of achieving improvement. The technology of regulation is such that its full costs outweigh by far any benefits that may be achieved.

The Austrian lessons drawn from the preceding survey of the debate about socialist economic calculation suggest that another set of considerations, until now not sufficiently emphasized in the literature, deserve to be included in the list of causes to which one might attribute the failures of regulation. These considerations constitute a separate line of criticism of government intervention, to be added to the other lines of criticism (where one or more of these may be relevant).[26]

Government Regulation and the Market Discovery Process

The perils associated with government regulation of the economy addressed here arise out of the *impact that regulation can be expected to have on the discovery process, which the unregulated market tends to generate*. Even if current market outcomes in some sense are judged unsatisfactory, intervention, and even intervention that can successfully achieve its immediate objectives, cannot be considered the obviously correct solution. After all, the very problems apparent in the market might generate processes of discovery and correction superior to those undertaken deliberately by government regulation; deliberate intervention by the state not only might serve as an imperfect substitute for the spontaneous market process of discovery; but also might impede desirable processes of discovery the need for which has *not* been perceived by the government. Again, government regulation itself may generate new (unintended and undesired), processes of market adjustments that produce a final outcome even less preferred than what might have emerged in the free market.

Here I discuss critically the impact of government regulation on the discovery process of the unregulated market at four distinct levels. First, I consider the likelihood that would-be regulators may not correctly assess the course the market might itself take in the absence of regulation. Second, I consider the likelihood that, because of the presumed absence of entrepreneurial incentives operating on government decision makers, government regulatory decisions will fail to exploit opportunities for social betterment waiting to be discovered. Third, I consider the likelihood that government regulation may stifle or inhibit desirable discovery processes which the market might have generated. Finally, I consider the likelihood that government regulation may influence the market by creating opportunities for new, and not necessarily desirable, market discovery processes which would not be relevant in an unregulated market.

The Undiscovered Discovery Process

We assumed earlier that regulation is demanded because of undesirable conditions that emerge in the market in the absence of regulation. But the urge to regulate, to control, to alter these outcomes must presume not only that these undesirable conditions are attributable to the absence of regulation, but also that the speedy removal of such conditions cannot be expected from the future course of unregulated market events. To attribute undesirable conditions to absence of regulation, moreover, also may require the denial of the proposition that were a better state of affairs indeed feasible, the market probably would have already discovered how to achieve it.

More specifically, many demands for government intervention into the market rest on one or both of two possible misunderstandings concerning the market discovery process. Demand for government intervention, on the one hand, might grow out of a failure to realize that the market already may have discovered virtually everything worth discovering (so that what appears to be obvious inefficiency might be able to be explained altogether satisfactorily if government officials had all the information the market has long since discovered and taken advantage of). Demand for regulation, on the other hand, may stem from the belief that unsatisfactory conditions will never be corrected unless by deliberate intervention. Such demands for regulation might be muted, that is, were it understood that genuine inefficiencies can be relied upon in the *future* to generate market processes for their own correction. (This second misunderstanding itself may rest on either of two bases. First, the tendency of markets to discover and eliminate inefficiency simply is not recognized. Second, by contrast, it is assumed, far too sanguinely, that market processes are *so* rapid that our awareness of an unmistakably unsatisfactory condition proves that some kind of market "failure" has occurred and that one cannot rely on future corrective processes.)

These misunderstandings, so often the foundation for demands for intervention, surely derive from an unawareness of several basic principles of the theory of market process. These principles show that, first, were knowledge perfect, it would be inconceivable that unexploited opportunities could yet remain for rearranging the pattern of input utilization or output consumption in such a way as to improve the well-being of all market participants; second, the existence of such unexploited opportunities, reflecting imperfect knowledge throughout the market, expresses itself in the unregulated market in the form of opportunities for pure entrepreneurial profit; and third, the tendency for such pure profit opportunities to be discovered and exploited tends more or less rapidly to eliminate unexploited opportunities for improving the allocation of resources.[27] These principles of the theory of market process suggest that if genuine inefficiency exists, then (perhaps because of a recent sudden change in conditions of resource supply, of technology, or of consumer tastes) the market has not yet discovered *all that it will surely soon tend to discover.*

These principles may be denied either by expressing a lack of confidence in the systematic tendency for imperfect knowledge to be spontaneously improved or by attributing to the market the ability to attain equilibrium instantaneously (that is, by assuming that ignorance is not merely a disequilibrium phenomenon, but that ignorance disappears the very instant it emerges). Both denials may lead to demands for government intervention. The denial based on a lack of confidence about improving knowledge leads to the belief that current inefficiencies will not tend to be corrected spontaneously (and also to the propensity to see inefficiency where the market *already* has made necessary corrections). The denial based on the belief in instantaneous correction of disequilibrium conditions leads to the view that existing inefficiencies somehow are consistent with market equilibrium and that therefore extramarket steps are called for to achieve correction.

The Unsimulated Discovery Process

Government regulation takes the general form of imposed price ceilings and floors, of mandated quality specifications, and of other restraints or requirements imposed in interpersonal market transactions. The hope surrounding such government impositions, I continue to assume, is that they will constrain market activities to desired channels and at desired levels. But what is the likelihood that government officials, with the best of intentions, will *know* what imposed prices, say, might evoke the "correct," desired actions by market participants? This question parallels that raised by Mises and Hayek with respect to "market" socialism.[28] Government officials in the regulated economy do enjoy the advantage (*not* shared by socialist planning officials) of making their decisions within the framework of genuine market prices. But the question remains: How do government officials know what prices to set (or qualities to require, and so forth)? Or to press the point further:

How will government officials know if their earlier decisions were in error and in what direction to make corrections? In other words, how will government officials *discover* those opportunities for improving the allocation of resources, which one cannot assume to be automatically known to them at the outset of a regulatory endeavor?

The compelling insight underlying these questions rests heavily on the circumstance that officials institutionally are precluded from capturing *pecuniary* profits in the market, in the course of their activities (even though they are as eager as anyone else for entrepreneurial "profit" in the broadest sense of the term). The regulators' estimates of the prices consumers are prepared to pay, or of the prices resource owners are prepared to accept, for example, *are not profit-motivated estimates*. The estimates are not profit motivated at the time of an initial government regulatory action, and they are not profit motivated at each subsequent date when modification of a regulation might be considered. But estimates of market demand conditions or market supply conditions that are not profit motivated cannot reflect the powerful, discovery-inspiring incentives of the entrepreneurial quest for profit.

Nothing in the course of the regulatory process suggests a tendency for as yet unperceived opportunities of resource allocation improvement to be discovered. Nothing ensures that government officials who might perceive market conditions more accurately than others will tend systematically to replace less competent regulators. There is no entrepreneurial process at work, and there is no proxy for entrepreneurial profit or loss that easily might indicate where errors have been made and how they should be corrected. What regulators know (or believe they know) at a given moment presumably remains only partly correct. No systematic process seems at work through which regulators might come to discover what they have not known, *especially since they have not known that they enjoy less than complete awareness of a particular situation.*

The problem raised here is not quite the same as the one identified in other literature critical of government intervention. It is often noted, for example, that government officials are not motivated to minimize costs, since they will not personally benefit from the resulting economies.[29] The problem raised here differs importantly from such questions of incentives for adopting known efficiencies. For even if one could imagine an official so dedicated to the citizenry that he would ensure the adoption of all known possible measures for cutting costs, one cannot yet imagine him somehow divining *as yet undiscovered* techniques for cutting costs. What the official knows, he knows, and what he knows that he does *not* know, one may imagine him diligently undertaking to find out, through appropriate cost-benefit-calculated search. But one can hardly imagine him discovering, except by the sheerest accident, those opportunities for increasing efficiency of which he is completely unaware. The official is not subject to the entrepreneurial profit incentive, which somehow appears continually and successfully to inspire discovery of hitherto undreamed of possibilities for eliminating unnecessary expenditures. Nothing within the regulatory process seems able to simulate even remotely well the discovery process that is so integral to the unregulated market.

The Stifled Discovery Process

The most serious effect of government regulation on the market discovery process well might be the likelihood that regulation, in a variety of ways, may discourage, hamper, and even completely stifle the discovery process of the unregulated market. Indeed, that much regulation is introduced as a result of unawareness of the market's discovery process already has been noted.

Government regulation plainly might bar exploitation of opportunities for pure entrepreneurial profit. A price ceiling, a price floor, an impeded merger, or an imposed safety requirement might block possibly profitable entrepreneurial actions. Such restraints and requirements may be designed to block *particular* activities. If so, the likelihood is that since the possibility of such activities is so clearly seen and feared, the blocked activity may provide standard rates of return, but *not* particularly profitable ones in the entrepreneurial sense. Regulated restraints and requirements, though, are also likely to block activities that have *not* yet been foreseen by anyone, including the regulatory authorities. Regulatory constraints, that is, are likely *to bar the discovery* of pure profit opportunities.

That government regulation diminishes competition is common knowledge. Tariffs, licensing requirements, labor legislation, airline regulation, and bank regulation reduce the number of potential participants in particular markets. Government regulation, therefore, is responsible for imposing monopoly like inefficiencies ("deadweight" welfare losses) upon the economy. But such losses by no means constitute the full impact of the countercompetitive measures often embodied in regulatory constraints.

The beneficent aspect of competition in the sense of a rivalrous process, as noted earlier, arises out of *freedom of entry*. What government regulations so often erect are *regulatory barriers to entry*. Freedom of "entry," for the Austrian approach, refers to the freedom of potential competitors to discover and to move to exploit existing opportunities for pure profit. If entry is blocked, such opportunities simply may never be discovered, either by existing firms in the industry, or by regulatory authorities, or for that matter by outside entrepreneurs who *might* have discovered such opportunities were they allowed to be exploited when found.

From *this* perspective on regulation's anticompetitive impact, it follows that much regulation introduced explicitly to *create* or *maintain* competition is no less hazardous to the competitive—entrepreneurial process than are other forms of regulation that restrict competition. Entry of competitors, in the dynamic sense, need not mean entry of firms of about equal size. For example, entry might imply the *replacement*, by merger or other means, of a number of relatively high-cost producers by a *single* low-cost producer. Antitrust activity designed ostensibly to protect competition might *block* this kind of entry. Such regulatory activity thus blocks the capture of pure profit, obtainable in this case by the discovery and implementation of the possibility of lowering the price to consumers by taking advantage of hitherto unexploited, and perhaps unsuspected, economies of scale.

The literature critical of government regulation often draws attention to the undesirable effects of imposed prices. A price ceiling for a particular product or service (rent control, for example) tends to generate artificial shortages (of housing). A price floor for a particular product or service, (minimum wages, for example) tends to generate an artificial surplus (teenage unemployment!. These important, well-recognized consequences of imposed prices flow from the efforts of the regulators to legislate prices at other than equilibrium levels.

Quite apart from the discoordination generated by such imposed prices in the markets for *existing* goods and services, price (and also quality) restraints also may well inhibit the discovery of wholly new opportunities. A price ceiling does not merely block the upper reaches of a given supply curve. Such a ceiling also may inhibit the discovery of as yet unsuspected sources of supply (which in the absence of the ceiling would have tended to shift the entire supply curve to the right) or of as yet wholly unknown new products (tending to create supply curves for wholly new graphs).[30] The lure of pure profit tends to uncover such as yet unknown opportunities.

Price and quality restraints and requirements and restrictions on organizational forms operate (in a generally understood but not precisely predictable way) to inhibit entrepreneurial discovery. Price ceilings, for example, not only restrict supply from known sources of natural gas (or from known prospects for search), but also inhibit the discovery of wholly unknown sources. Drug testing regulations, as another example, not only reduce the flow of new pharmaceutical drugs where successful research might have been more or less predictable, but also discourage the entrepreneurial discovery of wholly unknown research procedures. Against whatever benefits might be derived from government regulation and intervention, one is forced to weigh, as one of regulation's intrinsically immeasurable costs, the stifling of the market discovery process.

The Wholly Superfluous Discovery Process

There is yet one more aspect of government regulation's complex impact on the discovery process. Whether intended by the regulatory authorities or not and whether suspected by them or not, the imposition of regulatory restraints and requirements tends to create entirely new, and not necessarily desirable opportunities for entrepreneurial discovery.

That such opportunities may be created follows from the extreme unlikelihood that govern-ment-imposed price, quality, or quantity constraints introduce anything approaching an equilibrium configuration. These constraints, on the contrary, introduce pure profit opportunities that would otherwise have been absent, as they simultaneously reduce or possibly eliminate other opportunities for pure profit that might otherwise have existed. This rearrangement of opportunities for pure profits, of course, is unlikely to be the explicit aim of regulation; nor even, indeed, is such rearrangement ever likely to be fully *known* to the authorities. Market ignorance is a fact of economic life. It follows that the replacement of one set of (unregulated) prices by another set of (partly regulated) prices, simply means that regulation has generated a possibly major alteration in the pattern of the discovery process. The now regulated market will tend to pursue the altered discovery process.

This regulation-induced alteration in the pattern of market discovery is closely related to the often noticed circumstance that regulation may result in a different set of equilibrium market consequences. Such consequences, moreover, may not have been correctly foretold by the authorities and, indeed, may be wholly undesired by them. Regulation often imposes costs not immediately recognized.[31] Unless, quite fantastically, the regulatory authorities (somehow all acting in com-pletely coordinated fashion) are perfectly informed on all relevant data about the market, they will not generally be able to perceive what new profit opportunities they create by their own regulatory actions. Inevitably, therefore, the imposition of a set of regulatory constraints on a market must set in motion a series of entrepreneurial actions that have not been anticipated and, therefore, that may well lead to wholly unexpected and even undesired final outcomes.[32]

The one kind of new "profit" opportunity created by regulation that is by now well anticipated, though hardly desired of course, involves bribery and corruption of the regulators. There is widespread understanding of the unwholesome channels into which the entrepreneurial quest for pure profit inevitably tends to be attracted if arbitrary restraints on otherwise profitable activities are imposed.[33]

The basic insight underlying these conclusions, in sum, is a simple one. The competitive entrepreneurial process, being a process of discovery of the as yet unknown, can hardly be predicted in any but the broadest terms. The imposition of regulatory constraints necessarily results, therefore, in a pattern of consequences different from and, most plausibly, distinctly less desirable than what would have occurred in the unregulated market. One might therefore refer to this unplanned, undesired pattern of consequences of regulation as the wholly superfluous discovery process.

Discovery, Evidence, and Illustration

The preceding discussion is theoretical and general, providing no hints of possible verification of its conclusions. While this discussion relies on highly plausible insights into the character of human action, a reader may believe himself justified in demanding evidence that might support the discussion's rather strong conclusions. Yet such evidence can hardly be furnished, and it may be instructive to spell out the reasons.

Evidence About Discovery

Econometricians have endeavored to measure the consequences of particular economic policies. Much of their ingenuity and sophistication has been called forth to grapple with the formidable problem of describing *what might have occurred* in the absence of particular policies. The problem of describing concretely what might have happened but did not, it should be noted, exists even in situations in which all the alternatives before relevant decision makers are clearly defined, so that one at least knows the list of options from among which choices would have been forthcoming. The problem derives from the circumstance that it is not possible, without more or less sophisticated conjecture, to be confident as to which of an array of options a particular decision maker *might* have selected in hypothetical circumstances.

This problem becomes infinitely more formidable if one wishes to describe, in specified hypothetical circumstances, *what might have been spontaneously discovered.* Here the problem is not merely that a particular decision maker's preferences are unknown. The problem is that one cannot imagine what specific, now unknown opportunities might have been discovered in the relevant hypothetical circumstances.

One should not be surprised, therefore, that the losses from the regulatory stifling of market discovery processes are difficult to single out. Indeed, one should not be surprised that analysis, too, has tended to overlook such losses. Therefore one can only hope to draw brief attention to studies that perhaps can provide some illustrative flavor of the kinds of losses attributable to regulatory constraints, to which I have sought to direct attention. For purposes of such illustration, I draw on work focusing on the discovery process initiated by the lure of entrepreneurial profit in technological innovation and in corporate entrepreneurial endeavor.

Discoverers: Innovators

Much recent work by economists is devoted to gaining insight into the process of technological innovation. A small part of that work has considered the impact of government regulation on innovative activity at the technological frontiers. Although the authors of these studies are not primarily concerned with the impact of regulation upon entrepreneurial incentives, it is difficult to read their work without noticing its direct relevance to this essay's concerns.

A 1971 Brookings Institution volume, for example, was devoted to a symposium examining technological change in regulated industries (in particular electric power, telecommunications, and air and surface transportation).[34] In the analytical framework within which this examination was conducted, brief attention is paid to the thesis (attributed, perhaps too hastily, to Schumpeter) that it is "the incentive to earn very large profits" which "spurs entrepreneurs to introduce new techniques," so that the limits on possible profits imposed by regulatory commissions may inhibit such innovation.[35]

A similar possible link between regulatory constraints and the possible slowing down of the processes of technological discovery is noted particularly in the context of drug research in the pharmaceutical industry. The classic paper by Professor Peltzman, examining the impact of the 1962 drug amendments upon drug research, together with the work of others, has led to widespread discussion of the possibility that drug research in the United States lags seriously behind that of other countries.[36] Peltzman's results do not prove that regulation inhibits entrepreneurial discovery, which means the discovery of hitherto unknown opportunities, unknown even in the sense that it had not been known that they were there to be discovered. That is, Peltzman's findings would fit in equally well with a theory of search based on the assumption of awareness of discoverable opportunities waiting to be researched if the cost were not too high. Nonetheless, once attention is focused on entrepreneurial discovery, it is difficult to avoid linking Peltzman's results with the postulation of an entrepreneurial discovery process hampered by regulatory constraints.

Discoverers: Insiders

Another important area in which the role of entrepreneurial discovery has been explicitly explored is that of decision making by corporate managers. In his definitive study of the issue, Henry Manne discusses the impact upon the exercise of entrepreneurship in the corporate firm of regulatory restrictions on insider trading.[37] Manne's study thoroughly examines the entrepreneurial role and its expression in a world of corporations. The study identifies the incentives of entrepreneurial profit needed to evoke the entrepreneurial role and the part that insider trading, in the absence of regulatory prohibition, might play to provide profit opportunities to reward entrepreneurial success. Restrictions on insider trading, Manne shows, no matter how plausible the motives underlying the regulatory restrictions may appear, tend to inhibit the exercise of entrepreneurship in corporate firms.[38]

Conclusion

This essay draws attention to some less obvious drawbacks of government regulation of the market. These drawbacks are rooted in the way regulatory restrictions, restraints, and controls interfere with the spontaneous discovery process that the unregulated market tends to generate. These drawbacks are also to be clearly distinguished from other disadvantages that flow from government intervention.

The peculiar character of the perils of regulation identified here closely parallels certain economic problems associated with the operation of the socialist economy. The review of the Mises-Hayek criticisms of the possibility of economic calculation under socialism provides a classic source for an Austrian perspective on the market process, and simultaneously the review provides important lessons for an understanding of the dangers inherent in regulation.

Recognition of these dangers can be most helpful in explaining the inefficiencies and the stagnation that appear so consistently to beset modern interventionist economies. It is in the nature of the subject, however, that the recognition of these perils does not lead easily to the provision of clear-cut examples of such regulatory damage. Nonetheless, in a modest way it is possible to illustrate these perils from contemporary discussions of palpable problems.

An emphasis on the perils of regulation that arises out of concern for the market process does not, in and of itself, justify the absolute condemnation of government regulation of the market process. Such condemnation would require full consideration, in addition, not only of other perils than those discussed here, but also of the hoped-for benefits sought through regulation of the market. Ultimately, public policy must depend on the value judgments of the policymakers or of those they wish to serve. But, no policy decisions with respect to government regulation can be properly arrived at without a full understanding of all the dangers inherent in such regulation. And such a full understanding arises particularly out of studying the market process of entrepreneurial discovery.

Notes

1. For the literature on private incentives for public regulation, see George J. Stigler, "The Theory of Economic Regulation," *Bell Journal of Economics and Management Science* 2 (Spring 1971): 321; reprinted in Stigler, *The Citizen and the State* (Chicago: University of Chicago Press, 1975); Richard A. Posner, "Theories of Economic Regulation," *Bell Journal of Economics and Management Science* 5 (Autumn 1974): 335-58; Sam Peltzman, "Toward a More General Theory of Regulation," *Journal of Law and Economics* 19 (August 1976): 211-40.

2. The most trenchant recent criticisms of government regulation from this perspective include Ludwig von Mises, *Human Action* (New Haven: Yale University Press, 1949), part 6; Milton Friedman, *Capitalism and Freedom* (Chicago: University of Chicago Press, 1962); Friedman, *An Economist's Protest* (Glen Ridge, N.J.: Thomas Horton and Daughters, 1972).

3. Ludwig von Mises, "Die Wirtschaftsrechnung im sozialistischen Gemeinwesen," *Archiv für Sozialwissenschaften und Sozialpolitik* 47 (April 1920): 86-121; reprinted in *Collectivist Economic Planning*, trans. and ed. Friedrich A. Hayek (London: Routledge and Kegan Paul, 1935).

4. Ludwig von Mises, *Socialism: An Economic and Sociological Analysis*, trans. J. Kahane (New Haven: Yale University Press, 1951) part 2, sect. 1; this edition is translated from the second German edition (published 1932) of Mises's *Die Gemeinwirtschaft* (originally published in 1922); see also Mises, *Human Action*, part 5.

5. Hayek, *Collectivist Economic Planning.*

6. Friedrich A. Hayek, "Socialist Calculation: The Competitive 'Solution,'" *Economica* 7 (May 1940): 125-49; reprinted as "Socialist Calculation III: The Competitive 'Solution,'" in Hayek, *Individualism and Economic Order* (London: Routledge and Kegan Paul, 1949).

7. Oskar Lange, "On the Economic Theory of Socialism," in Oskar Lange and Fred M. Taylor, *On the Economic Theory of Socialism*, ed. Benjamin E. Lippincot (New York: McGraw-Hill, 1964).

8. Trygve J. B. Hoff, *Economic Calculation in the Socialist Society*; trans. M. A. Michael (London and Edinburgh: Hodge, 1949).

9. Dominic T. Armentano, "Resource Allocation Problems under Socialism," in *Theory of Economic Systems: Capitalism, Socialism, Corporatism*, ed. William P. Snavely (Columbus, Ohio: Merrill, 1969), pp. 133-34.

10. Hayek, "Socialist Calculation III." Reviewed particularly were Lange, "On the Economic Theory of Socialism," and Henry D. Dickinson, *Economics of Socialism* (London: Oxford University Press, 1939).

11. Thus they agreed with Mises and Hayek that efficiency is impossible without indicators of value and that any hope of solving the problem by direct mathematical methods (for example, by solving the Walrasian equation system) is illusory.

12. Hayek, *Individualism and Economic Order*, p. 187.

13. Abba P. Lerner, *The Economics of Control* (New York: Macmillan, 1944).

14. See most recently Murray N. Rothbard, "Ludwig von Mises and Economic Calculation under Socialism," in *Economics of Ludwig von Mises*, ed. Laurence S. Moss (Kansas City: Sheed and Ward, 1976).

15. Lange, "On the Economic Theory of Socialism," p. 70.

16. Ibid., pp. 70-71.

17. This assumption, of course, is vulnerable to serious question. See James M. Buchanan, *Cost and Choice* (Chicago: Markham, 1969), chap. 6; G. Warren Nutter, "Markets without Property: A Grand Illusion," in *Money, the Market, and the State: Essays in Honor of James Muir Waller*, ed. Nicholas A. Beadles and L. Aubrey Drewry, Jr. (Athens: University of Georgia Press, 1968). It is important to note that the argument stated in the text does *not* depend on any doubt concerning managers' ability and motivation to obey rules. Were socialist managers to be given price lists, then we may assume for the purposes of the present discussion that they *could* make decisions *as if* they were intent on maximizing "profits." (Of course, the profits maximized in equilibrium contexts are not pure entrepreneurial profits. This distinction is discussed later in this essay.)

18. Lange, "On the Economic Theory of Socialism," p. 65-72.

19. Particularly in Mises, *Human Action,* chap. 15.

20. Hayek, "Economics and Knowledge," "The Use of Knowledge in Society," and "The Meaning of Competition," all reprinted in *Individualism and Economic Order.* In this respect the work of Austrian-born Joseph A. Schumpeter is of considerable relevance for the Austrian view of the market; see particularly Schumpeter, *The Theory of Economic Development,* trans. Redvers Opie (New York: Oxford University Press, 1961); this work first appeared in German in 1912 and was first translated by Opie in 1934. See also Schumpeter, *Capitalism, Socialism and Democracy* (New York: Harper and Row, 1950), chap. 7.

21. This section draws freely from my *Competition and Entrepreneurship* (Chicago: University of Chicago Press, 1973), and *Perception, Opportunity, and Profit* (Chicago: University of Chicago Press, 1979).

22. Friedrich A. Hayek, ea., "Competition as a Discovery Procedure," in *New Studies in Philosophy, Politics, Economics and the History of Ideas* (Chicago: University of Chicago Press, 1978).

23. See Hayek, "Economics and Knowledge," "The Use of Knowledge in Society," and "The Meaning of Competition."

24. See Kirzner, *Perception, Opportunity, and Profit,* chaps. 2, 8, 9.

25. Once again, we assume away criticisms based on the view that regulation may be motivated not by the wish to benefit consumers, but by the wish to benefit the regulators and those they regulate.

26. While these considerations support a stance critical of regulation, in and of themselves they do not necessarily declare regulation to be wrong, or even inefficient. Given sufficiently strong value judgments on the part of would be regulators—whether in favor of environmental purity, of an egalitarian distribution of wealth, of freedom from pornography or disease, of national prestige, of the enrichment of the arts, or of whatever—criticism of intervention, from the perspective of these value judgments, may (properly) carry little weight. The economist's task, however, is to spell out as fully as possible the consequences of alternative policies, so that policy decisions at least will not be taken on the basis of erroneous assessments of their likely consequences. The discussion in the following pages does not offer an airtight case against intervention but draws attention to possibly grave perils of intervention, perils that seem to have been taken fully and explicitly into account neither by the literature critical of interventionist policies nor, a fortiori, by the uncritical proponents and supporters of government regulation.

27. Here an improvement in the allocation of resources (given the initial pattern of resource distribution) is defined as a change in the pattern of input utilization and/or input consumption that improves the well-being of each member of the economy. Although this definition is close to the norm of Paretian welfare economics, it does *not* invoke the notion of aggregate welfare.

28. "The Austrian finds no detailed explanation in welfare economics of how government is supposed to obtain the information necessary to carry out its assigned tasks. The knowledge required . . . is not to be found collected in one place, but rather dispersed throughout the many members of the economy." Stephen C. Littlechild, *The Fallacy of the Mixed Economy: An "Austrian" Critique of Economic Thinking and Policy* (London: Institute of Economic Affairs, 1978), p. 40. See also Gordon Tullock, *The Politics of Bureaucracy* (Washington, D.C.: Public Affairs Press 1965), p. 124: "Administrative problems . . . could . . . be of such complexity that the centralization of information necessary to make decisions effectively in a bureaucracy might not be possible."

29. It is even most cogently pointed out that the very notion of cost, seen from the perspective of the regulator, is unlikely to coincide with any notion of cost that one might wish to consider relevant to the quest for efficiency. See Buchanan, *Cost and Choice*, chaps. 5 and 6.

30. Professor Machlup valuably refers to the "fertility of freedom" in generating discovery of new possibilities. Fritz Machlup, "Liberalism and the Choice of Freedoms," in *Roads to Freedom: Essays in Honour of Friedrich A. von Hayek*, ed. Erich Streissler (London: Routledge and Kegan Paul, 1969), p. 130.

31. Murray L. Weidenbaum, "The Impact of Government Regulation" (study prepared for the Joint Economic Committee, Subcommittee on Economic Growth and Stabilization, United States Congress, July 1978). See also Ernest C. Pasour, "Hide and Seek: Hidden Costs of Government Regulation," *World Research INK* 2 (December 1978): 5.

32. "There is ample evidence that imagination and innovation are not stilled by restrictive legislation—only diverted to figuring out ways around it." Freidman, *Economist's Protest*, p. 149.

33. See, for example, Nicholas Sanchez and Alan R. Waters, "Controlling Corruption in Africa and Latin America," in *The Economics of Property Rights,* ed. Eirik Furubotn and Svetozar Pejovich (Cambridge, Mass.: Ballinger, 1974); Edward C. Banfield, "Corruption as a Feature of Governmental Organization," *Journal of Law and Economics* 18 (December 1975): 587-605; and Simon Rottenberg, "Comment," *Journal of Law and Economics* 18 (December 1975): 611-15.

34. William M. Capron et al., eds., *Technological Change in Regulated Industries* (Washington, D.C.: Brookings Institution, 1971).

35. Ibid., p. 8. See also chap. 2.

36. Sam Peltzman, "An Evaluation of Consumer Protection Legislation: The 1962 Drug Amendments," *Journal of Political Economy* 81 (September-October 1973): 1049-91. See also David Schwartzman, *Innovation in the Pharmaceutical Industry* (Baltimore: Johns Hopkins Press, 1976).

37. Henry G. Manne, *Insider Trading and the Stock Market* (New York: Free Press, 1966).

38. Although there are many other studies illustrating the hidden distortions generated by regulation, I do not cite them here, since they do not obviously call our attention to the market discovery process and its modification as a result of the regulatory constraints.

THE ANTITRUST ECONOMISTS' PARADOX

Thomas J. DiLorenzo

Today regulation is generally recognized as a mechanism by which special interests lobby the government to create barriers to entry or other special privileges. Research has shown, for example, that the Civil Aeronautics Board cartelized the airline industry, the Interstate Commerce Commission helped monopolize the railroad and the trucking industries, the Federal Deposit Insurance Corporation sharply limited entry into the banking business, and occupational licensing created entry barriers into hundreds of occupations. Much of the history of regulation chronicles monopoly privileges procured through the auspices of the state, as Adam Smith pointed out more than 200 years ago in *The Wealth of Nations.*

Oddly, antitrust regulation is still widely viewed as government's benevolent response to the "failures" and "imperfections" of the marketplace. Even economists who are usually skeptical of regulations enacted in the name of the public interest seem to lose their perspective when it comes to antitrust. George Stigler, for example, has stated: "So far as I can tell, [the Sherman Act] is a public interest law . . . in the same sense in which I think having private property, enforcement of contracts, and suppression of crime are public-interest phenomena. . . . I like the Sherman Act."[1]

A 1984 survey of professional economists revealed that 83 percent of the respondents believed that "antitrust laws should be used vigorously to reduce monopoly power from its current level."[2] This opinion is widespread despite common knowledge among antitrust scholars that in practice the antitrust laws restrain output and the growth of productivity have contributed to a deterioration of the competitive position of U.S. industry, and are routinely used to subvert competition.

Why then do the antitrust laws continue to command such powerful support among economists and legal scholars when the pervasive failures are so well known? There are several possible explanations. Antitrust consultants and expert witnesses often stand to make a good deal of money, so financial self-interest may preclude criticism of antitrust. Many economists are also unable to voice informed opinions on antitrust. If it is not their area of expertise, they may not have kept up with research over the past 30 years, or excessive concentration on mathematical models may have left some economists somewhat detached from economic reality. Finally, it is widely believed that there was once a "golden age of antitrust" during which the public was protected from rapacious monopolists by benevolent public servants. According to this perspective, although mistakes have been made, more knowledgeable and public-spirited regulators can successfully reform antitrust. Once reformed, antitrust policy can then perform its original purpose and defend competition and free enterprise.

Unfortunately, the Sherman Act was never intended to protect competition. It was a blatantly protectionist act designed to shield smaller and less efficient businesses from their larger competitors. There never was a golden age of antitrust. The standard account of the origins of antitrust is a myth.

Interest Group Politics and the Sherman Act

In the late 1880s, widespread economic change produced myriad pleas from relatively small—but politically active—farmers who sought protection from larger, corporate competitors. Historian Sanford Gordon offered an example: "Perhaps the most violent reaction [against industrial combinations] of any single special interest group came from farmers. . . . They singled out the jute bagging and alleged binder twine trust, and sent petitions to both their state legislators and to Congress demanding some relief. Cotton was suggested as a good substitute for jute to cover their cotton bales. In Georgia, Mississippi, and Tennessee the [farmers'] alliances passed resolutions condemning the jute bagging trust and recommended the use of cotton cloth."[3]

Southern farmers were annoyed that consumers increasingly preferred jute to the cotton cloth they produced, and they sought antitrust legislation that would dissolve their competition. Such special interest behavior was characteristic of the farm lobby. During the 51st Congress, Gordon notes that "64 petitions and memorials were recorded in the *Congressional Record*, all calling for action against combinations. These were almost exclusively from farm groups. . . . The greatest vehemence was expressed by representatives from the Midwest."[4]

Farmers complained to their national representatives that the products they bought from the trust were increasingly expensive relative to the prices of farm products, but the facts do not support this contention. From 1865 to 1900 farm prices were falling, but at a slower rate than the general price level. This produced real income gains for farmers. In addition, the rapidly increasing quality of manufactured goods further improved the farmers' standard of living. The volatility of farm prices caused the farmers to be politically active.

Many other groups joined the antitrust coalition— small business organizations, academics (though not economists), and journalists. They argued that the "giant monopolies" were creating a "dangerous concentration of wealth" among the capitalists of the day. Although the conspicuous wealth of entrepreneurs such as Rockefeller, Vanderbilt, Mellon, and Morgan added fuel to this charge, it does not appear to be true. In fact, economic historians have concluded that from 1840 to 1900, the division of national income between labor and property owners (capital and natural resource suppliers) remained in a 70-to-30 ratio.[5] Over the same time span, both capital and developed natural resources increased faster than the labor force. This means that labor income per unit of labor rose compared with profit and interest per unit of property input.

Although there was no significant redistribution of wealth from labor to capital owners in the aggregate, competitive markets always alter the distribution of income in ways that some do not like. There was no "dangerous concentration of wealth," but many supporters of antitrust legislation found that their own income had fallen (or not increased rapidly enough). The push for antitrust legislation was an attempt to use the powers of the government to improve their economic status.

Economic conditions were changing rapidly in the latter part of the nineteenth century. Expansion of the railroad and inland shipping industries greatly reduced the cost of transportation. Technological developments led to large-scale (and lower-cost) production of steel, cement, and other goods. Communications technology rapidly expanded, especially the use of the telegraph. And the capital markets became more sophisticated. The United States also underwent a rapid transition from a predominantly agrarian to an industrial society. In 1810 the ration of farm to nonfarm labor was approximately 4.0. This ratio fell to 1.6 by 1840, and by 1880 the labor force was about equally divided between farm and nonfarm endeavors. Meanwhile, individuals and groups uncomfortable with rapid change were becoming increasingly adept at using the regulatory powers of the state. In this increasingly mercantilist atmosphere, the Sherman Act was passed in 1890.

Were the Trusts Monopolistic?

In introducing federal "antitrust" legislation, Sen. Sherman and his congressional allies claimed that combinations or trusts tended to restrict output and thus drive up prices. If Sherman's claims were true, then there should be evidence that those industries allegedly being monopolized by the trusts had restricted output. By contrast, if the trust movement was part of the evolutionary process of competitive markets responding to technological change, one would expect an expansion of trade or output. In fact, there is no evidence that trusts in the 1880s were restricting output or artificially increasing prices.

The *Congressional Record* of the 51st Congress provides a list of industries that were supposedly being monopolized by the trusts. Those industries for which data are available are salt, petroleum, zinc, steel, bituminous coal, steel rails, sugar, lead, liquor, twine, iron nuts and washers, jute, castor oil, cotton seed oil, leather, linseed oil, and matches. The available data are incomplete, but in all but two of the 17 industries, output *increased*—not only from 1880 to 1890, but also to the turn of the century.[6] Matches and castor oil, the only exceptions to the general rule, hardly seem to be items that would cause a national furor, even if they were monopolized.

As a general rule, output in these industries expanded more rapidly than GNP during the 10 years preceding the Sherman Act. In the nine industries for which nominal output data are available, output increased on average by 62 percent; nominal GNP increased by 16 percent over the same period. Several of the industries expanded output by more than 10 times the increase in nominal GNP. Among the more rapidly expanding industries were cottonseed oil (151 percent), leather goods (133 percent), cordage and twine (166 percent), and jute (57 percent).

Real GNP increased by approximately 24 percent from 1880 to 1890. Meanwhile, the allegedly monopolized industries for which a measure of real output is available grew on average by 175 percent. The more rapidly expanding industries in real terms included steel (258 percent), zinc (156 percent), coal (153 percent), steel rails (142 percent), petroleum (79 percent), and sugar (75 percent).

These trends continued from 1890 to 1900 as output expanded in every industry but one for which we have data. (Castor oil was the exception.) On average, the allegedly monopolized industries continued to expand faster than the rest of the economy. Those industries for which nominal data are available expanded output by 99 percent, while nominal GNP increased by 43 percent. The industries for which we have data increased real output by 76 percent compared with a 46 percent increase in real GNP from 1890 to 1900.

As with measures of output, not all of the relevant price data are available, but the information that is at hand indicates that falling prices accompanied the rapid expansion of output in the "monopolized" industries. In addition, although the consumer price index fell by 7 percent from 1880 to 1890, prices in many of the suspect industries were falling even faster.

The average price of steel rails, for example, fell by 53 percent from $68 per ton in 1880 to $32 per ton in 1890. The price of refined sugar fell from 9 cents per pound in 1880, to 7 cents in 1890, to 4.5 cents in 1900. The price of lead dropped 12 percent, from $5.04 per pound in 1880 to $4.41 in 1890. The price of zinc declined by 20 percent, from $5.51 to $4.40 per pound from 1880 to 1890.

The sugar and petroleum trusts were among the most widely attacked, but there is evidence that these trusts actually reduced prices from what they otherwise would have been. Congress clearly recognized this. During the House debates over the Sherman Act, Congressman William Mason stated, *"Trusts have made products cheaper, have reduced prices;* but if the price of oil, for instance, were reduced to one cent a barrel, it would not right the wrong done to the people of this country by the 'trusts' which have destroyed legitimate competition and driven honest men from legitimate business enterprises."[7] Sen. Edwards, who played a key role in the debate, added, "Although for the time being *the sugar trust has perhaps reduced the price of sugar, and the oil trust certainly has reduced the price of oil immensely,* that does not alter the wrong of the principle of any trust."[8] Perhaps it would be more accurate to describe the Sherman Act as an anti-price-cutting law.

One final argument could be made that the trusts were practicing predatory pricing, that is, that they were pricing below their costs to drive out competitors. But in more than a century of looking for a proven real-world monopoly actually created by predatory pricing, an example has yet to be found. Moreover, prices charged by the nineteenth-century trusts continued to fall for more than a decade. What rational businessman would continue to price below cost for more than ten years?

In sum, the nineteenth-century trusts were not guilty of the charge levied against them by Sen. Sherman. There is no consistent evidence that they restricted output to raise prices.

Government: The True Source of Monopoly

It appears that one function of the Sherman Act was to divert public attention from a more certain source of monopoly—government. In the late nineteenth century, tariffs were a major source of trade restraints, but the Sherman Act made no provision for attacking tariffs or any other government-created barriers to competitive entry. In fact, evidence exists that a major political function of the Sherman Act was to serve as a smoke screen behind which politicians could grant tariff protection to their big business constituents while assuring the public that something was being done about the monopoly problem.

In a particularly revealing statement during the debates over the antitrust act, Sherman attacked the trusts on the ground that they "subverted the tariff system; they undermined the policy of government to protect . . . American industries by levying duties on imported goods."[9] This is certainly an odd statement from the author of the "Magna Carta of free enterprise." But increased output and reduced prices in these increasingly efficient industries apparently dissipated the monopoly profits previously generated by the tariffs. This worked against the objectives of the protected industries and their legislative champions, including Sen. Sherman.

Even more damning is the fact that just three months after the Sherman Act was passed, Sen. Sherman, as chairman of the Senate Finance Committee, sponsored legislation popularly known as the "Campaign Contributors' Tariff Bill" that sharply raised tariff rates. On October 1, 1890, the *New York Times* reported: "The Campaign Contributors' Tariff Bill now goes to the president for his signature, which will speedily be affixed to it, and the favored manufacturers, many of whom . . . proposed and made the [tariff] rates which affect their products, will begin to enjoy the profits of this legislation."

The *New York Times* further reported that "the speech of Mr. Sherman on Monday [September 29, 1890] should not be overlooked, for it was one of confession." Apparently, Sen. Sherman withdrew his speech from the *Congressional Record* for "revision," but a reporter obtained an unabridged copy of the original. The *New York Times* reported: "We direct attention to those passages [of Sherman's speech] relating to combinations of protected manufacturers designed to take full advantage of high tariff duties by exacting from consumers prices fixed by agreement after competition has been suppressed. . . . Mr. Sherman closed his speech with some words of warning and advice to the beneficiaries of the new tariff. He was earnest enough in his manner to indicate that he is not at all confident as to the outcome of the law. The great thing that stood in the way of the success of the bill, he said, was whether or not the manufacturers of this country would permit free competition in the American market. The danger was that the beneficiaries of the bill would combine and cheat the people out of the benefits of the law. They were now given reasonable and ample protection, and if they would resist the temptation attaching to great aggregations of capital to combine and advance prices, they might hope for a season of great prosperity. . . . He did hope, the Senator concluded, that the manufacturers would open the doors to fair competition and give its benefits to the people. . . . He hoped the manufacturers would agree to compete one with another and would refuse to take the high prices that are so easily obtained."

It was absurd, of course, for Sen. Sherman to say that a protective tariff would actually help consumers if only manufacturers could be trusted to refrain from raising prices. The whole purpose of tariff protection is to allow domestic manufacturers to raise prices, or at least to avoid reducing them. Such hypocrisy led the *New York Times* to withdraw its support of antitrust legislation. The *Times* concluded: "That so-called Anti-Trust law was passed to deceive the people and to clear the way for the enactment of this . . . law relating to the tariff. It was projected in order that the party organs might say to the opponents of tariff extortion and protected combinations, 'Behold! We have attacked the Trusts. The Republican party is the enemy of all such rings.' And now the author of it can only 'hope' that the rings will dissolve of their own accord." Thus, the Sherman Act seems to have been passed to help draw public attention away from the process of monopolization through tariff protection.

The Sherman Act won legislators votes and campaign contributions from farmers and small businessmen who thought antitrust regulation would protect them from their more efficient competitors, and the tariff bill was supported by all U.S. manufacturers, both large and small. In a political sense, then, the Sherman Act was very efficient. Congress itself seems to have been one of the principal special-interest groups to benefit from antitrust legislation.

Economists and the Emergence of Antitrust

Although most economists today favor stricter antitrust regulation, from the 1880s until the 1920s the economics profession expressed nearly unanimous opposition to antitrust. When Sanford Gordon surveyed professional journals in the social sciences and articles and books written by economists before 1890, he found, "A big majority of the economists conceded that the combination movement was to be expected, that high fixed costs made large-scale enterprises economical, that competition under these new circumstances frequently resulted in cutthroat competition, that agreements among producers was a natural consequence, and the stability of prices usually brought more benefit than harm to the society. They seemed to reject the idea that competition was declining, or showed no fear of decline."[10]

George Stigler has also noted economists' initial disapproval of antitrust: "For much too long a time students of the history of antitrust policy have been at least mildly perplexed by the coolness with which American economists greeted the Sherman Act. Was not the nineteenth century the period in which the benevolent effects of competition were most widely extolled? Should not a profession praise a Congress which seeks to legislate its textbook assumptions into practice?"[11] Stigler offered three possible explanations. First, economists did not appreciate the importance of tacit collusion. Second, they had too much confidence in other forms of regulation as a means of dealing with monopoly. Third, they underestimated the income they would receive as antitrust consultants.

These explanations are plausible, but there may be an even more important reason for the transformation of economists' attitudes toward antitrust. In the late nineteenth century most economists viewed competition as a dynamic, rivalrous process, similar to the theory of competition embodied in the work of Adam Smith and today's Austrian economists. Consequently, they tended to regard mergers as a natural consequence of the competitive struggle and not something that should be interfered with by antitrust legislation.[12] Although some industries were becoming more concentrated in the late nineteenth century, rivalry was still as strong as ever, as the rapid expansion of output and the decline in prices attest. Thus, the economists of the time saw no reason to interfere in market processes with antitrust regulation.

Beginning in the 1920s, mathematical economists developed the so-called perfect competition model, and it replaced the older theory. To economists competition no longer meant rivalry and enterprise. Instead, it meant the equation of price and marginal cost. Most important, it meant that there must be "many" firms in "unconcentrated" industries. Once economists began to define competition in terms of market structure, they became more and more enamored with antitrust regulation as a way of forcing the business world to conform to their admittedly unrealistic theory of competition.

Economist Paul McNulty has noted: "The two concepts [of competition] are not Only different; they are fundamentally incompatible. Competition came to mean, with the mathematical economists, a hypothetically realized situation in which business rivalry . . . was ruled out by definition."[13] F. A. Hayek has made an even stronger statement: "What the theory of perfect competition discusses has little claim to be called 'competition' at all and . . . its conclusions are of little use as guides to policy."[14] Moreover, wrote Hayek, "If the state of affairs assumed by the theory of perfect competition ever existed, it would not only deprive of their scope all the activities which the verb 'to compete' describes but would make them virtually impossible."[15] Advertising, product differentiation, and price undercutting, for example, are all excluded by definition from a state of "perfect" competition which, according to Hayek, "means indeed the absence of all competitive activities."

Those economists who use market structure to measure competition are likely to have a favorable attitude toward antitrust regulation. Stigler asserted more than 30 years ago, "One of the assumptions of perfect competition is the existence of a Sherman Act."[16] To the nineteenth-century economists, however, an antitrust law was incompatible with rivalry and free enterprise. The perfect competition model and its corollary, the structure-conduct-performance paradigm of industrial

---

354

organization theory, have seriously misled the economics profession, at least as far as antitrust policy is concerned.

Conclusion

The two principal reasons for the "antitrust economists' paradox," then, are the lack of historical knowledge—particularly about actual economic events in the late nineteenth century—and the failure to appreciate that competition is best viewed as a dynamic discovery procedure, as Hayek contends. Economists who believe that there was once a "golden age of antitrust" have never produced any evidence of such an age. As this paper has shown, the Sherman Act was a tool used to regulate some of the most competitive industries in America, which were rapidly *expanding* their output and *reducing* their prices, much to the dismay of their less efficient (but politically influential) competitors. The Sherman Act, moreover, was used as a political fig leaf to shield the real cause of monopoly in the late 1880s—protectionism. The chief sponsor of the 1890 tariff bill, passed just three months after the Sherman Act, was none other than Sen. Sherman himself.

In the late nineteenth century most economists viewed competition as a dynamic, rivalrous process, much like the contemporary Austrian theory. Accordingly, they nearly unanimously opposed antitrust on the grounds that such a law would be inherently incompatible with rivalry. Once the economics profession embraced the "perfect" competition theory which, as Hayek has said, means "the absence of all competitive activities," it also embraced antitrust regulation. For once competition came to mean "many" firms and the equation of price to marginal costs, rather than dynamic rivalry, most economists became convinced that antitrust laws were needed to force markets in the direction of their idealized model of "perfect" competition. Consequently, antitrust has for over a century been a tremendous drag on competition, rendering American industry less productive and less competitive in world markets. Robert Bork might not have been exaggerating when, writing in his book, *The Antitrust Paradox*, he remarked that if government were to somehow force the economy into "competitive equilibrium," it would have approximately the same effect on personal wealth as several strategically placed nuclear explosions.

Notes

1. Quoted in Thomas Hazlett, "Interview With George Stigler," *Reason* (January 1984): 46.

2. Bruno Frey, et al., "Consensus and Dissention Among Economists," *American Economic Review* (May 1984): 986-94.

3. Sanford Gordon, "Attitudes Toward the Trusts Prior to the Sherman Act," *Southern Economic Journal* (July 1963): 158.

4. Ibid., p. 162.

5. R. Gray, and J. Peterson, *Economic Development in the United States* (New York: Irwin, 1965).

6. The following discussion is based on Thomas J. DiLorenzo, "The Origins of Antitrust: An Interest Group Perspective," *International Review of Law and Economics* (June 1985).

7. *Congressional Record*, 51st Congress, House, 1st Session (June 20, 1890), p. 4100; emphasis added.

8. Ibid., p. 2558; emphasis added.

9. Ibid., p. 4100.

10. Sanford Gordon, "Attitudes Toward the Trusts," p. 158.

11. George Stigler, "The Economists and the Problem of Monopoly," *American Economic Review* (May 1982): 1.

12. The following discussion is based on Thomas J. DiLorenzo and Jack C. High, "Antitrust and Competition, Historically Considered," *Economic Inquiry* (Summer 1988).

13. Paul McNulty, "A Note on the History of Perfect Competition," *Journal of Political Economy* (August 1967): 398.

14. F.A. Hayek, "The Meaning of Competition," in F. A. Hayek, *Individualism and Economic Order* (Chicago: University of Chicago Press, 1948), p. 92.

15. Ibid.

16. George Stigler, "Perfect Competition, Historically Contemplated," *Journal of Political Economy* (February 1957): 1.

THE MYTH OF PREDATORY PRICING

Thomas J. DiLorenzo

> The attempt to reduce or to eliminate predatory pricing is also likely to reduce or
> eliminate competitive pricing beneficial to consumers.
>
> —*Harold Demsetz*

Predatory pricing is one of the oldest big business conspiracy theories. It was popularized in the late 19th century by journalists such as Ida Tarbell, who in *History of the Standard Oil Company* excoriated John D. Rockefeller because Standard Oil's low prices had driven her brother's employer, the Pure Oil Company, from the petroleum-refining business.[1] "Cutting to Kill" was the title of the chapter in which Tarbell condemned Standard Oil's allegedly predatory price cutting.

The predatory pricing argument is very simple. The predatory firm first lowers its price until it is below the average cost of its competitors. The competitors must then lower their prices below average cost, thereby losing money on each unit sold. If they fail to cut their prices, they will lose virtually all of their market share; if they do cut their prices, they will eventually go bankrupt. After the competition has been forced out of the market, the predatory firm raises its price, compensating itself for the money it lost while it was engaged in predatory pricing, and earns monopoly profits forever after.

The theory of predatory pricing has always seemed to have a grain of truth to it—at least to noneconomists—but research over the past 35 years has shown that predatory pricing as a strategy for monopolizing an industry is irrational, that there has never been a single clear-cut example of a monopoly created by so-called predatory pricing, and that claims of predatory pricing are typically made by competitors who are either unwilling or unable to cut their own prices. Thus, legal restrictions on price cutting, in the name of combatting "predation," are inevitably protectionist and anti-consumer, as Harold Demsetz noted.[2]

Predatory pricing is the Rodney Dangerfield of economic theory—it gets virtually no respect from economists. But it is still a popular legal and political theory for several reasons. First, huge sums of money are involved in predatory pricing litigation, which guarantees that the antitrust bar will always be fond of the theory of predatory pricing. During the 1970s AT&T estimated that it spent over $100 million a year defending itself against claims of predatory pricing. It has been estimated that the average cost to a major corporation of litigating a predation case is $30 million.[3]

Second, because it seems plausible at first, the idea of predatory pricing lends itself to political demagoguery, especially when combined with xenophobia. The specter of a foreign conspiracy to take over American industries one by one is extremely popular in folk myth. Protectionist members of Congress frequently invoke that myth in attempts to protect businesses in their districts from foreign competition.

Third, ideological anti-business pressure groups, such as Citizen Action, a self-styled consumer group, also employ the predatory pricing tale in their efforts to discredit capitalism and promote greater governmental control of industry. Citizen Action perennially attacks the oil industry for either raising or cutting prices. When oil and gas prices go up, Citizen Action holds a press conference to denounce alleged price gouging. When prices go down, it can be relied on to issue a "study" claiming that the price reductions are part of a grand conspiracy to rid the market of all competitors. And when prices remain constant, price-fixing conspiracies are frequently alleged.

Fourth, predatory pricing is a convenient weapon for businesses that do not want to match their competitors' price cutting. Filing an antitrust lawsuit is a common alternative to competing by cutting prices or improving product quality, or both.

Finally, some economists still embrace the theory of predatory pricing. But their support for the notion is based entirely on highly stylized "models," not on actual experience.

The Irrationality of Predatory Pricing

The classic article on predatory pricing was written by economist John McGee in 1958.[4] McGee examined the famous 1911 Standard Oil antitrust decision that required John D. Rockefeller to divest his company. Although at that time popular folklore held that Rockefeller had "monopolized" the oil refinery business by predatory pricing, McGee showed that Standard Oil did not engage in predatory pricing; it would have been irrational to have done so.

Judging from the record, Standard Oil did not use predatory price discrimination to drive out competing refiners, nor did its pricing practice have that effect. Whereas there may be a very few cases in which retail kerosene peddlers or dealers went out of business after or during price cutting, there is no real proof that Standard's pricing policies were responsible. I am convinced that Standard did not systematically, if ever, use local price cutting in retailing, or anywhere else, to reduce competition. To do so would have been foolish; and, whatever else has been said about them, the old Standard organization was seldom criticized for making less money when it could readily have made more.[5]

McGee was the first economist to think through the logic of predatory pricing, laying aside the emotional rhetoric that had always surrounded it. He concluded that not only would it have been foolish for Standard Oil to have engaged in predatory pricing; it would also be irrational for *any* business to attempt to monopolize a market in that way.

In the first place, such practices are very costly for the large firm, which is always assumed to be the predator. If price is set below average cost, the largest firm will incur the largest losses by virtue of having the largest volume of sales. Losing a dollar on each of 1,000 widgets sold per month is more costly than losing a dollar on each of 100 widgets.

Second, there is great uncertainty about how long a price war would last. The prospect of incurring losses indefinitely in the hope of someday being able to charge monopolistic prices will give any business person pause. A price war is an extremely risky venture.

Standard Oil was not the only trust accused of predatory pricing; antitrust folklore has it that virtually all of the late-19th-century trusts were guilty of the practice. However, as I have shown elsewhere, the industries accused of becoming monopolies during the congressional debates on the 1890 Sherman Antitrust Act all dropped their prices more rapidly than the general price level fell during the 10 years before the Sherman Act.[6] It would certainly have been irrational for those businesses to have engaged in predatory pricing *for an entire decade* in the dim hope of someday being able to charge prices slightly above the competitive market rate.

Third, there is nothing stopping the competition (or "prey") from temporarily shutting down and waiting for the price to return to profitable levels. If that strategy is employed, price competition will render the predatory pricing strategy unprofitable—all loss and no compensatory benefit. Alternatively, even if the preyed-upon firms went bankrupt, other firms could purchase their facilities and compete with the alleged predator. Such competition is virtually guaranteed if the predator is charging monopolistic prices and earning above-normal profits.

Fourth, there is the danger that the price war will spread to surrounding markets and cause the alleged predator to incur losses in those markets as well.

Fifth, the theory of predatory pricing assumes the prior existence of a "war chest of monopoly profits" that the predator can use to subsidize its practice of pricing below average cost. But how does that war chest come into being if the firm has not yet become a monopoly? That part of the theory is simply a non sequitur.

Finally, the opportunity cost of the funds allegedly used to try to bankrupt rivals must be taken into account. For predatory pricing to seem rational, the rate of return on predation must be higher than the market rate of interest; in fact, it must be higher than the expected rate of return on any other investment the predator might make, including "investment" in lobbying for protectionism, monopoly franchises, and the like. Predation is unlikely, given the great uncertainties about whether it would have any positive return at all.

Predatory Counterstrategies

The theory of predatory pricing has always assumed that a dominant firm is able to manipulate its smaller rivals. But the potential use of predatory counterstrategies by the smaller rivals makes the likelihood of successful predatory pricing extremely remote. Frank Easterbrook has produced a taxonomy of predatory counterstrategies that has led him to conclude that "the antitrust offense of predation should be forgotten."[7]

The predator can recoup its losses only if consumers cooperate. That is, the strategy will fail if consumers are able to stock up during the low-price predation period. If they do so, there can never be a post-predation recoupment period for the predator. And if the predator responds by limiting quantity, its rivals can step in and make up the difference by supplying additional quantities at a higher price. "A predator that puts a cap on sales thus [preys] against itself."[8]

Admittedly, consumer stockpiling is not always possible, and there is another problem related to the predator's ability to recoup his losses: the "victims" have strong incentives to ride out the price war, as discussed above, because of the lure of monopoly profits when the war is over. The capital markets, moreover, should be willing to finance the victims because they, after all, are not incurring as large a loss as is the predator. There is a risk, of course, in providing capital to the victims, but that risk can be attenuated by charging an appropriate interest rate. As George Stigler once described it, the victim of alleged predation, such as that supposedly engineered by Standard Oil, could go to a lender and say:

> There is a threat of a three-month price war, during which I will lose $10,000, which unfortunately I do not possess. If you lend me $10,000, I can survive the price war—and

once I show your certified check to Rockefeller the price war will probably never be embarked upon. Even if the price war should occur, we will earn more by cooperation afterward than the $10,000 loss, or Rockefeller would never embark upon the strategy.[9]

Thus, lenders may have a financial incentive to aid the prey. There is also the possibility that larger firms, which have their own "deep pockets," will acquire the victims if it seems profitable to do so.[10]

Even if the victim goes bankrupt, the predator is by no means guaranteed a monopoly. The bankrupt firm's resources do not simply disappear; they may be acquired by another firm (possibly at fire-sale prices). Because the acquiring firm has lower fixed costs than the predator, it may be able to underprice the predator.

The victim could also approach its customers and arrange for long-term contracts at a price above the predatory price. The customers would be willing to enter into such contracts if they realized that the current low price was to be followed by a monopolistic price.

Finally, it should be kept in mind that the anticipated monopoly profits of the predator must be discounted to their present value. The predator firm may realize that possible monopoly profits in the future are not worth lost profits today.[11] If that is the case, predatory pricing clearly does not pay.

Predation or Competition?

The theory of predatory pricing fails to recognize that price cutting—even below average cost—is a normal activity in competitive markets. That is because the theory is derived from the so-called perfect competition model of economic theory. In an ideal, or "perfectly competitive," market, every firm charges an identical price, and in equilibrium that price is equal to average total cost. Deviations from that benchmark are viewed as market "imperfections."

The perfect competition theory has its uses, but a more realistic way of thinking about competition—especially for public policy purposes—is that of the Austrian economists who view competition as dynamic rivalry. As Nobel laureate Friedrich Hayek has stated, "Competition is by its nature a dynamic process whose essential characteristics are assumed away by the assumptions underlying static analysis" (i.e., perfect competition theory).[12] Competition "is the action of endeavoring to gain what another endeavors to gain at the same time."[13] Thus, price cutting, product differentiation, and advertising are all important elements of a competitive market according to the

Austrian view, but those elements "are all excluded by definition" from perfect competition theory. "Perfect competition means the absence of all competitive activities."[14]

Once one thinks of competition as rivalry, the notion of predatory pricing seems bizarre. Cutting prices below cost is an important way for newer businesses to break into a market or for older, more established businesses to grab a larger market share. The former case is exemplified by the local pizza parlor that tries to lure customers away from older, more established businesses with a "two-for-one" special. It may lose money in the short run, but such temporary losses should be viewed as an investment in future business. The pizza parlor is using lower prices today to increase its clientele tomorrow. (*USA Today* lost money for years before it got off the ground.) The latter case—an established business that becomes more entrepreneurial and makes a grab for a larger market share—is exemplified by Henry Ford.

When Ford declared in 1908, "I will build a motor car for the great multitude" and produced the Model T, he at first lost money and market share to Buick, Oldsmobile, and other competitors.[15] The year 1910 was a good one for the automobile industry, and Ford's advisers told him to follow Buick and Oldsmobile by raising the price of the Model T significantly. Rather than take their advice, however, Ford *dropped* his price by 20 percent to $780, which was below his average total cost. He gambled that the lower price would greatly expand his sales volume and reduce his per unit costs, thereby enabling him to make a profit. The gamble paid off. As George Gilder explained:

> Ford set his price not on the basis of his existing costs or sales but on the basis of the much lower costs and much expanded sales that might become possible at the lower price. The effect in the case of Henry Ford in 1910 was a 60 percent surge in sales that swept the Model T far ahead of Buick. . . . In the recession year of 1914, he cut prices twice, and sales surged up while other companies failed. By 1916, he had reduced the price of a Model T to $360 and increased his market share from 10 percent to 40 percent. . . . After cutting prices 30 percent during the 1920 economic crisis, Ford commanded a 60 percent share of [the] market.[16]

Ford became the dominant firm in the automobile industry by offering a high-quality product at the lowest price available. Ford may have "harmed" his competitors by "preying" on them, but it was all to the benefit of consumers.

If Tarbell and other muckraking journalists had waged the kind of propaganda campaign against Henry Ford that they did against John D. Rockefeller, the Model T might never have been produced. Ford did not always receive favorable publicity, but neither was he sued for predatory pricing and forced to divest his company.

It is not an exaggeration to say that all of Henry Ford's success may have been linked to his below-cost pricing strategy. In his own words:

> Our policy is to reduce the price, extend the operations, and improve the article. You will note that the reduction of price comes first. We have never considered any costs as fixed. Therefore we first reduce the price to the point where we believe more sales will result. Then we go ahead and try to make the prices. We do not bother about the costs. The new price forces the costs down.[17]

Ford went on to note that "the more usual way is to take the costs and then determine the price," but he believed his way was better.[18] "No one knows what a cost ought to be," he said, but "one of the ways of discovering [it] . . . is to name a price so low as to force everybody in the place to the highest point of efficiency. The low price makes everybody dig for profits. We make more discoveries concerning manufacturing and selling under this forced method than by any method of leisurely investigation."[19]

As Hayek has said, competition is a "discovery procedure," and below-cost pricing has long been an important element of that procedure and of the benefits it produces for consumers.[20] Competition provides numerous reasons for price cutting. Sellers may be meeting their competitors' price cuts. They may be discounting their prices as a way of introducing their new and unknown products to consumers. The goods may be perishable or obsolescent and must therefore be sold at any price to avoid losses. The seller may have built a large-capacity plant that is more efficient because of higher volume; he charges low prices to stimulate demand, as did Henry Ford. Or there may be excess capacity in the market that prompts the seller to charge a price that minimizes losses until demand increases again.

Businesses that accuse their rivals of predation are simply unwilling or unable to produce efficiently enough to meet their rivals' lower prices.

The Futile Search for a Predatory Pricer

Even though predatory pricing was part of the theoretical underpinning of the original federal antitrust laws, and there have been hundreds of federal antitrust cases based on claims of predatory pricing, economists and legal scholars have to this day failed to provide an unambiguous example of a single monopoly created by predatory pricing. (In contrast, no such ambiguity exists in the case of government sanctioned monopolies created by protectionism, exclusive franchising, grandfather clauses, occupational licensing, and other government-imposed barriers to competition.)

The theory of predatory pricing is no longer widely accepted by economists, but it was the conventional wisdom before McGee's 1958 article. The economics profession—and antitrust practitioners—accepted the notion as a matter of faith even though no one (before McGee) had conducted a systematic economic analysis of predatory pricing.

By 1970 more than 120 federal (and thousands of private) antitrust cases in which predatory pricing was alleged had been brought under the 1890 Sherman Act. Yet in a 1970 study of the so-called gunpowder trust—43 corporations in the explosives industry—Kenneth Elzinga stated, after an extensive literature search, that "to my knowledge no one has ever examined in detail, as McGee did, other alleged incidents of predatory pricing."[21] Elzinga found no evidence that the gunpowder trust—which had been accused of predatory pricing—actually practiced it.

Shortly after Elzinga's work appeared, Ronald H. Koller examined the "123 federal antitrust cases since the passage of the Sherman Act in 1890 in which it was alleged that behavior generally resembling predation had played a significant role."[22] Ninety-five of those cases resulted in convictions, even though in only 26 of the cases was there a trial that "produced a factual record adequate for the kind of analysis employed" by Koller.[23] Apparently, many of the defendants decided it was cheaper to plead guilty than to defend themselves.

Even though no systematic analysis of predatory pricing was performed in any of the 123 cases, Koller established the following criteria for independently determining whether a monopoly was established by predatory pricing: Did the accused predator reduce its price to less than its short-run average total cost? If so, did it appear to have done so with a predatory intent? Did the reduction in price succeed in eliminating a competitor, precipitating a merger, or improving "market discipline"?

Koller's criteria give predatory pricing theory more credit than it deserves. As was explained earlier, below cost pricing per se is not necessarily a sign of predatory behavior; it is a normal feature of competitive markets. Moreover, determining predatory intent is an exercise that is far beyond the capabilities of any economist and for which mystics might be better suited. And "eliminating a competitor" is the very purpose of all competition.

Employing those criteria for determining predatory behavior, Koller found that below-cost pricing "seems to have been at least attempted" in only seven cases.[24] That, of course, proves nothing about monopolizing behavior, given the fact that below-cost pricing can be just as easily construed as competitive behavior. Koller claims that in four of the cases low prices seemed to have been motivated by the desire to eliminate a rival. One would hope so! The entire purpose of competitive behavior—whether cutting prices or improving product quality—is to eliminate one's rivals.

Even in the cases where a competitor seemed to have been eliminated by low prices, "in no case were all of the competitors eliminated."[25] Thus, there was no monopoly, just lower prices.

Three cases seem to have facilitated a merger, but mergers are typically an efficient alternative to bankruptcy, not a route to monopoly. In those cases, as in the others, the mergers did not result in anything remotely resembling a monopolistic industry, as defined by Koller (i.e., one with a single producer).

In sum, despite over 100 federal antitrust cases based on predatory pricing, Koller found absolutely no evidence of *any* monopoly having been established by predatory pricing between 1890 and 1970. Yet at the time Koller's study was published (1971), predatory pricing had long been part of the conventional wisdom. The work of McGee, Elzinga, and other analysts had not yet gained wide recognition.

The search for the elusive predatory pricer has not been any more successful in the two decades since Koller's study appeared. The complete lack of evidence of predatory pricing, moreover, has not gone unnoticed by the U.S. Supreme Court. In *Matsushita Electric Industrial Co. v. Zenith Radio* (1986), the court demonstrated knowledge of the above-mentioned research in declaring, effectively, that predatory pricing was about as common as unicorn sightings.

Zenith had accused Matsushita and several other Japanese microelectronics companies of engaging in predatory pricing—of using profits from the Japanese market to subsidize below-cost pricing of color television sets in the United States. The Supreme Court ruled against Zenith, recognizing in its majority opinion that

> a predatory pricing conspiracy is by nature speculative. Any agreement to price below the
> competitive level requires the conspirators to forgo profits that free competition would offer
> them. The forgone profits may be considered an investment in the future. For the investment
> to be rational, the conspirators must have a reasonable expectation of recovering, in the form
> of later monopoly profits, more than the losses suffered.[26]

The Court also noted that "the success of such schemes is inherently uncertain: the short-run loss is definite, but the long-run gain depends on successfully neutralizing the competition."[27] The Court continues, "There is a consensus among commentators that predatory pricing schemes are rarely tried, and even more rarely successful."[28]

In that case, Zenith and RCA were obviously attempting to use the antitrust laws, via their accusation of predatory pricing, to eliminate some of their foreign competition. The Court determined, for example, that "two decades after their conspiracy is alleged to have commenced, petitioners appear to be far from achieving their goal: the two largest shares of the retail market in television sets are held by RCA and . . . Zenith, not by any of the petitioners."[29] Moreover, the share of the market held by Zenith and RCA "did not decline . . . during the 1970s," which provides further evidence that "the conspiracy does not in fact exist."[30]

The Court concluded by warning potential litigants of the folly of bringing predatory pricing cases.

> Cutting prices in order to increase business often is the very essence of competition. Thus, mistaken inferences in cases such as this one are especially costly, because they chill the very conduct the antitrust laws are designed to protect.[31]

Since predatory pricing schemes "require conspirators to suffer losses in order eventually to realize . . . gains," the Court concluded that "economic realities tend to make predatory pricing conspiracies self-deterring."[32]

What predatory pricing comes down to is a theory and a legal doctrine that are still used by inefficient firms to try to get the coercive powers of government to attain for them what they cannot attain in the marketplace. As former Federal Trade Commission chairman James Miller has written, government has all too often used predatory pricing as a vehicle for instructing businesses to "stop competing, leave your competitors alone, raise your prices."[33]

"Dumping" on Competition

Even though predatory pricing is vacuous in both theory and reality, and has been viewed as such by the Supreme Court, the doctrine lives on. Special-interest groups that wish to undermine competition have no incentives to pay attention to the theory and reality of predatory pricing. In fact, as economist Gordon Tullock has written:

> Special interest groups normally have an interest in diminishing the information of the average voter. If they can sell him some false tale which supports their particular effort to rob the treasury, it pays. They have resources and normally make efforts to produce this kind of misinformation.[34]

Thus, the myth of predatory pricing will continue to be perpetrated in the courts and in the legislature. So-called anti-dumping laws are an example. In the context of international trade, "dumping" occurs when a foreign manufacturer sells a product in the United States at a lower price than is charged in the home market. Such price differentials can be easily explained by competition: New entrants in a foreign market must offer low prices to induce consumers to try their products. Fierce competition in the domestic market is also a reason for price differentials.

Anti-dumping laws ignore the competitive aspects of price cutting and invoke predatory pricing as a rationale for protectionism. For example, in November 1987 the U.S. Department of Commerce ruled that "Japanese companies violated international trade laws by failing to increase their prices to match the sharp rise in the value of the yen."[35] With the rise in the value of the yen, Japanese goods sold in the United States became relatively more expensive. The Japanese producers responded by cutting their costs, prices, and profit margins to remain competitive, to the great satisfaction of American consumers. According to the Commerce Department, Japanese export prices declined by 23 percent between 1985 and 1987.36 Despite significant benefits to American consumers, the Reagan administration's Commerce Department attempted to "force" Japanese companies to raise their prices.

Such a policy is absurd not only because it obviously harms American consumers but also because, under it, the American government effectively enforces a cartel pricing arrangement that benefits *foreign* manufacturers. The Japanese companies may have wanted to raise their prices and earn monopolistic profits, but competition prohibited it. Being prosecuted under the anti-dumping laws achieved for them what they were not able to achieve for themselves in the marketplace.

The same anti-consumer policies prevail today. In June 1991 the Bush Commerce Department launched an investigation of alleged dumping of Japanese minivans in the American market. If successful, the investigation could lead to "forcing up prices of Japanese . . . cars."[37] The Big Three domestic automakers were advocating Japanese price increases, which they hoped would "blunt the Japanese advance" in the minivan market.[38] The Big Three at that time controlled 88 percent of the minivan market, but they complained that their sales were "weakened by the unfair pricing."[39] They accused Japanese automakers of charging prices in the United States that were 30 percent lower than those charged in their home country. There could not be a more specious argument for using the coercive powers of government to thwart competition and to harm consumers.

On December 20, 1991, the Bush Commerce Department ruled in favor of the Big Three. It charged Mazda with the "crime" of selling minivans in the United States for 7.19 percent less than in Japan; Toyota was "guilty" of selling its minivans in America at 0.95 percent less than in Japan.[40] Because of that ruling, which is being appealed, the U.S. government will impose tariffs on Japanese products, which will enable the domestic automakers to charge even higher prices. Consumers will unequivocally be harmed.

Unfortunately, such anti-consumer policies, all adopted to punish "predatory pricing," are becoming increasingly prevalent. The United States Business and Industrial Council, a collection of protectionist businesses, is organized to "demand a tougher trade stance with Japan by raising tariffs on Japanese cars and electronic products."[41] A similar sentiment was voiced by Patrick J. Buchanan in December 1991 when he announced his candidacy for the Republican party's presidential nomination. In his announcement Buchanan spoke of "predatory traders of Europe and Asia who have targeted this or that American industry for dumping and destruction" and promised that, if he is elected, "they will find themselves on a collision course with the President of the United States."[42]

Regardless of Buchanan's personal political fate, special-interest groups seem to be increasingly dependent on the discredited predatory pricing argument for advancing the cause of protectionism. The national Democratic party is also stepping up its Japan-bashing efforts by proposing ever more restrictive trade legislation.

The myth of predatory pricing also threatens consumer welfare via the domestic policy route. One recent example is the latest of a long line of attacks on the oil industry by the self-described "consumer" group, Citizen Action. In a September 1991 report that warns ominously that "Big Oil" has allegedly "taken control of America's gasoline markets," Citizen Action singles out the Arco Oil Company for some unexpected praise. Arco, the report claims, is now "the dominant force in the refining and marketing of petroleum on the U.S. West Coast" because of "a combination of unexpected risk-taking, shrewd corporate planning and investment, [and] aggressive leadership."[43] The company "eliminated its credit cards, expanded its gasoline sales per station, created a chain of convenience stores on many of its gasoline station sites in order to maximize profits. . . . All of these actions made good economic sense. They reduced costs, increased efficiency and maximized profits."[44]

But Citizen Action's "praise" is not genuine. Rather than applauding its efficiencies, Citizen Action ascribes diabolical motivations to Arco, alleging "a ruthless determination to weaken, intimidate and eventually eliminate the independent refiners, wholesalers and marketers" with its low-cost, low-price strategy.[45] Arco is guilty of using its organizational efficiencies to "sharply lower the wholesale and retail price of gasoline," thereby "squeezing both independent refiners and marketers."[46]

The end result of the alleged monopolization of the West Coast market was that, according to Citizen Action's own data, "by 1990, Arco [was] number 1 with 19 percent of the market."[47] In other words, Arco was (and is) nothing close to a monopolist. Its efficiencies allowed it to become more competitive and improve its market position over the positions of Shell, Chevron, Unocal, and myriad other competitors, but it still has less than one-fifth of the market.

There are no entry barriers in the gasoline market; competition remains vigorous; and real gasoline prices have been *falling*. Citizen Action's claim that Arco has gained a monopoly through predatory pricing is simply preposterous. By Citizen Action's own admission, Arco's increased market share is due to its enhanced efficiency and lower prices. Nevertheless, Citizen Action tries to convince the readers of its report that black is white and white is black with the following horror stories.

Arco stations in two California towns north of San Bernardino are selling gas 20 [cents] below the market.

Motorists are queuing up at four recently-opened Arco stations in Victorville and Hisperia, Calif.

Arco's remodeled am/pm's post street prices of 58.9 [cents] for regular leaded; 68.9 [cents] for regular unleaded; 78.9 [cents] for premium unleaded.

Closest competition from a major: Shell whose regular leaded sells for 79.9 [cents] for premium unleaded—21 [cents]/gallon above Arco's.[48]

Worse yet, says Citizen Action, Arco's super-efficient, low-price strategies are being "quickly emulated by the other major companies."[49] One could only hope that all industries would emulate such strategies!

The Citizen Action report also warns that similar price-cutting strategies are being employed in Nevada and urges congressional action to put an end to them, all in the name of consumer protection! Oddly, there is very little mention of the impact on *consumers* of Arco's price cutting; the primary concern is "market share." The report reveals virtually no understanding on the part of its authors of the economic literature that shows that industrial concentration per se is by no means anti-competitive.[50] Becoming a "dominant" firm or rendering an industry more "concentrated" by cutting prices and improving product or service quality is desirable and should be encouraged. Citizen Action seems more concerned with ideological assaults on "big" business than with consumer protection, its ostensible purpose.

The logic and evidence of the Citizen Action report are laughable. But such "logic" has also been used by members of Congress who wish to protect businesses in their districts from competition. The proposed Petroleum Marketing Competition Enhancement Act (H.R. 2966), for example, claims to be designed to "prevent unfair competition," but eliminating the word "unfair" would probably reveal the true intent of the act.

Gasoline marketers who do not wish to compete in a free market and who want government to intervene to protect their profit margins are lobbying for that act. Ostensibly a response to alleged predatory pricing by the major oil companies, the act would make it "unlawful for a refiner to sell motor fuel, to any customer for resale, at a price which is higher than the refiner's adjusted retail price for the same or similar grade or quality of motor fuel from a direct operated outlet in the same geographic area." It would also make it "unlawful for a refiner to enter into any scheme or agreement to set, change, or maintain maximum retail prices of motor fuel provided, that this . . . shall not apply to a refiner's retail sales at its direct operated outlets."

By making it unlawful for a refiner to write a contract to maintain *maximum* retail prices, that provision would tend to *increase* prices. The objective of the bill is to "guarantee" the profit margins of gasoline middlemen by trying to isolate them from the forces of supply and demand, a futile objective if ever there was one. The effect of the law would be higher prices for consumers and a system of price controls. Any law that guarantees profit margins would have to do so by setting prices by governmental rules and regulations rather than by market forces. Price controls were, of course, a disaster when last implemented in the 1970s.

The purpose of this discussion is not necessarily to evaluate in detail the probable effects of the misnamed "Petroleum Marketing Competition Enhancement Act" but to make the point that the whole idea that gasoline middlemen need and deserve governmental protection from competition is rooted in the idea of predatory pricing. Similarly mischievous policies are found in many other industries.

Conclusion

The government's alleged right to tell citizens how they may use their legally and peacefully acquired property, and at what prices they may sell it, should be questioned. The question is, What right does government have to interfere with a business person who is peacefully striving to earn a living by cutting, raising, or maintaining stable prices? Are private property and individual freedom of choice desirable social institutions, or aren't they? To advocate a law regulating or eliminating "predatory" price cutting is to answer that question in the negative: Any proposal to interfere with voluntary market pricing arrangements is simply a denial of the legitimacy of private property rights and individual freedom of choice. From a natural rights perspective, laws designed to regulate predatory pricing—or any other kind of pricing—are improper. As Armentano has eloquently stated:

> This [natural rights] theory holds that individuals have inalienable rights to life, liberty, and property. These rights imply the liberty of any person or persons to enter into any noncoercive trading agreement on any terms mutually acceptable, to produce and trade any factor or good that they own, and to keep any property realized by such free exchange. This perspective would hold that it is right to own and use property; it is right to employ that property in any manner that does not infringe on anyone else's property rights; it is right to trade any or all of that property to anyone else on any terms mutually acceptable; and that it

is right to keep and enjoy the fruits of that effort. . . . Consequently, it would be wrong . . . to outlaw or regulate certain types of business contracts, organizational structures, or business cooperation.[51]

That perspective has a long history. In one of the most famous passages of *Wealth of Nations,* Adam Smith warns of the pervasiveness of business conspiracies: "People of the same trade seldom meet together, even for merriment and diversion, but the conversation ends in a conspiracy against the public, or in some contrivance to raise prices."[52] But in *the very next sentence* Smith added: "It is impossible indeed to prevent such meetings by any law which either could be executed, or would be consistent with liberty and justice." Smith clearly recognized the potential for business conspiracies; but whether they were likely or not, he believed that any government regulation of them was improper.

Harold Demsetz is right. The attempt to reduce or eliminate so-called predatory pricing will only eliminate competitive pricing, which is beneficial to consumers.[53] Predatory pricing is simply illogical, although there are some highly stylized economic models that claim that it is feasible under certain assumptions. Other research has shown, however, that predatory pricing cannot even be replicated under laboratory conditions by "experimental" economics.[54] In either case, an unambiguous example of a free-market monopoly that was established as a result of predatory pricing has yet to be found.

Unfortunately, the doctrine of predatory pricing still motivates antitrust suits and other protectionist pleadings. Significantly, it is legislation and regulation enacted in the name of predatory pricing (not predatory pricing itself) that are truly monopolizing. Government—not the free market—is the source of monopoly.

Notes

Thomas J. DiLorenzo holds the Scott L. Probasco, Jr., Chair of Free Enterprise at the University of Tennessee at Chattanooga.

1. Ida Tarbell, *The History of the Standard Oil Company* (New York: Peter Smith, 1950). Tarbell's brother, William, was treasurer of Pure Oil Company.

2. Harold Demsetz, "Barriers to Entry," *American Economic Review* 72 (May 1982): 52-56.

3. Frank Easterbrook, "Predatory Strategies and Counterstrategies," *University of Chicago Law Review* 48 (1981): 334.

4.   John McGee, "Predatory Price Cutting: The Standard Oil (N.J.) Case," *Journal of Law and Economics* 1 (April 1958): 137-69.

5.   Ibid., p. 168.

6.   Thomas J. DiLorenzo, "The Origins of Antitrust: An Interest Group Perspective," *International Review of Law and Economics* 5 (Fall 1985): 73-90.

7.   Easterbrook, p. 337.

8.   Ibid., p. 269.

9.   George Stigler, "Imperfections in the Capital Market," *Journal of Political Economy* 75 (June 1967): 116.

10. Easterbrook, p. 269.

11. Ibid.

12. Friedrich Hayek, "The Meaning of Competition," in his *Individualism and Economic Order* (Chicago: University of Chicago Press, 1974), p. 94.

13. Ibid., p. 96.

14. Ibid.

15. Quoted in George Gilder, *The Spirit of Enterprise* (New York: Simon and Schuster, 1984), p. 155.

16. Ibid., p. 157.

17. Ibid., p. 159.

18. Ibid.

19. Ibid.

20. Friedrich Hayek, "Competition as a Discovery Procedure," in his *New Studies in Philosophy, Politics, Economics and the History of Ideas* (Chicago: University of Chicago Press, 1978), pp. 179-90.

21. Kenneth G. Elzinga, "Predatory Pricing: The Case of the Gunpowder Trust," *Journal of Law and Economics* 13 (April 1970): 223.

22. Ronald H. Koller, "The Myth of Predatory Pricing: An Empirical Study," *Antitrust Law and Economics Review* 4 (Summer 1971): 110.

23. Ibid.

24. Ibid., p. 112.

25. Ibid., p. 113.

26. *Matsushita Electric Industrial Co. v. Zenith Radio* 475 U.S. 590, *Supreme Court Reporter,* 1986, p. 1357.

27. Ibid.

28. Ibid.

29. Ibid., p. 1358.

30. Ibid., p. 1359.

31. Ibid., p. 1360.

32. Ibid.

33. James C. Miller and Paul Pautler, "Predation: The Changing View in Economics and the Law," *Journal of Law and Economics* 28 (May 1985): 502.

34. Gordon Tullock, *Welfare for the Well-to-Do* (Dallas: Fisher Institute, 1983), p. 71.

35. Stuart Auerbach, "Japanese Companies Violated Trade Laws," *Washington Post,* November 20, 1987, p. D-1.

36. Ibid.

37. Eduardo Lachica and Joseph B. White, "Washington Is Expected to Investigate Alleged Dumping of Japanese Minivans," *Wall Street Journal,* June 20, 1991, p. B-3.

38. Ibid.

39. Frederick Standish, "Big Three Charge Japanese with 'Dumping' Minivans," *Washington Times*, June 7, 1991, p. G-4.

40. "Japanese Dumping Minivans," *Chattanooga Times*, December 21, 1991, p. B-8.

41. Stuart Auerbach, "Conservative Group Attacks Free Trade," *Washington Post,* November 26, 1991, p. C-1.

42. Hobart Rowen, "Forward into the Past," *Washinaton Post National Weekly Edition,* December 30-January 5, 1992, p. 5.

43. Citizen Action, "Destroying Competition and Raising Prices: How Big Oil Has Taken Control of America's Gasoline Markets," Washington, September 1991, p. 58.

44. Ibid., p. 59.

45. Ibid.

46. Ibid.

47.   Ibid., p. 60.

48.   Ibid., p. 61.

49.   Ibid., p. 60.

50.   Works they ignore include Yale Brozen, *Concentration. Mergers and Public Policy* (New York: MacMillan, 1983); John McGee, *In Defense of Industrial Concentration* (New York: Praeger, 1971); Harvey Goldschmidt, Patrick Mann, and Fred Weston, *Industrial Concentration: The New Learning* (Boston: Little, Brown, 1974).

51.   Dominick Armentano, *Antitrust and Monopoly* (New York: Wiley, 1982), p. 8. See also Roger Pilon, "Corporations and Rights: On Treating Corporate People Justly," *Georgia Law Review* 13, no. 4 (Summer 1979): 1245-1370.

52.   Adam Smith, *An Inquiry into the Nature and Causes of the Wealth of Nations* (Indianapolis: Liberty Fund, 1981), p. 145.

53.   Demsetz, pp. 47-57.

54.   R. Mark Isaac and Vernon L. Smith, "In Search of Predatory Pricing," *Journal of Political Economy*, April 1985, pp. 320-45.

ANTITRUST POLICY: REFORM OR REPEAL?

D.T. Armentano

T he current wave of business mergers raises the specter of increasing corporate monopoly power in the economy. Critics of industrial concentration claim that current merger trends are worrisome and that vigorous enforcement of the antitrust laws is necessary to preserve competition.

The critics are especially annoyed with antitrust chief William Baxter who, they argue, has essentially adopted a laissez faire attitude toward monopoly. Although Baxter was the major catalyst in the historic divestiture of the American Telephone and Telegraph Company, his critics contend that his policies in general have meant a less active antitrust policy.

What *is* existing antitrust policy and does it make economic sense? Is a vigorous enforcement of the antitrust laws necessary to preserve competition? Or would we all be better off without *any* antitrust policy?

The Theory Behind Antitrust

The economic case for free markets is said to depend on the existence of business competition. According to the conventional wisdom, the existence f competition ensures that scarce resources will be put to their most efficient use. Competition keeps costs low and induces firms to innovate and engage in technological development. Competition is the institutional vehicle through which private business self-interest is said to promote the public interest.

Business monopoly is seen as the antithesis of competition and has little utilitarian justification. The existence of monopoly and monopoly power misallocates economic resources and makes the economy less efficient than under competition. Monopolies reduce production and charge higher prices for their products. Moreover, monopolies are said to engage in socially wasteful product differentiation, and some restrict the pace of technological activity. When monopolists pursue their own business self-interest, they injure the public interest.

One important source of business monopoly is legal barriers to entry. It has been well recognized that government regulation can foster business monopoly by legally restricting entry and competition.[1] Government licensing, franchises, certificates of public convenience, and other legal restrictions can be a source of monopoly power for the firms that are protected from open competition. The social cure for this monopoly is deregulation.

It is also believed, however, that business monopoly can arise in a free market without any government support. The origin of this monopoly power is traced to certain *economic* barriers to entry that insulate existing firms from potential competition.[2] Product differentiation, economies of scale, predatory practices, and advertising are often identified as important barriers that limit competition and misallocate economic resources. In addition, collusion that restricts market output is said to be socially inefficient. And it is this private, antisocial monopoly power that the antitrust laws were allegedly intended to control.

Old Directions in Antitrust Policy

Antitrust law, especially the Sherman Antitrust Act of 1890, has always enjoyed widespread political and academic support in America. The existence and enforcement of the antitrust laws has rarely been a partisan political issue; Democrats and Republicans have endorsed the laws and have advocated "tough" enforcement. In addition, the bulk of the academic economists have always supported the Sherman Act and a vigorous enforcement policy.[3] While some scholars have written critically of the application of the law in specific areas, there has been little enthusiasm in the academic world for a complete repeal of the antitrust statutes.

Yet the actual history of antitrust enforcement has never warranted this widespread academic and political support. There is little in the classic antitrust cases to convince anyone—much less an economist—that monopoly power is a free market problem, or that the firms indicted (and convicted) under the antitrust laws were damaging the public interest. Indeed, the cases often demonstrate that the firms involved were reducing costs and prices and engaging in an intensely competitive process, and that the antitrust laws—whatever their alleged intent—were employed to restrict and restrain the competition process.[4]

Standard Oil (1911)

For example, in the classic Standard Oil case (1911), it is still widely believed that Standard of New Jersey was convicted because it had restricted production, raised prices, and engaged in ruthless predatory practices to destroy competition. Yet none of this was ever proven at court. Standard lost the decision in 1911 because a lower court in 1909 had determined that the formation of its holding company in 1899 was *prima facie* illegal since it ended the potentiality of competition between the (now) merged firms.[5] The Supreme Court, while *announcing* a rule of reason, simply reaffirmed the unanalytical decision of that lower court.

An objective study of the petroleum industry between 1859 and 1911 would reveal that Standard did *not* plunder consumers or competitors. The price of kerosene—the industry's major product—dropped from over 50 cents a gallon in the early 1860s to less than six cents in the late 1890s. While Standard always did a large share of the industry's business, they always had competition. When they were dissolved in 1911 for monopolizing in restraint of trade, there were at least 147 independent petroleum refining companies selling products in competition with the Standard Oil Company.[6] The industry was not monopolized.

American Tobacco (1911)

The American Tobacco Company (the Tobacco Trust) was ordered dissolved by the Supreme Court in 1911. Again, legend has it that American Tobacco ruthlessly raised cigarette prices, drove down the price of leaf tobacco, engaged in "predatory" wars with rivals, and generally acted like the abusive monopoly of antitrust theory.

The legend is sheer fantasy; none of this was ever proven.[7] The Supreme Court did not rule specifically on these charges, and the lower court, which had discussed the charges in some detail, concluded that they did not occur. Even a casual reading of the lower court decision would reveal that the prices of tobacco products were not arbitrarily increased (cigarette prices fell between 1895 and 1907), that leaf tobacco prices rose substantially, and that American Tobacco did not "dragoon" competitors into bankruptcy or merger with itself. There were hundreds of companies selling cigarettes in the market, and many thousands more selling smoking tobacco, plug, snuff, and cigars.

The American Tobacco Company was large and had a high percentage share in some tobacco markets, but it had not obtained a coercive monopoly position in the tobacco industry.

U.S. Steel (1920)

The United States Steel Company, the largest corporation in the country when it was formed as a holding company in 1901, was indicted by the Department of Justice in 1911. The corporation, however, was found innocent of monopolizing in 1915 and again in 1920. With the Supreme Court's newly enunciated rule of reason actually in effect, U.S. Steel demonstrated to a majority of judges and justices that it did have active competition, that the competitors were growing faster than the U.S. Steel Company, that essential raw materials were not being monopolized, and that the prices of steel products had *fallen* on average between 1901 and 1911.[8] Although U.S. Steel admittedly was of impressive size, the Supreme Court declared that "its power over price was not and is not commensurate with its power to produce." Since its economic conduct and performance were judged reasonable, and since mere size was *not* to be a legal offense, U.S. Steel (and many other large corporations in very similar trials) was declared innocent of any economic wrongdoing.

Alcoa (1945)

The 1945 *Alcoa* decision reversed the rule of reason approach and again made high market share a legal offense. Alcoa was convicted of monopolizing an artificially defined relevant market: primary ingot aluminum. Even though the special Court of Appeals admitted that secondary aluminum (scrap) competed pound for pound with primary ingot, they steadfastly refused to include it when measuring Alcoa's share of the market. Without scrap, Alcoa was doing almost 90 percent of the aluminum ingot business, and that in and of itself was enough to constitute a monopoly and a violation of the law. Alcoa may have been a "good trust," but the Congress had not meant to condone good trusts, said the court in 1945.

Alcoa was, indeed, a good trust, as the lower court decision of 193 had clearly demonstrated.[9] District Court Judge Caffey had found Alcoa innocent of more than 140 separate government charges. Caffey had laboriously determined that Alcoa had not monopolized bauxite, water power sites, aluminum ingot, castings, pistons, or many other items as the government had charged in its longwinded indictment. In addition, Alcoa had not illegally excluded competition, engaged in conspiracy, and charged "exorbitant" prices, or earned an "exorbitant" rate of return. Aluminum ingot prices had fallen from over $2.00 a pound in the 1890s to less than 22 cents a pound at the time of the trial, and Alcoa's average rate of return for 50 years was just over 10 percent on invested capital. Yet all of this was suddenly *irrelevant* in 1945. To maintain a high market share for a long period of time—an extraordinary business achievement—was to monopolize in violation of the antitrust law.

Actually Alcoa's efficient performance was legally *worse* than irrelevant and immaterial; it helped convict the company. Circuit Court Judge Learned Hand explained that it was Alcoa's "skill, energy, and initiative" that "excluded" competitors in aluminum production. If Alcoa had been less efficient there would have been "more competition" and no violation of the antitrust law. In one of the most outrageous statements in antitrust history, Alcoa's industrial virtues were condemned as an illegal restraint of trade.

> It was not inevitable that it [Alcoa] should always anticipate increases in the demand for ingot and be prepared to supply them. Nothing compelled it to keep doubling and redoubling its capacity before others entered the field. It insists that it never excluded competitors; but we can think of no more effective exclusion than progressively to embrace each new opportunity as it opened, and to face every newcomer with new capacity already geared into a great organization, having the advantage of experience, trade connections and the elite of personnel.[10]

The past irrationalities of antitrust enforcement have not been confined to the classic monopoly cases. Business mergers that would have increased efficiency and likely intensified competition have been legally prevented in the name of concern over increasing "concentration." Price discrimination, an important element of a rivalrous competitive process, has been vigorously and mistakenly prosecuted by the Federal Trade Commission since the early 1930s. And it is only too clear that in the thousands of *private* antitrust cases (where one corporation sues another), the law serves to restrain and restrict the competitive commercial activities of the defendant corporation. In these latter cases, at least, there is no pretense that the concern is "monopoly," or that the interest that is being served is the public interest.

New Directions in Antitrust Policy

Within the last 10 years the widespread support for traditional antitrust enforcement has eroded considerably. There is now an important group of scholars and policy officials that seriously doubt the wisdom of conventional enforcement. Antitrust critics such as Robert Bork, Yale Brozen, Harold Demsetz, and Robert Tollison are often associated with the view that much of our traditional enforcement has been misplaced and may have served to restrict competition and not enhance it.[11] Most of these critics tend to see a competitive process where antitrust enthusiasts saw monopolization and increasing concentration. Most would allow liberal amounts of price discrimination and tying agreements and would not impede conglomerate mergers or vertical integration in most markets. Internal growth that results in increasing concentration would generally be defended as efficient. In short, the critics would substantially reduce traditional enforcement efforts, and there is abundant evidence that most current policies and enforcement efforts reflect the "new directions" of the critics.[12]

It is clear that the recent abandonment by the Justice Department and Federal Trade Commission of landmark antitrust cases against IBM and the leading ready-to-eat cereal companies is entirely appropriate from the perspective of the antitrust critics. IBM was not a monopoly when the Department of Justice brought its antitrust suit in 1969, and it is certainly not a monopoly today. Likewise, the cereal industry personifies a condition of rivalrous competition, and the leading companies never "shared a monopoly" as the Federal Trade Commission had boldly asserted.[13] Both of these cases were premised on the misguided notion that efficiency ought to be attacked since it is exclusionary of potential competitors and results in substantial market share. Yet the defendants in these cases had *earned* their shares (and expanded them) through a rigorous competitive performance. Occasionally, smaller competitors found such a rigorous competitive process difficult. But the antitrust laws were not intended to protect less efficient competitors (or potential competitors) from the rigors of open competition. Almost 20 years of litigation was wasted on these cases.

Antitrust Revisionism: Theory and Evidence

The collapse of the intellectual support for traditional antitrust enforcement can be traced to a number of different developments. Most important is the disenchantment with the orthodox "barriers to entry" doctrine.[14] It is now widely admitted that most of these so-called barriers were in reality *economies and efficiencies* that business organizations had earned in the marketplace. Economies of scale only "limited competition" with high-cost firms—hardly a good reason to prosecute such barriers in the name of consumer welfare. Product differentiation only limited competition with firms unable to match the products and the experience of the existing firms. If advertising limited competition, it did so by reducing the cost and price of the product advertised. Advertising expenditures that increased costs and price would act as an *invitation to entry* and not as a barrier. In every instance efficiency broadly conceived, not market power, excluded the less efficient business organization.

Complementary to this theoretical revisionism have been numerous empirical investigations of the collusion/concentration/high profits hypothesis. The early work in this area had appeared to discover a slight positive correlation between high concentration and above-normal rates of return.[15] These studies assumed that barriers to entry limited competition in the concentrated industries, and that this restriction explained the persistence of monopoly profits. Critics of these early studies maintain, however, that persistently high profits can be more easily explained by greater efficiency on the part of the faster growing, high-market-share companies.[16] Moreover, the critics hold that the positive correlations between concentration and profit disappear with a longer time period under investigation and a larger industry sample size.[17] Finally, Yale Brozen has argued recently that the weight of the new empirical evidence is now overwhelming that market share and concentration reflect efficiency and not monopoly power.[18]

Antitrust and Output Restriction

While the current critics of antitrust policy favor a substantial reduction in traditional enforcement, they do not oppose all enforcement or favor a total repeal of the antitrust laws. Indeed, the critics generally see a continued need for constant surveillance and enforcement in the one area where they believe that antitrust can promote the public interest: the prevention of horizontal agreements that might restrict production. This, according to some of the critics, was the original mission of antitrust policy and the only mission consistent with sound economic analysis.[19] Enforcement that would prevent price fixing, large horizontal mergers, and division-of-market agreements would be consistent with this perspective.

Admittedly, current antitrust enforcement is slightly more rational than traditional enforcement, but the *"output restriction" hypothesis on which current policy is seriously flawed and cannot support even this minimalist antitrust policy.* Conventional monopoly theory holds that an "artificial" reduction in market output is inefficient and can lead to a reduction in consumer and social welfare. The antitrust laws are necessary, therefore, to prevent such restrictions. But is such an approach theoretically sound?

The Output Restriction Hypothesis

What is socially inefficient about a cooperative and voluntary market output? A traditional response to this question is that the reduction is inefficient when compared to the output level under *perfect competition*. In the traditional economics literature the perfectly competitive (equilibrium) output is widely regarded as the socially optimum level of production, and restrictions from that output are seen as inefficient.[20] Thus, any "collusion" that reduces market output reduces social welfare.

There are several difficulties with this position. The first is that the perfectly competitive equilibrium is a notoriously static framework from which to make welfare judgments concerning various levels of output. The perfectly competitive output is efficient *only if* perfect information is assumed, and only if preferences and technological information doesn't change. In a changing and dynamic world with imperfect information, it is unclear that outputs that are less than the static benchmark level are inefficient in any meaningful sense.[21] All real-world outputs are "restricted" and all firms (even hose that are not expressly colluding) produce less than they would if the world were perfectly competitive. This approach to output "restriction" could be employed to prosecute *all* firms regardless of whether their collusion was explicit or not. Yet this is an absurd policy position and serves to highlight the difficulty of this theoretical approach to monopoly power.

If the perfectly competitive output is not the relevant welfare benchmark, then what output level is the relevant one? If firms collude and restrict production, then we simply have less production after the collusion than before the collusion. Why is this an inefficient state of affairs? If buyers pay the higher prices associated with less production and if this generates — or promises to generate — higher profits for the producers, why is the "restriction" socially undesirable? On the other hand, if the higher prices generate — or promise to generate — lower profits for the producers, the restrictive agreement will likely be abandoned. In either case, it is the revealed preferences for the buyers that determine the socially optimum output level. What is the justification for regulation in either case?

It is important to note that consumers are sovereign over the entire length of their theoretical demand function. Higher prices are just as compatible with full consumer sovereignty as are lower prices. It is the buyers at each theoretical point on their demand curve that determine the "correct" level of production. Knowledge of that level cannot be known beforehand by economists who wish to assert that an output restriction must reduce consumer welfare (assuming for the moment that we could even measure welfare).

Some of the support for making horizontal agreements illegal is the belief that such agreements typically work to raise prices above previous levels and increase the profits of the conspirators. Yet there is accumulating theoretical and empirical evidence which suggests that market division agreements (in the absence of explicit government support) are tenuous at best, and tend to break apart naturally in open markets.[22] Restrictive agreements appear to be short-run, unable generally to withstand changing market conditions. If the markets are legally open to competition, entry and competition will normally defeat any long-run agreement to restrict production.

The public is easily misled about the effectiveness of price conspiracy since it often accepts indictment and conviction in price-fixing antitrust cases as evidence of effective restriction. This inference, however, is entirely mistaken. Price agreements are illegal *per se*; to have an agreement is enough to violate the law.[23] Whether the outputs have been successfully restricted or whether the prices have been increased is irrelevant and immaterial in the federal legal action (though not of course in the private treble damage suits). Firms indicted under the Sherman Act in this area often plead *nolo contendere* since they are aware that the existence of the agreement is sufficient for conviction. Yet it should be obvious that a federal conviction alone is insufficient evidence that there has been an actual output restriction or any higher prices in the marketplace.

Another difficulty with a flat prohibition on restrictive agreements is that such arrangements—even from the theoretical perspective of the critics — may lead to a net increase in social efficiency and welfare. The easy assumption has always been that the costs of collusion greatly outweigh the benefits (if any) that might flow from the agreement. Yet it is no longer obvious that such an assumption is valid.[24] Market division agreements may end costly (and wasteful) cross-hauling and advertising. In the trucking industry it is argued that agreements among "competitors" through rate bureaus actually reduce information and transactions costs and allow the services to be provided more efficiently.[25] Cooperative research and development, though it may limit competition in the traditional sense, may reduce future costs. Since even the critics admi that economies are often subtle and subjective, it is unclear—even from their own perspective—why they support a flat prohibition on restrictive agreements.

The Subjectivist Criticism

It has been assumed up to this point in the analysis, consistent with standard neoclassical theory, that social costs and benefits are measurable objective phenomena that are knowable to independent observers. Restrictive agreements are said to increase inefficiency, lower consumer welfare, and generate more net costs than benefits to society as a whole. Yet all of this calculation and measurement is open to serious criticism. The costs of an action are the subjective opportunities forgone by the person who makes the decision; the benefits are the subjective satisfactions. Certainly individuals can ordinally rank their own costs and benefits and choose, *ex ante*, an appropriate (efficient) course of action, but the costs and benefits cannot be known to any outside observer.[26] Further, since costs and benefits are subjective they are not cardinally measurable. There is no standard unit of value that would allow the summing up of individual costs and benefits into social aggregates for comparison.[27] Thus, it is misleading to suggest that a rational antitrust policy can weigh the costs against the gains of restrictive agreements and decide which are socially efficient and which are not. Although this approach pretends to be rigorous and scientific, such social calculations misconstrue the fundamental nature of economic information.

A Coordination Theory of Efficiency

There is an alternative approach to social efficiency that does not depend on interpersonal utility comparisons or on cost aggregation. This approach would regard *all* voluntary agreements, including so-called restrictive agreements, as socially efficient since they aim *ex ante* to coordinate the respective plans of the participants to the agreement. Social efficiency is to be associated with a society that allows full scope for all free and voluntary agreements. Social arrangements are efficient if they tend to provide the widest opportunity for private plan fulfillment and coordination.[28]

This theory of social efficiency has several advantages over the standard neoclassical approach. The first—as already mentioned—is that it does not depend on objective measurements of fundamentally subjective phenomena such as utility and cost. The second is that it can encompass all voluntary agreements—horizontal as well as vertical—as promoting efficiency, even if such agreements prove unworkable in the long run. Many marriages are not workable in the long run but this does not imply that such agreements were *ex ante* inefficient, or that a case can be made for government regulation. We can always look back with hindsight and say that a contract was unwise, but hindsight (with more information) is not the proper perspective for acting man. The fact remains that at the moment of decision the agreement appeared, *ex ante*, to be efficient and coordinating. Thus, the ultimate failure of (restrictive) agreements is no reason for their social prohibition or regulation. All voluntary agreements are efficient in a plan-coordinating sense and ought to be allowed in order that the relevant individual costs be minimized and relevant individual values maximized.

It should be apparent that we have now developed an economic justification for open markets and that we have made an economic condemnation of legal barriers to entry. Legal barriers are socially inefficient in a scientific sense since they artificially reduce the scope of mutually advantageous exchanges and plan coordinations for potential consumers and suppliers. Legal monopoly is harmful *not because we can measure the welfare loss in a neoclassical sense*, but because all such legal restrictions limit and restrict voluntary plan coordination. From this perspective, to remove such legal restrictions to coordination through deregulation would be the only appropriate antitrust policy.

Antitrust and Civil Liberties

A final argument against *any* antitrust regulation is that all such policies violate basic civil liberties,[29] which allow individuals to speak freely, associate freely, and make contractual agreements. Yet a flat prohibition of restrictive agreements is inherently invasive of these fundamental rights.

It might be argued that business people forgo their right to liberty when they collude and restrict production, since such behavior violates the "rights" of the buyers. But such a perspective on rights is misguided. Producers own their property and have *all of the rights to it*; likewise, consumers own their income, and they have all of the rights to that property. The rights of neither party can be violated by a refusal to deal or a partial refusal to deal. A consumer boycott of a manufacturers product will not violate the property rights of the manufacturer; the manufacturer has no right to the consumers income in the first place. Likewise, a restriction of production on the part of the manufacturer (a producer boycott) cannot violate the rights of consumers since they have no rights to the product. Thus, restrictive agreements, though unpopular, are not invasive of anyone's rights; indeed, a flat prohibition on their existence or enforcement must violate basic civil liberties.

The civil liberties issues become especially important in conscious parallelism antitrust cases where there may be no explicit evidence of any conspiracy to reduce production. In these cases the government *infers* illegal behavior from the fact that firms may have followed similar patterns of business behavior.[30] Company A lowered its prices; Company B followed. Company A innovated some new cereal brand; Company B introduced a similar brand a week later. If Company B adopts the delivered pricing system of Company A, this imitation may well be construed as an illegal conspiracy in restraint of trade with appropriate fines and jail sentences. Yet it should be clear that any such prohibition must violate the basic civil liberties of individuals to meet, associate, talk, and make agreements that do not involve fraud or violence against the person of another. Even Adam Smith did not favor such a law against price agreement since in Smiths cogent view, *such a law could not be "executed... in a manner consistent with liberty and justice."*[31]

Let us reiterate the criticism of antitrust policy discussed above. We maintain that the standard neoclassical monopoly theory is not internally consistent; that the standard cost/benefit methodology employed to calculate the social inefficiency of restricted agreements is inherently flawed; that legal barriers to entry *do* misallocate resources since they explicitly prevent voluntary plan coordination; and finally, that aside from purely scientific considerations, any antitrust policy is invasive of basic civil liberties.

Recent Issues in Antitrust

As an illustration of these criticisms and of the current ambiguity in antitrust policy, it might be appropriate to examine the recently announced merger guidelines and a recently concluded historic antitrust consent decree involving American Telephone and Telegraph Company.

The Department of Justice has issued revised guidelines on permissible horizontal mergers based on the so-called Herfindahl Index of market concentration.[32] Mergers that raise the Herfindahl by more than some stated numerical amount, or push the industry index beyond some stated number, will in all probability trigger legal action by the government in opposition to the merger. The guidelines have already been employed to restrain specific mergers in the beer industry and in the petroleum industry.

Aside from the accuracy of the Herfindahl Index, the fact remains that any measure of market concentration is irrelevant to the actual source of monopoly power in the economy: legal barriers to entry. Concern over specific levels of market concentration creates the misleading impression that private firms can control markets, restrict production, and injure consumers. But these impressions are erroneous and are based on theoretical notions that we have already examined—and rejected.

There are additional problems with the merger guidelines. The first is that since there is no unambiguous way to define any relevant market in the first place (used goods? foreign imports? inter-product competition?), *all* concentration ratios and indexes are arbitrary and subject to much statistical manipulation. Secondly, the Justice Department limits on concentration are themselves totally arbitrary numbers with no theoretical or empirical significance whatever. Finally, to legally limit mergers in markets already concentrated can serve to protect the market positions of the established firms. Certainly Anheuser Busch and Miller Brewing—the dominant beer companies—can now breathe easier knowing that the government will prevent consolidations large enough to threaten their market position.[33] In this instance the merger guidelines serve not to protect consumers from monopoly but to protect *some* firms from the competition of *other* firms.

The recently concluded antitrust case against AT&T provides an excellent illustration of the continuing confusion over monopoly theory. AT&T held monopoly power in precisely those areas where entry and competition were restricted by state public utility authorities and the Federal Communications Commission. In addition, and ironically, a 1956 consent decree had legally frozen AT&T out of certain markets. Government regulation, not vertical integration, was the problem in the telecommunications industry, and *deregulation*, not *divestiture*, should have been the appropriate public policy remedy. Divestiture of the local telephone companies will leave the real source of monopoly power unaffected, and will create the mistaken impression that Bells corporate size or the likelihood of cross-subsidization somehow restricted competition. Further, as has already been widely admitted, the breakup of AT&T will tend to increase the cost of local telephoning, and these increased costs will be passed along, under utility regulation, to residential users. Antitrust will have served, again, to obscure the issue of monopoly power in the economy.

Bad theory always results in inappropriate public policy. The most rational antitrust reform would be a thorough and complete business deregulation *and* the immediate repeal of the antitrust laws.

Notes

1.   Yale Brozen, "Is Government the Source of Monopoly?," *The Intercollegiate Review*, Winter 1968-1969. Reprinted in *Is Government the Source of Monopoly? and Other Essays*, Cato Institute, Washington, D.C., 1980.

2.   Philip Areeda, *Antitrust Analysis: Problems, Text Cases* (Boston: Little, Brown and Co., 1974), pp. 18-19.

3.   In a recent study of public policies attitudes, 85 percent of the professional economists sampled agreed with the proposition that "antitrust laws should be used vigorously to reduce monopoly power from its current level." See J. R. Kearl, Clayne L. Pope, Gordon C. Whiting, Larry T. Wimmer, "A Confusion of Economists?," *American Economic Review, Papers and Proceedings* 69 (May 1979): 30.

4.   Dominick T. Armentano, *Antitrust and Monopoly: Anato of a Policy Failure* (New York: John Wiley and Sons, 1982).

5.   *U.S. v. Standard Oil Company,* 173 Fed. Reporter 193.

6.   Gabriel Kolko, *The Triumph of Conservatism* (Glencoe, Ill.: Fee Press, 1963), p. 40.

7.   Armentano, pp. 91-95.

8.   *U.S. v. United States Steel Corporation*, 223 Fed. Reporter 81.

9.   *U.S. v. Aluminum Company of America*, 44 Fed. Supp. 107.

10.   *U.S. v. Aluminum Company of America*, 148 F.2d 430-431.

11.   For a representative view of the important critics, see Robert Bork, *The Antitrust Paradox: A Policy at War with Itself* (New York: Basic Books, 1978); Richard A. Posner, *Antitrust Law: An Economic Perspective* (Chicago: University of Chicago Press, 1976); and Goldschmid, Mann, and Weston, eds. *Industrial Concentration: The New Learning* (Boston: Little Brown and Co., 1974).

12.   In the *GTE Sylvania* (1977) case, for example, the court was explicitly mindful of the views of the critics. See 433, U.S. 36. See also Edward Meadows, "Bold Departures in Antitrust," *Fortune*, October 15, 1981.

13. The FTC complaint (Docket No. 8883) filed in 1972 against Kellogg, General Mills, General Foods, and Quaker Oats was dismissed without merit by the FTC in 1982.

14. Armentano, pp. 36-39. Also see Wesley J. Liebeler, "Market Power and Competitive Superiority in Concentrated Markets," *UCLA Law Review* 25 (1978): 1243-1250.

15. Joe S. Bain, "Relation of Profit Rates to Industry Concentration," *Quarterly Journal of Economics,* August 1951.

16. Harold Demsetz, "Industry Structure, Market Rivalry and Public Policy," *Journal of Law and Economics* 16 (April 1973).

17. Brozen, "Concentration and Profits: Does Concentration Matter?," *The Antitrust Bulletin* 19 (Summer 1974).

18. Brozen, *Concentration, Mergers and Public Policy* (New York: Macmillan Co., 1982).

19. Bork, "The Legislative Intent and the Policy of the Sherman Act," *Journal of Law and Economics* 9 (October 1966).

20. Areeda, pp. 6-23.

21. Israel Kirzner, "Competition, Regulation, and the Market Process: An Austrian Perspective," *Policy Analysis,* Cato Institute, Washington, D.C., September 1982.

22. P. Asch and R. Seneca, "Is Collusion Profitable?," *Review of Economics and Statistics* 58 (1976). See also, Armentano, pp. 133-166.

23. *U.S. v. Trenton Potteries*, 273, U.S. 397 (1927). Such was not the case under the common law. Prior to the Sherman Act, many restrictive agreements between competitors were allowed as a matter of right although they were not always enforceable. See Hans B. Thorelli, *The Federal Antitrust Policy* (Baltimore: Johns Hopkins Press, 1955), pp. 36-53.

24. Donald Dewey, "Information, Entry and Welfare: The Case for Collusion," *American Economic Review* 69 (September 1979).

25. Paul R. Duke, "The Impact of the Removal of Antitrust Immunity on Collective Ratemaking in the Motor Carrier Industry, statement before the Motor Carrier Ratemaking Study Commission, Boston, Mass., March 19, 1982.

26. James Buchanan, *Cost and Choice* (Chicago: Markham Publishing Co., 1969). See also, Thomas Sowell, *Knowledge and Decisions* (New York: Basic Books, 1980), pp. 50-52.

27. M. N. Rothbard, *Towards a Reconstruction of Utility and Welfare Economics*, Center for Libertarian Studies, New York, 1978.

28. Israel Kirzner, *Market Theory and the Price System* (New York: Van Nostrand Reinhold 1963).

29. Roger Pilon, "Corporations and Rights: On Treating Corporate People Justly," *Georgia Law Review* 13 (Summer 1979).

30. *American Tobacco v. U.S.*, 328 U.S. 781 (1946). See also the FTC "shared monopoly" case against Kellogg, General Mills, General Foods and Quaker Oats, Docket No. 8883, 1972.

31. Adam Smith, *The Wealth of Nations* (New York: Modern Library, Inc., 1937), p. 128. [Emphasis added]

32. For an explanation of this index, see David S. Weinstock, "Using the Herfindahl Index to Measure Concentration," *The Antitrust Bulletin* 22 (Summer 1982): 285-297.

33. Peter Brimelow, "Crippling Competition," *Barrons*, April 26, 1982, p. 11.

Published by the Cato Institute, *Policy Analysis* is a regular series evaluating government policies and offering proposals for reform. Nothing in *Policy Analysis* should be construed as necessarily reflecting the views of the Cato Institute or as an attempt to aid or hinder the passage of any bill before Congress.

Additional copies of *Policy Analysis* are $2.00 on an individual basis and $1.00 each in bulk. Orders and correspondence should be addressed to: Policy Analysis, Cato Institute, 224 Second Street S.E., Washington, D.C. 20003.

PLANNING AND DEMOCRACY

Friedrich A. Hayek

> The statesman who should attempt to direct private people in what manner they ought to employ their capitals, would not only load himself with a most unnecessary attention, but assume an authority which could safely be trusted to no council and senate whatever, and which would nowhere be so dangerous as in the hands of a man who had folly and presumption enough to fancy himself fit to exercise it.
>
> —*Adam Smith*

The common features of all collectivist systems may be described, in a phrase ever dear to socialists of all schools, as the deliberate organization of the labors of society for a definite social goal. That our present society lacks such "conscious" direction toward a single aim, that its activities are guided by the whims and fancies of irresponsible individuals, has always been one of the main complaints of its socialist critics.

In many ways this puts the basic issue very clearly. And it directs us at once to the point where the conflict arises between individual freedom and collectivism. The various kinds of collectivism, communism, fascism, etc., differ among themselves in the nature of the goal toward which they want to direct the efforts of society. But they all differ from liberalism and individualism in wanting to organize the whole of society and all its resources for this unitary end and in refusing to recognize autonomous spheres in which the ends of the individuals are supreme. In short, they are totalitarian in the true sense of this new word which we have adopted to describe the unexpected but nevertheless inseparable manifestations of what in theory we call collectivism.

The "social goal," or "common purpose," for which society is to be organized is usually vaguely described as the "common good," the "general welfare," or the "general interest." It does not need much reflection to see that these terms have no sufficiently definite meaning to determine a particular course of action. The welfare and the happiness of millions cannot be measured on a single scale of less and more. The welfare of a people, like the happiness of a man, depends on a great many things that can be provided in an infinite variety of combinations. It cannot be adequately expressed as a single end, but only as a hierarchy of ends, a comprehensive scale of values in which every need of every person is given its place. To direct all our activities according to a single plan presupposes that every one of our needs is given its rank in an order of values which must be complete enough to make it possible to decide among all the different courses which the planner has to choose. It presupposes, in short, the existence of a complete ethical code in which different human values are allotted their due place.

The conception of a complete ethical code is unfamiliar, and it requires some effort of imagination to see what it involves. We are not in the habit of thinking of moral codes as more or less complete. The fact that we are constantly choosing between different values without a social code prescribing how we ought to choose does not surprise us and does not suggest to us that our moral code is incomplete. In our society there is neither occasion nor reason why people should develop common views about what should be done in such situations. But where all the means to be used are the property of society and are to be used in the name of society according to a unitary plan, a "social" view about what ought to be done must guide all decisions. In such a world we should soon find that our moral code is full of gaps.

We are not concerned here with the question whether it would be desirable to have such a complete ethical code. It may merely be pointed out that up to the present the growth of civilization has been accompanied by a steady diminution of the sphere in which individual actions are bound by fixed rules. The rules of which our common moral code consists have progressively become fewer and more general in character. From the primitive man, who was bound by an elaborate ritual in almost every one of his daily activities, who was limited by innumerable taboos, and who could scarcely conceive of doing things in a way different from his fellows, morals have more and more tended to become merely limits circumscribing the sphere within which the individual could behave as he liked. The adoption of a common ethical code comprehensive enough to determine a unitary economic plan would mean a complete reversal of this tendency.

The essential point for us is that no such complete ethical code exists. The attempt to direct all economic activity according to a single plan would raise innumerable questions to which the answer could be provided only by a moral rule, but to which existing morals have no answer and where there exists no agreed view on what ought to be done. People will have either no definite views or conflicting views on such questions, because in the free society in which we have lived there has been no occasion to think about them and still less to form common opinions about them.

Not only do we not possess such an all-inclusive scale of values: it would be impossible for any mind to comprehend the infinite variety of different needs of different people which compete for the available resources and to attach a definite weight to each. For our problem it is of minor importance whether the ends for which any person cares comprehend only his own individual needs, or whether they include the needs of his closer or even those of his more distant fellows—that is, whether he is egoistic or altruistic in the ordinary senses of these words. The point which is so important is the basic fact that it is impossible for any man to survey more than a limited field, to be aware of the urgency of more than a limited number of needs. Whether his interests center round his own physical needs, or whether he takes a warm interest in the welfare of every human being he knows, the ends about which he can be concerned will always be only an infinitesimal fraction of the needs of all men.

This is the fundamental fact on which the whole philosophy of individualism is based. It does not assume, as is often asserted, that man is egoistic or selfish or ought to be. It merely starts from the indisputable fact that the limits of our powers of imagination make it impossible to include in our scale of values more than a sector of the needs of the whole society, and that, since, strictly speaking, scales of value can exist only in individual minds, nothing but partial scales of values exist—scales which are inevitably different and often inconsistent with each other. From this the individualist concludes that the individuals should be allowed, within defined limits, to follow their own values and preferences rather than somebody else's; that within these spheres the individual's system of ends should be supreme and not subject to any dictation by others. It is this recognition of the individual as the ultimate judge of his ends, the belief that as far as possible his own views ought to govern his actions, that forms the essence of the individualist position.

This view does not, of course, exclude the recognition of social ends, or rather of a coincidence of individual ends which makes it advisable for men to combine for their pursuit. But it limits such common action to the instances where individual views coincide; what are called "social ends" are for it merely identical ends of many individuals—or ends to the achievement of which individuals are willing to contribute in return for the assistance they receive in the satisfaction of their own desires. Common action is thus limited to the fields where people agree on common ends. Very frequently these common ends will not be ultimate ends to the individuals but means which different persons can use for different purposes. In fact, people are most likely to agree on common action where the common end is not an ultimate end to them but a means capable of serving a great variety of purposes.

When individuals combine in a joint effort to realize ends they have in common, the organizations, like the state, that they form for this purpose are given their own system of ends and their own means. But any organization thus formed remains one "person" among others, in the case of the state much more powerful than any of the others, it is true, yet still with its separate and limited sphere in which alone its ends are supreme. The limits of this sphere are determined by the extent to which the individuals agree on particular ends; and the probability that they will agree on a particular course of action necessarily decreases as the scope of such action extends. There are certain functions of the state on the exercise of which there will be practical unanimity among its citizens; there will be others on which there will be agreement of a substantial majority; and so on, until we come to fields where, although each individual might wish the state to act in some way, there will be almost as many views about what the government should do as there are different people.

We can rely on voluntary agreement to guide the action of the state only so long as it is confined to spheres where agreement exists. But not only when the state undertakes direct control in fields where there is no such agreement is it bound to suppress individual freedom. We can unfortunately not indefinitely extend the sphere of common action and still leave the individual free in his own sphere. Once the communal sector, in which the state controls all the means, exceeds a certain proportion of the whole, the effects of its actions dominate the whole system. Although the state controls directly the use of only a large part of the available resources, the effects of its decisions on the remaining part of the economic system become so great that indirectly it controls almost everything. Where, as was, for example, true in Germany as early as 1928, the central and local authorities directly control the use of more than half the national income (according to an official German estimate then, 53 per cent), they control indirectly almost the whole economic life of the nation. There is, then, scarcely an individual end which is not dependent for its achievement on the action of the state, and the "social scale of values" which guides the state's action must embrace practically all individual ends.

It is not difficult to see what must be the consequences when democracy embarks upon a course of planning which in is execution requires more agreement than in fact exists. The people may have agreed on adopting a system of directed economy because they have been convinced that it will produce great prosperity. In the discussions leading to the decision, the goal of planning will have been described by some such term as "common welfare," which only conceals the absence of real agreement on the ends of planning. Agreement will in fact exist only on the mechanism to be used. But it is a mechanism which can be used only for a common end; and the question of the precise goal toward which all activity is to be directed will arise as soon as the executive power has to translate the demand for a single plan into a particular plan. Then it will appear that the agreement on the desirability of planning is not supported by agreement on the ends the plan is to serve. The effect of the people's agreeing that there must be central planning, without agreeing on the ends, will be rather as if a group of people were to commit themselves to take a journey together without agreeing where they want to go: with the result that they may all have to make a journey which most of them do not want at all. That planning creates a situation in which it is necessary for us to agree on a much larger number of topics than we have been used to, and that in a planned system we cannot confine collective action to the tasks on which we can agree but are forced to produce agreement on everything in order that any action can be taken at all, is one of the features which contributes more than most to determining the character of a planned system.

It may be the unanimously expressed will of the people that its parliament should prepare a comprehensive economic plan, yet neither the people nor its representatives need therefore be able to agree on any particular plan. The inability of democratic assemblies to carry out what seems to be a clear mandate of the people will inevitably cause dissatisfaction with democratic institutions. Parliaments come to be regarded as ineffective "talking shops," unable or incompetent to carry out the tasks for which they have been chosen. The conviction grows that if efficient planning is to be done, the direction must be "taken out of politics" and placed in the hands of experts—permanent officials or independent autonomous bodies.

The difficulty is well known to socialists. It will soon be half a century since the Webbs began to complain of "the increased incapacity of the House of Commons to cope with its work."[1] More recently, Professor Laski has elaborated the argument:

"It is common ground that the present parliamentary machine is quite unsuited to pass rapidly a great body of complicated legislation. The National Government, indeed, has in substance admitted this by implementing its economy and tariff measures not by detailed debate in the House of Commons but by a wholesale system of delegated legislation. A Labour Government would, I presume, build upon the amplitude of this precedent. It would confine the House of Commons to the two functions it can properly perform: the ventilation of grievances and the discussion of general principles of its measures. Its Bills would take the form of general formulae conferring wide powers on the appropriate government departments; and those powers would be exercised by Order in Council which could, if desired, be attacked in the House by means of a vote of no confidence. The necessity and value of delegated legislation has recently been strongly reaffirmed by the Donoughmore Committee; and its extension is inevitable if the process of socialization is not to be wrecked by the normal methods of obstruction which existing parliamentary procedure sanctions."

And to make it quite clear that a socialist government must not allow itself to be too much fettered by democratic procedure, Professor Laski at the end of the same article raised the question"whether in a period of transition to Socialism, a Labour Government can risk the overthrow of its measures as a result of the next general election"—and left it significantly unanswered.[2]

It is important clearly to see the causes of this admitted ineffectiveness of parliaments when it comes to a detailed administration of the economic affairs of a nation. The fault is neither with the individual representatives nor with parliamentary institutions as such but with the contradictions inherent in the task with which they are charged. They are not asked to act where they can agree, but to produce agreement on everything—the whole direction of the resources of the nation. For such a task the system of majority decision is, however, not suited. Majorities will be found where it is a choice between limited alternatives; but it is a superstition to believe that there must be a majority view on everything. There is no reason why there should be a majority in favor of any one of the different possible courses of positive action if their number is legion. Every member of the legislative assembly might prefer some particular plan for the direction of economic activity to no plan, yet no one plan may appear preferable to a majority to no plan at all.

Nor can a coherent plan be achieved by breaking it up into parts and voting on particular issues. A democratic assembly voting and amending a comprehensive economic plan clause by clause, as it deliberates on an ordinary bill, makes nonsense. An economic plan, to deserve the name, must have a unitary conception. Even if a parliament could, proceeding step by step, agree on some scheme, it would certainly in the end satisfy nobody. A complex whole in which all the parts must be most carefully adjusted to each other cannot be achieved through a compromise between conflicting views. To draw up an economic plan in this fashion is even less possible than, for example, successfully to plan a military campaign by democratic procedure. As in strategy it would become inevitable to delegate the task to the experts.

Yet the difference is that, while the general who is put in charge of a campaign is given a single end to which, for the duration of the campaign, all the means under his control have to be exclusively devoted, there can be no such single goal given to the economic planner, and no similar limitation of the means imposed upon him. The general has not got to balance different independent aims against each other; there is for him only one supreme goal. But the ends of an economic plan, or of any part of it, cannot be defined apart from the particular plan. It is the essence of the economic problem that the making of an economic plan involves the choice between conflicting or competing ends—different needs of different people. But which ends do so conflict, which will have to be sacrificed if we want to achieve certain others, in short, which are the alternatives between which we must choose, can only be known to those who know all the facts; and only they, the experts, are in a position to decide which of the different ends are to be given preference. It is inevitable that they should impose their scale of preferences on the community for which they plan.

This is not always clearly recognized, and delegation is usually justified by the technical character of the task. But this does not mean that only the technical detail is delegated, or even that the inability of parliaments to understand the technical detail is the root of the difficulty.[3] Alterations in the structure of civil law are no less technical and no more difficult to appreciate in all their implications; yet nobody has yet seriously suggested that legislation there should be delegated to a body of experts. The fact is that in these fields legislation does not go beyond general rules on which true majority agreement can be achieved, while in the direction of economic activity the interests to be reconciled are so divergent that no true agreement is likely to be reached in a democratic assembly.

It should be recognized, however, that it is not the delegation of law-making power as such which is so objectionable. To oppose delegation as such is to oppose a symptom instead of the cause and, as it may be a necessary result of other causes, to weaken the case. So long as the power that is delegated is merely the power to make general rules, there may be very good reasons why such rules should be laid down by local rather than by the central authority. The objectionable feature is that delegation is so often resorted to because the matter in hand cannot be regulated by general rules but only by the exercise of discretion in the decision of particular cases. In these instances delegation means that some authority is given power to make with the force of law what to all intents and purposes are arbitrary decisions (usually described as "judging the case on its merits").

The delegation of particular technical tasks to separate bodies, while a regular feature, is yet only the first step in the process whereby a democracy which embarks on planning progressively relinquishes its powers. The expedient of delegation cannot really remove the causes which make all the advocates of comprehensive planning so impatient with the impotence of democracy. The delegation of particular powers to separate agencies creates a new obstacle to the achievement of a single coordinated plan. Even if, by this expedient, a democracy should succeed in planning every sector of economic activity, it would still have to face the problem of integrating these separate plans into a unitary whole. Many separate plans do not make a planned whole—in fact, as the planners ought to be the first to admit, they may be worse than no plan. But the democratic legislature will long hesitate to relinquish the decisions on really vital issues, and so long as it does so it makes it impossible for anyone else to provide the comprehensive plan. Yet agreement that planning is necessary, together with the inability of democratic assemblies to produce a plan, will evoke stronger and stronger demands that the government or some single individual should be given powers to act on their own responsibility. The belief is becoming more and more widespread that, if things are to get done, the responsible authorities must be freed from the fetters of democratic procedure.

The cry for an economic dictator is a characteristic stage in the movement toward planning. It is now several years since one of the most acute of foreign students of England, the late Élie Halévy, suggested that, "if you take a composite photograph of Lord Eustace Percy, Sir Oswald Mosley, and

Sir Stafford Cripps, I think you would find this common feature—you would find them all agreeing to say: 'We are living in economic chaos and we cannot get out of it except under some kind of dictatorial leadership.' "[4] The number of influential public men whose inclusion would not materially alter the features of the "composite photograph" has since grown considerably.

In Germany, even before Hitler came into power, the movement had already progressed much further. It is important to remember that, for some time before 1933, Germany had reached a stage in which it had, in effect, had to be governed dictatorially. Nobody could then doubt that for the time being democracy had broken down and that sincere democrats like Bruning were no more able to govern democratically than Schleicher or von Papen. Hitler did not have to destroy democracy; he merely took advantage of the decay of democracy and at the critical moment obtained the support of many to whom, though they detested Hitler, he yet seemed the only man strong enough to get things done.

The argument by which the planners usually try to reconcile us with this development is that, so long as democracy retains ultimate control, the essentials of democracy are not affected. Thus Karl Mannheim writes:

> The only [*sic*] way in which a planned society differs from that of the nineteenth century is that more and more spheres of social life, and ultimately each and all of them, are subjected to state control. But if a few controls can be held in check by parliamentary sovereignty, so can many . . . . In a democratic state sovereignty can be boundlessly strengthened by plenary powers without renouncing democratic control.[5]

This belief overlooks a vital distinction. Parliament can, of course, control the execution of tasks where it can give definite directions, where it has first agreed on the aim and merely delegates the working-out of the detail. The situation is entirely different when the reason for the delegation is that there is no real agreement on the ends, when the body charged with the planning has to choose between ends of whose conflict parliament is not even aware, and when the most that can be done is to present to it a plan which has to be accepted or rejected as a whole. There may and probably will be criticism; but as no majority can agree on an alternative plan, and the parts objected to can almost always be represented as essential parts of the whole, it will remain quite ineffective. Parliamentary discussion may be retained as a useful safety valve and even more as a convenient medium through which the official answers to complaints are disseminated. It may even prevent some flagrant abuses and successfully insist on particular shortcomings being remedied. But it cannot direct. It will at best be reduced to choosing the persons who are to have practically absolute power. The whole system will tend toward that plebiscitarian dictatorship in which the head of the government is from time to time confirmed in his position by popular vote, but where he has all the powers at his command to make certain that the vote will go in the direction he desires.

It is the price of democracy that the possibilities of conscious control are restricted to the fields where true agreement exists and that in some fields things must be left to chance. But in a society which for its functioning depends on central planning this control cannot be made dependent on a majority's being able to agree; it will often be necessary that the will of a small minority be imposed upon the people, because this minority will be the largest group able to agree among themselves on the question at issue. Democratic government has worked successfully where, and so long as, the functions of government were, by a widely accepted creed, restricted to fields where agreement among a majority could be achieved by free discussion; and it is the great merit of the liberal creed that it reduced the range of subjects on which agreement was necessary to one on which it was likely to exist in a society of free men. It is now often said that democracy will not tolerate "capitalism." If "capitalism" means here a competitive system based on free disposal over private property, it is far more important to realize that only within this system is democracy possible. When it becomes dominated by a collectivist creed, democracy will inevitably destroy itself.

We have no intention, however, of making a fetish of democracy. It may well be true that our generation talks and thinks too much of democracy and too little of the values which it serves. It cannot be said of democracy, as Lord Acton truly said of liberty, that it "is not a means to a higher political end. It is itself the highest political end. It is not for the sake of a good public administration that it is required, but for the security in the pursuit of the highest objects of civil society, and of private life." Democracy is essentially a means, a utilitarian device for safeguarding internal peace and individual freedom. As such it is by no means infallible or certain. Nor must we forget that there has often been much more cultural and spiritual freedom under an autocratic rule than under some democracies—and it is at least conceivable that under the government of a very homogeneous and doctrinaire majority democratic government might be as oppressive as the worst dictatorship. Our point, however, is not that dictatorship must inevitably extirpate freedom but rather that planning leads to dictatorship because dictatorship is the most effective instrument of coercion and the enforcement of ideals and, as such, essential if central planning on a large scale is to be possible. The clash between planning and democracy arises simply from the fact that the latter is an obstacle to the suppression of freedom which the direction of economic activity requires. But in so far as democracy ceases to be a guaranty of individual freedom, it may well persist in some form under a totalitarian regime. A true "dictatorship of the proletariat," even if democratic in form, if it undertook centrally to direct the economic system, would probably destroy personal freedom as completely as any autocracy has ever done.

The fashionable concentration on democracy as the main value threatened is not without danger. It is largely responsible for the misleading and unfounded belief that, so long as the ultimate source of power is the will of the majority, the power cannot be arbitrary. The false assurance which many people derive from this belief is an important cause of the general unawareness of the dangers which we face. There is no justification for the belief that, so long as power is conferred by democratic procedure, it cannot be arbitrary; the contrast suggested by this statement is altogether false: it is not the source but the limitation of power which prevents it from being arbitrary. Democratic control *may* prevent power from becoming arbitrary, but it does not do so by its mere existence. If democracy resolves on a task which necessarily involves the use of power which cannot be guided by fixed rules, it must become arbitrary power.

Notes

1. Sidney and Beatrice Webb, *Industrial Democracy* (1897), p. 800 n.

2. H.J. Laski, "Labour and the Constitution," *New Statesman and Nation*, No. 81 (new ser.), September 10, 1932, p. 277. In a book (*Democracy in Crisis* [1933], particularly p. 87) in which Professor Laski later elaborated these ideas, his determination that parliamentary democracy must not be allowed to form an obstacle to the realization of socialism is even more plainly expressed: not only would a socialist government "take vast powers and legislate under them by ordinance and decree" and "suspend the classic formulae of normal opposition" but the "continuance of parliamentary government would depend on its [i.e., the Labour government's] possession of guarantees from the Conservative Party that its work of transformation would not be disrupted by repeal in the event of its defeat at the polls"!

   As Professor Laski invokes the authority of the Donoughmore Committee, it may be worth recalling that Professor Laski was a member of that committee and presumably one of the authors of its report.

3. It is instructive in this connection briefly to refer to the government document in which in recent years these problems have been discussed. As long as thirteen years ago, that is before England finally abandoned economic liberalism, the process of delegating legislative powers had already been carried to a point where it was felt necessary to appoint a committee to investigate "what safeguards are desirable or necessary to secure the sovereignty of Law." In its report the Donoughmore Committee (*Report of the [Lord Chancellor's] Committee in Ministers' Powers,* Cmd. 4060 [1932]) showed that even at that date Parliament had resorted "to the practice of wholesale and indiscriminate delegation" but regarded this (it was before we had really glanced into the totalitarian abyss!) as an inevitably and relatively innocuous development. And it is probably true that delegation as such need not be a dan-

ger to freedom. The interesting point is why delegation had become necessary on such a scale. First place among the causes enumerated in the report is given to the fact that "Parliament nowadays passes so many laws every year" and that "much of the detail is so technical as to be unsuitable for Parliamentary discussion." But if this were all there would be no reason why the detail should not be worked out *before* rather than after Parliament passes a law. What is probably in many cases a much more important reason why, "if Parliament were not willing to delegate law-making power, Parliament would be unable to pass the kind and quantity of legislation which public opinion requires" is innocently revealed in the little sentence that "many of the laws affect people's lives so closely that elasticity is essential"! What does this mean if not conferment of arbitrary power—power limited by no fixed principles and which in the opinion of Parliament cannot be limited by definite and unambiguous rules?

4. "Socialism and the Problems of Democratic Parliamentarism," *International Affairs*, XIII, 501.

5. *Man and Society in an Age of Reconstruction* (1940), p. 340.

PLANNING AND THE RULE OF LAW

Friedrich A. Hayek

> Recent studies in the sociology of law once more confirm that the fundamental principle of formal law by which every case must be judged according to general rational precepts, which have a few exceptions as possible and are based on logical subsumptions, obtains only for the liberal competitive phase of capitalism.
>
> —*Karl Mannheim.*

Nothing distinguishes more clearly conditions in a free country from those in a country under arbitrary government than the observance in the former of the great principles known as the Rule of Law. Stripped of all technicalities, this means that government in all its actions is bound by rules fixed and announced beforehand—rules which make it possible to foresee with fair certainty how the authority will use its coercive powers in given circumstances and to plan one's individual affairs on the basis of this knowledge.[1] Though this ideal can never be perfectly achieved, since legislators as well as those to whom the administration of the law is intrusted are fallible men, the essential point, that the discretion left to the executive organs wielding coercive power should be reduced as much as possible, is clear enough. While every law restricts individual freedom to some extent by altering the means which people may use in the pursuit of their aims, under the Rule of Law the government is prevented from stultifying individual efforts by *ad hoc* action. Within the known rules of the game the individual is free to pursue his personal ends and desires, certain that the powers of government will not be used deliberately to frustrate his efforts.

The distinction we have drawn before between the creation of a permanent framework of laws within which the productive activity is guided by individual decisions and the direction of economic activity by a central authority is thus really a particular case of the more general distinction between the Rule of Law and arbitrary government. Under the first the government confines itself to fixing rules determining the conditions under which the available resources may be used, leaving to the individuals the decision for what ends they are to be used. Under the second the government directs the use of the means of production to particular ends. The first type of rules can be made in advance, in the shape of *formal rules* which do not aim at the wants and needs of particular people. They are intended to be merely instrumental in the pursuit of people's various individual ends. And they are, or ought to be, intended for such long periods that it is impossible to know whether they will assist particular people more than others. They could almost be described as a kind of instrument of production, helping people to predict the behavior of those with whom they must collaborate, rather than as efforts toward the satisfaction of particular needs.

Economic planning of the collectivist kind necessarily involves the very opposite of this. The planning authority cannot confine itself to providing opportunities for unknown people to make whatever use of them they like. It cannot tie itself down in advance to general and formal rules which prevent arbitrariness. It must provide for the actual needs of people as they arise and then choose deliberately between them. It must constantly decide questions which cannot be answered by formal principles only, and, in making these decisions, it must set up distinctions of merit between the needs of different people. When the government has to decide how many pigs are to be raised or how many busses are to be run, which coal mines are to operate, or at what prices shoes are to be sold, these decisions cannot be deduced from formal principles or settled for long periods in advance. They depend inevitably on the circumstances of the moment, and, in making such decisions, it will always be necessary to balance one against the other the interests of various persons and groups. In the end somebody's views will have to decide whose interests are more important; and these views must become part of the law of the land, a new distinction of rank which the coercive apparatus of government imposes upon the people.

The distinction we have just used between formal law or justice and substantive rules is very important and at the same time most difficult to draw precisely in practice. Yet the general principle involved is simple enough. The difference between the two kinds of rules is the same as that between laying down a Rule of the Road, as in the Highway Code, and ordering people where to go; or, better still, between providing signposts and commanding people which road to take. The formal rules tell people in advance what action the state will take in certain types of situation, defined in general terms, without reference to time and place or particular people. They refer to typical situations into which anyone may get and in which the existence of such rules will be useful for a great variety of individual purposes. The knowledge that in such situations the state will act in a definite way, or require people to behave in a certain manner, is provided as a means for people to use in making their own plans. Formal rules are the merely instrumental in the sense that they are expected to be useful to yet unknown people, for purposes for which these people will decide to use for them, and in circumstances which cannot be foreseen in detail. In fact, that we do *not* know their concrete effect, that we do *not* know what particular ends these rules will further, or which particular people they will assist, that they are merely given the form most likely on the whole to benefit all the people affected by them, is the most important criterion of formal rules in the sense in which we here use this term. They do not involve a choice between particular ends or particular people, because we just cannot know beforehand by whom and in what way they will be used.

In our age, with its passion for conscious control of everything, it may appear paradoxical to claim as a virtue that under one system we shall know less about the particular effect of the measures the state takes than would be true under most other systems and that a method of social control should be deemed superior because of our ignorance of its precise results. Yet this consideration is in fact the rationale of the great liberal principle of the Rule of Law. And the apparent paradox dissolves rapidly when we follow the argument a little further.

This argument is twofold; the first is economic and can here only briefly be stated. The state should confine itself to establishing rules applying to general types of situations and should allow the individuals freedom in everything which depends on the circumstances of time and place, because only the individuals concerned in each instance can fully know these circumstances and adapt their actions to them. If the individuals are to be able to use their knowledge effectively in making plans, they must be able to predict actions of the state which may affect these plans. But if the actions of the state are to be predictable, they must be determined by rules fixed independently of the concrete circumstances which can be neither foreseen nor taken into account beforehand: and the particular effects of such actions will be unpredictable. If, on the other hand, the state were to direct the individual's actions so as to achieve particular ends, its action would have to be decided on the basis of the full circumstances of the moment and would therefore be unpredictable. Hence the familiar fact that the more the state "plans," the more difficult planning becomes for the individual.

The second, moral or political, argument is even more directly relevant to the point under discussion. If the state is precisely to foresee the incidence of its actions, it means that it can leave those affected no choice. Wherever the state can exactly foresee the effects on particular people of alternative courses of action, it is also the state which chooses between the different ends. If we want to create new opportunities open to all, to offer chances of which people can make what use they like, the precise results cannot be foreseen. General rules, genuine laws as distinguished from specific orders, must therefore be intended to operate in circumstances which cannot be foreseen in detail, and, therefore, their effect on particular ends or particular people cannot be known beforehand. It is in this sense alone that it is at all possible for the legislator to be impartial. To be impartial means to have no answer to certain questions—to the kind of questions which, if we have to decide them, we decide by tossing a coin. In a world where everything was precisely foreseen, the state could hardly do anything and remain impartial.

Where the precise effects of government policy on particular people are known, where the government aims directly at such particular effects, it cannot help knowing these effects, and therefore it cannot be impartial. It must, of necessity, take sides, impose its valuations upon people and, instead of assisting them in the advancement of their own ends, choose the ends for them. As soon as the particular effects are foreseen at the time a law is made, it ceases to be a mere instrument to be used by the people and becomes instead an instrument used by the lawgiver upon the people and for his ends. The state ceases to be a piece of utilitarian machinery intended to help individuals in the fullest development of their individual personality and becomes a "moral" institution—where "moral" is not used in contrast to immoral but describes an institution which imposes on its members its views on all moral questions, whether these views be moral or highly immoral. In this sense the Nazi or any other collectivist state is "moral," while the liberal state is not.

Perhaps it will be said that all this raises no serious problem because in the kind of questions which the economic planner would have to decide he need not and should not be guided by his individual prejudices but could rely on the general conviction of what is fair and reasonable. This contention usually receives support from those who have experience of planning in a particular industry and who find that there is no insuperable difficulty about arriving at a decision which all those immediately interested will accept as fair. The reason why this experience proves nothing is, of course, the selection of the "interests" concerned when planning is confined to a particular industry. Those most immediately interested in a particular issue are not necessarily the best judges of the interests of society as a whole. To take only the most characteristic case: when capital and labor in an industry agree on some policy of restriction and thus exploit the consumers, there is usually no difficulty about the division of the spoils in proportion to former earnings or on some similar principle. The loss which is divided between thousands or millions is usually either simply disregarded or quite inadequately considered. It we want to test the usefulness of the principle of "fairness" in deciding the kind of issues which arise in economic planning, we must apply it to some question where the gains and the losses are seen equally clearly. In such instances it is readily recognized that no general principle such as fairness can provide an answer. When we have to choose between higher wages for nurses or doctors and more extensive services for the sick, more milk for children and better wages for agricultural workers, or between employment for the unemployed or better wages for those already employed, nothing short of a complete system of values in which every want of every person or group has a definite place is necessary to provide an answer.

In fact, as planning becomes more and more extensive, it becomes regularly necessary to qualify legal provisions increasingly by reference to what is "fair" or "reasonable"; this means that it becomes necessary to leave the decision of the concrete case more and more to the discretion of the judge or authority in question. One could write a history of the decline of the Rule of Law, the disappearance of the *Rechtsstaat*, in terms of the progressive introduction of these vague formulas into legislation and jurisdiction, and of the increasing arbitrariness and uncertainty of, and the consequent disrespect for, the law and the judicature, which in these circumstances could not but become an instrument of policy. It is important to point out once more in this connection that this process of the decline of the Rule of Law had been going on steadily in Germany for some time before Hitler came into power and that a policy well advanced toward totalitarian planning had already done a great deal of the work which Hitler completed.

There can be no doubt that planning necessarily involves deliberate discrimination between particular needs of different people, and allowing one man to do what another must be prevented from doing. It must lay down by a legal rule how well off particular people shall be and what different people are to be allowed to have and do. It means in effect a return to the rule of status, a reversal of the "movement of progressive societies" which, in the famous phrase of Sir Henry Maine, "has hitherto been a movement from status to contract." Indeed, the Rule of Law, more than the rule of contract, should probably be regarded as the true opposite of the rule of status. It is the Rule of Law, in the sense of the rule of formal law, the absence of legal privileges of particular people designated by authority, which safeguards that equality before the law which is the opposite of arbitrary government.

A necessary, and only apparently paradoxical, result of this is that formal equality before the law is in conflict, and in fact incompatible, with any activity of the government deliberately aiming at material or substantive equality of different people, and that any policy aiming directly at a substantive ideal of distributive justice must lead to the destruction of the Rule of Law. To produce the same result for different people, it is necessary to treat them differently. To give different people the same objective opportunities is not to give them the same subjective chance. It cannot be denied that the Rule of Law produces economic inequality—all that can be claimed for it is that this inequality is not designed to affect particular people in a particular way. It is very significant and characteristic that socialists (and Nazis) have always protested against "merely" formal justice, that they have always objected to a law which had no views on how well off particular people ought to be,[2] and that they have always demanded a "socialization of the law," attacked the independence of judges, and at the same time given their support to all such movements as the *Freirechtsschule* which undermined the Rule of Law.

It may even be said that for the Rule of Law to be effective it is more important that there should be a rule applied always without exceptions than what this rule is. Often the content of the rule is indeed of minor importance, provided the same rule is universally enforced. To revert to a former example: it does not matter whether we all drive on the left- or on the right-hand side of the road so long as we all do the same. The important thing is that the rule enables us to predict other people's behavior correctly, and this requires that it should apply to all cases—even if in a particular instance we feel it to be unjust.

The conflict between formal justice and formal equality before the law, on the one hand, and the attempts to realize various ideals of substantive justice and equality, on the other, also accounts for the widespread confusion about the concept of "privilege" and its consequent abuse. To mention only the most important instance of this abuse—the application of the term "privilege" to property as such. It would indeed be privilege if, for example, as has sometimes been the case in the past, landed property were reserved to members of the nobility. And it is privilege if, as is true in our time, the right to produce or sell particular things is reserved to particular people designated by authority. But to call private property as such, which all can acquire under the same rules, a privilege, because only some succeed in acquiring it, is depriving the word "privilege" of its meaning.

The unpredictability of the particular effects, which is the distinguishing characteristic of the formal laws of a liberal system, is also important because it helps us to clear up another confusion about the nature of this system: the belief that its characteristic attitude is inaction of the state. The question whether the state should or should not "act" or "interfere" poses an altogether false alternative, and the term "laissez faire" is a highly ambiguous and misleading description of the principles on which a liberal policy is based. Of course, every state must act and every action of the state interferes with something or other. But that is not the point. The important question is whether the individual can foresee the action of the state and make use of this knowledge as a datum in forming his own plans, with the result that the state cannot control the use made of its machinery and that the individual knows precisely how far he will be protected against interference from others, or whether the state is in a position to frustrate individual efforts. The state controlling weights and measures (or preventing fraud and deception in any other way) is certainly acting, while the state permitting the use of violence, for example, by strike pickets, is inactive. Yet it is in the first case that the state observes liberal principles and in the second that it does not. Similarly with respect to most of the general and permanent rules which the state may establish with regard to production, such as building regulations or factory laws: these may be wise or unwise in the particular instance, but they do not conflict with liberal principles so long as they are intended to be permanent and are not used to favor or harm particular people. It is true that in these instances there will, apart from the long-run effects which cannot be predicted, also be short-run effects on particular people which may be clearly known. But with this kind of laws the short-run effects are in general not (or at least ought not to be) the guiding consideration. As these immediate and predictable effects become more important compared with the long-run effects, we approach the border line where the distinction, however clear in principle, becomes blurred in practice.

The Rule of Law was consciously evolved only during the liberal age and is one of its greatest achievements, not only as a safeguard but as the legal embodiment of freedom. As Immanuel Kant put it (and Voltaire expressed it before him in very much the same terms), "Man is free if he needs to obey no person but solely the laws." As a vague ideal it has, however, existed at least since Roman times, and during the last few centuries it has never been so seriously threatened as it is today. The idea that there is no limit to the powers of the legislator is in part a result of popular sovereignty and democratic government. It has been strengthened by the belief that, so long as all actions of the state are duly authorized by legislation, the Rule of Law will be preserved. But this is completely to misconceive the meaning of the Rule of Law. This rule has little to do with the question whether all actions of government are legal in the juridical sense. They may well be and yet not conform to the Rule of Law. The fact that someone has full legal authority to act in the way he does gives no answer to the question whether the law gives him power to act arbitrarily or whether the law prescribes unequivocally how he has to act. It may well be that Hitler has obtained his unlimited powers in a strictly constitutional manner and that whatever he does is therefore legal in the juridical sense. But who would suggest for that reason that the Rule of Law still prevails in Germany?

To say that in a planned society the Rule of Law cannot hold is, therefore, not to say that the actions of the government will not be legal or that such a society will necessarily be lawless. It means only that the use of the government's coercive powers will no longer be limited and determined by preestablished rules. The law can, and to make a central direction of economic activity possible must, legalize what to all intents and purposes remains arbitrary action. If the law says that such a board or authority may do what it pleases, anything that board or authority does is legal—but its actions are certainly not subject to the Rule of Law. By giving the government unlimited powers, the most arbitrary rule can be made legal; and in this way a democracy may set up the most complete despotism imaginable.[3]

If, however, the law is to enable authorities to direct economic life, it must give them powers to make and enforce decisions in circumstances which cannot be foreseen and on principles which cannot be stated in generic form. The consequence is that, as planning extends, the delegation of legislative powers to divers boards and authorities becomes increasingly common. When before the last war, in a case to which the late Lord Hewart has recently drawn attention, Mr. Justice Darling said that "Parliament had enacted only last year that the Board of Agriculture in acting as they did should be no more impeachable than Parliament itself," this was still a rare thing. It has since become an almost daily occurrence. Constantly the broadest powers are conferred on new authorities which, without being bound by fixed rules, have almost unlimited discretion in regulating this or that activity of the people.

The Rule of Law thus implies limits to the scope of legislation: it restricts it to the kind of general rules known as formal law and excludes legislation either directly aimed at particular people or at enabling anybody to use the coercive power of the state for the purpose of such discrimination. It means, not that everything is regulated by law, but, on the contrary, that the coercive power of the state can be used only in cases defined in advance by the law and in such away that it can be foreseen how it will be used. A particular enactment can thus infringe the Rule of Law. Anyone ready to deny this would have to contend that whether the Rule of Law prevails today in Germany, Italy, or Russia depends on whether the dictators have obtained their absolute power by constitutional means.[4]

Whether, as in some countries, the main applications of the Rule of Law are laid down in a bill of rights or in a constitutional code, or whether the principle is merely a firmly established tradition, matters comparatively little. But it will readily be seen that, whatever form it takes, any such recognized limitations of the powers of legislation imply the recognition of the inalienable right of the individual, inviolable rights of man.

It is pathetic but characteristic of the muddle into which many of our intellectuals have been led by the conflicting ideals in which they believe that a leading advocate of the most comprehensive central planning like H. G. Wells should at the same time write an ardent defense of the rights of man. The individual rights which Mr. Wellshopes to preserve would inevitably obstruct the planning which he desires. To some extent he seems to realize the dilemma, and we find therefore the provisions of his proposed "Declaration of the Rights of Man" so hedged about with qualifications that they lose all significance. While, for instance, his declaration proclaims that every man "shall have the right to buy and sell without any discriminatory restrictions anything which may be lawfully bought and sold," which is admirable, he immediately proceeds to make the whole provision nugatory by adding that it applies only to buying and selling "in such quantities and with such reservations as are compatible with the common welfare." But since, of course, all restrictions ever imposed upon buying or selling anything are supposed to be necessary in the interest of the "common welfare," there is really no restriction which this clause effectively prevents and no right of the individual that is safeguarded by it.

Or, to take another basic clause, the declaration states that every man "may engage in any lawful occupation" and that "he is entitled to paid employment and to a free choice whenever there is any variety of employment open to him." It is not stated, however, who is to decide whether a particular employment is "open" to a particular person, and the added provision that "he may suggest employment for himself and have his claim publicly considered, accepted or dismissed," shows that Mr. Wells is thinking in terms of an authority which decides whether a man is "entitled" to a particular position— which certainly means the opposite of free choice of occupation. And how in a planned world "freedom of travel and migration" is to be secured when not only the means of communication and currencies are controlled but also the location of industries planned, or how the freedom of the press is to be safeguarded when the supply of paper and all the channels of distribution are controlled by the planning authority, are questions to which Mr. Wells provides as little answer as any other planner.

In this respect much more consistency is shown by the more numerous reformers who, ever since the beginning of the socialist movement, have attacked the "metaphysical" idea of individual right sand insisted that in a rationally ordered world there will be no individual rights but only individual duties. This, indeed, has become the much more common attitude of our socalled "progressives,"and few things are more certain to expose one to the reproach of being a reactionary than if one protests against a measure on the grounds that it is a violation of the rights of the individual. Even a liberal paper like the *Economist* was a few years ago holding up to us the example of the French, of all people, who had learned the lesson that "democratic government no less than dictatorship must always [*sic*] have plenary powers in *posse*, without sacrificing their democratic and representative character. There is no restrictive penumbra of individual rights that can never be touched by government in administrative matters whatever the circumstances. There is no limit to the power of ruling which can and should be taken by a government freely chosen by the people and can be fully and openly criticized by an opposition."

This may be inevitable in wartime, when, of course, even free and open criticism is necessarily restricted. But the "always" in the statement quoted does not suggest that the *Economist* regards it as a regrettable wartime necessity. Yet as a permanent institution this view is certainly incompatible with the preservation of the Rule of Law, and it leads straight to the totalitarian state. It is, however, the view which all those who want the government to direct economic life must hold.

How even a formal recognition of individual rights, or of the equal rights of minorities, loses all significance in a state which embarks on a complete control of economic life, has been amply demonstrated by the experience of the various Central European countries. It has been shown there that it is possible to pursue a policy of ruthless discrimination against national minorities by the use of recognized instruments of economic policy without ever infringing the letter of the statutory protection of minority rights. This oppression by means of economic policy was greatly facilitated by the fact that particular industries or activities were largely in the hands of a national minority, so that many a measure aimed ostensibly against an industry or class was in fact aimed at a national minority. But the almost boundless possibilities for a policy of discrimination and oppression provided by such apparently innocuous principles as "government control of the development of industries" have been amply demonstrated to all those desirous of seeing how the political consequences of planning appear in practice.

Notes

1. According to the classical exposition by A. V. Dicey in *The Law of the Constitution* (8th ed.), p.198, the Rule of Law "means, in the first place, the absolute supremacy or predominance of regular law as opposed to the influence of arbitrary power, and excludes the existence of arbitrariness, of prerogative, or even of wide discretionary authority on the part of government." Largely as a result of Dicey's work the term has, however, in England acquired a narrower technical meaning which does not concern us here. The wider and older meaning of the concept of the rule or reign of law, which in England had become an established tradition which was more taken for granted than discussed, has been most fully elaborated, just because it raised what were new problems there, in the early nineteenth century discussion in Germany about the nature of the *Rechtsstaat.*

2. It is therefore not altogether false when the legal theorist of National Socialism, Carl Schmitt, opposes to the liberal *Rechsttaaat* (i.e. the Rule of Law) the National Socialist ideal of the *gerechte Staat* ("the just state")—only that the sort of justice which is opposed to formal justice necessarily implies discrimination between persons.

3. The conflict is thus *not*, as it has often been misconceived in nineteenth-century discussions, one between liberty and law. As John Locke had already made clear, there can be no liberty without law. The conflict is between different kinds of law—law so different that it should hardly be called by the same name: one is the law of the Rule of Law, general principles laid down beforehand, the "rules of the game" which enable individuals to foresee how the coercive apparatus of the state will be used, or what he and his fellow-citizens will be allowed to do, or made to do, in stated circumstances. The other kind of law gives in effect the authority power to do what it thinks fit to do. Thus the Rule of Law could clearly not be preserved in a democracy that undertook to decide every conflict of interests not according to rules previously laid down but "on its merits."

4. Another illustration of an infringement of the Rule of Law by legislation is the case of the bill of attainder, familiar in the history of England. The form which the Rule of Law takes in criminal law is usually expressed by the Latin tag *nulla poena sine lege*—no punishment without a law expressly

prescribing it. The essence of this rule is that the law must have existed as a general rule before the individual case arose to which it is to be applied. Nobody would argue that, when in a famous case in Henry VIII's reign Parliament resolved with respect to the Bishop of Rochester's cook that "the said Richard Rose shall be boiled to death without having the advantage of his clergy," this act was performed under the Rule of Law. But while the Rule of Law had become an essential part of criminal procedure in all liberal countries, it cannot be preserved in totalitarian regimes. There, as E. B. Ashton has well expressed it, the liberal maxim is replaced by the principles *nullum crimen sine poena*—no "crime" must remain without punishment, whether the law explicitly provides for it or not. "The rights of the state do not end with punishing law breakers. The community is entitled to whatever may seem necessary to the protection of its interests—of which observance of the law, as it stands, is only one of the more elementary requirements" (E.B. Ashton, *The Fascist, His State and Mind* [1937], p. 119). What is an infringement of "the interests of the community" is, of course, decided by the authorities.

Part III

ENVIRONMENTAL, INTERNATIONAL, HEALTH CARE AND OTHER ISSUES: PROBLEMS AND SOLUTIONS

BUREAUCRACY VERSUS ENVIRONMENT

Terry Anderson and Donald Leal

Although efforts to reserve millions of acres in the political domain were underway during the late nineteenth century, Mr. and Mrs. W. W. Beck were doing their part to preserve one little corner of the world on the outskirts of Seattle, Washington. In 1887, they bought several parcels of land with giant fir trees reaching 400 feet in height and 20 feet in diameter. The Becks built a pavilion for concerts and nature lectures and added paths, benches, and totem poles. Ravenna Park soon became immensely popular. Visitors paid 25 cents a day or $5 a year ($3 and $60 in 1990 dollars) to enter the park. Even with the fees, 8,000 to 10,000 people visited the park on a busy day.[1]

As the Seattle population grew and conservationist sentiment developed, residents began to lobby for acquiring more public parklands, including Ravenna Park. In 1911, the city bought Ravenna from the Becks for $135,663 following condemnation proceedings. Shortly after the city's acquisition, according to newspaper accounts, the giant firs began disappearing. The Seattle Federation of Women's Clubs confronted Park Superintendent J. W. Thompson with reports of tree cutting. He acknowledged that the large "Roosevelt Tree" had been cut down because it had posed a "threat to public safety." It had been cut into cordwood and sold, Thompson conceded, but only to facilitate its removal and to defray costs. The federation asked a University of Washington forestry professor to investigate. When the women brought the professor's finding that a number of trees had been cut to the attention of the Park Board, the board expressed regret and promised that the cutting would stop. By 1925, however, all the giant fir trees in Ravenna had disappeared.[2]

Some people still blame the destruction of the trees on a 1925 windstorm; others blame automobiles and chimney smoke. But it was the bureaucracy that destroyed what the Becks had saved. Park employees took advantage of their access to the park and cut down trees to sell for firewood. Park Department records charge Superintendent Thompson with abuse of public funds, equipment, and personnel, plus the unauthorized sale of park property. Even if he and his subordinates were not the direct culprits, they had allowed the cutting to go on.

The Ravenna Park debacle occurred at a time when leaders of the early conservation movement were touting public ownership as the only way to conserve America's natural resources. In their view, the greed of private owners was an insurmountable obstacle to conservation. Yet, in Ravenna Park private owners protected natural treasures while public agents destroyed them. Even an outcry from public watchdogs could not prevent the eventual destruction of the giant fir trees. Today, Ravenna is just another city park with tennis courts and playgrounds.

Could similar controversies and results occur with political resources today? Unfortunately, the answer is yes, and on a much larger scale than the incident at Ravenna Park.

Timber Beasts Versus Tree Huggers

The U.S. Forest Service, with an annual budget of around $2 billion and roughly 39,000 full-time employees, is the largest natural resource agency in the federal government. It oversees natural resource use on 191 million acres of national forests and is required by law to manage its lands for multiple uses, which include timber production, livestock grazing, mineral and energy production, fish and wildlife habitat, wilderness protection, and public recreation. During the past two decades, the agency has come under a barrage of criticism from environmentalists who feel that the agency has over-emphasized commodity production at the expense of environmental amenities and commodity interests that believe the agency gives wilderness values too much attention.[3]

Such controversy is typical on the seven national forests that make up the 14 million-acre Greater Yellowstone ecosystem, the "largest relatively intact ecosystem remaining in the lower 48 states."[4] The forests are valued for their recreational opportunities and their commodity production, including timber, but environmentalists insists that the Forest Service's timber program is highly destructive. They argue that the region's harsh climate and steep terrain are not good for producing commercial stands of timber. Because reforestation is slow and costly, wildlife populations are disturbed. When timber is harvested, too little emphasis has been given to the visual effects of clear-cutting. Environmentalists also contend that logging in roadless areas threatens to displace Yellowstone's grizzly bear population and that the water quality in streams known worldwide for their fishing is likely to decline from sedimentation associated with road construction and clearcutting.[5] Logging interests counter that these problems will be worse if timber harvesting does not control the fuel load and minimize the effect of fires. They point out that the massive fires in the summer of 1988 had much smaller environmental effects and lower control costs in areas where logging had taken place.[6]

Added to the environmental debate are fiscal concerns. Virtually every aspect of national forest management loses money. The national forests surrounding Yellowstone National Park had losses from their timber programs ranging from $241,000 to $2.2 million per year from 1979 through 1984. According to Forest Service budgets, all seven national forests had losses in fiscal year 1988 totalling $7.15 million. Less well recognized are the losses on recreational services. The millions of people who fish, hike, and hunt on national forests generally do so for free. On the Gallatin National Forest alone, expenditures surpassed receipts in fiscal year 1988 by nearly $2 million, approximately twice the deficit from timber production.[7]

Yellowstone's ecosystem is not the only environmentally significant area mired in political controversy. Environmentalists argue that excessive logging and road building are also occurring on the Tongass National Forest in Alaska, the largest in the national forest system and "one of the last largely intact rain forests in the world's temperate latitudes."[8] Most of the trees in the Tongass are giant Sitka spruce and hemlock, some as old as 800 years. These trees also provide valuable habitat for Sitka blacktailed deer and for the greatest concentrations of bald eagles and grizzly bears in America. According to studies by the US. Fish and Wildlife Service and Alaska's Department of Fish and Game, it can take as long as 250 years before a logged area can provide suitable habitat for these species, so the Forest Service's planned harvest program will likely lead to substantial declines in these wildlife populations.[9] But the Forest Service continues to offer for sale nearly 450 million board feet a year, losing anywhere from fifteen to ninety-eight cents on every dollar spent.[10]

The fiscal and environmental problems that exist in the national forests are the result of institutions, not people. To expect forest managers in the bureaucracy to set aside self-interest and objectively weigh the benefits and costs of multiple-use management is to ignore the information and the incentives that confront them. Forest managers are not supposed to manage the public lands to maximize the economic return, but they can and do manage in ways that maximize their budgets. Bureaucrats in general have a propensity to expand their staffs and budgets because such expansions provide higher salaries, more prestige, and more power. In the case of the Forest Service, timber revenues are generated when trees are harvested with a percentage of the receipts retained by the bureaucracy. In addition, timber harvests mean larger road building staffs and more budget for timber management. With little revenue generated from recreational or environmental amenities and less staff required to manage wilderness, these values have received less attention than traditional commodities.

Organized wilderness advocates, however, are increasing pressure for making larger expenditures on recreational and environmental amenities and for devoting more land to these uses. The pendulum may swing toward these areas, but the controversy will not disappear. With the costs diffused among all taxpayers and with benefits concentrated, environmentalists consider no price to be too great for saving wilderness. For example, when a group of environmentalists and local landowners discovered that a timber company was planning to cut trees from four sections (2,560 acres) in the Greater Yellowstone ecosystem, they asked Congress to buy the property. With timberlands in the area worth approximately $500 per acre, the landowner was eager to sell if the group got the appropriation, which was equal to nearly $800 per acre. Such pressures will only increase Forest Service deficits and fuel the backlash from commodity interests whose jobs depend on the forests. The bureaucratic process does little to encourage either fiscal or environmental responsibility.

Plant Control on the Range

Like the national forests, our federal rangelands have multiple uses. They provide a seasonal or permanent home for some three thousand species of wildlife and fish, a source of energy reserves and hardrock minerals, rangeland for grazing livestock and wildlife, and free recreation for the public. And like our national forests, there is reason to question the government's management of these lands.

Consider the management tool known as chaining, where two crawler tractors drag 600 feet of anchor chain with links weighing 90 pounds between them to remove pinon pine and juniper trees. The BLM and the Forest Service used these tractors on hundreds of thousands of acres in the Southwest during the 1960s and 1970s and advocated chaining as an effective plant control program. Its application, they believed had a variety of benefits, including restoring an area to its original grassland state, improving wildlife habitat, increasing watershed values, and increasing livestock forage.[11]

With the financial backing of the federal treasury, the BLM chained more than 250,000 acres in Utah and 43,000 acres in Nevada. The Forest Service chained over 77,000 acres in Utah's national forests and 6,000 acres in Nevada's Humboldt Forest. Reports of the extent of chaining are not complete, but when lands in Arizona and New Mexico are included the total area cleared by chaining is about 3 million acres.[12]

Little research supports the federal land managers' contention that chaining has a multiplicity of values. There is no solid evidence that pinon-juniper woodland areas represent an invasion of original grassland habitat; therefore, chaining cannot be considered an act of restoration. In addition, Forest Service scientists have found that chaining has no significant effect on water quality and does not increase water yield. As far as wildlife is concerned, removing woodland habitat eliminates an area of security for mule deer and, while it creates forage for deer, it does little for the deer population, since the limiting factor in the chained areas is habitat security. Finally, chaining did not help the Shoshone and Paiute Indians of Nevada, who depended on pinon pine nuts as a traditional source of winter food. The only real benefit from chaining was the creation of additional forage for livestock, which allowed those holding grazing leases on chained lands to receive the benefits while making no investment.[13]

The "Water" Pork Barrel

While chaining accommodated a few leaseholders, it pales in comparison to what the Bureau of Reclamation has done on behalf of western irrigators. Even though federal dam construction practically ground to a halt during the 1980s, costs are still being exacted on the treasury and the environment. One example of the environmental cost was revealed when contaminated drainage water forced the closing of California's Kesterson Wildlife Refuge, an important stopover for millions of migrating waterfowl. The culprit was an unusually high level of selenium, a naturally occurring chemical, that is benign at low levels but lethal at high levels. Biologists found that as a result of the selenium poisoning, wild duck eggs often did not hatch and when they did grotesque deformities were common. The source of the seleniumlaced water that found its way to Kesterson was California's Central Valley Project, an irrigation project that provides subsidized water to farmers in the San Joaquin Valley. Further investigation has revealed that the selenium contamination extends to thousands of evaporation ponds in California's Central Valley and to the rivers that flow into San Francisco Bay.[14]

The effects of irrigation on wildlife are amplified when rivers and natural lakes are dewatered by subsidized federal water projects. In Nevada's Pyramid Lake and in the Stillwater National Refuge, for example, water levels have receded to unprecedented low levels. A system of dams and canals on the Carson and Truckee rivers has caused the drawdown by diverting water to irrigators in Nevada's Lahontan Valley. The water level at Pyramid Lake, home of the endangered cuiui fish and the threatened Lahontan cutthroat trout, has dropped by sixty feet. The Stillwater Refuge, which in good years harbored 200,000 ducks, 6,000 geese, and 8,000 tundra swans, has lost almost 68 percent of its productive marsh.[15] In 1938, Winnemucca Lake, once a paradise for waterfowl on the Pacific Flyway, dried up. The same fate may be in store for Pyramid Lake and the Stillwater Refuge.

The situations in California and Nevada are the byproducts of the federal government's water pork barrel. For eighty years, the Bureau of Reclamation, the federal agency responsible for making the "desert bloom like a rose," has spent tens of billions of taxpayers' dollars to bring subsidized water to western irrigators. Through interest-free loans and extended repayment schedules, western irrigators pay only a fraction of the cost of storing and delivering water. Irrigators whose runoff ended up in Kesterson, for example, pay less than 10 percent of the cost to store and deliver the water.[16] BuRec's efforts have resulted in engineering marvels like Glen Canyon Dam and Hoover Dam, but the water that continues to flow so cheaply into fields creates not only environmental tragedies, it also aggravates agricultural surpluses.

The fiscal and environmental problems inherent in federal water projects are not the fault of bad managers. They result from an institutional framework that does not discipline federal managers to be either fiscally or environmentally responsible. Moreover, the system builds an iron triangle among politicians, water users, and bureaucrats that is difficult to dismantle. If the discipline of free market environmentalism was at work, massive, subsidized projects would not be built, higher water prices would encourage efficiency, and polluters would be liable for the damage they produce.

A Bird's-Eye View of Farm Policy

For sixty years, federal farm policy has set the tone for land management on a major portion of the 300 to 340 million acres of private farmland in the United States. Unfortunately, the program's track record of wildlife conservation has been abysmal. During the last thirty years, the population of small game animals such as ring-necked pheasants, ducks, cottontail rabbits, and bobwhite quail has been reduced to only a small fraction of what it was.[17] These birds and animals once thrived on farms with shelterbelts, shrubs along fence rows, and thick growths of cattails along streams and marshes. Today, this kind of habitat is more the exception than the rule. Farmers are now growing the same crop year after year, draining the remaining wetlands, converting upland cover to row crops, and drenching their fields with pesticides and herbicides. The result is a bland, repetitious countryside that offers minimal habitat for wildlife.

Federal agricultural programs are the major cause of this sterile landscape. They induce farmers to increase production by cultivating otherwise uneconomic land. For example, agriculture was responsible for 87 percent of wetland conversion between 1950 and 1980, and direct government subsidies were the main reason the conversions were undertaken.[18] The negative impact on the environment has been exacerbated by programs that support commodity prices and reduce risks by subsidizing insurance. With returns higher and costs lower than they would be in a free market, farmers plant more acres and produce more crops. To reduce the surpluses, federal programs require farmers to cut back on the acreage planted, but farmers attempt to circumvent such efforts by using more pesticides and fertilizers to increase output per acre.

Federal programs have also tried to retire land from production, but the programs have had virtually nothing to do with conservation. For example, annual surveys by wildlife personnel in twelve midwestern states and in Colorado and Pennsylvania indicated that from 20 to 56 percent of idled cropland was without cover for entire summers, thus providing little protection for animals. Land that did have cover was frequently disturbed by early summer mowing during the critical nesting period for birds. Ironically, annual set-aside acreage in the Midwest includes more than two-thirds of the acres previously converted from wetlands through federally subsidized drainage programs.[19]

Equally bad for wildlife is the farm program's "base acreage" concept. A farmer's subsidy payments are computed as a percentage of average acres planted in the previous five years. The more land that a farmer has in his acreage base, the larger his government payments are. This gives farmers a tremendous incentive to bring even poorer land into production, because it enlarges the cropland base and qualifies them for bigger government payments in the future.

Following passage of the 1985 Farm Act and the establishment of the Conservation Reserve Program, there was hope that farmers would return to practicing environmentally sensitive agriculture. Under the program, taxpayers pay farmers to take land out of production for ten years and provide financial assistance for planting a cover crop. After five years and an annual cost of $1.5 billion, however, the program has had disappointing results. Only a small percentage of the 30 million retired acres provide enough diversity of vegetation to help wildlife survive the elements. Moreover, most of the acreage is in tame grass, which the Department of Agriculture continually lets farmers remove in drought-hit regions.[20]

The Conservation Reserve Program is an example of a well-intentioned but ineffective effort to accomplish soil and wildlife conservation. The farmers who receive the largest payments are those who have cultivated the most erodible soil; farmers who have practiced good land conservation receive very little. A far more effective approach would be to remove the subsidies that create the incentives to destroy habitat in the first place, saving taxpayers money and improving soil and wildlife conservation.

Conclusion

And so the story goes. The Forest Service, the Bureau of Land Management, the Bureau of Reclamation, and the Department of Agriculture carry out policies that exact heavy tolls on the environment. What is the problem? Some critics of environmental and natural resource policy focus on the personalities in administrations. But such an approach overlooks the fact that environmental travesties have occurred under both Democratic and Republican administrations. The volum of logging on national forests and the resulting budget shortfalls have increased in every decade since the 1950s; federal water projects underwritten by taxpayers have spanned nearly a century; and subsidies for farm products and other federal inducements for destroying habitat have been taking place since the 1930s. Other critics argue that more money should be spent on environmental amenities. Yet, spending for pollution control alone totaled $739 billion in constant 1982 dollars from 1972 through 1984.[21]

The perverse results described in this chapter occur because of institutional failure. In government agencies, bureaucrats have incentives to provide constituents with the products and services they want at little or no cost to them. Entrepreneurs in this arena are rewarded with larger staffs, more authority, and larger budgets, but they do not face the reality check of profitability. Moreover, to the extent that they have a single constituency, such as farmers in the Department of Agriculture, there is little incentive for the bureaucracy to consider other values. Increasing farmers' incomes becomes the primary goal, even if there are perverse environmental consequences. Where there are multiple constituencies, such as in the Forest Service, the political arena becomes a battleground where development interests are pitted against environmental interests in a zero-sum game. Unfortunately, the process is costly to the groups themselves, to the taxpayer, to the economy, and often to the environment.

Notes

1.   Terry L. Anderson and Jane Shaw, "Grass Isn't Always Greener in Public Park," *Wall Street Journal*, May 28, 1985, 30.

2.   Ibid.

3.   National Audubon Society, *Audubon Wildlife Report* 1968 (New York: National Audubon Society, 1986) 1156.

4. Rick Reese, *Greater Yellowstone: The National Park and Adjacent Lands* (Helena: Montana Magazine, 1984), 36.

5. The Wilderness Society, *Management Directions for the National Forests of the Greater Yellowstone Ecosystem* (Washington. D.C.: The Wilderness Society. 1987). 1314.

6. Letter to Donald Leal from Doug Crandall, March 4, 1990. Crandall is manager of Brand S. Corporation, a logging company in the Greater Yellowstone area.

7. The Wilderness Society, *Management Directions*, 22; U.S. Forest Service, *Timber Sale Program, Annual Report: Fiscal Year 1988* (Washington, D.C.: U.S. Forest Service, 1989); Gallatin National Forest recreational budget for fiscal year 1988.

8. The Wilderness Society, *America's Vanishing Rail Forest* (Executive Summary) (Washington, D.C.: The Wilderness Society, 1986), 1.

9. John W. Shoen, Matthew Kirchoff, and Michael Thomas, "Seasonal Distribution and Habitat Use by Sitka Blacktailed Deer in Southeastern Alaska (Alaska Department of Fish and Game, Juneau, 1985); J.I. Hodges, James G. King, and Fred C. Robards, "Resurvey of the Bald Eagle Breeding Population in Southeast Alaska," *Journal of Wildlife Management* 43 (January 1979): 219-21.

10. U.S. Forest Service, Region 10, "Statement of Obligations" (Juneau Alaska, 1984). See also U.S. Forest Service, *Timber Sale Program Annual Report*.

11. Ronald M. Lanner, "Chained to the Bottom" in *Bureaucracy vs. the Environment,* ed. John Baden and Richard L. Stroup (Ann Arbor: University of Michigan Press, 1981), 154-69. Although chaining is no longer practiced to the extent that it was, the disruption of thousands of acres remains.

12. Richard S. Aro, "Pinion-Juniper Woodland Manipulation with Mechanical Methods," *The Pinion-Juniper Ecosystem: A Symposium*, ed. Gerald Gifford and Frank E. Busby (Logan: Utah State University, 1975), 67-75, 156.

13. Lanner, "Chained to the Bottom" 158; Warren P. Clary et al., "Effects of Pinion-Juniper Removal on Natural Resource Products and Use in Arizona," Research Paper RM120 (Washington, .C.: U.S. Forest Service, 1974), 163.

14. Richard W. Wahl, *Markets for Federal Water: Subsidies, Property Rights, and the Bureau of Reclamation* (Washington, D.C.: Resources for the Future 1989), 197-219; Kathleen Rude, "Ponded Poisons," *Ducks Unlimited* 54 (January-February 1990): 1418.

15. Kathleen Rude, "Heavenly Water, Earthly Waste," *Ducks Unlimited* 50 (May-June 1986): 41-45.

16. Richard W. Wahl, "Cleaning Up Kesterson," *Resources* no. 83 (Spring 1986): 12.

17. Robert B. Dahlgren, "Distribution and Abundance of the RingNecked Pheasant in North America," in *Pheasants: Symptoms of Wildlife Problems on Agricultural Lands,* ed. D. L. Hallett, W. R. Edwards, and G. V. Burger (Bloomington, Ind.: North Central Section of The Wildlife Society, 1988), 29-43.

18. Secretary of the Interior, *The Impact of Federal Programs on Wetlands: Vol. 1. The Lower Mississippi Alluvial Plain and the Prairie Pothole Region* (Washington, D.C.: Government Printing Office, 1988), 3-5.

19. A. H. Berner, "Federal Pheasants: Impact of Federal Agricultural Programs on Pheasant Habitat, 19341985," in *Pheasants*, 60.

20. U.S. Department of Agriculture, Agricultural Stabilization and Conservation Service, *Conservation Reserve Program: Ninth Signup Results* (Washington, D.C.: Government Printing Office, January 1990); U.S. Department of Agriculture, News Division, "Yeutter Announced Additional Drought Assistance: CRP Opened for Haying and Grazing" (news release, Washington, D.C., July 1989).

21. *State of the Environment: A View Toward the Nineties* (Washington, D.C.: The Conservation Foundation, 1987), 23.

HOMESTEADING THE OCEANS

Terry Anderson and Donald Leal

As one of the world's largest commons, the oceans provide a challenge for free market environmental solutions. Outside the territorial limits of sovereign countries, only weak treaties limit the use of ocean resources for fishing, mineral or energy development, shipping, and garbage disposal. With few restrictions on entry, a tragedy of the commons occurs, resulting in pollution and the depletion of fish populations. Moreover, pressure on the commons is increasing, as new technologies raise the returns to exploiting ocean resources. For example, new drilling techniques make ocean oil exploration more feasible; shipping technologies are increasing the size of oil tankers and the potential for pollution; and refrigeration, sonar, and onboard processing allow fishing fleets to deplete fisheries.

Common fisheries are also being exploited by recreational fishing. The Sport Fishing Institute reported that the number of days devoted to marine recreational angling each year in the United States nearly tripled between 1955 and 1985. In fact, scientists contend that the catch of some species by sport fishermen has had a greater impact on population size than the activities of commercial fishermen. The growing influence of saltwater sport fishing coupled with commercial harvesting has intensified pressure on ocean fish.[1]

These rising demands and new technologies are creating pressures to change the rules governing access to ocean resources. Historically, access to resources beyond territorial waters was open to anyone for the taking. Gradually, however, coastal nations have begun to exert greater control over resources lying farther off their shores. The move to "fence" ocean resources began in 1945, when President Harry Truman claimed that the United States had exclusive rights to mineral and hydrocarbon resources lying on or under its continental shelf. What followed was a steady procession of declarations by coastal nations to extend claims to resources lying within 200 miles from shore. These claims have converted coastal waters "from a regime of largely open access and high seas freedoms to one with significant national controls over resource uses."[2]

Like the evolution of property rights to land and water on the American frontier, extending territorial limits is not the final solution to the problem of open access to ocean resources. As economist Ross Eckert pointed out, the conversion from strictly open access to limited access "does not guarantee the improved allocation of ocean resources" but is "only a first step for removing the inefficiencies that result from communal rights." Data from the National Marine Fisheries Service show that all major coastal fisheries in the United States continue to suffer from overexploitation. Fisheries off the Northeast coast, for example, have experienced some of the worst problems, with a 53 percent decrease in the stock of Atlantic cod and significant declines in haddock, flounder, and pollack.[3]

Table 9.1 lists species in United States coastal waters that were either fully utilized or overfished according to the criteria of maximum sustainable yield. Of the overfished species, seven were fished by foreign fleets and six by United States fleets. The declines can no longer be blamed on foreign vessels, however, because their numbers have dropped dramatically during the last eight years.[4] At the same time, total catch has risen, putting pressure on the reproductive capacity of fisheries. After decades of regulation, the striking result has been the continued decline of fish populations. As with reforms in land resource policy, the key to effective fishery policy lies in a property rights approach.

The Ocean Commons

Ocean fisheries provide the classic case of the tragedy of the commons because many species of fish are mobile and access is difficult to monitor. Therefore, the rule of capture dominates: any fish left by one fisherman is available to another. Rather than leaving fish to grow and reproduce, the incentive is to harvest the stock before others do. With each fisherman facing this incentive, the end result is for the fish stock to be overexploited. Whether the population of fish ends up becoming extinct ultimately depends on the cost of capturing the last fish in the stock. Because these costs tend to rise exponentially, declining fisheries have historically reached commercial extinction before biological extinction; that is, the additional costs of capturing the few remaining fish exceed the returns, so that it has become unprofitable to continue fishing.[5]

TABLE 9.1 Status of Selected United States Fisheries, June 1974

Fully Utilized	
Atlantic Mackerel	Pacific Hake
Red Hake	Atlantic Cod
Silver Hake	Atlantic Ocean Perch
Atlantic Herring	Bluefish
Atlantic Squid	Menhaden
Bering Sea Cod	American Lobster
King Crab	Gulf Shrimp
Tanner Crab	Eastern Tropical Pacific
Yellowfin Tuna	

Overfished	
Yellowfin Sole (Foreign)	Haddock (Foreign)
Alaska Pollock (Foreign)	Yellowtail Flounder (U.S. / Foreign)
Pacific Ocean Perch (Foreign)	California Sardine (U.S.)
Pacific Halibut (U.S.)	Pacific Mackerel (U.S.)
Atlantic Halibut (Foreign)	Atlantic Sea Scallop (U.S.)
Bering Sea Herring (Foreign)	Northwest Atlantic Shrimp (U.S.)
Bering Sea Shrimp (Foreign)	Atlantic Bluefin Tuna (U.S.)

Source: U.S. Senate, Committee on Commerce and National Ocean Policy Study, A *Legislative History of the Fishery Conservation and Management Act of 1976*, 94th Congress, 2d session (Washington, D.C., October 1976), pp. 358-59.

Nonetheless, open access to the resource results in a lower than optimal (if not total depletion of) stock and an overinvestment in fishing effort. As long as the cost of taking an additional fish is less than the value of the fish, a profit can be earned. But with open access, not all costs will be taken into account. Another fish taken from the stock can reduce the reproductive capacity of the fishery and raise search and capture costs for other fishermen. Because these added costs are external to an individual fisherman who considers only his costs and benefits, over time there will be too many fishermen in the fishery. In addition, open access encourages a rate of exploitation that will be too rapid. Being the first to exploit the fishery allows the highest returns, because the costs of finding and catching fish will be lowest. This race to the best fishing grounds is often manifest in the form of overcapitalization in radar, sonar, faster boats, and larger nets. The result is lower profits for the too many fishermen investing in too much capital to catch too few fish.

Economist Frederick Bell provided one of the first empirical verifications of overexploitation of an open-access fishery. In his examination of New England's northern lobster fishery in 1966, he found that an efficient output of lobster would have occurred at 17.2 million pounds. To attain this output, the efficient number of lobster traps would have been 433,000 traps. During 1966, the observed number of traps was roughly double this amount, leading Bell to conclude that "over 50 percent of the capital and labor employed in lobstering represent an uneconomic use of factors."[6]

Oyster fisheries along the United States coast offer a useful contrast of how property rights can improve resource allocation. Using data from oyster fisheries in Maryland, Virginia, Louisiana, and Mississippi from 1945 to 1970, economists Agnello and Donnelley tested the hypotheses that private ownership of oyster beds would generate more conservation and higher returns for fishermen than open-access beds.[7] Under open access, we would expect fishermen to take as many oysters as early as possible, with the result being diminishing returns later in the season. Agnello and Donnelley found that the ratio of harvest during the earlier part of the season to the later part was 1.35 for open-access oyster beds and 1.01 for private beds. After controlling for other variables, they also found that fishermen in the private leasing state of Louisiana earned $3,207, while their counterparts in the common-property state of Mississippi earned $807. These findings support the expectation that private property rights solve the open-access problem.

Could property rights be established for fisheries on the high seas? This kind of approach is not costless, and federal and state governments have overruled groups of fishermen who have attempted to limit entry to their fisheries. Economists Johnson and Libecap observed that even though private territorial rights were missing, fishermen have historically "resorted to informal contracting and the use of unions and trade associations to mitigate open access conditions."[8] Fishing unions were particularly active from the 1930s through the 1950s, implementing policies along the Gulf Coast to limit entry, conserve shrimp stocks, and increase members' incomes. Such efforts by unions and fishing associations eventually met their demise in the courts, which refused to exempt the collective actions of associations and unions from antitrust prosecution.

> A cooperative association of boat owners is not freed from the restrictive provisions of the Sherman Antitrust Act . . . because it professes, in the interest of the conservation of important food fish, to regulate the price and the manner of taking fish unauthorized by legislation and uncontrolled by proper authority.[9]

Although scarcity and competition limit the effectiveness of unions and associations, they can provide an alternative "to limit entry and negotiate price agreements with wholesalers and canneries."[10] For a short time, they succeeded in internalizing the cost of regulation and conserving shrimp stocks. But as this situation revealed, any agreement establishing property rights to resources is difficult to maintain if the government declares it illegal.

Regulating the Ocean Fishery

Instead of relying on a property rights solution, government regulation has been the traditional mechanism for controlling overexploitation of the ocean commons. Unfortunately, there are inherent problems with regulation, because the regulators do not own the resource and do not face economic incentives to manage it efficiently. For the fishery, most regulatory schemes have focused on sustaining the maximum yield of a fishery, that is, in allowing the largest quantity of fish that can be caught year after year without depleting the stock. Economists argue that this yield is usually not the yield that maximizes profits, however, because it ignores economic variables such as discounted returns of future catches and the costs of present and future extraction.[11]

On the whole, regulatory schemes focusing on maximum sustained yield and ignoring economic factors have led to lower profits and economic wastes in United States fisheries. Regulatory policies in the United States before 1976, for example, attempted to reduce catch and maximize sustainable yield by raising the cost of fishing. In the Pacific salmon fishery, regulators prohibited the use of traps that were first perfected by the Indians who caught the salmon when the fish returned to spawn. With the elimination of traps, fishermen turned to chasing the salmon in the open ocean. The substitute for traps became very expensive with sophisticated equipment that still allowed fishermen to over-exploit the resource. When the number of fishermen and the length of the season were restricted, entrepreneurs bought bigger boats, sonar, and more efficient nets. To plug these holes in the dike, regulators then established other layers of regulations controlling seasonal limits. The salmon catch was ultimately curtailed, but the approach generated economic inefficiency, as more labor and capital were applied to catch fewer fish. As fishermen were forced to fish longer in less productive areas with more expensive equipment, economic waste reduced the net value of the fishery. In 1965, Francis T. Christy, Jr., estimated that the overcapitalization and overuse of labor in American fisheries cost $300 million per year or, at a 6 percent interest rate, $5 billion in perpetuity.[12]

In addition to the over-capitalization caused by regulations, resources are invested in the regulatory process to favor one group of fishermen over another or owners of one type of equipment over another. The result is often absurd regulation. For example, Maryland oystermen at one time could use dredges but had to tow them behind sailboats on all but two days of the week, when motorized boats were allowed.[13] As economist James Crutchfield observed, the regulatory process has "generated an ever-increasing mass of restrictive legislation, most of it clothed in the shining garments of conservation, but bearing the clear marks of pressure politics."[14] The combined costs of regulations led Robert Higgs to conclude:

> The social resource waste has therefore grown steadily larger over time. Today from a comprehensive point of view, the Washington salmon fishery almost certainly makes a negative contribution to net national product. The opportunity costs of the socially unnecessary resources employed there, plus the socially unnecessary costs of governmental research, management, and regulation, are greater than the total value added by all the labor and capital employed in the fishery.[15]

Meanwhile, despite these costs, many fisheries in United States coastal waters during the early 1970s were either in trouble or on the verge of it.

The Magnuson Fishery Conservation and Management Act of 1976 tried to remove some of these regulatory inefficiencies by setting a new direction for fishery policy. It extended the nation's marine management jurisdiction from three to 200 miles offshore and encouraged the development of domestic fisheries. Eight regional councils were established with the authority to manage fisheries under their jurisdiction. Notably, the act does not mandate the standard of maximum sustainable yield, but rather stipulates that fishery management plans may "establish a system for limiting access to the fishery in order to achieve optimum yield."[16] Optimum yield in this case must take into account economic variables, such as interest rates, fish values, and the cost of alternative technologies.

While the Magnuson legislation was a step in the right direction, significant problems remain for regulators. The legislation encouraged licensing entrants as a way of limiting the number of fishermen or vessels in a fishery, but limiting entrants "cannot prevent crowding, congestion, strategic fishery behavior, racing, and capital stuffing." Controlling the intensity of effort remains a thorny problem, because fishermen are substituting fewer larger boats for more smaller sized boats. The result is that "rising fish prices constrained by a limited number of vessels, and unconstrained by any sort of territorial limit, has led to vastly increased individual fishing capacity." Even with licensing, regulators find that a few powerful fishing vessels can do in a few minutes what used to take days. The bottom line is that the Magnuson act has not rebuilt the declining fisheries in United States waters. According to the 1986 "Calio study" (named after Anthony Calio, then head of the National Oceanic and Atmospheric Administration), twenty-two fisheries have an allowable catch that could be caught by fewer vessels. This excess catch capacity has also resulted in many fisheries being severely overfished (see Table 9.2). The study also concluded that the ten most favored species, which have traditionally accounted for three-quarters of the total value of American commercial fisheries remain significantly below historical levels and continue to be over-fished.[17]

TABLE 9.2 Representative List of Stocks Under Management

Geographic Area	Overfished	Overcapitalized
New England	haddock, yellowtail flounder, sea scallops	haddock, yellowtail flounder, American lobster
Mid-Atlantic	swordfish, scallops	swordfish, scallops, surf clams, ocean quahogs
South Atlantic	Spanish mackerel	Atlantic shrimp
Gulf of Mexico	Spanish mackerel, king mackerel, Gulf of Mexico reef fish (notably red snapper)	spiny lobster, shrimp, stone crab
Caribbean	shallow water reef (Nassau grouper and possibly certain trunkfishes)	spiny lobster
Pacific	chinook and coho salmon (selected stocks), Pacific ocean perch	chinook and coho salmon, groundfish (except Pacific whiting)
North Pacific	red king and gulf croaker, Tanner crab, Pacific ocean perch	sablefish, halibut, high seas salmon, king and Tanner crab
Western Pacific	seamount groundfish	bottomfish, lobster

Source: U.S. Department of Commerce, *NOAA Fishery Management Study* (Washington, D.C., 1986).

Complicating the regulation of commercial fishing is recreational or sport fishing. With the recent rise in recreational fishing, several fish stocks have come under pressure, forcing regulators in some instances to take drastic action. For example, in 1987 the National Marine Fisheries Service banned commercial fishing of king mackerel after recreational fishermen from Texas through southeast Florida exceeded a 740,000-pound catch limit. Meanwhile, tension has grown between recreational fishermen and commercial interests. Commercial fishermen fear that recreational fishermen under the guise of conservation have become highly influential in setting policy at both the state and federal levels. Recreational fishermen complain that fisheries must not be managed solely for commercial interests and that they have as much right to the resource as commercial interests do. The management districts for both the South Atlantic and Gulf Coast fisheries are experiencing intense pressures from these the two groups.[18]

The conflicts between commercial and sport interests have led to concerted efforts by both groups to gain stronger footholds in regional fisheries management councils. Historically, the regional councils of the National Marine Fisheries Service were dominated by representatives from commercial fishing interests. This dominance may be changing as recreational interests have managed to gain more political influence. Meanwhile, the turf battles have left questions concerning the regional councils' effectiveness in managing fish stocks.

> As the battle between user groups has intensified, many observers have questioned whether NFMS and the councils, in their desire to satisfy every demand for a piece of the resource pie, have lost sight of their fundamental responsibility to protect the health of fish stocks.[19]

Policy Alternatives

The preferred free market environmentalism approach to the fishery problem is to allow the establishment of property rights. This approach is certainly not new. Robert Higgs found that Indians along the Columbia River had well-established rights to fishing sites long before whites came to the area.[20] The Indians developed effective technologies for catching the salmon and avoided over-exploitation through intertribal agreements to allow sufficient upstream migration and to ensure sustained spawning. "Legally induced technical regress" resulted from legislation that outlawed traps and effectively eliminated fishing rights. This legislation ran counter to British common law, which had a place for private rights to coastal fisheries.

> . . when we consider that there were already, in 1200 AD, in tidal waters, territorial fishing rights in England and a form of territorial salmon right throughout the world in the 19th century, the legislative process can only be said to have reduced the characteristics of individual fishing rights.[21]

The tradition of property rights is gaining popularity with the growth of aquaculture. With aquaculture, there is potential for increasing fish production while reducing pressure on wild stocks. Because investment in aquaculture requires secure property rights and because property rights are more likely to evolve where the costs of establishing rights are lower, sessile species, such as oysters, have the most promise. As noted earlier, private rights to oyster beds in some states have led to greater productivity.

The emergence of salmon ranching indicates that a solution based on property rights can also be applied to anadromous species that return to their original spawning ground. But before salmon ranching can realize its full potential, property rights problems have to be worked out. For example, a ranch operator has control over his stock only while the salmon are in captivity—before they are released and after they return for spawning. Otherwise, the salmon reside in the open sea beyond the rancher's control. Under conditions of the "open range," the rancher may lose a substantial portion of his investment to natural mortality and commercial and sport fishermen. Some of these problems can be overcome if there is better coordination between ranchers and commercial fishermen. For example, economists Anderson and Wilen demonstrated that "restrictive ocean fishing season, depleted stocks of other species and low public smolt release levels raise the profitability from private aquaculture." They concluded that salmon ranchers would be willing to pay for a reduced season length and for reduced public smolt releases in return for receiving compensation from those who catch ranch fish in the ocean.[22]

This problem is similar to the one faced by British salmon sport fishermen. In many cases, the fishermen own fishing rights on streams, but they are disturbed by the alarmingly depleted salmon stocks that return to spawn. The reductions are the result of increased commercial harvests, especially by fishermen who have netting rights at the mouths of rivers.[23] To combat the problem, the Atlantic Salmon Conservation Trust of Scotland has been buying up netting rights. Most have been purchased from private owners, but some have even come from the crown. The idea of this buyout program began in Canada, where the federal government bought and retired commercial netting rights in NewBrunswick, Nova Scotia, and Quebec. Because the buyout program is working so well, private interests in Iceland are exploring the possibility of buying the Greenland and Faeroese fisheries and shutting them down completely. The key to this solution is the transferability of fishing rights.

Another approach that eliminates interactions between fish ranchers and fishermen is based on raising salmon in pens. When the salmon reside in pens for their entire lives, there are no losses due to commercial and sport fishing in the open ocean. This method has proven highly successful for the Norwegians, who are the leading international producers of Atlantic salmon. Salmon farmers and ranchers in the United States still face political opposition from commercial fishermen who have sought government protection of their markets, and from environmentalists who fear that salmon farming will lead to more pollution of bays and inland waters. In 1987, commercial fishermen in the Pacific Northwest convinced the Alaskan government to impose a one-year moratorium on net-pen salmon farms, and protests from local environmentalists in Washington have led the state to impose stringent guidelines in siting salmon farms.[24]

Institutional roadblocks also stand in the way of other private operations. In Maryland, out of some 9,000 acres of privately leased oyster grounds, only 1,000 are in production, 280,000 acres remain public. Privatizing Maryland's Chesapeake Bay oyster fishery faces the problem of weak enforcement of private leases. "It's hard to find an oyster ground that hasn't been poached upon," complained a planter on the Tred Avon River. "It's the main reason why so many people are reluctant to take their ground and invest their money in it."[25] Obviously, to realize the full potential of aquaculture in the United States, institutional barriers must be removed and the defense of private property rights must be strengthened.

Japan has led the race in establishing private property rights in fisheries. The Japanese took bold steps to allow the privatization of the commons because access to foreign fishing grounds was being more and more restricted by legislation such as the Magnuson act. The Japanese government now initiates the property rights process by designating areas that are eligible for aquaculture. The fishermen's cooperative associations are then given the responsibility of partitioning these areas and assigning them to individual fishermen for their exclusive use. Exclusive use allows the owner to invest in improvements and to capture the benefits of their investment.

Another mechanism for assigning rights to fisheries is to establish individual tradable quotas, or ITQs. An individual quota entitles the holder to catch a specified percentage of the total allowable catch. This system is attractive for several reasons. First, each quota holder faces greater certainty that his share of the catch will not be taken by someone else. Under the current system, total allowable catch is established, but the share is determined by who is best at capturing the fugitive resources. With ITQs, holders do not compete for the shares, so there is less incentive to race other fishermen. Second, transferability allows quotas to end up in the hands of the most efficient fishermen—that is, those with the lowest costs and who can pay the highest price for the ITQs. Less efficient producers and inputs move to other industries. As a corollary, ITQs encourage progress in reducing the cost of catching fish. Fishermen who adopt new cost-reducing methods make more money with their quotas and are in a better position to purchase quotas from those who are less efficient. This is in marked contrast to the current regulatory system, which encourages over-investment in the race for fugitive resources.

Several countries, most notably Australia and New Zealand, have implemented ITQs for handling fisheries where regulations have failed. Australia is using the ITQ system for the southern bluefin tuna fishery. Globally. the southern bluefin tuna population had declined from an estimated 650,000 metric tons prior to 1950 to about 160,000 meric tons in 1980. Scientists have concluded that to maintain the 1980 level, the world catch of the fish needed to be stabilized at about 32,000 metric tons, down from the previous level of 40,000 metric tons. To achieve this level, given an expected Japanese catch of 15,000 metric tons, the Australian catch had to be reduced from 21,000 metric tons to less than 10,000 metric tons. In addition, the Australian southern bluefin tuna fishery had so much over-capacity and over-capitalization that it remained unprofitable while taking record catches.

The results from implementing ITQs were very positive. After six months, the fleet capacity in the fishery had been reduced by 60 percent, as those who intended to stay in the fishery bought quotas from those who could earn more by leaving. There was also an increase in the average size of the catch, as operators with access to larger fish bought out operators with access to smaller fish. After the government established the ITQs, the improvements were achieved in the marketplace, without the government determining who could fish, what size fish could be kept, and what methods could be used. As an indication of increased value of the fishery, ITQs began selling for just under $1,000 per ton on October 1, 1984; they sold for $2,000 per ton five and one-half months later.[26]

Conclusion

While ITQs offer considerable advantages, determining the size of the total catch remains a governmental function. Fishery regulators determine total catch based on biological sustainability and economic factors. Unfortunately, regulators are susceptible to political pressures from the special interest groups they regulate, who then become important bureaucratic constituents in the budgetary process. The incentive for pleasing such groups by maintaining an inefficient industry size can be strong enough to overshadow the objectives of efficient production and sustainable future catches.

Establishing property rights to the ocean commons will not be easy, but, like the frontier West, we can expect increasing efforts at definition and enforcement. ITQ systems offer a step toward facilitating property rights solutions. In New Zealand, ITQs for the abalone fishery off the Chatham Islands are showing signs of eliminating the commons problem that have plagued the fishery for years. With more secure rights to future harvests, the value of ITQs rose in value by nearly a factor of six from 1988 to 1989. Furthermore, fishermen with more secure rights have formed a cooperative into which its members put one percent of their annual sales for a program to rear and plant young abalone.[27] ITQs make it "easier and cheaper" for fishermen holding quotas "to act collectively" in managing the size of their catch.[28]

Unfortunately, the success of ITQs and collective action by fishing associations stimulate political action by special interest groups who want a share of the growing pie. In the New Zealand case, government officials argue that part of the income from the abalone fishery is a "windfall" to quota holders and belongs to the government. And several indigenous groups argue that their rights to the fishery supersede nonindigenous quota holders and, therefore, the quotas should be turned over to them.[29] Unfortunately, these conflicts focus only on how to carve up the pie, not how to make it even larger. Removing judicial roadblocks to collective action by voluntary fishing associations, implementing ITQ systems, and refraining from further governmental redistribution of fishing rights can move us a long way toward a free market environmental solution to the ocean commons problem.

Notes

1. Nelson Bryant, "Fishing Licenses Are At Issue," *New York Times,* February 5, 1989; Gina Maranto, "Caught in Conflict," *Sea Frontiers* 35 (May-June 1988): 144-51.

2. Ross Eckert, *The Enclosure of Ocean Resources* (Stanford, Calif.: Hoover Institution Press, 1979); 4.

3. Ibid.. 16; U.S. Department of Commerce, National Oceanic and Atmospheric Administration, National Marine Fisheries Service, *Fisheries of the United States,* 1986, Current Fishery Statistics no. 8385 (April 1987); Jennifer A. Kingston, "Northeast Fishermen Catch Everything, and That's a Problem," *New York Times,* November 13, 1988.

4. US. Department of Commerce, National Oceanic and Atmospheric Administration, National Marine Fisheries Service, *Fisheries of the United States, 1986 (Supplemental)* (Washington, D.C.: National Marine Fisheries Service, April 1987).

5. For a classic article on the commons problem, see H. Scott Gordon, "The Economic Theory of a Common Property Resource: The Fishery," *Journal of Political Economy* 62 (April 1954): 124-42. See also Colin W. Clark, "Profit Maximization and the Extinction of Animal Species," *Journal of Political Economy* 81 (August 1981): 950-60.

6. Frederick W. Bell, "Technological Externalities and Common-Property Resources: An Empirical Study of the U.S. Northern Lobster Fishery," *Journal of Political Economy* 80 (January-February 1972): 156.

7. Richard J. Agnello and Lawrence P. Donnelley, "Prices and Property Rights in the Fisheries," *Southern Economic Journal* 42 (October 1979): 253-62.

8. Ronald N. Johnson and Gary D. Libecap, "Contracting Problems and Regulation: The Case of the Fishery," *American Economic Review* 12 (December 1982): 1007.

9. *Gulf Coast Shrimpers and Oystermens Association v. United States*, 236 F. 2nd 658 (1956).

10. Johnson and Libecap, "Contracting Problems and Regulation," 1008.

11. See Tom Tietenberg, *Environmental and Natural Resource Economics,* 2d ed. (Glenview, Ill.: Scott, Foresman and Company, 1988), 258-64.

12. J. A. Crutchfield and G. Pontecovo. *The Pacific Salmon Fisheries: A Study of Irrational Conservation* (Baltimore: Johns Hopkins Press, for Resources for the Future, 1969); "The Flaw in the Fisheries Bill," *Washington Post*, April 13, 1976.

13. Francis T. Christy, Jr., and Anthony Scott, *The Common Wealth in Ocean Fisheries* (Baltimore: Johns Hopkins University Press, for Resources for the Future, 1965), 15-16.

14. James A. Crutchfield, "Resources from the Sea," in *Ocean Resources and Public Policy,* ed. T. S. English (Seattle: University of Washington Press, 1973), 115.

15. Robert Higgs, "Legally Induced Technical Regress in the Washington Salmon Fishery," *Research in Economic History* 7 (1982): 82.

16. U.S. Senate, Committee on Commerce, *A Legislative History of the Fishery Conservation and Management Act of 1976* (Washington, D.C.: U.S. National Marine Fisheries Service, October 1976).

17. Anthony Scott, "Market Solutions to Open-Access, Commercial Fisheries Problems" (paper presented at APPAM 10th Annual Research Conference, October 2729, 1988), 7-8. U.S. Department of Commerce, National Oceanic and Atmospheric Administration, National Marine Fisheries Service, *NOAA Fishery Management Study* (Washington, D.C.: Government Printing Office, 1986), 62.

18. Maranto, "Caught in Conflict," 145.

19. William J. Chandler, ed., *Audubon Wildlife Report,* 1988/1989 (San Diego: Academic Press, 1988), 48.

20. Higgs, "Legally Induced Technical Regress."

21. Scott, "Market Solutions," 19.

22. James L. Anderson and James E. Wilen, "Implications of Private Salmon Aquaculture on Prices, Production, and Management of Salmon Resources," *American Journal of Agricultural Economics* 68 (November 1986): 877.

23. Nelson Bryant, "A Scottish Group Protects Salmon," *New York Times,* January 8, 1990, 5-13.

24. Edwin S. Iversen and Jane Z. Iversen, "Salmon-farming Success in Norway," *Sea Frontiers* (November-October 1987): 355-61; Cheryl Sullivan, "Salmon 'Feedlots' in Northwest," *Christian Science Monitor,* July 23, 1987. See also Robert R. Stickney, "Commercial Fishing and Netpen Salmon Aquaculture: Turning Conceptual Antagonism Toward a Common Purpose," *Fisheries* 13 (July-August 1988): 9-13.

25. Merrill Leffler, "Killing Maryland's Oysters," *Washington Post,* March 29, 1987.

26. William L. Robinson, "Individual Transferable Quotas in the Australian Southern Bluefin Tuna Fishery," in *Fishery Access Control Programs Worldwide: Proceedings of the Workshop on Management Options for the North Pacific Longline Fishers,* Alaska Sea Grant Report no. 86-4 (Orca Island, Wash.: University of Alaska, 1986), 189-205.

27. Rodney P. Hide and Peter Ackroyd, *Depoliticising Fisheries Management: Chatham Islands' Paua (abalone) as a Case Study* (Christchurch, New Zealand: Centre for Resource Management, Lincoln University, March 1990), 42, 44.

28. Scott, "Market Solutions," 23. Scott argued that the individual quotas may lay the groundwork for fishermen to monitor and discourage violations of quotas for alleviating the problem of catching other species, known as the by-catch problem. The by-catch problem is addressed by the opportunity to trade mixed quotas among fishermen.

29. Hide and Ackroyd, *Depoliticising Fisheries Management,* 45-62.

A MARKET OF LANDSCAPE VISIONS

Karl Hess, Jr.

When Dayton Hyde first came to Chiloquin, Oregon, his private and permitted rangelands were dry expanses of pine trees and shrubby bitterbrush. Except for scattered grassy parks and a few small sagebrush openings, the landscape extended in all directions as forest. But Dayton had a personal landscape vision, a vision with enforceable limits that began and ended on his small forested ranch in southwestern Oregon. He believed that ranchers had an obligation to care for their lands—particularly their private lands, the ones over which they had greatest control. That was why he started Operation Stronghold, a voluntary landowner's alliance devoted to using private property for wildlife conservation. It was for a similar reason that he began the Institute of Range and the American Mustang (IRAM). Today, he is using IRAM to set up voluntary private reserves for wild horses in South Dakota.

Landscape visions are like charity, though: They are best begun and observed at home. For Dayton Hyde, the power and allure of his vision lie not in the four hundred members and several million acres of Operation Stronghold or in the good intentions of IRAM but in the beautiful, sculpted landscapes that his ethic of caring has brought to his small ranch.

One of those landscapes is a marshland. Dayton turned the dry valley bottom lying below his headquarters into a mosaic of clear streams, open pools, sedge and willow bogs, and lush meadows. He marshaled and stewarded the feeble headwaters of the Williamson River with holding ponds, water diversions, and proper grazing management. His efforts paid off in many ways. His family enjoyed a healthier and richer environment, fishermen angled for prize trout on formerly barren land, and plant and wildlife species thrived and flourished.

Cattle are part of Dayton's vision. He uses them to enhance the diversity of the marsh, grazing them carefully so that they do not disturb nesting birds or upset fish spawning grounds. Yet if livestock were not so vital to the health of the marsh, he might do just as well without them—at least dollarwise. During the summer, five fishermen per week pay more than $100 per day apiece for lodging and angling. And during the winter, the large number of mule deer and elk that rely on his marsh for water and food attract paying hunters. As it turns out, a judicious mix of recreation, wildlife, and cattle allows Dayton and his family to make their living off the land without overgrazing its plants, eroding its soils, or exhausting its other renewable resources. In fact, it enables them to give more to the land than they have taken.

They would like to give even more. Not long ago, Dayton asked the Forest Service for permission to reduce stocking on public lands adjacent to his marsh. He believed that deer and elk could graze and maintain the marsh just as well as livestock. To offset lost revenue, he offered to pay the same grazing bill as before, even though he would no longer be running as many cows. The Forest Service denied his request, telling him that his grazing permit was for cattle, not wildlife.

As important as the marsh is to Dayton, the pride and joy of his wildlife vision is a second landscape—a small lake that he carved out of the Oregon wilds. At most ten miles from his headquarters, it is a sanctuary where he can wile away hours writing naturalist and wildlife books and pass balmy afternoons running and hunting with the timber wolf he raised from a pup. It is also a special refuge for fish, birds, and mammals. On one of many boulders around the lake, Dayton and I sat and watched the wildlife, listened to the wolf's howl, and talked about the quarter-mile stretch of man-made water below us.

Before the lake existed, the land was well drained and densely timbered in pine. Wildlife was hardly visible and far from diverse. But Dayton arrived with his vision and built a dam to hold water. Over tire years, he watched as the lake filled, plant life changed, and wildlife appeared in greater numbers and species. He was especially pleased with the varieties of bird life that found homes on his newly made refuge. His first counts had shown only eight species. But after the lake was filled, he counted eighty three species of birds, including the American bald eagle.

When the Forest Service learned that the lake had attracted bald eagles, it closed a road that Dayton had long used to maintain the perimeter fence protecting his private refuge. The agency did not want him driving on the road because the noise might disturb nesting eagles. He was angered. He was the one who had brought the bald eagle to the Winema National Forest by spending $200,000 to build the lake. Why should he be viewed as a potential intruder?

Dayton was able to resolve part of the problem by swapping a portion of his marshland for Forest Service property adjacent to the lake. The new land made it easier for him to maintain fences, control access, and preserve the ecological integrity of the refuge. But he was saddened when he returned to the portion of the marshland that now belonged to the Forest Service and found it despoiled. Gone were the profusion of fish, the dense grasses, and the rich variety of mammals and birds.

Other disappointments have since marred what should have been an unblemished triumph of human will. Well-intentioned environmental zoning codes passed by the people of Oregon are making it difficult for Dayton to do as he wishes with his private sanctuary. Although he built the lake with his own money and labor, state planners are authorized to tell him what he can and cannot do with it. For example, Dayton would like to build a few fishing cabins on the far side of the lake to help cover the costs of maintaining its water level and conserving its wildlife. But doing that may not be possible, given Oregon's strict environmental regulations. The only option that state law allows him is to breach the dam and return the lake bed to its forested and relatively lifeless past.

Dayton is also disappointed that the Forest Service will not allow him to try his vision on public lands. He would like to heal eroding meadows and improve wildlife habitat by building a series of ponds and diversion lines to spread water evenly over the landscape. But he cannot. The best he can do is sit on the boulder next to me and ponder the options left him by state planners and land managers. We hear the unsettling howl of the lake's solitary wolf. Two endangered species make their stand: one a symbol of a world past, the other an agent of a world that might be—a world where visions are free and the likes of Dayton Hyde are tolerated.

Ecology, Markets, and Landscape Visions

Freeing the western range from the tyranny of single visions and the misrule of the visionary state begins with seeing and appreciating that nature is more complex and dynamic than intolerant visions have allowed. It tarts by envisioning the western range apart from the narrow constraints well-intentioned people have set and by entertaining possibilities beyond cultivated fields, engineered landscapes, and sacred places. And it means facing the shortcomings of agrarian, progressive, and environmental visions and understanding why they failed in their quest to capture and remold landscapes into a single, unchanging form.

Among those ideologies, the one that most threatens the relation of man and nature on the western range is the presumption that the land has a life and destiny independent of people and their communities. Today, that ideology lives in the lingering legacy of Clements's ecology. It colors progressive and environmental perceptions of the western range, pointing to an absolute standard for measuring the health and well-being of the land. And that single image of how the land once was, and should be again, tightens the regulatory grasp of the environmental welfare state and heightens the zeal of righteous managers. Yet beneath the certainty of visionary rhetoric, there is another reality—one that challenges the unnatural division of people and nature on the western range.

Three-quarters of a century of science has all but demolished Clements's vision of a deterministic world, where man is more intruder than welcomed member. A tradition of ecology anchored in the writings of H. A. Gleason and Robert Whittaker and continued at the cutting edge of patch dynamics theory paints a portrait of an altogether different world—a natural world characterized more by indeterminacy and disturbance than by climax and predictability. Clements's vision, it is argued, fails to account for the role of chance and accident in the sculpting of nature and its vegetation. And plant communities, far from being organisms evolving toward a preordained end point, are simply collages, collections, and patches of individual species as they occur along multiple environmental gradients.

Moreover, continuous change is the rule for plant communities. Shifting patterns of species within discrete patches of vegetation are the transient faces that landscapes assume in their ever-changing nature. Far from being the negative factor that Clements blamed for undermining vegetation structure and stability, disturbance is the essential feature of healthy and sound ecological systems. From this perspective, Clements's ecology is obsolete. As James Gleick notes in *Chaos,* "those looking to science for a general understanding of nature's habitats will be better served by the laws of chaos." Those laws teach the indeterminacy of nature—a revelation, Gleick observes, that forced ecologist William Schaffer to reconsider his basic assumptions on ecology:

> [He] found himself realizing that ecology based on a sense of equilibrium seems doomed to fail. The traditional models are betrayed by their linear bias. Nature is more complicated. Instead he sees chaos, "both exhilarating and a bit threatening." Chaos may undermine ecology's most enduring assumptions . . . [but] "what passes for fundamental concepts in ecology is as a mist before the fury of the storm—in this case, a full, nonlinear storm."

A "nonlinear storm" is already besieging those who have dared to assert and impose what is right and proper on the western range. By pinning their landscape ideals and hopes to the static, illusory world of Clements, land agencies and righteous managers have taken a path as far astray from ecological good as the course followed by the cattlemen who overgrazed and abused federal rangelands. Visions of engineered landscapes and sacred places have deluded progressive and environmental thinkers into believing that nature can be mastered and set on a straight and narrow course as dictated by the will of the state. Such inflexible visions, unfortunately, have steered well-intentioned people away from the standard and test of ecological right and wrong set by Aldo Leopold.

Whatever defects mar visionary portraits of the public lands, they are exacerbated by an underlying mistrust of people in general, a belief that men and women are disrupters of nature and interlopers on the western range. Only the environmental welfare state, staffed with right-thinking and properly caring people, can mitigate the worst effects of human presence and isolate public lands from the contagion they threaten.

Viewing people in such light, though, merely reinforces the reign of intolerant visions and the rule of the visionary state. To challenge the supremacy of both, we must discard simple formulas that describe humans as virulent agents eating away at the immense biological diversity and ecological health of western rangelands. In making that challenge, of course, we cannot overlook the environmental damage caused by modern man's assault on nature, nor can we forget that the biological richness of the earth has been diminished by human action. But it would be wrong to assume that people are bad or that man cannot live in harmony with nature.

People are an inescapable and necessary part of their environments. They are not, as Clements regretfully told us, intruders on virgin grasslands; they are not, as experts inform us, special interest constituencies who are properly managed and supervised by mammoth bureaucracies; and they are not, as Muir would have us believe, nondescript hordes of destroyers ravaging western forests. The role people play extends far beyond the handful of institutions that make up the environmental welfare state and the chosen few who staff the ranks of those holding encompassing visions.

Landscape ecology, a youthful discipline born in European rather than American ecology, has theory and evidence enough to substantiate the pivotal role of man in nature. The intricate patterns of vegetation—both civilized and wild—that clothe the earth's diverse terrains are as much the outcomes of historical human action as they are the products of climate, soils, species dispersal, genetic drift, and local topography. Landscape ecology accepts men and women as legitimate members of the natural world. Climax communities, in the sense perceived by Clements, are nonexistent. Possibility, rather than inevitability, characterizes the protean land communities of landscape ecology.

Ecological systems, like those on the western range, are envisioned by most ecologists as hierarchies of organization, starting with single organisms and extending onward through the levels of populations, communities, and ecosystems. For landscape ecologists, including such prominent American ecologists as Eugene and Howard Odum, the hierarchy culminates at what is termed the ninth level of integration—at the realm of landscapes and the total human ecosystem. It is there that people are included in the ecological picture, completing what in nature entails a viable and functioning human ecosystem. "By human ecosystem," writes ecologist Frank Egler,

> we certainly do not mean a virgin, climax, primeval wilderness which man has utilized, exploited, raped or ruined and which would return to its "balance of nature" if only man would "preserve" it. This is the archaic view of those scientists who are pegged at the Eighth (Ecosystem) Level, and have hit their intellectual ceiling. On the contrary, the idea of the Total Human Ecosystem [THE] is that *man-and-his-total-environment* form one single whole in nature that can be, should be and will be studied in its totality.

Merely asserting that man is an integral part of the natural world, of course, does not resolve the issue of whether his contributions and potential are weighed more heavily toward environmental destruction than toward benevolence. By some standards, human intervention in nature is necessarily bad; it can only blemish the harmony and perfection inherent in a pristine world. John Muir is an excellent example of this sentiment. He saw only the harmful and contaminating presence of man in the forests, mountains, and prairies that were once pristine and unpolluted. Muir made it clear that people add nothing to the complexity and beauty of nature; they only detract from its wonders. Such an assumption, so prevalent in the landscape visions that have dominated law and policy on public lands, is shortsighted and prejudicial. For all the environmental harm that men and women have brought to western rangelands, for all the varied and rich life that stockmen have left trampled and severely grazed in the wake of too many cattle and sheep, the human factor is nonetheless a crucial element in the overall diversity and ecological potential of federal rangelands.

This last point may be best understood by looking beyond the boundaries of the western range. For example, Raymond Coppinger and Charles Smith—both evolutionary ecologists—conclude in "The Domestication of Evolution" that man's modification of the natural world has enhanced the survivability of the human species and its domesticated plants and animals. They acknowledge that ecological systems are becoming simplified at an alarming rate—that species are disappearing and landscapes are becoming impoverished. Much of that loss, they concede, is the consequence of more solar energy, more open spaces, and more nutrients being dedicated to feeding and housing an ever-growing human population. This imminent loss of diversity should, by all accounts, threaten, not enhance, human survival.

Certainly, diversity is vital. It is the lifeblood of natural and social systems—an insurance policy of sorts that allows human and nonhuman life to weather the constant storm of environmental change. It is the network through which energy and information flow to animate life, and at the same time it is the source of the energy and information needed to maintain life. Every species, subspecies, and individual, including the immense variety of environments in which they thrive and flourish, is part of both the fabric and the process of diversity. Each and every one of these elements of diversity is linked to the survival and stability of both wild and civilized places. If diversity is understood in this manner, as the process whereby life sustains itself rather than simply the many forms that it assumes, then we can begin to understand the anomaly described by Coppinger and Smith.

Despite the accelerating rate of species extinction and the accompanying biological simplification of the global environment, humans have the potential to enhance diversity by creating and processing information—that is, by their ability to propagate through culture, community, science, and art a diversity upon which people and nature can thrive and coexist in harmony. Through such diversity, it is even conceivable that species extinction may be slowed or reversed. As long as humans are able to exercise their special informational skills and respond to their environments creatively and with dispatch, flourishing and viable landscapes are possible and probable. Clearly, of the many roles that people fill in the global ecosystem, that of communicator may be most crucial to the continuance of life.

Ideas and information, then, constitute the power and potential of human diversity—an ecological, as opposed to biological, diversity in which a single species by virtue of creativity is able to play a disproportionate and, with good fortune, a more benevolent role in the health and well-being of the earth. It may not be too farfetched to suggest that the human mind mimics the ecological role and function of a single species, or that the collectivity of minds is in many ways analogous to the diversity that comes with genetic variability and multiple species. The only difference between human and nonhuman diversity is choice. Only man has the option to act for better or worse, to turn his skills toward enriching or impoverishing his life and the lives of other species.

Most people would agree that given the option of choice, humans have an obligation to turn their creativity toward salvaging the elements of biological diversity that are currently threatened. And few would question that the overall quality of life, in both material and aesthetic terms, would be enhanced by preserving species and protecting environmental diversity. At the same time, it must be understood that rescuing the wild and pristine does not mean removing man and his creative influence from the natural world. Human diversity, as translated into innovative ideas and responsive information, is the key to viable and desirable landscapes on a planet so overwhelmingly populated by people. It is also the pivotal ecological factor in determining people's ability to live in peace and harmony among themselves and with nature.

Returning to the western range from our overview of global diversity and global ecosystems, it is clear that the problems of the federal estate are similar to those of more distant places. Diversity is endangered, and its restoration is crucial. What is needed to heal overgrazed lands and to enrich western landscapes is a market of landscape visions—an atmosphere of political and environmental tolerance in which individuals and groups are free to pursue their dreams and ambitions without the benefit of political force or the largesse of federal subsidy. In such an environment, the diversity that comes with many minds and as many visions will be unleashed, innovative ideas can be pursued, and new approaches and strategies for the use, conservation, and preservation of wild and tamed lands can be tried and tested.

Such a market will bring visions down to earth, making them answerable to the land, to the wildlife, and to the social communities that invariably bear many of the costs and benefits of environmental abuse and benevolence. The question is how to arrive at a market of landscape visions, how to unleash the power of diversity and the promise of many visions on the lands of the federal range.

Diversity, Process, and Environmental Gain

A market of landscape visions is not something tangible, like the market for automobiles or the thousands of flea markets that spring up every weekend across the country. It is not the millions of monetary transactions that shuffle resources, products, and people around the nation with dispatch. A market of landscape visions describes a political and social environment in which basic beliefs and underlying ideologies are left to the discretion of the individual and his community.

Choice and volunteerism are the key components of a market of landscape visions, just as they are the attributes of a freemarket economy. But between the two market types, there is a crucial difference in the emphasis placed on choice and voluntarism. The markets that concern economists have traditionally focused on products and services for people. Although such markets can and do affect the environment (quite often for the worse), they are not designed to address issues relating to environmental health and ecological well-being. Moreover, they are often departures from the free-market ideal, being regulated by laws and policies aimed at specific national goals. To the extent that choice and voluntarism are valued and relied upon, it is because they enhance society, not because they enrich nature.

The new resource economics (NRE), however, argues that traditional markets can serve the needs of the environment when government regulation is minimal and when property rights are identifiable, enforceable, and transferable. Under those conditions, it insists, incentives will exist to channel human action in more environmentally desirable directions. People will be more responsible toward the land because they will bear the financial risks of bad management and assume the potential benefits of superior management. Adam Smith's "invisible hand" will make choice and voluntarism the unwitting handmaidens of ecological good.

A growing body of evidence suggests that the NRE is right, that markets work for the environment when people are accountable and when human action is guided by choice and voluntarism. A market of landscape visions starts with those assumptions but goes one step further. It harnesses choice and voluntarism directly to the fate of the environment and its ecology. What counts is that people have the *opportunity* to ply their dreams where it matters most, on the land. Better incentives to deal kindly with nature are simply inadequate to correct all the problems that plague the federal estate. They might motivate ranchers to graze their lands more carefully; they might encourage agencies to be more cost-effective and they might inspire other land users to be more conscientious of the lands they rely on for recreation. But incentives alone would not unleash the potential that inevitably comes with having many landscape visions. To crack the political hegemony that rules the federal range, more than incentives is needed. The answer is diversity.

Diversity is the product of a market of landscape visions. Many minds and many visions generate the wealth of information needed to help keep environments healthy and ecological systems viable. And as long as those minds and visions operate by choice and through voluntary means, the market of landscape visions can become a proving ground. Like the services and products in traditional markets, which come and go according to how well they satisfy consumers, landscape visions will rise and fall to the extent that they meet the environmental and ecological demands of the land. There will be no need for taxpayer bailouts. Unworkable visions—like subsidized grazing and price-supported agriculture—will cease to exist. Rushing in to fill the vacuum left by failed visions will be those that are gentler to the land and more responsive to the needs of people.

In a very real sense, ecology and economics converge in the marketplace of landscape visions. The biological world of nature and the social universe of people meld together in the arena of many competing visions. And it is only proper that they should. Healthy landscapes and free markets are two sides of the same coin; one is the biological and the other is the human face of self-regulating ecological systems. Moreover, a concern for efficiency and conservation is central to both the economic and the ecological perspectives and establishes common ground between the two. Energy and information, whether in the currency of dollars, ideas, species, or sunlight, are stewarded by man and nature alike. Biological and economic systems must make do as best they can with the limited resources they have or face decline and death.

Ecology and economics (at least free-market economics) share an even greater affinity in diversity. The economic power of free markets, like the ecological strength of natural communities, comes from the profusion of diversity that emanates from both. Just as a diverse economy insulates a city or region from the full brunt of economic shock, so also does a diversity of species and habitats insulate landscapes from the full biological turmoil of environmental change. More important, diversity creates options. Consumers in free markets, when faced with a shortage of some vital product, are almost always able to find satisfactory substitutes. Likewise, deer or elk, when faced with the loss of favored forage due to disease or insects, are able to find substitute feed.

The allure of a market of landscape visions is that it unites the common features of ecology and economics under a single metaphoric roof. Landscape visions that are unfettered by state regulation and not shielded from the lessons of nature by subsidies and political intrusions will almost always offer more to man and nature than will single, encompassing visions. The presence of many visions is, in fact, as crucial to the health and soundness of the environment as are the nonhuman factors of soil, water, plants, and animals. Above all, a diversity of visions provides a modicum of assurance that human needs can be met while the integrity of the natural world is maintained or enhanced. A market of landscape visions, like the final stage of ecological integration at the level of the total human environment, is the interface between people and the land. There, man and nature work out their relations, for better or worse.

On the western range, those relations have been destructive. The evidence is overwhelming that the single visions that have imposed the policy hegemony of the environmental welfare state have been unworkable and ecologically flawed. There is, it would seem, no other direction to go but toward free and unfettered landscape visions—toward the marketplace, in which each individual and community decides how best to live with the land and nature becomes the final arbiter of ecological right and wrong. Such a direction leads to what Robert Nozick, in *Anarchy, State and Utopia*, calls "a framework for utopia." But to arrive at that point, where freedom and openness guide human action, conditions must be met.

For citizens and their communities to become fountainheads of diversity on public lands, power and control must be devolved. In the past, federal policy and land bureaucracy have encroached on local sovereignty and have negated whatever contributions the diversity of many minds and visions has had to offer. Laws, regulations, and policies requiring public input into Forest Service and BLM planning have forced land agencies to listen, but they have not made citizens and their communities masters in their own lands. The ecological possibility of many minds—the promise and potential of their creativity, culture, and visions—has been lost for want of the means of implementation: power and control.

Power and control translate potential human diversity into maximum ecological benefit when visions can be tried on landscapes where individuals and their communities are both responsible and accountable for what they do. This is the essence of a market of landscape visions. It does not mean that lands must be owned in the traditional sense or that property rights must be vested in the hands of single individuals. It requires only that people have secure control over the landscapes on which their visions are to be tested and that such control be attained by peaceful rather than forceful means.

Other conditions must also be met to ensure the workings of a market of landscape visions. In particular, the information that is vital to making visions work must be abundant, accessible, and sought after. Abundance of information, of course, is a natural outcome of a community of many minds and many visions. Opening the western range to more players than a handful of bureaucracies and a few powerful lobbying groups should expand ideas and information manyfold over what exists today. But making information accessible and sought after is another matter. In part, it comes with the expansion of opportunity and the inclusion of more players. Yet what facilitates it most is the removal of obstacles. Markets of information—or of visions—must be freed of the distortions that subsidies and political intrusions inevitably bring. People will be more likely to seek out superior information, and should have greater success in obtaining it, when spared the disincentives of federal handouts and freed of the bureaucratic middlemen who stand between themselves and their land. If these guidelines—decentralization of power, establishment of local control, and expansion of accessible information—are followed, the shortcomings and failures of intolerant visions will, at the very least, be sidestepped. At the most, those guidelines will help bring out the best of human nature, nurturing peace and harmony between people and the lands of the federal range.

The Forest Service and the BLM are obstacles to a market of landscape visions. They are the technologies of an age of arrogance, when elitism ruled the politics of public lands. And they are obsolete. Freeman Dyson, in his collection of essays titled *Infinite in All Directions,* offers a description of technological evolution that fits today's land agencies remarkably well. "During its phase of rapid growth and spectacular success," he notes, a technology "is usually small, quick and agile." As it ages, "it becomes settled and conservative, prevented by the inertia of size from reacting quickly to sudden shocks." Finally, Dyson writes, "when a technology has grown so big and sluggish that it can no longer bend with the winds of change, it is ripe for extinction." The Forest Service and the BLM are technologies that no longer bend with the wind.

Today, the Forest Service and the BLM are entangled in a web of laws, policies, and administrative requirements. Their time and budgets are spent increasingly on internal affairs and the *procedures* of land management. Layers of bureaucracy compounded with layers of competing interest groups have made land stewardship a small item on the agenda of public-land management. Aldo Leopold's fear that government conservation might share the fate of the mastodon is coming true. Land agencies are succumbing to the mass of their bureaucracies and the limits of their visions.

It is time to recognize that nature on the western range is too complex to be orchestrated by mammoth agencies or a handful of special interest groups. It is time to move beyond Pinchot's elite and Muir's righteous. By replacing the disproven technologies of centralized planning with a market of landscape visions, federal lands will reap the economic and ecological benefits of a free society and gain from the diversity of many minds and many visions.

Expanding the number of active players on the deserts, grasslands, and forests of the western range will do three things. First, it will buffer the environment against ill-advised visions. Human actions that are detrimental to the land will be limited in space and time. Fewer acres will be disturbed for much shorter periods of time. There will no longer be environmental mistakes on the scale of the homestead acts and federal grazing policies. Second, the possibility that highly desirable landscapes will be preserved or re-created will increase as more minds and visions find and try environmentally superior ideas. Third, the dreams and ambitions of all Americans will have more elbow room. There will be ample opportunities—landscape opportunities—for people to seek and fulfill their visions of how best to live on the western range.

To appreciate the significance of landscape opportunities, picture the "viable ecological space" of chapter 11 as the area bounded by an imaginary cube. Within the cube are any number of smaller spaces corresponding to the array of landscape possibilities in which people and nature can coexist in long-term harmony. These "subsets of the ecological space" may include such varied examples as an industrial or metropolitan complex, a wildlife preserve, or a well-managed farm. What is common to each of these landscape possibilities is that they can be sustained indefinitely. They are viable because they are self-supporting, and they are stable because they exist within the limits and constraints of their respective environments. Public-land grazing has never met any of these criteria—nor have the other activities on federal lands.

The point is that realistic landscape opportunities are finite, occurring within real but largely unexplored and untapped ecological spaces. The single visions that have dominated the western range have consistently fallen outside those spaces. They have been able to continue for so long only because taxpayers have paid the bill—and because the political clout needed to change public-land management has been divided and diluted by the maneuvering of land agencies and the bickering of special interest groups.

There is, unfortunately, no guarantee that a market of landscape visions will generate opportunities that fall consistently within the ecological cube. But there is certainty on three counts. The first is that visions that seek impossible landscapes are doomed to failure. Bereft of the forced generosity of American taxpayers and the politics of special interest groups, they must sink or swim. Second, a market of landscape visions virtually ensures that more rather than fewer of the cube's viable landscapes will be explored and tapped by those who wish to mix their labor and love with the land. Enough visions will find a place to flourish within the imaginary cube that the western range will at last meet the expectations of all Americans, not merely a privileged few. Opportunity will replace bureaucratic fiat, and diversity will supplant the visionary state.

Third, and most significant, a market of landscape visions will enlist all Americans in the destiny of their western lands. Today, a handful of trained experts and impassioned special interests exercise unchallenged dominion over one-third of the nation's land. Tomorrow, a market of landscape visions could open the western range to the historically disenfranchised. More people than ever would become part of the future of the nation's landed wealth. And even more people, through the invisible hand of the marketplace, would make their opinions heard. Visionaries and their visions, when focused on federal lands, would have to pay attention to more than the many messages of nature; they would have to listen and attend to the many voices of the American people.

Public-land ranchers would be less likely to overgraze their lands, or even to graze them at all, if the cues of the marketplace carried greater persuasion than the logic of the permit system or the dictates of bureaucracies. Stockmen would be able to see that their meadows and streams had value other than as feed for sheep and water for cattle. They would be able to respond to the wishes of the American public by doing things prohibited to them for over a century. And even if they did not, others with greater insight and ambition would. Under a market of landscape visions, the federal range would no longer be the protected province of ranchers and their livestock. Indeed, every acre of the Forest Service and the BLM estate would be freed from the multiple use mandates that have empowered special interest groups for decades to log, mine, ranch, and four wheel drive the nation's forests and rangelands into environmental depletion. There would be abundant room for other visions, ensuring that Americans would get what they increasingly want: open space, recreation, wildlife, and escape. People would gain, wildlife would benefit, and the land would blossom in almost infinite diversity.

Arising from the market of landscape visions is one truth: that ecological good as defined by Leopold's axiom is virtually indeterminate. There is no final answer on what is environmentally and ecologically proper. Within the bounds of the imaginary ecological cube or on the surface of healthy and thriving landscapes, what constitutes ecological good is as much a matter of opinion as it is a subject of science. If a landscape is viable—if a vision "tends to preserve the integrity, stability, and beauty of the biotic community"—then it is, by Leopold's test, right. On the western range, this means that multiple possibilities rather than single solutions will determine the destiny of the land and its people.

One crucially important sidelight to this "truth" of indeterminacy is that the form or structure of visions and the landscapes they forge is less important than the way in which they are realized. In other words, what matters is not the constellation of visions and the multiple landscapes that ultimately find sanctuary on federal lands. What counts is how people pursue their visions and, most important, how responsive their visions are to the ecological demands of the land and its varied life.

Process, in the final analysis, is what a market of landscape visions is all about. It entails hardly an iota of ideology except the simple dictum that the affairs of man and nature are best left to their own devices, free from the political intrusions that have for so long forced them down unwelcome and shortsighted paths. The trace of ideology that colors the market process does not, and cannot, dictate what should or should not be done with the lands of the western range. A market of landscape visions and its ounce of ideology merely provide the environment of tolerance and freedom in which visions can be mixed with the land. But mostly, they form the tribunal where visions are judged against reality and where visionaries are held accountable to society and nature. The many verdicts passed down by this court drive the process of landscape visions inexorably in the direction of diversity.

Yet not even diversity is the ultimate test of a market of landscape visions. The presence of many species and many visions is important, but importance does not lie in the aesthetic potential diversity offers, it lies in the ecological process it sustains. Everything comes back to process. Diversity is significant not because it offers a finished portrait of how nature should look but because it offers the way and means by which people can live in harmony with the environment. That is the lasting harvest of a market of landscape visions.

Democratization of the Western Range

An infinite number of factors can complicate the task of change and reform. This is particularly true for the western range. In the hundred and thirty years since the first homestead act, public lands have become encumbered by special interest claims and by injustices that call out for immediate attention. Ranchers and miners who see the federal estate as their personal domain proclaim their rights to its forage and minerals in the name of archaic and ecologically unsound laws. Logging communities and timber mills that have historical ties of dependence to national forests make compelling moral, if not legal, claims to the timber resources of public lands. And those Americans who want to use public lands for something other than minerals, beef, and timber have a long list of grievances. In their minds, they have been denied the legacy of the western range.

Given the complexity of the legal status of public lands, one must decide how best to address the region's woes. One solution is to dive headfirst into the complexity of laws, rights, claims, and injustices that weigh heavily on today's federal range. One could attempt to correct every law, address every grievance, and respect every right and claim. But by the time such a Herculean task were completed, the solution might well be more cumbersome than the original problem.

A simpler, cleaner approach is to recognize that what exists is beyond salvage. Cosmetic changes just will not work. George Coggins's idea of reforming the BLM by remaking it in the image of the Forest Service would only intensify the powers of a disproven and failed management monoculture. Randal O'Toole's proposal to reform the Forest Service by exposing individual forests to the forces of the marketplace would be only a half-step toward a market of landscape visions. Bureaucracies would still be entrenched on soil that is rightfully that of all citizens.

Environmentalist demands that multiple use be overhauled to give more standing to nontraditional values and uses on federal lands would only perpetuate more of the same mismanagement. Worst of all, legislative schemes like the proposed American Heritage Trust Act would pump billions of federal dollars into expanding the domain of land management bureaucracies. Not only would more lands be subject to the fate of the western commons, but people and nature would also be driven further apart. A land ethic based on living with the land would become that much less likely as layers of bureaucracy erected higher and mightier walls between Americans and their landed birthright.

What is needed on the western range is reform that strikes at the heart of the problem, not at the endless procession of symptoms that have come and gone in the region's tragic history. Meaningful reform must address the environmental harm of the past, promising something more hopeful than mediocrity and offering something better than stale visions and bureaucratic management. Above all, effective reform must address the inequity and injustice that have shrouded the federal range since it was opened to settlement.

Democracy lost is the legacy of past visions. Restoring that legacy is the aim of a market of landscape visions. What matters most is that reform tap the democratic sentiment that infuses the federal estate and direct it toward expanding opportunities for all Americans—making certain that this time, all citizens, not merely the wealthiest, most ambitious, best educated, and most righteous, have a role and place in the destiny of he western range. This means that public lands should no longer serve the interests of a few or suffer the consequences of their intolerant visions. It means that many minds and many visions must be given a chance to have their democratic say.

Change for the better is within reach if the fateful step is taken toward real public ownership of the federal estate—toward what amounts to democratization of the western range. Democratization requires creating a level playing field, where visions are free to flourish and citizens are free to pursue them. There are, I imagine, any number of ways to bring democracy to the western range, to reach at last the beginning point of a market of landscape visions. What I propose, however, is simply this: that the public lands managed by the Forest Service and the BLM be given back to the American people.

In 1982, Vernon L. Smith, professor of economics at the University of Arizona, wrote an intriguing article, "On Divestiture and the Creation of Property Rights in Public Lands," for the *Cato Journal*. Seven years later, as I traveled through the West, meeting and interviewing the people whose stories make up this book, I met Professor Smith. We discussed a wide range of ideas, but we always came back to his article and how it might be fashioned into a reform proposal in concert with the themes of democracy and the workings of many visions. What we concluded, and what formed in my mind in subsequent months, took me increasingly afield from his original plan. But one crucial feature of that plan stuck with me: that Americans were shareholders in the public lands and that the shares they held were the key to democratizing the western range.

With that thought in mind, I wondered, what if . . . what if those shares were made real and tangible, and what if they could then be used by people to create the environment for a market of landscape visions? The possibilities were exhilarating and endless. Here lay one path to reform, a direction toward an explosion of visions, tolerance, and diversity on the western range. And it was possible. It could be done in such a way that special interest groups, federal agencies, and the silent majority of Americans divorced from the fate of federal lands could benefit. Most of all, it would redress a long history of environmental trespass and provide the possibility of escaping the closing circle of an uncontrolled and uncared for western commons.

The proposal is simple and straightforward. Over a twenty-year period—the start and finish to be set by statute—the federal government would be required to divest itself of the surface rights to all lands managed by the Forest Service and the BLM. Five of those years would be set aside for laying the groundwork for what would be the most sweeping land reform in American history. The remaining fifteen years would be spent in the actual transfer of federal lands from managing agencies to an array of citizens, citizen groups, and local communities.

For simplicity's sake, federal lands managed by the National Park Service, the U.S. Fish and Wildlife Service, and other, less visible, agencies would be exempt, along with the subsurface estate of minerals and energy managed by the BLM. Parklands and refuges, for example, hold special meaning and significance for many Americans. Their inclusion with Forest Service and BLM lands would cloud the ecological issue of democratization with an excessive emotional outcry. Similarly, the subsurface estate is seen by many as being vital to the nation's well-being. To make it a key part of a plan of divestiture would pit perceived national interests against needed environmental reform.

To calm the fears of those who have already leaped to the conclusion that my proposal is merely a sellout of public lands to people wealthy enough to acquire them, I offer this reassurance. In the scenario to be laid out in the following pages, there would be no sudden blossoming of "For Sale" signs on federal property, no massive subdivision of the western range into private parcels and kingdoms, and no imminent takeover of public lands by foreign investors. Quite the contrary.

Every American holding a social security number at the time the proposal is implemented would receive one hundred shares in America's public lands. American citizens would be the immediate beneficiaries of divestiture. Each would be given a claim to the federal range and would then have the opportunity to determine its fate.

Each shareholder would have three options. The first would be to allow his or her shares to expire by not applying them against parcels of land before the end of the twenty-year period. This is unlikely, given the value that would be attached to them. For it would be shares, not dollars, that would determine how public lands would be democratized and in what ways they would be divested from bureaucracies to citizens. The other two options would require action. Americans would have to either sell their shares to others or apply the shares to the purchase of public lands. *All* Forest Service and BLM lands would, by law, be divested by the end of the twenty-year period. Unused shares would be, at the very least, lost income and, at the most, lost opportunity.

Whichever option people chose, one inviolable rule would hold sway: Only those individuals, groups, or communities (including towns, cities, and counties) holding shares would be allowed to negotiate in the marketplace of Forest Service and BLM lands. National and state governments would be expressly prohibited by law from holding or acquiring shares—or, for that matter, from holding or acquiring interests in shares. Retirement of federal lands would be the business of the American people, not the concern of their distant governments. The only active role to be played by the federal government would be in the transfer and interim management of public lands.

All shares would be electronically credited to individual tax accounts by the Internal Revenue Service. And only the IRS would have the power to move shares between accounts as citizens sold them for cash or exchanged them for land. Moreover, the Forest Service and the BLM would be given the task of surveying and appraising public lands and the public and private improvements existing within their boundaries. These inventory and surveying tasks, along with a one-year interim period for publicizing the divestiture plan and for educating the public on its operation, would last approximately five years. At the end of those five years, shares would be allotted to all citizens and a fifteen-year period would be set aside to transfer public lands from the bureaucratic sector to the public sector.

In addition, the land agencies would be directed to continue managing public lands for as long as they remained under federal control—at most twenty years after the passage of enabling legislation. During that period, there could be a hiring freeze within the Forest Service and the BLM. Staff remaining after the completion of the program could be given the option of early retirement or continued service in some other federal agency.

Citizens having legal claims to public lands and public resources (such as ranchers, loggers, and miners) would be given special consideration only to the extent that their leases, permits, and contracts would be honored during the plan's twenty-year transition period. Moreover, existing laws and policies governing licensed uses of public lands and resources would remain in effect for the duration, enforced by the Forest Service and the BLM.

Public-land ranchers would be allowed to graze livestock at current grazing fees within the existing constraints of public land law and management. Timber sales would be permitted to continue so long as harvests were scheduled within the twenty-year span and so long as standards already set by long-term Forest Service planning documents were followed. Energy and mineral leases would be honored up to the last day of the twentieth year. After that date, companies would have to negotiate with surface owners for the right to continue their below-ground activities. The surface estate would reign supreme. And after twenty years, there would be no more energy and mineral extraction, public-land grazing, or timber harvests on Forest Service and BLM lands. There would be no Forest Service and BLM lands left.

The mechanics of transferring federal lands into the hands of citizens would be handled by the free market. People wishing to acquire particular tracts would have to buy their shares on the stock exchange—again, with the IRS playing the role of middleman. It would not matter which shares they bought, since none of the shares would be tied to specific parcels of land. All that would count would be accumulating enough shares to make successful bids. For stock sellers, the process would be equally straightforward. Their tax accounts would be debited one or more shares and credited with the dollar amount set by that day's market transaction. And only the market value of each persons original shares (if sold) and the profit reaped from buying and selling the shares of others would be taxable. Tax receipts collected in this way could be earmarked to help pay the costs of the program.

Original shares used to acquire land, or simply allowed to expire, would be tax-exempt. More important, shares donated to nonprofit organizations—such as environmental groups—would be tax deductible. This could be accomplished in one of two ways. The market value of the donated shares could be subtracted from taxable net income or, more preferably, deducted directly from one's tax liability. In the second case, tax credits could be provided to citizens whose income was below taxable levels. The obvious benefit of doing this would be that citizens who might otherwise be reluctant to donate their shares to community or nonprofit organizations would have the option of doing so without bearing what could be a significant financial loss.

The transfer of discrete parcels of land could be handled in any number of ways. Buyers could initiate the process or agencies could proceed in some systematic manner consistent with keeping costs down while meeting the fifteen-year deadline that would follow interim surveys, appraisals, and publicity. In any event, minimum land areas would have to be set for disposal to ensure that administrative expenses did not get out of hand and to avoid divvying up the federal range into ecologically unsound parcels—as was done initially with the homestead acts.

Grazing allotments, some combination of them, or basic administrative units like Forest Service ranger districts and BLM resource areas might be used as the basis for identifying such land parcels. Because they already exist and because their boundaries often follow natural breaks in the landscape, their use would be convenient and ecologically sound. Only in the instance of small, isolated parcels of federal land might minimum size requirements be waived. Already, such scattered islands of the public estate have economic importance and ecological significance only to the extent that they are part of more substantial surrounding private or nonfederal holdings. It would be only natural for them to become permanent parts of those holdings.

Once a land area were identified and marked for transfer, notice of its impending sale would be published in the *Federal Register*. Local realtors and banks would work with the two land agencies by helping with surveys, inventories, and appraisals; by providing basic banking and real estate services to prospective buyers; and by handling the details of land auctions. Moreover, the public-land surveys, inventories, and appraisals made by local business and government officials could be used to set an initial monetary value on lands proposed for transfer or simply to provide information to potential bidders.

The marketplace would determine the final price of the land. At a predetermined time, buyers would convene, either physically or through the wonders of electronics. The market, not the government, would set the monetary value of shares and determine by open and competitive bidding whose landscape visions would prevail. And through such means as prudent people—shareholders holding on to their shares in anticipation of higher prices—and futures or options markets, shares would be distributed relatively evenly across the program horizon of fifteen years. The natural workings of a market of landscape visions would ensure that every acre of Forest Service and BLM land would be transferred into the hands of citizens as mandated by federal statute.

All bidders would be treated equally—there would be no right of first refusal. The only advantage some individuals or groups might have would lie in physical assets they owned or controlled on specific parcels of federal land. Public-land ranchers, for example, would receive credit for the discounted value of privately owned improvements such as fences and pipelines and for water rights filed with and recognized by the appropriate state authorities. During the bidding process of course, they would have to follow the same rules as everyone else. To control their historical grazing lands, they would have to outbid their competitors. If they succeeded, the value of their physical improvements and water rights would be tallied in the net shares debited from their IRS account. If they failed, they would be compensated for property lost.

Surface owners would have the right to enjoin federal lessees from extracting minerals and energy lying below their newly acquired lands following the plan's twenty-year transition period. A skeleton BLM staff would remain to administer the subsurface estate and to facilitate negotiations among landowners, miners, and energy developers. But there is no reason why the subsurface estate could not be dealt with in a manner similar to that for surface lands. Once democratization of the surface estate were complete, it would be only reasonable to proceed with divestiture of the rights that lie below. By that time, concerns of national interest might have given way to realization that free people and free markets *are* the country's best interest.

There is no way to tell what the landscapes of the federal range might look like at the end of the twenty-year program. But one thing is certain: All Americans would have had an *equal opportunity* to benefit from lands that are, by law and tradition, their birthright. Even those who might choose not to mix their visions with the land—to apply their shares to concrete parcels of the western range—would at least have been given the chance. And they would, in any case, enjoy the monetary dividend of having been a partner and shareholder in the federal estate. Indeed, families who sell their shares could expect a modest windfall of hundreds to thousands of dollars.

For those who decide to do something with their shares other than cash them in, the possibilities would be unlimited. Stockmen would have the option to purchase their ranches, and ownership would mean that they alone would be accountable and responsible for stewarding and protecting their lands. It would give them the opportunity to try different approaches to management and to explore new uses of their rangelands. They would be able to make a living off their ranches in ways that could be more beneficial to society and more gentle to plants and animals. Most important, the day of the welfare rancher would be over.

There would no longer be government subsidies to bail out uncaring or careless people whose primary concern lies with how much they can take from the land. Indeed, only stockmen committed to good stewardship would find a lasting home on a decentralized western range. And men and women from many different walks of life would have the chance to do something other than raise livestock on arid lands. In many cases, the values to be captured from public lands—such as traditional ways of living and the aesthetics of wild places—would not give the kinds of monetary return that profit-conscious investors seek. For that reason, ample enough opportunity would exist for people like Dayton Hyde to muster their resources and to create landscapes for wildlife, fisheries, and recreation.

Much of the federal range would become the domain of associations and communities. Single individuals or large for-profit corporations would simply lack the resources or the business interest to acquire many of the most desirable public lands—the landscapes holding the greatest promise for recreation, wildlife, and wilderness and the least potential for profitable logging and grazing. Moreover, even if those lands held economically valuable forage and timber resources (minerals and energy resources are excluded from the initial phase of divestiture), and even if individuals and corporations could raise substantial capital, there would still be no guarantee that they could obtain shares at reasonable prices. Just as wealthy individuals and corporations have not monopolized private lands in the United States in the past, it is just as likely that they would not strive to monopolize divested public lands in the future. In contrast, associations and communities would be able to tap the enormous wealth of shares held by their members and apply them toward commonly held goals. By the sheer weight of membership alone, they would be the biggest winners in the reshuffling of federal lands from bureaucracies to the American people.

Environmentalists—ranging from conservationists to wildlife enthusiasts to wilderness preservationists—would have the opportunity of a lifetime. Their organizations would be free to solicit tax-deductible shares from members and from other citizens supporting their visions of stewardship and protection. They could harness that public support to the cause of environmental good—all made possible because people's shares, not dollars, would control the destiny of the western range. They would be able to focus their efforts and shares where they might be most effective, in the acquisition of wilderness and in the making of wildlife sanctuaries. And the results would be a vision of environmental good defined by them, not by bureaucracy and special interest politics. They would be responsible and accountable for the land, bearing the costs of their errors and reaping the benefits of their successes.

Voluntary associations of citizens would also enjoy unparalleled opportunity on the western range. Sportsmen's clubs and bird-watchers' societies would be able to control landscapes crucial to their interests and their visions. They could establish public corporations in which members who donated shares of stock would be the true owners of the land. Even local communities would find new and exciting options. Towns and counties might solicit shares from their citizens or offer local tax credits in exchange for shares to acquire valuable parklands, to provide a diversity of recreation, or to establish greenbelts and wildlife preserves. And for the multitude of groups and organizations that seek a place and role on the western range, there would be a ready pool of former Forest Service and BLM employees to help them manage and protect their newfound lands.

Ranchers wishing to hold on to their historical grazing lands but lacking sufficient shares might benefit from the awakening of public interest in public lands. For example, they could negotiate conservation easements with local citizens or representatives of larger environmental groups. In this way, all parties could pool their shares to the mutual benefit of each. Ranchers would be able to continue their life-style, and environmentalists would have the satisfaction of knowing that streams, wildlife, and unique landscapes would be protected forever.

Oil and timber companies might enter into similar alliances with citizen organizations and environmental groups. They could combine their shares with those of other interests to buy surface lands with the mutual understanding that resources could be extracted only so long as the ecological needs of the land were met. In some instances, restrictive covenants might be set by the legislation enabling divestiture and placed on lands having unique ecological value. Old-growth forests in the Northwest, habitat for the northern spotted owl, are good examples. Loggers and environmentalists alike would be free to make their competitive bids. The winners would have to abide by congressional deed restrictions, harnessing their visions to the needs of ancient trees and endangered owls. Timber could be cut and recreation developed so long as the overall ecological integrity of the forests remained intact.

Emerging from the market of landscape visions would be a pattern of landownership and control limited only by the imagination and energy of many minds and many visions. Private property would undoubtedly remain a major component on the western range, complementing the already substantial private holdings now in existence. And ranching and logging would still be part of the region's culture and natural history—though this time, they would be practiced in a manner more attentive to the needs of the environment and more in tune with the ecology of the land. But there would be a new wrinkle to the land, its people, and their collective future.

Across the width and breadth of what was once the federal range, an infinite array of decentralized "little commons" would spring forth. These would be lands collectively held and enjoyed by groups of various sizes and diverse interests. They would differ from the western commons of the past in one crucial feature. Their memberships would be able to protect them, wielding effective control over their use and ensuring that the right people would be accountable for their well-being. A commons that people could be part of and take pride in would at last take shape on the vast deserts, prairies, and timbered mountain ranges that lie west of the 100th meridian. Democratization would end the tragedy of the commons and open the land to its unexplored possibilities.

Unfortunately, the decision of whether or not democratization will be tried will be made in the arena of politics, not on the even playing field of a market of landscape visions. But if the plan should come to pass, the western range would at long last be freed of the rule of single visions and opened to the promise of many minds. The reign of special interests, whether livestock, timber or environmental, would be over. The destiny of the western range would be in the hands of many, not few—and it would, more often than not, entail a partnership among friends and neighbors and between communities and associations.

Divesting bureaucracy of its landed estate, however, is only the starting point for realizing the ecological and environmental potential of a market of landscape visions. The potential that comes with human diversity would evolve with time and patience, as the new custodians of the western range plied their visions, corrected their errors, and strove with single-mindedness toward environmental excellence. Lands and people historically divided by unsound laws, distant bureaucracies, and damaging multiple use policies would be reconciled in a crescendo of environmental energy and in a contagious outbreak of democratic enthusiasm. Landscapes of diversity would replace the ailing landscapes of the Forest Service and the BLM. And people and nature could find healthier and more harmonious ways to coexist on the western range.

The politics of conflict and the policies of mediocrity would give way to the peaceful process of the marketplace and the workings of tolerance and diversity. Land reform on an unprecedented scale could finally achieve what Jefferson envisioned but the state never allowed. The second American Revolution would complete what the first sought but could not attain: a virtuous republic of independent, caring, and responsible stewards of the western range.

THE FAIR TRADE FRAUD

James Bovard

Introduction

Americans' freedom and prosperity are being sacrificed on an altar of fair trade. Protectionists have wrapped themselves in a cloak of fairness, and each year they discover new moral pretexts to further restrict how American citizens may spend their paychecks. Fair trade is a moral delusion that could be leading to an economic catastrophe.

Congressmen are calling for an "economic war" with our trading partners. Starkly protectionist legislation has been passed in recent years by both the House and Senate, only to be stopped by presidential vetoes. American corporations are now running advertisements that seek to inflame hostility to foreign companies. "Fair trade" is widely perceived as a panacea for the U.S.'s international economic problems.

But, "fair trade" is one of the great intellectual frauds of the twentieth century. The louder politicians have demanded fair trade, the more U.S. trade policies have become a travesty of fairness. The U.S. government has created a trade lynch law that can convict foreign companies almost regardless of how they operate. Between 1980 and 1989, the U.S. Commerce Department reached a "not guilty" verdict in only 5 percent of its investigations of foreign dumping.[1] Over three thousand foreign companies have been penalized since 1980 for selling their products to Americans at prices lower than the U.S. government approved.

When politicians call for "fair trade" with foreigners, they routinely use a concept of fairness that is diametrically opposed to the word's normal usage. In exchanges between individuals in contract law—the test of fairness is the voluntary consent of each party to the bargain: "the free will which constitutes fair exchanges," as Sen. John Taylor wrote in 1822.[2] When politicians speak of unfair trade, they do not mean that buyers and sellers did not voluntarily agree, but that U.S. government officials disapprove of the bargains American citizens chose to make. Fair trade, as the term is now used, usually means government intervention to direct, control, or restrict trade. Fair trade means government officials deciding what Americans should be allowed to buy, and what prices they should be forced to pay. Fair trade is paternalism applied to international commerce. Fair trade means subjugating the economic interests of private citizens to the moral and political values of government policymakers.

Fair trade often consists of some politician or bureaucrat picking a number out of thin air and imposing it on foreign businesses and American consumers. Fair trade means that Jamaica is allowed to sell the U.S. only 970 gallons of ice cream a year, that Mexico is allowed to sell Americans only 35,292 bras a year, that Poland is allowed to ship us only 350 tons of alloy tool steel, that Haiti is allowed to sell the U.S. only 8,030 tons of sugar. Fair trade means permitting each American citizen to consume the equivalent of only one teaspoon of foreign ice cream per year, two foreign peanuts per year, and one pound of imported cheese per year. Fair trade means the U.S. government imposing import quotas on tampons, typing ribbons, tents, twine, table linen, tapestries, and ties. Fair trade means that the U.S. Congress can dictate over 8,000 different taxes on imports, with tariffs as high as 458%.

Fair trade is generating a new economic scholasticism. Thirteenth-century theologians debated the doctrine of the "just price." Today, U.S. Commerce Department employees spend their lives ensnaring foreign companies in quibbles over what is a used forklift, how a company disposed of wilted flowers, and how to account for the costs of storing frozen raspberries. The Commerce Department recently penalized a Japanese company for selling typewriters in the U.S. for a fraction of a penny less than in Japan.[3] A federal judge criticized American TV manufacturers for using American trade law to conduct an "economic war" against their Japanese competitors.[4]

American trade negotiators have exerted far more effort to close the U.S. market than to open foreign markets. Since 1980, the U.S. government has negotiated over 170 bilateral trade agreements to restrict exports to the United States. If a Third World nation's exports of a clothing item equal 1 percent or more of U.S. production, the U.S. government almost automatically restricts that nation's exports. U.S. trade law has turned incompetence into an entitlement, as any lagging American company has a right to seek relief from foreign competition. Foreign nations are increasingly denounced as unfair unless they provide "affirmative action" programs to force foreign businesses to buy more American products.

Webster's *New World Dictionary* defines "fair" as "just and honest; impartial; unprejudiced." Yet, most of the foreign trade practices deemed to be unfair are not considered unfair if done by the U.S. government or by an American company. U.S. government officials loudly denounce Japan's beef import quota, though the U.S. also imposes import quotas on Australian and Argentine beef. The U.S. levied an import surtax on Thai rice in 1986 because of a small Thai government rice subsidythough the U.S. government was simultaneously providing a subsidy over a hundred times larger to American rice growers.[5] American trade law requires foreign companies to earn a significantly higher profit than American companies—or else the foreign companies are penalized as if they were selling at a loss. In federal unfair trade investigations, foreign companies are automatically assumed to be lying and American companies are automatically assumed to be telling the truth. The Commerce Department has used information provided by American firms to punish foreign competitors even when it knows that the allegations from the American firms are incorrect or false.

Fair trade consists largely of the U.S. government devising new ways to protect American consumers against the scourge of low prices. The U.S. government does not penalize foreign companies for charging high prices—only for charging low prices. Imported clothing that is priced lower than U.S. clothing is automatically assumed to threaten to disrupt the U.S. market. Fair trade aims not to safeguard competition, but to enrich American competitors. The most common foreign "unfair trade practice" is producing a better product at a lower price. In a nation with hundreds of federal, state, and local consumer protection agencies, consumers are explicitly denied a role in most trade proceedings of the U.S. International Trade Commission and Commerce Department.

Federal trade policy is increasingly sacrificing some industries to other industries. American manufacturers have been forced to beg Commerce Department officials for each ton of specialty steel they are allowed to import. The number of American manufacturing jobs destroyed since 1980 by sugar import quotas exceeds the total number of sugar farmers in the U.S.

American politicians are profiteering on allegations of foreign unfairness. For American trade policy, need is the basis of right, and political campaign contributions are the measure of need. Congressmen's solution to the problem of unfair foreigners is almost always to increase their own power over what Americans are allowed to buy. Every restriction on foreign competition means an increase in political control over the American consumer. And to control what a person is allowed to buy is indirectly to control how a person lives.

Though complaints about unfair trade are at a historic high, American protectionists have always found some moral pretext to denounce imports. In the 1820s, protectionists proclaimed that trade between England and America could not be fair because England was advanced and America was comparatively backward. In the 1870s, protectionists announced that trade between America and Latin America could not be fair because America was comparatively rich while Latin American countries were poor. In the 1880s, protectionists warned that trade could not be fair if the interest rate among the trading nations differed by more than 2 percent.[6] In 1922, Congress effectively defined "unfair competition" as any foreign cost of production advantage that existed for any reason on any product.[7]

In practice, fair trade means protectionism. Yet, every trade barrier undermines the productivity of capital and labor throughout the economy. A 1979 Treasury Department study estimated that trade barriers routinely cost American consumers eight to ten times as much as they benefit American producers.[8] A 1984 Federal Trade Commission study estimated that tariffs cost the American economy $81.00 for every $1.00 of adjustment costs saved.[9] Restrictions on clothing and textile imports cost consumers $ 1.00 for each 1 cent of increased earnings of American textile and clothing workers.[10] According to the Institute for International Economics, trade barriers are costing American consumers $80 billion a year—equal to over $1,200 per family.[11]

Conclusion

The myth of fair trade is that politicians and bureaucrats are fairer than markets that government coercion and restriction can create a fairer result than voluntary agreement and that prosperity is best achieved by arbitrary political manipulation, rather than allowing each individual and company to pursue their own interest. Government cannot make trade more fair by making it less free.

Our great-grandchildren may look back at the trade wars of the twentieth century with the same contempt that many people today look at the religious wars of the seventeenth century as a senseless conflict over issues that grown men should not fight about. Every voluntary trade transaction is mutually beneficial, otherwise the parties would not agree to trade. Most trade wars consist of politicians turning a squabble over the division of benefits into a schism that makes all the nations involved losers.

Many people consider the idea of fair trade in the abstract and judge trade policy simply by the question of whether fairness in itself is a good or bad thing. We need to understand the contrast between the ideals and the realities of fair trade. Fair trade can only be as fair as the trade laws and the restrictions that governments proclaim in the name of fairness. The best way to understand fair trade is to examine how our trade laws, trade agreements, and trade restrictions actually operate.

We will examine the U.S. tariff code, import quotas, how the dumping law operates, the U.S. government's judgments on foreign subsidies, the U.S. International Trade Commission's role in unfair trade investigations, the failure of trade retaliation, the nature of political control of trade, and the moral essence of trade restraints.

Notes

1. U.S. Congress, Senate Finance Committee, *Remedies Against Dumping of Imports*, July 18, 1986 (Washington: Government Printing Office, 1986), p. 37. (Testimony of Gilbert Kaplan). Also, see U.S. International Trade Commission, *Operations of the Trade Agreements Program,* annual reports 1987-1989.

2. John Taylor, *Tyranny Unmasked* (Washington: Davis and Force, 1822), p. 38.

3. *Federal Register,* November 13, 1989, p. 47249.

4. *Zenith Radio Corp. v. Matsushita Elec. Indus. Co.*, 513 F. Supp. 1100 (1981), p. 1333.

5. *Federal Register*, April 9, 1986, p. 12356.

6. William Graham Sumner, *Protectionism* (New York: Henry Holt & Co., 1888), p. 42.

7. E.E. Schattschneider, *Politics, Pressure, and the Tariff* (New York: Prentice Hall, 1935), p. 69.

8. Dave Larsons, "The Cost of Import Protection in the United States," U.S. Treasury Department, 1979; cited in Michael Finger, H. Keith Hall, and Douglas Nelson, "The Political Economy of Administrative Protectionism," *American Economic Review*, Vol. 72, No. 3, June 1982, p. 453.

9. David Tarr and Morris Morkre, "Aggregate Cost to the United States of Tariffs and Quotas in Imports," Federal Trade Commission, 1984.

10. Martin Wolf, "Why Voluntary Export Restraints? An Historical Analysis," *The World Economy*, 12, no. 3, September 1989, p. 284. Wolf was citing a 1984 study by the Trade Policy Research Centre.

11. Paul Blustein, "Unfair Traders: Does the U.S. Have Room to Talk?," *Washington Post,* May 24, 1989.

TARIFFS AND OTHER BORDER LAND MINES

James Bovard

The U.S. tariff code is the accumulated junk heap of over a hundred years of political payoffs and kickbacks. In 1790, the Tariff Code consisted of a single sheet of rates posted at U.S. Custom Houses; now, our tariff code occupies two hefty volumes with 8,753 different rates, a blizzard of arbitrary discriminations against and among products. This is equivalent to over 8,000 different industrial policies and—8,000 different entitlement programs for protected domestic industries.

The U.S. has the best tariff code that American industry could buy. While the average tariff is now around 5%, some tariffs are still in the stratosphere. Low-priced watch parts are hit with a 151.2% tariff,[1] tobacco stems must pay a 458.3% tariff,[2] and tariffs on some shoe imports are 67%.[3] The tariff code is a precise mathematical measure of the historical-political clout of various Washington lobbies.

The U.S. government complements the thousands of different tariff categories with constant revisions of its official definitions of products. This makes importing an especially exciting business. And the Customs Service in recent years appears intent on solving the federal budget deficit by increasing its arbitrary confiscations of imported goods.

Uplifting the Downtrodden

The U.S . Tariff Code is devoted to encouraging the poor to raise their standard of living. If someone buys an imported plastic school satchel, he pays a 20% duty.[4] But if he buys a school satchel made of reptile leather, he pays only a 4.7% duty. Footwear with outer soles of rubber or plastic, valued at not over $3 pair, is tariffed at 48%; but if it is valued over $12, the tariff is only 20%. Soda lime drinking glasses valued at less than 30 cents carry a 38% tariff; if valued over $5, the tariff is only 7.2%. Cheap jewelry, imported in lots worth less than $18 a dozen, is tariffed at 27.5%, while gold necklaces pay only 6.5%.

Mink furs are duty free. And with the money a mother saves on her mink, maybe she can afford a polyester sweater for her baby—which carries a 34.6% tariff. Lobster is duty free; with the savings, struggling parents may be able to afford infant food preparations, which carry a 17.2% tariff. Orange juice carries a 40% tariff, but Perrier water pays only 0.8%. Mushroom imports pay 11 cents a kilogram plus 25% ad valorem. But, happily, truffles are duty free.

Cheap brandy—valued at less than $2.38 a liter—is tariffed at 41.9%. Brandy valued between $2.38 and $3.43 a liter is tariffed at 9.6%, while the highest quality brandy pays only a 1.2% tariff. But, on imitation brandy the Customs Service levies a 97.7% tariff. This tariff policy has helped persuade street people to stop drinking imitation brandy.

Vice President Thomas Marshall observed in 1920, "What this country needs is a good five-cent cigar."[5] Regrettably, cigar tariffs are class warfare at its worst. Cigars valued at less than 15 cents each are tariffed at 23.6%, while cigars worth over 23 cents pay a tariff of only 7.0%.

America's tariff makers perceive the vast differences between similar products that ordinary mortals miss. The tariff on duck liver is sixteen times higher than the tariff on goose liver. The tariff on grape wine with low alcoholic content is six times higher than the tariff on grape wine with high alcoholic content. The tariff on vodka worth less than $2.05 a liter is thirteen times higher than the tariff on higher-priced vodka. Gjetost cheese, made from goat's milk, pays a 6.5% tariff, while goya cheese, made from cow's milk, pays a 25% tariff. (This proves that the dairy lobby is stronger than the goat lobby).

Looking at the tariff code, one might conclude that most congressmen have doctorates in chemistry, as the code makes over 700 molecule-splitting distinctions on chemicals. Boride of titanium is tariffed at 4.9%, boride of tungsten at 10.0%, and boride of vanadium at 16.0%. Dye tariffs display great judiciousness: dye Direct Black 51 pays a 9.5% levy while dye Black 672 pays a 14.2% tariff. Pigment Black 1 is tariffed at 8.3%, Acid Black is tariffed at 9.2%, and mordant Black 75 pays 9.0%.

Congress apparently believes that not all the malnourished should be treated equally. Vitamin B12, which is necessary to prevent anemia and is no longer produced in the U.S., is hit with a 16.2% tariff, while vitamin B2, vital for avoiding stunted growth, pays only a 7.8% rate. Vitamin C carries a 3% tariff, while vitamin E is hit with a 7% levy.

Looking at tariffs on medicine and medical equipment, one might think that tariff policy is secretly controlled by Christian Scientists. Aspirin carries a 10.2% tariff, which makes as much sense as providing a federal subsidy for headaches. The tariff on anti-depressants and tranquilizers is 16.6%—a full employment program for therapists. Congress deters the import of sulfathiazole, an anti-infective agent, with a 15% tariff.

"Death by tariff" results when higher prices caused by tariffs result in fewer people using lifesaving drugs or equipment. In 1984, a West German company developed a lithotripter that destroys kidney stones by shock waves from outside the body. Kidney stones are a common and often serious medical ailment: over 250,000 people a year are admitted to hospitals for kidney stone treatment, and 1,149 people died of kidney stone disease in 1985.[6] The new German machine was a vast improvement over existing methods of surgical removal of kidney stones. Although no American companies were producing competing machines, the U.S. levied a 7.9% tariff on the German product. The Saint Joseph Medical Center of Burbank, California, paid a $189,964.32 tariff on a single lithotripter. The high tariff strongly discouraged more American hospitals from importing the medically advanced German machine. As a result, thousands of Americans in the mid to late 1980s had to undergo painful surgery and relatively long recuperation.[7] (The recuperation time for shockwave treatment is less than half the recuperation time for traditional kidney surgery.) Many deaths from kidney stones and kidney stone surgery could have been avoided if American hospitals had not been deterred by the U.S. tariff code from quickly adopting this new technology.

U.S. tariff policy assumes that it is better that the poor go hungry than to allow them to eat foreign food. No price is too high to help Americans avoid the curse of cheap food. The U.S. imposes over 500 different tariffs to deter foreign food from invading American stomachs, including:

Yogurt	20%	Cucumbers	24.7%
Asparagus	25%	Olives	30.8%
Dried garlic	35%	Dates	35%
Avocados	21.6%	Grapefruit	16%
Grapefruit juice	41.3%	Grape juice	24.5%
Inshell peanuts	36.3%	Peanut oil	18.1%
Grain cereals	17.5%	Frozen chicken	28.6%
Milk powder	17.5%	Dried egg yolks	22.3%
Brussel sprouts	25%	Watermelon	20%
Sardines	15%	Limes	15%

Carrots	17.5%	Frozen corn	17.5%
Dried prunes	17.5%	Strawberries	14%
Tuna	35%	Fish sticks	15%

The U.S. government spends over $28 billion each year on thirteen different food assistance programs. Taxpayers are hit twice—once to pay salaries of Customs agents to keep low-priced foreign food out, and a second time to feed low-income Americans hurt by high food prices.

For some agricultural products, the "fair" tariff depends on the day of the year. Cantaloupe that invades the U.S. between August 1 and September 15 pays a 20% entry fee; cantaloupe entering any other time faces a 35% levy. Congress created a new tariff category in 1984: "Asparagus: If fresh or chilled; entered during the period from September 15 to November 15, inclusive, in any year; and transported to the United States by air: 5% ad valorem. Other: 25% ad valorem."[8] Congressmen believed either that asparagus arriving in a truck is five times more pernicious than airborne asparagus, or that the U.S. government should bail out the air freight business.

American ships must pay a 50% duty on the cost of any repairs that are done in a foreign port. This is designed to benefit domestic ship repair yards—but most domestic shipyards are too busy with lavish military contracts to stoop to repairing commercial ships. One American flag carrier recently sought bids on a ship repair and was told it must wait at least nine months before any domestic yard could even begin the work.[9]

The tariff on a special wool blend fabric used to make firefighters' protective garments is 33%.[10] When Rep. Richard Roe proposed in 1988 to reduce this tariff, the American Textile Manufacturers Institute (ATMI) objected. Even though American companies did not produce the special fabric, ATMI thought some companies might choose to make the product if the tariff were kept high. A few more singed or dead firemen is a small price to pay for the possibility that a domestic firm might deign to make a fabric already supplied by foreign companies.

The tariff code often helps one American industry by sacrificing another. The U.S. has 193,000 fishermen; by contrast, there are only 1,000 people employed in manufacturing fishnets in the U.S. U.S. fishermen must compete every day with foreign fishermen. Yet, the tariff on fishnets is 17%.[11] A 17% tariff on fishnets makes as much sense as a government decree that American fishermen must cut holes in their nets.

The U.S. tariff code looks like a variable value-added tax that was concocted in an lunatic asylum. The tariff on brooms is 42.3%, thereby safeguarding dust and dirt; the tariff on flashlights is 25%, thereby encouraging people to break their nose in the dark; the tariff on cheap scissors is 23.6%, thereby encouraging taxpayers to shred their IRS tax forms with their bare hands instead of cutting them neatly into little squares.

Although most tariff changes these days are reductions of tariffs on items no longer produced in the U.S., some federal policymakers retain their faith in the beneficence of high tariffs. In 1986, the U.S. raised the tariff on red cedar shakes and shingles to 35%. U.S. Deputy Trade Representative Michael Smith announced that the high tariff "will facilitate the [U.S. shake and shingles] industry's transition back to free market competition and will ultimately reduce consumer costs."[12] It was peculiar to describe imposing high tariffs as part of a "transition back to free market competition." The high tariff devastated the Canadian shakes and shingles industry; several Canadian mills shut down and many workers lost their jobs.[13] Canada retaliated to the unprovoked U.S. tariff hike by imposing high tariffs on U.S. computer parts, Christmas trees, tea bags, and cider.[14] The high tariff was supposed to spur "adjustment" in the U.S. industry; but a U.S. International Trade Commission (ITC) report concluded that "the most common 'adjustment' made by producers was the purchase of additional saws," and the industry did not increase its productivity.[15]

The higher tariffs turned some U.S. individuals who had contracts to purchase cedar at long-term, pre-tariff prices into instant millionaires.[16] The U.S. shakes and shingles industry reacted to the high tariff by sharply raising its prices; as a result, U.S. builders scorned shakes and shingles and used tile and asphalt for roofing instead. In the two years after the tariff was imposed, the U.S. market for shakes and shingles contracted by up to 45%.[17] The primary effect of the tariff, aside from boosting prices and disrupting the roofing market, was to encourage American timber companies to more quickly exhaust the extremely limited supply of red cedar. The high tariff was scheduled to last five years; the ITC reported that the U.S. red cedar supply could be exhausted within ten years.[18]

Tariff Reform Hearings

The Trade Policy Staff Committee (TPSC), a group of staffers from various federal agencies, held hearings on Uruguay Round tariff reform hearings in November, 1989. Some of the pleadings from protected industries were most instructive. Pimentos are tariffed at 9.5%; a domestic pimento manufacturer commented, "The present tariff on pimentos is not an impediment to imports and any reduction in the tariff would have an adverse—even a disastrous—effect on the domestic industry."[19]

The big threat was not the Japanese, but Mexican business barons who may soon monopolize the American market. Indiana Glass Company, "the largest employer in Jay County, Indiana," complained that glasses from Mexican companies were selling at K-Mart for $1.99 a set, while Indiana Glass sets were selling at K-Mart for $3.99. The company's brief warned consumers: "There is absolutely no difference in quality" between the Mexican product and the Indiana Glass product.[20]

Indiana Glass concluded that "this evidence of [foreign] price advantage under current tariffs compels at least the maintenance, if not increase, of tariffs [currently up to 38%] on soda lime drinking glasses." Any foreign advantage in cost of production is thus taken as proof of the need for imposing higher taxes on American consumers.

A second glass manufacturer, the Newell Company, demonstrated an excellent theoretical understanding of the value of international trade:

> The Newell Company wholeheartedly supports the broad trade liberalization goals of the Bush Administration in the ongoing round of trade negotiations. Reducing tariff and non-tariff barriers increases the size of the economic pie from which all civilized nations partake. Thus, trade liberalization enhances worldwide economic welfare. Nonetheless, Newell strongly urges the Trade Representative to maintain U.S. tariffs on glass products at their current rates.[21]

Free trade is sound policy for every product in the nation except those Newell manufactures.

Some advocates were carried away by their dedication to high tariffs. Bobby McKown of the Florida Citrus League declared, "Many of our foreign competitors receive important government assistance. U.S. producers receive none."[22] Actually, the U.S. Agriculture Department has given over $30 million to American citrus companies and organizations since 1986 to bankroll their brandname ads and promotions in foreign countries.[23]

A spokesman for Blue Diamond almond grower argued that American almond growers are entitled to have the 14.8% tariff on almond imports retained. Why? Because, "Over the years, the U.S. almond industry has dedicated substantial resources towards achieving liberalized access worldwide through bilateral and multilateral efforts."[24] Because the U.S. almond industry vigorously advocated lower foreign tariffs, it deserves a high tariff at home.

The National Juice Products Association warned against lowering the 40% tariff on orange juice: "In the long term, lowering the orange juice tariff would make U.S. consumers more vulnerable to anticompetitive pricing by Brazilian processors." Better a large price hike guaranteed by the U.S. Congress than needlessly risk the danger of a small price increase engineered by a Brazilian juice cartel.[25] The only way to assure competitive juice prices is to impose a 40% surcharge on the most efficient juice producer.

Some lobbies fielded impressive representatives to carry their "Buy American" banner. The Committee to Preserve American Color TV urged the TPSC to retain the 15% duty on color picture tubes, which hits primarily Asian producers. The person who gave the testimony was Joseph

Donohue, Senior Vice President of Thomson Consumer Electronics, a subsidiary of the Thomson, S.A., the French corporation that recently bought General Electric's TV production operation.[26]

Some advocates insisted that high tariffs are not a barrier to imports. One spokesman for the Rubber and Plastic Footwear Manufacturers Association asserted, "Rubber footwear duties are high, ranging from 20% to about 67% but they can hardly be considered protective in light of the ease of entry of imports to this market."[27] According to this reasoning, if foreigners can still export to the U.S. despite draconian tariffs, then tariffs cannot be too high.

The TPSC handled high-tariff advocates with tender loving care. Suzy Early, Assistant Trade Representative for Agriculture Policy, commented to the spokesman for Blue Diamond almond company, "Steve, your industry is really to be congratulated."[28] Betsy White of the Labor Department complimented one witness who was pursuing his self-interest, "I just sort of commend your support for maintaining that color television picture tube duty at 15%..."[29] A Commerce Department official demanded to know, "Why are the importers so interested in having duty rates reduced on nonrubber footwear when the amount of exports that are coming in are so dramatic already?"[30] The TPSC members showed almost no curiosity as to why tariffs were put at a certain level, devoting themselves instead to a careful and sympathetic study of the reasons not to lower them. The question was not "Why is this tariff so much higher than other tariffs?", but "What damage might we do if we lowered this tariff?" Each existing tariff was taken as a given as an entitlement to a domestic company that the government would need an exemplary reason to reduce.

Angels on a Pinhead: Tariff Classification Disputes

Few people realize that the U.S. Customs Service is perhaps the most philosophic of all government agencies. Each month, Customs Service employees wrestle with age-old questions such as "What is a popcorn popper?", "Can a tennis shoe have two sets of shoestrings?," and, "How transparent must a garment be before it is stimulating enough to be lingerie?" Since tariff classification rulings often result in a massive increase in tariff rates or in embargoes, these questions are disputed with a passion that would make St. Thomas Aquinas proud.

Tariff classification ruling 89-27(6) could have a major impact on some Americans' social lives. Customs decreed that condoms that are electronically tested must pay a higher import tax than condoms that are not tested.[31] Customs also ruled that condoms that include a spermicide must pay more to enter the U.S. than condoms without spermicide. (It is not known whether this decision was part of a secret Bush administration plan to boost the revenues of abortion clinics). While the Customs

Service happily collects a few extra dollars in condom taxes, other government agencies continue spending scores of millions of dollars a year for family planning programs.

On January 4, 1989, the Customs Service stunned the automotive world with a decree that, henceforth, jeeps and vans would be trucks, not automobiles. This announcement overturned numerous previous Customs rulings that declared that jeeps and minivans were automobiles. There is a ten-fold difference in the tariff on cars and trucks, 2.5% versus 25%. This surprise decision bushwhacked German, British, and Japanese companies exporting minivans and/or jeeps to the U.S. The tenfold higher tariff began to be collected on the day the announcement was made, seriously disrupting American automobile dealerships selling imported vehicles.

The redefinition of jeep was largely the result of heavy lobbying by Lee Iacocca, head of Chrysler Corporation, and other U.S. auto company officials. Customs' announcement sparked fierce controversy, and Iacocca warned, "It would be a national disgrace, and every American should feel ashamed and humiliated if [a reversal of the redefinition of jeep] takes place."[32] At the same time Iaccoca sought to save the national honor, he sent a private cable to Chrysler dealers, urging them to lobby the Treasury Department and noting that the new tariff classification "translates to a $2,000 per truck cost penalty to your competitors."[33] The new definition of jeep was widely ridiculed; one British diplomat observed, "Who in his right mind would say that people would pay $36,000 to buy a fully loaded luxury Range Rover to haul pigs to market?"[34] The Treasury Department eventually modified Customs' change, declaring that two-door vehicles like the Suzuki Samurai jeep were trucks and four-door sport vehicles and jeeps are automobiles.

Sometimes the only thing required to redefine a product is a few phone calls from a U.S. Senator. The U.S. imposes import quotas on sugar to safeguard Americans' constitutional right to pay double, triple, or quadruple the world price for their sugar.[35] In the early 1980s, Canadian firms were exporting sugarcorn sweetener blends to the U.S. that were roughly 35 percent cheaper than pure sugar. The U.S. government created a separate import quota for the blended product in 1985, recognizing it as a distinct product from sugar. Even though the quota limited Canadian sales to 2 percent of the U.S. market, the imports still gave heartburn to American sugar growers. In 1988, the Cane Sugar Refiners Association contacted their good friend, Sen. Jesse Helms, and asked him to help the Customs Service understand the true meaning of sugar. Helms repeatedly called his good friend, Customs Commissioner William von Raab, for sweet talk. In early 1989, the Customs Service redefined sugar and banned all Canadian blended imports. The first time Canadian companies learned of the new sugar definition was when four trucks carrying their products were stopped at the U.S.Canada border and prohibited from entering. The Customs Service change in definition devastated an Ohio firm that relied on the Canadian blend as its main product. Canada was outraged: One Canadian official complained, "You simply cannot wipe out $25 million of trade with the stroke of a pen in the dead of night and get away with it."[36] Helms denied receiving any honorariums from the sugar lobby, but journalist Greg Rushford revealed that the Cane Sugar Refiners gave Helms $2,000 for eating breakfast with them shortly after his efforts in their behalf.[37]

The Customs Service is continually discovering new meaning in old steel products. The U.S. government in the 1980s strong-armed 28 foreign nations into signing so-called Voluntary Restraint Agreements (VRAs) to restrict their steel exports. Each VRA specified which tariff classifications of steel would be restrained. Although happy with the VRAs, the U.S. steel industry was aghast at the prospect of any freely imported steel. The steel industry lobbied Customs to solve this problem by changing the official definition of steel products. On December 6, 1988, Customs reversed three previous rulings dating back to 1974 and announced that it was reclassifying steel wire rope with beckets from an uncontrolled tariff category into a tariff classification restricted by the VRAs.[38] Similarly, on August 31, 1989, at the suggestion of Bethlehem Steel, Customs reversed three rulings since 1978 and moved scrollcut tin free steel sheet from an unrestricted tariff category into a tightly controlled category.[39]

Customs claims the right to reverse its tariff classification decisions even after a product has been imported and used. As David J. Elliot of Proctor and Gamble told the House Ways and Means Committee, "We found a need to import a topping packet for our Duncan Hines Muffin Mixes from our plant in Pointe Claire, Canada, because of a supply unavailability in the United States. Someone that works for me carefully looked at the sugar quota provision, concluded these topping packets were not subject to sugar quotas, called the [Customs Service] import specialist at the port concerned, and he agreed with them."[40] Proctor and Gamble imported $400,000 worth of the muffin toppings and sold them as part of a muffin mix. Then, as the *Wall Street Journal* reported, "Some six weeks after [Customs] cleared the topping supply, it sent Proctor and Gamble a notice that it had to return the mix because officials had decided the topping mix was subject to the U.S. import quota on sugar. The company was forced to suspend [muffin mix] production for more than seven weeks, at a cost of more than $200,000, before the Customs Service again reversed itself... If the agency had stuck with the sugar classification, Proctor and Gamble would have had to pay a $750,000 penalty for topping that had a sugar content worth $30,000."[41]

On July 2, 1987, the Customs Service announced a surprise retroactive 2,500% tariff increase on computer parts. Customs ruled that a computer motherboard—a computer component laden with semiconductor chips—is actually a computer. (This would be a shock to anyone who tried to use a mother board as a computer.) The reclassification was politically motivated. At the time, the U.S. government was trying to punish Japan for alleged violations of the U.S. Japan Semiconductor Arrangement. (For more details, see chapter 8). In April 1987, the U.S. imposed 100% penalty tariffs on Japanese computers. Japanese companies ceased exporting computers but continued exporting high quality computer parts. The reclassification increased the tariff American computer makers paid on mother boards from 3.9% to 100%, retroactive to January 1, 1987. The Computer and Business Equipment Manufacturers Association estimated that this reclassification would cost its U.S. members hundreds of millions of dollars.[42] IBM alone lost $26 million due to Customs rulings.[43] The decision was unfortunate, as U.S. computer makers were already struggling in their competition against computer clones from Korea and Taiwan—nations that were able to buy the Japanese mother boards much cheaper.

Customs Service tariff classification decisions often end up in court. In 1988, a federal judge finally resolved an age-old question that has perplexed generations of solons: Why do people sleep in tents? Judge James Watson of the Court of International Trade settled the issue with a ruling that "camping out using tents is not a sport." If a tent is defined as sports equipment, it would pay a 10% duty; if the tent is a textile product, it must pay a duty of 25 cents per pound plus 15% and cannot be imported without a special textile quota license. In 1976, the Customs Service ruled that "certain light tents used in backpacking were sports equipment because the activity of backpacking was found to be a sport." But in the 1988 case, the tents weighed between 29 and 33 pounds. The judge pondered deeply and concluded that such tents were simply too heavy for backpacking. (Apparently, someone who transports a tent in his car to a camping site is engaged in a completely different activity than someone who hikes to the same campsite with his tent.) Judge Watson opined, "Although the court remains as firmly convinced as ever of the desirability of encouraging human beings to retain the skills needed to function in the natural outdoor environment, it cannot honestly say that the simple routine of setting up temporary quarter in the outdoors has the characteristics of a sport."[44] The Court's decision meant sharply higher tent prices—and fewer Americans going camping.

Customs Service definitions often spur product design changes. Mattel Corporation planned to import a Barbie doll case but discovered that if the case were imported by itself, it would be classified as luggage and subject to a 20% tariff. So, Mattel added a fold-down table, chairs, and other play features and persuaded Customs that the product was a toy, subject to only a 6.8% tariff.[45] Foreign manufacturers of ladies garments in 1989 began adding a water-resistant lining to light coats; the lining reduced the tariff from 29.5% to 7.6%. Sen. Richard Shelby was outraged at this foreign conniving, declaring, "Essentially, these water resistant linings serve no practical purpose other than to qualify the garment for a 21.9% [tariff] reduction." (It is not known whether Sen. Shelby has spent his entire life in a desert where it never rained.) Shelby proposed legislation to abolish the lower tariff rate for water resistant garments, assuring everyone that his proposal "has the interests of all American garment manufacturers in mind."[46]

The Customs Service in 1988 boosted the tariff on a shipment of 33,000 girls ski jackets from 10.6% to 35% because the ski jackets had small strips of corduroy on the sleeves.[47] The Customs ruled that the strips, amounting to 2 percent of the jacket's composition, changed the tariff category from "garments designed for rainwear, hunting, fishing, or similar uses" (such as skiing) to "other girls' wearing apparel, not ornamented." Famous Raincoat Company, the importer, appealed the Customs ruling to the U.S. Court of International Trade. Judge Kenton Musgrave observed, "During the trial, government counsel... relied on the 'philosophical' meaning of the word 'or'... as opposed to 'and.' "[48] The judge threw the government's case out and ordered Customs to refund the tariff surcharge.

The Customs Service is increasingly changing its classification of goods—and becoming more secretive about its decisions. Kenneth Kumm, manager for trade affairs for Minnesota Mining and Manufacturing (3M) complained, "Today, very few rulings are published. On the other hand, it appears that reversals of previous positions have become legion. Even if you know how the law is currently being interpreted today, it apparently can be changed tomorrow. This makes investment, production, sales, or contract decisions that must be right for an extended period (years, not weeks or months), extremely difficult."[49] Joseph Donohue, a trade lawyer, notes, "In recent years, many major changes affecting millions of dollars worth of imports have been made by internal Customs telex with no notice whatsoever to the importing public until after the fact... In many cases, importers are faced with the prospect of going out of business or circumventing the law in order to survive until they have the opportunity to adjust to the changes."[50]

Rules of Origin Schizophrenia

Trade flows are increasingly disrupted by changes in rules of origin. Rules of origin are the federal regulations that determine the national origin of an imported good. Any violation of the vague, continually changing, sometimes contradictory U.S. rules of origin can bar a shipment of foreign goods from the U.S. mainland. As lawyer David Palmeter observes, "Customs' more recent country of origin determinations smack more of protectionism than of consumer protection, as the agency contorts, gyrates, and twists its way to one restrictive ruling after another."[51]

Rule of origin changes have been especially disruptive in products covered by import quotas. Not only does the U.S. force foreign governments to sign agreements restricting their exports, but the U.S. government sometimes arbitrarily and unilaterally changes the terms long after an agreement is signed. On August 3, 1984, Customs fundamentally changed the rules for determining the national origin of textile and apparel products.[52] Previously, the country of origin for textile products was determined by whether a product had undergone "substantial transformation" in the country that exported it to the U.S. Customs. In an effort to derail the Chinese and Hong Kong sweater industries, it was ruled that certain operations involving looping together knit sweater panels would no longer be considered a substantial transformation—even though the looping process created a completely different product. The Chinese ambassador to the U.S. complained that the new rules harmed "over 100,000 [workers] throughout China and around $200$300 million of China's trade."[53] One Hong Kong manufacturer observed, "Our manufacturers had to start knitting these garments themselves in Hong Kong instead of in China—and because they could not find enough workers in Hong Kong to do that kind of job they had to buy an enormous amount of new, computerized knitting machinery. One stroke of Commissioner von Raab's pen forced the industry in Hong Kong to spend hundreds of millions of dollars."[54]

In 1983, Congress enacted the Caribbean Basin Initiative (CBI), granting duty-free access to many Caribbean products. The 1983 law declared that as long at least 35 percent of a product's value originated in the Caribbean, the product qualified as a Caribbean product. Encouraged by the CBI, several companies invested tens of millions of dollars to establish plants in Jamaica and Costa Rica to convert surplus European wine into ethanol. The Customs Service ruled in 1984 that ethanol production added more than 35 percent of the value to the finished product, thus qualifying the Caribbean-produced ethanol for duty-free entry into the U.S.[55]

The 35 percent rule stood until 2 AM one morning in early 1986 during a congressional tax conference. One congressman slipped in an amendment to the tax bill that raised the local value-added requirement for Caribbean ethanol from 35 percent to 70 percent, creating a different rule of origin for ethanol than for any other Caribbean product. This clause was a death sentence for Caribbean ethanol producers. The 70 percent requirement effectively mandated the use of local agricultural products for ethanol feedstock, but there were almost no surplus agricultural stocks in the Caribbean.

The new, prohibitory rule of origin was a surprise because Caribbean ethanol shipments posed no threat to American competitors; shipments never exceeded 3 percent of the U.S. ethanol supply.[56] U.S. ethanol producers, who have received over $7 bllion in federal benefits since 1980, were unable to meet domestic demand for ethanol, but still wanted to lock out foreigners. U.S. producers, led by Archer Daniels Midland (which produces 70 percent of U.S. ethanol), engineered the late night rule change to strangle any possible foreign competition in the crib.

The 1986 amendment allowed existing Caribbean ethanol producers in 1990 to reach the 70 percent local value requirement. In 1989, Congress again changed the rule of origin for Caribbean ethanol. The new rule decreed that there would be no Caribbean feedstock requirement on the first 60 million gallons of ethanol imports; a 30 percent local feedstock requirement on the next 35 million gallons; and a 50 percent requirement for any additional imports. This rule, which effectively prohibits a sharp increase in Caribbean exports, makes the national origin of ethanol dependent simply on the number of gallons of ethanol imported.[57]

In 1986, the U.S. pressured Taiwan and Japan into signing agreements to restrict their exports of machine tools. (Machine tools are automatic power-driven tools such as electric lathes and punch presses used to cut, drill, grind, and stamp the metal that is used in manufacturing processes.) In 1988, Taiwan began shipping some machine tool parts to Israel, where an Israeli company combined the Taiwanese parts with Israeli products, built the finished product, and exported it to the United States. Customs ruled in 1989 that since more than 35 percent of the value of the finished product originated in Israel, the machine tools were Israeli products. But the Commerce Department, following its protectionist instincts, created its own twelve-point test to determine national origin for machine tools and then announced that it would penalize Taiwan for Israel's exports. *Inside U.S. Trade* newsletter reported on February 16, 1990, "Commerce has apparently decided to count the Israeli machine tools against the VRA [voluntary restraint agreement] retroactively from 1989, according to one Israeli source. As a result, Taiwan has stopped shipping the machine tool parts to Israel, and the Israeli company that made the machine tools has gone out of business."[58] (At the same time the U.S. government torpedoed an Israeli company, the U.S. was providing $3 billion a year in aid to Israel.)

The rules of origin for steel have also become more protectionist. Under U.S. law, the origin of imported steel products controlled by the VRAs was determined by the nation which last substantially transformed the product. Shortly after the 1984 steel quotas, American steel companies began complaining that foreign steel producers were exporting their steel to third countries not covered by VRAs, which then further processed the steel and exported it to the U.S. The Commerce Department sent a letter to foreign embassies in Washington in 1986 warning them that they could be penalized for steel they exported from their nation to a third country that later exported a finished product to the U.S. The Customs Service thereafter began imposing a more stringent origin test for steel products. A Panamanian company imported Korean steel, manufactured it into oil pipes, and exported the pipes to the United States. Customs announced in 1987 that the Panamanian company might be violating the VRA for Korean steel and barred its products from the U.S. market. The Panamanian company challenged Customs' ruling, and later Customs reversed itself. But, by that time, the Panamanian company was bankrupt.[59]

Imports need violate the rule of only one federal agency to be banned from the entire United States. Palmeter notes, "The Commerce Department will do as it sees fit regardless of the position of Customs. Commerce declared in one ruling, 'The Department is not required to rely on U.S. Customs [rule of origin] rulings.' "[60] This occurred in semiconductors: "Semiconductors assembled and tested in third countries using processed wafers or dice fabricated in Taiwan were included in a final antidumping determination covering semiconductors from Japan, despite the fact that U.S. Customs previously had ruled that the assembly and testing operations—conferred origin on the country in which they occurred."[61] Such policy contradictions between U.S. government agencies place foreign companies in perpetual double jeopardy.

Confiscation: The Ultimate Tariff

In 1988, Customs seized over $1 billion worth of imports. The House Ways and Means Subcommittee on Investigations issued a report in early 1990 which concluded that the Customs Service had greatly abused its seizure authority. Subcommittee chairman Rep. J.J. Pickle denounced the " 'gung ho, macho' management in Customs which led to flagrant neglect and abuse in many Customs areas."[62]

In the 1970s, the Customs Service was widely criticized for its "seizure fever" regarding imports. Congress reined in the agency in 1978 by sharply curtailing its power to confiscate private property. Customs officials were unhappy that Congress spoiled their fun. In 1986, Congress expanded Customs' power to seize goods suspected of being involved in illicit drug traffic. Customs promptly started seizing products with no relation to drugs.[63] When Customs Commissioner William von Raab was asked why his agency was using its new seizure authority so frequently, he replied, "Because it's easier."[64]

In 1987, the Fingerhut Corporation imported a large shipment of sewing kits, including needles and spools of thread; the kits were seized by Customs, which claimed the sewing kits were actually luggage, which carried a tariff three times higher and required a quota import license. Fingerhut lost hundreds of orders as a result. In another case, Fingerhut received a verbal opinion from a Customs' import specialist that a sweaterjacket would be judged to be a sweater. After Fingerhut began importing the product, a second Customs specialist declared that the product was actually a jacket and ordered Customs inspectors to initiate seizure proceedings. (Under U.S. textile import quotas, companies must have a separate license for each type of clothing item they import.) Fingerhut's Michael Laden told the House Ways and Means Committee, "In 1987 seizures of Fingerhut merchandise conservatively cost our firm more than half a million dollars in penalties, cancelled orders, lost productivity, and other administrative charges and overhead."[65]

Many textile and clothing import quotas are measured by weight. As a 1990 House Ways and Means Committee report noted,

In a major policy shift, starting in 1987, Customs...purchased hundreds of portable scales to be used by inspectors in warehouses throughout the country. Inspectors began weighing thousands of shipments using un documented and unpublished sampling techniques and seized hundreds of the shipments for violating quota agreements, even if the shipment was allegedly overweight by only the smallest margin. As with most such enforcement efforts...national Customs officials gave little or no guidance to field inspectors and inconsistent enforcement efforts resulted. In some cases, Customs weighed shipments of commodities that were not controlled by weight. In other cases, Customs weighed inappropriate samples, leading to inaccurately calculated weights. In still other cases, Customs failed to allow for extraordinary moisture content in the material being weighed.

Once an alleged overweight shipment was seized, importers were denied access to their shipments and could not confirm Customs findings or make corrections. They were presented with only two options. The first option was to pay a penalty, obtain a new visa for the Customs-determined weight, pay for storage costs, waive all claims against Customs, and waive their rights to litigate the issue. The other option was to let Customs keep the shipment and go to court. The latter was never a viable option because, by the time the litigation could be completed, the value of the shipment would be lost.[66]

Some Customs inspectors appear to have been heavily influenced by the 1970s cult film classic, "The Texas Chainsaw Massacre." In Seattle, Customs inspectors chainsawed an imported cigar store wooden Indian to prove beyond a shadow of a doubt that the Indian did not contain any narcotics.[67] Customs agents used chainsaws to "inspect" a large container tightly packed with paper products. Congressman J.J. Pickle berated Customs Commission William von Raab: "We have had instances where you brought antique [teakwood] elephants in or articles like that and you chainsawed it. That doesn't leave that elephant with a heck-of-a-lot of value."[68]

Chainsaws are an attractive, efficient means of inspecting imports in part because the Customs Service never compensates property owners for damage it does during inspections. The House Ways and Means Committee investigation concluded, "The U.S. Customs Service has little or no incentive to avoid damaging cargo during examinations." Customs officials take apart airplanes during inspections and then the aircraft owner has to pay to put the plane back together.

The Customs Service increased its seizures partly in order to impress protectionist congressmen with the agency's zeal against imports. Customs employees got points toward promotion or salary bonuses for seizing property.[69] The congressional report noted, "Entire Customs offices have been rated by Customs regional or Headquarters offices based on their seizure statistics...In too many cases, the merchandise is seized improperly in the first place. The seizure reports are never updated to reflect these dispositions."[70]

Some congressmen have shown a strong personal concern over Customs' seizures. Sen. Dennis Deconcini of Arizona proposed an amendment in 1990 to require the Customs Service to donate a turboprop airplane it seized to the University of Arizona.[71] (Deconcini thought Arizona should have the plane in part because a 1988 bill had specifically donated an airplane Customs seized to the Marion County, Indiana sheriff's office.)

Von Raab defended Customs' inspection practices: "Our borders are very, very sensitive, and the long-standing practice of every country in the world including ours, is that you must make your car, your plane, or boat accessible to Customs for inspection."[72] Customs "inspected" one airplane by forcing the owner to land his plane, after which Customs officials pulled up close by in a Black Hawk helicopter, and a prop blast from the helicopter flipped the plane over and destroyed it. Customs then arrested the pilot on suspicion of drug smuggling. Customs found no drugs and the pilot was later released. But Customs refused to compensate the man for the plane it destroyed. The pilot, Gustavo Viera, complained to Washington; the federal government responded by denying any compensation and reminding Viera, "The war on drugs requires the full effort of Government forces in cooperation with each and every citizen and the loss of support of even one citizen is a serious matter."[73]

Von Raab proudly told the House Ways and Means Committee, "The Customs Service has come to the support of our domestic industry to try, for the time through this program, to enforce some of our laws to protect our domestic industry against illegal practices by foreign manufacturers."[74] Customs issued a press release in early 1988 bragging that the seizure of illegal imports had increased threefold. But the vast majority of the increase in seizures was the result of the Customs Service adopting a far more expansive definition of "illegal."[75]

With a typical Washington "King Midas touch", the Customs Service actually turns confiscated imports into a burden on the government. The Customs Service hired Northrup Corporation to auction off confiscated property, and Northrup charged more to administer the program than the total auction proceeds. In one case, Customs seized $91,000 in clothing imports; Northrup charged Customs $8,000 to store the apparel and then auctioned it off for only $56,000.[76] A Customs official defended the agency by asserting that "the government is not out to make money" on the program. Rep. Clay Shaw complained, "We seize hundreds of millions of dollars worth of assets, and then we throw it all away."[77] First a corporation loses property when the government seizes its import shipments, and then it must pay federal taxes to help the government recoup its losses from the property seizure program.

The Meaning of the Tariff Code

In the 1400s in Europe, wealthy nobles could go to Rome and purchase a Papal decree officially forgiving their most flagrant sins. Nowadays, American industries go to Washington to "atone" for their economic mistakes by purchasing an exemption from foreign competition. A tariff is simply a decree from Congress officially forgiving an industry for all its economic sins—its incompetence, mismanagement, lethargy, contempt for its customers, and so on. If the tariff is set high enough, Congress' economic holy water will wash away all of a company's earthly failings.

The U.S. tariff code rests on the idea that the government can enrich a people by selectively raising the prices of politically favored items. But as Henry George noted more than a hundred years ago, "A discriminating pirate, who would confine his seizures to goods which might be produced in the country to which they were being carried, would be as beneficial to that country as a tariff."[78] As John Maynard Keynes noted, a tariff can do nothing against unemployment that an earthquake cannot do better.[79]

Congress has great faith in its own ability to fine-tune the American economy. U.S. Customs law allows Americans returning from overseas to bring in one liter of alcohol duty-free. In the 1990 trade act, Congress resolved that, to help our Caribbean neighbors, American citizens coming home from the Caribbean would be allowed to bring in two liters of alcohol duty free. This is the kind of economic statesmanship that should make all advocates of a national industrial policy stand up and cheer.[80] In 1984, Congress performed a similar visionary act when it ruled that the Customs Service should not impose tariffs on articles returned from outer space, but only as long as "such articles were previously launched into space from the customs territory of the United States aboard a spacecraft operated by, or under the control of, United States persons and owned" by U.S. citizens.[81]

Congress will sometimes suspend tariffs on products that are no longer produced in the U.S. But if a single American company objects, via its congressman, Congress will generally perpetuate the existing tariff. In a 1990 debate over suspending a tariff on ulcer medicine, Sen. Lloyd Bentsen, the chairman of the Senate Finance Committee, declared, "I appreciate very much that the senators from North Carolina are doing their best to help a company located in their state, but given that there is a domestic competitor that raises objections, I must oppose the amendment."[82] Current tariff policy allows a single company to hold the entire nation hostage. Even if a U.S. company produces only 1 percent of the supply of a product consumed in the U.S.—or is only contemplating producing the item in the future—Congress forces everyone in the nation to pay a higher price.

For most congressmen, setting tariffs is an exercise in know-nothing industrial policy. Most congressmen who exercise control over the tariff code's hundreds of different chemical taxes probably could not play with a junior chemistry set without blowing themselves up. Probably not one congressmen in a hundred could give a plausible explanation of why the tariff on artificial eyes for stuffed animals is significantly higher than the tariff for artificial eyes for plastic baby dolls, or why the tariff on baby dolls is almost double the tariff on baby doll eyes. Most congressmen could not even describe the technical products contained in different tariff classifications, yet they acquiesce to maintaining thousands of different taxes on products they do not comprehend. About

---

all the average congressman understands regarding the current tariff code is that he will get more honorariums and campaign contributions for maintaining existing tariffs than for abolishing them.

The American tariff code is living proof of a political system's inability to correct its economic mistakes. The U.S. tariff code resembles an economic Stonehenge, a cluttered field of monuments to the ancient power of various congressmen and lobbyists. Our tariff code has inherited and perpetuated handouts for the biggest political contributors to previous generations of congressmen. Although few would support setting high levies on orange juice or footwear or brooms if Congress was making policy today from scratch, the sheer lethargy of the American political system allows high tariffs to remain long after the original payoff recipients have turned to dust.

Tariffs are either a bailout to perpetuate uncompetitive American industries, or a license for efficient American industries to gouge their customers. It makes no sense for the federal government to "improve" a level playing field by randomly inserting hundreds of bumps, boulders, and brick walls. Regardless of what tariffs a foreign country may have, it is not in our national interest for the Customs Service to selectively blockade our own ports.

Notes

1. Office of the U.S. Trade Representative, "U.S. Proposal for Uruguay Round Market Access Negotiations," March, 1990, p. 416 (tariff line 9108.91.20). The official *Harmonized Tariff Schedule of the United States* does not provide the ad valorem percentage for many tariff categories, listing instead only the kilogram or piece rate. The "U.S. Proposal for Uruguay Round Market Access negotiations" provides ad valorem rates for all tariff categories. This document, prepared for the Uruguay Round, was confidential.

2. Ibid., p. 88 (tariff line 2401.30.60).

3. Office of the U.S. Trade Representative, Trade Policy Staff Committee, Hearing on Uruguay Round Tariff Reduction Proposals, November 1, 1989, p. 2-237.

4. U.S. Customs Service, *Harmonized Tariff Schedule of the United States 1990* (Washington: Government Printing Office, 1990).

5. H.L. Mencken, *A Dictionary of Quotations*, (New York: Knopf, 1942), p. 181.

6. Interview with Mary Harris, information office, National Institute of Health, Washington, D.C., January 25, 1991; also, interview with Pat O'Connor, National Kidney Foundation, New York, January 25, 1991.

7. U.S. Congress, House Ways and Means Committee, *Written Comments on Certain Tariff and Trade Bills,* November 10, 1989 (Washington: Government Printing Office, 1989), p. 8.

8. U.S. Congress, House Ways and Means Committee, *Trade Legislation Enacted Into Public Law 1981 Through 1988* (Washington: Government Printing Office, 1989), p. 71.

9. U.S. Trade Representative, Trade Policy Staff Committee, Hearing on Uruguay Round Tariff Reduction Proposals, October 31, 1989, p. 1-31.

10. U.S. International Trade Commission, "Memorandum to the Committee on Ways and Means of the United States House of Representatives on H.R. 4411, A Bill to Reduce the Duty on Certain Fabrics for Use in Making Fire-Protective Garments for Firefighters," July 4, 1988.

11. U.S. Congress, Senate Finance Committee, *Miscellaneous Tariff Bills, 1986,* May 8, 1986, (Washington: Government Printing Office, 1986), p. 21.

12. Office of the U.S. Trade Representative, "President Grants Import Relief to U.S. Western Red Cedar Shakes and Shingles Industry," Press Release No. 86/21, May 22, 1986.

13. Kimberly Noble, "Effort to bar Canadian shingles backfires in U.S.," *Kennebec Journal* (Augusta, Maine), November 21, 1988.

14. U.S. International Trade Commission, "Western Red Cedar Shakes and Shingles," ITC Publication 2131, October 1988, p. A-43.

15. Ibid., p. 18.

16. *International Trade Reporter*, August 24, 1988, p. 1191.

17. Noble, "Effort to bar Canadian shingles backfires in U.S."

18. U.S. International Trade Commission, "Western Red Cedar Shakes and Shingles," p. 14.

19. Office of the U.S. Trade Representative, Trade Policy Staff Committee, Hearing on Uruguay Round Tariff Reduction Proposals, October 31, 1989, p. 1-201. (Statement of G. Albert Bloodworth, Jr.)

20. U.S. Trade Representative, Trade Policy Staff Committee, PreHearing Brief Submitted by Indiana Glass on Uruguay Round Tariff Reduction Proposals, October 16, 1989.

21. Office of the U.S. Trade Representative, Trade Policy Staff Committee, Hearing on Uruguay Round Tariff Reduction Proposals, October 31, 1989, p. 4-19.

22. Ibid., p. 1-257.

23. U.S. General Accounting Office, "Improvements Needed in Management of the Targeted Export Assistance Program" June, 1990.

24. U.S. Trade Representative, Trade Policy Staff Committee, PreHearing Brief of Blue Diamond Almond Growers on Uruguay Round Tariff Reduction Proposals, October 15, 1989, p. 6.

25. Ibid., p. 1-96.

26. U.S. Trade Representative, Trade Policy Staff Committee, Hearing on Uruguay Round Tariff Reduction Proposals, October 31, 1989, p. 143.

27. Office of the U.S. Trade Representative, Trade Policy Staff Committee, Hearing on Uruguay Round Tariff Reduction Proposals, November 1, 1989, p. 2-222. (Statement of Mitchell Cooper, Counsel for the Rubber and Plastic Footwear Manufacturers Association.)

28. Ibid., October 31, 1989, p. 1-71.

29. Ibid., p. 1-58.

30. Ibid., November 1, 1989, p. 2-245.

31. U.S. Customs Service, Tariff Classification Ruling C.S.D. 89-27(6), October 31, 1988.

32. James Bovard, "A Jeep is a Truck?," *Baltimore Sun*, February 15, 1989.

33. Ibid.

34. Greg Rushford, "Lee Iacocca's Bumpy Truck Ride," *Legal Times,* April 3, 1989.

35. *International Trade Reporter*, February 8, 1989, p. 176.

36. Greg Rushford, "Customs Switch on Sugar Tariffs Could Turn Sour for Helms," *Legal Times*, September 11, 1989, p. 1.

37. Greg Rushford, "Helms Advocacy for Sugar was Sweet for Him, Too," *Legal Times,* June 4, 1990.

38. *Federal Register*, December 6, 1988, p. 49118.

39. Customs Bulletin and Decisions, T.D. 8985, 23, no. 23, p. 6.

40. U.S. Congress, House Ways and Means Committee, *Review of U.S. Customs Service Operations,* June 9, 1988 (Washington: Government Printing Office, 1989), p. 122.

41. Shoba Puroshothaman, "Customs Classification Codes Confuse Importers, Who Cry 'Trivial Pursuit'," *Wall Street Journal*, September 27, 1988.

42. Michael Miller, "Tariffs Targeted at Japan will hurt U.S., Group Says," *Wall Street Journal,* August 26, 1987.

43. U.S. Congress, House Ways and Means Committee, *Written Comments on Certain Tariff and Trade Bills,* July 20, 1989 (Washington: Government Printing Office, 1989), p. 398.

44. *International Trade Reporter,* June 15, 1988, p. 892.

45. *International Trade Reporter,* May 2, 1990, pg. 625.

46. *Congressional Record,* April 20, 1990, p. S4706.

47. *Famous Raincoat Co. v. the United States, U.S. Court of International Trade*, Slip Op. 9078, Court No. 88-10-00769, August 15, 1990.

48. Ibid., pp. 9-10.

49. U.S. Congress, House Ways and Means Committee, *Review of U.S. Customs Service Operations*, June 9, 1988 (Washington: Government Printing Office, 1989), p. 105.

50. Ibid., p. 272.

51. N. David Palmeter, "The U.S. Rules of Origin Proposal to GATT: Monotheism or Polytheism?," *Journal of World Trade,* April 1990, p. 28+.

52. *Federal Register,* August 3, 1984, p. 31248.

53. U.S. International Trade Commission, "The Impact of Rules of Origin on U.S. Imports and Exports," March 1985, ITC Publication No. 1623, p. 84.

54. James Lardner, "The Sweater Trade," *New Yorker,* January 11, 1988, p. 60.

55. U.S. Congress, House Ways and Means Committee, *Fuel Ethanol Imports from Caribbean Basin Initiative Countries*, April 25, 1989 (Washington: Government Printing Office, 1989), p. 80.

56. Ibid., p. 36.

57. U.S. Congress, "Customs and Trade Act of 1990," Conference Report 101-650 July 30, 1990 p. 136.

58. *Inside U.S. Trade*, February 16, 1990, p. 1.

59. U.S. Congress, House Ways and Means Committee, *Steel Import Stabilization Extension Act and Other Proposals Related to the Steel Voluntary Restraint Agreement Program*, June 13, 1989 (Washington: Government Printing Office, 1989), p. 118.

60. N. David Palmeter, "The U.S. Rules of Origin Proposal to GATT: Monotheism or Polytheism?," *Journal of World Trade,* April 1990, pp. 28f.

61. N. David Palmeter, "The Antidumping Law: A Legal and Administrative Non-Tariff Barrier," paper presented to the Conference on Procedures and Methods in the Commerce Department's Administration of the Trade Remedy Law, Brookings Institution, Washington, D.C., November 29, 1990, p. 22.

62. *International Trade Reporter*, February 21, 1990, p. 256.

63. U.S. Congress, House Ways and Means Committee, *Review of U.S. Customs Service Operations,* June 9, 1988 (Washington: Government Printing Office, 1989), pp. 151f.

64. Ibid., p. 155.

65. Ibid., p. 36.

66. U.S. Congress, House Committee on Ways and Means, *Abuses and Mismanagement in U.S. Customs Service Commercial Operations*, February 8, 1990 (Washington: Government Printing Office, 1990), p. 7.

67. Ibid., p. 39.

68. U.S. Congress, House Ways and Means Committee, *Review of U.S. Customs Service Operations,* June 9, 1988 (Washington: Government Printing Office, 1989), p. 571.

69. Ibid., p. 153.

70. House Committee on Ways and Means, *Abuses and Mismanagement*, p. 7.

71. *Congressional Record,* April 24, 1990, p. S4910.

72. Ibid., p. 571.

73. Ibid., p. 244.

74. Ibid., p. 454.

75. N. David Palmeter, "Customs' Crime Data Misleading," *Journal of Commerce*, February 12, 1988.

76. Michael Isikoff, "An Embarrassment of Wasted Riches," *Washington Post*, November 28, 1989.

77. Rick Wartzman, "U.S. Loses Money on Confiscated Goods," *Wall Street Journal,* September 19, 1989.

78. Henry George, *Protectionism or Free Trade* (New York: Doubleday, 1905 [first published in 1886]), p. 35.

79. Quoted in Leland B. Yeager and David G. Tuerck, *Foreign Trade and U.S. Policy,* (New York: Praeger, 1976), p. 119.

80. U.S. Congress, "Customs and Trade Act of 1990," Conference Report 101-650, July 30, 1990, p. 132.

81. U.S. Congress, House Ways and Means Committee, *Trade Legislation Enacted into Public Law 1981 Through 1988* (Washington: Government Printing Office, 1989), pp. 88-89.

82. *Congressional Record*, April 24, 1990, p. S4891.

THE PROTECTIONIST MENTALITY

Robert W. McGee

> In every country it always is and must be the interest of the great body of the people to buy whatever they want of those who sell it cheapest. The proposition is so very manifest, that it seems ridiculous to take any pains to prove it; nor could it ever have been called in question, had not the interested sophistry of merchants and manufacturers confounded the common sense of mankind.[1]

Protectionism is not new. Proponents were found in ancient Greece.[2] Plato thought that trading with foreigners would allow undesirable characters to enter the polis, along with gold and silver, all of which corrupt the soul. Aristotle also thought exchanging products for money had a corrupting influence and thought that the best state was one that was self-sufficient, although both Plato and Aristotle recognized the benefits of the division of labor (but not comparative advantage).

The theories supporting protectionism have been refuted for well over 100 years—by Bastiat in France, Cobden and Bright in England and John Prince Smith in Germany.[3] Adam Smith's refutation, *The Wealth of Nations*, was published in 1776. Richard Cantillon's contribution to the debate, *Essai Sur la Nature Du Commerce en Géneral*, was written in the 1720s and 1730s and published in 1755.[4]

Protectionist sentiment remains strong. As Vilfredo Pareto pointed out in 1927, the benefits of protectionism are concentrated while the costs are diffused.

Even if it were very clearly demonstrated that protection always entails the destruction of wealth, if that were taught to every citizen just as they learn the abc's, protection would lose so small a number of partisans and free trade would gain so few of them that the effect can be almost, or even completely, disregarded. The motives which lead men to act are quite different.

In order to explain how those who champion protection make themselves heard so easily, it is necessary to add a consideration which applies to social movements generally. The intensity of the work of an individual is not proportionate to the benefits which that work may bring him nor to the harm which it may enable him to avoid. If a certain measure A is the case of the loss of one franc to each of a thousand persons, and of a thousand franc gain to one individual, the latter will expend a great deal of energy, whereas the former will resist weakly; and it is likely that, in the end, the person who is attempting to secure the thousand francs via A will be successful.

A protectionist measure provides large benefits to a small number of people, and causes a very great number of consumers a slight loss. This circumstance makes it easier to put a protectionist measure into practice.[5]

With this clear-cut enormous benefit to some people, it is no wonder that protectionist ideas refuse to die—and even flourish—because the only thing preventing their enactment is a Congress that both understands basic economics and is honest enough to resist a well-financed lobby that wants them to enact something that will be to the detriment of their constituents. Robert Nozick explains what makes this abuse possible: "The illegitimate use of a state by economic interests for their own ends is based upon a preexisting illegitimate power of the state to enrich some persons at the expense of others."[6]

W. M. Curtiss puts it somewhat differently: "Through the years, some men have discovered how to satisfy their wants at the expense of others without being accused of theft: they ask their government to do the stealing for them."[7]

If it is immoral for Ford or General Motors executives to personally prevent a willing U.S. consumer from entering into a contract to buy a foreign automobile from a willing seller, is it any less immoral to ask government to do the job for them? The effect is the same whether the corporate executives physically restrain a consumer from walking into a Toyota or Hyundai dealership or whether they let the government intervene in their behalf by not allowing the automobile into the country in the first place. Also, are corporate executives who ask for government protection not acting immorally, because their action denies the right of consumers to exercise their right to property—to choose the product of their choice? Such action is a perversion of the law, because it allows some citizens to exploit the person, liberty, and property of others.[8] Bastiat tells how to determine when the law is being perverted: "See if the law takes from some persons what belongs to them, and gives it to other persons to whom it does not belong. See if the law benefits one citizen at the expense of another by doing what the citizen himself cannot do without committing a crime."[9]

According to this proviso, the welfare state is a perversion of the law, and protectionist measures such as tariffs and quotas are merely examples of one form of welfare—corporate subsidies. Frank Chodorov provides one of the most succinct refutations of the protectionist mentality:

> Let us test the claims of "protectionists" with an experiment in logic. If a people prosper by the amount of foreign goods they are not permitted to have, then a complete embargo, rather than a restriction, would do them the most good. Continuing that line of reasoning, would it not be better all around if each community were hermetically sealed off from its neighbor, like Philadelphia from New York? Better still, would not every household have more on its table if it were compelled to live on its own production? Silly as this reductio ad absurdum is, it is no sillier than the "protectionist" argument that a nation is enriched by the amount of foreign goods it keeps out of its market, or the "balance of trade" argument that a nation prospers by the excess of its exports over imports.[10]

What Is An Import?

On the surface, it may seem simple to define an import, but a closer analysis reveals that defining what constitutes an import is not so cut and dried. For example, Sony makes televisions in San Diego. About half of U.S. Harley-Davidson motorcycles are made in Japan.[11] The Volvo 780 that is sold in the United States is the product of work done in several countries. The following are some of the countries involved:

France	Engine
Japan	Transmission
United States	Air conditioner
Germany	Electronic system
Singapore	Control valves
Canada	Exhaust system
Taiwan	Power antenna
South Korea	Electrical components
Sweden	Axles
Ireland	Tires
Italy	Design and assembly

How Swedish is this car, anyway? When you consider that some of the components that comprise the Volvo were made with machinery and equipment from other countries, the problem becomes even more difficult to determine. Part of the problem inherent in any attempt to restrict imports lies in the definition of an import. A whole body of literature has evolved around the concept of "domestic content" and domestic content legislation. In many ways, the definition is arbitrary, which causes problems that would not exist if trade were completely free.

Many arguments have been advanced in favor of regulating trade between consenting adults. The next few pages summarize and analyze these arguments.

The Subsidy Argument

This argument will not stand up under close accounting analysis. Consumers who must pay higher prices for the goods they want or who are not able to get the products they want because of restrictive trade policies are obviously hurt by protectionism. They are not as well off as they would be in the absence of protectionism. Yet, advocates of protectionism continue to insist that forcing consumers to pay higher prices for farm products, for example, does not really harm them because the farmers will spend their extra income in the nonfarm sector. In other words, the extra money the farmers receive as the result of the subsidy all comes back to the consumer anyway, so there is no net loss.

This faulty thinking can be exposed by reference to the story of the beggar who asked the restaurant owner to give him $20.[12] The beggar points out that the restauranteur will be no worse off because the beggar promises to spend the entire $20 in the restaurant. What is seen is the sumptuous meal the beggar receives. The restauranteur also receives $20, so it appears that both have gained by the trade. What is less obvious is that the restauranteur, rather than having $20 and $20 worth of food now has only the $20 but not the food. Even though the beggar spent the entire proceeds of the subsidy in the restauranteur's restaurant, the restauranteur is poorer as a result.

Although this example may seem absurd, the same argument is being advanced by elected government officials and lobbyists who advocate subsidizing some industry. U.S. sugar farmers need a subsidy to survive, for example, but we will get it all back because their increased purchasing power will increase demand for goods and services throughout the economy.

The same argument is advanced by those who try to justify foreign aid on self-interest grounds. Give country X $100 million, the argument goes. They promise to spend it all in the United States anyway, so we are getting it all back. Our exports increase and our trade imbalance decreases. What is seen is an extra $100 million in exports. What is more difficult to see is that the taxpayers are $100 million poorer in order to subsidize the purchases of some foreign country. In the case of aid to the Philippines, much of the aid found its way back to the United States in the form of prime Manhattan real estate, which is not an export at all, paid for by the U.S. taxpayer.

The Dumping Argument

"Dumping" can mean several things. It can mean that foreign producers are selling their products on domestic markets below cost. It also can mean that foreigners are selling their products in the United States for less than what they sell them for in their own country.[13] A corollary of this argument is that foreign governments are subsidizing these exports. In its extreme form, dumping has been likened to predatory pricing, whereby a foreign producer deliberately sells below domestic competitors with the intent of driving them out of business and gaining a monopoly for itself.

The popular view is that dumping is bad and those who dump should be penalized. Frédéric Bastiat pointed out the fallacy of this view in 1845, yet the view is still not only with us, but also widely believed to be true.[14] In Bastiat's example, foreigners flood the market with goods without asking for anything in return. Even if imports become infinite and exports shrink to zero, how can it be said that the economy, as a whole, is worse off?

Modern examples of dumping are only slightly less absurd. Rather than giving us free stereos and automobiles, the Japanese sell us their products at prices that are lower than what U.S. companies can afford to sell for. Such "dumping" saves U.S. consumers millions or even billions of dollars a year, thus raising their standards of living. The money we save on "dumped" goods can be spent on other goods and services that have a lower value on our subjective value scales. A few thousand United Auto Workers lose something because Americans choose to buy foreign motor vehicles, but 260 million Americans stand to benefit by being able to buy products of their choice rather than the products the United Auto Workers (and their friends in Congress) allow them to buy.

Actually, the domestic industry does not "lose" anything. It just does not gain, because U.S. consumers prefer to do business with someone else. U.S. producers would "lose" only if they did not receive something they were entitled to receive. Yet they have no right to sell their products to unwilling buyers, so it cannot be said that U.S. companies lose as a result of foreign competition.

The "below cost" argument does not hold up under analysis. Although it is sometimes necessary to sell a product below cost because the market says the product is not worth the cost of production, companies that make a practice of consistently selling below cost to gain market share usually go out of business. Some commentators respond to this argument by stating that foreign governments subsidize these exports, making it possible to sell below cost without going out of business.

Although some governments do indeed encourage exports, should the importing country complain? I, for one, would not complain if Japanese taxpayers want to pay for part of my Japanese automobile or stereo. The ones who should be complaining about such policies are the Japanese taxpayers.[15]

The predatory pricing argument also falls apart under analysis. For one thing, it is inefficient.[16] For another, predatory pricing is a myth.[17] In the few cases where it has been tried, it has been unsuccessful, at least from a consumer perspective, except in cases where government has stepped in to prevent competitors from entering the market.

Companies that try to drive their competitors out of the market by cutting prices must fail. First, they must sell below cost, which cannot go on indefinitely. As prices drop, demand increases, which means they must produce more to satisfy the increased demand, thus losing even more money. Second, even if a company does succeed in driving its competitors out of the market, it cannot keep them out. As soon as it starts to raise prices, competitors will start to reappear. If a company does engage in predatory pricing and manages to drive a competitor out of business, the bankrupt competitor will have its assets bought by another company, which will then be a low-cost producer, because it was able to acquire the bankrupt company's assets for perhaps ten cents on the dollar.

Even if a predator could drive all competitors into bankruptcy, it will not be able to charge a monopoly price. Once it raises prices, new competitors will come into the market. For example, assume General Motors was able to drive Ford and Chrysler out of business. First, it would still have to compete with Fiat, Volvo, Volkswagen, Toyota, Hyundai, Honda, and numerous other companies. Second, there are any number of other companies that could enter the market in the absence of barriers to entry. General Electric or IBM or hundreds of other companies could decide to pick up the pieces of a few bankrupt firms and compete against General Motors. All it takes is capital and know-how. Large companies have the capital, and they can purchase the know-how (perhaps by making better offers to a few top General Motors employees).

The only thing that can keep competitors out of the market is governmentally imposed barriers to entry. Congress can pass laws to prevent an IBM or General Electric from entering the automotive industry, it can use existing antitrust laws to do it, or it can prohibit foreign automobile manufacturers from competing with General Motors. In the absence of governmentally imposed entry barriers, competition occurs in the marketplace because entrepreneurs perceive profitable opportunities.

The United States and other countries have enacted legislation aimed at preventing dumping and penalizing those caught dumping. The number of antidumping and antisubsidy cases has increased dramatically since the late 1970s,[18] and one author asserts that "the dramatic rise of such unfair trade cases is itself prima facie evidence of their use for harassment of successful foreign suppliers."[19] Patrick Messerlin examined more than 500 European Economic Community (EEC) antidumping cases brought between 1970 and 1985 and found that the General Agreement on Tariffs and Trade (GATT) rules were often used to harass and discriminate.[20]

In effect, antidumping laws are used to protect domestic producers, often (always?) at the expense of the consumer. Antidumping laws are based on a vague concept of "fairness," but the effect of enforcing such laws is to treat both producers and consumers unfairly.

The Job Destruction Argument

One of the most frequent arguments raised against unrestricted imports is that U.S. jobs will be lost. It is fairly easy to estimate the number of jobs lost in the U.S. automobile or steel industry by allowing imports into the country. One need only look at the number of such workers collecting unemployment insurance or look at the statistical compilations that have been made of automobile and steel industry employment totals, then discount that figure by some percentage based on the number of jobs that have been destroyed for other reasons, such as domestic competition, automation, and a decrease in domestic demand, and add back a percentage to represent the number of workers who were able to find other jobs. That is what is seen. However, what is not seen is the new jobs that are created as a result of free trade.

One source of jobs is the foreign auto and steel producers themselves. Foreign steel producers and motor vehicle manufacturers cannot spend U.S. dollars in their own countries. Those dollars must eventually return to the United States. They are deposited in the bank accounts of U.S. businesses that have sold goods to foreigners. The benefits of these sales permeate through the economy, expanding employment in many industries. For example, a Japanese automobile manufacturer investing in U.S. widgets increases employment in the U.S. widget industry. Widget industry workers spend their money on homes autos, appliances, beer, food, and many other items, which expands employment in these areas as well. However, these benefits are impossible to trace back to their origin—the American who purchased a Japanese motor vehicle, who gave the Japanese auto company the money to spend on U.S. products. All that is seen is the jobs that are lost in the U.S. automobile industry. By allowing U.S. consumers to buy the car of their choice, 50,000 automobile industry jobs might be lost, but perhaps 70,000 jobs might be created in other industries. The exact number of jobs created is impossible to measure, but it is reasonable to conclude that it is better to let the free market create jobs than to protect auto industry jobs at an annual cost of $160,000 per job.[21]

Imports create jobs in other ways as well. The transportation, retail, wholesale, and service industries expand if imports are allowed into the country. Again, the exact number of jobs created in this manner is impossible to measure, but it is reasonable to assume that individuals must be hired to service all the imports that are entering the market.

There is also a cross-fertilization effect. If U.S. automobile companies can purchase foreign steel cheaper than U.S. steel, they may be able to sell their cars for less, thus making them more competitive with foreign automobile producers. U.S. consumers benefit by the import of foreign steel, as do U.S. automobile manufacturers.[22] If U.S. consumers do not have to spend as much on automobiles, they can spend more on other goods and services, such as home repairs, education, clothes, or any number of other things. All industries benefit by allowing foreign steel to "invade" our shores, with the possible exception of U.S. steel producers. However, even here, there may be some beneficiaries. U.S. steel producers that cannot compete will have an incentive to curtail steel production and channel their resources into areas where there is more demand. Some U.S. steelmakers have expanded into specialty steel and oil, for example, and their companies are now more healthy than before as a result.

Public officials and others view an excess of imports over exports as detrimental to the economy. Yet, although the U.S. current account deficit quadrupled between 1982 and 1987, more than 13 million jobs were created—more than were created in Europe and Japan combined in the past 10 years. Between 1982 and 1986, the United States created jobs 3 times as fast as Japan and 20 times as fast as West Germany.[23] Between 1983 and 1987, the U.S. unemployment rate declined by 28%, while Japan's rate increased by 17% and the common market's rate increased by over 20% at a time when both Japan and the common market showed a trade surplus with the United States.

Not only do imports create jobs, but also, placing restrictions on imports destroys jobs. One study found that imposing "voluntary" export restraints in the steel industry actually destroyed more jobs than it saved.[24] Although some jobs in the steel industry were saved, more jobs were lost in the industries that use steel products, which had to pay higher steel prices as the result of the "voluntary" restraints. As a result of the 1984 steel voluntary export restraints, the steel industry gained 16,900 jobs while steel-using companies lost 52,400 jobs, for a net loss of more than 35,000 jobs. One author goes even further and states that U.S. steel import policies destroy 50 jobs in other parts of the economy for each job saved in the steel industry.[25]

The Deindustrialization Argument

Another argument in the popular press (and in some academic circles) is that the United States is deindustrializing. Bluestone and Harrison[26] have been among the most frequently cited modern advocates of this notion, which Bhagwati[27] refers to as the "manufacturing matters muddle." Nicholas Kaldor[28] was one of the first modern commentators to spread the doctrine, although the doctrine is actually as old as mercantilism itself.[29] Yet, a simple analysis of the facts proves this charge to be untrue. Manufacturing employment, although fluctuating somewhat, has remained about the same over the past few decades. The decline is only in relative, not absolute, terms, because the service sector has been expanding. Furthermore, industrial production is increasing because of increased productivity.[30] Thomas DiLorenzo[31] attempted to measure the extent of industrial decline but found that there was none. In fact, between 1982 and 1986, the United States gained 406,000 manufacturing jobs, at a time when the trade deficit was increasing.[32] Yet arguments continue to be heard that the United States is deindustrializing,[33] and some even assert that the United States of the future will be devoid of manufacturing.[34]

The Hamburger Flipper Argument

The hamburger flipper argument is a variation of the deindustrialization argument. Walter Mondale used it in his presidential campaign to argue that unless the United States adopts protectionist measures, the only jobs we will be able to get are flipping hamburgers at McDonalds or sweeping up around Japanese computers.[35]

As individuals lose their jobs because of a plant closure, they get new jobs to replace the jobs they lost. The Congressional Budget Office estimated that of the 8 million workers who were unemployed in January 1983, for example, only 20% lost jobs in a declining industry and most of the job losses were caused by the recession rather than by a structural change. Only 240,000 of the 1.6 million unemployed workers in declining industries had been unemployed for 26 weeks or more and only 60,000—representing 0.05%—had been on the job for 10 years or more. So, although some workers are displaced, the number displaced is small, and those who are displaced are displaced only temporarily in most cases.[36]

Do workers who lose their jobs have to settle for lower wages when they eventually find another job? Yes and no. Obviously, a steel worker who is paid 20% to 50% more than he would be worth in a free market will find it difficult to match the previous, inflated income.[37] The steel company he worked for was able to pay an above-market wage and pass the cost on to consumers because the industry was protected from foreign competition. When the protection was removed, the steel company could no longer stay in business and continue to pay the inflated wage. However, this kind of unemployment represents only about 20% of total unemployment. Actually, there is a shift away from lower paying jobs into higher paying jobs.[38] Furthermore, many of the workers earning low incomes are individuals who recently entered the job market, such as students and housewives, as well as retirees who just want to work part-time. Many of these workers are not the primary earners in their families, and their earnings are regarded as supplements to family income rather than the main source of family income.[39]

The Low Wage Argument

Protectionists often cite the fact that workers in foreign countries earn lower wages than domestic employees and claim that lower wages give foreign producers an unfair advantage. Although foreign workers often are paid less than their U.S. counterparts, U.S. labor productivity is often higher, which offsets this wage differential. Capital-intensive industries can afford to pay higher wages because wage costs form a smaller percentage of total costs than in labor-intensive industries.

Even if foreigners can undersell U.S. companies in some labor-intensive industries, consumers benefit because they can buy what they want for less money, which means they will have more to spend on other goods and services. Jobs will expand in other industries because of this increase in consumer spending in these other areas. It may be easy to see that industry A lost 5,000 jobs because of cheap foreign imports. What is less easy to see is the 4,000 or 7,000 or 10,000 jobs that have been created in other industries because consumers have more to spend on the goods and services these other industries produce.

A corollary of this low wage argument is that, in the absence of protectionism, Americans will also have to work for low wages or be forced into unemployment. However, although lifting protection may result in some downward pressure on nominal wage rates, lack of protection will also exert downward pressure on prices as competition increases so Americans will be able to purchase the same amount of goods for less money. Overall, consumers will be better off under free trade because the price of goods will decline, quality will increase, and they will no longer have to pay the cost of enforcing restrictive trade legislation.

The Full Employment Argument

The full employment argument is a spin-off of the hamburger flipper and low wage arguments. Those who advocate it see full employment rather than consumption as the goal. However, employment is merely the means used to achieve the end. All production is ultimately for consumption.[40] A nation's standard of living depends on the amount of goods and services that are available for consumption, not on the number of people who are employed. If employment were the key to prosperity, China would be the richest nation on earth.

Creating full employment is easy. All one has to do is draft a few million men into the army or outlaw farm machinery. These actions will not raise the standard of living but will actually lower it. If full employment were the goal, then our modern technological society is headed in the wrong direction. Rather than working 14 or 16 hours a day, six days a week, as our ancestors did, we now work 7 or 8 hours a day, five days a week. Our children go to school until age 18 or 22, rather than work in dingy factories or mines. Women have the option of working or not, whereas before they had the option of working in a factory or on a spinning loom at home.[41]

The Fairness Argument

One of the most popular recent arguments in favor of protectionism is that trade should be "fair" rather than free. It is unfair that other countries protect their domestic producers or dump their products on the U.S. market at low prices. What advocates of this position fail to see is that fairness is a process, not an outcome. Because of this failure to see the nature of the fairness concept, they fall into any number of other fallacious arguments. They would argue that it is unfair that some individuals or countries are rich while others are poor. They would argue that it is unfair that women earn less than men, even though some women choose to become bookkeepers rather than accountants, nurses rather than doctors, and so forth or choose to stay at home raising a family rather than climb the corporate ladder during their most productive years. Would it also be logical to argue that it is unfair that blacks comprise only 12% of the population yet comprise 75% of all professional basketball players—and earn more than whites, on average, to boot?[42] The remedy to this "unfair" state of affairs would be to establish quotas for white and oriental basketball players, a solution that would be ridiculous as well as unfair to the blacks who would lose their jobs to less qualified members of other races. Yet those who see fairness as an outcome rather than a process must logically advocate positions that would lead to absurd (and unfair!) results such as this.

Fairness should be seen as a process. A transaction is fair if consenting adults are free to enter into it without being coerced. It is fair that consumers are able to buy foreign products without having to pay a higher price due to some government intervention such as a tariff or import quota. It is unfair if some special interest group such as the steel lobby or the United Auto Workers uses the force of government to increase the price that consumers must pay for the goods and services of their choice. We cannot determine fairness by looking at the way things are; we must look at how things got that way.[43] If the current arrangement is the result of coercion, such as tariffs or quotas, it is unfair. If it is the result of consumer choice, it is fair.

It is unfair that foreign governments erect trade barriers that prevent U.S. products from entering their countries. It is unfair to U.S. producers and to the consumers in the foreign country. Such coercive acts by government prevent consenting adults from entering into contracts or, at least, raise the cost of entering into voluntary agreements. It does not follow that the U.S. government should retaliate by erecting trade barriers of its own to punish foreign producers for their governments' unfair acts. Erecting trade barriers of our own is unfair to U.S. consumers, who must pay higher prices for foreign goods or who might have to settle for a product that would be their second or third choice, if they had to buy American. It is also unfair to foreign producers, who would prefer to sell their products to U.S. consumers at lower prices.

Two wrongs do not make a right. Although that conclusion might seem obvious, it is a fact that many individuals in positions of authority fail to see this simple point. If they did, they would not advocate retaliating against foreign manufacturers whose governments act unfairly regarding international trade.

A corollary of the fair trade argument is that we should reduce our trade barriers only for countries that reduce their trade barriers for us. Using this line of logic, we might also argue that the U.S. government should continue to make U.S. consumers pay an extra 10%, or 20% or 50% for a Japanese radio or automobile—by keeping our high tariff—until Japan drops its tariff barriers against U.S. beef or fish or textiles. Our government will, thereby, reduce the standard of living of the millions of Americans who buy Japanese products until Japan's government lowers its tariffs for U.S. textile and food companies.

Millions of U.S. consumers suffer needlessly as a result of this irrational trade policy. The intelligent thing to do would be to unilaterally abolish our trade barriers, regardless of what other nations choose to do. That way, our standard of living will increase immediately, and we will not have to wait for years of delicate negotiations that may produce a less desirable result. A beneficial side effect of such a policy might be that consumers in other nations would see the results of our action and put pressure on their government officials to adopt the same policy. However, even if other nations do not reciprocate, U.S. consumers will still benefit because the prices consumers will be paying for foreign products will have been reduced.

Walter Block and Michael Walker point out another fallacy in the fair trade argument.[44] It is usually someone in a modern, industrialized country (first-world) who argues for fair trade. It is unfair to expect a company in a first-world country to compete with a company in a third-world country that has the advantage of lower wage rates. Yet it is fair for one first-world country to trade with another first-world country. For example, it is acceptable for Americans to buy Canadian shirts but not shirts made in Asia. The logical conclusion is that first-world countries should compete with first-world countries and third world countries should compete with third-world countries. Yet if such a policy were followed to any great extent, the economies of the first-world countries would stagnate because they would have to pay more for many products, and third-world countries would also suffer because many of their major markets would be closed to them.

The Level Playing Field Argument

The level playing field argument is a variation of the fair trade and dumping arguments. Like the advocates of fair trade, those who advocate a level playing field fall victim to the fallacy that trade should be viewed as an outcome rather than a process. The level playing field argument starts with the premise that no country should have an "unfair" competitive advantage over another. However, as was pointed out above, fairness is a matter of voluntary exchange. Exchange is fair if it is voluntary and unfair if coercion (such as tariffs or quotas) is involved.

Advocates of the level playing field argument often point out that foreign governments subsidize their producers' exports. U.S. lumber producers are at a disadvantage over Canadian lumber producers because the Canadian government subsidizes the Canadian lumber industry. Of course, the U.S. government does the same thing for certain producers of agricultural products, but that is somehow different. The U.S. government (taxpayer) subsidizes wheat production to the point where the United States is driving Australian wheat farmers out of business by dumping U.S. wheat on the Australian market.

The way to analyze this subsidization policy is to look at who wins and who loses. U.S. wheat farmers win because they are able to sell their wheat to Australians, which they would not be able to do in the absence of a subsidy. U.S. taxpayers lose because they are the ones who pay the subsidy. In effect, U.S. taxpayers are picking up part of the tab for the average Australian's grocery bill. Australian wheat farmers lose because U.S. wheat farmers can undersell them. Australian consumers gain because they can buy wheat products at lower prices than would be possible without the U.S. taxpayer subsidy.

Overall, the U.S. economy loses and the Australian economy gains as a result of the wheat subsidy. The vast majority of Australians benefit because they can buy wheat products at a lower cost, which means they now have more money to spend on other goods and services. The resources that Australian farmers formerly used to produce wheat— land, labor, capital, and entrepreneurial time and effort—can now be used to produce something else that they were not able to produce before. The only Australians who lose are the wheat farmers, who must shift resources into the production of something else. From a utilitarian perspective, Australia benefits because the majority benefit and only a minority are less well-off. From a property rights perspective, Australia is also better-off because no one's property rights are infringed upon.

The result is just the opposite for the United States. A few wheat farmers benefit at the expense of the majority, who must subsidize their wheat sales. U.S. taxpayers have their standard of living reduced because they must use part of their income to subsidize wheat farmers (and Australian wheat eaters) rather than to purchase goods and services. The property rights of the vast majority (taxpayers) are infringed, while a small minority (wheat farmers) receive tax dollars that they are not entitled to receive. In effect, wheat farmers are receiving "stolen goods," inasmuch as taxpayers are forced to part with a portion of their income to subsidize the wheat farmers.

Those who argue for a level playing field are actually arguing against the best interests of the vast majority of the population, at least in cases where they want foreign governments to stop subsidizing the products that domestic consumers buy. Australians who argue for a level playing field in wheat are arguing against the best interests of the vast majority of Australians. The ones who should argue for a level playing field are the U.S. taxpayers, who must otherwise subsidize a tiny minority of wheat farmers (who control the powerful farm lobby).

One of the most illogical cases of this level playing field mentality is the case where an American advocates quotas or tariffs on the importation of Japanese video cassette recorders (VCRs). None of the VCRs sold in the United States are made in the United States. No U.S. company makes VCRs. The Japanese (and perhaps a few other foreign producers) are the only producers. Not a single U.S. job is lost as a result of the free importation of VCRs. The fact that U.S. companies do not manufacture VCRs means that their productive resources are available to produce other products that they can sell on domestic and foreign markets. Those who advocate restrictions on the importation of VCRs are, in effect, saying that U.S. consumers should pay higher prices for something with no corresponding benefit. If the higher price they are forced to pay is the result of a tariff, the U.S. government is, in effect, taxing consumers for buying a VCR. If the higher price is the result of the U.S. government forcing the Japanese manufacturer to raise the price of the VCR, the U.S. consumer is subsidizing the Japanese manufacturer with the assistance of the U.S. government. In either case, the U.S. government is working against the interests of its own citizens.

The level playing field argument is philosophically flawed for another reason as well. Protectionists see trade as a win-lose proposition, like a sporting event. If one party wins, another must lose. However, trade is a win-win proposition. If two parties enter into a trade agreement, it is because they both gain by the exchange. Otherwise, there would be no trade.

This fallacious view of trade is not new. Frederic Bastiat exploded this myth more than a century ago. Bastiat used the example of a horse race to highlight the protectionist argument of his day.

> We believe that our protective tariffs should simply represent the difference between the net cost of a commodity that we produce and the net cost of a similar commodity produced in a foreign country. . . . A protective tariff computed on this basis merely assures free competition; . . . free competition exists only where there is equality in the costs and conditions of production. In the case of a horse race, the weight that each of the horses is to carry is ascertained, and conditions are equalized; otherwise, the horses would no longer be competitors. In the case of commerce, if one of the sellers can bring his goods to market more cheaply than the others, he ceases to be a competitor and becomes a monopolist. . . . If you abolish this protection, which represents the difference in net costs, the foreigner will invade your market and acquire a monopoly.
>
> Each person ought to wish, for his own sake as well as for the sake of his fellow citizens, that the production of the country be protected against foreign competition, *whenever a foreigner can furnish goods at a lower price.*[45]

In his response to this argument, Bastiat points out that the protectionists who take this position are taking the position of the producers, whereas those who advocate free trade take the position of the poor consumers, who must pay the price of protectionist measures. If the goal is to find out which horse is the fastest runner, then it makes sense to equalize the weight each horse must carry. However, if the goal is to get an important and urgent piece of news to a particular destination, it makes no sense to weigh down the horse that has the best chance of arriving first. If the goal is to satisfy the consumer at the lowest price, it does not make sense to increase the cost that consumers must pay by placing a tariff on cheaper foreign goods.

Inequality in the conditions of production between a foreign and a domestic industry does not mean that the higher cost industry will have to shut down completely. Low cost domestic producers will still be able to compete with foreign competitors, and high cost producers will have an incentive to enter another line of business where their resources can be used more productively.

The Strong Dollar Argument

Another popular argument that has been advanced is that a strong dollar is a source of our trade problems. Aside from the fact that this argument starts with a faulty premise—that trade deficits are always bad—it also assumes that there can be such a thing as a dollar that is too strong. Although it is true that imported goods cost less when the dollar is high relative to foreign currencies, there is no way to determine the correct price of the dollar. As long as exchange rates are flexible, consumers determine the relative strength of various currencies. It is nonsense to talk in terms of what the dollar should be valued at, because this value fluctuates constantly, along with the relative value of every other product and service.

A variation on this theme is the belief that the dollar should be measured in terms of some historical value, although it is never explained why this should be so. One popular benchmark is the 1980 dollar.[46] Yet when comparisons between 1980 prices of other commodities are made, the use of such benchmarks is seen to be ridiculous. Using 1980 as a benchmark, it appears that gasoline in 1989 is undervalued and hamburgers are overvalued. If a different benchmark is chosen—for example, 1960 — then it appears that gasoline is overvalued, because gasoline costs more today (and in 1980) than in did in 1960. Furthermore, because the dollar's value in 1980 was at a low point after going through a decade of inflation, comparing the relative value of the dollar today, using 1980 as a base, with the value of other currencies or commodities will produce distortions.

Because there is no such thing as a dollar that is too strong or too weak, it follows that attempts to restore the dollar to its correct value are absurd. Yet that is exactly what some individuals are advocating. Shifts in exchange rates are caused by changes in consumer preferences, in the absence of governmental tampering with exchange rates or the money supply. Furthermore, the market is a self-adjusting mechanism. If dollars rise too high to be sustained, imports will increase and dollars will flow into the international currency markets, thus reducing their relative value. There is no need to correct the market because the market corrects itself.

Exchange rates fluctuate based on the relative quantities of the various currencies that are in the international marketplace. Placing restrictions on imports causes fewer dollars to find their way into the international currency market, making the dollar relatively stronger. However, making the dollar artificially stronger by restricting imports tends to make imports even more attractive, which is the exact opposite of the policymaker's intention.

The Infant Industry Argument

Economists (including Adam Smith) advocating protectionism have cited the infant industry argument as the prime reason for shielding some domestic industries from foreign competition. It is one of the most basic and pervasive arguments, as well. Alexander Hamilton advocated it in his 1791 Report on Manufactures.[47] However, even this argument is based on faulty reasoning. According to the infant industry argument, government should protect a new industry from foreign competition so that it can, in time, grow strong enough to hold its own. Protection and various forms of subsidy are intended to be temporary, just until the new industry can get on its feet. The problem is that once an industry is protected or subsidized, it is difficult or nearly impossible to take away the protection. Interests become vested. In many cases, infant industries become midgets and never reach full height.[48] Furthermore, even when protection can help an infant industry, it does so by diverting resources from other industries, weakening them, and if the infant industry argument is used on many infant industries, the result will be no protection for any of them, because of the fallacy of composition.[49] In some cases, the infant industry approach does not work even when it is applied to only one industry.[50]

There is really no need to protect any industry, whether infant or mature. If foreigners can produce something better or cheaper than the domestic industry, it is to our advantage to buy foreign products and use our scarce resources to produce other products that we can do better than the competition. David Ricardo's law of comparative advantage comes into play here. Because we cannot produce everything, we should concentrate on what we can do well and buy everything else from foreigners.[51]

The Breathing Room Argument

Another popular argument in favor of protectionism is that U.S. industry only needs temporary protection. These industries, it is asserted, must have some breathing room so they can cut costs and improve productivity and then be able to compete with foreign producers. The steel, automobile, and textile industries are especially noted for using this argument, which is a variation on the "infant industry" theme. Murray Rothbard[52] calls it the senile industry argument.

The breathing room (senile industry) argument has not worked in practice. The U.S. auto industry is an example.[53] In 1981, the United States entered into a voluntary restraint agreement with Japan. Yet today, U.S. auto companies are still unable to compete with the Japanese, and there is pressure to continue the voluntary restraints and even tighten auto import restrictions. Temporary measures have a tendency to become permanent, to the detriment of consumers.

The steel industry is another example of where this breathing room strategy has failed. The U.S. steel industry has been cushioned from foreign producers since 1969 through quota agreements and restrictions. If the breathing room argument held water, steel industry production would be expected to increase and unit costs to fall. Yet just the opposite has been the case. Labor productivity has declined, and cost-cutting techniques have not been implemented. Investment in the steel industry actually declined after import restrictions were imposed, while foreign investment rose steadily.[54]

There is strong evidence to suggest that voluntary export restraints (VER) actually destroy more jobs than they save. For example, in Reagan's 1984 VER, aimed at reducing steel imports from 26% to 22% of domestic sales, employment in the steel industry increased by 17,000. However, employment in steel user industries declined by 52,000 because of the higher prices they had to pay for steel.[55]

The breathing room argument is also theoretically unsound. Competition provides incentives to improve quality and reduce costs. Taking away this incentive by insulating an industry from foreign competition retards these improvements. In effect, government restrictions on foreign imports give U.S. producers a monopoly. When there is monopoly, there is far less incentive to innovate, cut costs, and improve quality because consumers have fewer choices in the marketplace.

The Tax Burden Argument

The tax burden argument states that foreign producers have a lower tax burden than do domestic producers, which gives them a built-in structural advantage. If foreign producers actually had a lower tax burden, the solution is simple—reduce domestic corporate tax rates to make U.S. industry more competitive. Yet this solution is seldom offered. An analysis of the tax burdens in various industrialized countries, however, reveals that the premise is incorrect. As a result of the various tax reform measures passed in the early 1980s, the United States has one of the lowest corporate tax burdens of any industrialized country. A Library of Congress study found that Japanese manufacturers pay an effective rate of 50.5%, compared with 27.7% for U.S. manufacturers.[56] The total tax burden of a Japanese automobile sold in the United States is actually slightly higher than the tax burden on a U.S. automobile sold in the United States. Furthermore, Japan does not impose a tariff on automobile imports, whereas the United States does.

The Voluntary Restraint Argument

A voluntary restraint agreement is an agreement between the United States and some other country to limit imports of a certain product. For example, Japan has agreed not to export more than a certain number of automobiles to the United States. A number of countries have agreed not to do the same for steel.

One major problem with "voluntary" restraints is that they are not voluntary. These agreements are not between companies but between governments. The Japanese government prevents its automobile manufacturers from sending automobiles to the United States even though there are willing customers waiting to buy their products. The U.S. government uses threats and intimidation to get foreign governments to agree to these "voluntary" restrictions, because the absence of an agreement could lead to even less desirable trade terms.[57] U.S. consumers are hurt as a result, because some of them must settle on a choice that is lower down on their subjective value scale. The fact that it is called "voluntary" does not change the fact that consumers are hurt.

Robert Crandall[58] estimates that the VER on automobiles with Japan increased the price of a Japanese automobile by $2,500 in 1984 and allowed domestic manufacturers to charge $1,000 more than they would have been able to obtain in the absence of the quota. He estimated that this VER cost U.S. consumers about $16 billion in 1984 and 1985.

Another problem with so-called voluntary agreements is that they do not do what they are supposed to do. For example, Japan and the United States entered into an orderly marketing agreement in 1977 that limited the number of color televisions that Japan could send to the United States. As a result, the number of Japanese color televisions exported to the United States dropped from 2.50 million units to 1.56 million. However, domestic producers did not benefit from this decline, because the reduced number of Japanese imports was offset by increased imports from South Korea, Taiwan, and Canada. Furthermore, the restrictions were circumvented by starting production in the United States and then shipping the parts abroad, where the bulk of the manufacturing and assembly took place. The nearly completed units were shipped back to the United States for final assembly. This roundabout process undoubtedly increased costs, which would not have been necessary in the absence of the trade restriction.[59]

Voluntary restraints in the steel industry provide a further example. In 1968, the United States entered into a voluntary restraint agreement with Japanese and European exporters. They agreed to reduce the import tonnage by 22%, which they did. However, rather than maintain the previous product mix, the exporters shifted their exports from low-value basic steel to higher-value specialty steel products, so that even though the tonnage total was reduced, the market value of the steel they exported remained at about the same level as before.[60]

The Debtor-Nation Argument

Those of the protectionist mentality point out that the United States is a debtor nation, meaning that Americans owe foreigners more than foreigners owe Americans. They think that being a debtor nation is harmful. Would they rather have it the other way? If so, then they must think that it would be better for Americans to invest overseas than at home. Do they also think that Americans should send their money overseas to buy foreign goods rather than buy American-made products?

This debtor-nation argument has a number of other weaknesses as well. Although borrowing to finance the federal deficit is irresponsible because it siphons off money that could be used for private investment and causes the nation's debt burden to increase, borrowing by business to finance growth is good business. If a company can borrow at 12% and invest the proceeds to earn 16% then it is good business to borrow from anyone who wants to lend the money. If interest rates rise to 80%, it still makes good sense to borrow if the proceeds can be plowed into something that yields more than 80%. The fact that a business owes money does not mean that the business is unhealthy. In fact, it often means just the opposite. Sick businesses cannot find anyone to lend them money. The federal government, however, can borrow money because of its taxing power and ability to print money to repay both principal and interest.

Lending to business makes the economy healthy. Businesses expand production, create jobs, and flood the market with products that consumers (foreign and domestic) want to buy. Foreign investment helps make the U.S. economy stronger, so why should anyone be against it? Both parties benefit, the lender and the borrower. Other parties also benefit, such as the workers who must be employed to fill the newly created jobs and the consumers who now have more product choices. No one loses.

Historically, the U.S. economy has been healthiest when it was a debtor nation. The United States was a debtor nation during the rapid expansion of the nineteenth century. It was also a debtor nation during the economic expansion of the 1980s. It was a creditor nation during the depression of the 1930s, when no one wanted to lend U.S. business any money.[61] The whole debtor nation argument is based on faulty logic. On the one hand, protectionists complain that too much money is leaving the country because Americans are buying foreign goods. Then, when it comes back in the form of investment, they complain again because foreigners are pouring their money into the national economy (and creating jobs for Americans in the process).

The Retaliation Argument

Those who pay lip service to free trade argue that the United States should use trade as a weapon. We should threaten to erect trade barriers against nations that have erected trade barriers against the United States.[62] Those who advocate such policies are under the false impression that only the exporting country benefits by trade. Trade is mutually beneficial, and curtailing it for any reason hurts both sides. Restricting foreign imports is the same as restricting consumer purchases. There is no way to restrict one without restricting the other. Erecting trade barriers restricts consumer choice and causes prices to rise, because there is less competition.

If the U.S. government erects trade barriers, it can expect other countries to do likewise as a retaliatory measure. The effect of such restrictive policies is to reduce trade even more, hurting consumers. U.S. companies that export are also harmed by such policies, along with the employees of the exporters, who risk losing their jobs because of the government's restrictive trade practices.

Erecting trade barriers also cuts the foreign demand for U.S. products. If less dollars flow overseas, less dollars can flow back into the country. Foreign countries cannot spend dollars they do not have.

There is much empirical evidence to support the view that trade wars reduce exports. The Smoot-Hawley Tariff of 1930, for example, resulted in a dramatic decline in U.S. imports. In return, foreign countries retaliated by erecting high trade barriers of their own.[63] This act and its aftermath deepened and lengthened the depression.

The National Defense Argument

Defense is more important than opulence.[64]

Another argument for protectionism is that we must protect Industry A or Industry B for reasons of national defense. The oil industry is often cited as an example.[65] The argument states that if the United States does not protect its oil industry by imposing quotas or import fees on foreign oil or by subsidizing the domestic industry, we will be overrun with foreign oil; our domestic oil industry will be devastated and unable to supply us with the needed oil if foreign supplies should be cut off in time of war.

Actually, the oil import restrictions the United States placed on oil during the 1960s drained domestic reserves and increased U.S. vulnerability in the 1970s.[66] Furthermore, a shortage of oil would make us think twice before getting involved in a foreign war, and lack of oil would be the least of our worries in the event of a nuclear war. If we really needed to fight a conventional war, there is enough oil in the ground to meet our needs, although it may take a few months to get the oil pumping. However, even this problem could be avoided by keeping a few months' worth of oil in reserve.[67] Conventional wars seldom start without warning, and if it appears that war might be on the horizon, the U.S. oil industry could make the necessary preparations. There is no need to protect the oil industry by placing trade restrictions on the importation or exportation of oil. Actually, refusing to protect the oil industry (or any other industry) against foreign competition will force it to become more efficient, which enhances national defense.

Another problem with the defense argument is that once one exception is made for one industry, there is no logical stopping point. Every industry in need of protection will assert national defense as a valid reason for government intervention. At one time in our history, a trade association for the U.S. glove industry stated that national defense required that Congress place a high tariff on the importation of gloves. U.S. soldiers needed gloves, and a future war effort would be imperiled if they could not get them because the foreign source was cut off. Section 104 of the 1952 Defense Production Act restricts peanut imports in the interests of national defense.[68] The cheese, fruit, watch manufacturing, railroad, airline, truck, and telephone industries have also used the defense argument when asking for protection.[69] Where does it all end?

A corollary of the idea that we should trade with our friends is that we should not trade with our enemies, but this second idea often does not hold water and harms us more than it harms our enemies. For example, the United States could decide not to sell wheat to the former Soviet Union, but that does not mean that the Soviets will not be able to obtain wheat. They can very easily get it from Canada or some other country. Also, if U.S. wheat sales are diverted to some other country, there is no guarantee that the wheat will not turn up in the Soviet Union eventually. The only predictable part of this restraint is that U.S. farmers will lose a sale to someone else.[70] Economic sanctions generally do not work.[71] At most, they will raise the price of the restricted goods for the country intended to be punished, and the countries that participate in the sanctions will lose sales without being able to show any corresponding benefit. In fact, sanctions often increase animosity between countries that are not currently on friendly terms.

A variation on the defense theme is the self-sufficiency theme. This argument calls for a country to be economically self-sufficient, because of nationalistic reasons, to encourage domestic employment, or because trading with others corrupts the soul. This latter reason was argued by Plato and Aristotle as sufficient reason for limiting trade with outsiders.[72] Durant[73] discusses Plato's thinking on this point. Schumacher[74] is a modern exponent of it. The problem with this position is that self-sufficiency greatly reduces the division of labor, which results in a reduced standard of living.[75] If every community has to make everything for itself, it cannot specialize in the things it does best and trade for everything else. It means that Canadian residents will not be able to eat bananas or pineapples and Honolulu residents will not be able to eat potato chips. This logic would have us believe that it is somehow bad to sell pineapples to Canadians but good to sell them to residents of Maine or New Hampshire, which is absurd. Free trade enhances harmony and peaceful cooperation, whereas self-sufficiency and trade restrictions lead to animosity between nations and actually increase the chance of war.

Rather than free trade being a threat to national defense, there is substantial evidence to suggest that lack of free trade is a threat to peace. Many wars were caused, at least in part, because of trade restrictions and the adoption of mercantilist trade policies. World Wars I and II are perfect examples. World War I was preceded by tariff and trade wars. The depression of the 1930s, which, along with the Treaty of Versailles, prepared the way for World War II, was aggravated by the erection of trade barriers such as the Smoot-Hawley Tariff that practically cut off the flow of imports into the United States.[76] Roosevelt's trade embargo of Japan, which hindered its invasion of Manchuria and crippled its domestic economy, practically forced it to bomb Pearl Harbor.[77]

One of the main causes of the American Revolution was England's mercantilist policies. The various Navigation Acts required cargo to be carried on English ships manned by English seamen. The Staple Act required goods that were imported to the colonies from Europe to first go through British ports. The Hat Act, the Woolens Act, and numerous other acts of Parliament prevented the colonies from exporting manufactured goods, making them dependent on British trade. High tariffs were placed on goods that did not come from Britain or a British colony, which increased their price to the point where British goods looked cheap by comparison.[78] Gold was not permitted to flow from England to the colonies, but a flow in the opposite direction was encouraged, under the mistaken mercantilist belief that wealth was measured by the amount of gold in the treasury rather than by the amount of goods and services the economy produced.[79]

Many other wars were caused, at least in part, by trade restrictions, which are often used as economic weapons—a substitute for military action. For example, the 1651 Navigation Act caused the First Anglo-Dutch War of 1652-54.[80] The second and third Anglo-Dutch wars were also caused by restrictive trade policies. Other wars in this era caused by nationalistic economic policies included King William's War, the French and Indian War (Seven Years' War), and the various other wars and skirmishes between England and France that did not end until the Congress of Vienna in 1815, various wars with Spain, including the War of Spanish Succession (Queen Anne's War) and the War of Jenkin's Ear, and the War of Austrian Succession.[81] All these wars had to be paid for, and the king and Parliament found it easier to finance them by borrowing than by taxing. The seeds of the American Revolution were sown in the 1760s, when England attempted to get the American colonists to help pay these war debts by taxing them. All these wars could have been prevented if England and the other European economic powers of the time had adopted free trade policies rather than mercantilism.

Notes

1. Adam Smith, *An Inquiry into the Nature and Causes of the Wealth of Nations* (1776/1937), p. 461.

2. Plato, *Laws*, IV, 705a; Aristotle, *The Politics*, I, VII, chap. 4.

3. For Bastiat's views on free trade, see *Sophismes Économiques*, which is in Volume I of *Oeuvres Complètes de Frédéric Bastiat,* fourth edition (Guillaumin et Cie, 1878). Many of Bastiat's works have been translated into English. For example, see his *Economic Sophisms; Selected Essays on Political Economy* (Irvington-on-Hudson, N.Y.: Foundation for Economic Education, 1964); *Economic Harmonies* (Irvington-on-Hudson, N.Y.: Foundation for Economic Education, 1964). For information about John Prince Smith, see Ralph Raico, "John Prince Smith and the German Free-Trade Movement," in *Man, Economy and Liberty: Essays in Honor of Murray N. Rothbard,* eds. Walter Block and Llewellyn Rockwell, Jr. (Auburn, Ala.: Ludwig von Mises Institute, 1988), pp. 341-51; J. Becker, *Das Deutsche Manchestertum* (1907); W. O. Henderson, "Prince Smith and Free Trade in Germany," *Economic History Review* 2 (1950): 295. Richard Cobden and John Bright have had literally hundreds of books and articles written about their work, many of which are in English. Literature on these two English economists is sometimes listed under "Anti-Corn Law League" or "The Manchester School" as well as under Cobden and Bright. Also see Francis W. Hirst (ed.), *Free Trade and Other Fundamental Doctrines of the Manchester School* (London and New York: Harper Brothers, 1903; New York: Augustus M. Kelley, 1968).

4. Richard Cantillon, *Essai Sur la Nature Du Commerce en Général* [Essay on the Nature of Commerce in General] (1755; 1931). There is some speculation that Cantillon got some of his ideas, such as the monetary approach to the balance of payments, from David Hume, but there are doubts as to the validity of this allegation, because early drafts of *Essai* were in circulation long before Hume's essays *Of Money and of the Balance of Trade* first appeared in 1752. See Antoine E. Murphy, "Richard Cantillon—Banker and Economist," *Journal of Libertarian Studies* 7 (1985): 203. In fact, there is some speculation that Hume read Cantillon before he wrote his own essays on the subject. See F. A. Hayek, *Prices and Production* (London: Routledge & Sons, 1931/2 and 1935/9). For more on Hume's balance of payments and trade theories, see D. K. Fausten, "The Humean Origin of the Contemporary Monetary Approach to the Balance of Payments," *Quarterly Journal of Economics* 93 (1979): 655, H. G. Grubel, "Ricardo and Thornton on the Transfer Mechanism", *Quarterly Journal of Economics* 75 (1961): 292; Robert W. McGee, "The Economic Thought of David Hume," *Hume Studies* 15 (1989): 184; F. Petrella, "Adam Smith's Rejection of Hume's Price-Specie-Flow Mechanism: A Minor Mystery Resolved," *Southern Economic Journal* 34 (1968): 365; C.E. Staley, "Hume and Viner on the International Adjustment Mechanism," *History of Political Economy* 8 (1976): 252; M.I. Duke, "David Hume and Monetary Adjustment," *History of Political Economy* 11 (1979): 572.

5. Vilfredo Pareto, *Manual of Political Economy* (1927), pp. 377, 379.

6. Robert Nozick, *Anarchy, State, and Utopia* (New York: Basic Books, 1974), p. 272.

7. W. M. Curtiss, *The Tariff Idea* (Irvington-on-Hudson, N.Y.: Foundation for Economic Education, 1953), p. 19.

8. Frederic Bastiat elaborates on this theme in *The Law* (Irvington-on-Hudson, N.Y.: Foundation for Economic Education, 1968). Dean Russell discusses the same phenomenon in *Government and Legal Plunder: Bastiat Brought Up to Date* (Irvington-on-Hudson, N.Y.: Foundation for Economic Education, 1985).

9. Bastiat, *The Law*, p. 21.

10. Frank Chodorov, "The Humanity of Trade," in *Free Trade: The Necessary Foundation for World Peace*, ed. J. K Taylor (Irvington-on-Hudson, N.Y.: Foundation for Economic Education, 1986), p. 7.

11. Bjorn Ahlstrom, "Protecting Whom from What?" *The Freeman* 39 (1989): 153.

12. Ludwig von Mises, *Human Action*, third revised edition (Chicago, Ill.: Henry Regnery Company, 1966), p. 317.

13. This second definition is the General Agreement on Tariffs and Trade (GATT), Article VII definition, but charging different prices in different markets is simply rational profit-maximizing behavior, as any student of price discrimination theory knows.

14. The example, in the original French, may be found in Oeuvres *Complètes de Frédéric Bastiat,* Volume I, 4th ed., p. 57. The English translation is in Bastiat's *Economic Sophisms*, p. 55.

15. (London: Trade Policy Research Centre, 1975), p. xxxiii, as cited in Melvyn. B. Krauss, *The New Protectionism: The Welfare State and International Trade* (New York: New York University Press, 1978), p. 86.

16. D. T. Armentano, *Antitrust Policy: The Case for Repeal* (Washington, D.C.: Cato Institute, 1986), p.43.

17. R. Koller, Jr., "The Myth of Predatory Pricing: An Empirical Study," *Antitrust Law & Economics Review* 4 (1971): 105; John McGee, "Predatory Price Cutting: The Standard Oil (N.J.) Case," *Journal of Law & Economics* 1 (1958): 137.

18. J. Finger and J. Nogues, "International Control of Subsidies and Countervailing Duties," *World Bank Economic Review* 9 (1987): 707.

19. Jagdish N. Bhagwati, *Protectionism* (Cambridge, Mass.: MIT Press, 1988), p. 48.

20. P. Messerlin, *The Long Term Evolution of the EC Anti-Dumping Law: Some Lessons for the New AD Laws in LDCs* (Washington, D.C.: World Bank, 1987), p. 21, as cited by Bhagwati, *Protectionism*, p. 51.

21. Robert Crandall, "Import Quotas and the Automobile Industry: The Costs of Protectionism," *Brookings Review* 2 (1984): 16.

22. Restrictions on imported steel cost U.S. auto companies $300 per auto, according to one estimate. A Federal Trade Commission study found that limiting foreign steel producers to 18% of the U.S. market would cost consumers $8.5 billion in direct price increases and decreased economic efficiency. See Wayne Gable, *Myths About International Trade* (Washington, D.C.: Citizens for a Sound Economy, n.d.), p. 4; Walter Williams, *All It Takes Is Guts: A Minority View* (Washington, D.C.: Regnery Gateway, 1987), p.78.

23. A. Shapiro, "Why the Trade Deficit Does Not Matter," *Journal of Applied Corporation Finance* 2 (1989): 87-95.

24. Arthur T. Denzau, *How Import Restraints Reduce Employment*, Publication No. 80 (St. Louis, Mo.: Washington University, Center for the Study of American Business, 1987).

25. J. Michael Finger, "The Political Economy of Trade Policy," *Cato Journal* 3 (Winter 1983/84): 743.

26. Barry Bluestone and Bennett Harrison, *The Deindustrialization of America* (New York: Basic Books, 1982).

27. Bhagwati, *Protectionism,* p. 110.

28. Nicholas Kaldor, *The Causes of the Slow Economic Growth of the United Kingdom* (Oxford: Oxford University Press, 1966).

29. M. Folsom and S. Lubar (eds.), *The Philosophy of Manufactures: Early Debates Over Industrialization in the United States* (New York: Kelley, 1980).

30. For more on this point, see Richard B. McKenzie, *Competing Visions: The Political Conflict Over America's Economic Future* (Washington, D.C.: Cato Institute, 1985), p. 38; Charles L. Schultze, "Industrial Policy: A Dissent," in *Plant Closings: Public or Private Choices?* ed. Richard B. McKenzie (Washington, D.C.: Cato Institute, 1984), p. 155; and William H. Branson, "The Myth of Deindustrialization," in *Plant Closings: Public or Private Choices?* ed. McKenzie, (1984), p.177.

31. Thomas DiLorenzo, *The Myth of America's Declining Manufacturing Sector,* Heritage Foundation Backgrounder (Washington, D.C.: Heritage Foundation, 1984).

32. A. Shapiro, "Why the Trade Deficit Does Not Matter."

33. T. White, "The Danger from Japan," *New York Times Magazine*, July 28, 1985, p.23, as cited in Bhagwati, *Protectionism*, p. 64.

34. S. Chaikin, "Trade, Investment, and Deindustrialization," *Foreign Affairs* 60 (1988): 836-48.

35. Bhagwati, *Protectionism*, p. 64; The *New York Times,* October 13, 1982, p. A3; M. Schram, " 'Big Fritz': Tough Talk and a Flag," *Washington Post,* October 7, 1982, p. 1; McKenzie, *Competing Visions: The Political Conflict over America's Economic Future,* p. 65.

36. Richard B. McKenzie, *National Industrial Policy* (Dallas, Tex.: The Fisher Institute, 1984), p. 67.

37. The rate of compensation in motor vehicles to that in all manufactures was about 165% in 1982. The ratio in iron and steel was 189%. Even if wages in these industries were cut to make them competitive with wages in Japan, the ratio would still be considerably above average, so it cannot be said that the tariff is needed to protect downtrodden labor. See M. Kreinin, "Wage Competitiveness in the U.S. Auto and Steel Industries," *Contemporary Policy Issues* 4 (January 1984): 39; Edward Tower, "Some Empirical Results on Trade and National Prosperity," *Cato Journal* 3 (Winter 1983/84): 639-40. However, the problem with the auto and steel industries is due to more than just excessive wages. Outmoded facilities and union work rules also play major roles. One study found that the group of nonfarm labor that would benefit most by unilateral tariff reductions would be unskilled labor. See J. Hartigan and E. Teller, "Trade Policy and the American Income Distribution," *Review of Economics & Statistics* 72 (May 1982): 261.

38. N. Rosenthal, "The Shrinking Middle Class: Myth or Reality?" *Monthly Labor Review* (March 1985): 4; Richard B. McKenzie, *The American Job Machine* (New York: Universe Books, 1988), p. 102.

39. McKenzie, *The American Job Machine,* pp. 108-12.

40. The idea that all production is ultimately for consumption is Say's Law, which John Maynard Keynes attacked in his *General Theory of Employment, Interest and Money* (New York: Harcourt Brace, 1936). However, Keynes attacked a straw man, as has been pointed out by Mises, Hutt, and Sowell, among others. See Keynes, *The General Theory of Employment, Interest and Money*, p. 25; Ludwig von Mises, "Lord Keynes and Say's Law," *Freeman* 1 (October 30, 1950): 83, reprinted in Henry Hazlitt (ed.), *The Critics of Keynesian Economics* (New York: D. Van Nostrand, 1960); W. H. Hutt, *Keynesianism—Retrospect and Prospect* (Chicago, Ill.: Henry Regnery Company, 1963); W. H. Hutt, *A Rehabilitation of Say's Law* (Athens: Ohio University Press, 1975); W. H. Hutt, *The Keynesian Episode: A Reassessment* (Indianapolis, Ind.: Liberty Press, 1979); and Thomas Sowell, *Say's Law* (Princeton, N.J.: Princeton University Press, 1972), pp. 201-18.

41. For more on this point, see Richard B. McKenzie, *The American Job Machine* (New York: Universe Books, 1988).

42. Williams, *All It Takes Is Guts: A Minority View*, p. 80.

43. Ibid., p. 81.

44. Walter Block and Michael Walker, *Lexicon of Economic Thought* (Vancouver: Fraser Institute, 1989), pp. 131-32.

45. Bastiat, *Economic Sophisms,* p. 28; *Sophismes Économiques*, pp. 27-28.

46. Gable, *Myths About International Trade*, p. 7.

47. Hamilton's report is reproduced in A. H. Cole (ed.), *Industrial and Commercial Correspondence of Alexander Hamilton* (New York: Kelley, 1968).

48. Charles P. Kindleberger, "International Trade and National Prosperity," *Cato Journal* 3 (Winter 1983/84): 631; W. M. Corden, *Trade Policy and Economic Welfare* (New York: Oxford University Press, 1974).

49. Kindleberger, "International Trade and National Prosperity," p. 630; Larry E. Westphal, *Empirical Justification for Infant Industry Protection,* World Bank Working Paper No. 445, Washington, D.C., March 1981; Tower, "Some Empirical Results on Trade and National Prosperity," p. 642.

50. Anne O. Krueger and Baran Tuncer, "An Empirical Test of the Infant Industry Argument," *American Economic Review* 75 (1982): 1142; Lila J. Truett and Dale B. Truett, *Economics* (St. Louis, Mo.: Times Mirror/Mosby College Publishing, 1987), p. 726.

51. However, comparative advantage is not the key here. Some economists have argued that because of modern technology or other reasons, the law of comparative advantage no longer applies. Although that view is questionable, the key is that it is better to buy cheap than to buy expensive, regardless of whether the law of comparative advantage still applies or not.

52. Murray N. Rothbard, "Protectionism and the Destruction of Prosperity" in *The Free Market Reader*, ed. Llewellyn H. Rockwell, Jr. (Burlingame, Calif.: The Ludwig von Mises Institute, 1988), pp. 148-59.

53. Gable, *Myths About International Trade*, p. 14.

54. Ibid.

55. Denzau, *How Import Restraints Reduce Employment,* pp. 56; McKenzie, *The American Job Machine,* pp. 148-49.

56. Gable, *Myths About International Trade*, p. 17.

57. Many voluntary restraint agreements are the result of an unfair trade practice petition. See J. Finger and J. Nogues, "International Control of Subsidies and Countervailing Duties"; J. Finger, H. Hall, and D. Nelson, "The Political Economy of Administered Protection," *American Economic Review* 72 (1982): 452; Bhagwati, *Protectionism*, p. 53. "Orderly marketing agreements" and "adjustment assistance programs," although different in form, also have a negative effect on employment and free trade. See Leland B. Yeager and David G. Tuerok, "Realism and Free-Trade Policy," *Cato Journal* 3 (Winter 1983/84): 645-48; James Dorn, "Trade Adjustment Assistance: A Case of Government Failure," *Cato Journal* 2 (1982): 865.

58. R. Crandall, "Detroit Rode Quotas to Prosperity," *Wall Street Journal,* January 29, 1986, p. 30.

59. Victor A. Canto, "U.S. Trade Policy: History and Evidence," *Cato Journal* 3 (Winter 1983/84): 679-93; Victor A. Canto and Arthur Laffer, "The Effectiveness of Orderly Marketing Agreements: The Color TV Case," *Business Economics* 18 (January 1983): 38.

60. Canto, "U.S. Trade Policy: History and Evidence"; V. Canto, R. Eastin, and A. Laffer, "Failure of Protectionism: A Study of the Steel Industry," *Columbia Journal of World Business* 17 (1982): 43.

61. Gable, *Myths About International Trade*, p. 23.

62. "Talking Loudly and Carrying a Crowbar," *The Economist,* April 29, 1989, pp. 23-24, "The Myth of Managed Trade," *The Economist,* May 6, 1989, pp. 11-12; "Trade: Mote and Beam," *The Economist,* May 6, 1989, pp. 2223; A. Dowd, "What To Do About Trade Policy," *Fortune*, May 8, 1989, p. 106.

63. Benjamin M. Anderson, *Economics and the Public Welfare* (New York: D. Van Nostrand, 1949 Indianapolis, Ind.: Liberty Press, 1979), p. 225; Hans F. Sennholz, *Age of Inflation* (Belmont, Mass.: Western Islands, 1979), pp. 52, 128; Gable, *Myths About International Trade*, pp. 24-25; The Smoot-Hawley Tariff Act of 1930, Pub. L. No. 71-361, 46 Stat. 590.

64. Smith, *An Inquiry into the Nature and Causes of the Wealth of Nations,* p. 431.

65. Robert L. Bradley, Jr., *The Mirage of Oil Protection* (Lanham, Md.: University Press of America, 1989).

66. Thomas D. Willett and Mehrdad Jalalighajar, "U.S. Trade Policy and National Security," *Cato Journal* 3 (Winter 1983/84): 717-18, 721; J. Cox and A. Wright, "A Tariff Policy for Independence from Oil Embargoes," *National Tax Journal* 28 (March 1975): 29.

67. J. Plummer, "United States Oil Stockpiling Policy," *Journal of Contemporary Studies* 4 (1981): 5; G. Horwich and E. Mitchell (eds.), *Policies for Coping with Oil-Supply Disruptions* (New York: Praeger, 1982).

68. Curtiss, *The Tariff Idea*, p. 65.

69. Robert B. Ekelund, Jr., and Robert D. Tollison, *Economics*, second edition (Glenview, Ill., and Boston, Mass.: Scott, Foresman and Company, 1988), p. 868.

70. Earl Ravenal, "The Economic Claims of National Security," *Cato Journal* 3 (Winter 1983/84): 729-30.

71. There is ample empirical evidence to support this claim. For example, see M. Doxey, *Economic Sanctions and International Enforcement* (Washington, D.C.: Institute for International Economics, 1980); K. Knorr, *The Power of Nations* (New York: Macmillan, 1975); Willett and Jalalighajar, "U.S. Trade Policy and National Security," pp. 723-26.

72. Plato, *Laws*; Aristotle, *The Politics*; Lewis H. Haney, *History of Economic Thought* (New York: Macmillan, 1949), pp. 56-59. Walter Olson points out the irony of this "dependency" argument. Americans are dependent on foreigners for things like towels and tape decks, and foreigners are dependent on us

for things like food and raw materials. See Walter Olson, "Don't Slam the Door," *National Review* 35 (March 4, 1983): 248.

73. Will Durant, *The Story of Philosophy* (New York: Washington Square Press, 1952), pp. 19-20, 37-38.

74. E. Schumacher, *Small Is Beautiful* (Englewood Cliffs, NJ: Prentice-Hall, 1973).

75. V. Canto, A. Laffer, and J. Turney, "Trade Policy and the U.S. Economy," *Financial Analyst Journal* (September/October 1982): 237.

76. Murray N. Rothbard, *America's Great Depression* (Los Angeles, Calif.: Nash Publishing, 1963).

77. Willett and Jalalighajar, "U.S. Trade Policy and National Security," p. 725; Y. Wu, *Economic Warfare* (New York: Macmillan, 1952), p. 267; James J. Martin, "Pearl Harbor: Antecedents, Background and Consequences," in *The Saga of Hog Island* (Colorado Springs, Colo.: Ralph Myles, Publisher, 1977), p. 114. Discussing the economic factors leading to war in general, or to World Wars I and II in particular, would take another chapter, if not a book. For the causes of World War I, see L. C. F. Turner, *Origins of the First World War* (New York: W.W. Norton, 1970); Sidney Bradshaw Fay, *The Origins of the World War* (New York: Macmillan, 1939); Harry Elmer Barnes, *In Quest of Truth and Justice* (Chicago, Ill.: National Historical Society, 1928; Colorado Springs, Colo.: Ralph Myles, Publisher, 1972). For the causes of World War II, see A. J. P. Taylor, *The Origins of the Second World War* (New York: Athenium, 1983); Henry Elmer Barnes, "A. J. P. Taylor and the Causes of World War II," *New Individualist Review* 2 (1962): 3; William Henry Chamberlin, *America's Second Crusade* (Chicago, Ill.: Henry Regnery Company, 1950/62). For an in-depth study of 967 wars occurring between 500 B.C. and 1925 A.D., see Pitirim A. Sorokin, *The Crisis of Our Age: The Social and Cultural Outlook* (New York: Dutton, 1941). For an analysis of the relationship between economic nationalism and war, see Ludwig von Mises, *Omnipotent Government* (New Rochelle, N.Y.: Arlington House, 1969); Ludwig von Mises, "The Economics of War," in *Free Trade: The Necessary Foundation for World Peace*, ed. J. K. Taylor (Irvington-on-Hudson, N.Y.: Foundation for Economic Education, 1986), pp. 77-83; David Osterfeld, "The Nature of Modern Warfare," in Taylor (ed.), *Free Trade: The Necessary Foundation for World Peace*, pp. 84-90, Hans F. Sennholz, "Welfare States at War," in Taylor (ed.), *Free Trade: The Necessary Foundation for World Peace*, pp. 91-96; S. Husbands, "Free Trade and Foreign Wars," in Taylor (ed.), *Free Trade: The Necessary Foundation for World Peace*, pp. 97-105.

78. Clarence B. Carson, "The Mercantile Impasse," in Clarence B. Carson, *The Rebirth of Liberty: The Founding of the American Republic, 1760-1800* (Greenville, Ala.: American Textbook Committee, 1973/76), reprinted in Taylor (ed.), *Free Trade: The Necessary Foundation for World Peace,* pp. 41-51

79. Adam Smith pointed out this fallacy in *The Wealth of Nations* in 1776, yet the fallacy persists. The modern version of this mercantilist fallacy is that Americans are spending too much on imports, causing

dollars to flow overseas, or that the United States is becoming a debtor nation. There is no such thing as spending "too much" on imports or on anything else. As long as consumers are free to choose what to spend their money on, they are always spending precisely the right amount. Also, what difference does it make whether the United States is a debtor nation or a creditor nation, as long as the result came about by consenting adults freely choosing to enter into the transactions that led to the current status?

80. Carson, "The Mercantile Impasse"; C. Nettels, *The Roots of American Civilization* (Irvington-on-Hudson, N.Y.: Foundation for Economic Education, 1963), p. 281.

81. Carson, "The Mercantile Impasse."

THE MEDICAL MONOPOLY

PROTECTING CONSUMERS OR LIMITING COMPETITION?

Sue A. Blevins

Executive Summary

Nonphysician providers of medical care are in high demand in the United States. But licensure laws and federal regulations limit their scope of practice and restrict access to their services. The result has almost inevitably been less choice and higher prices for consumers.

Safety and consumer protection issues are often cited as reasons for restricting nonphysician services. But the restrictions appear not to be based on empirical findings. Studies have repeatedly shown that qualified nonphysician providers—such as midwives, nurses, and chiropractors—can perform many health and medical services traditionally performed by physicians—with comparable health outcomes, lower costs, and high patient satisfaction.

Licensure laws appear to be designed to limit the supply of health care providers and restrict competition to physicians from nonphysician practitioners. The primary result is an increase in physician fees and income that drives up health care costs.

At a time government is trying to cut health spending and improve access to health care, it is imperative to examine critically the extent to which government policies are responsible for rising health costs and the unavailability of health services. Eliminating the roadblocks to competition among health care providers could improve access to health services, lower health costs, and reduce government spending.

Introduction

> I am myself persuaded that licensure has reduced both the quantity and quality of medical practice. . . . It has forced the public to pay more for less satisfactory medical service.
> —*Milton Friedman*

Although broad-based health care reform has temporarily moved to the back of the public agenda, there remain serious problems of cost and access in the American health care system. The underlying reason for those problems is the lack of a functioning free market in health care in this country. There is privately owned health care, but there is not a living, vibrant free marketplace in health care like there is in other products and services.

Healthy markets have certain common characteristics. On the supply side, there is a choice of providers, in competition with one another, trying to gain customers on the basis of price and quality. And on the demand side, there are consumers seeking the best deal for their dollar. In today's health care system, neither of those conditions obtains.

During the 1994 health care reform debate, much attention was given to the demand side of the market.[1] That attention led to the development of ideas such as medical savings accounts to make health care consumers more cost conscious.[2]

However, true reform requires that the supply side of the health care market be addressed as well. Currently, a wide variety of licensing laws and other regulatory restrictions limits the scope of practice of nonphysician professionals and restricts access to their services. Moreover, at the same time that it is restricting the practices of nontraditional health care professionals, government is providing subsidies for the education and training of physicians who fit the medical orthodoxy. The result has been the creation of a de facto medical monopoly, leading to less choice and higher prices for consumers.

Therefore, true health care reform must involve ending the government-imposed medical monopoly and providing consumers with a full array of health care choices.

The Demand for Alternative Therapies

Every year millions of Americans seek providers who offer health care therapies that are neither widely taught in medical schools nor generally available in U.S. hospitals. Researchers from Harvard Medical School studied the health care practices of U.S. adults and estimated that 22 million Americans sought providers of unconventional care in 1990. The study, reported in the *New England Journal of Medicine*, estimates that in 1990 Americans made more visits to providers who offered unconventional therapies than to all primary care physicians—425 million compared to 388 million visits.[3]

Researchers estimate that 34 percent of Americans used at least 1 of 16 unconventional therapies, such as chiropractic, herbal, and megavitamin therapies, in 1990.[4] Back problems were the most commonly reported "bothersome or serious" health problem for which consumers sought nontraditional services.[5]

There is a great willingness to pay out-of-pocket for providers who offer unconventional health services. The Harvard researchers found that total projected expenditures on providers of unconventional care amounted to $11.7 billion in 1990. Nearly 70 percent—$8.2 billion—of that amount was paid by the consumer, rather than insurers or government. By contrast, only 17 percent of the bill for total physician services was paid out-of-pocket in 1990 .[6]

According to U.S Census data, receipts for nonphysician providers[7] grew by 83 percent—from $10.3 billion to $18.9 billion—between 1987 and 1992,[8] while physician receipts increased by 56 percent, from $90 billion to $141 billion. Census data show that employment by nonphysician establishments grew by 50 percent, while jobs in hospitals and physician offices increased less than 20 percent between 1987 and 1992.

Medical schools are responding to the consumer demand for unconventional health services. To date, 34 out of the 126 medical schools nationwide have started or are developing courses that focus on "alternative medical practices."[9]

It should be noted, however, that medical schools rely heavily on federal subsidies, while training for nonphysician providers is predominantly funded with private money. For example, all of the 17 chiropractic schools in the United States are privately funded; none are state owned.[10] By contrast, 76 of the 126 medical schools are state owned.[11]

At a time when government is looking for ways to reduce health spending, it should examine closely the supply side of health care reform. Some experts have raised concerns about an oversupply of highly trained specialists who rely heavily on government funding for training, while at the same time licensure laws and federal reimbursement regulations restrict nonphysician providers from entering the health care marketplace. An overview of the current supply of selected health care providers is presented in Table 1.

TABLE 1: Supply of Selected Health Care Providers, United States

Type of Provider	Number
Acupuncturists (nonphysician)	6,500
Chiropractors	45,000
Doctors of osteopathy	32,000
Homeopathists[a]	3,000
Massage therapists	9,000
Midwives	
Certified nurse	4,000
Lay	6,000
Total	10,000
Medical doctors	
Primary care	195,300
Nonprimary care	391,700
Total	587,000
Naturopathic doctors	1,000
Nurse practitioners	21,000

Source: Data on acupuncturists, homeopathy, N.D.s (1992), chiropractors, D.O.s (1993) and massage therapists (1994) from Office of Alternative Medicine, NIH, *Alternative Medicine: Expanding Medical Horizons*, NIH publication no. 94-066 (Washington: Government Printing Office, December 1994); data for M.D.s (1992) from Martin Gonzalez, *Socioeconomic Characteristics of Medical Practice 1994* (Chicago: AMA, 1994); data for midwives (1995) from Diana Korte, "Midwives on Trial," *Mothering*, (Fall 1995); and data for N.P.s (1991) from Mullan et al., p. 145.

[a]The estimated 3,000 health care practitioners who are licensed to use homeopathy include acupuncturists, chiropractors, dentists, naturopaths, nurse practitioners, osteopaths, physicians, physician assistants, and veterinarians. Office of Alternative Medicine, National Institute of Health, p. 82.

Any serious reform of the U.S. health care system must address the medical monopoly. Barriers to entry into the health care marketplace are partially responsible for high health costs and lack of access to primary and preventive health care.

Individual Choice and Freedom to Contract

Professional licensure laws and other regulatory restrictions impose significant barriers to Americans' freedom of choice in health care. Clark Havighurst, the William Neal Reynolds Professor of Law at Duke University, has pointed out, "Professional licensure laws have long made the provision of most personal health services the exclusive province of physicians. Obviously, such regulation limits consumers' options by forcing them to use highly trained, expensive personnel when other types might serve quite well."[12]

Yet the freedom to contract—the right of individuals to decide with whom and for what services they will dispose of their earning—is one of the fundamental rights of man. As Chief Justice John Marshall said in *Ogden v. Saunders*, "Individuals do not derive from government their right to contract, but bring that right with them into society . . . [e]very man retains [the right] to . . . dispose of [his] property according to his own judgment." Indeed, legal philosophers and ethicists, such as Roger Pilon, Richard Epstein, and Stephen Mecado, convincingly argue that the rights of property and contract are fundamental rights upon which all others are based.[13]

Accordingly, individuals should have the legal right to decide with whom they will contract for the provision and coordination of their health care services: doctors, midwives, nurse practitioners, chiropractors, spiritual healers, or other health care providers. Any restriction denies Americans the right to make decisions about their own bodies.

The Rise of Medical Licensure

Although protection of the public is often cited as the reason for medical licensing and limiting access to unconventional therapies, history indicates that professional interest was more of an overriding concern in the early enactment of those laws. The latter theory reflects economist Paul Feldstein's perspective that health associations act like firms: they try to maximize the interests of their existing membership.[14]

Medical licensure was first introduced in England in 1442 when London barbers were granted charters to perform certain procedures. The charters authorized "barbers" to treat wounds, let blood, and draw teeth.[15]

In the United States, the earliest health professional licensure law was enacted by Virginia in 1639. That law dealt with the collection of physician fees, vaccination, the quarantine of certain diseases, and the construction and management of isolation hospitals. Other early colonial acts denied nonphysician practitioners any standing in civil courts to collect fees. In 1760 New York City became the first American jurisdiction to prohibit practice by unlicensed physicians. Subsequently, many other cities and states introduced licensing requirements.[16]

During the early part of the 19th century, the United States experienced an era known as "free trade in medicine." A historical vignette in the *Journal of the American Medical Association* explains that during the mid-1800s, botanics and homeopathy were in great demand.[17] Those alternative health practices were a powerful counterforce to regular medicine. Most state licensure laws that granted special privileges to physicians were repealed because of the widespread consumer demand for botanicals. During the period, the United States was one of the healthiest nations, with the world's lowest infant mortality rate.[18]

However, the self-interest of physicians soon began to assert itself. The repeal of licensure laws "triggered a movement that led directly to the formation of the American Medical Association."[19] The AMA was determined to protect physicians from competition by nonphysician health care providers. Consequently, licensure laws arose again, beginning about 1870. By 1895 nearly every state had created some type of administrative board to examine and license physicians.[20]

Another study of the early development of medical licensing laws in the United States reports that the goals of the AMA in supporting licensing appear to have been to (1) restrict entry into the profession and thereby secure a more stable financial climate for physicians, (2) destroy for-profit medical schools and replace them with nonprofit institutions, and (3) eliminate other medical sects such as homeopaths and chiropractors.[21]

History reveals that the AMA was influential in linking physician licensure with strict educational standards that (1) restricted entry into the health care marketplace and (2) increased the cost of medical education.[22]

Paul Starr, in his Pulitzer prize-winning *The Social Transformation of American Medicine*, examined the consolidation of medical authority between 1850 and 1930. Starr notes that before 1870, requirements for physician training were minimal and that many medical schools were for-profit.[23]

Medical education began to be reformed around the late 19th century. Starr describes the competitive climate of the period: "Despite the new licensing laws, the ports of entry into medicine were still wide open, and the unwelcome passed through in great numbers. . . . From the viewpoint of established physicians, the commercial schools were undesirable on at least two counts: for the added competition they were creating and for the low image of the physician that their graduates fostered. Medicine would never be a respected profession—so its most vocal spokesman declared until it sloughed off its coarse and common elements."[24]

In 1904 the AMA established a Council on Medical Education with a mandate to elevate the standards of medical education. Two years later the council inspected the 160 medical schools throughout the United States and approved of only 82 schools: 46 were found imperfect, and 32 were declared "beyond salvage." But organized medicine's professional code of ethics "forbade physicians from taking up cudgels against each other in public," and the report was never published.[25]

Instead, the AMA commissioned an outside consultant to investigate and report on the status of medical education in the United States. Abraham Flexner of the Carnegie Foundation for the Advancement of Teaching was commissioned to do a study of medical education. Flexner, an educator with a bachelor's degree from Johns Hopkins, visited each of the 160 U.S. medical schools and released his recommendations in 1910.

Flexner decided that the great majority of medical schools should be closed and the remainder should be modeled after Johns Hopkins.[26] The AMA used the Flexner report in its campaign to abolish medical schools outside its control. With physician licensure already in place, it was relatively easy for the AMA-dominated state examination boards to consider only graduates of medical schools approved by the AMA or the Association of American Colleges, whose lists were identical. In many states the requirement was statutory.[27]

One result was a significant decline in the number of proprietary schools, which had been very prominent until the early 1900s. Although the number of medical colleges had decreased from 160 to 131 between 1900 and 1910, the release of the Flexner report facilitated the closure of an additional 46 medical schools between 1910 and 1920.[28]

By 1930 only 76 medical schools remained in the United States. In 1932 the chairman of the Commission on Medical Education—Harvard University president A. Lawrence Lowell—reported that "the definition of standards and the efforts of leaders in the medical profession were very influential in eliminating the proprietary and commercial medical schools."[29] Lowell also concluded in the 1932 report on medical education that "the budgets of many schools have increased from 200 to 1,000 percent during the last 15 years."[30]

Women and African-Americans were disproportionately affected by Flexner's recommendations. In 1905 and 1910 women medical students numbered 1,073 and 907, respectively. Five years after the Flexner report was released, the number of women medical students had been cut nearly in half from 907 to 592.[31] Starr notes, "As places in medical school became more scarce, schools that previously had liberal policies toward women increasingly excluded them."[32]

There were seven predominantly black medical schools in existence before the Flexner report, but only two remained after its release.[33] As a result, the number of doctors serving African-American communities declined. For example, blacks in Mississippi had 1 doctor for every 14,634 persons[34] compared to 1 doctor for every 2,563 persons nationwide in 1930.[35]

Many small towns and rural communities were affected by the new educational standards and associated licensure laws. AMA president William Pusey concluded that "as you increase the cost of the license to practice medicine you increase the price at which medical service must be sold and you correspondingly decrease the number of people who can afford to buy this medical service."[36]

The Flexner report also had a significant impact on nonphysician health care providers. Within 10 years after the Flexner report, approximately 130 laws were passed regulating at least 14 health-related occupations.[37] Some nontraditional specialties were virtually wiped out. Take homeopathy, for example. By the end of the 19th century, an estimated 15 percent of physicians practiced homeopathy, the use of natural remedies to stimulate the body's natural healing responses. There were 22 homeopathic medical schools and over 100 homeopathic hospitals in the United States.[38] Early supporters of homeopathy included Thomas Edison, John D. Rockefeller, and Mark Twain.[39] Four years after the Flexner report, the President of the Institute of Homeopathy, Dr. DeWitt Wilcox, shared his perception of organized medicine:

TABLE 2: Graduates of Selected Medical Schools and Nationwide Total Examined by State Boards in 1931

Medical School	Number Examined	Percentage of Failures
Albany Medical College	8	14.3
Boston University School of Medicine	55	10.9
Cornell University Medical College	59	6.8
Georgetown University School of Medicine	139	17.3
Hahnemann Medical College and Hospital of Philadelphia	89	3.4
Howard University College of Medicine	63	11.1
New York Homeopathic Medical College & Flower Hospital	88	11.4
Syracuse University College of Medicine	46	8.7
Total examined nationwide and percentage of failures	5,576	6.3

Source: A. Lawrence Lowell et al., *Final Report of the Commission on Medical Education* (New York: Association of American Medical Colleges, 1932), appendix, Table 87.

The American Medical Association is fast degenerating into a political machine bent on throttling everything which stands in its way for obtaining medical supremacy. It has made an unholy alliance with the Army and Navy Medical Departments, and together they propose to own and control every medical college in this country, all the State, municipal and university hospitals, and get within their grasp all the examining and licensing boards in the United States.[40]

By the late 1930s the practice of homeopathy had largely disappeared from the United States. The new rating system for medical schools was influential in eliminating homeopathic colleges nationwide.[41]

It is commonly thought that homeopathy disappeared because of its poor quality of education. But history shows that physicians graduating from two of the last homeopathic colleges—Hahnemann Medical College and New York Homeopathic College—passed examinations at a rate comparable to physicians from schools that were maintained (see Table 2).

Medical Licensing Today

Today states use three mechanisms for regulating health professionals: (1) licensure, the most restrictive form of regulation, makes it illegal to practice a profession without meeting state-imposed standards; (2) certification, granting title protection to persons meeting predetermined standards (those without the title may perform services, but may not use the title); and (3) registration, the least restrictive form of regulation, requiring individuals to file their names, addresses, and qualifications with a government agency before practicing.[42]

Professional health care associations have been influential in setting the standards for licensure laws in the United States. Feldstein has identified ways in which health care associations limit competition: the first approach, Feldstein notes, is simply to have substitute providers declared illegal.[43] If substitute providers are prohibited, or if they are severely limited in the tasks they are legally permitted to perform, then there will be a shift in demand away from their services. That approach has been used with lay midwives. In addition, states impose professional "scope-of-practice" regulations that prevent nurse practitioners from functioning independently as primary care providers.[44]

Another approach to limiting health care competition—used when licensure and scope-of-practice restrictions fail—is to restrict or limit substitute providers' services from payment by government health programs. That approach has been used by organized medicine, for example, to limit access to chiropractic treatment. Medicare regulations prohibit reimbursement to chiropractors for services they are licensed to perform in all 50 states. The federal reimbursement regulations appear not to be based on empirical evidence: the federal government's Agency for Health Care Policy and Research recently released national guidelines that recommend spinal manipulation as a safe and cost-effective treatment for acute back problems.[45]

The following examples show how the medical monopoly has used the power of government to restrict the practice of a variety of nonphysician health care providers.

Midwifery

At least 36 states restrict or outright prohibit the practice of lay midwifery.[46] Consequently, only 5 percent of all births are attended by midwives in this country,[47] compared with 75 percent of all births in European countries.[48] Americans' low usage of midwifery does not correlate with high-quality birth outcomes: the United States has the second highest caesarean rate in the world[49] and the fifth highest infant mortality rate among Western industrialized nations.[50]

There are an estimated 10,000 midwives in this country who fall into two categories: the certified nurse-midwife and the lay midwife (or "direct-entry" midwife). Certified nurse-midwives are registered nurses with two years of advanced training who most often work under the supervision of a physician and practice in clinic or hospital settings. Certified nurse-midwives represent approximately 4,000 of the 10,000 midwives nationwide.

By contrast, lay midwives enter the profession directly from independent midwifery schools or through apprenticeship. They are trained to meet individual state requirements for licensure, registration, or certification. But unlike certified nurse midwives, most lay midwives practice independently in consultation with physicians, not under direct physician supervision. About half the 6,000 lay midwives are associated with religious groups,[51] and a majority of home births in the United States are attended by lay midwives.[52]

Safety is most commonly cited as the reason for prohibiting or restricting lay midwifery in 36 states. Those licensure laws and regulatory restrictions, however, do not appear to be based on empirical findings of childbirth outcomes.[53] For example, the National Birth Center study on nearly 12,000 nonhospital births found a neonatal mortality rate for midwife-assisted births comparable to that of hospital births.[54] Another study examined 1,700 home births attended by lay midwives in rural Tennessee. Researchers found at-home midwife-assisted births to be as safe as physician-attended hospital deliveries.[55]

Many people attribute midwives' record of success to the fact that they do not assist with high-risk deliveries. To address that issue, researchers excluded physicians' high-risk cases from their study of lay midwives in rural Tennessee. The *American Journal of Public Health* reports that even with comparable low-risk deliveries, lay midwife-assisted home births were as safe as physician-assisted hospital births. Moreover, physician-attended hospitals births were 10 times more likely to require intervention (forceps, vacuum extractor, or caesarean section) than midwife-assisted home births.[56]

Those findings are supported by international studies. In the Netherlands—where more than 32 percent of births are attended by lay midwives at home-research shows that the perinatal mortality rate was lowest in cities that had the highest proportion of home births.[57] A study on Dutch births by the British journal *Midwifery* concluded that perinatal mortality was "much lower under the noninterventionist care of midwives than under the interventionist management of obstetricians."[58]

Midwives are considerably less expensive than traditional obstetric care providers. According to the Health Insurance Association of America, the average physician-attended birth costs $4,200; Midwives Alliance of North America reports that the average cost of a midwife-assisted birth is $1,200.[59] Americans could save $2.4 billion annually if only 20 percent of American women increased their access to midwives.[60]

Most important, though, is that women report significant personal and psychological benefits from midwife-assisted births. Since the early 1970s, a home birth renaissance has been sparked by feminist politics, the women's health and holistic health movements, back-to-nature ideology, and health consumerism.[61] A study of the home birth movement in the United States concludes, "Members have chosen their alternative form of care not through faulty understanding of medical principles and practices, but as a result of active and reasoned disagreement with them. The home birth movement is one of a number of lay health belief systems currently flourishing among middle class populations."[62]

As a result of midwives' success, a wide range of health organizations, including the American Public Health Association, National Commission to Prevent Infant Mortality, and World Health Organization, advocates the expanded use of midwives. The strongest advocacy has come from the women's health movement with support from the Boston Women's Health Book Collective, National Black Women's Health Project, National Women's Health Network, and Women's Institute for Childbearing Policy. The benefits of a low-intervention approach to childbirth are also supported by the General Accounting Office and the Office of Technology Assessment.[63]

Despite midwives' record of safety and mothers' reports of psychological and personal benefits, the medical community continues to enforce licensure laws that restrict women's birthing options.[64] A past president of the American College of Obstetrics and Gynecology (ACOG) denounced home birth as a form of "maternal trauma" and "child abuse" during the late 1970s.[65] A decade later, ACOG released statements that "discouraged the use of birth centers until better data were available."[66]

Midwives are continually placed under considerable legal and biomedical scrutiny. An award-winning women's health writer, Diana Korte, recently examined the number of midwives on trial across the country. According to Korte, at least 145 midwives in 36 states have had legal altercations with the medical authorities. One case involved the arrest of a rural Missouri midwife.

> At 2:00 a.m. on a January morning in 1991, seven law enforcement officers in bulletproof vests ransacked the birth center of a rural Missouri midwife, removed all of her computer disks, and destroyed files and other materials. Although the Missouri Nursing Board had previously authorized the birth center, the county prosecutor charged the midwife with eight felonies and several misdemeanors for practicing medicine without a license.[67]

Parents rarely make complaints about midwives: most legal altercations stem from the medical community.[68] Archie Brodsky, a senior research associate at the Harvard Medical School's Program in Psychiatry and the Law, noted that 71 percent of obstetrician-gynecologists had been named in one or more liability claims as of 1987. By comparison, only 10 percent of midwives had experienced legal claims at that time; lay midwives are even more rarely sued.[69]

The medical community often refuses to provide backup support to women who choose to deliver at home, despite midwives' record of safety and low malpractice claims. A recent pilot study of childbirth choices found that 20 percent of mothers delivering in the hospital setting would have preferred a nonhospital delivery, but no medical backup support was readily available.[70] Another study at the Medical College of Pennsylvania found that women met forceful resistance from physicians when they disclosed their plans for home delivery. Accordingly, the study notes,

> A number of women found it ironic, and even unconscionable, that physicians who criticized home birth as unsafe also refused to provide the prenatal care which all would agree would increase the safety of pregnancy and birth under any circumstances. Some concluded on these grounds that these physicians' motivation must have more to do with self-interest (in terms of power, authority, and money) than with interest in the health and safety of their patients and their babies.[71]

It should be noted, however, that fear of malpractice may have played a large part in the physicians' decisions to refuse backup support. Further, as Figure 1 illustrates, medical attitudes about midwifery and home births vary greatly among physicians and geographical areas. States that grant legal status to lay midwives in the form of licensure, certification, or registration include Alaska, Arkansas, Arizona, Colorado, Florida, Louisiana, New Hampshire, New Mexico, Montana, Oregon, South Carolina, Texas, Washington, and Wyoming.[72]

Nurse Practitioners

Particularly in underserved areas and long-term care facilities, registered nurses with advanced training—nurse practitioners—are able to provide most basic health services provided by physicians, and at lower costs. The American Nurses Association estimates that of the 2.1 million registered nurses nationwide, approximately 400,000 deliver primary care.[73] Many of them are practicing in managed-care organizations under the supervision of physicians. Some 21,000 nurses have received advanced training at graduate schools of nursing and are licensed nurse practitioners.

FIGURE 1: Legal Status of Direct-Entry Midwifery in the United States, April 1995

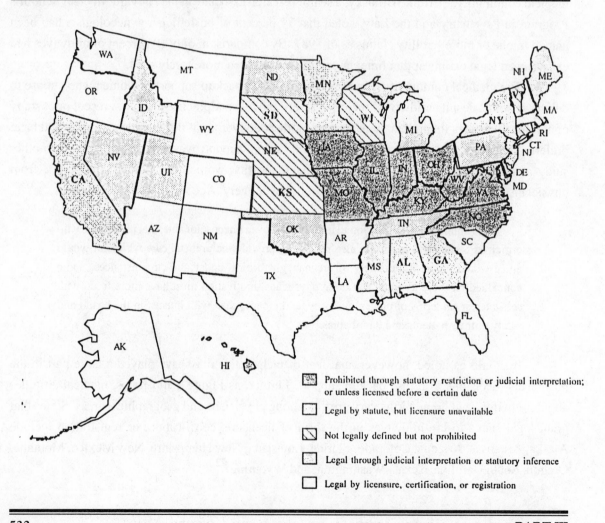

Prohibited through statutory restriction or judicial interpretation; or unless licensed before a certain date

Legal by statute, but licensure unavailable

Not legally defined but not prohibited

Legal through judicial interpretation or statutory inference

Legal by licensure, certification, or registration

Research shows that between 75 and 80 percent of adult primary care, and up to 90 percent of pediatric primary care, services could be safely provided by nurse practitioners.[74] A study by the Office of Technology Assessment found that the outcomes of nurse practitioner care were equivalent to those of services provided by physicians, and that nurse practitioners were actually more adept in communication and preventive care. The Office of Technology Assessment study also indicates that increasing access to nurse practitioner services could be especially advantageous for the home-bound elderly.[75]

Another study examined the outcomes of a nurse-managed clinic that was opened to provide primary care services to more than 2,000 low-income children and their families in an underserved Texas community. Research shows that after the clinic was opened in 1991, emergency room visits by pediatric Medicaid recipients decreased by 27 percent at the largest emergency room in the county. In addition, the pregnancy-induced hypertension rate was reduced from 7 to 3.3 percent over a three-year period, preventing costly hospitalizations.[76]

The economic loss from inefficient use of primary care nurse practitioners is estimated to be between $6.4 billion and $8.75 billion.[77] A meta-analysis conducted by the American Nurses Association in 1993 showed that nurse practitioner care resulted in fewer hospitalizations, higher scores on patient satisfaction, and lower cost per visit—$12.36 compared to $20.11 for physicians.[78] In addition to projected savings on direct health services, the taxpayer burden for training nurse practitioners is approximately one-fifth the cost of training physicians.[79]

Despite empirical evidence that nurse practitioners can safely provide primary care, many states impose scope-of-practice regulations that prevent nurses from practicing independently as primary care providers. Nurse practitioners derive their authority from various state nurse practice acts.[80] However, some states give their medical boards regulatory control over boards of nursing. That gives one profession full veto power over the rules and regulations of its competitors.

Moreover, scope-of-practice regulations often dictate that nurses must work in coordination with physicians. For example, 48 states grant nurse practitioners prescriptive authority but mandate that nurses must have a written practice agreement or work in collaboration with a physician.

As of January 1995, only 10 states granted nurse practitioners the legal right to prescribe drugs independent of a physician.[81] Moreover, even some of those states limited the independent nurse practitioner's prescription authority by law to 72 hours.[82] What that means for competition is that consumers—for example, elderly Medicare recipients who live in rural areas—would have to visit independent nurse practitioners every three days to renew prescriptions. Barbara Safriet, associate dean of Yale Law School, argues,

Medical practice acts remain overly broad and indeterminate, with concomitant and unnecessary restrictions in the licensure and practice acts of nonphysician providers. If we are to achieve our goal of offering high-quality care, at an affordable cost, to everyone who needs it, we must ensure that all health care providers are able to practice within the full scope of their professional competencies.[83]

States' scope-of-practice regulations shield the full market demand for nurse practitioner services because nurses are not legally free to compete in the health care market. A 1993 Gallup poll found that 86 percent of consumers would be willing to use nurse practitioners for basic health care services. Only 12 percent stated that they would be unwilling to see a nurse practitioner.[84]

This analysis does not in any manner call for increased government regulations that would force Medicaid or Medicare recipients to substitute nurse practitioner care for physician services. Instead, it argues that Americans should not be restricted from choosing low-cost alternative practitioners and forced to subsidize an oversupply of highly specialized physicians. Let nurse practitioners legally compete in the health care market and allow consumers to choose among qualified health providers on the basis of quality and cost.

Chiropractic

The chiropractic profession has faced significant challenges by organized medicine for over 100 years. For example, between 1963 and 1974 the AMA operated a Committee on Quackery with an intent to "expose the charlatanism of chiropractic." The AMA urged members to lend "their full support to the continuing vigorous attack on medical quackery and to the education program on the cult of chiropractic."[85]

Although the AMA certainly had every right to criticize medical practices with which it disagreed, the organization soon resorted to lobbying the government for restrictions on chiropractic practice. Today, chiropractors are subject to numerous restrictions on their scope of practice.[86]

In addition, the AMA recommended that Congress exclude payment for chiropractic services from federally supported health programs.[87] As a result, Medicare recipients are restricted from using the full range of chiropractic services. Medicare policy limits patient access to chiropractors this way: Medicare reimburses chiropractors for performing "spinal manipulation" but requires that a diagnostic spinal xray be taken before chiropractic treatment. The catch is that Medicare does not reimburse chiropractors for performing x-rays, even though they have the training and are licensed to perform x-rays in all 50 states.[88] That policy gives the medical profession control over managing back problems among elderly Americans.

Ironically, the federal government's Agency for Health Care Policy and Research (AHCPR) recently released national pain guidelines that recommend spinal manipulation for the common complaint of acute low back pain.[89] It is estimated that 80 percent of all adults suffer from back pain at some time in their lives,[90] and an estimated 91 percent of older adults (ages 65 to 74) report back problems.[91] The AHCPR estimates that Americans could save over $1 billion annually by using noninterventionist approaches for managing back pain, even if only 20 percent of practitioners followed the agency's recommendations.[92]

International research supports the U.S. findings that chiropractic is a safe and cost-effective method for managing back pain. A study published by the *British Medical Journal* reports that chiropractic treatment was more effective than outpatient hospital management of low back pain. British researchers estimate that if the 72,000 patients who show no contraindications to manipulation but are referred to hospitals for back care each year were instead referred to chiropractors, the British health system could reduce days of sickness absence by 290,000 and could save 2.9 million pounds in social security payments over a two-year period.[93]

Consumers are quite satisfied with chiropractic treatment. The *Western Journal of Medicine* reports that patients of chiropractors were three times more likely than patients of family physicians to report that they were very satisfied with their treatment for low back pain—by a score of 66 to 22 percent.[94] A 1991 Gallup poll found that 90 percent of patients regard their chiropractic care as effective and that approximately 80 percent consider the treatment costs reasonable.[95]

In 1976 four chiropractors filed an antitrust lawsuit against the AMA, 5 of its officers, and 10 other medical organizations including the American Hospital Association, charging them with criminal conspiracy to destroy chiropractic. Plaintiffs alleged a conspiracy that included (1) preventing medical doctors and doctors of osteopathy from associating professionally with chiropractors, (2) defining it as unethical for MDs to accept referrals from chiropractors, and (3) prohibiting chiropractors from using hospital diagnostic laboratory and radiological facilities, among other things.

In 1987 the AMA was found guilty of illegal conspiracy: the AMA's anti-quackery activity was in violation of U.S. antitrust laws,[96] yet restrictions on chiropractic scope of practice and reimbursement remain in place.

Vitamins and Herbs

For years mainstream medicine has suggested that individuals who use unconventional therapies—such as vitamin therapies and herbal products—are not acting according to scientific rationale and therefore need to be protected by the government.[97] The president of the National Council Against Health Fraud (NCAHF), William Jarvis, has suggested that regulators are failing to protect the public against quackery. Jarvis explains that "the real issues in the war against quackery are the principles, including scientific rationale, encoded into consumer protection laws, primarily by the U.S. Food, Drug, and Cosmetic Act. More such laws are badly needed."[98]

Jarvis suggests that promoters of a free-enterprise society are paving the way for organized quackery. He notes that "in recent years, a free-market ideology, advanced by Friedman in his book *Free to Choose*, has gained an influential following" and that "the only way to enjoy both the benefits of a free-enterprise health marketplace and avoid the abuses of quackery is to balance the situation with sound consumer protection laws, enforcement, and education."[99] More recently, a member of NCAHF and president of the Consumer Health Information Research Institute has received a special citation from the FDA for combating health fraud.[100]

One way the FDA combats health fraud is to pull herbal products from the shelf if manufacturers make specific health claims about their usefulness without first obtaining FDA approval. Some providers have even been subject to criminal prosecution. But getting herbal remedies through the drug approval process is unrealistic. Botanicals are not patentable (although they can be patented for use); and the cost of their approval as drugs would be difficult to recover. The total cost of taking a new drug to the market in the United States is close to $400 million, and it takes nearly 15 years to complete the procedure.[101]

Meanwhile, Americans are expressing an increased interest in nutritional and herbal therapies. And according to the World Health Organization, about 4 billion people—80 percent of the world population—use herbal remedies for some aspect of their health care. Yet in the United States the FDA often considers herbal remedies to be worthless or potentially dangerous.[102]

Health care regulators defend their position as necessary to protect consumers. But contrary to conventional expectation, users of unconventional therapies are well educated and have higher-than-average incomes.[103] Even in countries with socialized health systems that provide access to conventional medical care for all citizens, users of unconventional therapies and practitioners are usually from higher social classes.[104] A study of complementary medicine in the United Kingdom suggests that patients from higher social classes presumably have the opportunity to research and explore the possibilities of complementary medicine and to pay for it.[105]

Protecting Consumers or Limiting Competition?

There is little actual evidence that medical licensing improves quality or protects the public.[106] Medical economist Gary Gaumer, reviewing all the available literature on medical licensing, concluded,

> Research evidence does not inspire confidence that wide-ranging systems for regulating health professionals have served the public interest. Though researchers have not been able to observe the consequences of a totally unregulated environment, observation of incremental variations in regulatory practice generally supports the view that tighter controls do not lead to improvements in the quality of service.[107]

Even the Federal Trade Commission has concluded that "occupational licensing frequently increases prices and imposes substantial costs on consumers. At the same time, many occupational licensing restrictions do not appear to realize the goal of increasing the quality of professionals' services."[108]

Licensing laws may actually put the public more at risk by lulling consumers into a false sense of security. Terree Wasley points out in *What Has Government Done to Our Health Care?* that most state licensing laws permit all licensed physicians to perform all types of medical services, even those for which they are not specifically trained.[109] For example, in Massachusetts physicians are licensed to perform acupuncture even though they may not have received special training.[110] That situation disturbs nonphysician acupuncturists who receive more hours of acupuncture training than do most licensed physicians.[111]

Feldstein points out that licensure laws focus at the point of entry into the medical profession, not on continuous monitoring. Once medical professionals are licensed, there are no requirements for proving that they are fully trained to perform the most up-to-date procedures.[112] Some states do not require continuing education, so there is no guarantee that a physician is current with the most recent techniques and information.[113] Feldstein points out that

> state licensing boards are responsible for monitoring physicians' behavior and for penalizing physicians whose performance is inadequate or whose conduct is unethical. Unfortunately, this approach for assuring physician quality and competence is completely inadequate. . . . Monitoring the care provided by physicians through the use of claims and medical records data would more directly determine the quality and competence of a physician.[114]

In his 1987 Cato Institute book, *The Rule of Experts: Occupational Licensing in America*, S. David Young, a professor of accounting and finance at Tulane University, reviewed the literature on a wide variety of occupational licensing restrictions, including medical licensing, and found that "licensing has, at best, a neutral effect on quality and may even cause harm to consumers."[115]

While the public safety benefits of medical licensure are clearly questionable, nearly all economists recognize that professional licensure laws act as a barrier to entry that decreases competition and increases price. As Victor Fuchs wrote in 1974, "Most economists believe that part [of physician's high incomes] represents a monopoly return to physicians from restrictions on entry to the profession and other barriers to competition."[116]

One of the earliest studies of the impact of licensure on physician income was done in 1945 by Nobel Prize-winning economist Milton Friedman and Simon Kuznets. Friedman and Kuznets found that the difference in income between professional and nonprofessional health care workers was larger than could be explained by the extra skill and training of the professionals. A large portion of the variation, they concluded, was due to licensing restrictions. In addition, they concluded that the difference in mean income of physicians and dentists was caused by greater difficulty of entry into medicine than into dentistry.[117]

Friedman and Kuznets's conclusions have been confirmed by numerous other studies. For example, William White examined the effect of licensure on the income of clinical laboratory personnel and found that in cities with stringent licensing restrictions income was 16 percent higher than in cities with less stringent restrictions, with no variation in the quality of testing.[118]

Lawrence Shepard examined the fees of dentists in states that recognized out-of-state licenses and those that did not. He found that in states that did not recognize out-of-state licenses, dental fees were 12 to 15 percent higher.[119] A study of Canadian health care indicated that occupational licensing, combined with mobility restrictions and advertising restrictions, increased health care costs by as much as 27 percent.[120] Gaumer found that both fees and provider incomes were higher in states with more restrictive licensure requirements.[121]

Interesting confirmation that physician licensure is related more to a desire to increase physician incomes than to concern over public health and safety can be found in a 1984 study by medical economist Chris Paul, who found that the year that a state enacted physician licensing was related to the number of AMA members in the state.[122] Paul concluded that decisions by states to require licensing of physicians were more likely a result of special interests than of the public interest.

As the Friedmans note, "The *justification* [for licensure] is always the same: to protect the consumer. However, the *reason* is demonstrated by observing who lobbies at the state legislatures for imposition or strengthening of licensure. The lobbyists are invariably representatives of the occupation in question rather than its customers."[123]

Subsidies and the Medical Monopoly

In addition to using government to restrict competition, the medical monopoly also turns to government for subsidies. For example, most physician training is subsidized by the federal government.

In 1927 student fees accounted for 34 percent of medical school revenues.[124] Today less than 5 percent of medical school revenues comes from tuition and fees. Instead, medical schools rely heavily on federal and state support.[125] In 1992 total medical school revenues amounted to $23 billion.[126] State and local governments provided $2.7 billion.[127] The federal government paid at least $10.3 billion to medical schools and hospitals for medical education and training (Table 3). Additional revenues were obtained from charges for services, endowments, and private grants.

Medicare payments to hospitals represent the largest source of federal funding for medical education and training.[128] Medicare pays for physician education and training in two ways: First, hospitals receive direct payments from Medicare based on the number of full-time-equivalent residents employed at each hospital. Second, Medicare increases a hospital's diagnostic-related group payments according to an "indirect" medical education factor, based on the ratio of residents to hospital beds.[129]

The average Medicare payment to hospitals was more than $70,000 per resident for both direct and indirect education subsidies in 1992. An estimated 69,900 full-time-equivalent interns, residents, and fellows were eligible for Medicare reimbursement in 1991.[130]

TABLE 3: Taxpayer Support for Physician Education and Training, 1991-92

Source	Billions of Dollars
Medicare	5.2
Federal research, training, and teaching	5.1
State and local governments	2.7
Total	13.0

Sources: Fitzhugh Mullan et al., "Doctors, Dollars, and Determination: Making Physician Work-Force Policy," *Health Affairs* Supplement (1993), p. 142; and Janice Ganem et al., "Review of U.S. Medical School Finances 1992-93," *Journal of the American Medical Association* 274 (1995): 724.

Medicare paid hospitals $1.6 billion for direct medical education expenses and dispensed $3.6 billion for indirect medical education adjustments in 1992.[131] Of the total $5.2 billion that Medicare paid to hospitals for training, approximately $0.3 billion was appropriated for training nurses and allied health professionals.[132]

Medical schools and teaching hospitals receive additional federal funding from the National Institutes of Health, the Department of Veterans Affairs, the Department of Defense, and the Health Resources and Services Administration (Title VII) program. Federal funding for research, training, and teaching amounted to at least $5.1 billion in 1992.[133] That money was awarded to medical schools and affiliated hospitals in the form of grants and contracts. Supporting biomedical research in medical schools is one way the federal government supports medical education without appearing to do so directly.[134]

As Feldstein has pointed out, "There is no reason why medical students should be subsidized to a greater extent than students in other graduate or professional schools."[135] That point has also been suggested by Uwe Reinhardt, a professor of political economy at Princeton University, who recently noted,

> In the context of academic medicine, this inquiry should begin with the question of why the education of physicians is now so heavily supported with public funds, when similar support has never been extended to other important professions, for example, students in law schools or graduate programs in business. . . . In truth, the case for the traditional heavy public subsidies to medical education and training has simply been taken for granted . . . it never has been adequately justified.[136]

A less direct form of subsidy is the ability of the health care establishment to direct government payments from the Medicare and Medicaid programs to "approved" providers and hospitals. As already discussed, chiropractors and other nontraditional providers have generally been excluded from Medicare reimbursement. Furthermore, in order to be eligible to participate in Medicare, a hospital must be accredited by the Joint Commission on Accreditation of Health Care Organizations (or the American Osteopathic Association in the case of osteopathic hospitals). The JCAHO, which the *Wall Street Journal* describes as "one of the most powerful and secretive groups in all of health care,"[137] is a private organization with a board dominated by members representing the AMA and the American Hospital Association.

As several medical economists studying the issue have warned, in as much as Medicare is a major source of hospital revenues, "the influence of the JCAHO can be used to limit hospital competition and to protect physicians [against competition] from other groups of providers by denying them access to hospitals or influence within hospitals."[138] Thus the medical monopoly is able to use federal funds to reward its members and restrain its competitors.

Conclusion

What should government do if it is serious about cutting health spending and improving access to affordable health care? The first step should be to eliminate the anti-competitive barriers that restrict access to low-cost providers, namely licensure laws and federal reimbursement regulations. Americans should not be forced to substitute providers against their will; rather, they should be free to choose among all types of health care providers.

Instead of imposing strict licensure laws that focus on entry into the market but do not guarantee quality control, states should hold professionals equally accountable for the quality of their outcomes. That will reduce the need for strict licensure laws and other regulations that are purported to protect the public at large.

The time is right for eliminating barriers to nonphysician health care providers. Many Americans are seeking low-cost nontraditional providers and even choose to pay out-of-pocket for their services. Breaking the anti-competitive barriers of licensure laws and federal reimbursement regulations will provide meaningful health reform, increase consumer choice, and reduce health care costs.

Notes

This study was supported, in part, by the Institute for Humane Studies, George Mason University.

1. For a detailed discussion of the demand side of health care reform, see Stan Liebowitz, "Why Health Care Costs Too Much," *Cato Institute Policy Analysis* no. 211, June 23, 1994.

2. For a complete discussion of medical savings accounts, see John C. Goodman and Gerald L. Musgrave, *Patient Power: Solving America's Health Care Crisis* (Washington: Cato Institute 1992).

3. David Eisenberg et al., "Unconventional Medicine in the United States: Prevalence, Costs, and Patterns of Use," *New England Journal of Medicine* 328, no. 4 (1993): 246-52.

4. Eisenberg et al. examined therapies not widely taught in U.S. medical schools nor generally available in U.S. hospitals. Therapies included acupuncture, biofeedback, chiropractic, commercial weight-loss programs, energy healing, exercise, folk remedies, homeopathy, hypnosis, imagery, lifestyle diets

(e.g., macrobiotics), massage, megavitamin therapy, prayer, relaxation techniques, self-help groups, and spiritual healing.

5. Daniel Q. Haney, "Study Finds Adults Pay $14 Billion Annually on Offbeat Medicine," *Philadelphia Inquirer,* January 28, 1993, p. A6.

6. Estimate based on amount spent out-of-pocket for all physicians' services in 1990 = $23.5 billion, cited by Eisenberg et al., p. 251; and total amount (out-of-pocket, private insurance, and government) for all physicians' services in 1990 = $140.5 billion, cited by Katharine R. Levitt et al., "National Health Spending Trends, 1960-1993," *Health Affairs* (Winter 1994): 15.

7. Office of Management and Budget, *Standard Industrial Classification Manual* (Washington: National Technical Information Center, 1987). Nonphysician providers include acupuncturists, audiologists, chiropractors, Christian Science practitioners, dental hygienists, dieticians, hypnotists, inhalation therapists, midwives, naturopaths, nurses (not practicing in hospitals, clinics, or offices of medical doctors, nursing homes, HMOs, or home health care), nutritionists, occupational therapists, optometrists, paramedics, physical therapists, physicians' assistants, podiatrists, psychiatric social workers, psychologists, psychotherapists, speech clinicians, and speech pathologists.

8. U.S. Department of Commerce, Economics and Statistics Administration, Bureau of the Census, *1992 Census of Service Industries: Geographic Area Services, United States,* publication no SC92-A-52.

9. Joseph Jacobs, "Building Bridges between Two Worlds: The NIH's Office of Alternative Medicine," *Academic Medicine* 70 (January 1995): 41.

10. Paul Brown, "Chiropractic: A Medical Perspective," *Minnesota Medicine* 77 (1994): 21; National Center for Health Statistics, *Health, United States,* 1992, p. 149.

11. Fitzhugh Mullan et al., "Doctors, Dollars, and Determination: Making Physician Work-Force Policy," *Health Affairs*, Supplement 1993, pp. 138-51.

12. Clark Havighurst, "The Changing Locus of Decision Making in the Health Care Sector," *Journal of Health Politics, Policy and Law* 11 (1986): 700.

13. See, for example, James Dorn and Henry Manne, eds., *Economic Liberties and the Judiciary* (Fairfax, Va.: George Mason University Press, 1987).

14. Paul J. Feldstein, *Health Associations and the Demand for Legislation* (Cambridge, Mass.: Ballinger, 1977), p. 15.

15. A. Lawrence Lowell et al., *Final Report of the Commission on Medical Education* (New York: Association of American Medical Colleges, 1932), pp. 151-53.

16. Ibid.

17. Lester S. King, "Medical Sects and Their Influence," *Journal of the American Medical Association* 248 (1982).

18. Lawrence Wilson, "The Case against Medical Licensing," in *The Dangers of Socialized Medicine*, ed. Jacob Hornberger and Richard Ebeling (Fairfax, Va.: Future of Freedom Foundation, 1994), p. 59.

19. King, p. 1222.

20. Lowell, p. 156.

21. Ronald Hamowy, "The Early Development of Medical Licensing Laws in the United States, 1875-1900," *Journal of Libertarian Studies* (1979).

22. Reuben Kessel, "Price Discrimination in Medicine," *Journal of Law and Economics* 1 (1958): 20-53.

23. Paul Starr, *The Social Transformation of American Medicine* (New York: HarperCollins, 1982), pp. 79-144.

24. Ibid., pp. 116-17.

25. Ibid., p. 118.

26. Flexner called for the adoption of five principles that reflect the model of education developed at Johns Hopkins University School of Medicine in 1893. Those include (1) a minimum of two years of under-graduate college; (2) a four-year curriculum, with two years in the basic medical sciences followed by two years of supervised clinical work in both inpatient and outpatient hospital services; (3) regular laboratory teaching exercises; (4) a high level of quality instruction be maintained through the use of full-time faculty; and (5) that medical schools be university based. Anthony R. Kovner, *Health Care Delivery in the United States* (New York: Springer, 1990), p. 73.

27. A. R. Pruit, "The Medical Marketplace," in *Politicized Medicine* (Irvington-on-Hudson, N.Y.: Foundation for Economic Education, 1993), pp. 23-33; Milton Friedman and Rose Friedman, *Free to Choose* (New York: Harcourt, Brace, Jovanovich, 1979).

28. Lowell, appendix, Table 104.

29. Ibid., p. 11.

30. Ibid., p. 283.

31. Ibid., appendix, Table 116.

32. Starr, p. 124.

33. Ibid.

34. Ibid.

35. Estimate of 1 doctor per 2,563 persons nationwide based on U.S. Census data, total U.S. population = 122,775,046 in 1930; and the total number of physicians in 1932 = 47,914. Lowell, appendix, Tables 62, 63.

36. Starr, p. 126.

37. Charles Baron, "Licensure of Health Care Professionals: The Consumer's Case for Abolition," *American Journal of Law and Medicine* 9 (Fall 1983): 388.

38. Office of Alternative Medicine, NIH, *Alternative Medicine: Expanding Medical Horizons*, NIH publication no. 940-66 (Washington: Government Printing Office, December 1994), p. 82.

39. Burton Goldberg, *Alternative Medicine: The Definitive Guide* (Puyallup, Wash.: Future Medicine, 1993), p. 277.

40. Editorial, "Medical Organizations in Annual Session: The AMA Meeting," *Journal of American Osteopathic Association* 13 (1914): 650.

41. Goldberg, p. 277.

42. Pamela L. Brinegar and Kara L. Schmitt, "State Occupational and Professional Licensure," in *The Book of States* (Lexington, Ky.: Council of State Governments, 1992), p. 567.

43. Paul J. Feldstein, *The Politics of Health Legislation: An Economic Perspective* (Ann Arbor: Health Administration Press, 1988), p. 81.

44. Colleen Kochman, "Nurse Managed Clinics: Improving Access to Health Care for Children," *Invitation to Change: Better Government Competition Winners, 1993* (Boston: Pioneer Institute for Public Policy Research, 1993), pp. 3-22.

45. Mark L. Schoene, "Federal Acute Back Pain Guideline Recommends Medication, Spinal Manipulation, and Exercise: Most Patients Can Safely Defer Specialized Diagnostic Testing," *Back Letter* 10 (January 1995): 1.

46. Diana Korte, "Midwives on Trial," *Mothering* (Fall 1995): 52-59.

47. Stephanie J. Ventura et al., "Advance Report of Final Natality Statistics, 1992," *Monthly Vital Statistics Report: Final Data from the Centers for Disease Control and Prevention—National Center for Health Statistics* 43 (October 1994): 17-18.

48. Chris Hafner-Eaton and Laurie Pearce, "Birth Choices, the Law, and Medicine: Balancing Individual Freedoms and Protection of the Public's Health," *Journal of Health Politics, Policy and Law* 19 (Winter 1994): 815.

49. Francis Notzon et al., "International Differences in the Use of Obstetric Interventions, *Journal of the American Medical Association* 263 (1990): 3287.

50. George Schieber et al., "Health System Performance in OECD Countries, 1980-1992," *Health Affairs* (Fall 1994): 102-8.

51. Korte, p. 57.

52. Ventura, p. 71.

53. Hafner-Eaton, pp. 817-19.

54. Judith Rooks et al., "Outcomes of Care in Birth Centers: The National Birth Center Study," *New England Journal of Medicine* 321 (1989): 1804.

55. A. Mark Durand, "The Safety of Home Birth: The Farm Study," *American Journal of Public Health* 82 (March 1992): 450-53.

56. Ibid.

57. Hafner-Eaton, p. 818.

58. Archie Brodsky, "Home Delivery," *Reason*, March 1992, pp. 28-31.

59. Hafner-Eaton, p. 831.

60. Estimate based on 20 percent of 4,065,000 births in 1992 and savings of $3,000 from midwife-assisted services. Ventura et al.

61. Bonnie B. O'Connor, "The Home Birth Movement in the United States," *Journal of Medicine and Philosophy* 18 (1993): 150-51.

62. Ibid., pp. 152, 171.

63. Brodsky, p. 33.

64. P. A. Stephenson and M. G. Wagner, "Reproductive Rights and the Medical Care System: A Plea for Rational Health Policy," *Journal of Public Health Policy* (Summer 1993): 174-82.

65. O'Connor, p. 167.

66. Rooks, p. 1804.

67. Korte, pp. 54-55.

68. Ibid., p. 55.

69. Brodsky, p. 32.

70. Hafner-Eaton, p. 814.

71. O'Connor, p. 170.

72. Korte, p. 57.

73. Steve Sternberg, "Introducing—Dr. Nurse," *Atlanta Journal/Atlantic Constitution*, August 15, 1993.

74. Kochman, p. 8.

75. Office of Technology Assessment, *Nurse Practitioners, Physician Assistants, and Certified Nurse-Midwives*, Health Technology Case Study 37, OTA-HCS-37 (Washington: U.S. Government Printing Office, December 1986), pp. 5-10.

76. Kochman, p. 11; P. Capan et al., "Nurse-Managed Clinics Provide Access and Improved Health Care," *Nurse Practitioner* 18 (1993): 53-55.

77. Len M. Nichols, "Estimating Costs of Underusing Advanced Practice Nurses," *Nursing Economics* 10 (September-October 1994): 350.

78. Kochman, p. 9.

79. Barbara Safriet, "Health Care Dollars and Regulatory Sense: The Role of Advanced Practice Nursing," *Yale Journal on Regulation* 9 (1992): 437.

80. J. W. Gilliam II, "A Contemporary Analysis of Medicolegal Concerns for Physician Assistants and Nurse Practitioners," *Legal Medicine* (1994): 133-80.

81. Jurisdictions that grant nurse practitioners prescriptive authority independent of physicians include Alaska, Arizona, Iowa, Montana, New Mexico, Oregon, Vermont, Wisconsin, Wyoming, and the District of Columbia. Linda J. Pearson, "Annual Update of How Each State Stands on Legislative Issues Affecting Advanced Nursing Practice," *Nurse Practitioner* 20 (1995): 16.

82. Linda Minich, American Nurses Association, Washington, Personal communication, September 1995.

83. Barbara Safriet, "Impediments to Progress in Health Care Workforce Policy: License and Practice Laws," *Inquiry* 31 (1994): 310-17.

84. Candice Owley, "Broadside against Nurses," *Washington Post,* December 27, 1993.

85. American Medical Association, *Digest of Official Actions: 1959-1968* (Chicago: AMA, 1971), pp. 334-36; "Quackery Persists," editorial, *Journal of the American Medical Association* 221 (1972): 914.

86. "Chiropractic Scope of Practice," American Chiropractic Association, Washington, March 1993.

87. American Medical Association, *Digest of Official Actions: 1969-1978* (Chicago: American Medical Association, 1980), p. 248.

88. American Chiropractic Association, Arlington, Va., Personal communication, September 1995.

89. Schoene, p. 1.

90. Daniel Cherkin et al., "Patient Evaluations of Low Back Pain Care from Family Physicians and Chiropractors," *Western Journal of Medicine* 150 (1989): 351.

91. Robin A. Cohen et al., "Trends in the Health of Older Americans: United States, 1994," *Vital and Health Statistics from the Centers for Disease Control and Prevention/National Center for Health Statistics*, series 3, no. 30 (April 1995): 79.

92. Richard A. Knox, "Agency on Medical Cost-Effectiveness Fighting for Life," *Boston Globe*, July 23, 1995, p. 16.

93. T. W. Meade et al., "Low Back Pain of Mechanical Origin: Randomized Comparison of Chiropractic and Hospital Patient Treatment," *British Medical Journal* 300 (1990): 1435.

94. Cherkin, p. 351.

95. Richard Leviton, "Hands on the Back May Be the Best Treatment, Says U.S. Government Study," *Alternative Medicine Digest* 1 (1995): 33.

96. Brown, pp. 2125; Editor, ACA Journal of Chiropractic, *American Medical Association Issues Revised Ethics Opinion on Chiropractic as Litigation on Antitrust Suit Is Concluded* (Arlington, Va.: American Chiropractic Association, 1992).

97. See, for example, Julian B. Roebuck and Bruce Hunter, "The Awareness of Health-Care Quackery as Deviant Behavior," *Journal of Health and Social Behavior* 13 (1972): 166; James H. Young, "The Persistence of Medical Quackery in America," *American Scientist* 60 (1972): 324; Lois D. McBean et al., "Food Faddism: A Challenge to Nutritionists and Dietitians," *American Journal of Clinical Nutrition* 27 (1974): 1071-78; Faith T. Fitzgerald, "Science and Scam: Alternative Thought Patterns in Alternative Health Care," *New England Journal of Medicine* 309 (1983): 1066; Marc Galanter, "Cults and Zealous Self-Help Movements: A Psychiatric Perspective," *American Journal of Psychiatry* 147 (1990): 54351; Andrew A. Skolnick, "FDA Petitioned to 'Stop Homeopathy Scam,' " *Journal of the American Medical Association* 272 (1994): 1154-56; Thomas L. Delbanco, "Bitter Herbs: Mainstream, Magic, and Menace," *Annals of Internal Medicine* 121 (1994): 803-4.

98. William T. Jarvis, "Quackery: A National Scandal," *Clinical Chemistry* 38 (1992): 1574-86.

99. Ibid., p. 1575.

100. Tim Beardsley, "Fads and Feds: Holistic Therapy Collides with Reductionist Science," *Scientific American* (September 1993): 39-44.

101. Thomas M. Lenard et al., *Interim Report: The Future of Medical Innovation* (Washington: Progress and Freedom Foundation, 1995), p. 7.

102. Office of Alternative Medicine, pp. 183-206.

103. K. Danner Clouser and David Hufford, "Nonorthodox Healing Systems and Their Knowledge Claims," *Journal of Medicine and Philosophy* 18 (1993): 102; David J. Hufford, "Epistemologies in Religious Healing," *Journal of Medicine and Philosophy* 18 (1993): 175-94.

104. Stephen Fulder and Robin Munro, "Complementary Medicine in the United Kingdom: Patients, Practitioners, and Consultations," *Lancet* (1985): 542; Mathilde Boissett and Mary-Ann Fitzcharles, "Alternative Medicine Use by Rheumatology Patients in a Universal Health Care Setting," *Journal of Rheumatology* 21 (1994): 148.

105. Fulder and Munro, p. 542.

106. See, for example, Sidney Carroll and Robert Gaston, "Occupational Licensing and the Quality of Service: An Overview," *Law and Human Behavior*, September 1983.

107. Gary Gaumer, "Regulating Health Professionals: A Review of Empirical Literature," *Milbank Memorial Fund Quarterly* (1984).

108. Carolyn Cox and Susan Foster, "The Costs and Benefits of Occupational Regulation," Federal Trade Commission, October 1990.

109. Terree Wasley, *What Has Government Done to Our Health Care?* (Washington: Cato Institute, 1992).

110. The Commonwealth of Massachusetts's Acupuncture Statute (M.G.L. c, 112 ss. 148-62) states that "nothing contained herein shall prevent licensed physicians from practicing acupuncture."

111. Judy Foreman, "Acupuncture: An Ancient Medicine Is Making Its Point," *Boston Globe*, May 22, 1995, p. 25. Foreman reports that the national organization for physician-acupuncturists (American Academy of Medical Acupuncture) requires 200 hours of acupuncture training for membership. The national organization for nonphysician-acupuncturists (National Commission for the Certification of Acupuncturists) requires more than 1,000 hours of acupuncture training before candidates take the exam for national certification.

112. Paul J. Feldstein, *Health Policy Issues: An Economic Perspective on Health Reform* (Ann Arbor: Health Administration Press, 1994), p. 189.

113. Wasley, p. 42.

114. Feldstein, *Health Policy Issues,* pp. 189-90.

115. S. David Young, *The Rule of Experts: Occupational Licensing in America* (Washington: Cato Institute, 1987), p. 53.

116. Victor Fuchs, *Who Shall Live?* (New York: Basic Books, 1974), p. 20.

117. Milton Friedman and Simon Kuznets, *Income from Independent Professional Practice* (New York: National Bureau of Economic Research, 1945).

118. William White, "The Impact of Occupational Licensure on Clinical Laboratory Personnel," *Journal of Human Resources* (Winter 1978).

119. Lawrence Shepard, "Licensing Restrictions and the Cost of Dental Care," *Journal of Law and Economics* (April 1978).

120. Timothy Muzondo and Pazderka Bohumir, "Occupational Licensing and Professional Incomes in Canada," *Canadian Journal of Economics* (November 1990).

121. Gaumer, p. 397.

122. Chris Paul, "Physician Licensure and the Quality of Medical Care," *Atlantic Economic Journal* 12 (1984): 18-30.

123. Friedman and Friedman, p. 240. Emphasis in original.

124. Medical school revenues totaled $11,983,863 in 1932. Sources of income were as follows: student fees, $4,057,304; endowment income, $2,784,527; state and city, $2,574,973; and other, $2,567,059. Lowell et al., Table 104 and p. 283.

125. Uwe Reinhardt, "Planning the Nation's Health Workforce: Let the Market In," *Inquiry* 31 (Fall 1994): 250-63; Janice L. Ganem et al., "Review of US Medical School Finances, 1993-1994," *Journal of the American Medical Association* 274 (September 6, 1995): 724, Table 1.

126. Janice L. Ganem et al., "Review of U.S. Medical School Finances," *Journal of the American Medical Association* 274 (1995): 723-30.

127. Mullan et al., p. 142.

128. Congressional Budget Office, *Medicare and Graduate Medical Education* (Washington: Government Printing Office, 1995), p. 10.

129. Ibid.

130. Mullan et al., p. 143.

131. Ibid.

132. Ibid., pp. 142-43.

133. Ganem, p. 724, Table 1.

134. Kovner, p. 73.

135. Feldstein, *Health Policy Issues*, p. 189.

136. Reinhardt, pp. 253-54.

137. "Prized by Hospitals, Accreditation Hides Perils Patients Face," *Wall Street Journal*, October 12, 1988.

138. Sherman Follard, Allen Goodman, and Miran Stano, *The Economics of Health and Health Care* (New York, Macmillan, 1993), p. 583.

THE LAW OF THE MICROCOSM AND THE END OF SOCIALISM

George Gilder

The Information Revolution

Every era achieves a cultural pinnacle. In the Middle Ages it was probably the giant cathedral, whether Gothic or Byzantine. Wrought of rock and sand and glass, these cathedrals stand today as a cultural and religious epitome, a beacon of faith and aspiration reaching forth over the centuries—issuing a reproach to most of the architecture and art of the current epoch.

Nonetheless, our own age, I believe, has summoned a monument of aspiration and faith, devotion, diligence, and art as formidable as the great cathedrals of the past.

The cathedral of the 20th century is the microchip, a tiny computer inscribed on a small piece of semiconductor material. Like the medieval cathedrals, the microchip is wrought of the commonest elements in the earth, being earth itself. But seen through a microscope, that semiconductor shape emerges with the opalescent symmetry of a cathedral window.

I would sum it up in a vision of sand and glass. The sand is the substance of microelectronics. It comes in the form of a silicon sliver the size of a thumbnail that bears a pattern of wires and logic as complex as a street map of America, switching traffic in trillionths of seconds. At the heart of a microchip is the microswitch: the transistor. Twenty years ago transistors cost $7 dollars apiece and were plugged into circuit boards one at a time by hand. Today far better, faster, and more useful transistors cost a few ten thousandths of a cent.

Current chips contain as many as 20 million transistors. Scores can be placed not on the head of a pin but on the point of a pin. Switched in trillionths of seconds, these devices transcend all the normal constraints of time and space. Their development is by far the most important event of the current era.

The microchip of sand, however, joins with another amazing technology made of glass. The glass in the vision is so pure that if it were a window, you could see through miles. But it comes in fiberoptic threads the width of a human hair and as long as the rails to Leningrad. It is fed by laser diodes the size of a grain of salt and brighter than the sun. Today these threads flash information between the East Coast of America and Chicago at a pace of 8.6 gigabits a second: a thousand bibles a second. This technology represents a vast leap ahead of the copper wires that transmit most phone calls around the globe. For example, the U.S. Congress maintains a library holding all the publications of the nation over the last 100 years. Using copper wires would take 500 years to transmit the contents of the Library of Congress. Using fiberoptic threads would take just eight hours.

As this technology moves into homes and offices over the next decade, it will hugely enhance the powers of individuals to send and receive communications of all kinds, from movies and other digital video products to whole libraries of data and text. In the process it will replace the dumb television terminal with a telecomputer that can not only receive but also shape and send digital data and images.

As fast as fiberoptic technology is advancing, however, chip technology is keeping pace. Within the next 10 years, it will be possible to put as many as one billion transistors on a single sliver of silicon. One billion transistors is equivalent to the computing resources of perhaps 20 of the world's largest supercomputers, whether Crays in the United States or Elbus machines in the Soviet Union. Within the next 10 years or so, this computer power will be inscribed on a single chip that will cost less than $100 dollars to manufacture. Such an advance will mean approximately a millionfold rise in the cost-effectiveness of computing in 10 years.

Together these two technologies will create a global ganglion of computers and cables, a worldwide web of glass and light and sand that leaves all history in its wake. For good or ill, this technology will shape the future of all nations through the 21st century.

A New Economic Structure

The rise of these miraculous tools, I believe, both necessitates a radical change in the economic structure of the USSR and makes such a change possible. These microelectronic tools will allow the Soviet Union to move toward capitalism without suffering the pains and setbacks that economists often prescribe. However, the use of these new tools utterly requires the abandonment of all dreams of a centralized economy.

The Wealth of Knowledge

Mikhail Gorbachev pronounced a crucial insight regarding this new era. He pointed to the most valuable resource of the age. He did not mention oil or gas or gold, missiles or nuclear power. Instead he declared: "In the age of information sciences, the most valuable asset is knowledge, which is a creation of human imagination and creativity. We were among the last to comprehend this truth and we will be paying for this oversight for many years to come."

Gorbachev may be too pessimistic. The Soviet Union is full of the most valuable asset of the information age, full of well-trained and resourceful men and women. It faces no inherently difficult problem of transition. It merely faces the challenge of liberating its crucial resources of knowledge, now incarcerated in a million mazes of bureaucracy.

The Spirit of Enterprise

T. J. Rodgers of Cypress Semiconductor, one of the leading American microchip entrepreneurs, recently discovered how rich Russia is in the crucial resources of this new age. He visited the USSR in the summer of 1990 intent on licensing a graphics chip design. He expected to find the Soviet Union far behind the United States in semiconductors. In many ways he was right. In manufacturing and selling chips, the Soviet Union is indeed far behind. Compared to state-of-the-art American chips, Soviet devices are big and slow. But in a crucial way, T. J. discovered that he had greatly underestimated the Soviets.

Rodgers found that the Soviet failure to develop advanced hardware had induced great creativity in computer architecture and software. The absence of leading edge computer technology impelled Soviet engineers to an early mastery of the algorithms of parallel processing: using many low-performance microprocessors in parallel to emulate the most-advanced single processors. Soviet computer architects and chip designers, Rodgers discovered, emerged from their crucible of privation as some of the best in the world.

Some Americans making such a discovery would have hastened back to the Pentagon to report the terrible news of a new Soviet threat in microelectronics. Some American businessmen might have petitioned the government for new subsidies and supports to help keep pace with the Soviet designs. Even in America, many people see the world as a zero sum game, with every gain for one country or company a loss for someone else. Prevailing through the centuries, this attitude the view that the success of others is a threat rather than an opportunity—has blighted most of human history. The view that creators of wealth somehow oppress the poor is the most crippling prejudice of Marxism. T. J. Rodgers, however, is embued with a different spirit: the spirit of enterprise.

Being an entrepreneur, T. J. on the spot decided to buy licenses to all the salable technologies he found. He bought licenses for nine chip designs from such Soviet firms as INTEREVM, Mikron, Angstrem, Progress, and Elas. He launched a major computer project with a Soviet team. Entitled "Mir," it will be executed by a 50-man team in the USSR. Today some 15 leading Soviet engineers are working at Cypress in the United States.

Gains from Trade

T. J. was thrilled with the computer people he met in the Soviet Union. As an entrepreneur he could launch mutual projects with them almost immediately. Did he exploit the Soviet designers he dealt with? No. They all will gain hard currency royalties from any chips sold in the United States. Some of their designs were too complex even to be manufactured in the Soviet Union. They will have their chips produced on the best semiconductor production lines in the world. They will gain financially, and they will gain from the experience of having their ideas realized in hardware and sold widely to customers.

The Soviet Union will gain technologies that were previously unavailable to them and markets that were previously beyond their reach. Thus they will gain guidance about where to focus future efforts. The Soviet computer experts who dealt with T. J. Rodgers came away as big winners.

How about T. J.? He gained access to the most valuable resource of the information age: human creativity and imagination. He extended his product line into the important fields of digital signal processing and image processing, which his company had previously neglected. He won the rights to the output of an important new computer product. He gained entrance to what will be a tremendous new market for high technology devices. He too was a big winner in the Soviet Union.

That is the key secret of capitalism: win-win rivalry. Everybody wins; no one is exploited. Because every deal is voluntary, both sides gain; every transaction is a positive sum. If anyone feels unsatisfied with the terms, the deal cannot go through. Since each side improves its position through the transaction, the very process of free capitalist trading ensures that national wealth increases with every exchange.

Gross national product (GNP) rises even without the creation of any new product. The free market enhances the value of all the production of the nation by ensuring that it will go the people who want it most and can use it best.

Until T. J . showed up in Zelenograd, many of the great chip designs and computer architectures of the USSR were valueless because they could not find customers or manufacturers. His entrepreneurial vision lent value to intellectual properties that were valueless in the Soviet economy.

The Use of Knowledge under Socialism and Capitalism

In contrast to chip designs deemed worthless in the USSR, T. J. also visited a great center of wealth and power as judged by Soviet authorities. He visited the office of the man he said "has the worst job in Moscow." That is saying a lot. That man is a noted physicist named Yuri Pavlov. He does not sweep the streets or clean the public toilets. His job is "General Director of Moscow City Council Scientific Development Conglomerate for Automated Control Systems." He runs Moscow's governmental computer center.

The wonders of central planning mean Yuri has to plan the movement of bread and milk. He tries to make the lines shorter. He also keeps track of health care, drug prescriptions, retirement payments, water bills, apartment rents and allocations, and a long list of other services for nine million people.

Pavlov is a man of great relative wealth and power in the Soviet Union. He commands arrays of seemingly valuable computers. He helps rule the lives of millions. Unlike the chip designs deemed worthless in the USSR, Pavlov's establishment is supremely valuable in the planned economy.

In a market system, however, all Pavlov's panoply of powers and machines is less than worthless. The old IBM compatible computers he uses could hardly be sold as scrap in the United States. The work he does is irrelevant in an economy where economic planning is performed voluntarily by millions of individuals.

It is often said that the Soviet Union cannot prosper without huge inflows of capital from the outside world. That is an absurd assumption. The Soviet Union is already glutted with capital: roads, factories, weapons, mines, tractors, schools. For decades, the Soviet Union has invested a hugely greater proportion of its wealth than the United States. Communist systems are nearly always awash with useless capital. But without freedom, capital is blind and sterile.

In a capitalist system, you do not need new capital to create wealth. Freedom in itself creates wealth just as T. J. created new wealth at Zelenograd. By allowing the perpetuation of economic planning outside capital may even reduce the real wealth of Russia. It may plunge the real capital of the nation—its creative citizens—into the darkness of production without free customers.

Freedom means the right to fail. The key reason the U.S. economy is more successful than the Soviet economy is that the United States allows more failure. U.S. scientists and engineers outproduce Soviet scientists and engineers not because they are more numerous or better trained or more talented. In fact, there are many times more highly trained scientists and engineers in the USSR than in the United States, and Soviet students outperform American students on international tests.

U.S. scientists and engineers create more value because they collaborate with millions in the marketplace around the world. Soviet scientists and engineers collaborate only with each other and their political bosses. U.S. scientists and entrepreneurs can prevail because they can fail.

Bankruptcies play the same role in economic progress that falsification plays in the progress of ideas. The eminent philosopher of science Karl Popper identifies a valid scientific proposition chiefly by whether it is stated in a form in which it could possibly be disproved or rejected. If a theory—such as that people born in August under the sign of Leo tend to be temperamental—is too general or flexible to be proven wrong, it is incapable of generating new knowledge. Similarly, if an economic plan cannot be rejected by the marketplace, it cannot generate new value.

Every new business, however, provides an entrepreneurial test of a new idea. Unlike a national plan, a business plan is falsifiable. Because it can fail, it can also generate new knowledge. In fact entrepreneurs often learn more from their failures than from their successes.

By the very process of acquiring profits, entrepreneurs learn how to use them. By the very process of building businesses, entrepreneurs gain the discipline to avoid waste and the knowledge to see value. By the process of creating and responding to markets, entrepreneurs orient their lives toward the service of others. Entrepreneurs who hoard their wealth or seek governmental protection from rivals or revel in vain consumption or retreat to selfish isolation betray the very essence of their role and responsibility in the world. To that degree, they are no longer entrepreneurs or capitalists but relics of the feudal and static societies of the precapitalist era.

Every capitalist investment has a dual yield: a financial profit and an epistemological profit. One without the other is barren. Economies progress when the process of investment is informed by the results of previous investment. Entrepreneurs like T. J. Rodgers spread wealth because they constantly accumulate new knowledge by risking failure. This new knowledge is the most crucial capital they wield.

For many years, Marxists have believed that they could solve the knowledge problem of socialism through the creation of ever-large knowledge machines: computers. Giant computers could simulate markets and thus render freedom unnecessary and obsolete.

I believe however, that it is the computer that makes communism obsolete. Tile microchip may indeed offer the solution to the problem of socialist bureaucracy. But it is also the dissolution of socialism and all other centralized systems.

The Problem of Complexity

The key problem of the planned economy is the explosion of complexity. In the planned economy only the bureaucrats can plan But their plans inevitably break down in the nearly infinite complexities of a large economy. In a free economy, all citizens and businesses can make plans.

Because individual businesses face manageable complexities, they can actually carry out their plans. The paradox of the planned economy is that it prohibits all practical planning.

The Law of the Macrocosm

This problem can be summed up as the law of the macrocosm or the law of complexity. It shows that complexity rises by the square of the number of entities to be organized—whether phones in a network, chips on printed circuit boards, or prices and quantities in an urban economy. This law even confounds computations in physics, where the so-called many-body problem afflicts all analysis of relations between large numbers of entities.

Arno Penzias, the Nobel laureate physicist, explains the problem in terms of the impact of an additional child arriving at a party. The noise level does not rise by the increment of one more child; it rises exponentially in proportion to the additional child and all the other children he may shout at and interact with. This is another form of the many-body (and vocal chord) problem. That is, it is an example of the law of the macrocosm.

The Law of the Microcosm

In the microcosm of silicon chips, however, a completely different law applies: the law of the microcosm. On silicon, it is not complexity but efficiency that rises by the square of the number of entities to be organized. The more transistors crammed on each microchip, the cheaper, faster, cooler, more powerful, and more valuable they are. This relationship is measured in the industry as the power-delay product, relating the power consumption (and heat) to the speed of operation of a microelectronic device.

On individual microchips the power-delay product improves exponentially with the increase in the number of transistors and thus the closer they are packed together. As electrons moving in a transistor approach their mean free path—the distance they can travel without colliding with the structure of the silicon crystal—they move faster and more efficiently. It is as if a million more children arrived at the party and the noise level went down.

These gains in efficiency, however, apply only on individual chips. You begin combining lots of chips together and the law of complexity takes hold again. That is why the Elbus strategy for saving socialism—the big computer dream—will inevitably fail. All computers will eventually become single chip systems, basically equal in power and cheap enough for anyone to buy. Any top-down structure of organization—any hierarchy—will eventually collapse into a heterarchy, where equal processors, or individuals, communicate with one another on an essentially equal basis.

Once again, this is not an optional outcome; it is inherent in the very physics of computation. As chips rise toward a billion transistors each, their processing power will rise even faster. But the communications power from the chip, by contrast, will eke up slowly; it will depend on the circumference or in some cases on the area of the chip. Thus the premium on single chip systems will steadily increase. The penalty for master slave systems will rise acutely.

What is happening is the overthrow of the previous relationship between the cost of wires and the cost of switches. Wires are the communications medium between chips, and switches are the transistors that give the computer logical powers. When wires are cheap and switches expensive, it makes sense to centralize. It pays to run a few more wires to an expensive central processing unit dominated by switches. This was the case at the beginning of the computer era when switches were fragile and expensive vacuum tubes. Today however, switches are virtually free—infinitesimal transistors on a chip—while wires are relatively expensive. Under these conditions it pays to distribute intelligence on single chips.

The End of Socialism

The obsolescence of the big computer is already evident. For example, in 1977 nearly 100 percent of all the computer power in the world was commanded by large machines with dumb terminals attached. Just 13 years later, that figure had dropped to well under 1 percent. There are now over 100 million personal computers in the world, and they command virtually all the globe's computer power.

It is this change that dooms socialism. It is this change that permanently overthrows Marxism. Although Marx was wrong about many things, he did sense a crucial fact about the past industrial order. In the past, machines were hostile to human values. Factories worked best when individual workers adapted themselves to the machine. Industrial analysts would actually measure the movements of workers and attempt to adjust them to the requirements of the equipment they used. Even in freemarket economies, the factory or assembly line tended to be a top-down hierarchy.

This system resulted in huge gains of human productivity. But whether in the East or West, it was deeply inimical to the nature of human beings. Human beings are far more like chips than like assembly lines. We have the most powerful processors in the world between our ears. Two human eyes, for example, can do more image processing than all the supercomputers in the world put together. But as in the case of chips, our communications power is strictly limited. About 50 bits per second is the estimate of the experts.

The chemist, Michael Polanyi, has explained the effects of this relationship. It means that the bulk of human learning is tacit knowledge: It is literally incommunicable. For example, there is no way to explain how an individual reaches out and picks up a glass of water and brings it to his lips. Most of what we know about our jobs is this kind of tacit knowledge. Although the industrial era enhanced the productive power of human beings by raising their physical strength, this gain came at the cost of a loss of tacit knowledge.

The nature of human beings means that an organization functions best when individuals can be coupled as closely as possible to specific problems. Leaders can offer general goals and directions. But specific guidance and controls will cost far more in tacit learning than they will gain in efficiency. Workers must have common visions but not detailed supervision. Top-down bureaucracy, private or public, obliterates the crucial mental powers of human beings that elevate us above the apes and give us mastery of the world.

The microchip is the first technology that accords fully with the nature of human beings as thinking creatures. Favoring heterarchy over hierarchy, it overthrows all top-down systems.

As the chip reorganizes industry and commerce so also will it reorganize the powers of states and nations. The law of the microcosm subverts any attempt to capture, intimidate, confine, or overwhelm the exertions of mind by the tyranny of matter.

The mobility and ascendancy of mind among all the forms of capital deeply undermines the power of the state. Quantum technology devalues what the state is good at controlling—material resources geographic ties, physical wealth. Quantum technology exalts the one domain the state can never finally reach or even read: mind. Thus the move from the industrial era to the quantum era takes the world from a technology of control to a technology of freedom.

The New Industrial Revolution

The most evident effect of the change is a sharp decline in the value of natural resources. The first industrial revolution vastly increased the value of materials. All the dirt, rock, and gunk that had been ignored for centuries suddenly acquired worth in the age of mass manufacturing. The new industrial revolution is a revolution of mind over matter, and it is rapidly returning what used to be called "precious natural resources" to their previous natural value as dirt, rocks, and gunk.

The use of steel, coal, oil, and other materials is plummeting as a share of value added in the economy. As a symbol of the shift, consider two smelting processes. When smelting iron, you banish silicon in the slag as dirt; when "smelting" silicon, you get rid of the iron as conductive waste. A silicon chip is less than 2 percent raw materials. A few pounds of fiberoptic cable, also made essentially of sand, will soon carry as much information as a ton of copper. A single satellite now displaces many tons of copper wire.

This change has transformed the very foundations of geopolitics. Raw materials have long constituted a leading reason and reward for military aggression. In the past, ownership of particular regions imparted great political and economic power. The balance of power in Europe depended in part on who controlled the coal and steel in the Ruhr Basin. The Ruhr Basin is now a European sink of government subsidies.

We live in an epoch when desert-bound Israel can use computerized farming to supply 80 percent of the cut flowers in some European markets and compete in selling avocados in Florida, when barren Japan can claim to be number one, and when tiny islands like Singapore and Hong Kong can far outproduce Argentina or Indonesia.

To comprehend the change, consider a steel mill, the exemplary industry of the previous epoch: a huge manufacturing plant entrenched near iron and coal mines, anchored by a grid of railways and canals, and served by an army of regimented workers, all attended by an urban infrastructure of physical systems and services. At every step the steel mill can be regulated, taxed, and controlled by government.

Compare this massive array of measurable inputs and outputs to a person at a computer work station, with access to data bases around the world, designing microchips of a complexity exceeding the entire steel facility, to be manufactured from pattern generation tapes. Even the tape, the one physical manifestation of his product, has become optional. Without any fixed physical manifestation at all, the computer design can flow through the global ganglion into another computer attached to a production line anywhere in the world.

Even observers who comprehend the nature of information technology, however, often fail to understand its radical effect on international economics. The decline in the value of raw materials entails an equal decline in the value of geography. In an age when individuals can inscribe new worlds on grains of sand, particular territories are fast losing economic significance.

Not only are the natural resources under the ground rapidly declining in value, but the companies and capital above the ground can rapidly leave. Commanding a worldwide network of transport and communications, the modern business firm can send wealth flashing down fiberoptic cables and caroming off satellites at the speed of thought rather than of things.

Capital is no longer manacled to machines and places, nations and jurisdictions. Capital markets are now global and on line 24 hours a day. People—scientists, workers, and entrepreneurs—can leave at the speed of a 747, or even a Concorde. Companies can move in weeks. Ambitious persons need no longer stand still to be fleeced or exploited by bureaucrats. Geography has become economically trivial.

Empowering Individuals: A Microeconomics of Liberty

The global microcosm has permanently shifted the world balance of power in favor of entrepreneurs. Using the planetary utility, they can avoid most of the exactions of the state. Without their fully voluntary cooperation, a government cannot increase revenues, enhance military strength, provide for the public welfare, or gain economic clout.

This good news for individuals and entrepreneurs, however, is bad news for socialism. The state can dig iron or pump oil, mobilize manpower and manipulate currencies, tax and spend. The state can expropriate the means of production. But when it does, it will find that the most productive members of society—the entrepreneurs—will run for the daylight of liberty. One way or another, most of the time, the entrepreneurs take their money with them or send it on ahead. But always they take their minds, and knowledge is their crucial power.

Ideas are subjective events and always arise in individual minds and ultimately repose in them. The movement toward a quantum economy necessarily means a movement toward an economy of mind. Collective institutions will survive only to the extent that they can serve the individuals and families whom they comprise.

This is the age of the individual. Governments cannot take power by taking control or raising taxes, by mobilizing people or heaping up trade surpluses, or by seizing territory or stealing technology. By imperialism, protectionism, and mercantilism, nations eventually wither and weaken into third worldly stagnation.

In the modern world, the chief source of the new wealth of nations is free immigrants. Today nations have to earn power by attracting immigrants and by liberating their people, their workers, and their entrepreneurs.

The gains of the quantum era could yet be destroyed by some thug offering a final horrible holocaust to the Moloch of matter. But the logic of the technology, the logic of the microcosm, which is becoming the logic of history, runs the other way. History has capsized every prophecy of triumphant bureaucracy.

Rather than a New Industrial State, this era will disclose the new impotence of the state. Rather than the Revolt of the Masses under the leadership of demagogues, this era will see the revolt of the venturers against all forms of tyranny. Systems of national command and control will wither away. Systems of global emancipation will carry the day. The dismal science of the economics of aggregates—capital, labor, and land—will give way to a microeconomics of liberty. The beggar-thy-neighbor strategies of mercantilism—of trade as a weapon of the state—will collapse before the strategies of global wealth creation under the leadership of entrepreneurs.

The new technologies—themselves largely the creation of promethean individuals—completely transform the balance of power between the entrepreneur and the state. Inventive individuals have burst every link in the chain of constraints that once bound the entrepreneur and made him a servant of parliaments and kings. He is no longer entangled in territory, no longer manacled to land, capital, or nationality.

These developments are no special American monopoly. Indeed much of the benefit will be lost if only the United States and a few Asian capitalist countries follow the crucial lessons of the new technology. For the central lesson is that information technology is not a zero sum game to be won by some governmentally supported monopolist. Information technology constantly redistributes its own powers as it is used. The final and most flexible source and vessel of these powers is the individual human mind. The power of information always ultimately gravitates to individuals.

Conclusion

All the world will benefit from the increasing impotence of imperialism, mercantilism, and statism. In this new economy of freedom, Americans must hope for the prosperity and freedom of Russians and Chinese. We must celebrate the successes of Koreans and Japanese. We must hail the increasing wealth and power of the Third World. Depending on an altruistic spirit, the microcosm requires not only a technological renaissance but also a moral renewal. Following in the steps of T. J. Rodgers, all Americans will cheer the success of the Soviet Union in its great adventure of reform. Within the spiraling gains of capitalism, impelled by the spread of information technology subverting all tyrannies, there is room at the top for all.

Notes

Cato Journal, Vol. 11, No. 2 (Fall 1991). Copyright © Cato Institute. All rights reserved.

The author is a Senior Fellow of the Discovery Institute and the author of *Microcosm* and *Recapturing the Spirit of Enterprise.*